National Forest Camping

Directory of 3,704 Camping Areas in 41 States

Copyright Notice

Published by:

Roundabout Publications
P.O. Box 569
LaCygne, KS 66040

Phone: 800-455-2207
Internet: www.RoundaboutPublications.com

Library of Congress Control Number: 2021939666

ISBN-10: 1-885464-80-0
ISBN-13: 978-1-885464-80-4

Table of Contents

Abbreviations

Below is a list of abbreviations used throughout this directory.

Abbreviation	Description
ALA	Allagash National River
AMC	Appalachian Mountain Club
AR GFC	Arkansas Game & Fish Commission
ARB	Reserve Base
ASTL	Arizona State Trust Lands
AT	Appalachian Trail
BBRCD	Big Blue River Conservancy District
BLM	Bureau of Land Management
BMU	Basin Management Unit
BR	Bureau of Reclamation
BRA	Brazos River Authority
CDW	Colorado Division of Wildlife
CG	Campground
CGC	Colorado River - Grand Canyon
CID	Carlsbad Irrigation District
Co	County
COE	US Armp Corps of Engineers
COL	Colorado River
Cons	Conservation
CP	County Park
CTC	Cumberland Trail Conference
CUA	Concentrated Use Area
DEC	Department of Conservation
DEL	Delaware River
DEP	Department of Environmental Protection
DES	Deschutes River
DFWR	Department of Fish & Wildlife Resource
DGF	Department of Game and Fish
DNR	Department of Natural Resources
DNRC	Department of Natural Resources & Conservation
DOW	Divison of Wildlife
DSF	Demonstration State Forest
DWC	Department of Wildlife Conservation
DWR	Division of Wildlife Resources
EB	East-Bound
FAS	Fishing Access Site
FFS	Florida Forest Service
FG	Fish and Game

Abbreviation	Description
FHU	Full hookups (E/W/S)
FLT	Florida Trail
FM	Farm to Market Road
FPT	Florida Paddle Trail
FWC	Fish and Wildlife Conservation
FWS	US Fish & Wildlife Service
GFD	Game & Fish Department
GPC	Game & Parks Commission
GRE	Green River
GRR	Grande Ronde River
GSM	Great Smokey Mountains
HMU	Habitat Management Unit
HP	Historical Park
HSP	Historical State Park
IFG	Idaho Fish & Game
JDR	John Day River
KRMB	Kickapoo Reserve Management Board
LBNRD	Little Blue Natural Resources District
LBTL	Land Between the Lakes
LCRA	Lower Colorado River Authority
LECA	Lake Eau Claire Association
LENRD	Lower Elkhorn Natural Resources District
LKRWCD	Little Kentucky River Watershed Conservancy District
LNRA	Lavaca-Navidad River Authority
LPN NRD	Lower Platte North Natural Resource District
LSR	Lower Salmon River
LTVA	Long Term Visitors Area
LUA	Lakeside Use Area
MDC	Missouri Department of Conservation
MDWFP	Mississippi Department of Wildlife, Fisheries & Parks
MFS	Middle Fork Salmon River
MRA	Motorized Recreational Area
MRCA	Mountains Recreation and Conservation Authority
MU	Management Unit
MUA	Multiple Use Area
MWCD	Muskingum Watershed Conservancy District
NCA	National Conservation Area
NDOW	Neveada Dept of Wildlife
NG	National Grassland
NHP	National Historic Park
NM	National Monument
NMGF	New Mexico Department of Game & Fish
NMW	North Main Woods

Abbreviation	Description
NNL	National Natural Location
NNRD	Nemaha Natural Resources District
NP	National Park
NPS	National Park Service
NR	National River
NRA	National Recreation Area
NRD	Natural Resources District
NRRA	National River & Recreation Area
NRT	National Recreation Trail
NU	Northern Unit
NWFP	Northwest Forest Permit
NWR	National Wild River
NWR	National Wildlife Refuge
OHV	Off-Highway Vehicle
OHVA	Off-Highway Vehicle Area
ORA	Outdoor Recreation Area
PCT	Pacific Crest Trail
PDRA	Palo Duro River Authority
PFA	Public Fishing Access
PHWD	Pat Harrison Waterway District
PRBDD	Pearl River Basin Development District
NP	Non-Profit
PRL	Public Reserved Lands
PUF	Public Use Facility
PWD	Pawnee Watershed District
RA	Recreation Area
RBWCD	Rio Blanco Water Conservancy District
Reg	Regional
Res	Reservation
RMC	Randolph Mountain Club
RLCSD	Ruth Lake Community Services District
ROG	Rogue River
RRWC	Red River Waterway Commission
SAL	Salmon River
SB	State Beach
SCR	St Croix River
SEL	Selway River
SEP	Southeast Paddle Trail
SF	State Forest
SFA	State Fishing Area
SFC	State Forest Campground
SFWA	State Fish and Wildlife Area
SGMA	State Game Management Area

Abbreviation	Description
SGR	State Game Refuge
SHP	State Historic Park
SHS	State Historic Site
SJR	San Juan River
SMI	Smith River
SNA	State Natural Area
SNA	Snake River
SP	State Park
SRA	State Recreation Area
SRP	State Resort Park
SRS	State Recreation Site
SRSP	Scenic River State Park
ST	State Trail
SU	Southern Unit
SVRA	State Vehicular Recreation Area
SWA	State Wildlife Area
SWFA	State Wildlife and Fishing Area
SWRA	State Wildlife Recreation Area
TC	Trail Camp
TH	Trail Head
TMA	Travel Management Area
TRA	Trinity River Authority
TRDA	Tellico Reservoir Development Agency
TVA	Tennessee Valley Authority
TWRA	Tennessee Wildlife Resources Agency
UFN	Until Further Notice
Unk	Unknown
USBR	US Bureau of Reclamation
USFS	US Forest Service
WA	Wildlife Area
WB	West-Bound
WCA	Wildlife Conservation Area
WCFPD	Winnebago County Forest Preserve District
WDFW	Washington Department of Fish & Wildlife
WEA	Wildlife and Environmental Area
WGF	Wyoming Game & Fish
WHMA	Wildlife Habitat Management Area
WMA	Wildlife Management Area
WRD	Wildlife Resource Division
WRWA	White River Water Authority
WSA	Wilderness Study Area
Y-G	Yampa-Green Rivers
YP	Yellow Post (USFS term for dispersed sites)

Introduction

About The Ultimate Public Campground Project

The Ultimate Public Campground Project was conceived in 2008 to provide a consolidated and comprehensive source for public campgrounds of all types. It all began with a simple POI (Point of Interest) list of GPS coordinates and names, nothing more, totaling perhaps 5,000 locations. As the list grew in size and information provided, a website was designed to display the data on a map. Next came mobile apps, first iOS and Mac apps and more recently Android versions.

Ultimate Campgrounds is NOT the product of some large company with deep pockets. We are a team of three, all working on this as a part-time avocation: Ted is the founder of Ultimate Campgrounds and its Data Meister, Bill is our iOS and Mac developer and Geoff is our Android guy. Both Ted and Bill have been camping for many years and Ultimate Campgrounds reflects their interest in accurate and useful campground information.

Please note that despite our best efforts, there will always be errors to be found in the data. With over 43,000 records in our database, it is impossible to ensure that each one is always up-to-date. Ted tries to work his way through the data at least once a year to pick up things like increased fees and URL's that always seem to be changing. On an annual basis, it requires reviewing over 115 locations each and every day of the year – that's a pretty tall order.

Thus we always appreciate input from users who have found errors…or would like to submit a new location. Our goal is accuracy and we will gratefully accept any and all input.

We decided some years ago to focus on just one thing, publicly-owned camping locations, and try to be the best at it.

You can find a lot more information about Ultimate Campgrounds on our website: www.ultimatecampgrounds.com.

Feel free to address any questions or comments to us at info@ultimatecampgounds.com.

Happy Camping!

National Forest Camping

This book features select U.S. Forest Service camping areas in 41 states. Currently there are more than 19,000 camping areas within *The Ultimate Public Campground Project* database managed by the Forest Service. The majority are dispersed camping areas and are too numerous to include in one book. Various selection criteria was used to reduce the total number of camping areas included in this book to 3,704.

If you are interested in learning about *all* of the U.S. Forest Service camping areas (and other public land agencies, too), we recommend looking at our 17 volume series, *The Ultimate Public Campground Project*. Refer to our website, roundaboutpublications.com, for more information.

State Maps

A state map is provided to aid you in locating camping areas. All locations are shown with an identifying reference number allowing you to quickly locate in the *Camping Area Details* section.

Camping Area Details

Camping area details include various information about the public camping areas within the state. Preceding each camping area's name is an Entry ID number. This is used when cross-referencing with the map. Details of each camping area generally include the following:

- Total number of sites or dispersed camping
- Number of RV sites
- Sites with electric hookups
- Full hookup sites, if available
- Water (central location or spigots at site)
- Showers
- RV dump station
- Toilets (flush, pit/vault, or none)
- Laundry facilities
- Camp store
- Maximum RV size limits (if any)
- Reservation information (accepted, not accepted, recommended or required)
- Generator use and hours (if limited)
- Operating season
- Camping fees charged
- Length of stay limit
- Elevation in feet and meters
- Telephone number
- Nearby city or town
- Miscellaneous notes
- GPS coordinates

Alabama

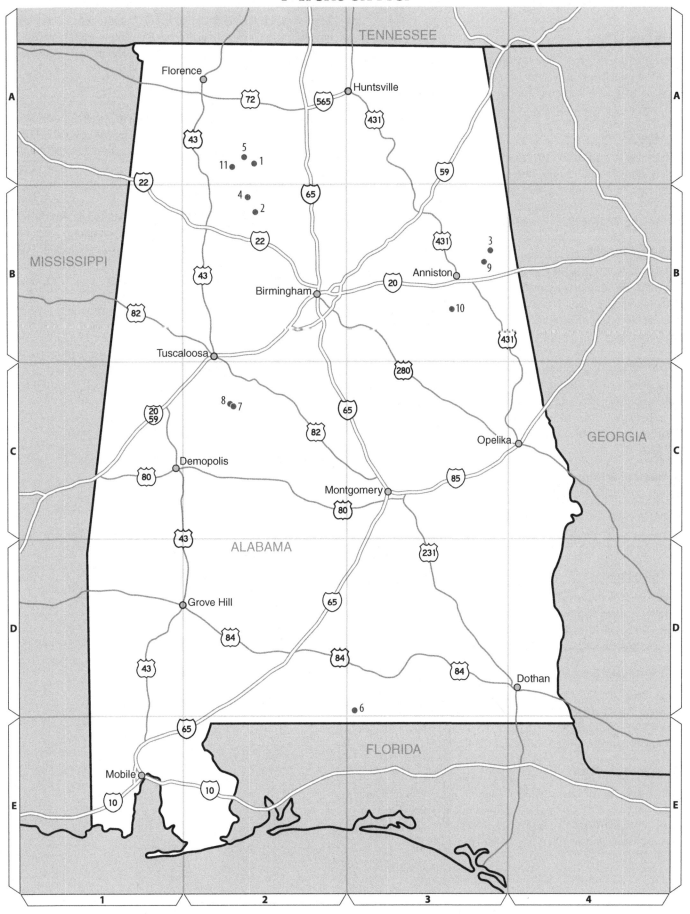

Alabama Camping Areas

1 • Brushy Lake

Total sites: 13; RV sites: 13; Central water; Flush toilets; Showers; No RV dump; Reservations not accepted; Max length: 18ft; Open all year; Tent & RV camping: $5; Elev: 682ft/208m; Tel: 205-489-5111; Nearest town: Moulton. GPS: 34.297225, -87.272131

2 • Clear Creek

Total sites: 102; RV sites: 102; Elec sites: 18; Water at site; Flush toilets; Showers; RV dump; Reservations accepted; Open Mar-Oct; Tent & RV camping: $24-26; Elev: 725ft/221m; Tel: 205-384-4792; Nearest town: Jasper; Notes: Group site: $50. GPS: 34.014404, -87.265625

3 • Coleman Lake

Total sites: 39; RV sites: 39; Elec sites: 39; Water at site; Flush toilets; Showers; RV dump; Reservations not accepted; Max length: 35ft; Open Mar-Dec; Tents: $8/RVs: $16; Elev: 1220ft/372m; Tel: 256-463-2272; Nearest town: Jacksonville. GPS: 33.784180, -85.557617

4 • Corinth

Total sites: 52; RV sites: 52; Elec sites: 52; Water at site; Flush toilets; Showers; RV dump; Reservations not accepted; Open Mar-Oct; Tents: $17/RVs: $28; Elev: 630ft/192m; Tel: 205-489-3165; Nearest town: Double Springs; Notes: 52 FHU. GPS: 34.101279, -87.320193

5 • McDougle Hunt Camp

Total sites: 10; RV sites: 10; Central water; Vault toilets; No showers; No RV dump; Max length: 22ft; Open all year; Tent & RV camping: Free; Elev: 945ft/288m; Tel: 205-489-5111; Nearest town: Moulton. GPS: 34.338000, -87.346000

6 • Open Pond

Total sites: 74; RV sites: 65; Elec sites: 65; Water at site; Flush toilets; Showers; RV dump; Reservations not accepted; Open all year; Tents: $8/RVs: $16; Elev: 236ft/72m; Tel: 334-222-2555; Nearest town: Lockhart. GPS: 31.089101, -86.549068

7 • Payne Lake Eastside

Total sites: 30; RV sites: 30; Central water; Vault toilets; No showers; No RV dump; Reservations not accepted; Open all year; Tents: $5/RVs: $12; Elev: 351ft/107m; Tel: 205-926-9765; Nearest town: Duncanville. GPS: 32.885577, -87.440597

8 • Payne Lake West

Total sites: 18; RV sites: 18; Elec sites: 7; Water at site; Flush toilets; Showers; RV dump; Reservations not accepted; Open all year; Tents: $5/RVs: $12-18; Elev: 299ft/91m; Tel: 205-926-9765; Nearest town: Duncanville. GPS: 32.888498, -87.443565

9 • Pine Glen

Total sites: 21; RV sites: 21; No water; Vault toilets; Reservations not accepted; Open all year; Tent & RV camping: $3; Elev: 1037ft/316m; Tel: 256-463-2272; Nearest town: Heflin. GPS: 33.724609, -85.603271

10 • Turnipseed

Total sites: 8; RV sites: 8; No water; Vault toilets; Reservations not accepted; Open Mar-Nov; Tent & RV camping: $5; Elev: 1184ft/361m; Tel: 256-362-2909; Nearest town: Oxford. GPS: 33.444041, -85.841401

11 • Wolf Pen Hunters Camp

Total sites: 9; RV sites: 9; Central water; Vault toilets; No showers; No RV dump; Open all year; Tent & RV camping: Free; Elev: 902ft/275m; Tel: 205-489-5111; Nearest town: Haleyville. GPS: 34.281641, -87.435219

Arizona

NEVADA

UTAH

CO

NM

ARIZONA

15

61 ●

60 ●   ● 39   **89**   **160**

122 ●

89

93

Kingman ●   **40**

71 ●   ● 16
64 ●   44 ●   ● 70
41 ●   132 ●   ● Flagstaff
24,87   23 ●   68 ●
80 ●   7,43,88 ●
37,42 ●

40

191

91 ● ● 82
4 ●   136 ●   92 ●   14 ●   25 ●   **A** 8,33,83   **77**
134 ●   53,79 ●   28 ●   29 ●   98 ●   96,112,115
77 ●   65 ●   66 ●   **260**
52 ●   76,129 ●   22 ●
58 ●   90 ●   **A** 11,46   Springerville ●
26,111   2,50   130   1,126   72 ●
32   109 ●   10,99 ●
27 ●   56 ●   135 ●   3 ●
17 ●   81 ●   105 ●   107 ●   5,18,35,49,94 ●   ● 78
97 ●   **87**   101 ●   **60**   9,19,38,40,55,93 ●   125 ●
100 ●   103 ●   108 ●   123 ●   67 ●   51 ●
75 ●   20 ●   102 ●   63 ●   54 ●   13 ●
21,124 ●   118 ●

Phoenix ●

85 ●   73,127 ●
74,119 ●   89,128 ●   **70**   48 ●   30 ●
12 ●

10

8   **79**   **77**

95 ● 113 ●
34,57,110 ●   ● 6
86 ●   117 ●

Yuma ●

10   114 ● 104 ●   **10**
47 ● ● 45
84 ●

Tucson ●

19   106 ● 59,116,120 ●
31 ●   121,131 ●   62 ●
15 ●   36 ●

133 ●   ● 69

Gulf of
California

MEXICO

NEVADA

1   2   3   4

Arizona Camping Areas

1 • Airplane Flat

Total sites: 12; RV sites: 12; No water; Vault toilets; Reservations not accepted; Max length: 16ft; Stay limit: 14 days; Open May-Oct; Tent & RV camping: Free; Elev: 6608ft/2014m; Tel: 928-462-4300; Nearest town: Young. GPS: 34.283375, -110.809621

2 • Alderwood

Total sites: 5; RV sites: 5; No water; Vault toilets; Reservations not accepted; Max length: 16ft; Stay limit: 14 days; Open all year; Tent & RV camping: Free; Elev: 5243ft/1598m; Tel: 928-474-7900; Nearest town: Young; Notes: 4x4 advised after storms. GPS: 34.205825, -110.980587

3 • Alpine Divide

Total sites: 12; RV sites: 12; No water; Vault toilets; Reservations not accepted; Max length: 12ft; Open May-Sep; Tent & RV camping: $10; Elev: 8550ft/2606m; Tel: 928-339-5000; Nearest town: Alpine. GPS: 33.893311, -109.153320

4 • Alto Pit OHV

Total sites: 11; RV sites: 11; No toilets; No showers; No RV dump; Reservations not accepted; Max length: 40ft; Open all year; Tent & RV camping: $14; Elev: 6089ft/1856m; Tel: 928-443-8000; Nearest town: Prescott. GPS: 34.588819, -112.561023

5 • Apache Trout

Total sites: 124; RV sites: 44; Elec sites: 44; Water at site; Flush toilets; Showers; RV dump; Reservations accepted; Max length: 80ft; Open May-Sep; Tents: $26/RVs: $42; Elev: 9147ft/2788m; Tel: 928-333-6200; Nearest town: Eagar; Notes: 44 FHU, Group sites $50-$350. GPS: 33.868887, -109.416307

6 • Arcadia

Total sites: 19; RV sites: 19; No water; Vault toilets; Reservations not accepted; Max length: 22ft; Stay limit: 14 days; Open all year; Tent & RV camping: $10; Elev: 6673ft/2034m; Tel: 928-428-4150; Nearest town: Safford; Notes: Reservable group site. GPS: 32.648247, -109.819429

7 • Ashurst Lake

Total sites: 25; RV sites: 25; Central water; Vault toilets; No showers; No RV dump; Reservations not accepted; Max length: 35ft; Stay limit: 14 days; Generator hours: 0600-2200; Open May-Oct; Tent & RV camping: $20; Elev: 7136ft/2175m; Tel: 928-774-1147; Nearest town: Flagstaff; Notes: Open fee-free with no amenities Nov-Apr when road is open. GPS: 35.019377, -111.408529

8 • Aspen

Total sites: 148; RV sites: 148; Central water; Vault toilets; No showers; RV dump; Reservations accepted; Open May-Oct; Tent & RV camping: $22; Elev: 7628ft/2325m; Tel: 928-535-9233; Nearest town: Payson. GPS: 34.327085, -110.945989

9 • Aspen

Total sites: 6; RV sites: 6; Central water; Vault toilets; No showers; No RV dump; Reservations not accepted; Tent & RV camping: $14; Elev: 7858ft/2395m; Tel: 928-339-5000; Nearest town: Heber. GPS: 33.807617, -109.314573

10 • Benny Creek

Total sites: 24; RV sites: 24; Central water; Vault toilets; No showers; RV dump; Reservations not accepted; Max length: 24ft; Stay limit: 14 days; Open May-Sep; Tent & RV camping: $12; Elev: 8274ft/2522m; Tel: 928-735-7313; Nearest town: Greer; Notes: Reservable group sites $40-$50. GPS: 34.044379, -109.449777

11 • Black Canyon Rim

Total sites: 21; RV sites: 21; Central water; Vault toilets; No showers; No RV dump; Reservations accepted; Max length: 40ft; Open May-Oct; Tent & RV camping: $18; Elev: 7572ft/2308m; Tel: 928-535-7300; Nearest town: Forest Lakes. GPS: 34.304365, -110.743654

12 • Blackjack

Total sites: 10; RV sites: 10; No water; Vault toilets; Reservations not accepted; Stay limit: 14 days; Open all year; Tent & RV camping: Free; Elev: 6276ft/1913m; Tel: 928-687-8600; Nearest town: Clifton. GPS: 33.056422, -109.080427

13 • Blue Crossing

Total sites: 4; RV sites: 4; No water; Vault toilets; Reservations not accepted; Max length: 16ft; Stay limit: 14 days; Open Apr-Nov; Tent & RV camping: Free; Elev: 5824ft/1775m; Tel: 928-339-5000; Nearest town: Alpine; Notes: 2 sites with Adirondack shelters. GPS: 33.627892, -109.098102

14 • Blue Ridge

Total sites: 10; RV sites: 10; Central water; Vault toilets; No showers; No RV dump; Reservations not accepted; Max length: 22ft; Generator hours: 0600-2200; Open May-Sep; Tent & RV camping: $16; Elev: 6962ft/2122m; Tel: 928-477-2255; Nearest town: Winslow. GPS: 34.591574, -111.200928

15 • Bog Springs

Total sites: 13; RV sites: 13; Potable water; Vault toilets; No showers; No RV dump; Reservations not accepted; Max length: 22ft; Stay limit: 14 days; Generator hours: 0600-2200; Open all year; Tent & RV camping: $10; Elev: 5121ft/1561m; Tel: 520-281-2296; Nearest town: Green Valley. GPS: 31.726807, -110.875000

16 • Bonito

Total sites: 44; RV sites: 44; Central water; Flush toilets; No showers; No RV dump; Reservations not accepted; Stay limit: 14 days; Open May-Oct; Tent & RV camping: $26; Elev: 6952ft/2119m; Tel: 928-526-0866; Nearest town: Flagstaff; Notes: Concession. GPS: 35.369513, -111.541524

17 • Bronco Trailhead

Total sites: 40; RV sites: 40; No water; Vault toilets; Max length: 32ft; Open all year; Tent & RV camping: Free; Elev: 3707ft/1130m;

Tel: 480-595-3300; Nearest town: Carefree; Notes: Horse corrals, stock water. GPS: 33.934822, -111.820501

18 • Brookchar

Total sites: 13; Central water; Flush toilets; No showers; RV dump; Reservations accepted; Open May-Oct; Tents only: $16; Elev: 9012ft/2747m; Tel: 928-735-7313; Nearest town: Eagar. GPS: 33.875303, -109.414358

19 • Buffalo Crossing

Total sites: 16; RV sites: 16; No water; Vault toilets; Reservations not accepted; Stay limit: 14 days; Open May-Oct; Tent & RV camping: $14; Elev: 7648ft/2331m; Tel: 928-339-5000; Nearest town: Alpine. GPS: 33.767822, -109.355225

20 • Burnt Corral Main

Total sites: 82; RV sites: 82; Central water; Vault toilets; No showers; No RV dump; Reservations not accepted; Max length: 22ft; Stay limit: 14 days; Open all year; Tent & RV camping: $20; Elev: 1959ft/597m; Tel: 602-225-5395; Nearest town: Roosevelt; Notes. Not recommended for trailers over 22ft. GPS: 33.626573, -111.204764

21 • Canyon Lake Marina

Total sites: 46; RV sites: 28; Elec sites: 28; Water at site; Flush toilets; Showers; No RV dump; Reservations accepted; Open all year; Tents: $35-40/RVs: $60-65; Elev: 1670ft/509m; Tel: 480-610-3300; Nearest town: Apache Jct; Notes: Concessionaire, RV pump-out available - $20. GPS: 33.534424, -111.422119

22 • Canyon Point

Total sites: 113; RV sites: 113; Elec sites: 32; Central water; Flush toilets; Pay showers; RV dump; Reservations accepted; Max length: 75ft; Open May-Oct; Tents: $25/RVs: $25-30; Elev: 7703ft/2348m; Tel: 928-535-9233; Nearest town: Greer; Notes: Dump fee $7, Group sites $71-$225. GPS: 34.323288, -110.825644

23 • Canyon Vista

Total sites: 11; RV sites: 11; Central water; Vault toilets; No showers; No RV dump; Reservations not accepted; Max length: 22ft; Stay limit: 14 days; Open May-Oct; Tent & RV camping: $22; Elev: 6841ft/2085m; Tel: 928-774-1147; Nearest town: Flagstaff; Notes: Concession. GPS: 35.123901, -111.598352

24 • Cave Springs

Total sites: 82; RV sites: 82; Central water; Flush toilets; Pay showers; No RV dump; Reservations accepted; Max length: 36ft; Stay limit: 14 days; Open Apr-Oct; Tent & RV camping: $22; Elev: 5472ft/1668m; Tel: 928-282-1629; Nearest town: Safford; Notes: Concession. GPS: 34.996437, -111.739522

25 • Chevelon Crossing

Total sites: 6; No water; Vault toilets; Reservations not accepted; Max length: 16ft; Stay limit: 14 days; Open all year; Tents only: Free; Elev: 6224ft/1897m; Tel: 928-535-7300; Nearest town: Heber. GPS: 34.590746, -110.787833

26 • Christopher Creek

Total sites: 43; RV sites: 43; Central water; No toilets; No showers; No RV dump; Reservations accepted; Max length: 22ft; Open Apr-Oct; Tent & RV camping: $22; Elev: 5715ft/1742m; Tel: 928-474-7900; Nearest town: Payson; Notes: Group site: $70. GPS: 34.307747, -111.035638

27 • Civilian Conservation Corps

Total sites: 10; RV sites: 10; No water; No toilets; Max length: 16ft; Stay limit: 14 days; Open all year; Tent & RV camping: $16; Elev: 3373ft/1028m; Tel: 480-595-3300; Nearest town: Carefree. GPS: 33.970625, -111.865476

28 • Clear Creek

Total sites: 18; RV sites: 18; Central water; Vault toilets; No showers; No RV dump; Reservations not accepted; Max length: 32ft; Open all year; Tent & RV camping: $18; Elev: 3240ft/988m; Tel: 928-204-0028; Nearest town: Camp Verde. GPS: 34.516072, -111.767313

29 • Clint's Well

Total sites: 7; RV sites: 7; No water; Vault toilets; Reservations not accepted; Max length: 22ft; Generator hours: 0600-2200; Open all year; Tent & RV camping: $8; Elev: 6900ft/2103m; Tel: 928-477-2255; Nearest town: Flagstaff. GPS: 34.554162, -111.311846

30 • Coal Creek

Total sites: 5; RV sites: 5; No water; Vault toilets; Reservations not accepted; Max length: 16ft; Stay limit: 14 days; Open all year; Tent & RV camping: Free; Elev: 5814ft/1772m; Tel: 928-687-8600; Nearest town: Clifton. GPS: 33.103033, -109.060386

31 • Cochise Stronghold

Total sites: 10; RV sites: 10; No water; Vault toilets; Reservations not accepted; Max length: 22ft; Stay limit: 14 days; Open Sep-May; Tent & RV camping: $10; Elev: 4934ft/1504m; Tel: 520-364-3468; Nearest town: Sunsites. GPS: 31.922616, -109.967567

32 • Colcord Ridge

Total sites: 8; RV sites: 8; No water; Vault toilets; Reservations not accepted; Max length: 32ft; Stay limit: 14 days; Open May-Oct; Tent & RV camping: Free; Elev: 7615ft/2321m; Tel: 928-462-4300; Nearest town: Young. GPS: 34.262172, -110.843822

33 • Crook

Total sites: 26; RV sites: 26; Central water; Vault toilets; No showers; No RV dump; Reservations not accepted; Max length: 32ft; Open May-Oct; Tent & RV camping: $20; Elev: 7631ft/2326m; Tel: 928-535-7300; Nearest town: Forest Lakes; Notes: 2 reservable group sites $270, Single sites available if not in use by group. GPS: 34.317763, -110.942401

34 • Cunningham

Total sites: 10; RV sites: 10; No water; Vault toilets; Reservations not accepted; Max length: 22ft; Stay limit: 14 days; Open Apr-Nov; Tent & RV camping: $10; Elev: 8884ft/2708m; Tel: 928-428-4150; Nearest town: Safford. GPS: 32.678151, -109.894197

35 • Cutthroat

Total sites: 18; Central water; Flush toilets; Showers; RV dump; Reservations accepted; Open Apr-Sep; Tents only: $16; Elev: 9094ft/2772m; Tel: 928-735-7313; Nearest town: Eagar. GPS: 33.873049, -109.418091

36 • Cypress Park

Total sites: 7; RV sites: 7; No water; Vault toilets; Reservations not accepted; Max length: 16ft; Stay limit: 14 days; Open Mar-Oct; Tent & RV camping: $10; Elev: 6201ft/1890m; Tel: 520-364-3468; Nearest town: Douglas. GPS: 31.775325, -109.312022

37 • Dairy Springs

Total sites: 30; RV sites: 30; Central water; Vault toilets; No showers; No RV dump; Reservations accepted; Max length: 35ft; Open May-Oct; Tent & RV camping: $22; Elev: 7162ft/2183m; Tel: 928-226-0493; Nearest town: Flagstaff; Notes: Group fee: $110. GPS: 34.955878, -111.484565

38 • Deer Creek (East Fork Black River)

Total sites: 6; Central water; Vault toilets; No showers; No RV dump; Reservations not accepted; Stay limit: 14 days; Open May-Sep; Tents only: $14; Elev: 7864ft/2397m; Tel: 928-339-5000; Nearest town: Alpine. GPS: 33.805526, -109.319258

39 • Demotte

Total sites: 38; RV sites: 38; Central water; Vault toilets; No showers; No RV dump; Reservations accepted; Max length: 22ft; Open Apr-Oct; Tent & RV camping: $22; Elev: 8806ft/2684m; Tel: 520-643-7395; Nearest town: Jacob Lake. GPS: 36.410465, -112.134742

40 • Diamond Rock

Total sites: 12; RV sites: 12; Central water; Vault toilets; No showers; No RV dump; Reservations not accepted; Max length: 12ft; Open May-Oct; Tent & RV camping: $14; Elev: 7930ft/2417m; Tel: 928-339-5000; Nearest town: Alpine; Notes: 3 sites with shelters. GPS: 33.818843, -109.300594

41 • Dogtown Lake

Total sites: 54; RV sites: 54; Central water; Vault toilets; No showers; No RV dump; Reservations accepted; Max length: 35ft; Open May-Sep; Tent & RV camping: $24; Elev: 7096ft/2163m; Tel: 928-699-1239; Nearest town: Williams; Notes: Group site: $276. GPS: 35.211545, -112.123084

42 • Double Springs

Total sites: 15; RV sites: 15; Central water; Vault toilets; No showers; No RV dump; Reservations not accepted; Max length: 35ft; Open May-Oct; Tent & RV camping: $20; Elev: 7208ft/2197m; Tel: 928-774-1147; Nearest town: Flagstaff. GPS: 34.942117, -111.493817

43 • Forked Pine

Total sites: 25; RV sites: 25; Central water; Vault toilets; No showers; No RV dump; Reservations not accepted; Max length: 35ft; Stay limit: 14 days; Open Jun-Oct; Tent & RV camping: $20; Elev: 7129ft/2173m; Tel: 928-774-1147; Nearest town: Flagstaff; Notes: No water in winter. GPS: 35.021240, -111.398926

44 • Freidlein Prairie

Total sites: 14; RV sites: 14; No water; No toilets; Reservations not accepted; Tent & RV camping: Free; Elev: 7552ft/2302m; Tel: 928-526-0866; Nearest town: Flagstaff; Notes: Small RVs/Tents. GPS: 35.282792, -111.718957

45 • General Hitchcock

Total sites: 11; No water; Vault toilets; Reservations not accepted; Stay limit: 14 days; Open May-Oct; Tents only: $20; Elev: 6037ft/1840m; Tel: 520-749-8700; Nearest town: Tucson. GPS: 32.377408, -110.686011

46 • Gentry

Total sites: 5; RV sites: 5; No water; Vault toilets; Reservations accepted; Max length: 15ft; Stay limit: 14 days; Open all year; Tent & RV camping: $18; Elev: 7694ft/2345m; Tel: 928-535-7300; Nearest town: Payson; Notes: Reservable as 1 group site: $90. GPS: 34.301271, -110.713246

47 • Gordon Hirabayashi

Total sites: 12; RV sites: 12; No water; Vault toilets; Reservations not accepted; Max length: 22ft; Stay limit: 14 days; Open Nov-Apr; Tent & RV camping: $20; Elev: 4872ft/1485m; Tel: 520-749-8700; Nearest town: Tucson; Notes: Horse corral. GPS: 32.338069, -110.718719

48 • Granville

Total sites: 11; RV sites: 11; Central water; Vault toilets; No showers; No RV dump; Reservations not accepted; Max length: 16ft; Stay limit: 14 days; Open Apr-Nov; Tent & RV camping: Free; Elev: 6713ft/2046m; Tel: 928-687-8600; Nearest town: Clifton. GPS: 33.188315, -109.383288

49 • Grayling

Total sites: 23; RV sites: 23; Central water; Flush toilets; Showers; RV dump; Reservations accepted; Max length: 22ft; Open May-Oct; Tent & RV camping: $20; Elev: 9068ft/2764m; Tel: 928-537-8888; Nearest town: Eagar. GPS: 33.872859, -109.413159

50 • Haigler Canyon

Total sites: 14; RV sites: 14; No water; Vault toilets; RV dump; Reservations not accepted; Max length: 20ft; Stay limit: 14 days; Open May-Oct; Tent & RV camping: $16; Elev: 5325ft/1623m; Tel: 928-462-4300; Nearest town: Young; Notes: Tonto Pass required: $8/day or $80/year, Dump fee (Ponderosa CG): $5. GPS: 34.219551, -110.963584

51 • Hannagan

Total sites: 8; RV sites: 8; Central water; Vault toilets; No showers; No RV dump; Reservations not accepted; Max length: 16ft; Stay limit: 14 days; Open May-Sep; Tent & RV camping: Donation; Elev: 9262ft/2823m; Tel: 928-339-5000; Nearest town: Alpine. GPS: 33.635859, -109.322315

52 • Hazlett Hollow

Total sites: 15; Central water; Vault toilets; No showers; No RV dump; Reservations not accepted; Stay limit: 14 days; Generator hours: 0600-2200; Open May-Sep; Elev: 6047ft/1843m; Tel: 928-443-8000; Nearest town: Crown King; Notes: Shelter: $10, High clearance vehicle recommended. GPS: 34.175399, -112.276664

53 • Hilltop

Total sites: 38; RV sites: 38; Central water; Vault toilets; No showers; No RV dump; Reservations not accepted; Max length: 40ft; Stay limit: 14 days; Generator hours: 0600-2200; Open Apr-Oct; Tent & RV camping: $18; Elev: 5627ft/1715m; Tel: 928-443-8000; Nearest town: Prescott. GPS: 34.510464, -112.380867

54 • Honeymoon

Total sites: 4; RV sites: 4; No water; Vault toilets; Reservations not accepted; Max length: 16ft; Stay limit: 14 days; Open all year; Tent & RV camping: Free; Elev: 5456ft/1663m; Tel: 928-687-8600; Nearest town: Clifton. GPS: 33.475351, -109.481205

55 • Horse Springs

Total sites: 27; RV sites: 27; Central water; Vault toilets; No showers; No RV dump; Reservations not accepted; Stay limit: 14 days; Open May-Oct; Tent & RV camping: $16; Elev: 7664ft/2336m; Tel: 928-339-5000; Nearest town: Alpine. GPS: 33.787814, -109.345291

56 • Horseshoe

Total sites: 12; RV sites: 12; No water; Vault toilets; Reservations not accepted; Max length: 16ft; Stay limit: 14 days; Open all year; Tent & RV camping: $16; Elev: 1916ft/584m; Tel: 480-595-3300; Nearest town: Carefree. GPS: 33.977571, -111.716941

57 • Hospital Flat

Total sites: 10; Vault toilets; Reservations not accepted; Stay limit: 14 days; Open Apr-Nov; Tents only: $10; Elev: 9042ft/2756m; Tel: 928-428-4150; Nearest town: Safford; Notes: Group site: $25. GPS: 32.665624, -109.874801

58 • Houston Mesa

Total sites: 45; RV sites: 28; Central water; Flush toilets; Pay showers; RV dump; Reservations accepted; Max length: 40ft; Open all year; Tent & RV camping: $27; Elev: 5056ft/1541m; Tel: 928-468-7135; Nearest town: Payson; Notes: RV water: $2, Dump fee: $3. GPS: 34.270706, -111.319481

59 • Idlewilde

Total sites: 9; RV sites: 9; No water; Vault toilets; Reservations not accepted; Max length: 16ft; Stay limit: 14 days; Open all year; Tent & RV camping: $20; Elev: 4944ft/1507m; Tel: 520-364-3468; Nearest town: Portal; Notes: No water in winter. GPS: 31.898233, -109.161968

60 • Indian Hollow

Total sites: 3; RV sites: 3; No water; Vault toilets; Reservations not accepted; Open all year; Tent & RV camping: Free; Elev: 6332ft/1930m; Tel: 928 643-7395; Nearest town: Grand Canyon; Notes: Not suitable for large RVs. GPS: 36.461789, -112.484467

61 • Jacob Lake

Total sites: 51; RV sites: 51; Central water; Vault toilets; No showers; No RV dump; Reservations accepted; Max length: 32ft; Open May-Oct; Tent & RV camping: $22; Elev: 7936ft/2419m; Tel: 928-643-7395; Nearest town: Jacob Lake; Notes: Group sites: $90-$165. GPS: 36.716112, -112.214947

62 • John Hands

Total sites: 6; No water; Vault toilets; Reservations not accepted; Open all year; Tents only: Free; Elev: 5610ft/1710m; Tel: 520-364-3468; Nearest town: Rodeo NM. GPS: 31.878000, -109.222000

63 • Jones Water

Total sites: 12; RV sites: 12; No water; Vault toilets; Reservations not accepted; Max length: 20ft; Stay limit: 14 days; Open all year; Tent & RV camping: Free; Elev: 4193ft/1278m; Tel: 928-402-6200; Nearest town: Globe. GPS: 33.592046, -110.642811

64 • Kaibab Lake

Total sites: 63; RV sites: 63; Central water; Vault toilets; No showers; RV dump; Reservations accepted; Max length: 40ft; Open May-Sep; Tent & RV camping: $24; Elev: 6841ft/2085m; Tel: 928-635-5600; Nearest town: Williams; Notes: 3 group sites $80-$204. GPS: 35.281498, -112.157068

65 • Kehl Springs Camp

Total sites: 8; RV sites: 8; No water; Vault toilets; Reservations not accepted; Max length: 22ft; Generator hours: 0600-2200; Open all year; Tent & RV camping: Free; Elev: 7477ft/2279m; Tel: 928-477-2255; Nearest town: Clints Well. GPS: 34.435053, -111.317574

66 • Knoll Lake

Total sites: 33; RV sites: 33; Central water; Vault toilets; No showers; No RV dump; Reservations not accepted; Max length: 32ft; Generator hours: 0600-2200; Open May-Sep; Tent & RV camping: $20; Elev: 7503ft/2287m; Tel: 928-477-2255; Nearest town: Blue Ridge. GPS: 34.426539, -111.093542

67 • KP Cienega

Total sites: 5; RV sites: 5; Central water; Vault toilets; No showers; No RV dump; Reservations not accepted; Max length: 16ft; Stay limit: 14 days; Open May-Sep; Tent & RV camping: Free; Elev: 8986ft/2739m; Tel: 928-339-5000; Nearest town: Alpine. GPS: 33.576183, -109.355957

68 • Lakeview

Total sites: 30; RV sites: 30; Central water; Vault toilets; No showers; No RV dump; Reservations not accepted; Max length: 28ft; Generator hours: 0600-2200; Open May-Oct; Tent & RV camping: $24; Elev: 6992ft/2131m; Tel: 928-774-1147; Nearest town: Flagstaff. GPS: 35.066959, -111.496548

69 • Lakeview

Total sites: 65; RV sites: 23; Central water; Vault toilets; No showers; No RV dump; Reservations not accepted; Max length: 36ft; Open all year; Tent & RV camping: $20; Elev: 5489ft/1673m; Tel: 520-378-0311; Nearest town: Sonoita. GPS: 31.427734, -110.450684

70 • Little Elden Springs Horsecamp

Total sites: 15; RV sites: 15; Central water; No toilets; No showers; No RV dump; Reservations accepted; Max length: 35ft; Open May-Oct; Tent & RV camping: $24; Elev: 7316ft/2230m; Tel: 928-226-0493; Nearest town: Page; Notes: Equestrian use only. GPS: 35.280117, -111.585505

71 • Lockett Meadow

Total sites: 17; RV sites: 19; No water; Vault toilets; Reservations not accepted; Max length: 18ft; Stay limit: 14 days; Generator hours: 0600-2200; Open Jun-Oct; Tent & RV camping: $18; Elev: 8563ft/2610m; Tel: 928-774-1147; Nearest town: Flagstaff. GPS: 35.358046, -111.620580

72 • Los Burros

Total sites: 10; RV sites: 10; No water; Vault toilets; Reservations not accepted; Max length: 22ft; Stay limit: 14 days; Open May-Oct; Tent & RV camping: Free; Elev: 7890ft/2405m; Tel: 928-368-2100; Nearest town: Lakeside. GPS: 34.140878, -109.777324

73 • Lower Juan Miller

Total sites: 4; RV sites: 4; No water; Vault toilets; Reservations not accepted; Max length: 16ft; Stay limit: 14 days; Open all year; Tent & RV camping: Free; Elev: 5718ft/1743m; Tel: 928-687-8600; Nearest town: Clifton. GPS: 33.267362, -109.340611

74 • Lower Pinal

Total sites: 16; RV sites: 16; Central water; Vault toilets; No showers; No RV dump; Reservations not accepted; Max length: 20ft; Stay limit: 14 days; Open May-Nov; Tent & RV camping: Free; Elev: 7539ft/2298m; Tel: 928-402-6200; Nearest town: Globe; Notes: Narrow winding mountain gravel road. GPS: 33.287354, -110.830322

75 • Lower Salt River RA - Coon Bluff

Total sites: 5; RV sites: 5; No water; Vault toilets; Reservations not accepted; Max length: 40ft; Open Oct-Apr; Tent & RV camping: Free; Elev: 1332ft/406m; Tel: 602-225-5200; Nearest town: Mesa; Notes: Overnight camping allowed Oct-Apr on Friday and Saturday nights and Sunday nights before holidays, Requires a Tonto pass - $8/day. GPS: 33.547274, -111.646137

76 • Lower Tonto Creek

Total sites: 9; RV sites: 9; Central water; Vault toilets; No showers; No RV dump; Reservations not accepted; Max length: 16ft; Stay limit: 14 days; Open all year; Tent & RV camping: $19; Elev: 5473ft/1668m; Tel: 928 474-7900; Nearest town: Payson. GPS: 34.338524, -111.096145

77 • Lower Wolf Creek

Total sites: 20; RV sites: 20; No water; Vault toilets; Reservations not accepted; Max length: 32ft; Stay limit: 14 days; Generator hours: 0600-2200; Open May-Oct; Tent & RV camping: $10; Elev: 6165ft/1879m; Tel: 928-443-8000; Nearest town: Prescott. GPS: 34.454839, -112.454613

78 • Luna Lake

Total sites: 50; RV sites: 50; Central water; Vault toilets; No showers; No RV dump; Reservations accepted; Max length: 32ft; Open May-Oct; Tent & RV camping: $16; Elev: 8038ft/2450m; Tel: 928-537-8888; Nearest town: Alpine; Notes: Group site: $60-$125. GPS: 33.835957, -109.081978

79 • Lynx Lake

Total sites: 36; RV sites: 36; Central water; Flush toilets; Reservations accepted; Max length: 40ft; Open Apr-Oct; Tent & RV camping: $18; Elev: 5620ft/1713m; Tel: 928-443-8000; Nearest town: Prescott. GPS: 34.517308, -112.389036

80 • Manzanita

Total sites: 18; Central water; Vault toilets; No showers; No RV dump; Reservations accepted; Open all year; Tents only: $22; Elev: 4801ft/1463m; Tel: 928-204-2034; Nearest town: Red Rock; Notes: Tents and small sleep-in vehicles only - no trailers or RVs allowed. GPS: 34.936279, -111.744873

81 • Mesquite

Total sites: 12; RV sites: 6; No water; Vault toilets; Reservations not accepted; Stay limit: 14 days; Open all year; Tent & RV camping: $16; Elev: 1890ft/576m; Tel: 480-595-3300; Nearest town: Carefree; Notes: Trailers not recommended. GPS: 33.964174, -111.716373

82 • Mingus Mountain

Total sites: 30; RV sites: 19; Elec sites: 19; No water; Vault toilets; Reservations not accepted; Max length: 24ft; Stay limit: 14 days; Generator hours: 0600-2200; Open May-Oct; Tents: $10/RVs: $14; Elev: 7477ft/2279m; Tel: 928-567-4121; Nearest town: Clarkdale. GPS: 34.691942, -112.117915

83 • Mogollon

Total sites: 26; RV sites: 26; Central water; Vault toilets; No showers; No RV dump; Reservations accepted; Max length: 32ft; Open May-Oct; Tent & RV camping: $18; Elev: 7658ft/2334m; Tel: 928-535-7300; Nearest town: Forest Lakes. GPS: 34.321425, -110.956745

84 • Molino Basin

Total sites: 37; RV sites: 37; No water; Vault toilets; Reservations not accepted; Max length: 22ft; Open Oct-Apr; Tent & RV camping: $20; Elev: 4396ft/1340m; Tel: 520-749-8700; Nearest town: Tucson. GPS: 32.337091, -110.693196

85 • Oak Flat

Total sites: 16; RV sites: 16; Vault toilets; Reservations not accepted; Max length: 30ft; Stay limit: 14 days; Open all year; Tent & RV camping: Free; Elev: 3934ft/1199m; Tel: 928-402-6200; Nearest town: Superior. GPS: 33.307879, -111.050359

86 • Peppersauce

Total sites: 17; RV sites: 17; Central water; Vault toilets; No showers; No RV dump; Reservations not accepted; Max length:

22ft; Stay limit: 14 days; Open all year; Tent & RV camping: $15; Elev: 4626ft/1410m; Tel: 520-749-8700; Nearest town: Oracle. GPS: 32.538424, -110.716501

87 • Pine Flat

Total sites: 56; RV sites: 56; Central water; Vault toilets; No showers; No RV dump; Reservations accepted; Max length: 30ft; Open Apr-Oct; Tent & RV camping: $22; Elev: 5722ft/1744m; Tel: 928-282-3233; Nearest town: Sedona. GPS: 35.012575, -111.737288

88 • Pinegrove

Total sites: 46; RV sites: 46; Central water; Flush toilets; Pay showers; RV dump; Reservations accepted; Max length: 45ft; Generator hours: 0600-2200; Open May-Oct; Tent & RV camping: $26; Elev: 6939ft/2115m; Tel: 928-226-0493; Nearest town: Flagstaff. GPS: 35.027479, -111.462044

89 • Pioneer Pass

Total sites: 23; RV sites: 23; No water; Vault toilets; Reservations not accepted; Max length: 18ft; Stay limit: 14 days; Open May-Nov; Tent & RV camping: Free; Elev: 5886ft/1794m; Tel: 928-4-2-6200; Nearest town: Globe. GPS: 33.279701, -110.796712

90 • Ponderosa

Total sites: 48; RV sites: 48; Central water; Vault toilets; No showers; No RV dump; Reservations accepted; Max length: 34ft; Open Apr-Oct; Tent & RV camping: $20; Elev: 5728ft/1746m; Tel: 928-468-7135; Nearest town: Payson; Notes: 2 group sites: $100. GPS: 34.298919, -111.114209

91 • Potato Patch

Total sites: 40; RV sites: 40; Elec sites: 12; Central water; Vault toilets; No showers; No RV dump; Reservations accepted; Max length: 40ft; Stay limit: 14 days; Generator hours: 0600-2200; Open May-Oct; Tents: $14/RVs: $14-18; Elev: 7011ft/2137m; Tel: 928-567-4121; Nearest town: Clarkdale; Notes: May not fill RV water tanks. GPS: 34.709264, -112.155644

92 • Powell Springs

Total sites: 11; RV sites: 11; No water; Vault toilets; Reservations not accepted; Max length: 40ft; Stay limit: 14 days; Generator hours: 0600-2200; Open all year; Tent & RV camping: Free; Elev: 5331ft/1625m; Tel: 928-567-4121; Nearest town: Camp Verde. GPS: 34.578051, -112.068914

93 • Raccoon

Total sites: 10; Central water; Vault toilets; No showers; No RV dump; Reservations not accepted; Stay limit: 14 days; Open May-Oct; Tents only: $14; Elev: 7785ft/2373m; Tel: 928-339-5000; Nearest town: Alpine. GPS: 33.798679, -109.329398

94 • Rainbow

Total sites: 161; RV sites: 161; Central water; Flush toilets; Showers; RV dump; Reservations accepted; Max length: 32ft; Open May-Oct; Tent & RV camping: $20-22; Elev: 9157ft/2791m;

Tel: 928-333-6200; Nearest town: Greer; Notes: Group site: $80. GPS: 33.875583, -109.402529

95 • Riggs Flat

Total sites: 31; RV sites: 31; No water; Vault toilets; Reservations not accepted; Max length: 22ft; Stay limit: 14 days; Open Apr-Nov; Tent & RV camping: $20; Elev: 8832ft/2692m; Tel: 928-428-4150; Nearest town: Safford. GPS: 32.708013, -109.962759

96 • Rim

Total sites: 26; RV sites: 26; No water; Vault toilets; Reservations accepted; Max length: 40ft; Open May-Sep; Tent & RV camping: $18; Elev: 7576ft/2309m; Tel: 928-535-7300; Nearest town: Forest Lakes. GPS: 34.304711, -110.908293

97 • Riverside

Total sites: 12; RV sites: 12; No water; Vault toilets; Reservations not accepted; Max length: 16ft; Stay limit: 14 days; Open all year; Tent & RV camping: $16; Elev: 1604ft/489m; Tel: 480-595-3300; Nearest town: Carefree. GPS: 33.809098, -111.647379

98 • Rock Crossing

Total sites: 36; RV sites: 36; Central water; Vault toilets; No showers; No RV dump; Reservations not accepted; Max length: 32ft; Generator hours: 0600-2200; Open May-Oct; Tent & RV camping: $16; Elev: 7323ft/2232m; Tel: 928-477-2255; Nearest town: Blue Ridge. GPS: 34.562585, -111.218878

99 • Rolfe C. Hoyer

Total sites: 91; RV sites: 91; Central water; Vault toilets; Pay showers; No RV dump; Reservations accepted; Max length: 32ft; Open May-Oct; Tent & RV camping: $24; Elev: 8324ft/2537m; Tel: 928-333-6200; Nearest town: Greer. GPS: 34.033936, -109.453857

100 • Roosevelt Lake - Cholla

Total sites: 206; RV sites: 194; Central water; Flush toilets; Showers; No RV dump; Reservations not accepted; Max length: 32ft; Stay limit: 14 days; Open all year; Tent & RV camping: $25; Elev: 2198ft/670m; Tel: 928-467-3200; Nearest town: Roosevelt; Notes: Dump station open Thu & Fri from 12pm - 2pm. GPS: 33.729631, -111.204619

101 • Roosevelt Lake - Indian Point

Total sites: 54; RV sites: 54; Central water; No toilets; No showers; No RV dump; Reservations not accepted; Max length: 16ft; Stay limit: 14 days; Open all year; Tent & RV camping: Free; Elev: 2185ft/666m; Tel: 928-467-3200; Nearest town: Roosevelt. GPS: 33.767051, -111.239973

102 • Roosevelt Lake - Schoolhouse

Total sites: 211; RV sites: 211; Central water; Vault toilets; No showers; No RV dump; Reservations not accepted; Max length: 32ft; Stay limit: 14 days; Open all year; Tent & RV camping: $20; Elev: 2159ft/658m; Tel: 928-467-3200; Nearest town: Roosevelt. GPS: 33.648392, -111.011187

103 • Roosevelt Lake - Windy Hill

Total sites: 347; RV sites: 347; Central water; Flush toilets; Showers; RV dump; Reservations accepted; Max length: 32ft; Stay limit: 14 days; Open all year; Tent & RV camping: $25; Elev: 2206ft/672m; Tel: 928-467-3200; Nearest town: Roosevelt. GPS: 33.663223, -111.090631

104 • Rose Canyon

Total sites: 73; RV sites: 73; Central water; Vault toilets; No showers; No RV dump; Reservations not accepted; Max length: 22ft; Open Apr-Oct; Tent & RV camping: $24; Elev: 7159ft/2182m; Tel: 520-749-8700; Nearest town: Tucson; Notes: Reservable group site: $39. GPS: 32.394584, -110.697445

105 • Rose Creek

Total sites: 5; RV sites: 5; No water; Vault toilets; Reservations not accepted; Max length: 16ft; Stay limit: 14 days; Open May-Oct; Tent & RV camping: Free; Elev: 5472ft/1668m; Tel: 928-462-4300; Nearest town: Young. GPS: 33.829667, -110.979623

106 • Rustler Park

Total sites: 25; RV sites: 25; No water; Vault toilets; Reservations not accepted; Max length: 22ft; Stay limit: 14 days; Open Apr-Oct; Tent & RV camping: $15; Elev: 8478ft/2584m; Tel: 520-364-3468; Nearest town: Rodeo NM; Notes: Group site: $5 + $5/car. GPS: 31.905282, -109.280066

107 • Salt River Canyon - Second CG

Total sites: 25; RV sites: 25; No water; No toilets; Tent & RV camping: Fee unknown; Elev: 3337ft/1017m; Tel: 928-402-6200; Notes: Also boat-in sites, $125 permit per group. GPS: 33.826566, -110.546043

108 • Sawmill Flats

Total sites: 5; RV sites: 5; Vault toilets; Reservations not accepted; Max length: 16ft; Stay limit: 14 days; Open May-Oct; Tent & RV camping: Free; Elev: 5817ft/1773m; Tel: 928-462-4300; Nearest town: Young. GPS: 33.813672, -110.983472

109 • Scott Reservoir

Total sites: 12; RV sites: 12; No water; Vault toilets; Reservations not accepted; Stay limit: 5 days; Open Apr-Oct; Tent & RV camping: Free; Elev: 6742ft/2055m; Tel: 928-368-2100; Nearest town: Lakeside; Notes: Rough access road. GPS: 34.176715, -109.961051

110 • Shannon

Total sites: 11; RV sites: 11; No water; Vault toilets; Reservations not accepted; Max length: Trlr-22ft/RV-16ft; Stay limit: 14 days; Open Apr-Nov; Tent & RV camping: $15; Elev: 9052ft/2759m; Tel: 928-428-4150; Nearest town: Safford. GPS: 32.658379, -109.857961

111 • Sharp Creek

Total sites: 28; RV sites: 28; Central water; Vault toilets; No showers; No RV dump; Reservations accepted; Max length: 40ft; Stay limit: 14 days; Open Apr-Oct; Tent & RV camping: $27; Elev: 5971ft/1820m; Tel: 928-468-7135; Nearest town: Payson; Notes: Group site: $150. GPS: 34.300952, -110.998056

112 • Sinkhole

Total sites: 26; RV sites: 26; Central water; Vault toilets; No showers; No RV dump; Reservations accepted; Max length: 32ft; Stay limit: 14 days; Open Apr-Oct; Tent & RV camping: $20; Elev: 7572ft/2308m; Tel: 928-535-7300; Nearest town: Forest Lakes. GPS: 34.305158, -110.885495

113 • Soldier Creek

Total sites: 12; RV sites: 12; No water; Vault toilets; Reservations not accepted; Max length: 22ft; Stay limit: 14 days; Open Apr-Nov; Tent & RV camping: $20; Elev: 9386ft/2861m; Tel: 928-428-4150; Nearest town: Safford. GPS: 32.698958, -109.920357

114 • Spencer Canyon

Total sites: 60; RV sites: 60; Central water; Vault toilets; No showers; No RV dump; Reservations not accepted; Max length: 22ft; Open Apr-Oct; Tent & RV camping: $22; Elev: 7923ft/2415m; Tel: 520-576-1492; Nearest town: Tucson. GPS: 32.414339, -110.739034

115 • Spillway

Total sites: 26; RV sites: 26; Central water; Flush toilets; No showers; No RV dump; Reservations accepted; Max length: 16ft; Open May-Oct; Tent & RV camping: $25; Elev: 7513ft/2290m; Tel: 928-535-7300; Nearest town: Heber; Notes: Group fee: $150. GPS: 34.332424, -110.937214

116 • Stewart

Total sites: 6; RV sites: 6; Central water; Vault toilets; No showers; No RV dump; Reservations not accepted; Max length: 16ft; Stay limit: 14 days; Open all year; Tent & RV camping: $20; Elev: 5102ft/1555m; Tel: 520-364-3468; Nearest town: Portal; Notes: No water in winter, Susceptible to flooding. GPS: 31.891146, -109.167715

117 • Stockton Pass

Total sites: 7; RV sites: 7; No water; Vault toilets; Reservations not accepted; Max length: 22ft; Stay limit: 14 days; Open all year; Tent & RV camping: $15; Elev: 5705ft/1739m; Tel: 928-428-4150; Nearest town: Safford; Notes: Group site. GPS: 32.591697, -109.850151

118 • Strayhorse

Total sites: 7; RV sites: 7; Central water; Vault toilets; No showers; No RV dump; Reservations not accepted; Max length: 16ft; Open Apr-Nov; Tent & RV camping: Free; Elev: 7802ft/2378m; Tel: 928-687-8600; Nearest town: Alpine. GPS: 33.550321, -109.318093

119 • Sulphide Del Ray

Total sites: 10; RV sites: 10; No water; Vault toilets; Max length: 20ft; Stay limit: 14 days; Open all year; Tent & RV camping: Free; Elev: 6024ft/1836m; Tel: 928-402-6200; Nearest town: Globe. GPS: 33.292725, -110.867920

120 • Sunny Flat

Total sites: 14; RV sites: 14; Central water; Vault toilets; No showers; No RV dump; Reservations not accepted; Max length: 28ft; Stay limit: 14 days; Open all year; Tent & RV camping: $20; Elev: 5112ft/1558m; Tel: 520-364-3468; Nearest town: Rodeo NM; Notes: Susceptible to flooding. GPS: 31.884766, -109.176025

121 • Sycamore

Total sites: 7; RV sites: 7; No water; Vault toilets; Reservations not accepted; Max length: 16ft; Stay limit: 14 days; Open all year; Tent & RV camping: $15; Elev: 6355ft/1937m; Tel: 520-364-3468; Nearest town: Douglas. GPS: 31.859799, -109.334303

122 • Ten X

Total sites: 70; RV sites: 70; Central water; Vault toilets; No showers; No RV dump; Reservations accepted; Max length: 22ft; Open May-Oct; Tent & RV camping: $10; Elev: 6670ft/2033m; Tel: 928-638-2443; Nearest town: Tusayan; Notes: Group sites $75-$125. GPS: 35.937012, -112.123047

123 • Timber Camp Rec Area

Total sites: 13; RV sites: 13; No water; Vault toilets; Reservations accepted; Max length: 45ft; Stay limit: 14 days; Open all year; Tent & RV camping: $16; Elev: 5699ft/1737m; Tel: 928-402-6200; Nearest town: Globe; Notes: Group site: $75-$150. GPS: 33.687924, -110.571446

124 • Tortilla

Total sites: 76; RV sites: 76; Water at site; No showers; RV dump; Reservations accepted; Max length: 30ft; Stay limit: 14 days; Open Oct-Mar; Tent & RV camping: $20; Elev: 1706ft/520m; Tel: 480-610-3300; Nearest town: Apache Junction; Notes: Narrow road with sharp curves. GPS: 33.529232, -111.397548

125 • Upper Blue

Total sites: 3; RV sites: 3; No water; Vault toilets; Reservations not accepted; Max length: 16ft; Stay limit: 14 days; Open Apr-Nov; Tent & RV camping: Free; Elev: 6335ft/1931m; Tel: 928-339-5000; Nearest town: Alpine. GPS: 33.694001, -109.071863

126 • Upper Canyon Creek

Total sites: 10; RV sites: 10; No water; Vault toilets; Reservations not accepted; Max length: 16ft; Stay limit: 14 days; Open May-Oct; Tent & RV camping: Free; Elev: 6591ft/2009m; Tel: 928-462-4300; Nearest town: Young. GPS: 34.288308, -110.803339

127 • Upper Juan Miller

Total sites: 4; No water; Vault toilets; Reservations not accepted; Open all year; Tents only: Free; Elev: 5889ft/1795m; Tel: 928-687-8600; Nearest town: Clifton. GPS: 33.268996, -109.348063

128 • Upper Pinal

Total sites: 3; RV sites: 3; Reservations not accepted; Max length: 20ft; Stay limit: 14 days; Open May-Nov; Tent & RV camping: Free; Elev: 7687ft/2343m; Tel: 928-402-6200; Nearest town: Globe; Notes: Narrow winding mountain gravel road. GPS: 33.284227, -110.821267

129 • Upper Tonto Creek

Total sites: 9; RV sites: 9; Central water; Vault toilets; No showers; No RV dump; Reservations not accepted; Stay limit: 14 days; Open Apr-Oct; Tent & RV camping: $19; Elev: 5505ft/1678m; Tel: 928-474-7900; Nearest town: Payson. GPS: 34.340016, -111.095469

130 • Valentine Ridge

Total sites: 10; RV sites: 10; No water; Vault toilets; Reservations not accepted; Max length: 16ft; Stay limit: 14 days; Open May-Oct; Tent & RV camping: Free; Elev: 6647ft/2026m; Tel: 928-462-4300; Nearest town: Heber. GPS: 34.244005, -110.798245

131 • West Turkey Creek

Total sites: 7; No water; No toilets; Reservations not accepted; Stay limit: 14 days; Open all year; Tents only: Free; Elev: 5981ft/1823m; Tel: 520-388-8300; Nearest town: Douglas. GPS: 31.864589, -109.359279

132 • White Horse Lake

Total sites: 94; RV sites: 94; Central water; Vault toilets; No showers; RV dump; Reservations accepted; Max length: 38ft; Stay limit: 14 days; Open May-Sep; Tent & RV camping: $24; Elev: 6565ft/2001m; Tel: 928-635-5600; Nearest town: Williams; Notes: Group site: $168, Dump fee: $10. GPS: 35.115825, -112.017024

133 • White Rock

Total sites: 15; RV sites: 15; Central water; Vault toilets; No showers; No RV dump; Reservations not accepted; Max length: 22ft; Stay limit: 14 days; Open all year; Tent & RV camping: $15; Elev: 3930ft/1198m; Tel: 520-281-2296; Nearest town: Nogales. GPS: 31.394631, -111.089591

134 • White Spar

Total sites: 56; RV sites: 56; Central water; Vault toilets; No showers; No RV dump; Reservations accepted; Max length: 32ft; Generator hours: 0600-2200; Open all year; Tent & RV camping: $14; Elev: 5656ft/1724m; Tel: 928-443-8000; Nearest town: Prescott; Notes: 12 sites open all year - $10 Nov-Mar. GPS: 34.509334, -112.476753

135 • Winn

Total sites: 63; RV sites: 63; Central water; Vault toilets; No showers; No RV dump; Reservations accepted; Max length: 45ft; Stay limit: 14 days; Open May-Oct; Tent & RV camping: $14; Elev: 9350ft/2850m; Tel: 928-333-6200; Nearest town: Greer; Notes: Group sites $125. GPS: 33.965653, -109.485118

136 • Yavapai

Total sites: 21; RV sites: 21; Elec sites: 1; Central water; Vault toilets; No showers; No RV dump; Reservations accepted; Max length: 25ft; Open May-Oct; Tent & RV camping: $18; Elev: 5827ft/1776m; Tel: 928-443-8000; Nearest town: Prescott. GPS: 34.602181, -112.539569

Arkansas

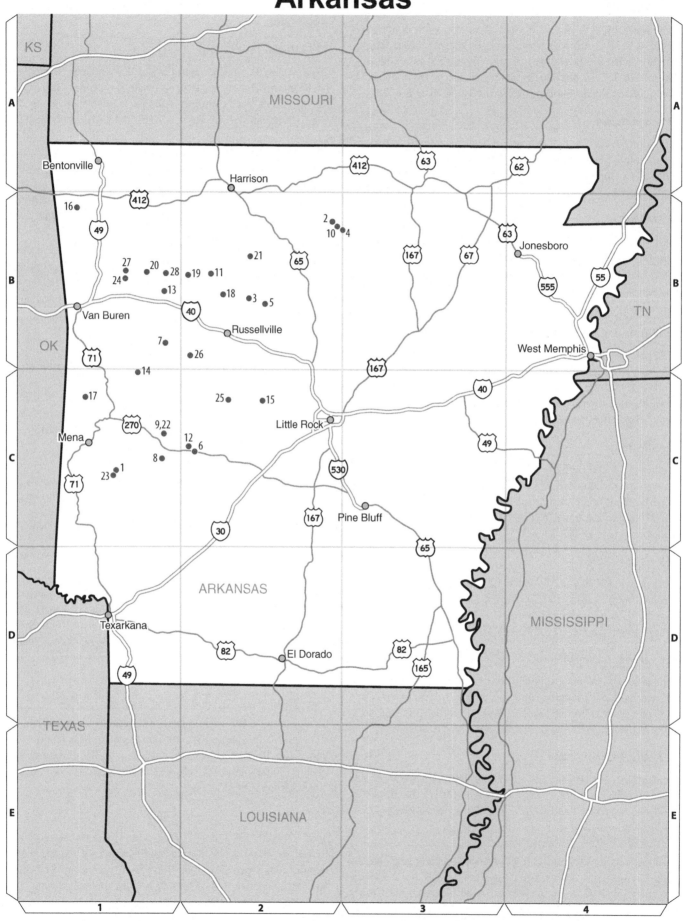

Arkansas Camping Areas

1 • Bard Springs

Total sites: 5; No water; Vault toilets; Reservations not accepted; Open all year; Tents only: $8; Elev: 1326ft/404m; Tel: 501-321-5202; Nearest town: Athens; Notes: Adirondack-type shelters. GPS: 34.391011, -94.010514

2 • Barkshed

Total sites: 5; RV sites: 1; No water; Vault toilets; Reservations not accepted; Open all year; Tent & RV camping: $3; Elev: 548ft/167m; Tel: 870 757 2211; Nearest town: Mountain View; Notes: No large RVs. GPS: 36.018687, -92.250417

3 • Bayou Bluff

Total sites: 7; RV sites: 7; Central water; Vault toilets; No showers; No RV dump; Reservations not accepted; Open Mar-Dec; Tent & RV camping: $7; Elev: 673ft/205m; Tel: 479-284-3150; Nearest town: Jerusalem; Notes: No large RVs, No water in winter, CCC rock shelters $10. GPS: 35.523691, -92.944059

4 • Blanchard Springs

Total sites: 32; RV sites: 32; Central water; Flush toilets; Showers; RV dump; Reservations not accepted; Max length: 32ft; Open all year; Tent & RV camping: $15; Elev: 420ft/128m; Tel: 870-757-2211; Nearest town: Fifty Six; Notes: Reservable group sites $35-$60, May be closed during high water. GPS: 35.969104, -92.172821

5 • Brock Creek Lake

Total sites: 6; RV sites: 6; No water; Vault toilets; Reservations not accepted; Open all year; Tent & RV camping: Fee unknown; Elev: 787ft/240m; Tel: 479-284-3150; Nearest town: Jerusalem. GPS: 35.491575, -92.805673

6 • Charlton

Total sites: 58; RV sites: 58; Central water; Flush toilets; Showers; RV dump; Reservations not accepted; Open Apr-Nov; Tents: $15/RVs: $25; Elev: 705ft/215m; Tel: 870-867-2101; Nearest town: Mt. Ida. GPS: 34.516294, -93.382615

7 • Cove Lake

Total sites: 36; RV sites: 36; Central water; Flush toilets; Showers; No RV dump; Open all year; Tent & RV camping: $15; Elev: 1050ft/320m; Tel: 479-963-6421; Nearest town: Paris; Notes: Cabin(s). GPS: 35.224778, -93.624113

8 • Crystal

Total sites: 9; RV sites: 9; No water; Vault toilets; Reservations not accepted; Open all year; Tent & RV camping: Free; Elev: 1034ft/315m; Tel: 870-356-4186; Nearest town: Norman; Notes: No large RVs. GPS: 34.479411, -93.638484

9 • Dragover Float Camp

Total sites: 7; No water; No toilets; Tents only: Free; Elev: 659ft/201m; Tel: 870-867-2101; Nearest town: Mt Ida; Notes: Also boat-in sites. GPS: 34.641438, -93.631262

10 • Gunner Pool

Total sites: 27; RV sites: 27; Central water; Vault toilets; No showers; No RV dump; Tent & RV camping: $7; Elev: 486ft/148m; Tel: 870-269-3228; Nearest town: Fifty Six. GPS: 35.994335, -92.212323

11 • Haw Creek Falls

Total sites: 9; RV sites: 9; No water; Vault toilets; Reservations not accepted; Open Mar-Dec; Tent & RV camping: $4; Elev: 892ft/272m; Tel: 479-284-3150; Nearest town: Pelsor; Notes: Closed when heavy rain forecast. GPS: 35.679235, -93.259637

12 • Hickory Nut Mt

Total sites: 8; RV sites: 8; No water; Vault toilets; Open all year; Tent & RV camping: Free; Elev: 1220ft/372m; Tel: 870-867-2101; Nearest town: Bismarck. GPS: 34.561521, -93.422959

13 • Horsehead Lake

Total sites: 10; RV sites: 10; Central water; Flush toilets; Showers; No RV dump; Reservations not accepted; Max length: 30ft; Open all year; Tent & RV camping: $10; Elev: 705ft/215m; Tel: 479-754-2864; Nearest town: Clarksville; Notes: Group site $15. GPS: 35.565619, -93.639625

14 • Jack Creek

Total sites: 5; RV sites: 5; No water; Vault toilets; Reservations not accepted; Open Apr-Nov; Tent & RV camping: Free; Elev: 699ft/213m; Tel: 479-637-4174; Nearest town: Booneville. GPS: 35.033855, -93.845912

15 • Lake Sylvia

Total sites: 27; RV sites: 19; Elec sites: 19; Water at site; Flush toilets; Showers; RV dump; Reservations not accepted; Max length: 30ft; Open Apr-Oct; Tents: $15/RVs: $20; Elev: 646ft/197m; Tel: 501-984-5313; Nearest town: Perryville; Notes: 2 group sites $25. GPS: 34.867894, -92.822738

16 • Lake Wedington

Total sites: 18; RV sites: 18; Central water; Flush toilets; Showers; No RV dump; Reservations accepted; Open Apr-Nov; Tent & RV camping: $20; Elev: 1191ft/363m; Tel: 479-442-3527; Nearest town: Fayettville; Notes: Cabin(s). GPS: 36.091707, -94.372054

17 • Little Pines

Total sites: 9; RV sites: 9; Elec sites: 9; Water at site; Flush toilets; Showers; RV dump; Reservations not accepted; Open all year; Tent & RV camping: $20-25; Elev: 833ft/254m; Tel: 479-637-4174; Nearest town: Waldron. GPS: 34.869629, -94.268555

18 • Long Pool

Total sites: 40; RV sites: 40; Elec sites: 20; Water at site; Flush toilets; Showers; RV dump; Tents: $7/RVs: $7-13; Elev: 568ft/173m; Tel: 479-284-3150; Nearest town: Dover. GPS: 35.548828, -93.160645

19 • Ozone

Total sites: 8; RV sites: 8; No water; Vault toilets; Open all year; Tent & RV camping: $3; Elev: 1896ft/578m; Tel: 479-754-2864; Nearest town: Clarksville. GPS: 35.671144, -93.448932

20 • Redding

Total sites: 27; RV sites: 27; Central water; Flush toilets; Showers; No RV dump; Reservations not accepted; Open all year; Tent & RV camping: $10; Elev: 807ft/246m; Tel: 479-754-2864; Nearest town: Ozark. GPS: 35.682129, -93.785645

21 • Richland Creek

Total sites: 11; No water; Vault toilets; Reservations not accepted; Open all year; Tents only: $10; Elev: 1046ft/319m; Tel: 870-446-5122; Nearest town: Pelsor; Notes: Very rough road. GPS: 35.797232, -92.934054

22 • River Bluff Float Camp

Total sites: 6; No water; Vault toilets; Reservations not accepted; Tents only: Free; Elev: 686ft/209m; Tel: 870-867-2101; Nearest town: Mt Ida; Notes: Also boat-in sites. GPS: 34.640186, -93.625715

23 • Shady Lake

Total sites: 65; RV sites: 65; Elec sites: 20; Water at site; Flush toilets; Showers; RV dump; Reservations not accepted; Max length: 32ft; Open Mar-Nov; Tents: $15/RVs: $20-25; Elev: 1214ft/370m; Tel: 479-394-2382; Nearest town: Athens. GPS: 34.365234, -94.027832

24 • Shores Lake

Total sites: 23; RV sites: 23; Central water; Flush toilets; Showers; No RV dump; Reservations not accepted; Open all year; Tents: $8/RVs: $12; Elev: 712ft/217m; Tel: 479-667-2191; Nearest town: Mulberry; Notes: No water Dec-Mar - $6-$10. GPS: 35.639648, -93.960205

25 • South Fourche

Total sites: 6; RV sites: 6; Central water; Vault toilets; No showers; No RV dump; Reservations not accepted; Open all year; Tent & RV camping: $5; Elev: 508ft/155m; Tel: 501-984-5313; Nearest town: Hollis; Notes: No large RVs. GPS: 34.869769, -93.109238

26 • Spring Lake

Total sites: 13; RV sites: 13; Central water; Flush toilets; Showers; No RV dump; Reservations not accepted; Open May-Sep; Tent & RV camping: $9; Elev: 548ft/167m; Tel: 479-963-3076; Nearest town: Belleville. GPS: 35.150574, -93.424561

27 • White Rock Mt

Total sites: 8; RV sites: 8; Central water; Vault toilets; No showers; No RV dump; Reservations not accepted; Open all year; Tent & RV camping: $10; Elev: 2342ft/714m; Tel: 479-667-2191; Nearest town: Mulberry; Notes: Cabin(s). GPS: 35.691434, -93.956608

28 • Wolf Pen

Total sites: 6; RV sites: 6; No water; Vault toilets; Reservations not accepted; Max length: 18ft; Open all year; Tent & RV camping: $10; Elev: 965ft/294m; Tel: 479-754-2864; Nearest town: Oark. GPS: 35.675598, -93.630554

California

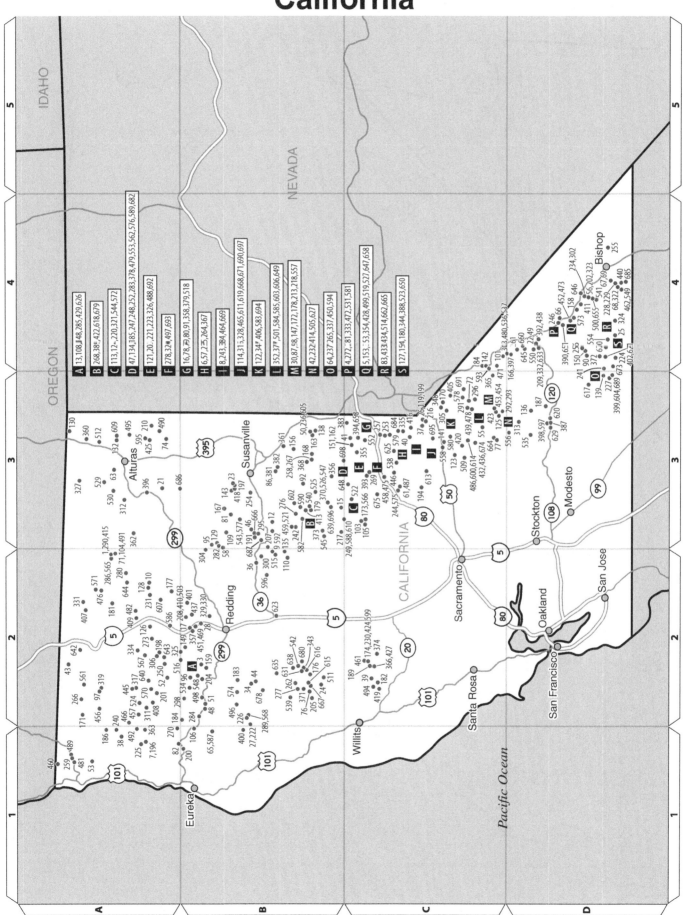

A 13,108,148,285,429,626
B 268,38,422,618,679
C 113,12,220,321,544,572
D 47,134,185,247,248,252,283,378,479,553,562,576,589,682
E 121,20,221,223,326,488,692
F 278,324,497,693
G 16,78,80,91,358,379,518
H 6,57,25,264,367
I 8,243,384,464,669
J 114,31,328,465,611,619,668,671,690,697
K 122,34,406,583,694
L 352,37,501,584,585,603,606,649
M 30,87,58,147,172,178,213,218,557
N 42,232,414,505,627
O 64,237,265,337,450,594
P 4,272,81,333,472,531,581
Q 5,153,53,354,428,499,519,527,647,658
R 83,43,434,514,662,665
S 127,154,180,344,388,523,650

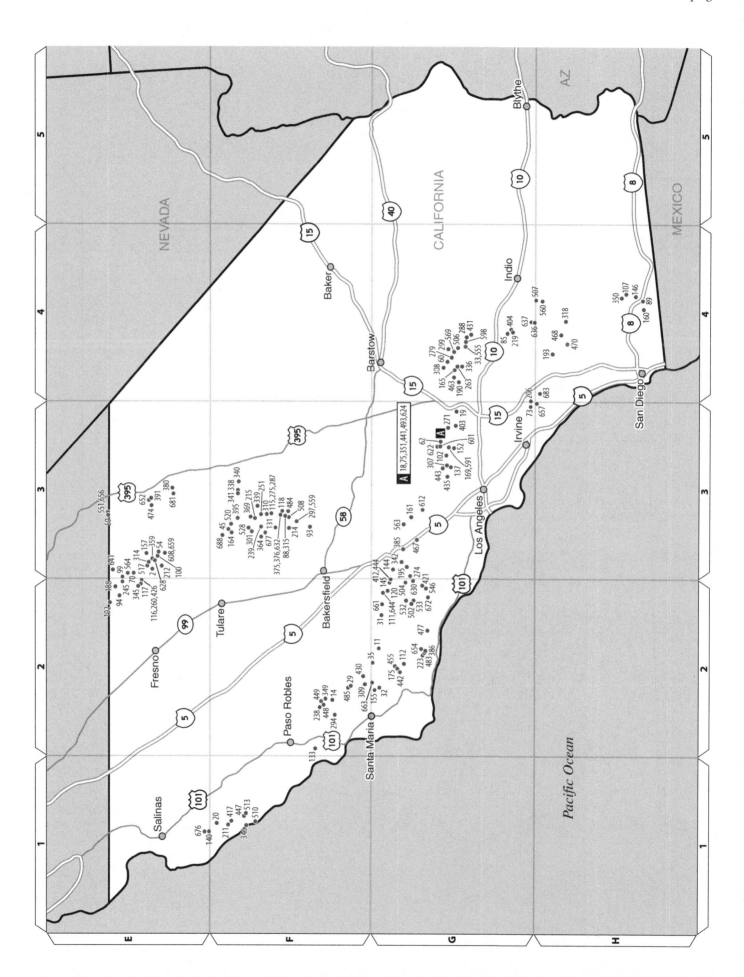

California Camping Areas

1 • A H Hogue

Total sites: 24; RV sites: 24; Central water; Vault toilets; No showers; No RV dump; Reservations accepted; Max length: 30ft; Stay limit: 14 days; Open Jul-Sep; Tent & RV camping: $14; Elev: 6758ft/2060m; Tel: 530-233-5811; Nearest town: Tionesta. GPS: 41.586282, -121.592038

2 • Abbott Creek

Total sites: 2; RV sites: 2; No water; No toilets; Reservations not accepted; Tent & RV camping: Free; Elev: 6004ft/1830m; Nearest town: Miramonte. GPS: 36.768003, -118.974786

3 • Ackerman

Total sites: 51; RV sites: 51; Central water; Flush toilets; No showers; RV dump; Reservations accepted; Max length: 40ft; Open all year; Tent & RV camping: $18; Elev: 1946ft/593m; Tel: 530-623-2121; Nearest town: Lewiston; Notes: Dump station open Apr-Oct. GPS: 40.785889, -122.771973

4 • Aerie Crag

Total sites: 10; RV sites: 10; No water; Vault toilets; Reservations not accepted; Stay limit: 14 days; Open Jun-Nov; No tents/RVs: $14; Elev: 7221ft/2201m; Tel: 760-647-3044; Nearest town: June Lake; Notes: Open only when nearby CG's full. GPS: 37.802895, -119.113406

5 • Agnew Meadows

Total sites: 20; RV sites: 14; Central water; Vault toilets; No showers; No RV dump; Reservations not accepted; Stay limit: 14 days; Open Jun-Sep; Tent & RV camping: $23-25; Elev: 8376ft/2553m; Tel: 760-924-5500; Nearest town: Mammoth Lakes; Notes: Reservable group site: $75, Narrow, single lane road, 3 equestrian sites, Must use bear boxes. GPS: 37.682056, -119.086593

6 • Ahart

Total sites: 12; RV sites: 12; No water; Vault toilets; Reservations not accepted; Open May-Oct; Tent & RV camping: $20; Elev: 5387ft/1642m; Tel: 530-265-4531; Nearest town: Foresthill. GPS: 39.145752, -120.407471

7 • Aikens Creek West

Total sites: 10; RV sites: 10; Central water; No toilets; No showers; RV dump; Reservations not accepted; Max length: 35ft; Open May-Sep; Tent & RV camping: Free; Elev: 312ft/95m; Tel: 530-627-3291; Nearest town: Orleans. GPS: 41.228795, -123.654856

8 • Airport Flat

Total sites: 16; RV sites: 16; No water; Vault toilets; Reservations not accepted; Stay limit: 14 days; Open May-Oct; Tent & RV camping: Free; Elev: 5407ft/1648m; Tel: 530-644-2349; Nearest town: Pollock Pines. GPS: 38.985357, -120.380174

9 • Alder Creek (Lassen)

Total sites: 6; No water; Vault toilets; Reservations not accepted; Open May-Oct; Tents only: $10; Elev: 3904ft/1190m; Tel: 530-258-2141; Nearest town: Chester. GPS: 40.209134, -121.496721

10 • Algoma

Total sites: 8; No water; Vault toilets; Reservations not accepted; Max length: 24ft; Open May-Oct; Tent & RV camping: Free; Elev: 3848ft/1173m; Tel: 530-964-2184; Nearest town: McCloud. GPS: 41.256047, -121.883773

11 • Aliso

Total sites: 10; RV sites: 10; No water; Vault toilets; Reservations not accepted; Max length: 28ft; Generator hours: 0600-2200; Open all year; Tent & RV camping: $5; Elev: 2884ft/879m; Tel: 661-245-3731; Nearest town: New Cuyama; Notes: Adventure Pass required ($5/day or $30/year) or Interagency Pass. GPS: 34.907715, -119.768555

12 • Almanor

Total sites: 104; RV sites: 104; Central water; Vault toilets; No showers; No RV dump; Reservations accepted; Max length: 22ft; Open May-Sep; Tents: $15-18/RVs: $18; Elev: 4619ft/1408m; Tel: 530-258-2141; Nearest town: Chester. GPS: 40.215576, -121.173828

13 • Alpine View

Total sites: 54; RV sites: 54; Central water; Flush toilets; No showers; No RV dump; Reservations accepted; Open May-Sep; Tent & RV camping: $23; Elev: 2523ft/769m; Tel: 530-623-2121; Nearest town: Trinity Center. GPS: 40.886475, -122.767334

14 • American Canyon

Total sites: 14; RV sites: 14; No water; Vault toilets; Reservations not accepted; Max length: 25ft; Open Aug-Sep; Tent & RV camping: $5; Elev: 1801ft/549m; Tel: 805-925-9538; Nearest town: San Luis Obispo; Notes: Open only during deer season, Adventure Pass required ($5/day or $30/year) or Interagency Pass. GPS: 35.283691, -120.266357

15 • American House OHV Camp

Total sites: 5; No water; No toilets; Tents only: Free; Elev: 4534ft/1382m; Nearest town: La Porte. GPS: 39.628499, -121.002283

16 • Annie McCloud

Total sites: 10; RV sites: 10; No water; Vault toilets; Max length: 20ft; Tent & RV camping: Free; Elev: 5833ft/1778m; Nearest town: Truckee. GPS: 39.380723, -120.135419

17 • Antlers

Total sites: 45; RV sites: 45; Central water; Flush toilets; No showers; No RV dump; Reservations accepted; Open all year; Tent & RV camping: $20; Elev: 1148ft/350m; Tel: 530-275-8113; Nearest town: Lakehead; Notes: Senior Pass cannot be used for double sites, Concessionaire. GPS: 40.887451, -122.378662

18 • Appletree

Total sites: 8; Central water; Vault toilets; No showers; No RV dump; Reservations not accepted; Stay limit: 14 days; Open all year; Tents only: $5; Elev: 6214ft/1894m; Tel: 619-249-3483; Nearest town: Big Pines; Notes: Adventure Pass required ($5/day or $30/year) or Interagency Pass. GPS: 34.386334, -117.713723

19 • Applewhite

Total sites: 44; RV sites: 44; Central water; Flush toilets; No showers; No RV dump; Reservations not accepted; Max length: 30ft; Open all year; Tent & RV camping: $10; Elev: 3369ft/1027m; Tel: 909-382-2851; Nearest town: Lytle Creek; Notes: No wood or charcoal fires. GPS: 34.259975, -117.493207

20 • Arroyo Seco

Total sites: 39; RV sites: 24; Central water; Flush toilets; Pay showers; No RV dump; Reservations accepted; Open all year; Tents: $25-30/RVs: $30; Elev: 932ft/284m; Tel: 831-674-5726; Nearest town: Greenfield; Notes: Group site: $125. GPS: 36.233207, -121.484963

21 • Ash Creek

Total sites: 5; RV sites: 5; No water; Vault toilets; Reservations not accepted; Max length: 22ft; Stay limit: 14 days; Open all year; Tent & RV camping: Free; Elev: 4895ft/1492m; Tel: 530-299-3215; Nearest town: Adin; Notes: Rough road. GPS: 41.160959, -120.828823

22 • Aspen

Total sites: 56; RV sites: 56; Central water; Vault toilets; No showers; No RV dump; Reservations not accepted; Max length: 40ft; Stay limit: 14 days; Tent & RV camping: $14; Elev: 7536ft/2297m; Tel: 760-873-2400; Nearest town: Lee Vining; Notes: Bear boxes must be used for food storage. GPS: 37.939000, -119.188000

23 • Aspen Grove

Total sites: 28; Central water; Flush toilets; No showers; No RV dump; Reservations accepted; Generators prohibited; Open May-Oct; Tents only: $20; Elev: 5151ft/1570m; Tel: 530-310-1245; Nearest town: Lee Vining; Notes: Bear boxes must be used for food storage. GPS: 40.556146, -120.772536

24 • Atchison Camp

Total sites: 6; RV sites: 6; No water; Vault toilets; Reservations not accepted; Open May-Oct; Tent & RV camping: Free; Elev: 4452ft/1357m; Tel: 707-983-6118. GPS: 39.750227, -122.924974

25 • Badger Flat

Total sites: 15; RV sites: 15; No water; Vault toilets; Reservations not accepted; Max length: 25ft; Stay limit: 14 days; Open Jun-Oct; Tent & RV camping: $22; Elev: 8294ft/2528m; Tel: 559-855-5355; Nearest town: Lakeshore. GPS: 37.270598, -119.115989

26 • Badger's Den

Total sites: 84; Central water; Flush toilets; Showers; No RV dump; Generators prohibited; Open all year; Tents only: $45; Elev: 6242ft/1903m; Tel: 530-541-1801; Nearest town: South Lake Tahoe; Notes: No pets, Concessionaire. GPS: 38.934102, -120.037878

27 • Bailey Canyon

Total sites: 25; RV sites: 20; Central water; Vault toilets; No showers; No RV dump; Reservations not accepted; Max length: 22ft; Open May-Sep; Tent & RV camping: $12; Elev: 2762ft/842m; Tel: 707-574-6233; Nearest town: Mad River. GPS: 40.340597, -123.400673

28 • Bailey Cove

Total sites: 7; RV sites: 7; Central water; Flush toilets; No showers; No RV dump; Reservations accepted; Max length: 40ft; Open all year; Tent & RV camping: $23; Elev: 1105ft/337m; Tel: 530-275-8113; Nearest town: Redding. GPS: 40.799847, -122.318372

29 • Baja

Total sites: 1; RV sites: 1; No water; Vault toilets; Reservations not accepted; Tent & RV camping: Free; Elev: 1411ft/430m; Tel: 805-925-9538; Nearest town: Santa Maria. GPS: 35.139186, -120.137827

30 • Baker

Total sites: 44; RV sites: 33; Central water; Vault toilets; No showers; No RV dump; Reservations not accepted; Open Apr-Oct; Tent & RV camping: $20; Elev: 6309ft/1923m; Tel: 209-965-3434; Nearest town: Mi-Wuk. GPS: 38.324213, -119.752648

31 • Ballinger

Total sites: 20; RV sites: 20; No water; Vault toilets; Reservations accepted; Generator hours: 0600-2200; Open all year; Tent & RV camping: $20; Elev: 3123ft/952m; Tel: 661-245-3731. GPS: 34.884078, -119.445027

32 • Barrel Springs

Total sites: 6; RV sites: 6; No water; Vault toilets; Reservations not accepted; Tent & RV camping: $5; Elev: 1034ft/315m; Tel: 805-925-9538; Nearest town: Santa Maria; Notes: Adventure Pass required ($5/day or $30/year) or Interagency Pass. GPS: 34.901276, -120.142303

33 • Barton Flats

Total sites: 52; RV sites: 52; Central water; Flush toilets; Showers; RV dump; Reservations accepted; Open May-Oct; Tent & RV camping: $33-35; Elev: 6391ft/1948m; Tel: 909-866-8550; Nearest town: Angelus Oaks. GPS: 34.171288, -116.875518

34 • Basin Gulch

Total sites: 13; RV sites: 13; No water; Vault toilets; Reservations not accepted; Max length: 20ft; Tent & RV camping: Fee unknown; Elev: 2590ft/789m; Tel: 530-352-4211; Nearest town: Platina. GPS: 40.352178, -122.960844

35 • Bates Canyon

Total sites: 6; RV sites: 6; No water; Vault toilets; Reservations not accepted; Open all year; Tent & RV camping: $5; Elev: 2858ft/871m; Tel: 805-925-9538; Nearest town: Santa Maria; Notes:

Adventure Pass required ($5/day or $30/year) or Interagency Pass. GPS: 34.953642, -119.907721

36 • Battle Creek

Total sites: 50; RV sites: 50; Central water; Vault toilets; No showers; No RV dump; Reservations not accepted; Max length: 24ft; Open Apr-Oct; Tent & RV camping: $18; Elev: 4859ft/1481m; Tel: 530-258-2141; Nearest town: Mineral. GPS: 40.348408, -121.627657

37 • Bayview

Total sites: 13; RV sites: 13; No water; Vault toilets; Reservations not accepted; Max length: 20ft; Open May-Oct; Tent & RV camping: $17; Elev: 6850ft/2088m; Tel: 530-543-2600; Nearest town: South Lake Tahoe. GPS: 38.945801, -120.099121

38 • Beans Camp

Total sites: 6; RV sites: 6; No water; Vault toilets; Reservations not accepted; Open May-Oct; Tent & RV camping: Free; Elev: 4324ft/1318m; Tel: 530-627-3291; Nearest town: Orleans. GPS: 41.443717, -123.613089

39 • Bear Creek

Total sites: 16; RV sites: 16; No water; Vault toilets; Reservations not accepted; Tent & RV camping: Free; Elev: 2274ft/693m; Tel: 707-275-2361; Nearest town: Upper Lake. GPS: 39.322687, -122.836399

40 • Bear Lake

Total sites: 5; No water; No toilets; Reservations not accepted; Open Jun-Oct; Tents only: Free; Elev: 7625ft/2324m; Nearest town: Tahoe City. GPS: 39.048626, -120.224918

41 • Bear Valley

Total sites: 10; RV sites: 5; Central water; Vault toilets; No showers; No RV dump; Reservations not accepted; Tent & RV camping: Free; Elev: 6608ft/2014m; Tel: 530-994-3401; Nearest town: Truckee. GPS: 39.557373, -120.236816

42 • Beardsley Dam

Total sites: 16; RV sites: 16; Central water; Vault toilets; No showers; No RV dump; Reservations not accepted; Open May-Oct; Tent & RV camping: $20; Elev: 3350ft/1021m; Tel: 209-965-3434. GPS: 38.210000, -120.075000

43 • Beaver Creek

Total sites: 8; RV sites: 8; No water; Vault toilets; Reservations not accepted; Stay limit: 14 days; Open May-Oct; Tent & RV camping: Free; Elev: 2246ft/685m; Tel: 530-493-2243; Nearest town: Happy Camp. GPS: 41.927669, -122.829174

44 • Beegum Gorge

Total sites: 2; No water; Vault toilets; Reservations not accepted; Tents only: Free; Elev: 2497ft/761m; Tel: 530-352-4211. GPS: 40.313890, -122.933330

45 • Belknap

Total sites: 13; Central water; Vault toilets; Reservations accepted; Open May-Oct; Tents only: $26-28; Elev: 5059ft/1542m; Tel: 559-539-2607; Nearest town: Springville. GPS: 36.141699, -118.599704

46 • Benner Creek

Total sites: 9; RV sites: 9; No water; Vault toilets; Reservations not accepted; Open May-Oct; Tent & RV camping: Free; Elev: 5614ft/1711m; Tel: 530-258-2141; Nearest town: Chester. GPS: 40.395335, -121.268047

47 • Berger

Total sites: 8; RV sites: 8; No water; Vault toilets; Reservations accepted; Max length: 18ft; Open May-Oct; Tent & RV camping: $18; Elev: 5928ft/1807m; Tel: 530-862-1368; Nearest town: Bassett. GPS: 39.627930, -120.643555

48 • Big Bar

Total sites: 3; No water; Vault toilets; Reservations not accepted; Open all year; Tents only: Free; Elev: 1220ft/372m; Tel: 530-623-2121; Nearest town: Big Bar. GPS: 40.738124, -123.251602

49 • Big Bend

Total sites: 17; RV sites: 17; Central water; Vault toilets; No showers; No RV dump; Reservations not accepted; Max length: 30ft; Stay limit: 14 days; Open Jun-Oct; Tent & RV camping: $22; Elev: 7936ft/2419m; Tel: 760-647-3044; Nearest town: Lee Vining; Notes: Bear boxes must be used for food storage. GPS: 37.945451, -119.203181

50 • Big Cove

Total sites: 42; RV sites: 42; Central water; Flush toilets; Showers; No RV dump; Reservations accepted; Open May-Sep; Tent & RV camping: $25; Elev: 5633ft/1717m; Tel: 530-258-7606; Nearest town: Chilcoot. GPS: 39.902588, -120.175049

51 • Big Flat

Total sites: 10; RV sites: 10; Central water; Vault toilets; No showers; No RV dump; Reservations not accepted; Max length: 22ft; Tent & RV camping: $12; Elev: 1350ft/411m; Tel: 530-623-2121; Nearest town: Junction City. GPS: 40.739246, -123.204172

52 • Big Flat

Total sites: 9; RV sites: 9; No water; Vault toilets; Reservations not accepted; Stay limit: 14 days; Open May-Oct; Tent & RV camping: Free; Elev: 5184ft/1580m; Tel: 530-468-5351; Nearest town: Fort Jones. GPS: 41.068035, -122.934505

53 • Big Flat

Total sites: 28; RV sites: 28; No water; Vault toilets; Reservations not accepted; Open May-Sep; Tent & RV camping: $8; Elev: 742ft/226m; Tel: 707-457-3131; Nearest town: Crescent City. GPS: 41.687228, -123.909183

54 • Big Meadow

Total sites: 38; RV sites: 38; No water; Vault toilets; Reservations accepted; Tent & RV camping: $23; Elev: 7598ft/2316m; Tel: 559-338-2251; Nearest town: Cedarbrook; Notes: Bear boxes must be used for food storage. GPS: 36.721027, -118.820668

55 • Big Meadow

Total sites: 20; RV sites: 10; Central water; Vault toilets; No showers; No RV dump; Reservations not accepted; Max length: 27ft; Open Jun-Sep; Tent & RV camping: $19; Elev: 6578ft/2005m; Tel: 209-795-1381; Nearest town: Arnold; Notes: Group fee: $50. GPS: 38.416857, -120.106415

56 • Big Meadow

Total sites: 11; RV sites: 11; Central water; Flush toilets; No showers; No RV dump; Reservations not accepted; Stay limit: 14 days; Open Jun-Sep; Tent & RV camping: $25; Elev: 8537ft/2602m; Tel: 760-873-2500; Nearest town: Mammoth Lakes. GPS: 37.509824, -118.714269

57 • Big Meadows

Total sites: 54; RV sites: 48; Central water; Vault toilets; No showers; No RV dump; Reservations not accepted; Stay limit: 14 days; Open May-Oct; Tent & RV camping: $10; Elev: 5417ft/1651m; Tel: 530-333-4312; Nearest town: Foresthill; Notes: Water may not be available. GPS: 39.074631, -120.428536

58 • Big Pine

Total sites: 19; RV sites: 19; Central water; Vault toilets; No showers; No RV dump; Reservations not accepted; Open May-Oct; Tent & RV camping: $12; Elev: 4669ft/1423m; Tel: 530-336-5521; Nearest town: Old Station. GPS: 40.633658, -121.466419

59 • Big Pine Creek

Total sites: 25; RV sites: 21; No water; Vault toilets; No showers; No RV dump; Reservations accepted; Stay limit: 14 days; Open Apr-Oct; Tent & RV camping: $21; Elev: 7759ft/2365m; Tel: 760-872-7018; Nearest town: Big Pine. GPS: 37.125683, -118.433418

60 • Big Pine Flat

Total sites: 19; RV sites: 19; Central water; Vault toilets; Reservations not accepted; Max length: 30ft; Open May-Oct; Tent & RV camping: $26; Elev: 6857ft/2090m; Tel: 909-382-2790; Nearest town: Big Bear Lake; Notes: Water is limited/please fill up trailers/RVs before arriving. GPS: 34.320086, -117.011653

61 • Big Reservoir

Total sites: 100; RV sites: 100; Central water; Flush toilets; Showers; RV dump; Reservations accepted; Tent & RV camping: $25-35; Elev: 4131ft/1259m; Tel: 530-367-2129; Nearest town: Foresthill; Notes: Group sites: $100-$160, Pet fee: $5, Reservations through phone number shown, Concessionaire. GPS: 39.143534, -120.755594

62 • Big Rock

Total sites: 8; RV sites: 8; No water; Vault toilets; Reservations not accepted; Max length: 20ft; Stay limit: 14 days; Open all year; Tent & RV camping: $5; Elev: 5433ft/1656m; Tel: 805-944-

2187; Nearest town: Pearblossom; Notes: Hike-in-only in winter, Adventure Pass required ($5/day or $30/year) or Interagency Pass. GPS: 34.388000, -117.777000

63 • Big Sage

Total sites: 11; RV sites: 11; No water; Vault toilets; Reservations not accepted; Max length: 22ft; Stay limit: 14 days; Open May-Oct; Tent & RV camping: Free; Elev: 4905ft/1495m; Tel: 530-233-5811; Nearest town: Alturas. GPS: 41.579841, -120.629174

64 • Big Sandy

Total sites: 18; RV sites: 18; No water; Vault toilets; Reservations not accepted; Max length: 20ft; Stay limit: 14 days; Open May-Sep; Tent & RV camping: $24-27; Elev: 5856ft/1785m; Tel: 559-877-2218; Nearest town: Fresno. GPS: 37.467395, -119.582956

65 • Big Slide

Total sites: 8; No water; Vault toilets; Reservations not accepted; Tents only: Free; Elev: 1213ft/370m; Tel: 530-628-5227; Nearest town: Hyampom. GPS: 40.663444, -123.495538

66 • Big Springs

Total sites: 26; RV sites: 26; No water; Vault toilets; Reservations not accepted; Stay limit: 21 days; Open Jun-Oct; Tent & RV camping: Free; Elev: 7290ft/2222m; Tel: 760-647-3044; Nearest town: Mammoth Lakes; Notes: Bear boxes must be used for food storage. GPS: 37.748779, -118.940918

67 • Big Trees

Total sites: 16; RV sites: 10; Central water; Flush toilets; No showers; No RV dump; Reservations not accepted; Stay limit: 7 days; Open May-Sep; Tent & RV camping: $26; Elev: 7451ft/2271m; Tel: 760-873-2500; Nearest town: Bishop; Notes: Bear boxes must be used for food storage. GPS: 37.264893, -118.578857

68 • Bishop Park

Total sites: 21; RV sites: 21; Central water; Flush toilets; No showers; No RV dump; Reservations not accepted; Stay limit: 14 days; Open May-Sep; Tent & RV camping: $26; Elev: 8360ft/2548m; Tel: 760-873-2500; Nearest town: Bishop; Notes: Small RVs only, Bear boxes must be used for food storage. GPS: 37.243941, -118.597241

69 • Bitterbrush

Total sites: 30; RV sites: 30; Central water; Vault toilets; No showers; No RV dump; Reservations not accepted; Stay limit: 14 days; Open all year; Tent & RV camping: $23; Elev: 6795ft/2071m; Tel: 760-873-2400; Nearest town: Bishop; Notes: Use bear boxes for food storage, Free in winter - no services. GPS: 37.286722, -118.558207

70 • Black Rock Reservoir/PGE

Total sites: 10; No water; Vault toilets; Reservations not accepted; Stay limit: 14 days; Open all year; Tents only: $14; Elev: 4190ft/1277m; Tel: 559-855-5355; Notes: Pet fee: $2/night. GPS: 36.921428, -119.021229

71 • Blanche Lake

Total sites: 6; RV sites: 6; No water; Vault toilets; Reservations not accepted; Stay limit: 14 days; Open Jul-Oct; Tent & RV camping: Free; Elev: 6818ft/2078m; Tel: 530-667-2246; Nearest town: Bug Station. GPS: 41.557000, -121.570000

72 • Bloomfield

Total sites: 20; RV sites: 10; Central water; Vault toilets; No showers; No RV dump; Reservations not accepted; Open Jun-Sep; Tent & RV camping: $12; Elev: 7989ft/2435m; Tel: 209-795-1381; Nearest town: Arnold; Notes: Trailers not recommended, No services in winter - limited access. GPS: 38.537958, -119.825041

73 • Blue Jay

Total sites: 50; RV sites: 50; Central water; Vault toilets; No showers; No RV dump; Reservations not accepted; Max length: 20ft; Stay limit: 14 days; Open all year; Tent & RV camping: $20; Elev: 3373ft/1028m; Tel: 619-673-6180; Nearest town: Lake Elsinore. GPS: 33.651741, -117.453185

74 • Blue Lake

Total sites: 35; RV sites: 35; Central water; Vault toilets; No showers; No RV dump; Reservations not accepted; Stay limit: 14 days; Open May-Oct; Tent & RV camping: $14; Elev: 6119ft/1865m; Tel: 530-279-6116; Nearest town: Likely. GPS: 41.142129, -120.279564

75 • Blue Ridge

Total sites: 8; RV sites: 8; No water; Vault toilets; Reservations not accepted; Max length: 20ft; Stay limit: 14 days; Open all year; Tent & RV camping: $5; Elev: 7950ft/2423m; Tel: 805-944-2187; Nearest town: Wrightwood; Notes: No winter road access, Adventure Pass required ($5/day or $30/year) or Interagency Pass. GPS: 34.359426, -117.686751

76 • Boardman Camp

Total sites: 3; RV sites: 3; No water; Vault toilets; Reservations not accepted; Tent & RV camping: Free; Elev: 4525ft/1379m; Nearest town: Covelo. GPS: 39.847079, -123.012889

77 • Boards Crossing

Total sites: 5; No water; Vault toilets; Reservations not accepted; Tents only: Free; Elev: 3864ft/1178m; Tel: 209-795-1381; Nearest town: Boards Crossing; Notes: Narrow steep road. GPS: 38.301109, -120.235969

78 • Boca

Total sites: 23; RV sites: 20; No water; Vault toilets; Reservations accepted; Open May-Oct; Tent & RV camping: $20; Elev: 5646ft/1721m; Tel: 530-587-9281; Nearest town: Truckee. GPS: 39.394461, -120.105268

79 • Boca Rest

Total sites: 34; RV sites: 34; Central water; Vault toilets; No showers; No RV dump; Reservations accepted; Open May-Oct; Tent & RV camping: $20; Elev: 5617ft/1712m; Tel: 530-587-9281; Nearest town: Truckee. GPS: 39.418953, -120.087298

80 • Boca Spring

Total sites: 13; RV sites: 13; Central water; Vault toilets; No showers; No RV dump; Reservations accepted; Open May-Oct; Tent & RV camping: $20; Elev: 5961ft/1817m; Tel: 530-587-9281; Nearest town: Truckee; Notes: Group site: $66. GPS: 39.428179, -120.075184

81 • Bogard

Total sites: 10; RV sites: 10; Central water; Vault toilets; No showers; No RV dump; Reservations not accepted; Max length: 25ft; Stay limit: 14 days; Open all year; Tent & RV camping: Free; Elev: 5692ft/1735m; Tel: 530-257-4188; Nearest town: Susanville; Notes: Not maintained in winter - often inaccessible. GPS: 40.575297, -121.098381

82 • Boise Creek

Total sites: 17; RV sites: 14; No water; Vault toilets; No showers; No RV dump; Reservations accepted; Open May-Sep; Tent & RV camping: $10; Elev: 906ft/276m; Tel: 530-629-2118; Nearest town: Willow Creek. GPS: 40.944779, -123.658528

83 • Bolsillo

Total sites: 3; RV sites: 3; Central water; Vault toilets; No showers; No RV dump; Reservations not accepted; Open Jun-Oct; Tent & RV camping: Free; Elev: 7461ft/2274m; Tel: 559-855-5355; Nearest town: Clovis; Notes: Large RVs or motorhomes not recommended for travel on the Kaiser Pass Road. GPS: 37.315273, -119.042126

84 • Bootleg

Total sites: 63; RV sites: 63; Central water; Flush toilets; No showers; No RV dump; Reservations not accepted; Max length: 35ft; Stay limit: 14 days; Open May-Sep; Tent & RV camping: $22; Elev: 6437ft/1962m; Tel: 760-932-7070; Nearest town: Coleville. GPS: 38.416602, -119.450095

85 • Boulder Basin

Total sites: 16; RV sites: 7; No water; Vault toilets; Reservations accepted; Open May-Oct; Tent & RV camping: $10; Elev: 7513ft/2290m; Tel: 909-382-2922; Nearest town: Idyllwild; Notes: High clearance vehicles recommended. GPS: 33.826395, -116.755803

86 • Boulder Creek

Total sites: 44; RV sites: 44; Central water; Vault toilets; No showers; No RV dump; Reservations accepted; Generator hours: 0600-2200; Open May-Sep; Tent & RV camping: $25; Elev: 5062ft/1543m; Tel: 530-283-0555; Nearest town: Taylorsville. GPS: 40.191650, -120.613037

87 • Boulder Flat

Total sites: 20; RV sites: 20; Central water; Vault toilets; No showers; No RV dump; Reservations not accepted; Stay limit: 14 days; Open May-Sep; Tent & RV camping: $15; Elev: 5656ft/1724m; Tel: 209-965-3434; Nearest town: Mi-Wuk. GPS: 38.354321, -119.861582

88 • Boulder Gulch

Total sites: 78; RV sites: 78; Potable water; Flush toilets; Showers; No RV dump; Reservations accepted; Max length: 45ft; Open Apr-

Sep; Tent & RV camping: $28; Elev: 2618ft/798m; Tel: 760-376-3781; Nearest town: Lake Isabella. GPS: 35.672363, -118.470215

89 • Boulder Oaks Horse Camp

Total sites: 30; RV sites: 30; Central water; Vault toilets; No showers; No RV dump; Reservations accepted; Max length: 27ft; Stay limit: 14 days; Open all year; Tent & RV camping: $16; Elev: 3182ft/970m; Tel: 619-445-6235; Nearest town: Pine Valley; Notes: One loop has 17 equestrian sites and corrals - the other loop has family campsites. GPS: 32.729064, -116.483295

90 • Bowler

Total sites: 12; RV sites: 12; No water; Vault toilets; Reservations not accepted; Max length: 20ft; Stay limit: 14 days; Open Jul-Oct; Tent & RV camping: Free; Elev: 7110ft/2167m; Tel: 559-877-2218; Nearest town: Oakhurst. GPS: 37.509257, -119.328103

91 • Boyington Mill

Total sites: 11; RV sites: 11; No water; Vault toilets; Reservations accepted; Open May-Oct; Tent & RV camping: $20; Elev: 5709ft/1740m; Tel: 530-587-9281; Nearest town: Truckee. GPS: 39.437591, -120.090497

92 • Bradys Camp

Total sites: 6; No water; Vault toilets; Reservations not accepted; Open all year; Tents only: Free; Elev: 7057ft/2151m; Tel: 530-283-0555; Nearest town: Quincey; Notes: Uphill gravel road not recommended for RVs or trailers. GPS: 39.956403, -120.753499

93 • Breckenridge

Total sites: 8; No water; Vault toilets; Reservations not accepted; Open May-Nov; Tents only: Free; Elev: 6616ft/2017m; Tel: 760-376-3781; Nearest town: Lake Isabella. GPS: 35.468132, -118.582102

94 • Bretz Mill

Total sites: 10; RV sites: 10; No water; Vault toilets; Reservations not accepted; Max length: 24ft; Stay limit: 14 days; Open all year; Tent & RV camping: Free; Elev: 3356ft/1023m; Tel: 559-855-5355; Nearest town: Shaver Lake. GPS: 37.037897, -119.240066

95 • Bridge

Total sites: 25; RV sites: 25; No water; Vault toilets; Reservations not accepted; Stay limit: 14 days; Open Apr-Oct; Tent & RV camping: $10; Elev: 3878ft/1182m; Tel: 530-336-5521; Nearest town: Old Station. GPS: 40.730831, -121.438691

96 • Bridge Camp

Total sites: 10; RV sites: 10; No water; Vault toilets; No showers; No RV dump; Reservations not accepted; Max length: 20ft; Open all year; Tent & RV camping: $10; Elev: 2936ft/895m; Tel: 530-623-2121; Nearest town: Weaverville; Notes: Limited services Nov-May. GPS: 40.873535, -122.917969

97 • Bridge Flat

Total sites: 4; RV sites: 4; No water; Vault toilets; Reservations not accepted; Open May-Oct; Tent & RV camping: Free; Elev:

2205ft/672m; Tel: 530-468-5351; Nearest town: Fort Jones. GPS: 41.650108, -123.113116

98 • Brightman Flat

Total sites: 32; RV sites: 32; Central water; Vault toilets; No showers; No RV dump; Reservations not accepted; Stay limit: 14 days; Open May-Oct; Tent & RV camping: $19; Elev: 5725ft/1745m; Tel: 209-965-3434; Nearest town: Mi-Wuk. GPS: 38.352651, -119.848712

99 • Buck Meadow

Total sites: 10; RV sites: 10; No water; Vault toilets; Reservations not accepted; Max length: 35ft; Stay limit: 14 days; Open May-Sep; Tent & RV camping: $22; Elev: 6837ft/2084m; Tel: 559-855-5355; Nearest town: Shaver Lake. GPS: 37.010791, -119.063861

100 • Buck Rock

Total sites: 8; RV sites: 8; No water; Vault toilets; Reservations not accepted; Max length: 16ft; Tent & RV camping: Free; Elev: 7779ft/2371m; Tel: 559-338-2251; Nearest town: Grant Grove. GPS: 36.722406, -118.850873

101 • Buckeye

Total sites: 65; RV sites: 65; No water; Flush toilets; No showers; No RV dump; Reservations not accepted; Max length: 22ft; Stay limit: 14 days; Open May-Nov; Tent & RV camping: $20; Elev: 7205ft/2196m; Tel: 760-932-7070; Nearest town: Bridgeport; Notes: Non-potable water, Hot springs nearby. GPS: 38.236665, -119.346065

102 • Buckhorn

Total sites: 38; RV sites: 38; Central water; Vault toilets; No showers; No RV dump; Reservations not accepted; Max length: 18ft; Stay limit: 14 days; Generator hours: 0600-2200; Open Apr-Nov; Tent & RV camping: $12; Elev: 6466ft/1971m; Tel: 818-899-1900; Nearest town: La Canada. GPS: 34.346158, -117.912838

103 • Bullards Lakeshore

Total sites: 60; RV sites: 60; No water; No toilets; Reservations not accepted; Tent & RV camping: $22; Elev: 2198ft/670m; Tel: 530-692-3200; Nearest town: Camptonville. GPS: 39.449196, -121.132965

104 • Bullseye Lake

Total sites: 10; RV sites: 10; No water; Vault toilets; Reservations not accepted; Max length: 22ft; Stay limit: 14 days; Open May-Oct; Tent & RV camping: Free; Elev: 6798ft/2072m; Tel: 530-667-2246; Nearest town: McCloud. GPS: 41.554672, -121.573793

105 • Burnt Bridge

Total sites: 31; RV sites: 13; Central water; Vault toilets; No showers; No RV dump; Reservations not accepted; Tent & RV camping: Free; Elev: 2264ft/690m; Tel: 530-534-6500; Nearest town: Nevada City. GPS: 39.420342, -121.172944

106 • Burnt Ranch

Total sites: 16; RV sites: 16; Central water; Vault toilets; No showers; No RV dump; Reservations not accepted; Max length:

25ft; Tent & RV camping: $12; Elev: 1257ft/383m; Tel: 530-623-2121; Nearest town: Big Bar. GPS: 40.827414, -123.482634

107 • Burnt Rancheria

Total sites: 109; RV sites: 69; Central water; Flush toilets; Pay showers; No RV dump; Reservations accepted; Max length: 50ft; Stay limit: 14 days; Open Mar-Oct; Tent & RV camping: $27; Elev: 5948ft/1813m; Tel: 619-473-0120; Nearest town: Pine Valley. GPS: 32.859995, -116.417898

108 • Bushytail

Total sites: 11; RV sites: 11; Elec sites: 9; Central water; Flush toilets; Pay showers; No RV dump; Reservations accepted; Open May-Sep; Tents: $23/RVs: $23-25; Elev: 2441ft/744m; Tel: 530-623-2121; Nearest town: Trinity Center. GPS: 40.851583, -122.813096

109 • Butte Creek

Total sites: 10; No water; Vault toilets; Reservations not accepted; Open all year; Tents only: Free; Elev: 5599ft/1707m; Tel: 530-257-4188; Nearest town: Susanville. GPS: 40.611882, -121.297703

110 • Butte Meadows

Total sites: 13; RV sites: 13; Central water; Vault toilets; No showers; No RV dump; Reservations not accepted; Open May-Oct; Tent & RV camping: $12; Elev: 4403ft/1342m; Tel: 530-258-2141; Nearest town: Chester. GPS: 40.079316, -121.558265

111 • Caballo

Total sites: 5; No water; Vault toilets; Reservations not accepted; Generator hours: 0600-2200; Tents only: Free; Elev: 6092ft/1857m; Tel: 661-245-3731; Notes: High clearance vehicles recommended. GPS: 34.868783, -119.226375

112 • Cachuma

Total sites: 6; RV sites: 6; No water; No toilets; Reservations not accepted; Tent & RV camping: Free; Elev: 2254ft/687m; Notes: No longer maintained by USFS, primitive camping only. GPS: 34.697687, -119.912886

113 • Cal-Ida

Total sites: 14; RV sites: 7; Central water; Vault toilets; Reservations accepted; Open Apr-Oct; Tent & RV camping: $24; Elev: 2369ft/722m; Tel: 530-862-1368; Nearest town: Camptonville. GPS: 39.520896, -120.997117

114 • Camino Cove

Total sites: 32; RV sites: 32; No water; Vault toilets; Stay limit: 14 days; Open Jun-Oct; Tent & RV camping: Free; Elev: 4905ft/1495m; Tel: 530-644-2324; Nearest town: Pollock Pines. GPS: 38.880347, -120.428115

115 • Camp 3

Total sites: 52; RV sites: 52; Central water; Vault toilets; No showers; No RV dump; Reservations accepted; Max length: 30ft; Open May-Sep; Tent & RV camping: $30-32; Elev: 2920ft/890m; Tel: 760-376-3781; Nearest town: Kernville. GPS: 35.809926, -118.454458

116 • Camp 4

Total sites: 5; RV sites: 5; No water; Vault toilets; Reservations not accepted; Max length: 25ft; Open all year; Tent & RV camping: Free; Elev: 1129ft/344m; Tel: 559-338-2251; Nearest town: Fresno; Notes: Unsuitable for trailers. GPS: 36.856728, -119.107775

117 • Camp 4 1/2

Total sites: 4; RV sites: 4; No water; Vault toilets; Reservations not accepted; Max length: 25ft; Open all year; Tent & RV camping: Free; Elev: 1027ft/313m; Tel: 559-338-2251; Nearest town: Fresno. GPS: 36.861834, -119.122033

118 • Camp 9

Total sites: 109; RV sites: 109; Central water; Flush toilets; No showers; RV dump; Reservations accepted; Open all year; Tent & RV camping: $17; Elev: 2618ft/798m; Tel: 760-376-3781; Nearest town: Kernville; Notes: Dump fee: $10, 11 reservable group sites: $90-$160. GPS: 35.695409, -118.431927

119 • Camp Richardson RV Park

Total sites: 103; RV sites: 103; Elec sites: 103; Water at site; Flush toilets; Showers; RV dump; Open all year; No tents/RVs: $50; Elev: 6280ft/1914m; Tel: 530-541-1801; Nearest town: South Lake Tahoe; Notes: FHU sites, No pets, Concessionaire. GPS: 38.934171, -120.040136

120 • Campo Alto

Total sites: 15; RV sites: 15; No water; Vault toilets; Reservations accepted; Max length: 30ft; Generator hours: 0600-2200; Open May-Oct; Tent & RV camping: $20; Elev: 8209ft/2502m; Tel: 661-245-3731; Nearest town: Pine Mountain Club; Notes: 2 group sites: $100. GPS: 34.831393, -119.209368

121 • Canyon Creek

Total sites: 20; No water; Vault toilets; Reservations not accepted; Tents only: Free; Elev: 6010ft/1832m; Tel: 530-265-4531; Notes: Very rough/rocky/narrow road requiring high clearance vehicle. GPS: 39.436929, -120.579614

122 • Caples Lake

Total sites: 34; RV sites: 13; Central water; Vault toilets; No showers; No RV dump; Reservations not accepted; Max length: 30ft; Stay limit: 14 days; Open Jun-Oct; Tent & RV camping: $24; Elev: 7874ft/2400m; Tel: 209-295-4251; Nearest town: Kit Carson; Notes: Also walk-to sites. GPS: 38.705116, -120.053349

123 • Capps Crossing

Total sites: 11; RV sites: 4; Central water; Vault toilets; No showers; No RV dump; Reservations not accepted; Stay limit: 14 days; Open May-Sep; Tent & RV camping: $23; Elev: 5154ft/1571m; Tel: 530-644-2324; Nearest town: Pollock Pines; Notes: Group site: $105, Individual sites available if not reserved by group. GPS: 38.650969, -120.407095

124 • Carlton

Total sites: 19; RV sites: 7; Central water; Vault toilets; No showers; No RV dump; Reservations accepted; Open Apr-Oct; Tent & RV camping: $24; Elev: 2359ft/719m; Tel: 530-862-1368; Nearest town: Downieville. GPS: 39.519204, -121.000247

125 • Cascade Creek

Total sites: 14; RV sites: 14; No water; Vault toilets; Reservations not accepted; Stay limit: 14 days; Open May-Oct; Tent & RV camping: $8; Elev: 6125ft/1867m; Tel: 209-965-3434; Nearest town: Mi-Wuk. GPS: 38.279871, -119.971522

126 • Castle Lake

Total sites: 6; RV sites: 6; No water; Vault toilets; Reservations not accepted; Stay limit: 3 days; Open all year; Tent & RV camping: Free; Elev: 5331ft/1625m; Tel: 530-926-4511; Nearest town: Mt Shasta; Notes: Not recommended for large RVs. GPS: 41.235280, -122.378890

127 • Catavee

Total sites: 23; RV sites: 23; Central water; Flush toilets; No showers; No RV dump; Reservations accepted; Max length: 30ft; Stay limit: 14 days; Open May-Sep; Tent & RV camping: $34-36; Elev: 7103ft/2165m; Tel: 559-893-2111; Nearest town: Lakeshore. GPS: 37.252695, -119.180675

128 • Cattle Camp

Total sites: 27; RV sites: 27; No water; Vault toilets; Reservations not accepted; Max length: 32ft; Tent & RV camping: $15; Elev: 3720ft/1134m; Tel: 530-964-2184; Nearest town: McCloud. GPS: 41.262114, -121.940786

129 • Cave

Total sites: 46; RV sites: 46; Central water; Vault toilets; No showers; No RV dump; Reservations not accepted; Max length: 22ft; Stay limit: 14 days; Open Apr-Oct; Tent & RV camping: $16; Elev: 4354ft/1327m; Tel: 530-336-5521; Nearest town: Old Station. GPS: 40.685053, -121.422711

130 • Cave Lake

Total sites: 3; RV sites: 3; No water; Vault toilets; Reservations not accepted; Stay limit: 14 days; Open Jul-Oct; Tent & RV camping: Free; Elev: 6801ft/2073m; Tel: 530-279-6116; Nearest town: New Pine Creek. GPS: 41.978187, -120.205818

131 • Cedar Creek

Total sites: 11; No water; Vault toilets; No showers; No RV dump; Reservations not accepted; Open all year; Tents only: Free; Elev: 4944ft/1507m; Tel: 760-376-3781; Nearest town: Kernville; Notes: Not suitable for trailers. GPS: 35.748978, -118.582784

132 • Cedar Pass

Total sites: 17; RV sites: 17; No water; Vault toilets; Reservations not accepted; Max length: 17ft; Stay limit: 14 days; Open May-Oct; Tent & RV camping: Free; Elev: 5791ft/1765m; Nearest town: Cedarville. GPS: 41.559055, -120.298784

133 • Cerro Alto

Total sites: 22; RV sites: 10; Central water; Vault toilets; No showers; No RV dump; Reservations accepted; Max length: 30ft; Generator hours: 0600-2200; Open all year; Tent & RV camping: $25; Elev: 1083ft/330m; Tel: 805-434-1996; Nearest town: Atascadero. GPS: 35.424881, -120.740302

134 • Chapman Creek

Total sites: 27; RV sites: 20; Central water; Vault toilets; No showers; No RV dump; Reservations accepted; Max length: 22ft; Open May-Oct; Tent & RV camping: $24; Elev: 5899ft/1798m; Tel: 530-862-1368; Nearest town: Sierra City. GPS: 39.631104, -120.544678

135 • Cherry Hill

Total sites: 25; RV sites: 19; Central water; Vault toilets; No showers; No RV dump; Reservations not accepted; Max length: 22ft; Open Apr-Oct; Tent & RV camping: $14; Elev: 4816ft/1468m; Tel: 530-258-2141; Nearest town: Chester. GPS: 40.102731, -121.497471

136 • Cherry Valley

Total sites: 45; RV sites: 45; Central water; Vault toilets; No showers; No RV dump; Reservations accepted; Max length: 22ft; Stay limit: 14 days; Open May-Sep; Tent & RV camping: $24; Elev: 4997ft/1523m; Tel: 209-962-7825; Nearest town: Groveland; Notes: Water source unreliable. GPS: 37.986286, -119.920279

137 • Chilao

Total sites: 83; RV sites: 83; Central water; Vault toilets; No showers; No RV dump; Reservations not accepted; Max length: 40ft; Stay limit: 14 days; Open Apr-Sep; Tent & RV camping: $12; Elev: 5328ft/1624m; Tel: 626-574-1613; Nearest town: La Canada. GPS: 34.322023, -118.017209

138 • Chilcoot

Total sites: 40; RV sites: 40; Central water; Flush toilets; Showers; No RV dump; Reservations accepted; Max length: 22ft; Open May-Sep; Tent & RV camping: $25; Elev: 5223ft/1592m; Tel: 530-258-7606; Nearest town: Chilcoot. GPS: 39.866455, -120.167480

139 • Chilkoot

Total sites: 14; RV sites: 14; No water; Vault toilets; Reservations accepted; Stay limit: 14 days; Open May-Nov; Tent & RV camping: $26; Elev: 4767ft/1453m; Tel: 559-642-3212; Nearest town: Oakhurst. GPS: 37.367705, -119.538104

140 • China Camp

Total sites: 9; RV sites: 9; No water; Vault toilets; Reservations accepted; Max length: 20ft; Stay limit: 14 days; Generator hours: 0600-2200; Open Apr-Oct; Tent & RV camping: $20; Elev: 4557ft/1389m; Tel: 831-385-5434; Nearest town: Carmel. GPS: 36.295503, -121.566901

141 • China Flat

Total sites: 18; RV sites: 11; Central water; Vault toilets; No showers; No RV dump; Reservations not accepted; Max length: 22ft; Stay limit: 14 days; Open May-Sep; Tent & RV camping: $23; Elev: 4852ft/1479m; Tel: 530-644-2324; Nearest town: Kyburz. GPS: 38.754267, -120.267991

142 • Chris Flat

Total sites: 15; RV sites: 15; Central water; Vault toilets; No showers; No RV dump; Reservations not accepted; Stay limit: 14 days; Open Apr-Oct; Tent & RV camping: $20; Elev: 6555ft/1998m; Tel: 760-932-7070; Nearest town: Walker. GPS: 38.394511, -119.452009

143 • Christie

Total sites: 69; RV sites: 69; Central water; Flush toilets; No showers; No RV dump; Reservations accepted; Generator hours: 0800-2200; Open May-Sep; Tent & RV camping: $20; Elev: 5148ft/1569m; Tel: 530-825-3212; Nearest town: Susanville; Notes: Group sites: $30. GPS: 40.568115, -120.837891

144 • Chuchupate

Total sites: 30; RV sites: 30; No water; Vault toilets; Reservations accepted; Max length: 24ft; Generator hours: 0600-2200; Open May-Oct; Tent & RV camping: $20; Elev: 6230ft/1899m; Tel: 661-245-3731; Nearest town: Frazier Park. GPS: 34.786171, -119.001228

145 • Chula Vista

Total sites: 12; RV sites: 12; No water; Vault toilets; Reservations not accepted; Generator hours: 0600-2200; Tent & RV camping: Free; Elev: 8324ft/2537m; Tel: 661-245-3731; Nearest town: Frazier Park; Notes: 500 yard walk-in to tent CG, Self-contained vehicles only in parking lot, favored star-gazing spot. GPS: 34.813591, -119.123699

146 • Cibbets Flat

Total sites: 25; RV sites: 25; Central water; Vault toilets; No showers; No RV dump; Reservations not accepted; Max length: 27ft; Stay limit: 14 days; Tent & RV camping: $14; Elev: 4167ft/1270m; Tel: 858-673-6180; Nearest town: Pine Valley. GPS: 32.777217, -116.446916

147 • Clark Fork

Total sites: 88; RV sites: 88; Central water; Flush toilets; Showers; RV dump; Reservations not accepted; Stay limit: 14 days; Open May-Sep; Tent & RV camping: $22; Elev: 6114ft/1864m; Tel: 209-965-3434; Nearest town: Mi-Wuk. GPS: 38.397099, -119.800469

148 • Clark Springs

Total sites: 20; RV sites: 20; Central water; No toilets; No showers; No RV dump; Reservations not accepted; Open May-Oct; Tent & RV camping: $15; Elev: 2477ft/755m; Tel: 530-623-2121; Nearest town: Trinity Center. GPS: 40.857561, -122.814652

149 • Clear Creek

Total sites: 6; RV sites: 6; No water; Vault toilets; Reservations not accepted; Max length: 22ft; Open all year; Tent & RV camping: Free; Elev: 3540ft/1079m; Tel: 530-623-2121; Nearest town: Weaverville. GPS: 40.931275, -122.586341

150 • Clover Meadow

Total sites: 7; RV sites: 7; Central water; Vault toilets; No showers; No RV dump; Reservations not accepted; Max length: 20ft; Stay limit: 14 days; Open Jun-Oct; Tent & RV camping: Free; Elev: 7047ft/2148m; Tel: 209-966-3638; Nearest town: Fresno. GPS: 37.527022, -119.277625

151 • Cold Creek

Total sites: 6; RV sites: 6; No water; Vault toilets; Reservations accepted; Open May-Oct; Tent & RV camping: $16; Elev: 5712ft/1741m; Tel: 530-862-1030; Nearest town: Sierraville. GPS: 39.542725, -120.315674

152 • Coldbrook

Total sites: 20; RV sites: 20; No water; Vault toilets; Reservations not accepted; Max length: 22ft; Stay limit: 14 days; Tent & RV camping: $12; Elev: 3350ft/1021m; Tel: 818-335-1251; Nearest town: Big Bear City. GPS: 34.291889, -117.840607

153 • Coldwater

Total sites: 74; RV sites: 74; Central water; Flush toilets; No showers; No RV dump; Reservations accepted; Stay limit: 14 days; Open Jun-Sep; Tent & RV camping: $22-24; Elev: 9006ft/2745m; Tel: 760-924-5500; Nearest town: Mammoth Lakes; Notes: Bear boxes must be used for food storage. GPS: 37.598445, -118.995575

154 • College

Total sites: 11; Central water; Flush toilets; No showers; No RV dump; Reservations accepted; Stay limit: 14 days; Open Jun-Oct; Tents only: $33; Elev: 7014ft/2138m; Tel: 559-893-2308; Nearest town: Lakeshore. GPS: 37.251872, -119.169828

155 • Colson

Total sites: 5; RV sites: 5; No water; No toilets; Reservations not accepted; Generator hours: 0600-2200; Tent & RV camping: Free; Elev: 2067ft/630m; Tel: 805-925-9538; Nearest town: Santa Maria. GPS: 34.940000, -120.170000

156 • Conklin Park

Total sites: 9; RV sites: 9; No water; Vault toilets; Reservations not accepted; Stay limit: 14 days; Open all year; Tent & RV camping: Free; Elev: 5974ft/1821m; Tel: 530-836-2575; Nearest town: Portola. GPS: 40.047000, -120.368000

157 • Convict Flat

Total sites: 5; RV sites: 5; No water; Vault toilets; Reservations not accepted; Max length: 24ft; Open May-Nov; Tent & RV camping: Free; Elev: 3225ft/983m; Tel: 559-338-2251; Nearest town: Grant Grove Village. GPS: 36.818497, -118.832174

158 • Convict Lake

Total sites: 86; RV sites: 86; Central water; Flush toilets; No showers; RV dump; Reservations accepted; Stay limit: 14 days; Open May-Oct; Tent & RV camping: $27; Elev: 7552ft/2302m; Tel: 760-924-5500; Nearest town: Mammoth Lakes; Notes: Bear boxes must be used for food storage. GPS: 37.595459, -118.848633

159 • Cooper Gulch

Total sites: 5; RV sites: 5; Central water; Vault toilets; No showers; No RV dump; Reservations not accepted; Max length: 16ft; Open

Apr-Oct; Tent & RV camping: $20; Elev: 2018ft/615m; Tel: 530-623-2121; Nearest town: Weaverville. GPS: 40.745848, -122.806377

160 • Corral Canyon

Total sites: 20; RV sites: 20; Central water; Vault toilets; No showers; No RV dump; Reservations not accepted; Max length: 27ft; Stay limit: 14 days; Tent & RV camping: $5; Elev: 3474ft/1059m; Tel: 619-445-6235; Nearest town: Pine Valley; Notes: Adventure Pass required ($5/day or $30/year) or Interagency Pass. GPS: 32.712442, -116.572208

161 • Cottonwood

Total sites: 22; RV sites: 22; No water; Vault toilets; Reservations not accepted; Max length: 22ft; Stay limit: 14 days; Open all year; Tent & RV camping: $5; Elev: 2736ft/834m; Tel: 661-269-2808; Nearest town: Lake Hughes; Notes: Adventure Pass required ($5/day or $30/year) or Interagency Pass. GPS: 34.640025, -118.503028

162 • Cottonwood Creek

Total sites: 57; RV sites: 57; Central water; Vault toilets; No showers; No RV dump; Reservations accepted; Max length: 22ft; Open May-Oct; Tent & RV camping: $20; Elev: 5659ft/1725m; Tel: 530-862-1030; Nearest town: Sierraville. GPS: 39.548828, -120.318848

163 • Cottonwood Springs

Total sites: 20; RV sites: 20; Central water; Flush toilets; Showers; RV dump; Reservations accepted; Open May-Sep; Tent & RV camping: $25; Elev: 5705ft/1739m; Tel: 530-836-2575; Nearest town: Chilcoot; Notes: Group sites: $100-$140. GPS: 39.890869, -120.211426

164 • Coy Flat

Total sites: 20; RV sites: 20; No water; Vault toilets; Reservations accepted; Max length: 26ft; Open May-Nov; Tent & RV camping: $26; Elev: 4764ft/1452m; Tel: 559-539-2607; Nearest town: Springville. GPS: 36.126955, -118.619043

165 • Crab Flats

Total sites: 27; RV sites: 27; Central water; Vault toilets; No showers; No RV dump; Reservations accepted; Max length: 28ft; Open Apr-Oct; Tent & RV camping: $24-26; Elev: 5961ft/1817m; Tel: 909-867-2165; Nearest town: Lake Arrowhead; Notes: Due to washouts (potholes) access road to the campground is very narrow and may not accept large RVs. GPS: 34.263372, -117.086402

166 • Crags

Total sites: 27; RV sites: 27; Central water; Flush toilets; No showers; No RV dump; Reservations accepted; Stay limit: 14 days; Open May-Oct; Tent & RV camping: $23; Elev: 7113ft/2168m; Tel: 760-932-7070; Nearest town: Bridgeport; Notes: Group site: $125. GPS: 38.172225, -119.321468

167 • Crater Lake

Total sites: 17; RV sites: 17; Central water; Vault toilets; No showers; No RV dump; Reservations not accepted; Max length: 18ft; Generator hours: 0800-2200; Open May-Oct; Tent & RV camping: $10; Elev: 7024ft/2141m; Tel: 530-257-4188; Nearest town: Susanville. GPS: 40.626664, -121.042071

168 • Crocker

Total sites: 10; RV sites: 10; No water; Vault toilets; Reservations not accepted; Stay limit: 14 days; Open May-Oct; Tent & RV camping: Free; Elev: 5771ft/1759m; Tel: 530-836-2572; Nearest town: Portola. GPS: 39.891000, -120.423000

169 • Crystal Lake

Total sites: 191; RV sites: 191; Central water; Vault toilets; No showers; No RV dump; Reservations not accepted; Stay limit: 14 days; Open May-Dec; Tent & RV camping: $12; Elev: 5725ft/1745m; Tel: 626-335-1251; Nearest town: Azusa. GPS: 34.321846, -117.845689

170 • Crystal Springs

Total sites: 19; RV sites: 19; Central water; Vault toilets; No showers; No RV dump; Reservations not accepted; Stay limit: 14 days; Open Apr-Sep; Tent & RV camping: $18; Elev: 5994ft/1827m; Tel: 775-882-2766; Nearest town: Bridgeport. GPS: 38.765169, -119.845986

171 • Curly Jack

Total sites: 12; RV sites: 12; Central water; Vault toilets; No showers; No RV dump; Reservations accepted; Stay limit: 14 days; Open May-Dec; Tent & RV camping: $15; Elev: 1070ft/326m; Tel: 530-493-2243; Nearest town: Happy Camp; Notes: Group site: $50. GPS: 41.785682, -123.389859

172 • Dardanelle

Total sites: 28; RV sites: 28; Central water; Vault toilets; No showers; No RV dump; Reservations not accepted; Max length: 22ft; Stay limit: 14 days; Open May-Sep; Tent & RV camping: $19; Elev: 5771ft/1759m; Tel: 209-965-3434; Nearest town: Dardanelle. GPS: 38.341592, -119.833284

173 • Dark Day

Total sites: 9; Central water; Vault toilets; No showers; No RV dump; Reservation required; Open May-Sep; Tents only: $22; Elev: 2087ft/636m; Tel: 530-692-3200; Nearest town: Camptonville. GPS: 39.428564, -121.109806

174 • Davis Flat

Total sites: 20; RV sites: 20; No water; Vault toilets; Reservations not accepted; Open all year; Tent & RV camping: $5; Elev: 1591ft/485m; Tel: 530-963-3128; Nearest town: Stonyford. GPS: 39.362587, -122.654348

175 • Davy Brown

Total sites: 13; RV sites: 13; No water; Vault toilets; Reservations accepted; Max length: 25ft; Stay limit: 14 days; Generator hours: 0600-2200; Open Apr-Oct; Tent & RV camping: $20; Elev: 2087ft/636m; Tel: 805-925-9538; Nearest town: Santa Ynez. GPS: 34.757969, -119.953501

176 • Dead Mule

Total sites: 2; RV sites: 2; No water; Vault toilets; Reservations not accepted; Open Jun-Oct; Tent & RV camping: Free; Elev: 5148ft/1569m; Nearest town: Paskenta. GPS: 39.846136, -122.828245

177 • Deadlun

Total sites: 25; RV sites: 25; No water; Vault toilets; Reservations not accepted; Max length: 24ft; Open all year; Tent & RV camping: Free; Elev: 2746ft/837m; Tel: 530-275-1587; Nearest town: Round Mountain. GPS: 41.061087, -121.975684

178 • Deadman

Total sites: 17; RV sites: 15; Central water; Vault toilets; No showers; No RV dump; Reservations not accepted; Stay limit: 14 days; Open Apr-Oct; Tent & RV camping: $20; Elev: 6309ft/1923m; Tel: 209-965-3434; Nearest town: Pinecrest; Notes: Also walk-to sites. GPS: 38.317350, -119.748970

179 • Deanes Valley

Total sites: 7; RV sites: 7; No water; Vault toilets; Reservations not accepted; Open Apr-Sep; Tent & RV camping: Free; Elev: 4322ft/1317m; Tel: 530-283-0555; Nearest town: Quincy. GPS: 39.889545, -121.024617

180 • Deer Creek

Total sites: 28; RV sites: 28; Central water; Flush toilets; No showers; No RV dump; Reservations accepted; Max length: 40ft; Stay limit: 14 days; Open Jun-Oct; Tent & RV camping: $33; Elev: 7047ft/2148m; Tel: 559-893-2111; Nearest town: Clovis. GPS: 37.251807, -119.177016

181 • Deer Mt Snowpark

Total sites: 8; RV sites: 8; No water; Vault toilets; Reservations not accepted; Max length: 30ft; Stay limit: 14 days; Open all year; Tent & RV camping: Free; Elev: 5763ft/1757m; Tel: 530-398-4391; Nearest town: Weed; Notes: Winter RV parking in lot. GPS: 41.570447, -122.132071

182 • Deer Valley

Total sites: 13; RV sites: 13; No water; Vault toilets; Reservations not accepted; Open all year; Tent & RV camping: $6; Elev: 3553ft/1083m; Tel: 707-275-2361; Nearest town: Upper Lake. GPS: 39.266006, -122.883218

183 • Deerlick Springs

Total sites: 13; No water; Vault toilets; Reservations not accepted; Tents only: Free; Elev: 3043ft/928m; Tel: 530-352-4211; Nearest town: Platina. GPS: 40.470743, -122.927329

184 • Denny

Total sites: 5; RV sites: 5; No water; Vault toilets; Reservations not accepted; Max length: 22ft; Tent & RV camping: Fee unknown; Elev: 1598ft/487m; Tel: 530-623-2121; Nearest town: Denny. GPS: 40.932917, -123.394487

185 • Diablo

Total sites: 19; RV sites: 12; No water; Vault toilets; Reservations accepted; Open May-Oct; Tent & RV camping: $18; Elev: 5890ft/1795m; Tel: 530-862-1368; Nearest town: Bassett. GPS: 39.631754, -120.638539

186 • Dillon Creek

Total sites: 21; RV sites: 21; No water; Vault toilets; No showers; No RV dump; Reservations accepted; Open May-Sep; Tent & RV camping: $10; Elev: 863ft/263m; Tel: 530-627-3291; Nearest town: Orleans; Notes: Food storage lockers. GPS: 41.573525, -123.542816

187 • Dimond 'O'

Total sites: 40; RV sites: 40; Central water; Vault toilets; No showers; No RV dump; Reservations accepted; Stay limit: 14 days; Open Apr-Oct; Tent & RV camping: $26; Elev: 4482ft/1366m; Tel: 209-379-2258; Nearest town: Groveland. GPS: 37.863233, -119.870422

188 • Dinkey Creek

Total sites: 128; RV sites: 128; Central water; Flush toilets; Pay showers; No RV dump; Reservations accepted; Max length: 35ft; Open May-Sep; Tent & RV camping: $34-38; Elev: 5876ft/1791m; Tel: 559-841-2705; Nearest town: Dinkey Creek; Notes: Group site: $202. GPS: 37.072703, -119.155741

189 • Dixie Glade

Total sites: 7; RV sites: 7; No water; Vault toilets; Reservations not accepted; Open Apr-Nov; Tent & RV camping: $5; Elev: 3077ft/938m; Tel: 530-963-3128; Nearest town: Stonyford. GPS: 39.335324, -122.703154

190 • Dogwood

Total sites: 93; RV sites: 93; Central water; Flush toilets; Showers; RV dump; Reservations accepted; Max length: 22ft; Open Apr-Oct; Tents: $37-39/RVs: $47-49; Elev: 5673ft/1729m; Tel: 909-336-6717; Nearest town: Rimforest. GPS: 34.235575, -117.213083

191 • Domingo Springs

Total sites: 18; RV sites: 18; Central water; Vault toilets; No showers; No RV dump; Reservations not accepted; Open May-Sep; Tent & RV camping: $14; Elev: 5167ft/1575m; Tel: 530-258-2141; Nearest town: Chester. GPS: 40.360428, -121.347114

192 • Dorabelle

Total sites: 68; RV sites: 68; Central water; Vault toilets; No showers; No RV dump; Reservations accepted; Max length: 40ft; Stay limit: 14 days; Open May-Oct; Tent & RV camping: $31-33; Elev: 5430ft/1655m; Tel: 559-841-3533; Nearest town: Shaver Lake. GPS: 37.113016, -119.309746

193 • Dripping Springs

Total sites: 34; RV sites: 34; Central water; Vault toilets; No showers; No RV dump; Reservations accepted; Max length: 27ft; Stay limit: 14 days; Open all year; Tent & RV camping: $15; Elev: 1673ft/510m; Tel: 760-788-0250; Nearest town: Aguanga; Notes: 9 equestrian sites - 20' trailer limit. GPS: 33.460689, -116.970862

194 • Dru Barner Park

Total sites: 47; RV sites: 47; Central water; Flush toilets; No showers; No RV dump; Reservations not accepted; Stay limit: 14

days; Open all year; Tent & RV camping: $8; Elev: 3228ft/984m; Tel: 916-333-4312; Nearest town: Georgetown; Notes: Access road not plowed in winter. GPS: 38.942000, -120.765000

195 • Dutchman

Total sites: 8; No water; Vault toilets; Reservations not accepted; Generator hours: 0600-2200; Tents only: $5; Elev: 6752ft/2058m; Tel: 661-245-3731; Notes: High clearance vehicles recommended, Adventure Pass required ($5/day or $30/year) or Interagency Pass. GPS: 34.674162, -118.977229

196 • E-Ne-Nuck

Total sites: 10; RV sites: 10; Central water; Vault toilets; No showers; No RV dump; Reservations not accepted; Max length: 30ft; Open Jun-Oct; Tent & RV camping: $10; Elev: 420ft/128m; Tel: 530-627-3291; Nearest town: Orleans. GPS: 41.240357, -123.656291

197 • Eagle

Total sites: 50; RV sites: 41; Elec sites: 2; Central water; Flush toilets; No showers; No RV dump; Reservations accepted; Open May-Dec; Tent & RV camping: $20; Elev: 5190ft/1582m; Tel: 530-257-4188; Nearest town: Susanville; Notes: 2 group sites: $30, Additional fee for electric. GPS: 40.548615, -120.781277

198 • Eagle Creek

Total sites: 17; RV sites: 17; Central water; Vault toilets; No showers; No RV dump; Reservations not accepted; Max length: 35ft; Open May-Oct; Tent & RV camping: $15; Elev: 2799ft/853m; Tel: 530-623-2121; Nearest town: Trinity Center. GPS: 41.151855, -122.669922

199 • Eagle's Nest

Total sites: 31; Central water; Vault toilets; No showers; No RV dump; Reservations not accepted; Open all year; Tents only: $45; Elev: 6259ft/1908m; Tel: 530-541-1801; Nearest town: South Lake Tahoe; Notes: No pets, Concessionaire. GPS: 38.932697, -120.037278

200 • East Fork

Total sites: 10; RV sites: 10; No water; Vault toilets; Reservations not accepted; Max length: 22ft; Open Jun-Sep; Tent & RV camping: $8; Elev: 1808ft/551m; Tel: 530-629-2118; Nearest town: Willow Creek. GPS: 40.907083, -123.706798

201 • East Fork (Grasshopper Ridge)

Total sites: 6; RV sites: 6; No water; Vault toilets; Reservations not accepted; Stay limit: 14 days; Open May-Oct; Tent & RV camping: Free; Elev: 2461ft/750m; Tel: 530-468-5351; Nearest town: Cecilville. GPS: 41.153992, -123.108632

202 • East Fork (Mount Morgan)

Total sites: 133; RV sites: 108; Central water; Flush toilets; No showers; RV dump; Reservations accepted; Stay limit: 21 days; Open May-Oct; Tent & RV camping: $27; Elev: 8917ft/2718m; Tel: 760-935-4339; Nearest town: Bishop. GPS: 37.487604, -118.719779

203 • East Meadow

Total sites: 44; RV sites: 44; Central water; Flush toilets; No showers; Reservations accepted; Max length: 22ft; Open May-Sep; Tent & RV camping: $24; Elev: 6142ft/1872m; Tel: 530-265-8861; Nearest town: Truckee. GPS: 39.500488, -120.533936

204 • East Weaver

Total sites: 11; RV sites: 11; Central water; Vault toilets; No showers; No RV dump; Reservations not accepted; Max length: 25ft; Open all year; Tent & RV camping: $15; Elev: 2723ft/830m; Tel: 530-623-2121; Nearest town: Weaverville. GPS: 40.772039, -122.922091

205 • Eel River

Total sites: 15; RV sites: 15; No water; Vault toilets; Reservations not accepted; Open Apr-Nov; Tent & RV camping: $8; Elev: 1519ft/463m; Tel: 707-983-6118; Nearest town: Willits. GPS: 39.824381, -123.085472

206 • El Cariso

Total sites: 24; RV sites: 24; Central water; Vault toilets; No showers; No RV dump; Reservations not accepted; Max length: 22ft; Stay limit: 14 days; Open all year; Tent & RV camping: $15; Elev: 2641ft/805m; Tel: 619-673-6180; Nearest town: Lake Elsinore. GPS: 33.652474, -117.410197

207 • Elam Creek

Total sites: 15; RV sites: 12; Central water; Vault toilets; No showers; No RV dump; Reservations not accepted; Open Apr-Oct; Tent & RV camping: $14; Elev: 4452ft/1357m; Tel: 530-258-2141; Nearest town: Chester. GPS: 40.247559, -121.448486

208 • Ellery Creek

Total sites: 19; RV sites: 19; Central water; Vault toilets; No showers; No RV dump; Reservations accepted; Max length: 30ft; Open May-Sep; Tent & RV camping: $20; Elev: 1073ft/327m; Tel: 530-275-8113; Nearest town: Lakehead; Notes: Food storage lockers. GPS: 40.915334, -122.242636

209 • Ellery Lake

Total sites: 12; RV sites: 12; Central water; Vault toilets; No showers; No RV dump; Reservations not accepted; Max length: 30ft; Stay limit: 14 days; Open Jun-Oct; Tent & RV camping: $22-24; Elev: 9564ft/2915m; Tel: 760-647-3044; Nearest town: Lee Vining; Notes: Bear boxes must be used for food storage. GPS: 37.937073, -119.243189

210 • Emerson

Total sites: 4; RV sites: 4; No water; Vault toilets; Reservations not accepted; Max length: 16ft; Stay limit: 14 days; Open Jul-Oct; Tent & RV camping: Free; Elev: 5817ft/1773m; Tel: 530-279-6116; Nearest town: Eagleville; Notes: Narrow, steep, rough, dirt access road. GPS: 41.263166, -120.139048

211 • Escondido

Total sites: 9; RV sites: 9; No water; Vault toilets; Reservations accepted; Stay limit: 14 days; Generator hours: 0800-2200; Open

Apr-Oct; Tent & RV camping: $20; Elev: 2176ft/663m; Tel: 831-385-5434; Nearest town: Tassajara Hot Springs. GPS: 36.141337, -121.493933

212 • Eshom

Total sites: 24; RV sites: 24; Central water; Vault toilets; No showers; No RV dump; Reservations accepted; Max length: 25ft; Open May-Sep; Tent & RV camping: $25; Elev: 4915ft/1498m; Tel: 559-338-2251; Nearest town: Woodlake; Notes: 7 double sites. GPS: 36.689143, -118.950277

213 • Eureka Valley

Total sites: 28; RV sites: 24; Central water; Vault toilets; No showers; No RV dump; Reservations not accepted; Max length: 22ft; Stay limit: 14 days; Open Apr-Oct; Tent & RV camping: $18; Elev: 6142ft/1872m; Tel: 209-965-3434; Nearest town: Dardanelle; Notes: Also walk-to sites, 4 walk-to sites, Cash only. GPS: 38.340088, -119.791016

214 • Evans Flat

Total sites: 20; RV sites: 20; No water; Vault toilets; Reservations not accepted; Max length: 20ft; Tent & RV camping: Free; Elev: 6145ft/1873m; Tel: 760-379-5646; Nearest town: Wofford Heights; Notes: 4 horse sites. GPS: 35.642804, -118.589455

215 • Fairview

Total sites: 55; RV sites: 55; Central water; Vault toilets; No showers; RV dump; Reservations accepted; Max length: 45ft; Open Apr-Nov; Tent & RV camping: $25-27; Elev: 3560ft/1085m; Tel: 760-376-3781; Nearest town: Kernville. GPS: 35.929188, -118.490697

216 • Fallen Leaf

Total sites: 200; RV sites: 180; Central water; Flush toilets; Pay showers; No RV dump; Reservations accepted; Open May-Oct; Tent & RV camping: $36-38; Elev: 6391ft/1948m; Tel: 530-544-0426; Nearest town: Lake Tahoe Basin MU. GPS: 38.928605, -120.048461

217 • Feather Falls Trailhead

Total sites: 5; Central water; Vault toilets; No showers; No RV dump; Reservations not accepted; Stay limit: 14 days; Open all year; Tents only: Free; Elev: 2572ft/784m; Tel: 530-534-6500; Nearest town: Feather Falls. GPS: 39.613891, -121.266663

218 • Fence Creek

Total sites: 38; RV sites: 38; Central water; Vault toilets; No showers; No RV dump; Reservations not accepted; Stay limit: 14 days; Open May-Oct; Tent & RV camping: $8; Elev: 5669ft/1728m; Tel: 209-965-3434; Nearest town: Mi-Wuk. GPS: 38.367000, -119.871000

219 • Fern Basin

Total sites: 21; RV sites: 21; Central water; Vault toilets; No showers; No RV dump; Reservations accepted; Open May-Nov; Tent & RV camping: $10; Elev: 6322ft/1927m; Tel: 909-382-2922; Nearest town: Idyllwild. GPS: 33.789195, -116.736757

220 • Fiddle Creek

Total sites: 15; Central water; Vault toilets; No showers; No RV dump; Reservations accepted; Open Apr-Sep; Tents only: $24; Elev: 2276ft/694m; Tel: 530-862-1368; Nearest town: Camptonville. GPS: 39.518234, -120.992443

221 • Findley

Total sites: 11; RV sites: 11; Central water; Vault toilets; No showers; No RV dump; Reservations accepted; Open May-Sep; Tent & RV camping: $24; Elev: 6296ft/1919m; Tel: 530-862-1030; Nearest town: Sierraville. GPS: 39.483643, -120.554688

222 • Fir Cove

Total sites: 19; RV sites: 19; Central water; Vault toilets; No showers; No RV dump; Reservations accepted; Max length: 22ft; Open May-Sep; Tent & RV camping: $12; Elev: 2815ft/858m; Tel: 707-574-6233; Nearest town: Mad River. GPS: 40.342529, -123.404541

223 • Fir Top

Total sites: 10; RV sites: 10; Central water; Flush toilets; No showers; No RV dump; Reservations accepted; Open May-Sep; Tent & RV camping: $24; Elev: 6073ft/1851m; Tel: 530-862-1030; Nearest town: Sierraville. GPS: 39.485697, -120.550015

224 • Fish Creek (Mammoth Pool)

Total sites: 7; RV sites: 7; No water; Vault toilets; Reservations accepted; Max length: 20ft; Stay limit: 14 days; Open Jun-Nov; Tent & RV camping: $27-29; Elev: 4695ft/1431m; Tel: 559-642-3212; Nearest town: North Fork. GPS: 37.261226, -119.353379

225 • Fish Lake

Total sites: 24; RV sites: 24; No water; Vault toilets; No showers; No RV dump; Reservations accepted; Open Jun-Sep; Tent & RV camping: $10; Elev: 1752ft/534m; Tel: 530-627-3291; Nearest town: Orleans. GPS: 41.266453, -123.683239

226 • Forest Glen

Total sites: 15; RV sites: 15; Central water; Vault toilets; No showers; No RV dump; Reservations not accepted; Max length: 16ft; Open May-Sep; Tent & RV camping: $12; Elev: 2526ft/770m; Tel: 530-628-5227; Nearest town: Hayfork. GPS: 40.376221, -123.327637

227 • Forks (Bass Lake)

Total sites: 31; RV sites: 27; Central water; Flush toilets; No showers; No RV dump; Reservations accepted; Open Apr-Sep; Tent & RV camping: $36-38; Elev: 3461ft/1055m; Tel: 559-642-3212; Nearest town: Oakhurst. GPS: 37.313111, -119.568991

228 • Forks (Tungsten Hills)

Total sites: 21; RV sites: 21; Central water; Flush toilets; No showers; No RV dump; Reservations not accepted; Stay limit: 14 days; Open May-Sep; Tent & RV camping: $26; Elev: 7858ft/2395m; Tel: 760-873-2500; Nearest town: Bishop; Notes: Bear boxes must be used for food storage. GPS: 37.253226, -118.578598

229 • Four Jeffrey

Total sites: 106; RV sites: 106; Central water; Flush toilets; No showers; RV dump; Reservations accepted; Stay limit: 14 days; Open May-Oct; Tent & RV camping: $28; Elev: 8143ft/2482m; Tel: 760-935-4339; Nearest town: Bishop; Notes: Bear boxes must be used for food storage. GPS: 37.248772, -118.570709

230 • Fouts Springs

Total sites: 11; RV sites: 11; No water; Vault toilets; Reservations not accepted; Max length: 40ft; Open all year; Tent & RV camping: $5; Elev: 1627ft/496m; Tel: 530-963-3128; Nearest town: Stonyford. GPS: 39.358977, -122.653437

231 • Fowlers Camp

Total sites: 39; RV sites: 39; Central water; Vault toilets; No showers; No RV dump; Reservations accepted; Max length: 32ft; Stay limit: 14 days; Open May-Nov; Tent & RV camping: $15; Elev: 3376ft/1029m; Tel: 530-964-2184; Nearest town: McCloud. GPS: 41.245361, -122.022949

232 • Fraser Flat

Total sites: 38; RV sites: 38; Central water; Vault toilets; No showers; RV dump; Reservations not accepted; Stay limit: 14 days; Open Apr-Oct; Tent & RV camping: $19; Elev: 4869ft/1484m; Tel: 209-586-3234; Nearest town: Cold Springs. GPS: 38.169814, -120.071219

233 • Fremont

Total sites: 15; RV sites: 8; Central water; Flush toilets; No showers; No RV dump; Reservations accepted; Generator hours: 0600-2200; Open Mar-Nov; Tent & RV camping: $30; Elev: 955ft/291m; Tel: 805-967-8766; Nearest town: Santa Barbar. GPS: 34.543213, -119.821289

234 • French Camp

Total sites: 85; RV sites: 83; Central water; Flush toilets; No showers; RV dump; Reservations accepted; Max length: 30ft; Stay limit: 21 days; Open Apr-Oct; Tent & RV camping: $27; Elev: 7333ft/2235m; Tel: 760-935-4339; Nearest town: Bishop; Notes: Bear boxes must be used for food storage. GPS: 37.551987, -118.683793

235 • French Meadows

Total sites: 75; RV sites: 75; Central water; Flush toilets; No showers; No RV dump; Reservations accepted; Open May-Oct; Tent & RV camping: $24; Elev: 5354ft/1632m; Tel: 530-478-0248; Nearest town: Foresthill. GPS: 39.113972, -120.421427

236 • Frenchman

Total sites: 38; RV sites: 38; Central water; Vault toilets; No showers; RV dump; Reservations accepted; Max length: 22ft; Open May-Sep; Tent & RV camping: $30; Elev: 5636ft/1718m; Tel: 530-258-7606; Nearest town: Chilcoot. GPS: 39.900635, -120.187744

237 • Fresno Dome

Total sites: 15; No water; Vault toilets; Reservations not accepted; Stay limit: 14 days; Open May-Oct; Tents only: $27; Elev: 6542ft/1994m; Tel: 559-877-2218; Nearest town: Oakhurst. GPS: 37.455248, -119.549334

238 • Friis

Total sites: 3; RV sites: 3; No water; Vault toilets; Reservations not accepted; Stay limit: 14 days; Generator hours: 0600-2200; Open all year; Tent & RV camping: $5; Elev: 2280ft/695m; Tel: 805-925-9538; Nearest town: Pozo; Notes: Adventure Pass required ($5/day or $30/year) or Interagency Pass. GPS: 35.380795, -120.326748

239 • Frog Meadow

Total sites: 10; RV sites: 10; No water; Vault toilets; Reservations not accepted; Max length: 16ft; Open Jun-Oct; Tent & RV camping: Free; Elev: 7710ft/2350m; Tel: 559-539-2607; Nearest town: Glenville; Notes: Cabin(s), Cabin can be reserved. GPS: 35.874118, -118.575265

240 • Frog Pond

Total sites: 3; RV sites: 3; No water; Vault toilets; Reservations not accepted; Open May-Oct; Tent & RV camping: Free; Elev: 1932ft/589m; Tel: 530-627-3291; Nearest town: Orleans. GPS: 41.487464, -123.541769

241 • Gaggs Camp

Total sites: 11; RV sites: 11; No water; Vault toilets; Reservations not accepted; Max length: 22ft; Open Jun-Nov; Tent & RV camping: $26; Elev: 5902ft/1799m; Tel: 559-877-2218; Nearest town: Oakhurst. GPS: 37.361452, -119.468405

242 • Gansner Bar

Total sites: 16; RV sites: 16; Central water; Flush toilets; No showers; No RV dump; Reservations not accepted; Open May-Oct; Tent & RV camping: $30; Elev: 2418ft/737m; Tel: 530-283-0555; Nearest town: Quincy. GPS: 40.019775, -121.222412

243 • Gerle Creek

Total sites: 50; RV sites: 25; Central water; Vault toilets; No showers; No RV dump; Reservations accepted; Stay limit: 14 days; Open May-Sep; Tent & RV camping: $28; Elev: 5312ft/1619m; Tel: 530-647-5415; Nearest town: Pollock Pines. GPS: 38.975583, -120.392478

244 • Giant Gap

Total sites: 25; RV sites: 25; Central water; Vault toilets; No showers; No RV dump; Reservations accepted; Max length: 30ft; Open May-Oct; Tent & RV camping: $24; Elev: 3698ft/1127m; Tel: 530-478-0248; Nearest town: Foresthill; Notes: Food storage lockers. GPS: 39.137672, -120.793366

245 • Gigantea

Total sites: 10; RV sites: 10; No water; Vault toilets; Reservations not accepted; Max length: 35ft; Stay limit: 14 days; Open May-Oct; Tent & RV camping: $24; Elev: 6404ft/1952m; Tel: 559-855-5355; Nearest town: Shaver Lake. GPS: 37.015739, -119.106713

246 • Glass Creek

Total sites: 50; RV sites: 50; No water; Vault toilets; Reservations not accepted; Max length: 45ft; Open Jun-Oct; Tent & RV camping: Free; Elev: 7546ft/2300m; Tel: 760-647-3044; Nearest town: June Lake. GPS: 37.752693, -118.990749

247 • Gold Lake

Total sites: 37; RV sites: 37; No water; Vault toilets; Reservations not accepted; Stay limit: 14 days; Open May-Sep; Tent & RV camping: $20; Elev: 6457ft/1968m; Tel: 530-836-2575; Nearest town: Graeagle. GPS: 39.679924, -120.645945

248 • Gold Lake 4X4

Total sites: 16; RV sites: 16; No water; No toilets; Reservations not accepted; Tent & RV camping: Free; Elev: 6450ft/1966m; Tel: 530-836-2575; Nearest town: Graeagle; Notes: Also boat-in sites. GPS: 39.668632, -120.662843

249 • Golden Trout Crossing

Total sites: 15; Central water; Vault toilets; No showers; No RV dump; Reservations not accepted; Stay limit: 14 days; Open all year; Tents only: $15; Elev: 3986ft/1215m; Tel: 530-534-6500; Nearest town: Strawberry Valley. GPS: 39.615871, -121.142119

250 • Goldfield

Total sites: 6; RV sites: 6; No water; Vault toilets; Reservations not accepted; Max length: 16ft; Open all year; Tent & RV camping: Free; Elev: 3032ft/924m; Tel: 530-623-2121; Nearest town: Weaverville. GPS: 41.100000, -122.779000

251 • Goldledge

Total sites: 37; RV sites: 24; Central water; Vault toilets; No showers; No RV dump; Reservations accepted; Max length: 30ft; Open May-Sep; Tent & RV camping: $30-32; Elev: 3238ft/987m; Tel: 760-376-3781; Nearest town: Kernville. GPS: 35.874317, -118.457273

252 • Goose Lake

Total sites: 14; RV sites: 14; No water; Vault toilets; Reservations not accepted; Stay limit: 14 days; Open Jun-Oct; Tent & RV camping: $20; Elev: 6686ft/2038m; Tel: 530-836-2575; Nearest town: Graeagle. GPS: 39.675558, -120.636295

253 • Goose Meadow

Total sites: 21; RV sites: 21; Central water; Vault toilets; No showers; No RV dump; Reservations accepted; Open May-Sep; Tent & RV camping: $22; Elev: 5988ft/1825m; Tel: 530-587-9281; Nearest town: Truckee. GPS: 39.259481, -120.209617

254 • Goumaz

Total sites: 6; RV sites: 6; Central water; Vault toilets; No showers; No RV dump; Reservations not accepted; Max length: 18ft; Open May-Sep; Tent & RV camping: Free; Elev: 5249ft/1600m; Tel: 530-825-3212; Nearest town: Susanville; Notes: No water in winter. GPS: 40.413916, -120.862025

255 • Grandview

Total sites: 26; RV sites: 26; No water; Vault toilets; Reservations not accepted; Max length: 35ft; Stay limit: 14 days; Open all year; Tent & RV camping: $5; Elev: 8537ft/2602m; Tel: 760-873-2500; Nearest town: Big Pine; Notes: Popular star-gazing spot, may be closed by snow. GPS: 37.332602, -118.189632

256 • Granite Creek

Total sites: 20; RV sites: 20; No water; Vault toilets; Reservations not accepted; Max length: 20ft; Open Jun-Sep; Tent & RV camping: Free; Elev: 6982ft/2128m; Tel: 559-877-2218; Nearest town: Fresno. GPS: 37.538647, -119.263963

257 • Granite Flat

Total sites: 65; RV sites: 58; Central water; Vault toilets; No showers; No RV dump; Reservations accepted; Open May-Oct; Tent & RV camping: $22; Elev: 5892ft/1796m; Tel: 530-587-9281; Nearest town: Truckee. GPS: 39.298628, -120.204732

258 • Grasshopper Flat

Total sites: 70; RV sites: 70; Central water; Flush toilets; Pay showers; RV dump; Reservations accepted; Max length: 35ft; Stay limit: 14 days; Open May-Oct; Tent & RV camping: $30; Elev: 5863ft/1787m; Tel: 530-832-1076; Nearest town: Portola; Notes: Group site $100, Dump station within 1 mi. GPS: 39.890381, -120.478027

259 • Grassy Flat

Total sites: 19; RV sites: 15; No water; Vault toilets; No showers; No RV dump; Reservations accepted; Open May-Sep; Tent & RV camping: $10; Elev: 718ft/219m; Tel: 707-457-3131; Nearest town: Crescent City. GPS: 41.856434, -123.888093

260 • Green Cabin Flat

Total sites: 5; RV sites: 5; No water; Vault toilets; Reservations not accepted; Max length: 25ft; Open all year; Tent & RV camping: Free; Elev: 1063ft/324m; Tel: 559-338-2251; Nearest town: Fresno. GPS: 36.859925, -119.102895

261 • Green Creek

Total sites: 11; RV sites: 11; Central water; Vault toilets; No showers; No RV dump; Reservations not accepted; Stay limit: 14 days; Open May-Oct; Tent & RV camping: $20; Elev: 7979ft/2432m; Tel: 760-932-7070; Nearest town: Bridgeport; Notes: Group sites: $60-$75. GPS: 38.111457, -119.275508

262 • Green Springs Trailhead

Total sites: 6; RV sites: 6; No water; Vault toilets; Reservations not accepted; Max length: 22ft; Open Jun-Nov; Tent & RV camping: Free; Elev: 6047ft/1843m; Tel: 707-983-6118; Notes: No large RVs, Sites not level. GPS: 39.972523, -122.932274

263 • Green Valley

Total sites: 23; RV sites: 23; Central water; Flush toilets; No showers; No RV dump; Reservations accepted; Max length: 22ft; Open Apr-Oct; Tent & RV camping: $26-28; Elev: 7159ft/

2182m; Tel: 909-867-2165; Nearest town: Lake Arrowhead. GPS: 34.244727, -117.062757

264 • Green Valley TC

Total sites: 1; No water; No toilets; Reservations not accepted; Stay limit: 14 days; Open all year; Tents only: Free; Elev: 5804ft/1769m; Tel: 661-296-9710. GPS: 39.120439, -120.474091

265 • Greys Mountain

Total sites: 26; RV sites: 26; No water; Vault toilets; Reservations not accepted; Max length: 20ft; Open May-Sep; Tent & RV camping: $30; Elev: 5318ft/1621m; Tel: 559-877-2218; Nearest town: Oakhurst. GPS: 37.397079, -119.564989

266 • Grider Creek

Total sites: 10; RV sites: 10; No water; Vault toilets; Max length: 16ft; Stay limit: 14 days; Open May-Oct; Tent & RV camping: Free; Elev: 1708ft/521m; Tel: 530-493-2243; Nearest town: Seiad Valley. GPS: 41.806631, -123.217908

267 • Grizzly

Total sites: 57; RV sites: 57; Central water; Flush toilets; No showers; RV dump; Reservations accepted; Max length: 32ft; Stay limit: 14 days; Open May-Sep; Tent & RV camping: $30; Elev: 5909ft/1801m; Tel: 530-832-1076; Nearest town: Portola. GPS: 39.887207, -120.473633

268 • Grizzly Creek

Total sites: 11; RV sites: 8; No water; Vault toilets; Reservations not accepted; Open Apr-Oct; Tent & RV camping: $25; Elev: 5318ft/1621m; Tel: 530-283-0555; Nearest town: Quincy. GPS: 39.867047, -121.206948

269 • Grouse Ridge

Total sites: 9; RV sites: 5; No water; Vault toilets; Reservations not accepted; Max length: 16ft; Open May-Sep; Tent & RV camping: Free; Elev: 7492ft/2284m; Tel: 530-265-4531; Nearest town: Nevada City; Notes: Rough road. GPS: 39.390704, -120.609703

270 • Groves Prairie

Total sites: 5; RV sites: 5; No water; Vault toilets; Reservations not accepted; Open May-Oct; Tent & RV camping: Free; Elev: 4268ft/1301m; Tel: 530-629-2118; Nearest town: Arcata. GPS: 40.966182, -123.487157

271 • Guffy

Total sites: 6; No water; Vault toilets; Reservations not accepted; Stay limit: 14 days; Open all year; Tents only: $5; Elev: 8225ft/2507m; Tel: 661-269-2808; Nearest town: Big Pines; Notes: Rough road, Gate at Inspiration Point closed to vehicles during the winter months, Adventure Pass required ($5/day or $30/year) or Interagency Pass. GPS: 34.341126, -117.655404

272 • Gull Lake

Total sites: 11; RV sites: 11; Potable water; Flush toilets; No showers; No RV dump; Reservations not accepted; Max length: 30ft; Open Jun-Oct; Tent & RV camping: $23; Elev: 7638ft/2328m; Tel: 760-647-3044; Nearest town: June Lake; Notes: Bear boxes must be used for food storage. GPS: 37.773193, -119.081543

273 • Gumboot Lake

Total sites: 6; RV sites: 4; No water; Vault toilets; Reservations not accepted; Max length: 12ft; Open Jun-Oct; Tent & RV camping: Free; Elev: 6082ft/1854m; Tel: 530-926-4511; Nearest town: Mount Shasta; Notes: No large RVs. GPS: 41.212699, -122.509292

274 • Halfmoon

Total sites: 10; RV sites: 10; No water; Vault toilets; Reservations not accepted; Generator hours: 0600-2200; Tent & RV camping: $5; Elev: 4731ft/1442m; Tel: 661-245-3731; Nearest town: Frazier Park; Notes: Adventure Pass required ($5/day or $30/year) or Interagency Pass. GPS: 34.651000, -119.068000

275 • Halfway Group

Total sites: 5; No water; Vault toilets; Reservations not accepted; Open all year; Tent & RV camping: Fee unknown; Elev: 2825ft/861m; Tel: 760-379-1815; Nearest town: Kernville; Notes: Group sites: $42-$174. GPS: 35.802563, -118.451971

276 • Hallsted

Total sites: 20; RV sites: 20; Elec sites: 8; Central water; Flush toilets; Showers; No RV dump; Reservations accepted; Open Jun-Sep; Tents: $30/RVs: $30-40; Elev: 2851ft/869m; Tel: 530-283-0555; Nearest town: Quincy. GPS: 40.017127, -121.073213

277 • Hammerhorn Lake

Total sites: 9; RV sites: 9; Central water; Vault toilets; No showers; No RV dump; Reservations not accepted; Open May-Oct; Tent & RV camping: $8; Elev: 3619ft/1103m; Tel: 707-983-6118; Nearest town: Willits; Notes: No large RVs. GPS: 39.948853, -122.991495

278 • Hampshire Rocks

Total sites: 15; RV sites: 10; Central water; Vault toilets; No showers; No RV dump; Reservations accepted; Max length: 22ft; Open May-Sep; Tent & RV camping: $24; Elev: 5928ft/1807m; Tel: 530-478-0248; Nearest town: Big Bend. GPS: 39.310419, -120.497435

279 • Hanna Flat

Total sites: 88; RV sites: 88; Central water; Vault toilets; No showers; No RV dump; Reservations accepted; Max length: 26ft; Open Apr-Oct; Tent & RV camping: $30-34; Elev: 7159ft/2182m; Tel: 909-382-2790; Nearest town: Fawnskin. GPS: 34.287801, -116.974538

280 • Harris Spring

Total sites: 15; RV sites: 15; No water; Vault toilets; Reservations not accepted; Max length: 32ft; Open Aug-Oct; Tent & RV camping: Free; Elev: 4882ft/1488m; Tel: 530-964-2184; Nearest town: McCloud. GPS: 41.454346, -121.785156

281 • Hartley Springs

Total sites: 25; RV sites: 25; No water; Vault toilets; Reservations not accepted; Stay limit: 14 days; Open May-Oct; Tent & RV camping: Free; Elev: 8448ft/2575m; Tel: 760-647-3044; Nearest town: Mammoth Lakes; Notes: No bear lockers are available at this site. GPS: 37.771921, -119.037386

282 • Hat Creek

Total sites: 72; RV sites: 72; Central water; Flush toilets; No showers; No RV dump; Reservations not accepted; Max length: 22ft; Stay limit: 14 days; Open Apr-Oct; Tent & RV camping: $16; Elev: 4485ft/1367m; Tel: 530-335-7517; Nearest town: Old Station; Notes: RV dump in Old Station, Caving nearby. GPS: 40.667725, -121.446533

283 • Haven Lake

Total sites: 4; RV sites: 4; No water; Vault toilets; Reservations not accepted; Stay limit: 14 days; Open May-Sep; Tent & RV camping: $20; Elev: 6690ft/2039m; Tel: 530-836-2575; Nearest town: Graeagle. GPS: 39.672723, -120.631198

284 • Hayden Flat

Total sites: 35; RV sites: 35; Central water; Vault toilets; No showers; No RV dump; Reservations not accepted; Max length: 25ft; Open all year; Tent & RV camping: $12; Elev: 1207ft/368m; Tel: 530-623-2121; Nearest town: Del Loma; Notes: Group site: $40. GPS: 40.784545, -123.342827

285 • Haywood Flat

Total sites: 98; RV sites: 87; Central water; Flush toilets; No showers; No RV dump; Reservations accepted; Max length: 40ft; Open May-Sep; Tent & RV camping: $23; Elev: 2388ft/728m; Tel: 530-623-2121; Nearest town: Trinity Center; Notes: Group site $23-$30, Bear boxes. GPS: 40.872848, -122.767331

286 • Headquarters

Total sites: 16; RV sites: 16; No water; Vault toilets; Reservations accepted; Max length: 18ft; Stay limit: 14 days; Open Jul-Oct; Tent & RV camping: $14; Elev: 6745ft/2056m; Tel: 530-667-2246; Nearest town: McCloud. GPS: 41.585738, -121.615343

287 • Headquarters

Total sites: 44; RV sites: 31; Central water; Vault toilets; No showers; No RV dump; Reservations accepted; Max length: 27ft; Open all year; Tent & RV camping: $28-30; Elev: 2930ft/893m; Tel: 760-376-3781; Nearest town: Kernville. GPS: 35.797084, -118.451221

288 • Heart Bar

Total sites: 54; RV sites: 54; Central water; Vault toilets; No showers; No RV dump; Reservations accepted; Max length: 50ft; Open Apr-Nov; Tent & RV camping: $26-28; Elev: 6926ft/2111m; Tel: 909-866-8550; Nearest town: Angelus Oaks. GPS: 34.158919, -116.786185

289 • Hell Gate

Total sites: 17; RV sites: 17; Central water; Vault toilets; No showers; No RV dump; Reservations not accepted; Max length: 16ft; Open May-Sep; Tent & RV camping: $6; Elev: 2341ft/714m; Tel: 530-628-5227; Nearest town: Hayfork. GPS: 40.370681, -123.313807

290 • Hemlock

Total sites: 19; RV sites: 19; Central water; Vault toilets; No showers; No RV dump; Reservations accepted; Max length: 22ft; Stay limit: 14 days; Open Jul-Oct; Tent & RV camping: $14; Elev: 6772ft/2064m; Tel: 530-233-5811; Nearest town: Tionesta. GPS: 41.585917, -121.589553

291 • Hermit Valley

Total sites: 25; RV sites: 25; No water; Vault toilets; Reservations not accepted; Stay limit: 14 days; Open Jun-Oct; Tent & RV camping: Free; Elev: 7136ft/2175m; Tel: 209-795-1381; Nearest town: Bear Valley; Notes: Rough road. GPS: 38.538285, -119.899536

292 • Herring Creek

Total sites: 7; RV sites: 7; No water; Vault toilets; Reservations not accepted; Stay limit: 14 days; Open May-Oct; Tent & RV camping: Donation; Elev: 7392ft/2253m; Tel: 209-965-3434; Nearest town: Bumblebee. GPS: 38.244461, -119.932471

293 • Herring Reservoir

Total sites: 42; RV sites: 42; No water; Vault toilets; Reservations not accepted; Stay limit: 14 days; Open May-Sep; Tent & RV camping: Donation; Elev: 7448ft/2270m; Tel: 209-965-3434; Nearest town: Bumblebee. GPS: 38.248961, -119.934786

294 • Hi Mountain

Total sites: 11; RV sites: 11; No water; Vault toilets; Reservations not accepted; Max length: 16ft; Generator hours: 0600-2200; Tent & RV camping: $5; Elev: 2224ft/678m; Tel: 805-025-9538; Nearest town: San Luis Obispo; Notes: Adventure Pass required ($5/day or $30/year) or Interagency Pass. GPS: 35.261475, -120.413818

295 • High Bridge

Total sites: 12; RV sites: 12; No water; Vault toilets; No showers; No RV dump; Reservations not accepted; Generator hours: 0600-2200; Open May-Sep; Tent & RV camping: $12; Elev: 4893ft/1491m; Tel: 530-258-2141; Nearest town: Chester. GPS: 40.337839, -121.308098

296 • Highland Lakes

Total sites: 35; RV sites: 35; Central water; Vault toilets; Reservations not accepted; Stay limit: 14 days; Open Jun-Oct; Tent & RV camping: $12; Elev: 8635ft/2632m; Tel: 209-795-1381; Nearest town: Arnold. GPS: 38.488604, -119.807709

297 • Hobo

Total sites: 35; RV sites: 25; No water; Vault toilets; Reservations not accepted; Max length: 22ft; Open Apr-Sep; Tent & RV camping: $23-25; Elev: 2326ft/709m; Tel: 760-376-3781; Nearest town: Lake Isabella; Notes: Unsuitable for trailers. GPS: 35.574285, -118.529196

298 • Hobo Gulch

Total sites: 10; No water; Vault toilets; Reservations not accepted; Tents only: Free; Elev: 3182ft/970m; Tel: 530-623-2121; Nearest town: Junction City; Notes: Very rough road. GPS: 40.924198, -123.155012

299 • Holcomb Valley

Total sites: 19; RV sites: 19; No water; Vault toilets; Reservations not accepted; Open all year; Tent & RV camping: $24-26; Elev: 7385ft/2251m; Tel: 909-382-2790; Nearest town: Big Bear City. GPS: 34.302573, -116.896108

300 • Hole In The Ground

Total sites: 13; RV sites: 5; Central water; Vault toilets; No showers; No RV dump; Reservations not accepted; Open May-Oct; Tent & RV camping: $12; Elev: 4266ft/1300m; Tel: 530-258-2141; Nearest town: Mineral; Notes: Not recommended for large RVs. GPS: 40.309482, -121.562485

301 • Holey Meadow

Total sites: 10; No water; Vault toilets; Reservations accepted; Open May-Oct; Tents only: $26-28; Elev: 6483ft/1976m; Tel: 559-539-5230; Nearest town: California Hot Springs. GPS: 35.953817, -118.618639

302 • Holiday

Total sites: 35; RV sites: 35; Central water; Vault toilets; No showers; No RV dump; Reservations not accepted; Open all year; Tent & RV camping: $25; Elev: 7192ft/2192m; Tel: 760-873-2500; Nearest town: Mammoth Lakes; Notes: Used as overflow only, Free in winter - no services, Bear boxes must be used for food storage. GPS: 37.552641, -118.675952

303 • Honeymoon Flat

Total sites: 28; RV sites: 21; Central water; Vault toilets; No showers; No RV dump; Reservations accepted; Max length: 45ft; Stay limit: 14 days; Open May-Sep; Tent & RV camping: $20; Elev: 6932ft/2113m; Tel: 760-932-7070; Nearest town: Bridgeport. GPS: 38.198782, -119.320436

304 • Honn Creek

Total sites: 6; No water; Vault toilets; Reservations not accepted; Stay limit: 14 days; Open Apr-Oct; Tents only: $10; Elev: 3425ft/1044m; Tel: 530-336-5521; Nearest town: Old Station. GPS: 40.779204, -121.503206

305 • Hope Valley

Total sites: 28; RV sites: 28; Central water; Vault toilets; No showers; No RV dump; Reservations accepted; Stay limit: 14 days; Open May-Sep; Tent & RV camping: $22; Elev: 7159ft/2182m; Tel: 530-694-1002; Nearest town: Woodfords. GPS: 38.730341, -119.929845

306 • Horse Flat

Total sites: 10; RV sites: 10; No water; Vault toilets; Reservations not accepted; Max length: 16ft; Open May-Oct; Tent & RV camping: Free; Elev: 3458ft/1054m; Tel: 530-623-2121; Nearest town: Callahan. GPS: 41.165968, -122.691955

307 • Horse Flats

Total sites: 26; RV sites: 26; No water; Vault toilets; No showers; No RV dump; Reservations not accepted; Max length: 20ft; Stay limit: 14 days; Generator hours: 0600-2200; Open Apr-Nov; Tent & RV camping: $12; Elev: 5709ft/1740m; Tel: 818-899-1900; Nearest town: La Canada. GPS: 34.342445, -118.010042

308 • Horse Springs

Total sites: 11; RV sites: 11; No water; Vault toilets; Reservations not accepted; Open all year; Tent & RV camping: $10; Elev: 5732ft/1747m; Tel: 909-382-2790; Nearest town: Fawnskin; Notes: Road conditions may prevent or hinder access during winter/spring. GPS: 34.352124, -117.070488

309 • Horseshoe Springs

Total sites: 3; RV sites: 3; No water; Vault toilets; Reservations not accepted; Stay limit: 14 days; Generator hours: 0600-2200; Open all year; Tent & RV camping: $5; Elev: 1521ft/464m; Tel: 805-925-9538; Nearest town: Santa Maria; Notes: Adventure Pass required ($5/day or $30/year) or Interagency Pass. GPS: 35.021076, -120.114467

310 • Hospital Flat

Total sites: 40; RV sites: 29; Central water; Vault toilets; No showers; No RV dump; Reservations accepted; Max length: 30ft; Open May-Sep; Tent & RV camping: $30-32; Elev: 2979ft/908m; Tel: 760-376-3781; Nearest town: Kernville. GPS: 35.828383, -118.458453

311 • Hotelling

Total sites: 4; RV sites: 4; No water; Vault toilets; Stay limit: 14 days; Open May-Oct; Tent & RV camping: Free; Elev: 1401ft/427m; Tel: 530-468-5351; Nearest town: Callahan. GPS: 41.239544, -123.275314

312 • Howards Gulch

Total sites: 6; RV sites: 6; Central water; Vault toilets; No showers; No RV dump; Reservations not accepted; Max length: 27ft; Stay limit: 14 days; Open May-Oct; Tent & RV camping: $12; Elev: 4728ft/1441m; Tel: 530-233-5811; Nearest town: Canby. GPS: 41.485407, -120.969315

313 • Hull Creek

Total sites: 18; RV sites: 18; Central water; Vault toilets; No showers; No RV dump; Reservations not accepted; Stay limit: 14 days; Open Apr-Oct; Tent & RV camping: $12; Elev: 5523ft/1683m; Tel: 209-586-3234; Nearest town: Mi-Wuk. GPS: 38.094169, -120.042896

314 • Hume Lake

Total sites: 74; RV sites: 50; Central water; Flush toilets; No showers; No RV dump; Reservations accepted; Max length: 30ft; Open May-Sep; Tent & RV camping: $29-31; Elev: 5328ft/1624m; Tel: 559-338-2251; Nearest town: Hume. GPS: 36.794506, -118.907969

315 • Hungry Gulch

Total sites: 74; RV sites: 74; Central water; Flush toilets; No showers; No RV dump; Reservations accepted; Max length: 30ft; Open May-Sep; Tent & RV camping: $30-32; Elev: 2658ft/810m; Tel: 760-376-3781; Nearest town: Lake Isabella; Notes: Add $2 summer holiday weekends. GPS: 35.671875, -118.473145

316 • Ice House

Total sites: 81; RV sites: 69; Central water; Vault toilets; No showers; RV dump; Reservations accepted; Max length: 40ft; Stay limit: 14 days; Open May-Oct; Tent & RV camping: $28; Elev: 5426ft/1654m; Tel: 530-644-2349; Nearest town: Pollock Pines. GPS: 38.832953, -120.357644

317 • Idlewild

Total sites: 8; RV sites: 8; Central water; Vault toilets; No showers; No RV dump; Reservations not accepted; Max length: 24ft; Stay limit: 14 days; Open May-Oct; Tent & RV camping: $10; Elev: 2716ft/828m; Tel: 530-468-5351; Nearest town: Etna. GPS: 41.331527, -123.060039

318 • Indian Flats

Total sites: 17; RV sites: 17; No water; Vault toilets; Reservations not accepted; Max length: 15ft; Stay limit: 14 days; Open Jun-Mar; Tent & RV camping: $12; Elev: 3648ft/1112m; Tel: 858-673-6180; Nearest town: Warner Springs; Notes: Group site available. GPS: 33.349515, -116.659726

319 • Indian Scotty

Total sites: 27; RV sites: 27; Central water; Vault toilets; No showers; No RV dump; Reservations not accepted; Max length: 30ft; Stay limit: 14 days; Open May-Oct; Tent & RV camping: $10; Elev: 2503ft/763m; Tel: 530-468-5351; Nearest town: Fort Jones; Notes: Reservable group site $50. GPS: 41.634151, -123.079253

320 • Indian Springs

Total sites: 35; RV sites: 28; Central water; Vault toilets; No showers; No RV dump; Reservations accepted; Open May-Sep; Tent & RV camping: $24; Elev: 5577ft/1700m; Tel: 530-478-0248; Nearest town: Big Bend. GPS: 39.327935, -120.568112

321 • Indian Valley

Total sites: 17; RV sites: 17; Central water; Vault toilets; No showers; No RV dump; Reservations accepted; Open Apr-Oct; Tent & RV camping: $24; Elev: 2379ft/725m; Tel: 530-862-1368; Nearest town: Camptonville. GPS: 39.512883, -120.980797

322 • Intake 2

Total sites: 8; RV sites: 8; Central water; Flush toilets; No showers; No RV dump; Reservations not accepted; Open all year; Tent & RV camping: $26; Elev: 8192ft/2497m; Tel: 760-873-2500; Nearest town: Bishop; Notes: Bear boxes must be used for food storage. GPS: 37.245428, -118.589856

323 • Iris Meadow

Total sites: 14; RV sites: 14; Central water; Flush toilets; No showers; No RV dump; Reservations not accepted; Stay limit: 21 days; Open May-Sep; Tent & RV camping: $25; Elev: 8396ft/2559m; Tel: 760-873-2500; Nearest town: Mammoth Lakes. GPS: 37.518316, -118.712366

324 • Jackass Meadow

Total sites: 44; RV sites: 44; No water; Vault toilets; Reservations accepted; Max length: 25ft; Stay limit: 14 days; Open May-Sep; Tent & RV camping: $28-30; Elev: 7195ft/2193m; Tel: 559-893-2308; Nearest town: Lakeshore. GPS: 37.277105, -118.964304

325 • Jackass Spring

Total sites: 10; RV sites: 10; No water; Vault toilets; Reservations not accepted; Max length: 32ft; Open all year; Tent & RV camping: Free; Elev: 3501ft/1067m; Tel: 530-623-2121; Nearest town: Trinity Center. GPS: 40.961585, -122.646591

326 • Jackson Creek

Total sites: 14; No water; Vault toilets; Reservations not accepted; Tents only: Free; Elev: 5718ft/1743m; Notes: Very bad road, Bear proof food boxes available, Stream water. GPS: 39.457679, -120.601046

327 • Janes Reservoir

Total sites: 8; RV sites: 8; No water; Vault toilets; Reservations not accepted; Max length: 22ft; Stay limit: 14 days; Open May-Oct; Tent & RV camping: Free; Elev: 5121ft/1561m; Tel: 530-233-5811; Nearest town: Alturas. GPS: 41.880000, -120.764000

328 • Jones Fork

Total sites: 10; RV sites: 9; No water; Vault toilets; Reservations not accepted; Stay limit: 14 days; Open Jun-Oct; Tent & RV camping: $10; Elev: 5030ft/1533m; Tel: 530-647-5415; Nearest town: Pollock Pines. GPS: 38.859813, -120.384872

329 • Jones Valley (Lower)

Total sites: 9; RV sites: 9; Central water; Vault toilets; No showers; No RV dump; Reservations not accepted; Open all year; Tent & RV camping: $23; Elev: 1125ft/343m; Tel: 530-275-1587. GPS: 40.727558, -122.229083

330 • Jones Valley (Upper)

Total sites: 8; RV sites: 8; Central water; Vault toilets; No showers; No RV dump; Reservations not accepted; Max length: 16ft; Tent & RV camping: $22; Elev: 1066ft/325m; Tel: 530-275-1587; Notes: Overflow use only. GPS: 40.730544, -122.229793

331 • Juanita Lake

Total sites: 23; RV sites: 23; Central water; Vault toilets; No showers; No RV dump; Reservations not accepted; Max length: 55ft; Stay limit: 14 days; Open May-Oct; Tent & RV camping: $15; Elev: 5158ft/1572m; Tel: 530-398-4391; Nearest town: Macdoel; Notes: Reservable group: $50. GPS: 41.817139, -122.125488

332 • Junction

Total sites: 13; RV sites: 5; Central water; Vault toilets; No showers; No RV dump; Reservations not accepted; Max length: 40ft; Open

Jun-Oct; Tent & RV camping: $17-19; Elev: 9550ft/2911m; Tel: 760-647-3044; Nearest town: Lee Vining; Notes: Bear boxes must be used for food storage. GPS: 37.937858, -119.251219

333 • June Lake

Total sites: 28; RV sites: 28; Central water; Flush toilets; No showers; No RV dump; Reservations accepted; Stay limit: 14 days; Open Apr-Oct; Tent & RV camping: $23; Elev: 7658ft/2334m; Tel: 760-647-3044; Nearest town: June Lake. GPS: 37.782227, -119.075928

334 • Kangaroo Lake

Total sites: 18; RV sites: 13; Central water; Vault toilets; No showers; No RV dump; Reservations not accepted; Stay limit: 14 days; Open May-Oct; Tent & RV camping: $15; Elev: 6102ft/1860m; Tel: 530-468-5351; Nearest town: Etna; Notes: Also walk-to sites. GPS: 41.334717, -122.640625

335 • Kaspian

Total sites: 9; Central water; Flush toilets; No showers; No RV dump; Reservations accepted; Open May-Oct; Tents only: $22-24; Elev: 6184ft/1885m; Tel: 530-583-3642; Nearest town: South Lake Tahoe. GPS: 39.113926, -120.158708

336 • Keller Peak Yellow Post 3

Total sites: 9; No water; No toilets; Stay limit: 14 days; Tents only: Free; Elev: 6578ft/2005m; Tel: 909-382-2790; Nearest town: Running Springs. GPS: 34.208772, -117.065052

337 • Kelty Meadow

Total sites: 11; RV sites: 11; No water; Vault toilets; Reservations accepted; Max length: 30ft; Stay limit: 14 days; Open May-Sep; Tent & RV camping: $27-29; Elev: 5886ft/1794m; Tel: 559-642-3212; Nearest town: Oakhurst; Notes: Stock facilities - water for horses only. GPS: 37.440404, -119.544557

338 • Kern Plateau - Fish Creek

Total sites: 40; RV sites: 40; No water; Vault toilets; Reservations not accepted; Max length: 27ft; Open May-Oct; Tent & RV camping: $17; Elev: 7418ft/2261m; Tel: 760-376-3781; Nearest town: Inyokern. GPS: 36.059294, -118.219149

339 • Kern Plateau - Horse Meadow

Total sites: 33; RV sites: 15; No water; Vault toilets; Reservations not accepted; Max length: 22ft; Open May-Nov; Tent & RV camping: $17; Elev: 7451ft/2271m; Tel: 760-376-3781; Nearest town: Kernville. GPS: 35.902173, -118.371284

340 • Kern Plateau - Kennedy Meadows

Total sites: 38; RV sites: 38; Central water; Vault toilets; No showers; No RV dump; Reservations not accepted; Max length: 30ft; Stay limit: 14 days; Open all year; Tent & RV camping: $17; Elev: 6142ft/1872m; Tel: 760-376-3781; Nearest town: Pearsonville; Notes: Water as weather permits. GPS: 36.052734, -118.131348

341 • Kern Plateau - Troy Meadow

Total sites: 73; RV sites: 73; No water; Vault toilets; Reservations not accepted; Max length: 24ft; Open May-Nov; Tent & RV

camping: $17; Elev: 7792ft/2375m; Tel: 760-376-3781; Nearest town: Inyokern. GPS: 36.064675, -118.237255

342 • Kings Camp

Total sites: 7; RV sites: 7; Vault toilets; Reservations not accepted; Generator hours: 0600-2200; Open all year; Tent & RV camping: $5; Elev: 4344ft/1324m; Tel: 661-245-3731; Notes: Adventure Pass required ($5/day or $30/year) or Interagency Pass. GPS: 34.716072, -118.929554

343 • Kingsley Glade

Total sites: 6; RV sites: 6; No water; Vault toilets; Reservations not accepted; Open May-Nov; Tent & RV camping: Free; Elev: 4577ft/1395m; Tel: 530-934-3316; Nearest town: Paskenta; Notes: Horse corral. GPS: 39.903807, -122.764613

344 • Kinnikinnick

Total sites: 27; RV sites: 27; Central water; Flush toilets; No showers; No RV dump; Reservations accepted; Max length: 40ft; Open May-Sep; Tent & RV camping: $34-36; Elev: 7103ft/2165m; Tel: 559-893-2111; Nearest town: Lakeshore. GPS: 37.253231, -119.177800

345 • Kirch Flat

Total sites: 17; RV sites: 17; No water; Vault toilets; Max length: 30ft; Stay limit: 14 days; Open all year; Tent & RV camping: Free; Elev: 1047ft/319m; Tel: 559-885-5355; Nearest town: Prather. GPS: 36.879737, -119.150459

346 • Kirk Creek

Total sites: 33; RV sites: 33; No water; Vault toilets; Reservations accepted; Max length: 30ft; Stay limit: 14 days; Generator hours: 0600-2200; Open all year; Tent & RV camping: $35; Elev: 253ft/77m; Tel: 805-434-1996; Nearest town: Lucia. GPS: 35.989807, -121.495666

347 • Kirkwood Lake

Total sites: 12; Central water; Vault toilets; No showers; No RV dump; Reservations not accepted; Stay limit: 14 days; Open Jun-Sep; Tents only: $24; Elev: 7769ft/2368m; Tel: 209-295-4251; Nearest town: Pioneer. GPS: 38.707326, -120.087143

348 • Kit Carson

Total sites: 12; RV sites: 12; Central water; Vault toilets; No showers; No RV dump; Reservations accepted; Max length: 30ft; Stay limit: 14 days; Open Apr-Sep; Tent & RV camping: $18; Elev: 7001ft/2134m; Tel: 775-882-2766; Nearest town: Woodfords. GPS: 38.776661, -119.898597

349 • La Panza

Total sites: 15; RV sites: 15; No water; Vault toilets; Reservations accepted; Max length: 16ft; Generator hours: 0600-2200; Open all year; Tent & RV camping: $20; Elev: 2195ft/669m; Tel: 805-925-9538; Nearest town: Santa Maria. GPS: 35.353748, -120.262715

350 • Laguna

Total sites: 108; RV sites: 104; Central water; Flush toilets; Pay showers; No RV dump; Reservations accepted; Max length: 40ft;

Stay limit: 14 days; Open all year; Tent & RV camping: $27; Elev: 5545ft/1690m; Tel: 619-473-2082; Nearest town: Pine Valley; Notes: Star-gazing parties. GPS: 32.888638, -116.448821

351 • Lake

Total sites: 8; RV sites: 8; Central water; Vault toilets; No showers; No RV dump; Reservations accepted; Max length: 18ft; Stay limit: 14 days; Open May-Oct; Tent & RV camping: $23; Elev: 6106ft/ 1861m; Tel: 760-249-3526; Nearest town: Wrightwood. GPS: 34.391161, -117.722882

352 • Lake Alpine

Total sites: 25; RV sites: 20; Central water; Flush toilets; No showers; No RV dump; Reservations accepted; Max length: 27ft; Stay limit: 14 days; Open Jun-Sep; Tent & RV camping: $26; Elev: 7418ft/2261m; Tel: 209-795-1381; Nearest town: Arnold. GPS: 38.477295, -120.006104

353 • Lake George

Total sites: 15; RV sites: 15; Central water; Flush toilets; No showers; No RV dump; Reservations not accepted; Open May-Sep; Tent & RV camping: $24; Elev: 9058ft/2761m; Tel: 760-924-5500; Nearest town: Mammoth Lakes; Notes: Bear boxes must be used for food storage. GPS: 37.602051, -119.010254

354 • Lake Mary

Total sites: 48; RV sites: 48; Central water; Flush toilets; No showers; No RV dump; Reservations accepted; Open Jun-Sep; Tent & RV camping: $22-24; Elev: 8976ft/2736m; Tel: 650-322-1181; Nearest town: Mammoth Lakes. GPS: 37.606934, -119.007080

355 • Lake of the Woods

Total sites: 15; No water; Vault toilets; Reservations not accepted; Tents only: Free; Elev: 7426ft/2263m; Nearest town: Sierraville. GPS: 39.502925, -120.391289

356 • Lakes Basin

Total sites: 23; RV sites: 20; Central water; Vault toilets; No showers; No RV dump; Reservations accepted; Open May-Oct; Tent & RV camping: $30; Elev: 6332ft/1930m; Tel: 530-836-2575; Nearest town: Graeagle; Notes: Group tent site: $80. GPS: 39.703188, -120.661416

357 • Lakeshore East

Total sites: 23; RV sites: 15; Central water; Flush toilets; No showers; No RV dump; Reservations accepted; Open May-Sep; Tent & RV camping: $23; Elev: 1073ft/327m; Tel: 530-275-1587; Nearest town: Lakehead; Notes: Also shelters: $35. GPS: 40.875246, -122.388519

358 • Lakeside

Total sites: 32; RV sites: 29; Central water; Vault toilets; No showers; No RV dump; Reservations accepted; Open May-Oct; Tent & RV camping: $20; Elev: 5725ft/1745m; Tel: 530-587-9281; Nearest town: Truckee. GPS: 39.383846, -120.172139

359 • Landslide

Total sites: 9; RV sites: 3; No water; Vault toilets; Reservations not accepted; Max length: 16ft; Open May-Sep; Tent & RV camping: $25; Elev: 5840ft/1780m; Tel: 559-338-2251; Nearest town: Grant Grove. GPS: 36.763554, -118.882883

360 • Lassen Creek

Total sites: 4; RV sites: 4; No water; Vault toilets; Reservations not accepted; Stay limit: 14 days; Open May-Oct; Tent & RV camping: Free; Elev: 5463ft/1665m; Tel: 530-279-6116; Nearest town: Canby. GPS: 41.826733, -120.296228

361 • Laufman

Total sites: 6; RV sites: 6; No water; Vault toilets; Reservations not accepted; Stay limit: 14 days; Open Apr-Oct; Tent & RV camping: Free; Elev: 5098ft/1554m; Tel: 530-836-2575; Nearest town: Milford. GPS: 40.135000, -120.348000

362 • Lava Camp

Total sites: 12; RV sites: 12; Central water; Vault toilets; No showers; No RV dump; Reservations not accepted; Max length: 32ft; Stay limit: 14 days; Open May-Oct; Tent & RV camping: Free; Elev: 4426ft/1349m; Tel: 530-299-3215; Nearest town: Adin. GPS: 41.402091, -121.338554

363 • Le Perron Flat

Total sites: 4; Reservations not accepted; Tents only: Free; Elev: 2454ft/748m; Tel: 530-627-3291. GPS: 41.241730, -123.521530

364 • Leavis Flat

Total sites: 9; RV sites: 9; No water; Vault toilets; No showers; No RV dump; Reservations not accepted; Max length: 16ft; Open all year; Tent & RV camping: $23; Elev: 3143ft/958m; Tel: 559-539-2607; Nearest town: CA Hot Springs; Notes: Fire permit required. GPS: 35.879632, -118.676738

365 • Leavitt Meadows

Total sites: 16; RV sites: 16; Central water; Vault toilets; No showers; No RV dump; Reservations not accepted; Stay limit: 14 days; Open Apr-Sep; Tent & RV camping: $20; Elev: 7231ft/2204m; Tel: 760-932-7070; Nearest town: Walker. GPS: 38.333309, -119.553198

366 • Letts Lake

Total sites: 42; RV sites: 42; Central water; Vault toilets; No showers; No RV dump; Reservations not accepted; Max length: 24ft; Open May-Oct; Tent & RV camping: $12; Elev: 4574ft/1394m; Tel: 530-963-3128; Nearest town: Stonyford. GPS: 39.302913, -122.708736

367 • Lewis

Total sites: 40; RV sites: 40; Central water; Flush toilets; No showers; No RV dump; Reservations accepted; Max length: 22ft; Open May-Sep; Tent & RV camping: $20; Elev: 5280ft/1609m; Tel: 530-478-0248; Nearest town: Foresthill. GPS: 39.132043, -120.416345

368 • Lightning Tree

Total sites: 40; RV sites: 40; Central water; Vault toilets; No showers; Reservations accepted; Stay limit: 14 days; Open all year; Tent & RV camping: $30; Elev: 5797ft/1767m; Tel: 530-832-1076; Nearest town: Portola. GPS: 39.931152, -120.508057

369 • Limestone

Total sites: 19; No water; Vault toilets; Reservations accepted; Open Apr-Nov; Tents only: $26-28; Elev: 3875ft/1181m; Tel: 760-376-3781; Nearest town: Kernville. GPS: 35.963371, -118.479203

370 • Little Beaver

Total sites: 120; RV sites: 120; Central water; Flush toilets; No showers; No RV dump; Reservations accepted; Open May-Oct; Tent & RV camping: $23-25; Elev: 5115ft/1559m; Tel: 530-534-6500; Nearest town: La Porte. GPS: 39.729861, -120.968331

371 • Little Doe

Total sites: 13; RV sites: 13; No water; Vault toilets; Reservations not accepted; Open May-Oct; Tent & RV camping: $6; Elev: 3842ft/1171m; Tel: 707-983-6118; Nearest town: Covelo; Notes: No large RVs. GPS: 39.895575, -122.986747

372 • Little Jackass

Total sites: 5; No water; Vault toilets; Max length: 20ft; Open Jun-Sep; Tents only: Free; Elev: 4944ft/1507m; Tel: 559-877-2218; Nearest town: Fresno. GPS: 37.399069, -119.337111

373 • Little North Fork

Total sites: 8; RV sites: 8; Central water; Vault toilets; No showers; No RV dump; Reservations not accepted; Stay limit: 14 days; Tent & RV camping: $15; Elev: 4032ft/1229m; Tel: 530-534-6500; Nearest town: Berry Creek. GPS: 39.782000, -121.260000

374 • Little Stony

Total sites: 8; No water; Vault toilets; Reservations not accepted; Open all year; Tents only: $5; Elev: 1496ft/456m; Tel: 530-963-3128; Nearest town: Stonyford; Notes: Trailers not recommended. GPS: 39.286424, -122.577243

375 • Live Oak North

Total sites: 60; RV sites: 60; Central water; Flush toilets; Showers; No RV dump; Reservations not accepted; Max length: 30ft; Open May-Sep; Tent & RV camping: $24-26; Elev: 2710ft/826m; Tel: 760-376-3781; Nearest town: Wofford Heights. GPS: 35.702892, -118.460908

376 • Live Oak South

Total sites: 90; Central water; Flush toilets; Showers; No RV dump; Reservations not accepted; Open May-Sep; Tents only: $24; Elev: 2700ft/823m; Tel: 760-376-3781; Nearest town: Wofford Heights. GPS: 35.701501, -118.461421

377 • Lodgepole Overflow

Total sites: 30; RV sites: 30; Central water; Vault toilets; No showers; No RV dump; Reservations not accepted; Stay limit: 2 days; Open Jun-Sep; Tent & RV camping: $30; Elev: 7408ft/2258m; Tel: 209-795-1381; Nearest town: Bear Valley. GPS: 38.477504, -120.024149

378 • Loganville

Total sites: 18; Central water; Vault toilets; No showers; No RV dump; Reservations accepted; Open May-Oct; Tents only: $24; Elev: 4003ft/1220m; Tel: 530-862-1368; Nearest town: Sierra City; Notes: Pan for gold. GPS: 39.565142, -120.663208

379 • Logger

Total sites: 200; RV sites: 199; Central water; Vault toilets; No showers; No RV dump; Reservations accepted; Max length: 45ft; Open May-Oct; Tent & RV camping: $23; Elev: 6040ft/1841m; Tel: 530-587-9281; Nearest town: Truckee. GPS: 39.465148, -120.123856

380 • Lone Pine

Total sites: 42; RV sites: 39; Central water; Vault toilets; No showers; No RV dump; Reservations accepted; Max length: 40ft; Open Apr-Dec; Tent & RV camping: $24; Elev: 5846ft/1782m; Tel: 760-937-6070; Nearest town: Lone Pine; Notes: Group fee: $60, Bear boxes must be used for food storage. GPS: 36.597704, -118.184667

381 • Lone Rock

Total sites: 38; RV sites: 38; Central water; Vault toilets; No showers; No RV dump; Reservations accepted; Max length: 22ft; Open Jun-Sep; Tent & RV camping: $30; Elev: 5069ft/1545m; Tel: 530-283-0555; Nearest town: Taylorsville. GPS: 40.195068, -120.618164

382 • Long Point

Total sites: 38; RV sites: 38; Central water; Vault toilets; No showers; No RV dump; Reservations accepted; Stay limit: 30 days; Open May-Sep; Tent & RV camping: $30; Elev: 5062ft/1543m; Tel: 530-283-0555; Nearest town: Taylorsville; Notes: 4 group sites: $85. GPS: 40.178087, -120.578674

383 • Lookout

Total sites: 22; RV sites: 22; No water; Vault toilets; Reservations not accepted; Stay limit: 14 days; Open Jun-Sep; Tent & RV camping: $6; Elev: 6801ft/2073m; Tel: 775-882-2766; Nearest town: Reno NV. GPS: 39.589583, -120.073582

384 • Loon Lake

Total sites: 53; RV sites: 31; Central water; Vault toilets; No showers; No RV dump; Reservations accepted; Max length: 40ft; Stay limit: 14 days; Open Jun-Aug; Tent & RV camping: $28; Elev: 6450ft/1966m; Tel: 530-293-0827; Nearest town: Pollock Pines; Notes: Group sites: $130-$160. GPS: 38.979194, -120.319174

385 • Los Alamos

Total sites: 90; RV sites: 90; Central water; Vault toilets; No showers; RV dump; Reservations accepted; Max length: 26ft; Stay limit: 14 days; Open all year; Tent & RV camping: $20-35; Elev: 2894ft/882m; Tel: 805-434-1996; Nearest town: Gorman; Notes: Group sites: $85-$125. GPS: 34.702705, -118.810545

386 • Los Prietos

Total sites: 38; RV sites: 30; Central water; Flush toilets; No showers; No RV dump; Reservations accepted; Generator hours: 0600-2200; Open Mar-Nov; Tent & RV camping: $30; Elev: 1010ft/308m; Tel: 805-967-8766; Nearest town: Santa Barbara. GPS: 34.540527, -119.802002

387 • Lost Claim

Total sites: 10; RV sites: 10; No water; Vault toilets; No showers; No RV dump; Reservations accepted; Stay limit: 14 days; Open May-Oct; Tent & RV camping: $21; Elev: 3064ft/934m; Tel: 209-962-7825; Nearest town: Groveland. GPS: 37.821045, -120.048584

388 • Lower Billy Creek

Total sites: 15; RV sites: 15; Central water; Vault toilets; No showers; No RV dump; Reservations accepted; Max length: 30ft; Open May-Sep; Tent & RV camping: $34-38; Elev: 7064ft/2153m; Tel: 559-893-2111; Nearest town: Lakeshore. GPS: 37.237726, -119.228551

389 • Lower Bucks

Total sites: 7; RV sites: 7; No water; Vault toilets; Reservations not accepted; Tent & RV camping: $25; Elev: 5164ft/1574m; Tel: 530-283-0555; Nearest town: Quincy; Notes: Free with no services in winter. GPS: 39.902000, -121.215000

390 • Lower Deadman

Total sites: 15; RV sites: 15; No water; Vault toilets; Reservations not accepted; Stay limit: 14 days; Tent & RV camping: Free; Elev: 7818ft/2383m; Nearest town: Mammoth Lakes. GPS: 37.720485, -119.009028

391 • Lower Grays Meadow

Total sites: 31; RV sites: 31; Central water; Vault toilets; No showers; No RV dump; Reservations accepted; Open Apr-Oct; Tent & RV camping: $23; Elev: 5968ft/1819m; Tel: 760-937-6070; Nearest town: Independence; Notes: Bear boxes must be used for food storage. GPS: 36.781531, -118.284712

392 • Lower Lee Vining

Total sites: 60; RV sites: 60; No water; Vault toilets; Reservations not accepted; Stay limit: 14 days; Tent & RV camping: $14; Elev: 7317ft/2230m; Nearest town: Lee Vining; Notes: Bear boxes must be used for food storage. GPS: 37.928875, -119.153332

393 • Lower Lindsey Lake

Total sites: 12; No water; Vault toilets; Reservations not accepted; Open Jun-Sep; Tents only: $15; Elev: 6302ft/1921m; Tel: 530-265-4531; Nearest town: Nevada City; Notes: Very rough, narrow road, High-clearance vehicles recommended, Operated by PGE. GPS: 39.412654, -120.644323

394 • Lower Little Truckee

Total sites: 14; RV sites: 12; Central water; Vault toilets; No showers; No RV dump; Reservations accepted; Open May-Oct; Tent & RV camping: $20; Elev: 6168ft/1880m; Tel: 530-994-3401; Nearest town: Sierraville. GPS: 39.485605, -120.236477

395 • Lower Peppermint

Total sites: 17; RV sites: 10; Central water; Vault toilets; No showers; No RV dump; Reservations not accepted; Max length: 16ft; Open May-Nov; Tent & RV camping: $17; Elev: 5292ft/1613m; Tel: 559-539-2607; Nearest town: Kernville. GPS: 36.065994, -118.491243

396 • Lower Rush Creek

Total sites: 10; RV sites: 5; No water; Vault toilets; Reservations not accepted; Max length: 22ft; Stay limit: 14 days; Open all year; Tent & RV camping: Free; Elev: 4751ft/1448m; Tel: 530-299-3215; Nearest town: Adin; Notes: Also walk-to sites, 5 walk-in sites, Inaccessible during inclement weather. GPS: 41.292655, -120.878836

397 • Lower Twin Lakes

Total sites: 14; RV sites: 11; Central water; Flush toilets; No showers; No RV dump; Reservations accepted; Max length: 35ft; Stay limit: 14 days; Open Apr-Oct; Tent & RV camping: $26; Elev: 7119ft/2170m; Tel: 760-932-7070; Nearest town: Bridgeport. GPS: 38.170205, -119.323546

398 • Lumsden

Total sites: 10; No water; Vault toilets; Stay limit: 14 days; Open all year; Tents only: Free; Elev: 1460ft/445m; Tel: 209-962-7825; Nearest town: Groveland. GPS: 37.838096, -120.051586

399 • Lupine

Total sites: 51; RV sites: 48; Central water; Flush toilets; No showers; No RV dump; Reservations accepted; Max length: 40ft; Open May-Sep; Tent & RV camping: $36-38; Elev: 3402ft/1037m; Tel: 559-642-3212; Nearest town: Yosemite. GPS: 37.307655, -119.544244

400 • Mad River

Total sites: 40; RV sites: 40; Central water; Vault toilets; No showers; No RV dump; Reservations not accepted; Max length: 30ft; Stay limit: 14 days; Open May-Sep; Tent & RV camping: $12; Elev: 2602ft/793m; Tel: 707-574-6233; Nearest town: Fortuna. GPS: 40.402156, -123.466696

401 • Madrone

Total sites: 10; RV sites: 10; No water; Vault toilets; No showers; No RV dump; Reservations not accepted; Max length: 16ft; Open all year; Tent & RV camping: Free; Elev: 1552ft/473m; Tel: 530-275-1587; Nearest town: Redding; Notes: Bear boxes. GPS: 40.924361, -122.095473

402 • Mammoth Pool

Total sites: 47; RV sites: 47; Central water; Vault toilets; No showers; No RV dump; Reservations accepted; Max length: 30ft; Stay limit: 14 days; Open May-Sep; Tent & RV camping: $28-30; Elev: 3691ft/1125m; Tel: 559-642-3212; Nearest town: North Fork. GPS: 37.344157, -119.333965

403 • Manker

Total sites: 21; RV sites: 21; Central water; Vault toilets; No showers; No RV dump; Reservations not accepted; Max length:

16ft; Stay limit: 14 days; Open all year; Tent & RV camping: $14; Elev: 6092ft/1857m; Tel: 818-335-1251; Nearest town: Claremont. GPS: 34.264972, -117.630937

404 • Marion Mountain

Total sites: 24; RV sites: 24; Central water; Vault toilets; No showers; No RV dump; Reservations accepted; Open May-Nov; Tent & RV camping: $10; Elev: 6453ft/1967m; Tel: 909-382-2922; Nearest town: Idyllwild. GPS: 33.792174, -116.732121

405 • Markleeville

Total sites: 10; RV sites: 10; Central water; Vault toilets; No showers; No RV dump; Reservations not accepted; Stay limit: 14 days; Open Apr-Sep; Tent & RV camping: $18; Elev: 5502ft/1677m; Tel: 775-882-2766; Nearest town: Markleeville. GPS: 38.697759, -119.774064

406 • Martin Meadows

Total sites: 13; RV sites: 13; No water; Vault toilets; No showers; No RV dump; Reservations not accepted; Stay limit: 14 days; Tent & RV camping: Free; Elev: 7641ft/2329m; Nearest town: Kirkwood. GPS: 38.696476, -120.122656

407 • Martins Dairy

Total sites: 8; RV sites: 8; Central water; Vault toilets; No showers; No RV dump; Reservations not accepted; Stay limit: 14 days; Tent & RV camping: $10; Elev: 6030ft/1838m; Tel: 530-398-4391; Nearest town: Macdoel; Notes: No water in winter. GPS: 41.795897, -122.207735

408 • Matthews Creek

Total sites: 12; RV sites: 12; Central water; Vault toilets; No showers; No RV dump; Reservations not accepted; Open May-Oct; Tent & RV camping: $10; Elev: 1795ft/547m; Tel: 530-468-5351; Nearest town: Etna. GPS: 41.186768, -123.213867

409 • McBride Springs

Total sites: 10; RV sites: 10; Central water; Vault toilets; No showers; No RV dump; Reservations not accepted; Max length: 16ft; Stay limit: 7 days; Open May-Oct; Tent & RV camping: $10; Elev: 4938ft/1505m; Tel: 530-926-4511; Nearest town: Mt. Shasta. GPS: 41.352267, -122.283378

410 • McCloud Bridge

Total sites: 14; RV sites: 14; No water; Vault toilets; No showers; No RV dump; Reservations not accepted; Max length: 16ft; Open Apr-Oct; Tent & RV camping: $23; Elev: 1171ft/357m; Tel: 530-275-1589; Nearest town: Lakehead; Notes: Bear boxes. GPS: 40.935515, -122.246044

411 • McGee Creek

Total sites: 28; RV sites: 28; Central water; Flush toilets; No showers; No RV dump; Reservations accepted; Stay limit: 14 days; Open May-Oct; Tent & RV camping: $25; Elev: 7536ft/2297m; Tel: 760-935-4213; Nearest town: Mammoth Lakes; Notes: Bear boxes must be used for food storage. GPS: 37.563965, -118.785400

412 • McGill

Total sites: 78; RV sites: 78; No water; Vault toilets; Reservations accepted; Max length: 30ft; Generator hours: 0600-2200; Open May-Oct; Tent & RV camping: $20; Elev: 7480ft/2280m; Tel: 661-245-3731; Nearest town: Frazier Park; Notes: 2 Group sites: $100-$120. GPS: 34.813965, -119.101807

413 • Meadow Camp

Total sites: 7; RV sites: 7; No water; Vault toilets; Reservations not accepted; Open all year; Tent & RV camping: $15; Elev: 3747ft/1142m; Tel: 530-283-0555; Nearest town: Quincy; Notes: Free with no services in winter. GPS: 39.930435, -121.041738

414 • Meadowview

Total sites: 100; RV sites: 100; Central water; Flush toilets; No showers; No RV dump; Reservations not accepted; Max length: 22ft; Stay limit: 14 days; Open May-Oct; Tent & RV camping: $30; Elev: 5588ft/1703m; Tel: 209-965-3434; Nearest town: Mi-Wuk; Notes: Cash only. GPS: 38.186608, -120.004193

415 • Medicine Lake

Total sites: 22; RV sites: 22; No water; Vault toilets; Reservations accepted; Max length: 22ft; Stay limit: 14 days; Open Jul-Sep; Tent & RV camping: $14; Elev: 6732ft/2052m; Tel: 530-233-5811; Nearest town: McCloud. GPS: 41.587175, -121.596541

416 • Meeks Bay

Total sites: 36; RV sites: 20; Central water; Flush toilets; No showers; No RV dump; Reservations accepted; Max length: 20ft; Open May-Oct; Tent & RV camping: $31-33; Elev: 6240ft/1902m; Tel: 530-525-4733; Nearest town: Meeks Bay. GPS: 39.035889, -120.123535

417 • Memorial Park

Total sites: 8; RV sites: 8; No water; Vault toilets; Reservations accepted; Generator hours: 0600-2200; Open May-Oct; Tent & RV camping: $20; Elev: 2136ft/651m; Tel: 831-385-5434. GPS: 36.117845, -121.465255

418 • Merrill

Total sites: 173; RV sites: 173; Elec sites: 120; Water at site; Flush toilets; No showers; RV dump; Reservations accepted; Max length: 75ft; Open May-Oct; Tents: $20/RVs: $30-35; Elev: 5151ft/1570m; Tel: 530-825-3450; Nearest town: Susanville; Notes: Group sites $60, 57 FHU sites. GPS: 40.549072, -120.812256

419 • Middle Creek

Total sites: 23; RV sites: 23; Central water; Vault toilets; No showers; No RV dump; Reservations not accepted; Tent & RV camping: $8; Elev: 1493ft/455m; Tel: 707-275-2361; Nearest town: Upper Lake. GPS: 39.252897, -122.951044

420 • Middle Fork Cosumnes

Total sites: 19; RV sites: 4; No water; Vault toilets; Reservations not accepted; Stay limit: 14 days; Open May-Nov; Tent & RV camping: $16; Elev: 5279ft/1609m; Tel: 209-295-4251; Nearest town: Placerville. GPS: 38.583947, -120.301587

421 • Middle Lion

Total sites: 8; RV sites: 8; No water; Vault toilets; Reservations accepted; Generator hours: 0600-2200; Open all year; Tent & RV camping: $20; Elev: 3161ft/963m; Tel: 805-646-4348; Nearest town: Ojai. GPS: 34.549426, -119.166232

422 • Mill Creek

Total sites: 10; RV sites: 10; Central water; Vault toilets; No showers; No RV dump; Reservations not accepted; Open all year; Tent & RV camping: $30; Elev: 5194ft/1583m; Tel: 530-283-0555; Nearest town: Quincy; Notes: Free with no services in winter. GPS: 39.912773, -121.186946

423 • Mill Creek

Total sites: 17; RV sites: 17; No water; Vault toilets; Reservations not accepted; Stay limit: 14 days; Open May-Oct; Tent & RV camping: $8; Elev: 6312ft/1924m; Tel: 209-965-3434; Nearest town: Mi-Wuk. GPS: 38.301699, -119.938112

424 • Mill Creek

Total sites: 6; RV sites: 6; No water; Vault toilets; Reservations not accepted; Open all year; Tent & RV camping: $5; Elev: 1631ft/497m; Tel: 530-963-3128; Nearest town: Stonyford. GPS: 39.355691, -122.655123

425 • Mill Creek Falls

Total sites: 15; RV sites: 8; Central water; Vault toilets; No showers; No RV dump; Reservations not accepted; Max length: 22ft; Stay limit: 14 days; Open Jun-Oct; Tent & RV camping: $12; Elev: 5725ft/1745m; Tel: 530-279-6116; Nearest town: Likely. GPS: 41.276248, -120.289744

426 • Mill Flat

Total sites: 5; RV sites: 5; No water; Vault toilets; Reservations not accepted; Max length: 25ft; Open all year; Tent & RV camping: Free; Elev: 1083ft/330m; Tel: 559-338-2251; Nearest town: Fresno. GPS: 36.856581, -119.096994

427 • Mill Valley

Total sites: 15; RV sites: 15; No water; Vault toilets; Reservations not accepted; Max length: 32ft; Open May-Oct; Tent & RV camping: $10; Elev: 4065ft/1239m; Tel: 530-934-3316; Nearest town: Stonyford. GPS: 39.317354, -122.708252

428 • Minaret Falls

Total sites: 27; Central water; Vault toilets; No showers; No RV dump; Reservations not accepted; Open Jun-Sep; Tents only: $23; Elev: 7690ft/2344m; Tel: 760-924-5500; Nearest town: Mammoth Lakes; Notes: Narrow single lane road, Bear boxes must be used for food storage. GPS: 37.639648, -119.083252

429 • Minersville

Total sites: 14; RV sites: 14; Elec sites: 1; Central water; Flush toilets; No showers; No RV dump; Reservations accepted; Max length: 36ft; Open all year; Tents: $15/RVs: $20-25; Elev: 2356ft/718m; Tel: 530-623-1203; Nearest town: Trinity Center; Notes:

Also walk-to sites, 1/2 price in winter - reduced services. GPS: 40.849064, -122.811749

430 • Miranda Pine

Total sites: 3; RV sites: 3; No water; Vault toilets; Reservations not accepted; Generator hours: 0600-2200; Tent & RV camping: $5; Elev: 4006ft/1221m; Tel: 805-925-9538; Nearest town: Santa Maria; Notes: Adventure Pass required ($5/day or $30/year) or Interagency Pass. GPS: 35.035071, -120.037374

431 • Mission Springs TC

Total sites: 2; No water; No toilets; Tents only: Free; Elev: 7930ft/2417m; Tel: 909-382-2882; Nearest town: Angelus Oaks. GPS: 34.125608, -116.758241

432 • Mokelumne

Total sites: 13; RV sites: 8; No water; Vault toilets; Reservations not accepted; Stay limit: 14 days; Open Jun-Oct; Tent & RV camping: $20; Elev: 3343ft/1019m; Tel: 209-295-4251; Nearest town: Jackson. GPS: 38.478221, -120.270822

433 • Mono Creek

Total sites: 14; RV sites: 14; No water; Vault toilets; No showers; No RV dump; Reservations accepted; Max length: 25ft; Stay limit: 14 days; Open May-Sep; Tent & RV camping: $28-30; Elev: 7444ft/2269m; Tel: 559-893-2111; Nearest town: Lakeshore. GPS: 37.357131, -118.995552

434 • Mono Hot Springs

Total sites: 31; RV sites: 31; No water; Vault toilets; Reservations accepted; Max length: 25ft; Stay limit: 14 days; Open May-Sep; Tent & RV camping: $28-30; Elev: 6572ft/2003m; Tel: 559-893-2111; Nearest town: Lakeshore. GPS: 37.326181, -119.018758

435 • Monte Cristo

Total sites: 19; RV sites: 19; No water; Vault toilets; Reservations not accepted; Max length: 30ft; Stay limit: 14 days; Open all year; Tent & RV camping: $12; Elev: 3619ft/1103m; Tel: 818-899-1900; Nearest town: La Canada. GPS: 34.341018, -118.109526

436 • Moore Creek

Total sites: 8; Central water; Vault toilets; No showers; No RV dump; Reservations not accepted; Stay limit: 14 days; Open all year; Tents only: $20; Elev: 3297ft/1005m; Tel: 209-295-4251; Nearest town: Pollock Pines; Notes: Access blocked - road damage. GPS: 38.481588, -120.264961

437 • Moore Creek

Total sites: 12; RV sites: 12; Central water; Vault toilets; No showers; No RV dump; Reservations not accepted; Max length: 16ft; Open May-Sep; Tent & RV camping: $20; Elev: 1112ft/339m; Tel: 530-275-1587; Nearest town: Lakehead; Notes: Reservable group site $150, Bear boxes. GPS: 40.888478, -122.225007

438 • Moraine

Total sites: 25; RV sites: 25; No water; Vault toilets; Reservations not accepted; Tent & RV camping: $14; Elev: 7396ft/2254m;

Nearest town: Lee Vining; Notes: Open only as overflow. GPS: 37.930587, -119.161457

439 • Mosquito Lakes

Total sites: 11; No water; Vault toilets; Reservations not accepted; Stay limit: 14 days; Open Jun-Oct; Tents only: $8; Elev: 8114ft/2473m; Tel: 209-795-1381; Nearest town: Bear Valley. GPS: 38.515918, -119.914204

440 • Mountain Glen

Total sites: 5; No water; Vault toilets; Reservations not accepted; Stay limit: 7 days; Open May-Sep; Tents only: $24; Elev: 8534ft/2601m; Tel: 760-873-2500; Nearest town: Bishop; Notes: Bear boxes must be used for food storage. GPS: 37.223776, -118.566568

441 • Mountain Oak

Total sites: 17; RV sites: 17; Central water; Flush toilets; No showers; No RV dump; Reservations accepted; Max length: 18ft; Stay limit: 14 days; Open May-Nov; Tent & RV camping: $23; Elev: 6194ft/1888m; Tel: 661-269-2808; Nearest town: Wrightwood. GPS: 34.394748, -117.729488

442 • Mt Figueroa

Total sites: 32; RV sites: 32; No water; Vault toilets; No showers; No RV dump; Reservations not accepted; Max length: 25ft; Stay limit: 14 days; Generator hours: 0600-2200; Open all year; Tent & RV camping: $20; Elev: 3547ft/1081m; Tel: 805-925-9538; Nearest town: Los Olivos. GPS: 34.734447, -119.986548

443 • Mt. Pacifico

Total sites: 8; RV sites: 8; No water; Vault toilets; Reservations not accepted; Stay limit: 14 days; Open May-Sep; Tent & RV camping: $5; Elev: 6982ft/2128m; Tel: 818-899-1900; Nearest town: Pasadena; Notes: Adventure Pass required ($5/day or $30/year) or Interagency Pass, Road not maintained for passenger cars. GPS: 34.379407, -118.034394

444 • Mt. Pinos

Total sites: 19; RV sites: 19; No water; Vault toilets; Reservations accepted; Max length: 22ft; Generator hours: 0600-2200; Open May-Oct; Tent & RV camping: $20; Elev: 7822ft/2384m; Tel: 661-245-3731; Nearest town: Frazier Park; Notes: Good star-gazing. GPS: 34.810304, -119.108957

445 • Mulebridge

Total sites: 4; RV sites: 4; No water; Vault toilets; Stay limit: 14 days; Open May-Oct; Tent & RV camping: Free; Elev: 2907ft/886m; Tel: 530-468-5351; Nearest town: Etna. GPS: 41.356313, -123.075388

446 • Mumford Bar CG

Total sites: 4; RV sites: 4; No water; Vault toilets; Reservations not accepted; Tent & RV camping: Free; Elev: 5330ft/1625m; Tel: 530-367-2224; Notes: Hitching posts. GPS: 39.181627, -120.614456

447 • Nacimiento

Total sites: 9; RV sites: 9; No water; Vault toilets; Reservations not accepted; Max length: 25ft; Stay limit: 14 days; Generator hours: 0600-2200; Open all year; Tent & RV camping: $20; Elev: 1619ft/493m; Tel: 831-385-5434. GPS: 36.007518, -121.400767

448 • Navajo

Total sites: 2; RV sites: 2; No water; Vault toilets; Reservations not accepted; Tent & RV camping: Free; Elev: 2221ft/677m; Tel: 805-925-9538; Nearest town: Pozo. GPS: 35.368674, -120.312399

449 • Navajo Flat

Total sites: 5; RV sites: 5; No water; Vault toilets; Reservations accepted; Stay limit: 14 days; Generator hours: 0600-2200; Open all year; Tent & RV camping: $20; Elev: 1863ft/568m; Tel: 805-925-9538; Nearest town: Santa Margarita. GPS: 35.379157, -120.283997

450 • Nelder Grove

Total sites: 7; RV sites: 7; No water; Vault toilets; Reservations not accepted; Max length: 20ft; Open May-Dec; Tent & RV camping: Free; Elev: 5430ft/1655m; Tel: 559-877-2218; Nearest town: Fresno. GPS: 37.431043, -119.583468

451 • Nelson Point

Total sites: 8; RV sites: 8; No water; Vault toilets; Reservations not accepted; Open May-Sep; Tent & RV camping: $15; Elev: 1171ft/357m; Tel: 530-275-1587; Nearest town: O'Brien; Notes: Group site $100, Food storage lockers. GPS: 40.849249, -122.346455

452 • New Shady Rest

Total sites: 92; RV sites: 92; Central water; Flush toilets; No showers; RV dump; Reservations accepted; Open May-Nov; Tent & RV camping: $21-23; Elev: 7825ft/2385m; Tel: 760-924-5500; Nearest town: Mammoth Lakes; Notes: Bear boxes must be used for food storage. GPS: 37.648174, -118.961229

453 • Niagara Creek

Total sites: 10; RV sites: 10; No water; Vault toilets; Reservations not accepted; Stay limit: 14 days; Open May-Oct; Tent & RV camping: $8; Elev: 6585ft/2007m; Tel: 209-965-3434; Nearest town: Mi-Wuk. GPS: 38.324944, -119.915537

454 • Niagara OHV

Total sites: 10; RV sites: 10; No water; Vault toilets; Reservations not accepted; Stay limit: 14 days; Open May-Oct; Tent & RV camping: $8; Elev: 7054ft/2150m; Tel: 209-965-3434; Nearest town: Mi-Wuk. GPS: 38.311284, -119.890882

455 • Nira

Total sites: 11; RV sites: 6; No water; Vault toilets; Reservations accepted; Generator hours: 0600-2200; Open Apr-Oct; Tent & RV camping: $20; Elev: 2005ft/611m; Tel: 805-925-9538; Nearest town: Santa Ynez. GPS: 34.770508, -119.937744

456 • Norcross

Total sites: 6; RV sites: 6; No water; Vault toilets; Reservations not accepted; Stay limit: 14 days; Open May-Oct; Tent & RV camping: Free; Elev: 2428ft/740m; Tel: 530-493-2243; Nearest town: Happy Camp; Notes: Stock facilities - non-potable water. GPS: 41.647372, -123.311371

457 • Nordheimer

Total sites: 12; RV sites: 12; No water; Vault toilets; No showers; No RV dump; Reservations not accepted; Open Jun-Sep; Tent & RV camping: $8; Elev: 1109ft/338m; Tel: 530-627-3291; Nearest town: Orleans. GPS: 41.298542, -123.362666

458 • North Fork (Blue Canyon)

Total sites: 17; RV sites: 15; Central water; Vault toilets; No showers; No RV dump; Reservations accepted; Open Apr-Oct; Tent & RV camping: $24; Elev: 4836ft/1474m; Tel: 530-478-0248; Nearest town: Emigrant Gap. GPS: 39.270508, -120.658447

459 • North Fork (Caribou)

Total sites: 21; RV sites: 21; Elec sites: 21; Water at site; Flush toilets; Showers; Reservations not accepted; Tents: $30/RVs: $30-32; Elev: 2480ft/756m; Tel: 530-283-0555; Nearest town: Quincy. GPS: 40.039886, -121.219921

460 • North Fork (Six Rivers)

Total sites: 6; RV sites: 6; No water; Vault toilets; Reservations not accepted; Max length: 22ft; Open all year; Tent & RV camping: $8; Elev: 974ft/297m; Tel: 707-442-1721; Nearest town: Gasquet; Notes: No large RVs. GPS: 41.981108, -123.960317

461 • North Fork (St John)

Total sites: 10; RV sites: 10; No water; Vault toilets; Reservations not accepted; Open May-Nov; Tent & RV camping: $5; Elev: 1535ft/468m; Tel: 530-963-3128; Nearest town: Stonyford. GPS: 39.379101, -122.648233

462 • North Lake

Total sites: 11; Central water; Vault toilets; No showers; No RV dump; Reservations not accepted; Stay limit: 7 days; Open Jun-Sep; Tents only: $23; Elev: 9377ft/2858m; Tel: 760-873-2500; Nearest town: Bishop; Notes: Bear boxes must be used for food storage. GPS: 37.227404, -118.627367

463 • North Shore

Total sites: 27; RV sites: 27; Central water; Flush toilets; No showers; No RV dump; Reservations accepted; Open Apr-Sep; Tent & RV camping: $26-28; Elev: 5328ft/1624m; Tel: 909-866-8550; Nearest town: Running Springs. GPS: 34.267225, -117.164201

464 • Northshore

Total sites: 15; RV sites: 15; No water; Vault toilets; Reservations not accepted; Stay limit: 14 days; Open Jun-Oct; Tent & RV camping: $10; Elev: 6466ft/1971m; Tel: 530-644-2349; Nearest town: Pollock Pines. GPS: 38.999246, -120.318483

465 • Northwind

Total sites: 9; RV sites: 8; No water; Vault toilets; Reservations not accepted; Stay limit: 14 days; Open May-Oct; Tent & RV camping: $10; Elev: 5443ft/1659m; Tel: 530-644-2349; Nearest town: Placerville. GPS: 38.831945, -120.347821

466 • Oak Bottom

Total sites: 26; RV sites: 26; Central water; Vault toilets; No showers; No RV dump; Reservations accepted; Open Jun-Oct; Tent & RV camping: $10; Elev: 797ft/243m; Tel: 530-627-3291; Nearest town: Orleans. GPS: 41.376129, -123.452744

467 • Oak Flat (Whitaker Peak)

Total sites: 27; RV sites: 27; Central water; Vault toilets; No showers; No RV dump; Reservations not accepted; Max length: 18ft; Stay limit: 14 days; Open all year; Tent & RV camping: $5; Elev: 2782ft/848m; Tel: 661-269-2808; Nearest town: Castaic; Notes: Adventure Pass required ($5/day or $30/year) or Interagency Pass. GPS: 34.599941, -118.722024

468 • Oak Grove

Total sites: 75; RV sites: 75; Central water; Flush toilets; No showers; No RV dump; Reservations accepted; Max length: 32ft; Stay limit: 14 days; Open all year; Tent & RV camping: $15; Elev: 2772ft/845m; Tel: 760-788-0250; Nearest town: Warner Springs. GPS: 33.386925, -116.790428

469 • Oak Grove

Total sites: 10; RV sites: 5; No water; No toilets; Reservations not accepted; Tent & RV camping: Free; Elev: 1207ft/368m; Nearest town: Shasta Lake. GPS: 40.849476, -122.353343

470 • Observatory

Total sites: 43; RV sites: 43; Central water; Flush toilets; Pay showers; No RV dump; Reservations accepted; Max length: 32ft; Stay limit: 14 days; Open Apr-Nov; Tent & RV camping: $15; Elev: 4954ft/1510m; Tel: 760-788-0250; Nearest town: Palomar Mountain; Notes: Some sites have level cement pads for telescopes. GPS: 33.343002, -116.877867

471 • Obsidian

Total sites: 11; RV sites: 11; No water; Vault toilets; Reservations not accepted; Stay limit: 14 days; Open May-Oct; Tent & RV camping: $12; Elev: 7759ft/2365m; Tel: 760-932-7070; Nearest town: Walker. GPS: 38.297126, -119.447301

472 • Oh Ridge

Total sites: 135; RV sites: 130; Central water; Flush toilets; No showers; No RV dump; Reservations accepted; Max length: 40ft; Stay limit: 14 days; Open Apr-Oct; Tent & RV camping: $25-27; Elev: 7713ft/2351m; Tel: 760-647-3044; Nearest town: June Lake; Notes: Bear boxes must be used for food storage. GPS: 37.799136, -119.071392

473 • Old Shady Rest

Total sites: 47; RV sites: 47; Central water; Flush toilets; No showers; RV dump; Reservations accepted; Open May-Sep; Tent & RV camping: $21-23; Elev: 7851ft/2393m; Tel: 760-924-5500; Nearest town: Mammoth Lakes; Notes: Fee for RV dump, Bear boxes must be used for food storage. GPS: 37.650167, -118.962926

474 • Onion Valley

Total sites: 30; RV sites: 21; No water; Vault toilets; No showers; No RV dump; Reservations accepted; Max length: 25ft; Open Apr-Oct; Tent & RV camping: $23; Elev: 9173ft/2796m; Tel: 760-876-6200; Nearest town: Independence; Notes: Trailers not recommended - tent trailers OK, Bear boxes must be used for food storage. GPS: 36.771729, -118.340576

475 • Onion Valley

Total sites: 7; RV sites: 7; No water; Vault toilets; No showers; No RV dump; Open May-Oct; Tent & RV camping: $18; Elev: 4809ft/1466m; Tel: 530-265-4531; Nearest town: Emigrant Gap. GPS: 39.262902, -120.656668

476 • Orr Lake

Total sites: 8; RV sites: 8; No water; Vault toilets; No showers; No RV dump; Reservations not accepted; Stay limit: 14 days; Open May-Oct; Tent & RV camping: Free; Elev: 4682ft/1427m; Tel: 530-398-4391; Nearest town: Macdoel; Notes: Low-hanging branches. GPS: 41.667571, -121.992377

477 • P-Bar Flat

Total sites: 4; RV sites: 4; No water; Vault toilets; Reservations not accepted; Generator hours: 0600-2200; Tent & RV camping: $5; Elev: 1686ft/514m; Tel: 805-967-3481; Nearest town: Santa Barbara; Notes: High clearance vehicle recommended, Adventure Pass required ($5/day or $30/year) or Interagency Pass. GPS: 34.514995, -119.591085

478 • Pacific Valley

Total sites: 15; RV sites: 15; No water; Vault toilets; Reservations not accepted; Stay limit: 14 days; Open Jun-Oct; Tent & RV camping: $10; Elev: 7559ft/2304m; Tel: 209-795-1381; Nearest town: Bear Valley. GPS: 38.518541, -119.902269

479 • Packsaddle

Total sites: 14; RV sites: 14; Central water; Vault toilets; No showers; No RV dump; Reservations accepted; Open Jun-Oct; Tent & RV camping: $24; Elev: 6112ft/1863m; Tel: 530-862-1368; Nearest town: Sierra City; Notes: 2 equestrian sites. GPS: 39.623788, -120.649662

480 • Paha

Total sites: 21; RV sites: 21; Central water; Flush toilets; No showers; No RV dump; Reservations accepted; Max length: 35ft; Stay limit: 14 days; Open May-Sep; Tent & RV camping: $23; Elev: 7060ft/2152m; Tel: 760-932-7070; Nearest town: Bridgeport. GPS: 38.179632, -119.322969

481 • Panther Flat

Total sites: 39; RV sites: 39; Central water; Flush toilets; Pay showers; No RV dump; Reservations accepted; Open all year; Tent & RV camping: $15; Elev: 487ft/148m; Tel: 707-457-3131; Nearest town: Gasquet. GPS: 41.843799, -123.928833

482 • Panther Meadows Trail Overflow Lot

Total sites: 15; RV sites: 15; No water; No toilets; Reservations not accepted; Stay limit: 3 days; No tents/RVs: Free; Elev: 7725ft/2355m; Tel: 530-926-4511; Nearest town: Mt. Shasta. GPS: 41.359975, -122.202836

483 • Paradise

Total sites: 15; RV sites: 15; Central water; Flush toilets; No showers; No RV dump; Reservations accepted; Generator hours: 0600-2200; Open all year; Tent & RV camping: $30; Elev: 938ft/286m; Tel: 805-967-3481; Nearest town: Santa Barbara. GPS: 34.542166, -119.811844

484 • Paradise Cove

Total sites: 46; RV sites: 46; Central water; Flush toilets; No showers; RV dump; Reservations accepted; Open May-Oct; Tent & RV camping: $30-32; Elev: 2595ft/791m; Tel: 760-379-5646; Nearest town: Lake Isabella; Notes: $10 dump fee. GPS: 35.649817, -118.426828

485 • Paradise Spring

Total sites: 3; No water; Vault toilets; Reservations not accepted; Stay limit: 14 days; Tents only: Free; Elev: 1604ft/489m; Tel: 805-925-9538; Nearest town: Santa Maria. GPS: 35.152542, -120.144622

486 • Pardoes Point

Total sites: 10; Central water; Vault toilets; No showers; No RV dump; Reservations not accepted; Stay limit: 14 days; Open Jun-Sep; Tents only: $24; Elev: 5837ft/1779m; Tel: 209-295-4251; Nearest town: Pioneer. GPS: 38.537403, -120.240459

487 • Parker Flat Staging Area

Total sites: 6; RV sites: 6; No water; Vault toilets; Reservations not accepted; Max length: 20ft; Open Apr-Dec; Tent & RV camping: Free; Elev: 3940ft/1201m; Tel: 530-478-0248; Nearest town: Foresthill. GPS: 39.127425, -120.760353

488 • Pass Creek

Total sites: 25; RV sites: 25; Central water; Flush toilets; No showers; RV dump; Reservations accepted; Max length: 22ft; Open May-Oct; Tent & RV camping: $24; Elev: 6198ft/1889m; Tel: 530-265-8861; Nearest town: Truckee. GPS: 39.504971, -120.535096

489 • Patrick Creek

Total sites: 13; RV sites: 13; Central water; Flush toilets; No showers; No RV dump; Reservations accepted; Open May-Sep; Tent & RV camping: $14; Elev: 925ft/282m; Tel: 707-457-3131; Nearest town: Crescent City. GPS: 41.872252, -123.846282

490 • Patterson

Total sites: 6; RV sites: 6; Central water; Vault toilets; No showers; No RV dump; Reservations not accepted; Max length: 16ft; Stay limit: 14 days; Open May-Oct; Tent & RV camping: Free; Elev: 7274ft/2217m; Tel: 530-279-6116; Nearest town: Eagleville. GPS: 41.197916, -120.186206

491 • Payne Springs

Total sites: 5; RV sites: 5; No water; Vault toilets; Reservations not accepted; Max length: 20ft; Stay limit: 14 days; Open Jul-Oct; Tent & RV camping: Free; Elev: 6539ft/1993m; Tel: 530-667-2246; Nearest town: McCloud. GPS: 41.555082, -121.562137

492 • Pearch Creek

Total sites: 11; RV sites: 11; Central water; Vault toilets; No showers; No RV dump; Reservations accepted; Open all year; Tent & RV camping: $10; Elev: 554ft/169m; Tel: 530-627-3291; Nearest town: Orleans. GPS: 41.308871, -123.520853

493 • Peavine

Total sites: 4; Central water; Vault toilets; No showers; No RV dump; Reservations not accepted; Stay limit: 14 days; Open all year; Tents only: $5; Elev: 6040ft/1841m; Tel: 661-269-2808; Nearest town: Big Pines; Notes: Often inaccessible in winter, Adventure Pass required ($5/day or $30/year) or Interagency Pass. GPS: 34.389619, -117.718724

494 • Penny Pines

Total sites: 10; No water; Vault toilets; Reservations not accepted; Tents only: $6; Elev: 3665ft/1117m; Nearest town: Upper Lake. GPS: 39.300378, -122.930123

495 • Pepperdine

Total sites: 5; RV sites: 5; Central water; Vault toilets; No showers; No RV dump; Reservations not accepted; Stay limit: 14 days; Open Jul-Oct; Tent & RV camping: Free; Elev: 6844ft/2086m; Tel: 530-279-6116; Nearest town: Alturas; Notes: Not for large RVs, sites are uneven. GPS: 41.450229, -120.242219

496 • Philpot

Total sites: 6; No water; Vault toilets; Reservations not accepted; Tents only: Free; Elev: 2654ft/809m; Tel: 530-628-5227; Nearest town: Hayfork. GPS: 40.466000, -123.191000

497 • Pierce Creek

Total sites: 18; RV sites: 18; No water; Vault toilets; Reservations not accepted; Tent & RV camping: Free; Elev: 5163ft/1574m. GPS: 39.341284, -120.590881

498 • Pigeon Point

Total sites: 8; RV sites: 6; No water; Vault toilets; Reservations not accepted; Max length: 22ft; Open all year; Tent & RV camping: $12; Elev: 1545ft/471m; Tel: 530-623-2121; Nearest town: Junction City; Notes: Reservable group site: $75, Non-potable water. GPS: 40.767447, -123.132062

499 • Pine City

Total sites: 10; RV sites: 10; Central water; Flush toilets; No showers; No RV dump; Reservations not accepted; Open May-Sep; Tent & RV camping: $24; Elev: 9022ft/2750m; Tel: 760-924-5500; Nearest town: Mammoth Lakes; Notes: Bear boxes must be used for food storage. GPS: 37.604235, -119.000323

500 • Pine Grove

Total sites: 11; RV sites: 11; Central water; Vault toilets; No showers; No RV dump; Reservations not accepted; Stay limit: 21 days; Tent & RV camping: $25; Elev: 9386ft/2861m; Tel: 760-873-2400; Nearest town: Bishop; Notes: Bear boxes must be used for food storage. GPS: 37.470807, -118.724565

501 • Pine Marten

Total sites: 32; RV sites: 32; Central water; Flush toilets; No showers; No RV dump; Reservations accepted; Stay limit: 14 days; Open Jul-Sep; Tent & RV camping: $26; Elev: 7382ft/2250m; Tel: 209-795-1381; Nearest town: Bear Valley. GPS: 38.481173, -119.988917

502 • Pine Mountain

Total sites: 6; RV sites: 6; No water; Vault toilets; Reservations accepted; Generator hours: 0600-2200; Open May-Dec; Tent & RV camping: $20; Elev: 6739ft/2054m; Tel: 805-646-4348; Nearest town: Ojai. GPS: 34.638806, -119.326731

503 • Pine Point

Total sites: 14; RV sites: 14; Central water; Vault toilets; No showers; No RV dump; Reservations not accepted; Max length: 24ft; Open May-Sep; Tent & RV camping: $20; Elev: 1089ft/332m; Tel: 530-275-1587; Nearest town: Redding; Notes: Reservable group site $150, Bear boxes, Open holidays for overflow. GPS: 40.927541, -122.247374

504 • Pine Springs

Total sites: 12; RV sites: 12; No water; Vault toilets; Reservations not accepted; Generator hours: 0600-2200; Tent & RV camping: $5; Elev: 5812ft/1771m; Tel: 661-245-3731; Nearest town: Frazier Park; Notes: Adventure Pass required ($5/day or $30/year) or Interagency Pass. GPS: 34.691505, -119.132692

505 • Pinecrest

Total sites: 200; RV sites: 200; Central water; Flush toilets; Pay showers; RV dump; Reservations accepted; Stay limit: 14 days; Open May-Oct; Tent & RV camping: $32; Elev: 5682ft/1732m; Tel: 209-965 3434; Nearest town: Mi-Wuk. GPS: 38.191162, -119.993896

506 • Pineknot

Total sites: 52; RV sites: 52; Central water; Flush toilets; No showers; No RV dump; Reservations accepted; Open Apr-Oct; Tent & RV camping: $31-33; Elev: 6965ft/2123m; Tel: 909-866-8550; Nearest town: Big Bear City. GPS: 34.235772, -116.883829

507 • Pinyon Flat

Total sites: 18; RV sites: 18; Central water; Vault toilets; No showers; No RV dump; Reservations not accepted; Open all year; Tent & RV camping: $8; Elev: 4032ft/1229m; Tel: 909-659-2117; Nearest town: Palm Desert. GPS: 33.584877, -116.456766

508 • Pioneer Point

Total sites: 78; RV sites: 78; Central water; Flush toilets; No showers; No RV dump; Reservations accepted; Max length: 30ft; Open May-Sep; Tent & RV camping: $30; Elev: 2625ft/800m; Tel: 760-379-5646; Nearest town: Lake Isabella. GPS: 35.651611, -118.487061

509 • Pipi

Total sites: 51; RV sites: 31; Central water; Vault toilets; No showers; No RV dump; Reservations not accepted; Stay limit: 14 days; Open Jun-Nov; Tent & RV camping: $22; Elev: 4049ft/1234m; Tel: 209-295-4251; Nearest town: Pioneer. GPS: 38.567543, -120.431592

510 • Plaskett Creek

Total sites: 38; RV sites: 38; Central water; Flush toilets; No showers; No RV dump; Reservations accepted; Max length: 32ft; Open all year; Tent & RV camping: $35; Elev: 233ft/71m; Tel: 805-434-1996; Nearest town: Lucia; Notes: 1 group site $150. GPS: 35.917992, -121.466878

511 • Plaskett Meadows

Total sites: 31; RV sites: 31; Central water; Vault toilets; No showers; No RV dump; Reservations not accepted; Max length: 16ft; Open Jun-Oct; Tent & RV camping: $10; Elev: 6099ft/1859m; Tel: 530-963-3128; Nearest town: Elk Creek. GPS: 39.728415, -122.846684

512 • Plum Valley

Total sites: 7; RV sites: 7; No water; Vault toilets; Reservations not accepted; Max length: 16ft; Stay limit: 14 days; Open Jun-Oct; Tent & RV camping: Free; Elev: 5748ft/1752m; Tel: 530-279-6116; Nearest town: Davis Creek. GPS: 41.711837, -120.325772

513 • Ponderosa

Total sites: 22; RV sites: 22; Central water; Vault toilets; No showers; No RV dump; Reservations accepted; Max length: 35ft; Generator hours: 0600-2200; Open all year; Tent & RV camping: $25; Elev: 1549ft/472m; Tel: 805-434-1996; Nearest town: Pacific Valley; Notes: No water in winter. GPS: 35.997889, -121.383145

514 • Portal Forebay

Total sites: 11; RV sites: 11; No water; Vault toilets; Reservations not accepted; Open Jun-Sep; Tent & RV camping: $22; Elev: 7195ft/2193m; Tel: 559-855-5355; Nearest town: Lakeshore; Notes: Large RVs not recommended. GPS: 37.320217, -119.067034

515 • Potato Patch

Total sites: 32; RV sites: 32; Central water; Vault toilets; No showers; No RV dump; Reservations not accepted; Open Apr-Sep; Tent & RV camping: $14; Elev: 3534ft/1077m; Tel: 530-258-2141; Nearest town: Chester. GPS: 40.188477, -121.532227

516 • Preacher Meadow

Total sites: 45; RV sites: 45; Central water; Vault toilets; No showers; No RV dump; Reservations not accepted; Max length: 40ft; Open Jun-Oct; Tent & RV camping: $12; Elev: 2989ft/911m; Tel: 530-623-2121; Nearest town: Trinity Center. GPS: 40.963623, -122.731689

517 • Princess

Total sites: 88; RV sites: 69; Central water; Vault toilets; No showers; RV dump; Reservations accepted; Open May-Sep; Tent & RV camping: $29-31; Elev: 5948ft/1813m; Tel: 559-338-2251; Nearest town: Hume. GPS: 36.804237, -118.940967

518 • Prosser

Total sites: 23; RV sites: 23; Central water; Vault toilets; No showers; No RV dump; Reservations accepted; Open May-Oct; Tent & RV camping: $20; Elev: 5860ft/1786m; Tel: 530-587-9281; Nearest town: Truckee. GPS: 39.378662, -120.162354

519 • Pumice Flat

Total sites: 16; RV sites: 16; Central water; Flush toilets; No showers; No RV dump; Reservations not accepted; Open Jun-Sep; Tent & RV camping: $23; Elev: 7785ft/2373m; Tel: 760-924-5500; Nearest town: Mammoth Lakes; Notes: Narrow single lane road. GPS: 37.648529, -119.074577

520 • Quaking Aspen

Total sites: 34; RV sites: 30; Central water; Vault toilets; No showers; No RV dump; Reservations accepted; Max length: 24ft; Open May-Oct; Tent & RV camping: $28-30; Elev: 7070ft/2155m; Tel: 559-539-2607; Nearest town: Camp Nelson; Notes: Group sites $55-$203. GPS: 36.121342, -118.544539

521 • Queen Lily

Total sites: 12; RV sites: 12; Central water; Flush toilets; No showers; No RV dump; Reservations not accepted; Open Apr-Sep; Tent & RV camping: $30; Elev: 2520ft/768m; Tel: 530-283-0555; Nearest town: Quincy. GPS: 40.045718, -121.217863

522 • Ramshorn

Total sites: 14; Central water; Vault toilets; No showers; No RV dump; Reservations accepted; Open May-Sep; Tents only: $20; Elev: 2726ft/831m; Tel: 530-862-1368; Nearest town: Downieville. GPS: 39.539063, -120.909424

523 • Rancheria

Total sites: 149; RV sites: 149; Central water; Flush toilets; No showers; No RV dump; Reservations accepted; Max length: 40ft; Open May-Oct; Tent & RV camping: $34-36; Elev: 7103ft/2165m; Tel: 559-893-2111; Nearest town: Lakeshore. GPS: 37.247079, -119.162667

524 • Red Bank

Total sites: 5; RV sites: 5; No water; Vault toilets; Stay limit: 14 days; Open May-Oct; Tent & RV camping: Free; Elev: 1752ft/534m; Tel: 530-468-5351; Nearest town: Sawyers Bar. GPS: 41.297842, -123.230272

525 • Red Bridge

Total sites: 5; No water; Vault toilets; Reservations not accepted; Open all year; Tents only: Free; Elev: 5243ft/1598m; Nearest town: Quincy; Notes: No services in winter. GPS: 39.850248, -120.837219

526 • Red Feather

Total sites: 59; RV sites: 59; Central water; Flush toilets; No showers; RV dump; Reservations accepted; Stay limit: 14 days; Open May-Sep; Tent & RV camping: $23-25; Elev: 5148ft/1569m; Tel: 530-534-6500; Nearest town: La Porte. GPS: 39.734456, -120.968909

527 • Reds Meadow

Total sites: 56; RV sites: 56; Central water; Flush toilets; No showers; No RV dump; Reservations not accepted; Open Jun-Sep; Tent & RV camping: $23; Elev: 7710ft/2350m; Tel: 760-924-5500; Nearest town: Mammoth Lakes; Notes: Narrow single lane road, Bear boxes must be used for food storage, Campers may drive into area - shuttle fee applies. GPS: 37.618896, -119.073242

528 • Redwood Meadow

Total sites: 14; RV sites: 14; No water; Vault toilets; Reservations accepted; Max length: 16ft; Open May-Oct; Tent & RV camping: $30-32; Elev: 6158ft/1877m; Tel: 559-539-2607; Nearest town: Ducor. GPS: 35.977000, -118.592000

529 • Reservoir C

Total sites: 11; RV sites: 11; No water; Vault toilets; Reservations not accepted; Max length: 22ft; Stay limit: 14 days; Open May-Oct; Tent & RV camping: Free; Elev: 4954ft/1510m; Tel: 530-233-5811; Nearest town: Alturas. GPS: 41.660135, -120.775258

530 • Reservoir F

Total sites: 9; RV sites: 9; No water; Vault toilets; Reservations not accepted; Max length: 22ft; Stay limit: 14 days; Open May-Oct; Tent & RV camping: Free; Elev: 4961ft/1512m; Tel: 530-233-5811; Nearest town: Alturas. GPS: 41.580881, -120.874511

531 • Reversed Creek

Total sites: 16; RV sites: 16; Central water; Flush toilets; No showers; No RV dump; Reservations accepted; Max length: 30ft; Stay limit: 14 days; Open May-Oct; Tent & RV camping: $21-23; Elev: 7615ft/2321m; Tel: 760-647-3044; Nearest town: June Lake; Notes: Bear boxes must be used for food storage. GPS: 37.770315, -119.084611

532 • Reyes Creek

Total sites: 30; RV sites: 30; No water; Vault toilets; Reservations accepted; Max length: 22ft; Generator hours: 0600-2200; Open all year; Tent & RV camping: $20; Elev: 3983ft/1214m; Tel: 661-245-3731; Nearest town: Frazier Park. GPS: 34.679024, -119.308428

533 • Reyes Peak

Total sites: 6; RV sites: 6; No water; Vault toilets; Reservations accepted; Generator hours: 0600-2200; Open May-Dec; Tent & RV camping: $20; Elev: 7132ft/2174m; Tel: 661-245-3731; Nearest town: Ojai. GPS: 34.636939, -119.314442

534 • Ripstein

Total sites: 10; No water; Vault toilets; Reservations not accepted; Tents only: Free; Elev: 2825ft/861m; Tel: 530-623-2121; Nearest town: Junction City. GPS: 40.876709, -123.029297

535 • River Ranch

Total sites: 38; RV sites: 38; Central water; Vault toilets; No showers; No RV dump; Reservations not accepted; Stay limit: 14 days; Open Mar-Sep; Tent & RV camping: $28; Elev: 2518ft/767m; Tel: 209-586-3234; Nearest town: Tuolumne City; Notes: Part public/part private. GPS: 37.993645, -120.181522

536 • Robinson Creek North

Total sites: 30; RV sites: 27; Central water; Vault toilets; No showers; No RV dump; Reservations accepted; Max length: 35ft; Stay limit: 14 days; Open Apr-Oct; Tent & RV camping: $23; Elev: 7041ft/2146m; Tel: 760-932-7070; Nearest town: Bridgeport. GPS: 38.185216, -119.320946

537 • Robinson Creek South

Total sites: 26; RV sites: 18; Central water; Vault toilets; No showers; No RV dump; Reservations accepted; Stay limit: 14 days; Open May-Sep; Tent & RV camping: $23; Elev: 7044ft/2147m; Tel: 760-932-7092; Nearest town: Bridgeport. GPS: 38.183628, -119.321706

538 • Robinson Flat

Total sites: 14; Central water; Vault toilets; No showers; No RV dump; Reservations not accepted; Open all year; Tents only: Free; Elev: 6699ft/2042m; Nearest town: Foresthill; Notes: 7 equestrian sites, Narro winding road - trailers not recommended. GPS: 39.156263, -120.502227

539 • Rock Cabin Trailhead

Total sites: 3; RV sites: 3; No water; No toilets; Reservations not accepted; Max length: 20ft; Open Apr-Dec; Tent & RV camping: Free; Elev: 5059ft/1542m; Tel: 707-983-6118; Notes: No large RVs. GPS: 40.008229, -123.085231

540 • Rock Creek

Total sites: 3; RV sites: 3; No water; Vault toilets; Reservations not accepted; Open all year; Tent & RV camping: $15; Elev: 4508ft/1374m; Tel: 530-283-0555; Notes: No services in winter. GPS: 39.897488, -120.999234

541 • Rock Creek Lake

Total sites: 28; RV sites: 28; Central water; Flush toilets; Showers; No RV dump; Reservations accepted; Stay limit: 7 days; Open May-Oct; Tent & RV camping: $27; Elev: 9733ft/2967m; Tel: 760-873-2500; Nearest town: Toms Place; Notes: Bear boxes must be used for food storage. GPS: 37.450816, -118.735682

542 • Rocky Cabin

Total sites: 3; RV sites: 3; No water; Vault toilets; Reservations not accepted; Open Jun-Oct; Tent & RV camping: Free; Elev: 6246ft/1904m; Nearest town: Paskenta. GPS: 39.954494, -122.739613

543 • Rocky Knoll

Total sites: 18; RV sites: 18; Central water; Vault toilets; No showers; No RV dump; Reservations not accepted; Open May-Sep; Tent & RV camping: $12; Elev: 6493ft/1979m; Tel: 530-258-2141; Nearest town: Westwood. GPS: 40.498942, -121.155856

544 • Rocky Rest

Total sites: 8; RV sites: 8; Central water; Vault toilets; No showers; No RV dump; Reservations accepted; Open Apr-Sep; Tent & RV camping: $24; Elev: 2441ft/744m; Tel: 530-862-1368; Nearest town: Camptonville. GPS: 39.513084, -120.977263

545 • Rogers Cow Camp

Total sites: 6; RV sites: 6; Central water; Vault toilets; No showers; No RV dump; Reservations not accepted; Open all year; Tent & RV camping: $15; Elev: 4131ft/1259m; Tel: 530-534-6500; Nearest town: Berry Creek. GPS: 39.766905, -121.312547

546 • Rose Valley

Total sites: 9; RV sites: 9; No water; Vault toilets; Reservations accepted; Generator hours: 0600-2200; Open all year; Tent & RV camping: $20; Elev: 3425ft/1044m; Tel: 805-646-4348; Nearest town: Ojai. GPS: 34.531889, -119.182671

547 • Running Deer

Total sites: 40; RV sites: 40; Central water; Flush toilets; No showers; RV dump; Reservations accepted; Open May-Sep; Tent & RV camping: $23-25; Elev: 5226ft/1593m; Tel: 530-534-6500; Nearest town: La Porte. GPS: 39.738497, -120.967469

548 • Rush Creek

Total sites: 10; RV sites: 10; No water; Vault toilets; Reservations not accepted; Max length: 20ft; Open May-Sep; Tent & RV camping: $10; Elev: 2841ft/866m; Tel: 530-623-2121; Nearest town: Weaverville. GPS: 40.816834, -122.896343

549 • Sabrina

Total sites: 18; RV sites: 18; Central water; Vault toilets; No showers; No RV dump; Reservations not accepted; Max length: 16ft; Stay limit: 7 days; Open May-Sep; Tent & RV camping: $28; Elev: 8980ft/2737m; Tel: 760-873-2500; Nearest town: Bishop; Notes: Bear boxes must be used for food storage. GPS: 37.219463, -118.606592

550 • Saddlebag Lake

Total sites: 20; RV sites: 20; Central water; Vault toilets; No showers; No RV dump; Reservations not accepted; Max length: 16ft; Open Jun-Oct; Tent & RV camping: $22; Elev: 10202ft/3110m; Tel: 760-647-3044; Nearest town: Lee Vining; Notes: Reservable group site, Last 2 miles one-lane windy dirt road, Bear boxes must be used for food storage, No large RVs. GPS: 37.964357, -119.270883

551 • Sage Flat

Total sites: 28; RV sites: 28; Central water; Vault toilets; No showers; No RV dump; Reservations not accepted; Stay limit: 14 days; Open Apr-Oct; Tent & RV camping: $23; Elev: 7619ft/2322m; Tel: 760-873-2400; Nearest town: Big Pine; Notes: Bear boxes must be used for food storage. GPS: 37.130068, -118.412321

552 • Sagehen Creek

Total sites: 10; RV sites: 10; No water; Vault toilets; Reservations not accepted; Max length: 18ft; Open May-Nov; Tent & RV camping: Free; Elev: 6526ft/1989m; Tel: 530-994-3401; Nearest town: Truckee; Notes: Not suitable for large RVs. GPS: 39.434371, -120.257461

553 • Salmon Creek

Total sites: 31; RV sites: 26; Central water; Vault toilets; No showers; No RV dump; Reservations accepted; Open May-Oct; Tent & RV camping: $24; Elev: 5810ft/1771m; Tel: 530-862-1368; Nearest town: Sierra City. GPS: 39.623788, -120.613055

554 • Sample Meadow

Total sites: 16; RV sites: 16; No water; Vault toilets; Reservations not accepted; Max length: 20ft; Stay limit: 14 days; Open Jun-Oct; Tent & RV camping: Free; Elev: 7897ft/2407m; Tel: 559-855-5355; Nearest town: Lakeshore; Notes: Not recommended for large RVs or motorhomes. GPS: 37.335862, -119.156009

555 • San Gorgonio

Total sites: 51; RV sites: 51; Central water; Flush toilets; Showers; No RV dump; Reservations accepted; Open Apr-Sep; Tent & RV camping: $31-33; Elev: 6545ft/1995m; Tel: 909-866-8550; Nearest town: Angelus Oaks; Notes: 3 group sites $52-$56. GPS: 34.174437, -116.867463

556 • Sand Bar Flat

Total sites: 10; RV sites: 10; Central water; Vault toilets; No showers; No RV dump; Reservations not accepted; Max length: 35ft; Stay limit: 14 days; Open Apr-Nov; Tent & RV camping: $12; Elev: 2772ft/845m; Tel: 209-586-3234; Nearest town: Mi-Wuk; Notes: Road not suitable for large RVs. GPS: 38.184277, -120.155807

557 • Sand Flat

Total sites: 68; RV sites: 68; Central water; Vault toilets; No showers; No RV dump; Reservations not accepted; Max length: 22ft; Stay limit: 14 days; Open Apr-Oct; Tent & RV camping: $21; Elev: 6191ft/1887m; Tel: 209-965-3434; Nearest town: Kyburz; Notes: Cash only, May use RV dump at Clark Fork CG. GPS: 38.404219, -119.789774

558 • Sand Flat

Total sites: 29; RV sites: 27; Central water; Vault toilets; No showers; No RV dump; Reservations not accepted; Stay limit: 14 days; Open Jun-Sep; Tent & RV camping: $23; Elev: 3960ft/1207m; Tel: 530-644-2324; Nearest town: Placerville. GPS: 38.763516, -120.325835

559 • Sandy Flat

Total sites: 35; RV sites: 29; Central water; Vault toilets; No showers; No RV dump; Reservations accepted; Max length: 24ft; Open May-Oct; Tent & RV camping: $28-30; Elev: 2362ft/720m; Tel: 760-379-5646; Nearest town: Lake Isabella; Notes: Also walk-to sites, 6 walk-in sites. GPS: 35.582526, -118.524877

560 • Santa Rosa Yellow Post

Total sites: 14; No water; No toilets; Reservations not accepted; Open all year; Tents only: Fee unknown; Elev: 7999ft/2438m; Tel: 909-382-2922; Nearest town: Palm Springs. GPS: 33.536915, -116.461755

561 • Sarah Totten

Total sites: 9; RV sites: 9; Central water; Vault toilets; No showers; No RV dump; Reservations accepted; Stay limit: 14 days; Open May-Oct; Tent & RV camping: $10; Elev: 1568ft/478m; Tel: 530-493-2243; Nearest town: Happy Camp; Notes: 2 group sites $50. GPS: 41.786773, -123.053046

562 • Sardine Lake

Total sites: 27; RV sites: 27; Central water; Vault toilets; No showers; No RV dump; Reservations accepted; Max length: 16ft; Open May-Oct; Tent & RV camping: $24; Elev: 5751ft/1753m; Tel: 530-862-1368; Nearest town: Sierra City. GPS: 39.618896, -120.617432

563 • Sawmill

Total sites: 8; RV sites: 8; No water; Vault toilets; Reservations not accepted; Max length: 16ft; Stay limit: 14 days; Tent & RV camping: $5; Elev: 5187ft/1581m; Tel: 661-269-2808; Nearest town: Lake Hughes; Notes: Adventure Pass required ($5/day or $30/year) or Interagency Pass. GPS: 34.701083, -118.572056

564 • Sawmill Flat

Total sites: 15; No water; Vault toilets; Reservations not accepted; Stay limit: 14 days; Open Jun-Dec; Tents only: Free; Elev: 6811ft/2076m; Tel: 559-855-5355; Nearest town: Fresno. GPS: 36.969583, -119.017023

565 • Schonichin Springs

Total sites: 10; RV sites: 10; No water; Vault toilets; Reservations not accepted; Max length: 20ft; Stay limit: 14 days; Open Jul-Oct; Tent & RV camping: Free; Elev: 6782ft/2067m; Tel: 530-667-2246; Nearest town: McCloud. GPS: 41.591564, -121.617552

566 • Schoolhouse

Total sites: 56; RV sites: 56; Central water; Flush toilets; No showers; No RV dump; Reservation required; Max length: 22ft; Open May-Oct; Tent & RV camping: $22; Elev: 2310ft/704m; Tel: 530-288-3231; Nearest town: Camptonville; Notes: Reservation phone number is 530-692-3200. GPS: 39.417504, -121.121525

567 • Scott Mountain

Total sites: 7; RV sites: 7; No water; Vault toilets; Reservations not accepted; Max length: 15ft; Open all year; Tent & RV camping: Free; Elev: 5443ft/1659m; Tel: 530-623-2121; Nearest town: Weaverville. GPS: 41.275000, -122.698000

568 • Scotts Flat

Total sites: 10; RV sites: 10; No water; Vault toilets; Reservations not accepted; Max length: 20ft; Tent & RV camping: Free; Elev: 2354ft/717m; Tel: 530-628-5227; Nearest town: Hayfork. GPS: 40.365738, -123.309397

569 • Serrano

Total sites: 108; RV sites: 108; Elec sites: 29; Central water; Flush toilets; Showers; RV dump; Reservations accepted; Open Mar-Nov; Tents: $37-39/RVs: $37-49; Elev: 6844ft/2086m; Tel: 909-866-8021; Nearest town: Big Bear Lake. GPS: 34.263555, -116.917463

570 • Shadow Creek

Total sites: 5; RV sites: 5; No water; Vault toilets; Open May-Oct; Tent & RV camping: Free; Elev: 2976ft/907m; Tel: 530-468-5351; Nearest town: Cecilville. GPS: 41.201631, -123.069169

571 • Shafter

Total sites: 10; RV sites: 10; Central water; Vault toilets; No showers; No RV dump; Reservations not accepted; Stay limit: 14 days; Tent & RV camping: $10; Elev: 4393ft/1339m; Tel: 530-398-4391; Nearest town: Macdoel; Notes: Near railroad, No water in winter. GPS: 41.710225, -121.981279

572 • Shenanigan Flat

Total sites: 8; RV sites: 4; No water; Vault toilets; No showers; No RV dump; Tent & RV camping: Free; Elev: 2282ft/696m. GPS: 39.507064, -121.022796

573 • Sherwin Creek

Total sites: 85; RV sites: 70; Central water; Vault toilets; No showers; No RV dump; Reservations accepted; Open May-Sep; Tent & RV camping: $21-23; Elev: 7585ft/2312m; Tel: 760-924-5500; Nearest town: Mammoth Lakes; Notes: Bear boxes must be used for food storage. GPS: 37.630127, -118.937500

574 • Shiell Gulch

Total sites: 5; No water; Vault toilets; Reservations not accepted; Tents only: Free; Elev: 2806ft/855m. GPS: 40.470341, -123.060648

575 • Shirttail Creek

Total sites: 31; RV sites: 29; Central water; Vault toilets; No showers; No RV dump; Reservations accepted; Max length: 30ft; Open May-Oct; Tent & RV camping: $24; Elev: 3766ft/1148m; Tel: 530-478-0248; Nearest town: Foresthill; Notes: $6 dump fee, Use food storage lockers. GPS: 39.142441, -120.785152

576 • Sierra

Total sites: 16; No water; Vault toilets; Reservations accepted; Open May-Oct; Tents only: $18; Elev: 5742ft/1750m; Tel: 530-862-1368; Nearest town: Sierra City. GPS: 39.630615, -120.558594

577 • Silver Bowl

Total sites: 18; RV sites: 18; Central water; Vault toilets; No showers; No RV dump; Reservations not accepted; Open May-Oct; Tent & RV camping: $12; Elev: 6532ft/1991m; Tel: 530-258-2141; Nearest town: Westwood. GPS: 40.499326, -121.164112

578 • Silver Creek (Hwy 4)

Total sites: 27; RV sites: 27; No water; Vault toilets; No showers; No RV dump; Reservations accepted; Max length: 35ft; Stay limit: 14 days; Open Jun-Sep; Tent & RV camping: $18; Elev: 6821ft/2079m; Tel: 530-694-1002; Nearest town: Markleeville. GPS: 38.588057, -119.786696

579 • Silver Creek (Truckee)

Total sites: 23; RV sites: 16; Central water; Vault toilets; No showers; No RV dump; Reservations accepted; Max length: 24ft; Open May-Oct; Tent & RV camping: $20; Elev: 6060ft/1847m; Tel: 530-587-9281; Nearest town: Tahoe City; Notes: Also walk-to sites. GPS: 39.223389, -120.201904

580 • Silver Fork

Total sites: 35; RV sites: 22; Central water; Vault toilets; No showers; No RV dump; Reservations not accepted; Max length: 22ft; Stay limit: 14 days; Open Jun-Sep; Tent & RV camping: $23; Elev: 5587ft/1703m; Tel: 530-644-2324; Nearest town: Pioneer. GPS: 38.699023, -120.207537

581 • Silver Lake

Total sites: 62; RV sites: 62; Central water; Flush toilets; No showers; No RV dump; Reservations accepted; Open Apr-Nov; Tent & RV camping: $21-23; Elev: 7244ft/2208m; Tel: 760-647-3044; Nearest town: June Lake; Notes: Bear boxes must be used for food storage. GPS: 37.783165, -119.125897

582 • Silver Lake

Total sites: 7; No water; Vault toilets; Open May-Oct; Tents only: $20; Elev: 5794ft/1766m; Tel: 530-283-0555; Nearest town: Quincey. GPS: 39.959000, -121.135000

583 • Silver Lake East (Eldorado)

Total sites: 59; RV sites: 48; No water; Vault toilets; No showers; No RV dump; Reservations accepted; Stay limit: 14 days; Open Jun-Sep; Tent & RV camping: $24; Elev: 7306ft/2227m; Tel: 209-295-4251; Nearest town: Eldorado. GPS: 38.672352, -120.118262

584 • Silver Valley

Total sites: 21; RV sites: 21; No water; Flush toilets; No showers; No RV dump; Reservations accepted; Stay limit: 14 days; Open Jul-Sep; Tent & RV camping: $26; Elev: 7421ft/2262m; Tel: 209-753-6350; Nearest town: Arnold. GPS: 38.479980, -119.987549

585 • Silvertip

Total sites: 22; RV sites: 22; No water; Vault toilets; Reservations not accepted; Stay limit: 14 days; Open Jul-Sep; Tent & RV camping: $26; Elev: 7628ft/2325m; Tel: 209-795-1381; Nearest town: Bear Valley. GPS: 38.481505, -120.017942

586 • Sims Flat

Total sites: 19; RV sites: 19; Central water; Flush toilets; No showers; No RV dump; Reservations not accepted; Max length: 16ft; Open Apr-Nov; Tent & RV camping: $15; Elev: 1722ft/525m; Tel: 530-926-4511; Nearest town: Dunsmuir; Notes: Near railroad. GPS: 41.062012, -122.359619

587 • Slide Creek

Total sites: 5; No water; Vault toilets; Reservations not accepted; Tents only: Free; Elev: 1253ft/382m; Tel: 530-628-5227. GPS: 40.668217, -123.503351

588 • Sly Creek

Total sites: 23; RV sites: 23; Central water; Vault toilets; No showers; No RV dump; Reservations not accepted; Stay limit: 14 days; Open May-Oct; Tent & RV camping: $20; Elev: 3524ft/1074m; Tel: 530-534-1221; Nearest town: Strawberry Valley. GPS: 39.584455, -121.117436

589 • Snag Lake

Total sites: 12; RV sites: 12; No water; Vault toilets; Reservations not accepted; Open May-Sep; Tent & RV camping: Free; Elev: 6713ft/2046m; Tel: 530-265-4531; Nearest town: Bassetts. GPS: 39.670795, -120.626904

590 • Snake Lake

Total sites: 9; RV sites: 9; No water; Vault toilets; Reservations not accepted; Open all year; Tent & RV camping: $15; Elev: 4010ft/1222m; Tel: 530-283-0555; Nearest town: Quincy; Notes: No services in winter, Not plowed. GPS: 39.980787, -121.006064

591 • Snowslide Canyon

Total sites: 20; RV sites: 20; No water; Vault toilets; Reservations not accepted; Stay limit: 14 days; Tent & RV camping: Free; Elev: 5693ft/1735m; Nearest town: Azusa. GPS: 34.325396, -117.837086

592 • Soldier Meadows

Total sites: 15; RV sites: 15; No water; Vault toilets; Reservations not accepted; Open May-Oct; Tent & RV camping: $10; Elev: 4829ft/1472m; Tel: 530-258-2141; Nearest town: Chester. GPS: 40.213033, -121.273905

593 • Sonora Bridge

Total sites: 23; RV sites: 23; Central water; Vault toilets; No showers; No RV dump; Reservations not accepted; Max length: 35ft; Stay limit: 14 days; Open Apr-Oct; Tent & RV camping: $20; Elev: 6736ft/2053m; Tel: 760-932-7070; Nearest town: Walker. GPS: 38.364368, -119.476963

594 • Soquel

Total sites: 11; RV sites: 11; No water; Vault toilets; Reservations accepted; Max length: 20ft; Stay limit: 14 days; Open May-Sep; Tent & RV camping: $27-29; Elev: 5308ft/1618m; Tel: 559-642-3212; Nearest town: Oakhurst. GPS: 37.407226, -119.563106

595 • Soup Springs

Total sites: 8; RV sites: 8; Central water; Vault toilets; No showers; No RV dump; Reservations not accepted; Max length: 20ft; Stay limit: 14 days; Open Jun-Oct; Tent & RV camping: $12; Elev: 6854ft/2089m; Tel: 530-279-6116; Nearest town: Likely. GPS: 41.309013, -120.277433

596 • South Antelope

Total sites: 4; RV sites: 4; No water; Vault toilets; Reservations not accepted; Open all year; Tent & RV camping: Free; Elev: 2861ft/872m; Tel: 530-258-2141; Nearest town: Chester. GPS: 40.253027, -121.758434

597 • South Fork

Total sites: 9; No water; Vault toilets; Reservations not accepted; Stay limit: 14 days; Open all year; Tents only: Free; Elev: 1545ft/471m; Tel: 209-962-7825; Nearest town: Groveland; Notes: Burn area - use caution. GPS: 37.838865, -120.045299

598 • South Fork

Total sites: 24; RV sites: 24; Central water; Vault toilets; No showers; No RV dump; Reservations not accepted; Max length: 30ft; Open May-Sep; Tent & RV camping: $26; Elev: 6339ft/1932m; Tel: 909-382-2790; Nearest town: Angelus Oaks. GPS: 34.168616, -116.825184

599 • South Fork

Total sites: 10; RV sites: 10; Central water; Vault toilets; Reservations not accepted; Open all year; Tent & RV camping: $5; Elev: 1667ft/508m; Tel: 530-963-3128; Nearest town: Stonyford. GPS: 39.362311, -122.653389

600 • South Shore

Total sites: 22; RV sites: 7; Central water; Vault toilets; No showers; No RV dump; Reservations not accepted; Stay limit: 14 days; Open Jun-Sep; Tent & RV camping: $24; Elev: 5925ft/1806m; Tel: 209-295-4251; Nearest town: Pioneer. GPS: 38.533779, -120.243501

601 • Southfork

Total sites: 21; RV sites: 21; No water; Vault toilets; Reservations not accepted; Max length: 16ft; Stay limit: 14 days; Tent & RV camping: $5; Elev: 4646ft/1416m; Tel: 661-269-2808; Nearest town: Palmdale; Notes: Group site available, Adventure Pass required ($5/day or $30/year) or Interagency Pass. GPS: 34.395621, -117.820716

602 • Spanish Creek

Total sites: 24; RV sites: 20; Central water; Vault toilets; No showers; No RV dump; Reservations accepted; Open May-Sep; Tent & RV camping: $30; Elev: 3089ft/942m; Tel: 530-283-0555; Nearest town: Quincy; Notes: Near railroad. GPS: 40.027101, -120.965573

603 • Spicer Meadow Reservoir

Total sites: 43; RV sites: 43; Central water; Vault toilets; No showers; No RV dump; Reservations not accepted; Max length: 50ft; Stay limit: 14 days; Open Jun-Oct; Tent & RV camping: $24; Elev: 6686ft/2038m; Tel: 209-296-8895; Nearest town: Arnold; Notes: Group site: $140, No camping at boat ramp. GPS: 38.407539, -119.998164

604 • Spring Cove

Total sites: 63; RV sites: 63; Central water; Flush toilets; No showers; No RV dump; Reservations accepted; Max length: 30ft; Open May-Sep; Tents: $36-36/RVs: $36-38; Elev: 3471ft/1058m; Tel: 559-642-3212; Nearest town: Bass Lake. GPS: 37.301423, -119.542812

605 • Spring Creek

Total sites: 35; RV sites: 30; Central water; Vault toilets; No showers; RV dump; Reservations accepted; Max length: 22ft; Open May-Sep; Tent & RV camping: $30; Elev: 5627ft/1715m; Tel: 530-258-7606; Nearest town: Chilcoot. GPS: 39.896484, -120.178955

606 • Stanislaus River

Total sites: 24; RV sites: 10; Central water; Vault toilets; No showers; No RV dump; Reservations not accepted; Stay limit: 14 days; Open Jun-Sep; Tent & RV camping: $12; Elev: 6207ft/1892m; Tel: 209-795-1381; Nearest town: Arnold. GPS: 38.422319, -120.046767

607 • Star City

Total sites: 7; No water; No toilets; Reservations not accepted; Tents only: Free; Elev: 2708ft/825m; Tel: 530-964-2184; Nearest town: McCloud. GPS: 41.153805, -122.068762

608 • Stony Creek

Total sites: 49; RV sites: 49; Central water; Flush toilets; No showers; No RV dump; Reservations accepted; Max length: 22ft; Open May-Sep; Tent & RV camping: $29-31; Elev: 6522ft/1988m; Tel: 559-335-2232; Nearest town: Wilsonia. GPS: 36.665135, -118.833456

609 • Stough Reservoir

Total sites: 4; RV sites: 4; Central water; Vault toilets; No showers; No RV dump; Reservations not accepted; Max length: 22ft; Stay limit: 14 days; Open May-Oct; Tent & RV camping: Free; Elev: 6375ft/1943m; Tel: 530-279-6116; Nearest town: Cedar Pass. GPS: 41.562543, -120.255189

610 • Strawberry

Total sites: 17; RV sites: 17; Central water; Vault toilets; No showers; No RV dump; Reservations not accepted; Stay limit: 14 days; Open May-Sep; Tent & RV camping: $20; Elev: 3711ft/1131m; Tel: 530-534-6500; Nearest town: Strawberry Valley. GPS: 39.588508, -121.090271

611 • Strawberry Point

Total sites: 10; RV sites: 10; No water; Vault toilets; Reservations not accepted; Stay limit: 14 days; Open Jun-Oct; Tent & RV camping: $10; Elev: 5515ft/1681m; Tel: 530-644-2349; Nearest town: Placerville. GPS: 38.828635, -120.339103

612 • Streamside

Total sites: 9; No water; Vault toilets; Reservations not accepted; Stay limit: 14 days; Open all year; Tents only: $5; Elev: 2356ft/ 718m; Tel: 661-269-2808. GPS: 34.549421, -118.431984

613 • Stumpy Meadows

Total sites: 40; RV sites: 30; Central water; Vault toilets; No showers; No RV dump; Reservations accepted; Stay limit: 14 days; Open May-Oct; Tent & RV camping: $24; Elev: 4501ft/1372m; Tel: 530-333-4312; Nearest town: Georgetown. GPS: 38.904287, -120.591351

614 • Sugar Pine Point

Total sites: 8; No water; Vault toilets; Reservations not accepted; Stay limit: 14 days; Open May-Oct; Tents only: $24; Elev: 5882ft/1793m; Tel: 209-295-4251; Nearest town: Jackson. GPS: 38.544927, -120.241407

615 • Sugar Spring

Total sites: 3; No water; Vault toilets; Reservations not accepted; Open Jun-Nov; Tents only: Free; Elev: 5522ft/1683m; Tel: 530-934-3316; Nearest town: Paskenta. GPS: 39.859458, -122.918086

616 • Sugarfoot Glade

Total sites: 6; RV sites: 6; No water; Vault toilets; Reservations not accepted; Max length: 16ft; Open Jun-Nov; Tent & RV camping: Free; Elev: 3812ft/1162m; Tel: 530-934-3316; Nearest town: Red Bluff. GPS: 39.885038, -122.777093

617 • Summerdale

Total sites: 29; RV sites: 29; Central water; Vault toilets; No showers; No RV dump; Reservations accepted; Max length: 24ft; Stay limit: 14 days; Open May-Sep; Tent & RV camping: $34-36; Elev: 5023ft/1531m; Tel: 559-642-3212; Nearest town: Oakhurst; Notes: Water must be boiled. GPS: 37.490253, -119.632865

618 • Sundew

Total sites: 19; RV sites: 19; Central water; Vault toilets; No showers; No RV dump; Reservations not accepted; Open May-Sep; Tent & RV camping: $30; Elev: 5243ft/1598m; Tel: 530-283-0555; Nearest town: Quincy; Notes: Concessionaire managed. GPS: 39.900776, -121.200253

619 • Sunset - Union Valley

Total sites: 131; RV sites: 117; Central water; Vault toilets; No showers; RV dump; Reservations accepted; Stay limit: 14 days; Open May-Sep; Tent & RV camping: $28; Elev: 4957ft/1511m; Tel: 530-293-0827; Nearest town: Pollock Pines. GPS: 38.866554, -120.406895

620 • Sweetwater

Total sites: 12; RV sites: 12; Central water; Vault toilets; No showers; No RV dump; Reservations not accepted; Max length: 18ft; Stay limit: 14 days; Open all year; Tent & RV camping: $24; Elev: 3028ft/923m; Tel: 209-962-7825; Nearest town: Groveland; Notes: Filling RV water tank not allowed, No services in winter. GPS: 37.824179, -120.004424

621 • Sweetwater (Coarsegold)

Total sites: 7; RV sites: 7; No water; Vault toilets; Reservations accepted; Max length: 20ft; Stay limit: 14 days; Open Jun-Sep; Tent & RV camping: $27-29; Elev: 3835ft/1169m; Tel: 559-642-3212; Nearest town: Coarsegold. GPS: 37.364525, -119.352583

622 • Sycamore Flats

Total sites: 12; RV sites: 12; Central water; Vault toilets; No showers; No RV dump; Reservations not accepted; Max length: 18ft; Stay limit: 14 days; Open all year; Tent & RV camping: $5; Elev: 4429ft/ 1350m; Tel: 818-899-1900; Nearest town: Wrightwood; Notes: Adventure Pass required ($5/day or $30/year) or Interagency Pass. GPS: 34.413463, -117.825285

623 • Sycamore Grove (Red Bluff)

Total sites: 59; RV sites: 30; Elec sites: 10; Central water; Flush toilets; Pay showers; No RV dump; Reservations accepted; Stay limit: 14 days; Open all year; Tents: $16/RVs: $16-25; Elev: 272ft/ 83m; Tel: 530-934-3316; Nearest town: Red Bluff. GPS: 40.155554, -122.202022

624 • Table Mountain (Angeles)

Total sites: 38; RV sites: 38; Central water; Vault toilets; No showers; No RV dump; Reservations accepted; Max length: 32ft; Stay limit: 14 days; Open May-Oct; Tent & RV camping: $23; Elev: 7313ft/2229m; Tel: 760-249-3526; Nearest town: Wrightwood; Notes: Group fee: $92. GPS: 34.386471, -117.689954

625 • Talbot

Total sites: 5; No water; Vault toilets; Reservations not accepted; Tents only: Free; Elev: 5646ft/1721m; Tel: 530-265-4531; Nearest town: Truckee; Notes: River water. GPS: 39.188000, -120.373000

626 • Tannery Gulch

Total sites: 82; RV sites: 82; Central water; Flush toilets; No showers; No RV dump; Reservations accepted; Open May-Sep; Tent & RV camping: $23; Elev: 2513ft/766m; Tel: 530-623-2121; Nearest town: Weaverville; Notes: Group site $30. GPS: 40.834683, -122.846859

627 • TeleLi puLaya (Black Oak)

Total sites: 20; RV sites: 20; No water; Vault toilets; No showers; No RV dump; Reservations not accepted; Stay limit: 14 days; Open Apr-Oct; Tent & RV camping: $20; Elev: 5112ft/1558m; Tel: 209-965-3434; Notes: 2 group sites: $25, New in 2014. GPS: 38.186861, -120.057997

628 • Tenmile

Total sites: 13; RV sites: 13; No water; Vault toilets; Reservations accepted; Max length: 22ft; Open all year; Tent & RV camping: $25-27; Elev: 5938ft/1810m; Tel: 559-338-2251; Nearest town: Dunlap; Notes: No fees/services in winter. GPS: 36.754000, -118.892000

629 • The Pines

Total sites: 9; RV sites: 9; Central water; Vault toilets; No showers; No RV dump; Reservations not accepted; Stay limit: 14 days; Open all year; Tent & RV camping: $21; Elev: 3281ft/1000m; Tel: 209-379-2258; Nearest town: Groveland; Notes: Reservable group site $90, No water in winter. GPS: 37.818337, -120.095545

630 • Thorn Meadows

Total sites: 5; No water; Vault toilets; Reservations not accepted; Open May-Dec; Tents only: Free; Elev: 5007ft/1526m; Tel: 661-245-3731; Notes: Requires high clearance vehicles due to water crossings, 1 Pipe corral. GPS: 34.626996, -119.114117

631 • Three Prong

Total sites: 6; RV sites: 3; No water; Vault toilets; Reservations not accepted; Max length: RV-24ft/Trlr-16ft; Open Jun-Dec; Tent & RV camping: Free; Elev: 6014ft/1833m; Tel: 530-934-3316; Nearest town: Paskenta. GPS: 39.920713, -122.791721

632 • Tillie Creek

Total sites: 159; RV sites: 159; Central water; Flush toilets; No showers, RV dump; Reservations accepted; Max length: 45ft; Open May-Nov; Tent & RV camping: $30; Elev: 2638ft/804m; Tel: 760-379-5646; Nearest town: Wofford Heights; Notes: Group sites $243-$608. GPS: 35.701572, -118.456129

633 • Tioga Lake

Total sites: 13; RV sites: 13; Central water; Vault toilets; No showers; No RV dump; Reservations not accepted; Max length: 16ft; Open Jun-Oct; Tent & RV camping: $22; Elev: 9659ft/2944m; Tel: 760-647-3044; Nearest town: Lee Vining; Notes: Bear boxes must be used for food storage. GPS: 37.927207, -119.255054

634 • Toad Springs

Total sites: 5; Central water; Vault toilets; No showers; No RV dump; Reservations not accepted; Tents only: Free; Elev: 5676ft/1730m; Tel: 661-245-3731; Nearest town: Pine Mountain Club. GPS: 34.860721, -119.228178

635 • Tomhead Saddle

Total sites: 5; No water; Vault toilets; Reservations not accepted; Tents only: Free; Elev: 5686ft/1733m; Tel: 530-352-4211. GPS: 40.140152, -122.830288

636 • Tool Box Springs

Total sites: 6; RV sites: 6; No water; Vault toilets; Reservations not accepted; Open all year; Tent & RV camping: Free; Elev: 6122ft/1866m; Nearest town: Azusa. GPS: 33.611682, -116.661558

637 • Tool Box Springs Yellow Post

Total sites: 6; No water; No toilets; Reservations not accepted; Tents only: Free; Elev: 6014ft/1833m; Tel: 909-382-2922. GPS: 33.616043, -116.660679

638 • Toomes Camp

Total sites: 2; RV sites: 2; No water; Vault toilets; Reservations not accepted; Open Jun-Oct; Tent & RV camping: Free; Elev: 6001ft/1829m; Nearest town: Red Bluff. GPS: 40.002985, -122.759041

639 • Tooms RV Campground

Total sites: 20; RV sites: 20; Central water; Vault toilets; RV dump; Reservations not accepted; Stay limit: 14 days; No tents/RVs: $23; Elev: 5119ft/1560m; Tel: 530-534-6500; Nearest town: La Porte. GPS: 39.723847, -120.981948

640 • Trail Creek

Total sites: 12; RV sites: 12; Central water; Vault toilets; No showers; No RV dump; Reservations not accepted; Stay limit: 14 days; Tent & RV camping: $10; Elev: 4869ft/1484m; Tel: 530-468-5351; Nearest town: Etna. GPS: 41.229492, -122.972412

641 • Trapper Springs/PGE

Total sites: 75; RV sites: 75; No water; Vault toilets; Reservations not accepted; Max length: 35ft; Stay limit: 14 days; Open May-Oct; Tent & RV camping: $24; Elev: 8209ft/2502m; Tel: 559-855-5355; Nearest town: Clovis. GPS: 37.092337, -118.982691

642 • Tree of Heaven

Total sites: 20; RV sites: 20; Central water; Vault toilets; No showers; No RV dump; Reservations accepted; Stay limit: 14 days; Open May-Oct; Tent & RV camping: $15; Elev: 2057ft/627m; Tel: 530-493-2243; Nearest town: Yreka; Notes: Group site $20. GPS: 41.832147, -122.660438

643 • Trinity River

Total sites: 7; RV sites: 7; Central water; Vault toilets; No showers; No RV dump; Reservations not accepted; Max length: 35ft; Open May-Oct; Tent & RV camping: $10; Elev: 2608ft/795m; Tel: 530-623-2121; Nearest town: Weaverville. GPS: 41.108631, -122.705759

644 • Trout Creek

Total sites: 10; RV sites: 10; No water; Vault toilets; Reservations not accepted; Max length: 24ft; Generator hours: 0700-2200; Open Jun-Oct; Tent & RV camping: Free; Elev: 4941ft/1506m; Tel: 530-964-2184; Nearest town: McCloud. GPS: 41.445285, -121.885922

645 • Trumbull Lake

Total sites: 35; RV sites: 35; Central water; Vault toilets; No showers; No RV dump; Reservations accepted; Max length: 40ft; Stay limit: 14 days; Open Jun-Oct; Tent & RV camping: $23; Elev: 9688ft/2953m; Tel: 760-932-7070; Nearest town: Bridgeport. GPS: 38.051724, -119.256892

646 • Tuff

Total sites: 34; RV sites: 34; Central water; Vault toilets; No showers; RV dump; Reservations accepted; Stay limit: 21 days; Open Apr-Oct; Tent & RV camping: $25; Elev: 7021ft/2140m; Tel: 760-935-4026; Nearest town: Bishop; Notes: Bear boxes must be used for food storage. GPS: 37.562341, -118.668409

647 • Twin Lakes

Total sites: 94; RV sites: 94; Central water; Flush toilets; Showers; No RV dump; Reservations accepted; Open Jun-Oct; Tent & RV camping: $22-24; Elev: 8661ft/2640m; Tel: 760-924-5500; Nearest town: Mammoth Lakes; Notes: Bear boxes must be used for food storage. GPS: 37.615885, -119.006694

648 • Union Flat

Total sites: 11; RV sites: 7; Central water; Vault toilets; No showers; No RV dump; Reservations accepted; Open May-Oct; Tent & RV camping: $24; Elev: 3419ft/1042m; Tel: 530-862-1368; Nearest town: Downieville. GPS: 39.567383, -120.744629

649 • Union West

Total sites: 11; RV sites: 11; No water; Vault toilets; Reservations not accepted; Max length: 27ft; Stay limit: 14 days; Tent & RV camping: $16; Elev: 6906ft/2105m; Tel: 209-795-1381; Nearest town: Bear Valley. GPS: 38.428391, -119.991494

650 • Upper Billy Creek

Total sites: 44; RV sites: 44; Central water; Flush toilets; No showers; No RV dump; Reservations accepted; Max length: 30ft; Stay limit: 14 days; Open May-Sep; Tent & RV camping: $33-35; Elev: 7100ft/2164m; Tel: 559-893-2111; Nearest town: Eastwood. GPS: 37.238287, -119.227248

651 • Upper Deadman

Total sites: 15; RV sites: 15; No water; No toilets; Reservations not accepted; Max length: 45ft; Stay limit: 14 days; Tent & RV camping: Free; Elev: 7802ft/2378m; Tel: 760-873-2400; Nearest town: June Lake; Notes: No bear lockers available. GPS: 37.721182, -119.011747

652 • Upper Grays Meadow

Total sites: 35; RV sites: 35; Central water; Flush toilets; No showers; No RV dump; Reservations accepted; Max length: 40ft; Open Apr-Oct; Tent & RV camping: $23; Elev: 6125ft/1867m; Tel: 760-937-6070; Nearest town: Independence; Notes: Bear boxes must be used for food storage. GPS: 36.783591, -118.293652

653 • Upper Little Truckee

Total sites: 18; RV sites: 18; Central water; Vault toilets; No showers; No RV dump; Reservations accepted; Open May-Oct; Tent & RV camping: $20; Elev: 6220ft/1896m; Tel: 530-994-3401; Nearest town: Sierraville. GPS: 39.491107, -120.245067

654 • Upper Oso

Total sites: 25; RV sites: 25; Central water; Flush toilets; No showers; No RV dump; Reservations accepted; Generator hours: 0600-2200; Open all year; Tents: $30/RVs: $30-35; Elev: 1247ft/380m; Tel: 805-967-3481; Nearest town: Santa Barbara; Notes: 10 equestrian sites. GPS: 34.556621, -119.771756

655 • Upper Pine Grove

Total sites: 8; RV sites: 8; Central water; Vault toilets; No showers; No RV dump; Stay limit: 7 days; Open May-Sep; Tent & RV camping: $25; Elev: 9412ft/2869m; Tel: 760-873-2500; Nearest town: Crowley Lake; Notes: Small RVs only, Bear boxes must be used for food storage. GPS: 37.469195, -118.725567

656 • Upper Sage

Total sites: 28; RV sites: 28; Central water; Flush toilets; No showers; No RV dump; Reservations accepted; Stay limit: 14 days; Open May-Oct; Tent & RV camping: $25; Elev: 7515ft/2291m; Tel: 760-872-7018; Nearest town: Big Pine; Notes: Bear boxes must be used for food storage. GPS: 37.128852, -118.421355

657 • Upper San Juan

Total sites: 18; RV sites: 18; Central water; Vault toilets; No showers; No RV dump; Reservations not accepted; Max length: 32ft; Stay limit: 14 days; Open Jun-Sep; Tent & RV camping: $18; Elev: 1795ft/547m; Tel: 858-673-6180; Nearest town: Lake Elsinore. GPS: 33.607242, -117.432236

658 • Upper Soda Springs

Total sites: 28; RV sites: 28; Central water; Vault toilets; No showers; No RV dump; Reservations not accepted; Open Jun-Sep; Tent & RV camping: $23; Elev: 7779ft/2371m; Tel: 760-924-5500; Nearest town: Mammoth Lakes; Notes: Narrow single lane road, Bear boxes must be used for food storage, Campers may drive into area - shuttle fee applies. GPS: 37.653322, -119.077692

659 • Upper Stony Creek

Total sites: 11; RV sites: 11; Central water; Vault toilets; No showers; No RV dump; Reservations accepted; Open Jun-Sep; Tent & RV camping: $25-27; Elev: 6572ft/2003m; Tel: 559-338-2251; Nearest town: Dunlap. GPS: 36.667549, -118.831489

660 • Upper Virginia Creek

Total sites: 15; RV sites: 15; No water; Vault toilets; Reservations not accepted; Max length: 25ft; Stay limit: 14 days; Tent & RV camping: Free; Elev: 9373ft/2857m; Tel: 760-932-7070; Nearest town: Lee Vining; Notes: Bear boxes. GPS: 38.059815, -119.236567

661 • Valle Vista

Total sites: 7; RV sites: 7; Central water; Vault toilets; No showers; No RV dump; Reservations not accepted; Stay limit: 14 days; Generator hours: 0600-2200; Open all year; Tent & RV camping: $5; Elev: 4678ft/1426m; Tel: 661-245-3731; Nearest town: Frazier Park; Notes: Steep rutted sharply-curved entrance road, Adventure Pass required ($5/day or $30/year) or Interagency Pass. GPS: 34.878183, -119.341584

662 • Vermillion

Total sites: 31; RV sites: 31; Central water; Vault toilets; No showers; No RV dump; Reservations accepted; Max length: 25ft; Stay limit: 14 days; Open May-Sep; Tent & RV camping: $27-29; Elev: 7835ft/2388m; Tel: 559-893-2111; Nearest town: Lakeshore; Notes: Water should be boiled. GPS: 37.380937, -119.013317

663 • Wagon Flat

Total sites: 3; RV sites: 3; No water; Vault toilets; Reservations not accepted; Generator hours: 0600-2200; Tent & RV camping: $5; Elev: 1466ft/447m; Tel: 805-925-9538; Nearest town: Santa Margarita; Notes: Adventure Pass required ($5/day or $30/year) or Interagency Pass. GPS: 34.956645, -120.097924

664 • Wakalu Hep Yo

Total sites: 49; RV sites: 49; Central water; Flush toilets; No showers; No RV dump; Reservations not accepted; Stay limit: 14 days; Open Jun-Oct; Tent & RV camping: $20; Elev: 4101ft/1250m; Tel: 209-795-1381; Nearest town: Arnold. GPS: 38.322662, -120.217502

665 • Ward Lake

Total sites: 17; No water; Vault toilets; Reservations not accepted; Max length: 25ft; Open Jun-Oct; Tents only: $22-24; Elev: 7388ft/2252m; Tel: 559-855-5355; Nearest town: Lakeshore. GPS: 37.301068, -118.986093

666 • Warner Creek

Total sites: 13; RV sites: 13; No water; Vault toilets; Reservations not accepted; Open May-Oct; Tent & RV camping: $10; Elev: 5066ft/1544m; Tel: 530-258-2141. GPS: 40.362235, -121.308075

667 • Wells Cabin

Total sites: 25; RV sites: 15; No water; Vault toilets; Reservations not accepted; Open Jun-Nov; Tent & RV camping: Free; Elev: 6348ft/1935m; Tel: 530-934-3316; Nearest town: Covelo. GPS: 39.837652, -122.949882

668 • Wench Creek

Total sites: 100; RV sites: 83; Central water; Flush toilets; No showers; No RV dump; Reservations not accepted; Max length: 22ft; Stay limit: 14 days; Open Jun-Sep; Tent & RV camping: $28; Elev: 4944ft/1507m; Tel: 530-293-0827; Nearest town: Pollock Pines. GPS: 38.889454, -120.377183

669 • Wentworth Springs

Total sites: 8; No water; Vault toilets; Reservations not accepted; Stay limit: 14 days; Open Jun-Oct; Tents only: Free; Elev: 6207ft/1892m; Tel: 530-644-2349; Nearest town: Placerville. GPS: 39.011553, -120.325248

670 • West Kaiser

Total sites: 8; RV sites: 8; No water; Vault toilets; Reservations not accepted; Max length: 25ft; Open Jun-Dec; Tent & RV camping: Free; Elev: 5564ft/1696m; Tel: 559-855-5355; Nearest town: Shaver Lake. GPS: 37.344842, -119.240181

671 • West Point

Total sites: 8; RV sites: 8; No water; Vault toilets; Reservations not accepted; Stay limit: 14 days; Open Jun-Oct; Tent & RV camping: $25; Elev: 5016ft/1529m; Tel: 530-647-5415; Nearest town: Pollock Pines. GPS: 38.871111, -120.441168

672 • Wheeler Gorge

Total sites: 88; RV sites: 88; No water; Vault toilets; Reservations accepted; Max length: 35ft; Generator hours: 0600-2200; Open all year; Tent & RV camping: $25; Elev: 1857ft/566m; Tel: 805-640-1977; Nearest town: Ojai. GPS: 34.512939, -119.273438

673 • Whiskey Falls

Total sites: 14; RV sites: 14; No water; Vault toilets; Reservations not accepted; Open Jun-Nov; Tent & RV camping: Free; Elev: 5902ft/1799m; Tel: 559-877-2218; Nearest town: North Fork. GPS: 37.285756, -119.441554

674 • White Azelea

Total sites: 6; No water; Vault toilets; Reservations not accepted; Stay limit: 14 days; Open Jun-Oct; Tents only: $20; Elev: 3629ft/1106m; Tel: 209-295-4251; Nearest town: Jackson. GPS: 38.489766, -120.261885

675 • White Cloud

Total sites: 46; RV sites: 41; Central water; Vault toilets; Pay showers; No RV dump; Reservations accepted; Max length: 26ft; Open May-Oct; Tent & RV camping: $24; Elev: 4334ft/1321m; Tel: 530-478-0248; Nearest town: Nevada City. GPS: 39.319828, -120.845931

676 • White Oaks

Total sites: 8; RV sites: 8; No water; Vault toilets; No showers; No RV dump; Reservations accepted; Max length: 20ft; Generator hours: 0600-2200; Open May-Oct; Tent & RV camping: $20; Elev: 4114ft/1254m; Tel: 831-385-5434; Nearest town: Greenfield. GPS: 36.325959, -121.574882

677 • White River

Total sites: 12; Central water; Vault toilets; No showers; No RV dump; Reservations accepted; Open May-Oct; Tents only: $26; Elev: 4206ft/1282m; Tel: 559-539-2607; Nearest town: Wofford Heights. GPS: 35.844395, -118.635921

678 • White Rock

Total sites: 3; No water; No toilets; Tents only: Free; Elev: 5000ft/1524m; Tel: 530-352-4211. GPS: 40.253059, -123.023492

679 • Whitehorse

Total sites: 20; RV sites: 20; Central water; Vault toilets; No showers; No RV dump; Reservations accepted; Open Jun-Sep; Tent & RV camping: $30; Elev: 5305ft/1617m; Tel: 530-283-0555; Nearest town: Quincy. GPS: 39.888486, -121.142624

680 • Whitlock

Total sites: 5; RV sites: 5; No water; Vault toilets; Reservations not accepted; Open May-Nov; Tent & RV camping: Free; Elev: 4249ft/1295m; Tel: 530-934-3316; Nearest town: Paskenta. GPS: 39.920028, -122.687032

681 • Whitney Portal

Total sites: 43; RV sites: 43; Central water; Vault toilets; No showers; No RV dump; Reservations accepted; Open May-Oct; Tent & RV camping: $26; Elev: 8058ft/2456m; Tel: 760-937-6070; Nearest town: Lone Pine; Notes: Group site $80, Bear boxes must be used for food storage. GPS: 36.588887, -118.231704

682 • Wild Plum

Total sites: 47; RV sites: 23; Central water; Vault toilets; No showers; No RV dump; Reservations accepted; Max length: 22ft; Open May-Oct; Tent & RV camping: $24; Elev: 4495ft/1370m; Tel: 530-862-1368; Nearest town: Sierra City; Notes: Gold panning. GPS: 39.566406, -120.599121

683 • Wildomar

Total sites: 11; RV sites: 11; No water; Vault toilets; No showers; No RV dump; Reservations not accepted; Max length: 22ft; Stay limit: 14 days; Tent & RV camping: $15; Elev: 2487ft/758m; Tel: 858-673-6180; Nearest town: Lake Elsinore. GPS: 33.581419, -117.341497

684 • William Kent

Total sites: 86; RV sites: 86; Central water; Flush toilets; No showers; RV dump; Reservations accepted; Open May-Oct; Tent & RV camping: $31-33; Elev: 6302ft/1921m; Tel: 530-583-3642; Nearest town: Tahoe City. GPS: 39.139464, -120.156863

685 • Willow

Total sites: 8; No water; Vault toilets; Reservations not accepted; Stay limit: 7 days; Open May-Sep; Tents only: $23; Elev: 9354ft/2851m; Tel: 760-873-2500; Nearest town: Bishop; Notes: Bear boxes must be used for food storage. GPS: 37.194000, -118.561000

686 • Willow Creek

Total sites: 8; RV sites: 8; No water; Vault toilets; No showers; No RV dump; Reservations not accepted; Max length: 32ft; Stay limit: 14 days; Open May-Oct; Tent & RV camping: $12; Elev: 5118ft/1560m; Tel: 530-299-3215; Nearest town: Adin; Notes: Non-potable water available. GPS: 41.013056, -120.828056

687 • Willow Springs

Total sites: 14; RV sites: 14; No water; Vault toilets; Reservations not accepted; Open Apr-Oct; Tent & RV camping: Free; Elev: 5184ft/1580m; Tel: 530-258-2141; Nearest town: Chester. GPS: 40.306288, -121.377532

688 • Wishon

Total sites: 27; RV sites: 27; Central water; Vault toilets; No showers; No RV dump; Reservations accepted; Max length: 24ft; Open all year; Tent & RV camping: $26; Elev: 3947ft/1203m; Tel: 559-539-2607; Nearest town: Springville. GPS: 36.189388, -118.663885

689 • Wishon Point

Total sites: 31; RV sites: 31; Central water; Flush toilets; No showers; No RV dump; Reservations accepted; Stay limit: 14 days; Open Apr-Sep; Tent & RV camping: $34-36; Elev: 3428ft/1045m; Tel: 559-642-3212; Nearest town: Oakhurst. GPS: 37.297161, -119.534812

690 • Wolf Creek

Total sites: 42; RV sites: 10; Central water; Vault toilets; No showers; No RV dump; Reservations accepted; Max length: 22ft; Stay limit: 14 days; Open May-Sep; Tent & RV camping: $28; Elev: 4928ft/1502m; Tel: 530-293-0827; Nearest town: Placerville; Notes: Bear boxes must be used for food storage. GPS: 38.883836, -120.397768

691 • Wolf Creek

Total sites: 6; RV sites: 6; No water; Vault toilets; Reservations not accepted; Tent & RV camping: Free; Elev: 6535ft/1992m. GPS: 38.576713, -119.697261

692 • Woodcamp

Total sites: 16; RV sites: 16; Central water; Flush toilets; No showers; No RV dump; Reservations accepted; Open May-Sep; Tent & RV camping: $24; Elev: 6112ft/1863m; Tel: 530-265-8861; Nearest town: Sierraville. GPS: 39.486905, -120.547642

693 • Woodchuck

Total sites: 8; RV sites: 8; No water; Vault toilets; Reservations not accepted; Open May-Sep; Tent & RV camping: Free; Elev: 6299ft/1920m; Tel: 530-265-4531; Nearest town: Truckee. GPS: 39.332913, -120.519406

694 • Woods Lake

Total sites: 25; Central water; Vault toilets; No showers; No RV dump; Reservations not accepted; Max length: 16ft; Stay limit: 14 days; Open Jul-Oct; Tents only: $22-24; Elev: 8245ft/2513m; Tel: 209-295-4251; Nearest town: Kit Carson. GPS: 38.685451, -120.009233

695 • Wrights Lake

Total sites: 67; RV sites: 24; Central water; Vault toilets; No showers; No RV dump; Reservations accepted; Max length: 22ft; Stay limit: 14 days; Open Jun-Oct; Tent & RV camping: $20; Elev: 6998ft/2133m; Tel: 530-647-5415; Nearest town: Kyburz. GPS: 38.845828, -120.237113

696 • Wyandotte

Total sites: 28; RV sites: 28; Central water; Flush toilets; No showers; No RV dump; Reservations accepted; Stay limit: 14 days; Open May-Sep; Tent & RV camping: $23; Elev: 5125ft/1562m; Tel: 530-534-6500; Nearest town: La Porte. GPS: 39.726719, -120.984528

697 • Yellowjacket

Total sites: 40; RV sites: 29; Central water; Flush toilets; No showers; RV dump; Reservations accepted; Max length: 25ft; Stay limit: 14 days; Open May-Sep; Tent & RV camping: $28; Elev: 4974ft/1516m; Tel: 530-293-0827; Nearest town: Pollock Pines. GPS: 38.889728, -120.386388

698 • Yuba Pass

Total sites: 19; RV sites: 19; Central water; Vault toilets; No showers; No RV dump; Reservations accepted; Open Jun-Oct; Tent & RV camping: $24; Elev: 6717ft/2047m; Tel: 530-862-1368; Nearest town: Sierraville. GPS: 39.615838, -120.490467

Colorado

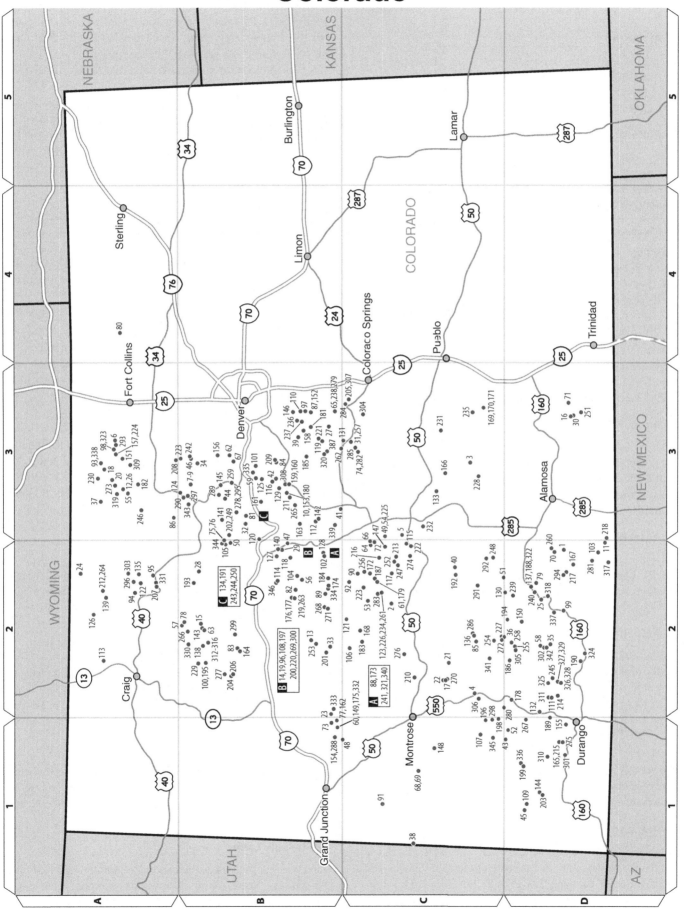

Colorado Camping Areas

1 • Alamosa

Total sites: 5; RV sites: 5; No water; No toilets; Reservations not accepted; Max length: 25ft; Open May-Sep; Tent & RV camping: Free; Elev: 8684ft/2647m; Tel: 719-274-8971; Nearest town: La Jara. GPS: 37.379395, -106.345215

2 • Almont

Total sites: 10; RV sites: 10; Central water; Vault toilets; No showers; No RV dump; Reservations not accepted; Open May-Sep; Tent & RV camping: $10; Elev: 8045ft/2452m; Nearest town: Almont. GPS: 38.653809, -106.858154

3 • Alvarado

Total sites: 50; RV sites: 43; Central water; Vault toilets; No showers; No RV dump; Reservations accepted; Max length: 35ft; Open May-Sep; Tent & RV camping: $22; Elev: 9036ft/2754m; Tel: 719-269-8500; Nearest town: Westcliffe. GPS: 38.079278, -105.563324

4 • Amphitheater

Total sites: 35; RV sites: 13; Central water; Vault toilets; No showers; No RV dump; Reservations accepted; Max length: 35ft; Open May-Sep; Tent & RV camping: $26; Elev: 8566ft/2611m; Tel: 970-874-6600; Nearest town: Ouray. GPS: 38.022802, -107.661376

5 • Angel of Shavano

Total sites: 20; RV sites: 20; No water; Vault toilets; Reservations not accepted; Max length: 30ft; Stay limit: 14 days; Open Jun-Sep; Tent & RV camping: $20; Elev: 9200ft/2804m; Tel: 719-553-1400; Nearest town: Maysville; Notes: Group site: $125. GPS: 38.583008, -106.220703

6 • Ansel Watrous

Total sites: 16; RV sites: 16; Central water; Vault toilets; No showers; No RV dump; Reservations accepted; Max length: 30ft; Open Jun-Oct; Tent & RV camping: $23; Elev: 5876ft/1791m; Tel: 970-295-6700; Nearest town: Rustic. GPS: 40.690042, -105.348751

7 • Arapaho Bay - Main

Total sites: 22; RV sites: 22; Central water; Vault toilets; No showers; No RV dump; Reservations accepted; Max length: 35ft; Open May-Oct; Tent & RV camping: $23; Elev: 8350ft/2545m; Tel: 970-887-4100; Nearest town: Granby. GPS: 40.119791, -105.756530

8 • Arapaho Bay - Moraine

Total sites: 29; RV sites: 29; Central water; Vault toilets; No showers; No RV dump; Reservations accepted; Open Jun-Oct; Tent & RV camping: $23; Elev: 8356ft/2547m; Tel: 970-887-4100; Nearest town: Granby. GPS: 40.124204, -105.762226

9 • Arapaho Bay - Roaring Fork

Total sites: 34; RV sites: 25; Central water; Vault toilets; No showers; No RV dump; Reservations accepted; Max length: 35ft; Open Jun-Oct; Tent & RV camping: $23; Elev: 8320ft/2536m; Tel: 970-887-4100; Nearest town: Granby. GPS: 40.129192, -105.767739

10 • Aspen (Jefferson)

Total sites: 12; RV sites: 9; Central water; Vault toilets; No showers; No RV dump; Reservations accepted; Max length: 25ft; Open May-Sep; Tent & RV camping: $17; Elev: 9955ft/3034m; Tel: 719-836-2031; Nearest town: Jefferson. GPS: 39.425518, -105.841832

11 • Aspen Glade

Total sites: 32; RV sites: 32; Central water; Vault toilets; No showers; No RV dump; Reservations accepted; Max length: 45ft; Open May-Sep; Tent & RV camping: $26; Elev: 8586ft/2617m; Tel: 719-376-2535; Nearest town: Antonito. GPS: 37.072998, -106.274658

12 • Aspen Glen

Total sites: 9; RV sites: 9; Central water; Vault toilets; No showers; No RV dump; Reservations not accepted; Max length: 35ft; Open May-Sep; Tent & RV camping: $19; Elev: 8707ft/2654m; Tel: 970-295-6700; Nearest town: Fort Collins. GPS: 40.619398, -105.818094

13 • Avalanche

Total sites: 13; RV sites: 13; Vault toilets; Reservations not accepted; Max length: 25ft; Open May-Sep; Tent & RV camping: Donation; Elev: 7507ft/2288m; Tel: 970-945-2521; Nearest town: Redstone. GPS: 39.235855, -107.202797

14 • Baby Doe

Total sites: 50; RV sites: 50; Central water; No toilets; No showers; No RV dump; Reservations accepted; Max length: 32ft; Open May-Sep; Tent & RV camping: $24-26; Elev: 9970ft/3039m; Tel: 719-486-0749; Nearest town: Leadville. GPS: 39.271396, -106.352558

15 • Bear Lake

Total sites: 43; RV sites: 43; Potable water; Vault toilets; No showers; No RV dump; Reservations not accepted; Stay limit: 14 days; Open May-Oct; Tent & RV camping: $10; Elev: 9780ft/2981m; Tel: 307-745-2300; Nearest town: Yampa. GPS: 40.046432, -107.068698

16 • Bear Lake (Trinchera Peak)

Total sites: 14; RV sites: 14; Central water; Vault toilets; No showers; No RV dump; Max length: 30ft; Open May-Sep; Tent & RV camping: $14; Elev: 10482ft/3195m; Nearest town: La Veta. GPS: 37.326172, -105.143311

17 • Beaver Lake

Total sites: 11; RV sites: 11; No water; Vault toilets; Reservations not accepted; Max length: 20ft; Open May-Sep; Tent & RV camping: $12; Elev: 8784ft/2677m; Tel: 970-240-5300; Nearest town: Cimarron. GPS: 38.250411, -107.543546

18 • Bellaire Lake

Total sites: 26; RV sites: 26; Elec sites: 21; Central water; No toilets; No showers; No RV dump; Reservations accepted; Max length: 60ft; Open Jun-Sep; Tents: $24/RVs: $24-32; Elev: 8717ft/2657m;

Tel: 970-295-6700; Nearest town: Red Feather Lakes. GPS: 40.768556, -105.622389

19 • Belle of Colorado

Total sites: 19; Central water; Vault toilets; No showers; No RV dump; Reservations not accepted; Open Jun-Sep; Tents only: $24; Elev: 9944ft/3031m; Tel: 719-553-1400; Nearest town: Leadville. GPS: 39.268071, -106.351983

20 • Big Bend

Total sites: 8; RV sites: 5; Central water; Vault toilets; No showers; No RV dump; Reservations not accepted; Max length: 20ft; Open May-Dec; Tent & RV camping: $19; Elev: 7720ft/2353m; Tel: 970-295-6700; Nearest town: Fort Collins. GPS: 40.707476, -105.724763

21 • Big Blue

Total sites: 11; RV sites: 11; No water; Vault toilets; Reservations not accepted; Open Jun-Sep; Tent & RV camping: Donation; Elev: 9652ft/2942m; Nearest town: Sapeniro. GPS: 38.217285, -107.385498

22 • Big Cimarron

Total sites: 10; RV sites: 10; No water; Vault toilets; Reservations not accepted; Open May-Sep; Tent & RV camping: $12; Elev: 8717ft/2657m; Tel: 970-240-5300; Nearest town: Cimarron. GPS: 38.257568, -107.545166

23 • Big Creek (Grand Mesa)

Total sites: 26; RV sites: 26; Central water; Vault toilets; No showers; No RV dump; Reservations not accepted; Max length: 30ft; Open Jul-Sep; Tent & RV camping: $14; Elev: 10144ft/3092m; Tel: 970-242-8211; Nearest town: Collbran. GPS: 39.078435, -107.882846

24 • Big Creek Lake

Total sites: 54; RV sites: 54; No water; Vault toilets; No showers; No RV dump; Reservations accepted; Max length: 45ft; Open Jun-Sep; Tent & RV camping: $10; Elev: 9035ft/2754m; Tel: 970-723-2700; Nearest town: Collbran. GPS: 40.935932, -106.610545

25 • Big Meadows

Total sites: 54; RV sites: 54; Central water; Vault toilets; No showers; No RV dump; Reservations accepted; Max length: 35ft; Open May-Sep; Tent & RV camping: $26; Elev: 9380ft/2859m; Tel: 719-657-3321; Nearest town: South Fork; Notes: Group site: $70. GPS: 37.539795, -106.795410

26 • Big South

Total sites: 4; RV sites: 4; No water; Vault toilets; Reservations not accepted; Max length: 25ft; Open Jun-Sep; Tent & RV camping: $19; Elev: 8560ft/2609m; Tel: 970-295-6700; Nearest town: Fort Collins. GPS: 40.632885, -105.807331

27 • Big Turkey

Total sites: 10; RV sites: 10; Central water; Vault toilets; No showers; No RV dump; Tent & RV camping: Free; Elev: 8032ft/2448m; Tel: 303-275-5610; Nearest town: West Creek. GPS: 39.119992, -105.227175

28 • Blacktail Creek

Total sites: 8; RV sites: 8; Central water; Vault toilets; No showers; No RV dump; Reservations not accepted; Max length: 18ft; Open May-Oct; Tent & RV camping: $10; Elev: 9127ft/2782m; Tel: 970-638-4516; Nearest town: Yampa. GPS: 40.067752, -106.579776

29 • Blodgett

Total sites: 6; RV sites: 6; Central water; Vault toilets; Max length: 30ft; Tent & RV camping: Fee unknown; Elev: 8855ft/2699m; Nearest town: Vail. GPS: 39.472238, -106.366498

30 • Blue Lake

Total sites: 15; RV sites: 15; Central water; Vault toilets; No showers; No RV dump; Reservations accepted; Max length: 40ft; Open May-Oct; Tent & RV camping: $21; Elev: 10554ft/3217m; Tel: 719-269-9719; Nearest town: La Veta. GPS: 37.313232, -105.138672

31 • Blue Mountain

Total sites: 21; RV sites: 21; No water; Vault toilets; Reservations accepted; Max length: 25ft; Open May-Sep; Tent & RV camping: $17; Elev: 8130ft/2478m; Tel: 719-836-2031; Nearest town: Florissant. GPS: 38.959156, -105.362002

32 • Blue River

Total sites: 24; RV sites: 24; Vault toilets; Reservations not accepted; Open May-Sep; Tent & RV camping: $20; Elev: 8471ft/2582m; Tel: 970-945-2521; Nearest town: Silverthorne. GPS: 39.726532, -106.131032

33 • Bogan Flats

Total sites: 36; RV sites: 36; Central water; Vault toilets; No showers; No RV dump; Reservations accepted; Max length: 40ft; Open May-Oct; Tent & RV camping: $27-29; Elev: 7605ft/2318m; Tel: 970-927-0107; Nearest town: Marble; Notes: Group site: $125. GPS: 39.100262, -107.261518

34 • Brainard Lake RA - Pawnee

Total sites: 47; RV sites: 47; Central water; Vault toilets; No showers; No RV dump; Reservations accepted; Max length: 100ft; Open Jun-Sep; Tent & RV camping: $23; Elev: 10368ft/3160m; Tel: 303-541-2500; Nearest town: Nederland. GPS: 40.078374, -105.569124

35 • Bridge

Total sites: 19; RV sites: 19; Central water; Vault toilets; No showers; No RV dump; Reservations not accepted; Max length: 50ft; Open May-Sep; Tent & RV camping: Fee unknown; Elev: 7930ft/2417m; Tel: 970-247-4874; Nearest town: Pagosa Springs. GPS: 37.465465, -107.196945

36 • Bristol Head

Total sites: 15; RV sites: 15; Central water; Vault toilets; No showers; No RV dump; Reservations not accepted; Max length: 45ft; Open May-Sep; Tent & RV camping: $19-23; Elev: 9508ft/2898m; Tel: 719-657-3321; Nearest town: Creede. GPS: 37.818115, -107.144287

37 • Browns Park

Total sites: 28; RV sites: 28; No water; Vault toilets; Reservations not accepted; Max length: 30ft; Open Jun-Sep; Tent & RV camping: $18; Elev: 8488ft/2587m; Tel: 970-295-6700; Nearest town: Gould. GPS: 40.796143, -105.927246

38 • Buckeye

Total sites: 48; RV sites: 48; No water; Vault toilets; Reservations accepted; Open May-Sep; Tent & RV camping: $10; Elev: 7640ft/2329m; Tel: 435-636-3360; Nearest town: Paradox; Notes: Group site: $50 - available for single use if no group, 18 sites are dispersed around lake. GPS: 38.446779, -109.045501

39 • Buffalo

Total sites: 37; RV sites: 35; No water; Vault toilets; No showers; No RV dump; Reservations accepted; Max length: 22ft; Open May-Sep; Tent & RV camping: $22; Elev: 7333ft/2235m; Tel: 303-275-5610; Nearest town: Buffalo Creek. GPS: 39.340687, -105.329825

40 • Buffalo Pass

Total sites: 19; RV sites: 19; No water; Vault toilets; Reservations not accepted; Max length: 60ft; Open May-Nov; Tent & RV camping: $5; Elev: 9140ft/2786m; Tel: 719 655-2547; Nearest town: Saguache. GPS: 38.184814, -106.517090

41 • Buffalo Springs

Total sites: 21; RV sites: 21; Central water; Vault toilets; No showers; No RV dump; Reservations accepted; Max length: 30ft; Open May-Sep; Tent & RV camping: $17; Elev: 9176ft/2797m; Tel: 719 836-2031; Nearest town: Fairplay. GPS: 39.032548, -105.985595

42 • Burning Bear

Total sites: 14; RV sites: 14; Central water; Vault toilets; No showers; No RV dump; Reservations accepted; Max length: 30ft; Open May-Dec; Tent & RV camping: $22; Elev: 9718ft/2962m; Tel: 303-275-5610; Nearest town: Jefferson. GPS: 39.513429, -105.710692

43 • Burro Bridge

Total sites: 12; RV sites: 12; Central water; Vault toilets; No showers; No RV dump; Reservations not accepted; Max length: 35ft; Open all year; Tent & RV camping: $16; Elev: 9137ft/2785m; Tel: 970-882-7296; Nearest town: Dolores; Notes: No services in winter, Steep road, Horse corral. GPS: 37.787329, -108.067456

44 • Byers Creek

Total sites: 6; RV sites: 6; Central water; Vault toilets; No showers; No RV dump; Reservations not accepted; Max length: 32ft; Stay limit: 14 days; Tent & RV camping: $14; Elev: 9360ft/2853m; Tel: 970-887-4100; Nearest town: Fraser. GPS: 39.878346, -105.896403

45 • Cabin Canyon

Total sites: 11; RV sites: 11; Central water; No toilets; No showers; RV dump; Reservations not accepted; Max length: 45ft; Tent & RV camping: Free; Elev: 6555ft/1998m; Nearest town: Cortez. GPS: 37.628199, -108.692988

46 • Camp Dick

Total sites: 41; RV sites: 41; Central water; Vault toilets; No showers; No RV dump; Reservations accepted; Max length: 45ft; Open Jun-Nov; Tent & RV camping: $23; Elev: 8681ft/2646m; Tel: 303-541-2500; Nearest town: Ward. GPS: 40.128913, -105.519664

47 • Camp Hale

Total sites: 15; RV sites: 15; No water; Vault toilets; No showers; No RV dump; Reservations accepted; Open May-Oct; Tent & RV camping: $22-24; Elev: 9308ft/2837m; Tel: 970-945-2521; Nearest town: Minturn. GPS: 39.420041, -106.314438

48 • Carson Lake

Total sites: 4; RV sites: 4; No water; Vault toilets; Reservations not accepted; Open Jul-Sep; Tent & RV camping: Free; Elev: 9915ft/3022m; Tel: 970-874-6600; Nearest town: Grand Junction. GPS: 38.997025, -108.111435

49 • Cascade

Total sites: 22; RV sites: 20; Central water; Vault toilets; No showers; No RV dump; Reservations accepted; Max length: 35ft; Open May-Oct; Tent & RV camping: $22; Elev: 9111ft/2777m; Tel: 719-539-3591; Nearest town: Nathrop. GPS: 38.710449, -106.244629

50 • Cataract Creek

Total sites: 5; RV sites: 5; No water; Vault toilets; Reservations not accepted; Max length: 25ft; Open May-Sep; Tent & RV camping: $18; Elev: 8579ft/2615m; Tel: 970-945-2521; Nearest town: Silverthorne. GPS: 39.838441, -106.307417

51 • Cathedral

Total sites: 22; RV sites: 22; No water; Vault toilets; Reservations not accepted; Max length: 45ft; Open Apr-Dec; Tent & RV camping: Free; Elev: 9475ft/2888m; Tel: 719-657-3321; Nearest town: Del Norte. GPS: 37.822266, -106.604980

52 • Cayton

Total sites: 27; RV sites: 27; Elec sites: 16; Central water; Vault toilets; No showers; RV dump; Reservations accepted; Open May-Sep; Tents: $24/RVs: $24-30; Elev: 9413ft/2869m; Tel: 970-882-7296; Nearest town: Rico. GPS: 37.771256, -107.977195

53 • Cement Creek

Total sites: 13; RV sites: 13; Central water; Vault toilets; No showers; No RV dump; Reservations not accepted; Open May-Oct; Tent & RV camping: $14; Elev: 9006ft/2745m; Tel: 970-874-6600; Nearest town: Crested Butte. GPS: 38.827881, -106.836914

54 • Chalk Lake

Total sites: 19; RV sites: 11; No water; Vault toilets; Reservations accepted; Max length: 35ft; Open May-Sep; Tent & RV camping: $22; Elev: 8721ft/2658m; Tel: 719-539-3591; Nearest town: Nathrop. GPS: 38.712731, -106.233744

55 • Chambers Lake

Total sites: 51; RV sites: 44; Central water; Vault toilets; No showers; No RV dump; Reservations accepted; Max length: 45ft; Open Jun-Sep; Tent & RV camping: $24; Elev: 9215ft/2809m; Tel: 970-295-6700; Nearest town: Rustic. GPS: 40.594014, -105.849422

56 • Chapman

Total sites: 84; RV sites: 84; Central water; Vault toilets; No showers; No RV dump; Reservations accepted; Max length: 22ft; Open May-Oct; Tent & RV camping: $26-28; Elev: 8553ft/2607m; Tel: 970-927-0107; Nearest town: Basalt. GPS: 39.315657, -106.642786

57 • Chapman Reservoir

Total sites: 12; RV sites: 12; No water; Vault toilets; Reservations not accepted; Open May-Oct; Tent & RV camping: $10; Elev: 9360ft/2853m; Nearest town: Yampa. GPS: 40.187198, -107.086844

58 • Cimarrona

Total sites: 21; RV sites: 21; Central water; Vault toilets; No showers; No RV dump; Reservations not accepted; Max length: 35ft; Tent & RV camping: Fee unknown; Elev: 8425ft/2568m; Nearest town: Pagosa Springs. GPS: 37.538955, -107.210274

59 • Clear Lake

Total sites: 8; RV sites: 8; Central water; Vault toilets; No showers; No RV dump; Reservations not accepted; Max length: 15ft; Open Jun-Sep; Tent & RV camping: $19; Elev: 10039ft/3060m; Tel: 303-567-3000; Nearest town: Georgetown. GPS: 39.651053, -105.708443

60 • Cobbett Lake

Total sites: 20; RV sites: 20; No water; Vault toilets; No showers; No RV dump; Reservations accepted; Max length: 40ft; Open Jun-Sep; Tent & RV camping: $16; Elev: 10279ft/3133m; Tel: 970-874-6600; Nearest town: Cedaredge. GPS: 39.041491, -107.983347

61 • Cold Spring (Taylor Canyon)

Total sites: 6; RV sites: 6; No water; Vault toilets; Reservations not accepted; Open May-Sep; Tent & RV camping: $10; Elev: 8966ft/2733m; Tel: 970-874-6600; Nearest town: Almont. GPS: 38.767216, -106.643087

62 • Cold Springs (Black Hawk)

Total sites: 36; RV sites: 31; Central water; Vault toilets; No showers; No RV dump; Reservations accepted; Max length: 50ft; Open Jun-Sep; Tent & RV camping: $22; Elev: 9396ft/2864m; Tel: 303-567-3000; Nearest town: Black Hawk. GPS: 39.841958, -105.495678

63 • Cold Springs (Orno Peak)

Total sites: 5; RV sites: 5; Potable water; Vault toilets; No showers; No RV dump; Reservations not accepted; Open May-Oct; Tent & RV camping: $10; Elev: 10266ft/3129m; Nearest town: Yampa. GPS: 40.030262, -107.119496

64 • Collegiate Peaks

Total sites: 56; RV sites: 56; Potable water; Vault toilets; No showers; No RV dump; Reservations accepted; Max length: 50ft; Open Jun-Sep; Tent & RV camping: $22; Elev: 9820ft/2993m; Tel: 719-539-3591; Nearest town: Buena Vista. GPS: 38.811241, -106.319324

65 • Colorado

Total sites: 81; RV sites: 81; Potable water; No toilets; No showers; No RV dump; Reservations accepted; Max length: 30ft; Open May-Sep; Tent & RV camping: $23; Elev: 7854ft/2394m; Tel: 719-636-1602; Nearest town: Woodland Park. GPS: 39.080255, -105.093878

66 • Colorado Pass

Total sites: 10; RV sites: 10; No water; No toilets; Tent & RV camping: Free; Elev: 9364ft/2854m; Nearest town: Buena Vista. GPS: 38.813189, -106.283709

67 • Columbine (Central City)

Total sites: 46; RV sites: 41; Central water; Vault toilets; No showers; No RV dump; Reservations accepted; Max length: 20ft; Open Jun-Sep; Tent & RV camping: $21; Elev: 9039ft/2755m; Tel: 303-567-3000; Nearest town: Central City. GPS: 39.816895, -105.549072

68 • Columbine Pass (New)

Total sites: 16; RV sites: 16; No water; Vault toilets; Tent & RV camping: Fee unknown; Elev: 9104ft/2775m; Nearest town: Montrose. GPS: 38.427473, -108.374749

69 • Columbine Pass (Old)

Total sites: 6; No water; Vault toilets; Reservations not accepted; Open Jun-Sep; Tents only: Free; Elev: 9101ft/2774m; Tel: 970-874-6600; Nearest town: Montrose. GPS: 38.424939, -108.381813

70 • Comstock

Total sites: 7; RV sites: 7; No water; Vault toilets; Reservations not accepted; Max length: 35ft; Open all year; Tent & RV camping: Free; Elev: 9718ft/2962m; Tel: 719-657-3321; Nearest town: Monte Vista; Notes: Winter access may be limited. GPS: 37.445309, -106.362832

71 • Cordova Pass

Total sites: 3; No water; Vault toilets; Reservations not accepted; Open May-Sep; Tents only: $12; Elev: 11276ft/3437m; Tel: 719-269-8500; Nearest town: La Veta. GPS: 37.348612, -105.025088

72 • Cottonwood Lake

Total sites: 24; RV sites: 24; Central water; Vault toilets; No showers; No RV dump; Reservations not accepted; Max length: 35ft; Generator hours: 0600-2200; Tent & RV camping: $11; Elev: 9613ft/2930m; Tel: 719-539-3591; Nearest town: Buena Vista; Notes: No water for RV tanks. GPS: 38.782629, -106.291934

73 • Cottonwood Lake

Total sites: 36; RV sites: 36; No water; Vault toilets; No showers; No RV dump; Reservations not accepted; Max length: 40ft; Open Jul-Sep; Tent & RV camping: $14; Elev: 10240ft/3121m; Tel: 970-242-8211; Nearest town: Collbran. GPS: 39.072525, -107.962775

74 • Cove

Total sites: 4; RV sites: 2; Central water; Vault toilets; No showers; No RV dump; Reservations accepted; Max length: 16ft; Open May-Oct; Tent & RV camping: $17; Elev: 8586ft/2617m; Tel: 719-836-2031; Nearest town: Lake George. GPS: 38.910017, -105.460614

75 • Cow Creek North

Total sites: 15; RV sites: 15; No water; Vault toilets; No showers; No RV dump; Reservations not accepted; Open May-Sep; Tent & RV camping: $18; Elev: 7992ft/2436m; Tel: 970-945-2521; Nearest town: Silverthorne. GPS: 39.883384, -106.288359

76 • Cow Creek South

Total sites: 40; RV sites: 40; No water; Vault toilets; No showers; No RV dump; Reservations accepted; Open May-Oct; Tent & RV camping: $18; Elev: 8005ft/2440m; Tel: 970-945-2521; Nearest town: Silverthorne. GPS: 39.877377, -106.284952

77 • Crag Crest

Total sites: 11; RV sites: 8; No water; Vault toilets; No showers; No RV dump; Reservations not accepted; Max length: 25ft; Open Jun-Sep; Tent & RV camping: $12; Elev: 10187ft/3105m; Nearest town: Grand Mesa. GPS: 39.048999, -107.937543

78 • Crosho Lake

Total sites: 10; RV sites: 10; No water; Vault toilets; Reservations not accepted; Open May-Nov; Tent & RV camping: Free; Elev: 8914ft/2717m; Tel: 307-745-2300; Nearest town: Yampa. GPS: 40.170000, -107.052000

79 • Cross Creek

Total sites: 12; RV sites: 5; Central water; Vault toilets; No showers; No RV dump; Reservations not accepted; Max length: 20ft; Open all year; Tents: $24/RVs: $24-29; Elev: 8901ft/2713m; Tel: 719-657-3321; Nearest town: South Fork; Notes: Very unlevel sites, No water in winter. GPS: 37.581055, -106.650146

80 • Crow Valley

Total sites: 10; RV sites: 10; Central water; Vault toilets; No showers; No RV dump; Reservations accepted; Max length: 35ft; Open Apr-Oct; Tent & RV camping: $14; Elev: 4846ft/1477m; Tel: 970-346-5000; Nearest town: Fort Collins; Notes: Group fee: $61. GPS: 40.644021, -104.336561

81 • Crown Point

Total sites: 10; RV sites: 10; No water; Vault toilets; Tent & RV camping: Free; Elev: 9088ft/2770m; Tel: 970-468-5400. GPS: 39.726532, -106.061482

82 • Dearhamer

Total sites: 13; RV sites: 13; Central water; Vault toilets; No showers; No RV dump; Reservations accepted; Max length: 35ft; Open May-Oct; Tent & RV camping: $25-27; Elev: 7812ft/2381m; Tel: 970-945-2521; Nearest town: Basalt. GPS: 39.360596, -106.737793

83 • Deep Lake

Total sites: 35; RV sites: 35; No water; Vault toilets; Reservations not accepted; Max length: 35ft; Open Jul-Oct; Tent & RV camping: $6; Elev: 10505ft/3202m; Tel: 970-945-2521; Nearest town: Gypsum. GPS: 39.772168, -107.295248

84 • Deer Creek

Total sites: 13; RV sites: 13; No water; Vault toilets; Reservations not accepted; Max length: 30ft; Open all year; Tent & RV camping: $22; Elev: 9272ft/2826m; Tel: 303-275-5610; Nearest town: Bailey. GPS: 39.508057, -105.553711

85 • Deer Lakes

Total sites: 15; RV sites: 15; Central water; Vault toilets; No showers; No RV dump; Reservations not accepted; Max length: 30ft; Open May-Sep; Tent & RV camping: $12; Elev: 10496ft/3199m; Tel: 970-641-0471; Nearest town: Lake City. GPS: 38.020649, -107.187411

86 • Denver Creek

Total sites: 22; RV sites: 22; Central water; Vault toilets; No showers; No RV dump; Reservations not accepted; Max length: 45ft; Open May-Sep; Tent & RV camping: $21; Elev: 8635ft/2632m; Tel: 970-887-4100; Nearest town: Granby. GPS: 40.254975, -106.079463

87 • Devils Head

Total sites: 21; RV sites: 21; No water; Vault toilets; Reservations not accepted; Max length: 30ft; Open May-Nov; Tent & RV camping: $22; Elev: 8883ft/2708m; Tel: 303-275-5610; Nearest town: Sedalia. GPS: 39.271822, -105.102558

88 • Dexter

Total sites: 24; RV sites: 24; No water; Vault toilets; No showers; No RV dump; Reservations not accepted; Max length: 37ft; Open May-Sep; Tent & RV camping: $20; Elev: 9291ft/2832m; Tel: 719-486-0749; Nearest town: Twin Lakes. GPS: 39.088436, -106.367351

89 • Difficult

Total sites: 47; RV sites: 47; Central water; Vault toilets; No showers; No RV dump; Reservations accepted; Max length: 40ft; Open May-Sep; Tent & RV camping: $28-30; Elev: 8202ft/2500m; Tel: 970-945-2521; Nearest town: Aspen; Notes: Group site $94, Campground roads are tight for large RVs, Vehicles over 35' prohibited over Independence Pass but can access CG via Aspen. GPS: 39.141701, -106.772787

90 • Dinner Station

Total sites: 22; RV sites: 22; Central water; Vault toilets; No showers; No RV dump; Reservations accepted; Open May-Sep;

Tent & RV camping: $18; Elev: 9616ft/2931m; Tel: 970-642-0566; Nearest town: Almont. GPS: 38.906172, -106.586152

91 • Divide Fork

Total sites: 11; RV sites: 11; No water; Vault toilets; Reservations not accepted; Max length: 20ft; Open Apr-Nov; Tent & RV camping: Free; Elev: 8740ft/2664m; Tel: 970-874-6600; Nearest town: Grand Junction. GPS: 38.684429, -108.689542

92 • Dorchester

Total sites: 10; RV sites: 10; No water; Vault toilets; Reservations not accepted; Open May-Oct; Tent & RV camping: Donation; Elev: 9933ft/3028m; Tel: 970-874-6600; Nearest town: Almont. GPS: 38.965683, -106.660955

93 • Dowdy Lake

Total sites: 70; RV sites: 60; Elec sites: 60; Central water; Vault toilets; No showers; No RV dump; Reservations accepted; Max length: 40ft; Open all year; Tents: $24/RVs: $24-32; Elev: 8163ft/2488m; Tel: 970-295-6700; Nearest town: Fort Collins. GPS: 40.792425, -105.554924

94 • Dry Lake

Total sites: 8; RV sites: 8; No water; Vault toilets; Reservations not accepted; Max length: 20ft; Open Jun-Oct; Tent & RV camping: $10; Elev: 8324ft/2537m; Tel: 307-745-2300; Nearest town: Steamboat Springs. GPS: 40.536264, -106.781954

95 • Dumont Lake

Total sites: 22; RV sites: 22; Potable water; Vault toilets; No showers; No RV dump; Reservations accepted; Max length: 40ft; Open Jun-Sep; Tent & RV camping: $12; Elev: 9537ft/2907m; Tel: 970-870-2299; Nearest town: Steamboat Springs. GPS: 40.401855, -106.624268

96 • Dunn Ditch

Total sites: 3; No water; No toilets; Tents only: Free; Elev: 9690ft/2954m; Nearest town: Leadville. GPS: 39.249374, -106.376933

97 • Dutch Fred

Total sites: 11; RV sites: 11; No water; Vault toilets; Reservations not accepted; Open May-Sep; Tent & RV camping: Free; Elev: 8501ft/2591m; Nearest town: Sedalia. GPS: 39.290192, -105.092383

98 • Dutch George Flats

Total sites: 20; RV sites: 20; Central water; Vault toilets; No showers; No RV dump; Reservations not accepted; Max length: 33ft; Open Jun-Sep; Tent & RV camping: $23; Elev: 6526ft/1989m; Tel: 970-295-6700; Nearest town: Fort Collins. GPS: 40.695965, -105.445352

99 • East Fork

Total sites: 26; RV sites: 26; Central water; Vault toilets; No showers; No RV dump; Reservations accepted; Max length: 35ft; Open May-Sep; Tent & RV camping: $22; Elev: 7776ft/2370m;

Tel: 661-702-1420; Nearest town: Pagosa Springs. GPS: 37.374442, -106.887304

100 • East Marvine

Total sites: 7; RV sites: 7; No water; Vault toilets; Reservations not accepted; Open May-Nov; Tent & RV camping: $20; Elev: 8225ft/2507m; Tel: 970-945-2521; Nearest town: Meeker; Notes: Corral fee: $5. GPS: 40.011581, -107.427279

101 • Echo Lake

Total sites: 17; RV sites: 11; Central water; Vault toilets; No showers; No RV dump; Reservations accepted; Max length: 20ft; Open Jun-Sep; Tent & RV camping: $21; Elev: 10718ft/3267m; Tel: 801-226-3564; Nearest town: Idaho Springs. GPS: 39.656787, -105.594636

102 • Elbert Creek

Total sites: 17; RV sites: 17; Central water; Vault toilets; No showers; No RV dump; Reservations not accepted; Max length: 16ft; Generator hours: 0600-2200; Open May-Sep; Tent & RV camping: $15; Elev: 10076ft/3071m; Nearest town: Leadville. GPS: 39.152512, -106.413376

103 • Elk Creek

Total sites: 31; RV sites: 31; Central water; Vault toilets; No showers; No RV dump; Reservations accepted; Max length: 25ft; Open May-Sep; Tent & RV camping: $26; Elev: 8704ft/2653m; Tel: 719-274-8971; Nearest town: Antonito. GPS: 37.125465, -106.367577

104 • Elk Wallow

Total sites: 7; RV sites: 7; No water; Vault toilets; Reservations not accepted; Max length: 20ft; Open May-Sep; Tent & RV camping: $13; Elev: 8924ft/2720m; Tel: 970-945-2521; Nearest town: Basalt. GPS: 39.344215, -106.613768

105 • Elliott Creek

Total sites: 15; RV sites: 15; Vault toilets; Reservations not accepted; Open May-Sep; Tent & RV camping: $18; Elev: 7940ft/2420m; Tel: 970-945-2521; Nearest town: Silverthorne. GPS: 39.874958, -106.325289

106 • Erickson Springs

Total sites: 18; RV sites: 18; Central water; Vault toilets; No showers; No RV dump; Reservations not accepted; Max length: 35ft; Open May-Sep; Tent & RV camping: $14; Elev: 6811ft/2076m; Nearest town: Paonia. GPS: 38.954778, -107.270283

107 • Fall Creek

Total sites: 2; RV sites: 2; No water; Vault toilets; Max length: 25ft; Tent & RV camping: Fee unknown; Elev: 7721ft/2353m; Nearest town: Placerville. GPS: 37.979311, -108.030513

108 • Father Dyer

Total sites: 26; RV sites: 26; Central water; No toilets; No showers; No RV dump; Reservations accepted; Max length: 32ft; Open

May-Sep; Tent & RV camping: $24; Elev: 9993ft/3046m; Tel: 719-486-0749; Nearest town: Leadville. GPS: 39.274617, -106.350874

109 • Ferris Canyon

Total sites: 7; RV sites: 7; No water; Vault toilets; No showers; No RV dump; Reservations not accepted; Max length: 45ft; Open all year; Tent & RV camping: Free; Elev: 6604ft/2013m; Nearest town: Cortez. GPS: 37.615246, -108.635597

110 • Flat Rocks

Total sites: 19; RV sites: 19; Central water; Vault toilets; No showers; No RV dump; Reservations not accepted; Max length: 30ft; Open May-Sep; Tent & RV camping: $22; Elev: 8136ft/2480m; Nearest town: Sedalia. GPS: 39.327944, -105.094008

111 • Florida

Total sites: 20; RV sites: 20; Central water; Vault toilets; No showers; No RV dump; Reservations not accepted; Max length: 35ft; Generator hours: 0600-2200; Open May-Sep; Tent & RV camping: $24; Elev: 8369ft/2551m; Tel: 970-884-2512; Nearest town: Bayfield. GPS: 37.452655, -107.682091

112 • Fourmile

Total sites: 14; RV sites: 14; Central water; Vault toilets; No showers; No RV dump; Reservations not accepted; Max length: 22ft; Open May-Sep; Tent & RV camping: $17; Elev: 10889ft/3319m; Tel: 719-836-2031; Nearest town: Leavick. GPS: 39.208966, -106.104361

113 • Freeman Reservoir

Total sites: 18; RV sites: 18; Potable water; Vault toilets; No showers; No RV dump; Reservations not accepted; Max length: 25ft; Tent & RV camping: $12; Elev: 8865ft/2702m; Tel: 307-745-2300; Nearest town: Craig. GPS: 40.762395, -107.421546

114 • Fulford Cave

Total sites: 7; RV sites: 7; Vault toilets; Reservations not accepted; Max length: 25ft; Open Jun-Sep; Tent & RV camping: $8; Elev: 9482ft/2890m; Tel: 970-945-2521; Nearest town: Eagle; Notes: Narrow and rough rocky road. GPS: 39.491638, -106.658953

115 • Garfield

Total sites: 11; RV sites: 11; Central water; Vault toilets; No showers; No RV dump; Max length: 30ft; Tent & RV camping: Fee unknown; Elev: 9872ft/3009m; Nearest town: Poncha Springs. GPS: 38.547283, -106.303846

116 • Geneva Park

Total sites: 26; RV sites: 25; Central water; Vault toilets; No showers; No RV dump; Reservations accepted; Max length: 20ft; Open May-Sep; Tent & RV camping: $22; Elev: 9810ft/2990m; Tel: 303-275-5610; Nearest town: Jefferson. GPS: 39.531126, -105.736681

117 • Gold Creek

Total sites: 6; RV sites: 6; No water; Vault toilets; Reservations not accepted; Max length: 25ft; Open May-Oct; Tent & RV camping: Donation; Elev: 10069ft/3069m; Tel: 970-874-6600; Nearest town: Gunnison; Notes: Campers are required to store food and other items in a hard sided vehicle or camping unit constructed of solid non-pliable material. GPS: 38.655175, -106.574499

118 • Gold Park

Total sites: 11; RV sites: 11; No water; Vault toilets; Reservations not accepted; Max length: 40ft; Open May-Sep; Tent & RV camping: $21; Elev: 9350ft/2850m; Tel: 970-945-2521; Nearest town: Red Cliff. GPS: 39.403320, -106.440674

119 • Goose Creek

Total sites: 10; Central water; Vault toilets; No showers; No RV dump; Reservations not accepted; Max length: 20ft; Open May-Sep; Tents only: $22; Elev: 7776ft/2370m; Tel: 303-275-5610; Nearest town: Woodland Park. GPS: 39.170187, -105.358562

120 • Gore Creek

Total sites: 24; RV sites: 16; No water; Vault toilets; Reservations accepted; Max length: 35ft; Open May-Oct; Tent & RV camping: $25-27; Elev: 8822ft/2689m; Tel: 970-945-2521; Nearest town: Vail; Notes: Also walk-to sites. GPS: 39.627231, -106.272103

121 • Gothic

Total sites: 4; RV sites: 4; No water; Vault toilets; Reservations not accepted; Open Jun-Oct; Tent & RV camping: $12; Elev: 9626ft/2934m; Tel: 970-874-6600; Nearest town: Crested Butte. GPS: 38.982000, -107.006000

122 • Granite

Total sites: 8; RV sites: 8; No water; Vault toilets; Reservations not accepted; Max length: 22ft; Open Jul-Oct; Tent & RV camping: $10; Elev: 9944ft/3031m; Tel: 307-745-2300; Nearest town: Steamboat Springs. GPS: 40.495512, -106.691759

123 • Granite (Taylor Canyon)

Total sites: 7; No water; Vault toilets; Reservations not accepted; Open May-Sep; Tents only: $12; Elev: 8406ft/2562m; Tel: 970-874-6600; Nearest town: Almont. GPS: 38.726061, -106.768228

124 • Green Ridge

Total sites: 78; RV sites: 78; Central water; Vault toilets; No showers; RV dump; Reservations accepted; Max length: 35ft; Open May-Oct; Tent & RV camping: $23; Elev: 8399ft/2560m; Tel: 970-887-4100; Nearest town: Granby. GPS: 40.206196, -105.844369

125 • Guanella Pass

Total sites: 17; RV sites: 10; Central water; Vault toilets; No showers; No RV dump; Reservations not accepted; Max length: 35ft; Open Jun-Sep; Tent & RV camping: $21; Elev: 10784ft/3287m; Tel: 303-567-3000; Nearest town: Georgetown. GPS: 39.611816, -105.717665

126 • Hahns Peak Lake

Total sites: 26; RV sites: 26; No water; Vault toilets; Reservations accepted; Max length: 40ft; Open Jun-Sep; Tent & RV camping:

$10; Elev: 8432ft/2570m; Tel: 970-870-2299; Nearest town: Steamboat Springs. GPS: 40.839433, -106.996528

127 • Halfmoon

Total sites: 7; RV sites: 7; No water; Vault toilets; Reservations not accepted; Max length: 15ft; Open May-Sep; Tent & RV camping: $15; Elev: 10315ft/3144m; Tel: 970-945-2521; Nearest town: Leadville; Notes: Food storage order. GPS: 39.500697, -106.432557

128 • Halfmoon West

Total sites: 10; RV sites: 10; No water; Vault toilets; Reservations not accepted; Open May-Sep; Tent & RV camping: $20; Elev: 9967ft/3038m; Tel: 719-486-0749; Nearest town: Leadville. GPS: 39.156744, -106.398192

129 • Hall Valley

Total sites: 9; RV sites: 9; No water; Vault toilets; Reservations not accepted; Max length: 20ft; Open May-Sep; Tent & RV camping: $22; Elev: 9828ft/2996m; Tel: 303-275-5610; Nearest town: Webster. GPS: 39.482264, -105.804858

130 • Hansons Mill

Total sites: 3; RV sites: 3; No water; Vault toilets; Reservations not accepted; Tent & RV camping: Free; Elev: 10935ft/3333m; Tel: 719-658-2556; Nearest town: Creede. GPS: 37.813000, -106.737000

131 • Happy Meadows

Total sites: 10; RV sites: 10; Central water; Vault toilets; No showers; No RV dump; Reservations accepted; Max length: 22ft; Open May-Sep; Tent & RV camping: $17-21; Elev: 7897ft/2407m; Tel: 719-748-3619; Nearest town: Woodland Park. GPS: 39.014104, -105.362831

132 • Haviland Lake

Total sites: 43; RV sites: 43; Elec sites: 17; Central water; Vault toilets; No showers; No RV dump; Reservations accepted; Max length: 45ft; Open Jun-Sep; Tents: $24/RVs: $24-32; Elev: 8178ft/2493m; Tel: 970-884-2512; Nearest town: Durango. GPS: 37.533804, -107.806769

133 • Hayden Creek

Total sites: 11; RV sites: 11; Potable water; Vault toilets; No showers; No RV dump; Reservations not accepted; Max length: 30ft; Open Jun-Sep; Tent & RV camping: $18; Elev: 7831ft/2387m; Tel: 719-539-3591; Nearest town: Salida. GPS: 38.329771, -105.823903

134 • Heaton Bay

Total sites: 81; RV sites: 81; Central water; Vault toilets; No showers; No RV dump; Reservations accepted; Max length: 32ft; Open May-Oct; Tents: $25-27/RVs: $25-32; Elev: 9068ft/2764m; Tel: 970-945-2521; Nearest town: Frisco. GPS: 39.602231, -106.077442

135 • Hidden Lakes

Total sites: 9; RV sites: 9; Potable water; Vault toilets; No showers; No RV dump; Reservations not accepted; Max length: 20ft; Open all year; Tent & RV camping: $10; Elev: 8947ft/2727m; Tel: 307-745-2300; Nearest town: Walden. GPS: 40.506609, -106.608701

136 • Hidden Valley

Total sites: 4; No water; Vault toilets; Reservations not accepted; Open Jun-Sep; Tents only: Donation; Elev: 9692ft/2954m; Tel: 970-641-0471; Nearest town: Lake City. GPS: 38.040979, -107.132788

137 • Highway Springs

Total sites: 13; RV sites: 13; No water; Vault toilets; Reservations not accepted; Max length: 35ft; Open May-Sep; Tent & RV camping: $20; Elev: 8415ft/2565m; Tel: 719-657-3321; Nearest town: South Fork. GPS: 37.621826, -106.685059

138 • Himes Peak

Total sites: 11; RV sites: 11; Vault toilets; Reservations not accepted; Open May-Nov; Tent & RV camping: $20; Elev: 8871ft/2704m; Tel: 970-945-2521; Nearest town: Buford. GPS: 40.028195, -107.272591

139 • Hinman

Total sites: 13; RV sites: 13; Potable water; Vault toilets; No showers; No RV dump; Reservations not accepted; Max length: 22ft; Open Jun-Oct; Tent & RV camping: $12; Elev: 7723ft/2354m; Tel: 307-745-2300; Nearest town: Steamboat Springs. GPS: 40.748584, -106.834213

140 • Hornsilver

Total sites: 7; RV sites: 7; Vault toilets; Reservations not accepted; Max length: 30ft; Open Jun-Sep; Tent & RV camping: $20; Elev: 8812ft/2686m; Tel: 970-945-2521; Nearest town: Minturn; Notes: Food storage order. GPS: 39.489077, -106.367731

141 • Horseshoe

Total sites: 7; RV sites: 7; No water; Vault toilets; Reservations not accepted; Max length: 50ft; Open Jun-Oct; Tent & RV camping: $18; Elev: 8497ft/2590m; Tel: 970-887-4100; Nearest town: Parshall. GPS: 39.900129, -106.095786

142 • Horseshoe (Fairplay West)

Total sites: 18; RV sites: 16; Central water; Vault toilets; No showers; No RV dump; Reservations accepted; Max length: 25ft; Open May-Oct; Tent & RV camping: $17; Elev: 10533ft/3210m; Tel: 719-836-2031; Nearest town: Fairplay. GPS: 39.199557, -106.084121

143 • Horseshoe (Omo Peak)

Total sites: 7; RV sites: 7; Central water; Vault toilets; No showers; No RV dump; Reservations not accepted; Open Jun-Sep; Tent & RV camping: $10; Elev: 10194ft/3107m; Tel: 970-620-2399; Nearest town: Yampa. GPS: 40.034667, -107.112924

144 • House Creek

Total sites: 65; RV sites: 65; Elec sites: 12; Central water; Vault toilets; No showers; RV dump; Reservations accepted; Open Jun-Sep; Tents: $24/RVs: $24-32; Elev: 6975ft/2126m; Nearest town: Dolores; Notes: Group site: $80. GPS: 37.516252, -108.535274

145 • Idlewild

Total sites: 24; RV sites: 24; Central water; Vault toilets; No showers; No RV dump; Reservations not accepted; Max length: 30ft; Open May-Sep; Tent & RV camping: $22; Elev: 8934ft/ 2723m; Tel: 970-887-4100; Nearest town: Winter Park. GPS: 39.903764, -105.779307

146 • Indian Creek

Total sites: 18; RV sites: 18; Central water; Vault toilets; No showers; No RV dump; Reservations not accepted; Max length: 20ft; Generator hours: 0600-2200; Open May-Sep; Tent & RV camping: $22; Elev: 7571ft/2308m; Tel: 303-275-5610; Nearest town: Sedalia. GPS: 39.381372, -105.097065

147 • Iron City

Total sites: 15; RV sites: 15; Potable water; Vault toilets; No showers; No RV dump; Reservations not accepted; Max length: 25ft; Generator hours: 0600-2200; Tent & RV camping: $20; Elev: 9954ft/3034m; Tel: 719-539-3591; Nearest town: Nathrop. GPS: 38.708564, -106.336335

148 • Iron Springs

Total sites: 8; RV sites: 8; No water; Vault toilets; Reservations not accepted; Open Jun-Oct; Tent & RV camping: Free; Elev: 9606ft/ 2928m; Tel: 970-240-5300; Nearest town: Montrose; Notes: Small RVs only. GPS: 38.316744, -108.164465

149 • Island Lake

Total sites: 41; RV sites: 41; Central water; Vault toilets; No showers; No RV dump; Reservations accepted; Max length: 40ft; Open Jun-Sep; Tents: $22/RVs: $22-30; Elev: 10321ft/3146m; Tel: 970-874-6600; Nearest town: Cedaredge. GPS: 39.030651, -108.008983

150 • Ivy Creek

Total sites: 4; RV sites: 2; No water; Vault toilets; Reservations not accepted; Max length: 25ft; Open all year; Tent & RV camping: Free; Elev: 9264ft/2824m; Tel: 719-657-3321; Nearest town: Creede; Notes: Winter access may be limited. GPS: 37.682097, -106.999589

151 • Jacks Gulch

Total sites: 56; RV sites: 56; Elec sites: 27; Central water; Vault toilets; No showers; No RV dump; Reservations not accepted; Max length: 80ft; Open May-Nov; Tents: $24/RVs: $24-32; Elev: 8199ft/2499m; Tel: 970-295-6700; Nearest town: Rustic; Notes: 5 equestrian sites, Reservable group site $170. GPS: 40.636618, -105.527367

152 • Jackson Creek

Total sites: 9; RV sites: 9; No toilets; Reservations not accepted; Max length: 16ft; Tent & RV camping: Free; Elev: 8212ft/2503m; Tel: 303-275-5610; Nearest town: Denver; Notes: Trailers not recommended. GPS: 39.251000, -105.089000

153 • Jefferson Creek

Total sites: 17; RV sites: 16; Central water; Vault toilets; No showers; No RV dump; Reservations accepted; Max length: 25ft; Open May-Sep; Tent & RV camping: $17; Elev: 10037ft/3059m; Tel: 719-836-2031; Nearest town: Jefferson. GPS: 39.434182, -105.853026

154 • Jumbo

Total sites: 26; RV sites: 26; Elec sites: 21; Central water; Vault toilets; No showers; No RV dump; Reservations accepted; Max length: 60ft; Open Jun-Sep; Tents: $22/RVs: $30; Elev: 9792ft/ 2985m; Tel: 970-874-6600; Nearest town: Mesa. GPS: 39.053226, -108.093569

155 • Junction Creek

Total sites: 44; RV sites: 44; Elec sites: 14; Central water; Vault toilets; No showers; No RV dump; Reservations accepted; Max length: 32ft; Open May-Sep; Tents: $24/RVs: $24-35; Elev: 7431ft/2265m; Tel: 970-884-2512; Nearest town: Durango; Notes: Group site: $100, Water at nearby Idlewild CG. GPS: 37.339469, -107.917407

156 • Kelly Dahl

Total sites: 46; RV sites: 46; Central water; Vault toilets; No showers; No RV dump; Reservations accepted; Max length: 50ft; Open Jun-Oct; Tent & RV camping: $23; Elev: 8632ft/2631m; Tel: 303-541-2500; Nearest town: Nederland. GPS: 39.932373, -105.497803

157 • Kelly Flats

Total sites: 29; RV sites: 25; Central water; Vault toilets; No showers; No RV dump; Reservations not accepted; Max length: 40ft; Open Jun-Sep; Tent & RV camping: $24; Elev: 6811ft/2076m; Tel: 970-295-6700; Nearest town: Rustic. GPS: 40.682376, -105.483854

158 • Kelsey

Total sites: 16; RV sites: 14; No water; Vault toilets; Reservations accepted; Max length: 30ft; Open May-Sep; Tent & RV camping: $22; Elev: 8081ft/2463m; Tel: 303-275-5610; Nearest town: Pine. GPS: 39.305628, -105.265721

159 • Kenosha Pass

Total sites: 24; RV sites: 24; Central water; Vault toilets; No showers; No RV dump; Reservations accepted; Max length: 20ft; Open May-Sep; Tent & RV camping: $22; Elev: 10016ft/3053m; Tel: 303-275-5610; Nearest town: Jefferson. GPS: 39.413894, -105.761112

160 • Kenosha Pass East

Total sites: 12; RV sites: 12; No water; Vault toilets; Reservations not accepted; Open May-Nov; Tent & RV camping: $20; Elev: 10036ft/3059m; Tel: 303-275-5610; Nearest town: Jefferson. GPS: 39.415312, -105.755481

161 • Keystone/Loveland Pass

Total sites: 6; RV sites: 6; No water; No toilets; Max length: 25ft; Tent & RV camping: Free; Elev: 9670ft/2947m; Nearest town: Keystone. GPS: 39.616912, -105.929926

162 • Kiser Creek

Total sites: 12; RV sites: 12; Vault toilets; Max length: 16ft; Open Jul-Sep; Tent & RV camping: Free; Elev: 10121ft/3085m; Nearest town: Grand Mesa. GPS: 39.037473, -107.948123

163 • Kite Lake

Total sites: 5; No water; Vault toilets; Reservations not accepted; Open May-Sep; Tents only: $15; Elev: 12083ft/3683m; Tel: 719-836-2031; Nearest town: Alma. GPS: 39.329425, -106.128549

164 • Klines Folly

Total sites: 4; No water; Vault toilets; Reservations not accepted; Open Jun-Nov; Tents only: Free; Elev: 10742ft/3274m; Tel: 970-328-6388; Nearest town: Eagle. GPS: 39.759584, -107.310712

165 • Kroeger

Total sites: 10; RV sites: 10; Central water; Vault toilets; No showers; No RV dump; Reservations not accepted; Max length: 35ft; Open May-Sep; Tent & RV camping: $20; Elev: 8927ft/2721m; Tel: 970-247-4874; Nearest town: Durango; Notes: Only 1 site for larger RV. GPS: 37.376231, -108.077104

166 • Lake Creek

Total sites: 11; RV sites: 11; Central water; Vault toilets; No showers; No RV dump; Reservations not accepted; Max length: 29ft; Open May-Sep; Tent & RV camping: $21; Elev: 8261ft/2518m; Tel: 719-553-1400; Nearest town: Westcliffe. GPS: 38.264367, -105.661113

167 • Lake Fork (Red Mt)

Total sites: 19; RV sites: 19; No water; Vault toilets; Reservations accepted; Max length: 25ft; Open May-Sep; Tent & RV camping: $23; Elev: 9550ft/2911m; Tel: 719-852-5941; Nearest town: Antonito. GPS: 37.309326, -106.477295

168 • Lake Irwin

Total sites: 32; RV sites: 32; Central water; Vault toilets; No showers; No RV dump; Reservations accepted; Max length: 45ft; Open Jun-Sep; Tent & RV camping: $20; Elev: 10417ft/3175m; Tel: 970-641-0471; Nearest town: Crested Butte. GPS: 38.881104, -107.107666

169 • Lake Isabel - La Vista

Total sites: 29; RV sites: 23; Elec sites: 14; Central water; Vault toilets; No showers; No RV dump; Reservations accepted; Open May-Sep; Tents: $24/RVs: $28; Elev: 8609ft/2624m; Tel: 719-269-8500; Nearest town: Canon City. GPS: 37.984556, -105.060025

170 • Lake Isabel - Southside

Total sites: 8; RV sites: 8; Central water; Vault toilets; No showers; No RV dump; Reservations accepted; Max length: 30ft; Open May-Sep; Tent & RV camping: $20; Elev: 8497ft/2590m; Tel: 719-269-8500; Nearest town: Canon City. GPS: 37.983106, -105.056316

171 • Lake Isabel - St Charles

Total sites: 15; RV sites: 14; Central water; No toilets; No showers; No RV dump; Reservations accepted; Open May-Oct; Tent & RV camping: $22; Elev: 8701ft/2652m; Tel: 719-269-8500; Nearest town: Canon City. GPS: 37.981028, -105.067415

172 • Lakeview (Gunnison)

Total sites: 64; RV sites: 64; Elec sites: 9; Central water; Vault toilets; No showers; RV dump; Reservations accepted; Max length: 32ft; Open May-Sep; Tents: $22/RVs: $22-30; Elev: 9511ft/2899m; Tel: 970-642-0566; Nearest town: Almont. GPS: 38.818498, -106.579836

173 • Lakeview (Pike)

Total sites: 33; RV sites: 33; Central water; Vault toilets; No showers; No RV dump; Reservations accepted; Open May-Sep; Tent & RV camping: $24; Elev: 9534ft/2906m; Tel: 719-486-0749; Nearest town: Leadville. GPS: 39.097911, -106.365233

174 • Lincoln Gulch

Total sites: 7; RV sites: 7; Vault toilets; Reservations not accepted; Max length: 35ft; Open May-Oct; Tent & RV camping: $20; Elev: 9692ft/2954m; Tel: 970-945-2521; Nearest town: Aspen. GPS: 39.117184, -106.695913

175 • Little Bear

Total sites: 36; RV sites: 36; Central water; No toilets; No showers; No RV dump; Reservations not accepted; Max length: 45ft; Open Jul-Sep; Tent & RV camping: $16; Elev: 10312ft/3143m; Tel: 970-874-6600; Nearest town: Delta. GPS: 39.035327, -107.997032

176 • Little Mattie

Total sites: 20; RV sites: 20; Central water; Vault toilets; No showers; No RV dump; Reservations not accepted; Max length: 22ft; Open May-Oct; Tent & RV camping: $26; Elev: 7910ft/2411m; Tel: 970-945-2521; Nearest town: Basalt. GPS: 39.376577, -106.807379

177 • Little Maud

Total sites: 22; RV sites: 22; Central water; Vault toilets; No showers; No RV dump; Reservations accepted; Max length: 35ft; Open May-Sep; Tent & RV camping: $28-30; Elev: 7953ft/2424m; Tel: 970-945-2521; Nearest town: Basalt. GPS: 39.377119, -106.814947

178 • Little Molas Lake

Total sites: 10; RV sites: 5; No water; Vault toilets; Reservations not accepted; Tent & RV camping: Free; Elev: 11004ft/3354m; Nearest town: Silverton. GPS: 37.744656, -107.709869

179 • Lodgepole (Gunnison)

Total sites: 16; RV sites: 16; Central water; Vault toilets; No showers; No RV dump; Reservations accepted; Max length: 40ft; Open May-Sep; Tent & RV camping: $18; Elev: 8901ft/2713m; Tel: 970-642-0566; Nearest town: Almont. GPS: 38.761230, -106.661865

180 • Lodgepole (Pike)

Total sites: 34; RV sites: 34; Central water; Vault toilets; No showers; No RV dump; Reservations accepted; Max length: 30ft; Open May-Sep; Tent & RV camping: $17; Elev: 9964ft/3037m; Tel: 719-836-2031; Nearest town: Jefferson. GPS: 39.422187, -105.842612

181 • Lone Rock

Total sites: 18; RV sites: 15; Central water; Vault toilets; No showers; No RV dump; Reservations accepted; Max length: 30ft; Open all year; Tent & RV camping: $22; Elev: 6444ft/1964m; Tel: 303-275-5610; Nearest town: Woodland Park. GPS: 39.252188, -105.235733

182 • Long Draw

Total sites: 25; RV sites: 25; Central water; Vault toilets; No showers; No RV dump; Reservations not accepted; Max length: 30ft; Open Jul-Sep; Tent & RV camping: $20; Elev: 10026ft/3056m; Tel: 970-295-6700; Nearest town: Gould. GPS: 40.515554, -105.767083

183 • Lost Lake

Total sites: 19; RV sites: 19; Central water; Vault toilets; No showers; No RV dump; Reservations not accepted; Max length: 28ft; Open Jun-Sep; Tent & RV camping: $20; Elev: 9656ft/2943m; Tel: 970-527-4131; Nearest town: Paonia; Notes: 5 equestrian sites. GPS: 38.869873, -107.208496

184 • Lost Man

Total sites: 10; RV sites: 10; Vault toilets; Reservations not accepted; Max length: 30ft; Open Jun-Sep; Tent & RV camping: $20; Elev: 10535ft/3211m; Tel: 970-945-2521; Nearest town: Aspen. GPS: 39.121595, -106.625098

185 • Lost Park

Total sites: 12; RV sites: 12; No water; Vault toilets; Reservations not accepted; Max length: 22ft; Open May-Sep; Tent & RV camping: $15; Elev: 9984ft/3043m; Tel: 719 836-2031; Nearest town: Jefferson. GPS: 39.284927, -105.507396

186 • Lost Trail

Total sites: 7; RV sites: 7; Central water; Vault toilets; No showers; No RV dump; Reservations not accepted; Max length: 20ft; Tent & RV camping: Free; Elev: 9619ft/2932m; Tel: 719-657-3321; Nearest town: Creede. GPS: 37.768619, -107.349813

187 • Lottis Creek

Total sites: 45; RV sites: 45; Elec sites: 38; Central water; Vault toilets; No showers; No RV dump; Reservations accepted; Open May-Sep; Tents: $22/RVs: $22-30; Elev: 9094ft/2772m; Tel: 970-874-6600; Nearest town: Almont. GPS: 38.775811, -106.628221

188 • Lower Beaver Creek

Total sites: 18; RV sites: 18; Central water; Vault toilets; No showers; No RV dump; Reservations not accepted; Open all year; Tent & RV camping: $18-24; Elev: 8481ft/2585m; Tel: 719-657-3321; Nearest town: South Fork; Notes: No services in winter. GPS: 37.616251, -106.676569

189 • Lower Hermosa

Total sites: 20; RV sites: 20; No water; Vault toilets; Reservations not accepted; Tent & RV camping: $18; Elev: 7779ft/2371m; Tel: 970-247-4874; Nearest town: Durango; Notes: Some sites for horse use only. GPS: 37.454503, -107.856779

190 • Lower Piedra

Total sites: 17; RV sites: 17; Central water; Vault toilets; No showers; No RV dump; Reservations not accepted; Max length: 35ft; Open May-Sep; Tent & RV camping: Fee unknown; Elev: 6627ft/2020m; Tel: 970-247-4874; Nearest town: Pagosa Springs. GPS: 37.241943, -107.342773

191 • Lowry

Total sites: 30; RV sites: 27; Elec sites: 23; No water; Vault toilets; Reservations accepted; Max length: 32ft; Open May-Sep; Tents: $23-25/RVs: $23-30; Elev: 9360ft/2853m; Tel: 970-945-2521; Nearest town: Dillon. GPS: 39.597113, -106.026813

192 • Luders Creek

Total sites: 6; RV sites: 6; No water; Vault toilets; Reservations not accepted; Max length: 25ft; Open May-Nov; Tent & RV camping: $5; Elev: 10056ft/3065m; Tel: 719 655-2547; Nearest town: Saguache; Notes: Stock facilities. GPS: 38.181194, -106.583802

193 • Lynx Pass

Total sites: 11; RV sites: 11; Potable water; Vault toilets; No showers; No RV dump; Reservations not accepted; Max length: 18ft; Open May-Oct; Tent & RV camping: $10; Elev: 8976ft/2736m; Tel: 307-745-2300; Nearest town: Toponas. GPS: 40.105713, -106.683105

194 • Marshall Park

Total sites: 16; RV sites: 16; Central water; Vault toilets; No showers; No RV dump; Reservations accepted; Max length: 32ft; Open May-Sep; Tent & RV camping: $23; Elev: 8766ft/2672m; Tel: 719-658-0829; Nearest town: Creede. GPS: 37.790499, -106.981491

195 • Marvine

Total sites: 24; RV sites: 24; No water; Vault toilets; Reservations accepted; Open May-Oct; Tent & RV camping: $23-25; Elev: 8148ft/2484m; Tel: 970-945-2521; Nearest town: Buford; Notes: 4 sites with corrals: $5 extra. GPS: 40.008762, -107.426031

196 • Mary E

Total sites: 15; RV sites: 15; No water; Vault toilets; No showers; No RV dump; Reservations not accepted; Max length: 22ft; Tent & RV camping: Free; Elev: 8061ft/2457m; Nearest town: Telluride; Notes: No fires. GPS: 37.940273, -107.897701

197 • Matchless

Total sites: 50; RV sites: 35; Central water; Vault toilets; No showers; No RV dump; Reservations not accepted; Generator hours: 0600-2200; Open May-Sep; Tent & RV camping: $24; Elev: 9909ft/3020m; Tel: 719-553-1404; Nearest town: Leadville; Notes: A large parking lot, No filling RV water tanks. GPS: 39.257317, -106.360397

198 • Matterhorn

Total sites: 28; RV sites: 28; Elec sites: 4; Central water; Flush toilets; Showers; No RV dump; Reservations accepted; Max length: 45ft; Open May-Oct; Tents: $24/RVs: $24-36; Elev: 9498ft/2895m; Tel: 970-249-4552; Nearest town: Telluride. GPS: 37.844941, -107.881359

199 • Mavreeso

Total sites: 19; RV sites: 19; Elec sites: 4; Central water; Vault toilets; No showers; No RV dump; Reservations accepted; Max length: 35ft; Open May-Sep; Tents: $24/RVs: $24-32; Elev: 7733ft/2357m; Tel: 970-882-7296; Nearest town: Dolores; Notes: Group site $80. GPS: 37.650827, -108.297028

200 • May Queen

Total sites: 27; RV sites: 23; Central water; Vault toilets; No showers; No RV dump; Reservations accepted; Max length: 32ft; Open May-Sep; Tent & RV camping: $24; Elev: 10046ft/3062m; Tel: 719-486-0749; Nearest town: Leadville. GPS: 39.278016, -106.431886

201 • McClure

Total sites: 10; RV sites: 10; No water; Vault toilets; Reservations not accepted; Max length: 35ft; Open May-Nov; Tent & RV camping: Free; Elev: 8205ft/2501m; Tel: 970-527-4131; Nearest town: Redstone. GPS: 39.123713, -107.313118

202 • McDonald Flats

Total sites: 13; RV sites: 13; No water; Vault toilets; Reservations not accepted; Open May-Oct; Tent & RV camping: $18; Elev: 7933ft/2418m; Tel: 970-945-2521; Nearest town: Silverthorne. GPS: 39.850084, -106.237011

203 • McPhee

Total sites: 71; RV sites: 71; Elec sites: 24; Central water; Flush toilets; No showers; No RV dump; Reservations accepted; Max length: 40ft; Open May-Sep; Tents: $24/RVs: $24-32; Elev: 7192ft/2192m; Tel: 970-247-4874; Nearest town: Dolores; Notes: Group site: $80. GPS: 37.497071, -108.552896

204 • Meadow Lake

Total sites: 20; RV sites: 20; Vault toilets; Reservations not accepted; Open May-Oct; Tent & RV camping: $20; Elev: 9626ft/2934m; Tel: 970-945-2521; Nearest town: New Castle. GPS: 39.817866, -107.542701

205 • Meadow Ridge

Total sites: 19; RV sites: 19; Potable water; Vault toilets; No showers; No RV dump; Reservations accepted; Max length: 30ft; Open May-Sep; Tent & RV camping: $23; Elev: 9203ft/2805m; Tel: 970-945-2521; Nearest town: Woodland Park. GPS: 38.977554, -104.986877

206 • Meadow Ridge

Total sites: 20; RV sites: 20; Vault toilets; Reservations not accepted; Max length: 16ft; Open May-Oct; Tent & RV camping: $20; Elev: 9639ft/2938m; Tel: 970-945-2521; Nearest town: Buford. GPS: 39.810648, -107.536772

207 • Meadows

Total sites: 30; RV sites: 20; No water; Vault toilets; Reservations not accepted; Open Jun-Oct; Tent & RV camping: $10; Elev: 9331ft/2844m; Tel: 970-870-2299; Nearest town: Steamboat Springs. GPS: 40.373791, -106.723288

208 • Meeker Park Overflow

Total sites: 29; RV sites: 29; No water; Vault toilets; Reservations not accepted; Max length: 25ft; Open May-Sep; Tent & RV camping: $13; Elev: 8638ft/2633m; Tel: 303-541-2500; Nearest town: Estes Park; Notes: Better suited for tents. GPS: 40.242525, -105.534311

209 • Meridian

Total sites: 18; RV sites: 18; Central water; Vault toilets; No showers; No RV dump; Reservations not accepted; Open May-Sep; Tent & RV camping: $22; Elev: 9026ft/2751m; Tel: 303-275-5610; Nearest town: Bailey. GPS: 39.511242, -105.535159

210 • Mesa Creek

Total sites: 4; RV sites: 4; No toilets; Reservations not accepted; Tent & RV camping: Free; Elev: 8995ft/2742m; Nearest town: Crawford. GPS: 38.475338, -107.523574

211 • Michigan Creek

Total sites: 12; RV sites: 12; Central water; Vault toilets; No showers; No RV dump; Reservations not accepted; Max length: 25ft; Open May-Oct; Tent & RV camping: $15; Elev: 10131ft/3088m; Tel: 719 836-2031; Nearest town: Jefferson. GPS: 39.410514, -105.882698

212 • Middle Fork Elk River

Total sites: 8; RV sites: 8; No water; Vault toilets; Tent & RV camping: Free; Elev: 8076ft/2462m; Nearest town: Steamboat Springs. GPS: 40.772756, -106.767631

213 • Middle Quartz

Total sites: 7; RV sites: 7; No water; Vault toilets; Reservations not accepted; Open May-Sep; Tent & RV camping: Donation; Elev: 10348ft/3154m; Tel: 970-641-0471; Nearest town: Monarch. GPS: 38.623000, -106.425000

214 • Miller Creek

Total sites: 12; RV sites: 12; Central water; Vault toilets; No showers; No RV dump; Reservations not accepted; Max length: 35ft; Open May-Sep; Tent & RV camping: $22; Elev: 8264ft/2519m; Tel: 970-247-4874; Nearest town: Bayfield. GPS: 37.405029, -107.661133

215 • Miners Cabin

Total sites: 7; RV sites: 7; No water; Vault toilets; Tent & RV camping: Free; Elev: 8959ft/2731m; Nearest town: Mayday. GPS: 37.381294, -108.076952

216 • Mirror Lake

Total sites: 10; RV sites: 10; No water; Vault toilets; Reservations not accepted; Open May-Sep; Tent & RV camping: $12; Elev: 10988ft/3349m; Tel: 970-641-0471; Nearest town: Almont. GPS: 38.747559, -106.432129

217 • Mix Lake

Total sites: 22; RV sites: 22; No water; Vault toilets; Reservations not accepted; Max length: 25ft; Open Jun-Sep; Tent & RV camping: $23; Elev: 10076ft/3071m; Tel: 719-274-8971; Nearest town: Antonito. GPS: 37.358544, -106.546835

218 • Mogote

Total sites: 59; RV sites: 59; Central water; Vault toilets; No showers; No RV dump; Reservations accepted; Max length: 25ft; Open May-Sep; Tent & RV camping: $26; Elev: 8428ft/2569m; Tel: 719-376-2535; Nearest town: Antonito; Notes: Group site $150. GPS: 37.065649, -106.231882

219 • Mollie B (White River)

Total sites: 26; RV sites: 26; Central water; Vault toilets; No showers; No RV dump; Reservations accepted; Max length: 32ft; Open May-Sep; Tent & RV camping: $28-30; Elev: 7868ft/ 2398m; Tel: 970-945-2521; Nearest town: Basalt. GPS: 39.375330, -106.812678

220 • Molly Brown

Total sites: 49; RV sites: 48; Central water; No toilets; No showers; RV dump; Reservations accepted; Max length: 32ft; Open May-Sep; Tents: $24/RVs: $24-26; Elev: 9957ft/3035m; Tel: 719-486-0749; Nearest town: Leadville. GPS: 39.263737, -106.353162

221 • Molly Gulch

Total sites: 15; Central water; Vault toilets; No showers; No RV dump; Reservations not accepted; Tents only: Free; Elev: 7551ft/ 2302m; Tel: 303-275-5610; Nearest town: Deckers; Notes: Rough road. GPS: 39.194985, -105.344668

222 • Monarch Park

Total sites: 37; RV sites: 35; Potable water; Vault toilets; No showers; No RV dump; Reservations accepted; Max length: 45ft; Open May-Sep; Tent & RV camping: $18; Elev: 10492ft/3198m; Tel: 719-539-3591; Nearest town: Poncha Springs. GPS: 38.516258, -106.325131

223 • Mosca

Total sites: 16; RV sites: 16; No water; Vault toilets; Reservations not accepted; Max length: 45ft; Open May-Oct; Tent & RV camping: $14; Elev: 9993ft/3046m; Tel: 970-641-0471; Nearest town: Almont. GPS: 38.860107, -106.710205

224 • Mountain Park

Total sites: 55; RV sites: 55; Elec sites: 32; Central water; Flush toilets; Pay showers; No RV dump; Reservations accepted; Max length: 45ft; Open May-Sep; Tents: $24/RVs: $24-32; Elev: 6676ft/2035m; Tel: 970-295-6700; Nearest town: Rustic; Notes: Group fee: $132. GPS: 40.682251, -105.466636

225 • Mt Princeton

Total sites: 17; RV sites: 17; No water; Vault toilets; Reservations accepted; Max length: 45ft; Open May-Sep; Tent & RV camping: $22; Elev: 8625ft/2629m; Tel: 719-539-3591; Nearest town: Nathrop. GPS: 38.713911, -106.223672

226 • North Bank

Total sites: 17; RV sites: 17; Central water; Vault toilets; No showers; No RV dump; Reservations not accepted; Open May-Sep; Tent & RV camping: $14; Elev: 8530ft/2600m; Tel: 970-641-0471; Nearest town: Almont. GPS: 38.730182, -106.757965

227 • North Clear Creek

Total sites: 21; RV sites: 21; Central water; Vault toilets; No showers; No RV dump; Reservations not accepted; Max length: 30ft; Open May-Sep; Tent & RV camping: $19; Elev: 9569ft/2917m; Tel: 719-657-3321; Nearest town: Creede. GPS: 37.835217, -107.139025

228 • North Crestone Creek

Total sites: 13; RV sites: 13; No water; Vault toilets; Reservations not accepted; Max length: 25ft; Open May-Nov; Tent & RV camping: $7; Elev: 8573ft/2613m; Tel: 719-655-2547; Nearest town: Crestone. GPS: 38.018539, -105.686026

229 • North Fork (Lost Park)

Total sites: 40; RV sites: 40; Central water; Vault toilets; No showers; No RV dump; Reservations accepted; Max length: 22ft; Open May-Nov; Tent & RV camping: $24-26; Elev: 7874ft/2400m; Tel: 970-945-2521; Nearest town: Buford. GPS: 40.058752, -107.434534

230 • North Fork Poudre

Total sites: 9; RV sites: 9; No water; Vault toilets; Reservations not accepted; Max length: 30ft; Open Jun-Sep; Tent & RV camping: $15; Elev: 9190ft/2801m; Tel: 970-295-6700; Nearest town: Livermore. GPS: 40.814232, -105.710238

231 • Oak Creek

Total sites: 15; RV sites: 15; No water; Vault toilets; Reservations not accepted; Open all year; Tent & RV camping: Free; Elev: 7680ft/2341m; Tel: 719-553-1400; Nearest town: Canon City. GPS: 38.296335, -105.267209

232 • Ohaver Lake

Total sites: 30; RV sites: 30; Potable water; Vault toilets; No showers; No RV dump; Reservations accepted; Max length: 45ft; Open May-Oct; Tent & RV camping: $22; Elev: 9216ft/2809m; Tel: 719-539-3591; Nearest town: Poncha Springs. GPS: 38.426495, -106.143914

233 • Olive Ridge

Total sites: 56; RV sites: 56; No water; Vault toilets; No showers; No RV dump; Reservations accepted; Max length: 30ft; Open May-Sep; Tent & RV camping: $23; Elev: 8350ft/2545m; Tel: 303-541-2500; Nearest town: Estes Park. GPS: 40.208394, -105.523728

234 • One Mile

Total sites: 25; RV sites: 25; Elec sites: 25; Central water; Vault toilets; No showers; No RV dump; Reservations accepted; Open May-Sep; Tent & RV camping: $30; Elev: 8444ft/2574m; Tel: 970-642-0566; Nearest town: Almont. GPS: 38.730168, -106.754684

235 • Ophir Creek

Total sites: 31; RV sites: 12; Central water; Vault toilets; No showers; No RV dump; Reservations not accepted; Max length: 30ft; Open May-Oct; Tent & RV camping: $21; Elev: 8924ft/2720m; Tel: 719-553-1400; Nearest town: Colorado City. GPS: 38.060059, -105.107422

236 • Osprey

Total sites: 13; No water; Vault toilets; Reservations not accepted; Generator hours: 0600-2200; Open all year; Tents only: $18; Elev: 6223ft/1897m; Tel: 719-553-1400; Nearest town: Woodland Park; Notes: No services in winter. GPS: 39.349000, -105.177000

237 • Ouzel

Total sites: 13; No water; Vault toilets; Reservations not accepted; Stay limit: 14 days; Generator hours: 0600-2200; Open all year; Tents only: $18; Elev: 6306ft/1922m; Tel: 719-553-1400; Nearest town: Woodland Park. GPS: 39.320000, -105.188000

238 • Painted Rocks

Total sites: 18; RV sites: 15; Potable water; Vault toilets; No showers; No RV dump; Reservations accepted; Max length: 30ft; Generator hours: 0600-2200; Open May-Sep; Tent & RV camping: $23; Elev: 7868ft/2398m; Tel: 719-553-1400; Nearest town: Woodland Park . GPS: 39.084473, -105.105957

239 • Palisade

Total sites: 12; RV sites: 12; Central water; Vault toilets; No showers; No RV dump; Reservations not accepted; Max length: 32ft; Open May-Sep; Tent & RV camping: $22-26; Elev: 8399ft/2560m; Tel: 719-657-3321; Nearest town: South Fork. GPS: 37.750732, -106.764648

240 • Park Creek

Total sites: 13; RV sites: 13; Central water; Vault toilets; No showers; No RV dump; Reservations not accepted; Max length: 35ft; Open May-Sep; Tent & RV camping: $24; Elev: 8547ft/2605m; Tel: 719-657-3321; Nearest town: South Fork. GPS: 37.591553, -106.729248

241 • Parry Peak

Total sites: 26; RV sites: 26; No water; Vault toilets; No showers; No RV dump; Reservations not accepted; Max length: 32ft; Generator hours: 0600-2200; Open May-Sep; Tent & RV camping: $22; Elev: 9514ft/2900m; Tel: 719-553-1400; Nearest town: Twin Lakes. GPS: 39.068115, -106.409912

242 • Peaceful Valley

Total sites: 17; RV sites: 17; Central water; Vault toilets; No showers; No RV dump; Reservations accepted; Max length: 45ft; Open May-Oct; Tent & RV camping: $23; Elev: 8573ft/2613m; Tel: 303-541-2500; Nearest town: Nederland. GPS: 40.131546, -105.506674

243 • Peak One

Total sites: 74; RV sites: 74; Central water; Vault toilets; No showers; No RV dump; Reservations accepted; Max length: 32ft; Open May-Sep; Tent & RV camping: $24-26; Elev: 9043ft/2756m; Tel: 970-945-2521; Nearest town: Frisco. GPS: 39.584199, -106.071483

244 • Pine Cove

Total sites: 56; RV sites: 56; Central water; Vault toilets; No showers; No RV dump; Reservations accepted; Max length: 35ft; Open May-Sep; Tent & RV camping: $20; Elev: 9036ft/2754m; Tel: 970-945-2521; Nearest town: Frisco. GPS: 39.588008, -106.068794

245 • Pine River

Total sites: 6; RV sites: 6; No water; No toilets; Reservations not accepted; Max length: 20ft; Tent & RV camping: Free; Elev: 7946ft/2422m; Tel: 970-247-4874; Nearest town: Durango; Notes: No large RVs. GPS: 37.447224, -107.505056

246 • Pines

Total sites: 11; RV sites: 11; Central water; Vault toilets; No showers; No RV dump; Reservations not accepted; Max length: 20ft; Open all year; Tent & RV camping: $10; Elev: 9236ft/2815m; Tel: 307-745-2300; Nearest town: Rustic; Notes: Snowmobile/ski access in winter. GPS: 40.491213, -106.007064

247 • Pitkin

Total sites: 22; RV sites: 22; Central water; Vault toilets; No showers; No RV dump; Reservations not accepted; Max length: 35ft; Open May-Sep; Tent & RV camping: $16; Elev: 9400ft/2865m; Tel: 970-641-0471; Nearest town: Pitkin. GPS: 38.610596, -106.501221

248 • Poso

Total sites: 11; RV sites: 11; No water; Vault toilets; Reservations not accepted; Max length: 25ft; Open May-Nov; Tent & RV camping: $5; Elev: 8917ft/2718m; Tel: 719-655-2547; Nearest town: Saguache. GPS: 37.908051, -106.427505

249 • Prairie Point

Total sites: 33; RV sites: 33; Central water; Vault toilets; No showers; No RV dump; Reservations not accepted; Max length: 20ft; Open May-Sep; Tent & RV camping: $18; Elev: 8035ft/2449m; Tel: 970-945-2521; Nearest town: Dillon. GPS: 39.843380, -106.232020

250 • Prospector

Total sites: 106; RV sites: 105; No toilets; Reservations accepted; Max length: 32ft; Open May-Sep; Tent & RV camping: $23-25; Elev: 9137ft/2785m; Tel: 970-945-2521; Nearest town: Dillon. GPS: 39.600101, -106.042848

251 • Purgatoire

Total sites: 23; RV sites: 13; Central water; Vault toilets; No showers; No RV dump; Reservations accepted; Max length: 22ft; Open Jun-Sep; Tent & RV camping: $21; Elev: 9741ft/2969m; Tel: 719-269-8500; Nearest town: La Veta; Notes: 6 equestrian sites. GPS: 37.253372, -105.109783

252 • Quartz

Total sites: 10; RV sites: 10; Central water; Vault toilets; No showers; No RV dump; Reservations not accepted; Open Jun-Sep; Tent & RV camping: $10; Elev: 9888ft/3014m; Tel: 970-641-0471; Nearest town: Pitkin. GPS: 38.638696, -106.468909

253 • Redstone

Total sites: 37; RV sites: 37; Elec sites: 19; Central water; Flush toilets; Showers; No RV dump; Reservations accepted; Open May-Oct; Tents: $32-34/RVs: $32-43; Elev: 7192ft/2192m; Tel: 970-945-2521; Nearest town: Redstone. GPS: 39.200642, -107.231527

254 • Rito Hondo

Total sites: 30; RV sites: 30; No water; Vault toilets; Reservations not accepted; Open all year; Tent & RV camping: Free; Elev: 10253ft/3125m; Tel: 719-852-5941; Nearest town: Creede. GPS: 37.892353, -107.178379

255 • River Hill

Total sites: 23; RV sites: 23; Central water; Vault toilets; No showers; No RV dump; Reservations accepted; Max length: 32ft; Open May-Sep; Tent & RV camping: $26; Elev: 9256ft/2821m; Tel: 719-657-3321; Nearest town: Creede. GPS: 37.730036, -107.228105

256 • Rivers End

Total sites: 15; RV sites: 15; Central water; Vault toilets; No showers; No RV dump; Reservations not accepted; Open May-Sep; Tent & RV camping: $14; Elev: 9360ft/2853m; Tel: 970-641-0471; Nearest town: Almont. GPS: 38.857422, -106.569092

257 • Riverside

Total sites: 18; RV sites: 7; Central water; Vault toilets; No showers; No RV dump; Reservations accepted; Max length: 30ft; Open May-Sep; Tent & RV camping: $17; Elev: 8064ft/2458m; Tel: 719-836-2031; Nearest town: Florissant. GPS: 38.960181, -105.375222

258 • Road Canyon

Total sites: 6; RV sites: 6; No water; Vault toilets; Max length: 25ft; Tent & RV camping: Free; Elev: 9318ft/2840m; Tel: 719-657-3321; Nearest town: Creede. GPS: 37.754996, -107.192111

259 • Robbers Roost

Total sites: 11; RV sites: 11; No water; Vault toilets; Reservations not accepted; Max length: 25ft; Tent & RV camping: $20; Elev: 9797ft/2986m; Tel: 970-887-4100; Nearest town: Winter Park. GPS: 39.831377, -105.756656

260 • Rock Creek (Greenie Mt)

Total sites: 10; RV sites: 10; No water; Vault toilets; Reservations not accepted; Max length: 40ft; Open Apr-Dec; Tent & RV camping: Free; Elev: 9219ft/2810m; Tel: 719-657-3321; Nearest town: Monte Vista. GPS: 37.468506, -106.332275

261 • Rosy Lane

Total sites: 20; RV sites: 20; Elec sites: 1; Central water; Vault toilets; No showers; No RV dump; Reservations accepted; Open May-Sep; Tents: $18/RVs: $18-24; Elev: 8478ft/2584m; Tel: 970-641-0471; Nearest town: Almont. GPS: 38.730671, -106.747618

262 • Round Mountain

Total sites: 15; RV sites: 15; Central water; Vault toilets; No showers; No RV dump; Reservations accepted; Max length: 35ft; Open May-Oct; Tent & RV camping: $17; Elev: 8573ft/2613m; Nearest town: Florissant. GPS: 39.030735, -105.431971

263 • Ruedi Marina

Total sites: 8; RV sites: 8; Central water; Vault toilets; No showers; No RV dump; Reservations accepted; Open May-Sep; Tent & RV camping: $25-27; Elev: 7805ft/2379m; Tel: 970-945-2521; Nearest town: Basalt. GPS: 39.373831, -106.813506

264 • Seedhouse

Total sites: 24; RV sites: 24; Central water; Vault toilets; Reservations accepted; Max length: 22ft; Open Jun-Sep; Tent & RV camping: $12; Elev: 8054ft/2455m; Tel: 970-870-2299; Nearest town: Steamboat Springs. GPS: 40.771809, -106.771771

265 • Selkirk

Total sites: 15; RV sites: 15; No water; Vault toilets; Reservations not accepted; Max length: 25ft; Open May-Sep; Tent & RV camping: $15; Elev: 10522ft/3207m; Tel: 719-836-2031; Nearest town: Fairplay. GPS: 39.371985, -105.951096

266 • Sheriff Reservoir

Total sites: 6; RV sites: 6; No water; Vault toilets; Reservations not accepted; Max length: 18ft; Open Jun-Oct; Tent & RV camping: $10; Elev: 9797ft/2986m; Tel: 307-745-2300; Nearest town: Yampa; Notes: Numerous dispersed sites located along access road suitable for larger RVs. GPS: 40.143685, -107.138939

267 • Sig Creek

Total sites: 9; RV sites: 9; Central water; Vault toilets; No showers; No RV dump; Reservations not accepted; Tent & RV camping: Free; Elev: 9331ft/2844m; Tel: 970-247-4874; Nearest town: Durango. GPS: 37.633704, -107.883662

268 • Silver Bell

Total sites: 14; RV sites: 14; Central water; Vault toilets; No showers; No RV dump; Reservations accepted; Open May-Oct; Tent & RV camping: $15; Elev: 8507ft/2593m; Tel: 970-925-3445; Nearest town: Aspen; Notes: Also walk-to sites. GPS: 39.142579, -106.895261

269 • Silver Dollar

Total sites: 43; RV sites: 43; No toilets; RV dump; Reservations accepted; Max length: 22ft; Open May-Sep; Tent & RV camping: $24; Elev: 9928ft/3026m; Tel: 719-553-1400; Nearest town: Leadville. GPS: 39.259328, -106.352091

270 • Silver Jack

Total sites: 60; RV sites: 60; Central water; Vault toilets; No showers; No RV dump; Reservations not accepted; Max length: 30ft; Open Jun-Sep; Tent & RV camping: $14; Elev: 9121ft/2780m; Tel: 970-874-6600; Nearest town: Cimarron. GPS: 38.236075, -107.537647

271 • Silver Queen

Total sites: 6; RV sites: 6; Central water; Vault toilets; No showers; No RV dump; Reservations accepted; Open May-Oct; Tent & RV camping: $15; Elev: 8727ft/2660m; Tel: 970-945-2521; Nearest town: Aspen. GPS: 39.129071, -106.901885

272 • Silver Thread

Total sites: 10; RV sites: 10; Central water; Vault toilets; No showers; No RV dump; Reservations not accepted; Max length: 30ft; Open all year; Tent & RV camping: $23; Elev: 9739ft/2968m; Tel: 719-657-3321; Nearest town: Creede. GPS: 37.827616, -107.156227

273 • Sleeping Elephant

Total sites: 15; RV sites: 15; No water; Vault toilets; Reservations not accepted; Max length: 20ft; Open Jun-Sep; Tent & RV camping: $19; Elev: 7871ft/2399m; Tel: 970-295-6700; Nearest town: Rustic. GPS: 40.682821, -105.773218

274 • Snowblind

Total sites: 23; RV sites: 23; Central water; Vault toilets; No showers; No RV dump; Reservations not accepted; Max length: 35ft; Open May-Sep; Tent & RV camping: $12; Elev: 9311ft/2838m; Tel: 970-874-6600; Nearest town: Sargents. GPS: 38.520752, -106.415283

275 • Snowslide

Total sites: 13; RV sites: 13; No water; Vault toilets; Reservations not accepted; Max length: 35ft; Tent & RV camping: $16; Elev: 8846ft/2696m; Tel: 970-247-4874; Nearest town: Durango. GPS: 37.370908, -108.078197

276 • Soap Creek

Total sites: 21; RV sites: 21; Central water; Vault toilets; No showers; No RV dump; Reservations not accepted; Open May-Sep; Tent & RV camping: $12; Elev: 7733ft/2357m; Tel: 970-641-0471; Nearest town: Sapeniro. GPS: 38.548103, -107.317784

277 • South Fork (Meadow Creek Lake)

Total sites: 18; RV sites: 18; No water; No toilets; Reservations not accepted; Open May-Oct; Tent & RV camping: $20; Elev: 7753ft/2363m; Tel: 970-945-2521; Nearest town: Meeker. GPS: 39.866699, -107.533936

278 • South Fork (Ute Peak)

Total sites: 21; RV sites: 21; Central water; Vault toilets; No showers; No RV dump; Reservations not accepted; Max length: 23ft; Open Jun-Oct; Tent & RV camping: $19; Elev: 8983ft/2738m; Tel: 970-887-4100; Nearest town: Parshall; Notes: Small corral, Group site $55. GPS: 39.795382, -106.029779

279 • South Meadows

Total sites: 64; RV sites: 62; Central water; Vault toilets; No showers; No RV dump; Reservations accepted; Max length: 36ft; Open May-Oct; Tent & RV camping: $23; Elev: 7907ft/2410m; Tel: 719-686-8816; Nearest town: Woodland Park; Notes: Reduced services in winter. GPS: 39.064711, -105.094156

280 • South Mineral

Total sites: 26; RV sites: 26; Central water; Vault toilets; No showers; No RV dump; Reservations not accepted; Max length: 25ft; Tent & RV camping: Fee unknown; Elev: 9856ft/3004m; Nearest town: Silverton. GPS: 37.804958, -107.775231

281 • Spectacle Lake

Total sites: 24; RV sites: 24; Central water; Vault toilets; No showers; No RV dump; Reservations not accepted; Max length: 25ft; Open May-Sep; Tent & RV camping: $19-23; Elev: 8796ft/2681m; Tel: 719-274-8971; Nearest town: Antonito. GPS: 37.167097, -106.438893

282 • Spillway

Total sites: 23; RV sites: 13; Central water; Vault toilets; No showers; No RV dump; Reservations accepted; Max length: 25ft; Open May-Oct; Tent & RV camping: $17; Elev: 8563ft/2610m; Tel: 719-836-2031; Nearest town: Lake George. GPS: 38.906635, -105.469217

283 • Spring Creek

Total sites: 12; RV sites: 12; Central water; Vault toilets; No showers; No RV dump; Reservations not accepted; Open May-Sep; Tent & RV camping: $14; Elev: 8592ft/2619m; Tel: 970-874-6600; Nearest town: Almont. GPS: 38.749756, -106.767090

284 • Springdale

Total sites: 12; RV sites: 11; No water; Vault toilets; Reservations not accepted; Max length: 25ft; Generator hours: 0600-2200; Open May-Sep; Tent & RV camping: $18; Elev: 9309ft/2837m; Nearest town: Woodland Park. GPS: 38.997422, -105.023611

285 • Springer Gulch

Total sites: 15; RV sites: 12; Central water; Vault toilets; No showers; No RV dump; Reservations accepted; Max length: 25ft; Open May-Sep; Tent & RV camping: $17; Elev: 8304ft/2531m; Tel: 719-836-2031; Nearest town: Lake George. GPS: 38.927216, -105.425345

286 • Spruce

Total sites: 9; RV sites: 9; Central water; Vault toilets; No showers; No RV dump; Reservations not accepted; Max length: 15ft; Open Jun-Oct; Tent & RV camping: Free; Elev: 9346ft/2849m; Tel: 970-641-0471; Nearest town: Lake City. GPS: 38.047277, -107.117029

287 • Spruce Grove (McCurdy Mt)

Total sites: 26; RV sites: 15; Central water; Vault toilets; No showers; No RV dump; Reservations accepted; Max length: 35ft; Open May-Oct; Tent & RV camping: $17; Elev: 8534ft/2601m; Tel: 719-836-2031; Nearest town: Florissant. GPS: 39.137829, -105.462068

288 • Spruce Grove (Mesa Lakes)

Total sites: 16; RV sites: 16; Central water; Vault toilets; No showers; No RV dump; Reservations not accepted; Max length: 45ft; Open May-Sep; Tent & RV camping: $12; Elev: 10033ft/3058m; Tel: 970-874-6600; Nearest town: Mesa. GPS: 39.049064, -108.079269

289 • St Louis Creek

Total sites: 16; RV sites: 16; Central water; Vault toilets; No showers; No RV dump; Reservations not accepted; Max length: 25ft; Open May-Oct; Tent & RV camping: $22; Elev: 8871ft/2704m; Tel: 970-887-4100; Nearest town: Fraser. GPS: 39.924001, -105.859081

290 • Stillwater

Total sites: 129; RV sites: 129; Elec sites: 20; Water at site; Flush toilets; Showers; RV dump; Reservations accepted; Max length: 40ft; Open May-Sep; Tents: $26/RVs: $26-34; Elev: 8340ft/2542m; Tel: 970-887-4100; Nearest town: Granby. GPS: 40.179856, -105.888521

291 • Stone Cellar

Total sites: 6; RV sites: 6; Central water; Vault toilets; No showers; No RV dump; Reservations not accepted; Max length: 25ft; Open May-Nov; Tent & RV camping: $5; Elev: 9498ft/2895m; Tel: 719-655-2547; Nearest town: Saguache. GPS: 38.019018, -106.677487

292 • Storm King

Total sites: 6; RV sites: 6; No water; Vault toilets; Reservations not accepted; Max length: 25ft; Open May-Nov; Tent & RV camping: $5; Elev: 9406ft/2867m; Tel: 719-655-2547; Nearest town: Saguache. GPS: 37.959229, -106.431152

293 • Stove Prairie

Total sites: 9; RV sites: 5; Central water; Vault toilets; No showers; No RV dump; Reservations accepted; Max length: 55ft; Open Jun-Oct; Tent & RV camping: $23; Elev: 6240ft/1902m; Tel: 970-295-6700; Nearest town: Fort Collins; Notes: Also walk-to sites. GPS: 40.683851, -105.396935

294 • Stunner

Total sites: 5; No water; Vault toilets; Reservations not accepted; Max length: 25ft; Open May-Sep; Tents only: Free; Elev: 9866ft/3007m; Tel: 719-274-8971; Nearest town: La Jara. GPS: 37.377803, -106.574129

295 • Sugarloaf

Total sites: 11; RV sites: 11; No water; Vault toilets; Reservations not accepted; Max length: 35ft; Open Jun-Oct; Tent & RV camping: $19; Elev: 8993ft/2741m; Tel: 970-887-4100; Nearest town: Hot Sulphur Springs. GPS: 39.788574, -106.023438

296 • Summit Lake

Total sites: 15; RV sites: 9; No water; Vault toilets; Reservations not accepted; Max length: 18ft; Open Jul-Oct; Tent & RV camping: $10; Elev: 10397ft/3169m; Tel: 307-745-2300; Nearest town: Walden. GPS: 40.546701, -106.683168

297 • Sunset Point

Total sites: 25; RV sites: 25; Central water; Vault toilets; No showers; No RV dump; Reservations not accepted; Max length: 50ft; Open May-Sep; Tent & RV camping: $26; Elev: 8284ft/2525m; Tel: 970-887-4100; Nearest town: Granby. GPS: 40.153827, -105.873874

298 • Sunshine

Total sites: 15; RV sites: 15; Central water; Vault toilets; No showers; No RV dump; Reservations not accepted; Max length: 35ft; Open May-Sep; Tent & RV camping: $18; Elev: 9600ft/2926m; Tel: 970-874-6600; Nearest town: Telluride. GPS: 37.889404, -107.890137

299 • Sweetwater Lake

Total sites: 9; RV sites: 9; Vault toilets; Reservations not accepted; Max length: 30ft; Open Jun-Oct; Tent & RV camping: $8; Elev: 7776ft/2370m; Tel: 970-945-2521; Nearest town: Dotsero. GPS: 39.797000, -107.161000

300 • Tabor

Total sites: 44; RV sites: 44; No toilets; RV dump; Reservations not accepted; Max length: 37ft; Open May-Sep; Tent & RV camping: $24; Elev: 9948ft/3032m; Tel: 719-553-1400; Nearest town: Leadville; Notes: No filling RV tanks. GPS: 39.273561, -106.354795

301 • Target Tree

Total sites: 25; RV sites: 25; Central water; Vault toilets; No showers; No RV dump; Reservations not accepted; Max length: 35ft; Tent & RV camping: $20; Elev: 7805ft/2379m; Tel: 970-882-6800; Nearest town: Mancos; Notes: 5 sites for horse users, 1 group site. GPS: 37.340781, -108.188129

302 • Teal

Total sites: 16; RV sites: 16; Central water; Vault toilets; No showers; No RV dump; Reservations not accepted; Max length: 35ft; Tent & RV camping: Fee unknown; Elev: 8304ft/2531m; Tel: 970-247-4874; Nearest town: Pagosa Springs. GPS: 37.510010, -107.229736

303 • Teal Lake

Total sites: 17; RV sites: 17; No water; Vault toilets; Reservations not accepted; Max length: 25ft; Open Jun-Sep; Tent & RV camping: $10; Elev: 8865ft/2702m; Tel: 307-745-2300; Nearest town: Walden. GPS: 40.585059, -106.607064

304 • The Crags

Total sites: 17; RV sites: 17; Potable water; Vault toilets; No showers; No RV dump; Reservations not accepted; Max length: 20ft; Generator hours: 0600-2200; Open May-Sep; Tent & RV camping: $18; Elev: 10141ft/3091m; Tel: 719-636-1602; Nearest town: Divide; Notes: Small RVs only. GPS: 38.871049, -105.121673

305 • Thirty Mile

Total sites: 39; RV sites: 39; Central water; Vault toilets; No showers; No RV dump; Reservations accepted; Max length: 32ft;

Open May-Sep; Tent & RV camping: $26; Elev: 9334ft/2845m; Tel: 719-852-5941; Nearest town: Creede. GPS: 37.723389, -107.258057

306 • Thistledown

Total sites: 9; No water; Vault toilets; Open May-Oct; Tents only: Free; Elev: 8775ft/2675m; Nearest town: Ouray; Notes: Nothing larger than van/pickup truck, Food storage order. GPS: 37.993402, -107.700366

307 • Thunder Ridge

Total sites: 21; RV sites: 21; Potable water; Vault toilets; No showers; No RV dump; Reservations accepted; Max length: 30ft; Open May-Oct; Tent & RV camping: $23; Elev: 9226ft/2812m; Tel: 719-553-1400; Nearest town: Woodland Park. GPS: 38.977201, -104.982588

308 • Timberline

Total sites: 24; RV sites: 24; No water; Vault toilets; No showers; No RV dump; Reservations accepted; Open May-Sep; Tent & RV camping: $22; Elev: 9854ft/3003m; Tel: 303-275-5610; Nearest town: Denver. GPS: 39.437253, -105.763363

309 • Tom Bennett

Total sites: 10; RV sites: 10; No water; Vault toilets; Reservations not accepted; Max length: 20ft; Open May-Oct; Tent & RV camping: $15; Elev: 8931ft/2722m; Tel: 970-295-6700; Nearest town: Rustic. GPS: 40.575715, -105.584243

310 • Transfer

Total sites: 12; RV sites: 12; Central water; Vault toilets; No showers; No RV dump; Reservations not accepted; Max length: 35ft; Open May-Sep; Tent & RV camping: $20; Elev: 8937ft/2724m; Nearest town: Mancos. GPS: 37.467396, -108.209666

311 • Transfer Park

Total sites: 25; RV sites: 25; Central water; Vault toilets; No showers; No RV dump; Max length: 35ft; Tent & RV camping: Fee unknown; Elev: 8500ft/2591m; Nearest town: Bayfield. GPS: 37.462908, -107.681508

312 • Trappers Lake - Bucks

Total sites: 10; RV sites: 10; Central water; Vault toilets; No showers; RV dump; Reservations not accepted; Open May-Sep; Tent & RV camping: $20; Elev: 9721ft/2963m; Tel: 970-945-2521; Nearest town: Meeker. GPS: 39.993972, -107.239579

313 • Trappers Lake - Cutthroat

Total sites: 14; RV sites: 14; Central water; Vault toilets; No showers; RV dump; Reservations not accepted; Open Jun-Nov; Tent & RV camping: $20-22; Elev: 9787ft/2983m; Tel: 970-945-2521; Nearest town: Meeker. GPS: 39.992656, -107.241705

314 • Trappers Lake - Horse Thief

Total sites: 7; RV sites: 7; Central water; Vault toilets; No showers; RV dump; Reservations not accepted; Max length: 22ft; Open May-Nov; Tent & RV camping: $20-25; Elev: 9784ft/2982m; Tel: 970-945-2521; Nearest town: Meeker; Notes: Horse corrals. GPS: 39.995335, -107.237913

315 • Trappers Lake - Shepherds Rim

Total sites: 16; RV sites: 15; Central water; Vault toilets; No showers; RV dump; Reservations accepted; Open Jun-Oct; Tent & RV camping: $20-22; Elev: 9741ft/2969m; Tel: 970-945-2521; Nearest town: Meeker. GPS: 39.994695, -107.242843

316 • Trappers Lake - Trapline

Total sites: 12; RV sites: 12; Central water; Vault toilets; No showers; RV dump; Reservations not accepted; Open Jun-Sep; Tent & RV camping: $20; Elev: 9767ft/2977m; Tel: 970-945-2521; Nearest town: Meeker. GPS: 39.993389, -107.240825

317 • Trujillo Meadows

Total sites: 50; RV sites: 50; Central water; Vault toilets; No showers; No RV dump; Reservations not accepted; Max length: 25ft; Open Jun-Sep; Tent & RV camping: $26; Elev: 10134ft/3089m; Tel: 719-274-8971; Nearest town: Chama. GPS: 37.046387, -106.449219

318 • Tucker Ponds

Total sites: 16; RV sites: 16; Central water; Vault toilets; No showers; No RV dump; Reservations not accepted; Max length: 35ft; Open Jun-Sep; Tent & RV camping: $19-23; Elev: 9685ft/2952m; Tel: 719-657-3321; Nearest town: South Fork. GPS: 37.494141, -106.761719

319 • Tunnel

Total sites: 49; RV sites: 49; Central water; Vault toilets; No showers; No RV dump; Reservations not accepted; Max length: 40ft; Open Jun-Sep; Tent & RV camping: $22; Elev: 8606ft/2623m; Tel: 970-295-6700; Nearest town: Rustic. GPS: 40.673695, -105.855942

320 • Twin Eagles

Total sites: 9; RV sites: 5; No water; Vault toilets; Reservations not accepted; Max length: 22ft; Open all year; Tent & RV camping: $15; Elev: 8579ft/2615m; Tel: 719 836-2031; Nearest town: Lake George; Notes: Reduced services in winter. GPS: 39.152446, -105.478753

321 • Twin Peaks

Total sites: 39; RV sites: 39; Central water; Vault toilets; Reservations not accepted; Max length: 32ft; Generator hours: 0600-2200; Open May-Sep; Tent & RV camping: $23; Elev: 9682ft/2951m; Tel: 719-553-1400; Nearest town: Twin Lakes; Notes: No filling of RV water tanks allowed. GPS: 39.067871, -106.421387

322 • Upper Beaver Creek

Total sites: 14; RV sites: 14; Central water; Vault toilets; No showers; No RV dump; Reservations not accepted; Max length: 35ft; Open May-Sep; Tent & RV camping: $20-24; Elev: 8632ft/2631m; Tel: 719-657-3321; Nearest town: South Fork. GPS: 37.606235, -106.676941

323 • Upper Narrows

Total sites: 7; RV sites: 7; Central water; Vault toilets; No showers; No RV dump; Reservations accepted; Max length: 30ft; Open May-Sep; Tent & RV camping: $23; Elev: 6539ft/1993m; Tel: 970-295-6700; Nearest town: Fort Collins. GPS: 40.691295, -105.432298

324 • Ute

Total sites: 26; RV sites: 26; Central water; Vault toilets; No showers; No RV dump; Reservations accepted; Open Jun-Sep; Tent & RV camping: $20; Elev: 6870ft/2094m; Nearest town: Pagosa Springs. GPS: 37.215000, -107.273000

325 • Vallecito

Total sites: 80; RV sites: 80; Elec sites: 3; Central water; Vault toilets; No showers; No RV dump; Reservations accepted; Open May-Sep; Tents: $24-25/RVs: $24-32; Elev: 7972ft/2430m; Tel: 970-247-4874; Nearest town: Vallecito. GPS: 37.476391, -107.547461

326 • Vallecito Reservoir - Graham Creek

Total sites: 25; RV sites: 25; Central water; No toilets; No showers; No RV dump; Reservations accepted; Open May-Nov; Tent & RV camping: $22; Elev: 7782ft/2372m; Tel: 970-884-2512; Nearest town: Bayfield; Notes: Steep entrance/exit roads. GPS: 37.390017, -107.539944

327 • Vallecito Reservoir - Middle Mountain

Total sites: 24; RV sites: 24; Central water; Vault toilets; No showers; No RV dump; Reservations not accepted; Max length: 22ft; Tent & RV camping: Fee unknown; Elev: 7812ft/2381m; Tel: 970-884-2512; Nearest town: Bayfield. GPS: 37.409041, -107.536211

328 • Vallecito Reservoir - North Canyon

Total sites: 21; RV sites: 21; No water; Vault toilets; Reservations accepted; Max length: 22ft; Open May-Sep; Tent & RV camping: $20; Elev: 7772ft/2369m; Tel: 970-884-2512; Nearest town: Bayfield. GPS: 37.394158, -107.539195

329 • Vallecito Reservoir - Pine Point

Total sites: 30; RV sites: 30; Central water; Vault toilets; No showers; No RV dump; Reservations accepted; Max length: 22ft; Open May-Sep; Tent & RV camping: $22-25; Elev: 7772ft/2369m; Tel: 970-884-2512; Nearest town: Bayfield. GPS: 37.400009, -107.535291

330 • Vaughn Lake

Total sites: 6; RV sites: 6; No water; Vault toilets; Reservations not accepted; Max length: 18ft; Open all year; Tent & RV camping: $10; Elev: 9518ft/2901m; Tel: 970-638-4516; Nearest town: Yampa; Notes: Reachable only by snowmobile in winter. GPS: 40.134055, -107.261397

331 • Walton Creek

Total sites: 14; RV sites: 14; No toilets; Reservations not accepted; Max length: 22ft; Open Jun-Sep; Tent & RV camping: $12; Elev: 9384ft/2860m; Tel: 970-870-2299; Nearest town: Steamboat Spring. GPS: 40.381896, -106.684823

332 • Ward Lake

Total sites: 27; RV sites: 27; Central water; Vault toilets; No showers; No RV dump; Reservations not accepted; Max length: 45ft; Open May-Sep; Tent & RV camping: $16; Elev: 10143ft/3092m; Tel: 970-874-6600; Nearest town: Cedaredge; Notes: Food storage order. GPS: 39.036837, -107.984478

333 • Weir and Johnson

Total sites: 12; RV sites: 12; No water; Vault toilets; Reservations not accepted; Max length: 22ft; Open May-Sep; Tent & RV camping: $14; Elev: 10508ft/3203m; Tel: 970-874-6600; Nearest town: Collbran. GPS: 39.066162, -107.831787

334 • Weller

Total sites: 11; RV sites: 11; Central water; Vault toilets; No showers; No RV dump; Reservations not accepted; Open May-Sep; Tent & RV camping: $21; Elev: 9485ft/2891m; Tel: 970-945-2521; Nearest town: Aspen. GPS: 39.121205, -106.720218

335 • West Chicago Creek

Total sites: 15; RV sites: 15; Central water; Vault toilets; No showers; No RV dump; Reservations accepted; Max length: 30ft; Open May-Sep; Tent & RV camping: $20; Elev: 9629ft/2935m; Tel: 303-567-3000; Nearest town: Idaho Springs. GPS: 39.678708, -105.657846

336 • West Dolores

Total sites: 18; RV sites: 18; Elec sites: 7; Central water; Vault toilets; No showers; No RV dump; Reservations accepted; Max length: 35ft; Open May-Sep; Tents: $24/RVs: $24-32; Elev: 7825ft/2385m; Tel: 970-882-7296; Nearest town: Dolores. GPS: 37.659668, -108.275635

337 • West Fork

Total sites: 28; RV sites: 28; Central water; Vault toilets; No showers; No RV dump; Reservations accepted; Max length: 35ft; Open May-Sep; Tent & RV camping: $22; Elev: 7930ft/2417m; Tel: 661-702-1420; Nearest town: Pagosa Springs. GPS: 37.446045, -106.908447

338 • West Lake

Total sites: 36; RV sites: 31; Elec sites: 31; Central water; Vault toilets; No showers; No RV dump; Reservations accepted; Max length: 50ft; Open May-Sep; Tents: $24/RVs: $24-32; Elev: 8238ft/2511m; Tel: 970-295-6700; Nearest town: Red Feather Lakes. GPS: 40.789795, -105.567627

339 • Weston Pass

Total sites: 14; RV sites: 12; Central water; Vault toilets; No showers; No RV dump; Reservations not accepted; Max length: 25ft; Open May-Sep; Tent & RV camping: $15; Elev: 10302ft/3140m; Tel: 719 836-2031; Nearest town: Fairplay. GPS: 39.078119, -106.136385

340 • Whitestar

Total sites: 68; RV sites: 68; Central water; No toilets; No showers; No RV dump; Reservations accepted; Max length: 32ft; Open May-Sep; Tent & RV camping: $23-24; Elev: 9258ft/2822m; Tel: 719-486-0749; Nearest town: Twin Lakes. GPS: 39.090031, -106.366723

341 • Williams Creek (Mesa)

Total sites: 23; RV sites: 23; Central water; Vault toilets; No showers; RV dump; Reservations not accepted; Max length: 32ft; Open May-Oct; Tent & RV camping: $14; Elev: 9219ft/2810m; Nearest town: Pagosa Springs. GPS: 37.921942, -107.335923

342 • Williams Creek (San Juan)

Total sites: 61; RV sites: 58; Central water; Vault toilets; No showers; RV dump; Reservations accepted; Open May-Sep; Tents: $25/RVs: $25-32; Elev: 8228ft/2508m; Tel: 970-585-1200; Nearest town: Pagosa Springs. GPS: 37.495559, -107.226359

343 • Willow Creek Reservoir

Total sites: 35; RV sites: 35; Central water; Vault toilets; No showers; No RV dump; Reservations not accepted; Max length: 25ft; Open May-Oct; Tent & RV camping: $23; Elev: 8173ft/2491m; Tel: 970-887-4100; Nearest town: Granby. GPS: 40.143308, -105.952198

344 • Willows

Total sites: 35; RV sites: 35; Central water; Vault toilets; No showers; No RV dump; Reservations not accepted; Open May-Oct; Tent & RV camping: $18; Elev: 7966ft/2428m; Tel: 970-945-2521; Nearest town: Silverthorne. GPS: 39.889284, -106.309259

345 • Woods Lake

Total sites: 41; RV sites: 41; Central water; Vault toilets; No showers; No RV dump; Reservations not accepted; Open May-Oct; Tent & RV camping: $16-18; Elev: 9403ft/2866m; Tel: 970-874-6600; Nearest town: Placerville; Notes: 5 horse sites. GPS: 37.886284, -108.055604

346 • Yeoman Park

Total sites: 24; RV sites: 24; Central water; Vault toilets; No showers; No RV dump; Reservations not accepted; Max length: 30ft; Open Jun-Sep; Tent & RV camping: $8; Elev: 9078ft/2767m; Tel: 970-945-2521; Nearest town: Eagle; Notes: Food storage order. GPS: 39.501671, -106.677029

Florida

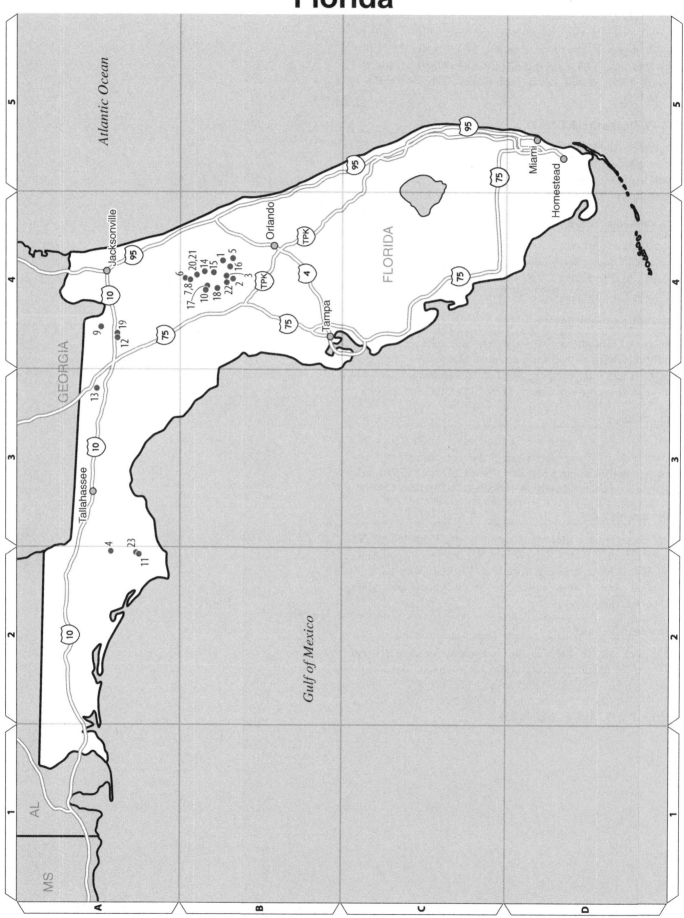

Florida Camping Areas

1 • Alexander Springs

Total sites: 66; RV sites: 66; Central water; Flush toilets; Showers; RV dump; Reservations accepted; Open all year; Tent & RV camping: $24; Elev: 59ft/18m; Tel: 352-669-3522; Nearest town: Altoona. GPS: 29.080078, -81.578125

2 • Big Bass Lake Rec Area

Total sites: 34; RV sites: 34; Central water; Vault toilets; No showers; RV dump; Reservations not accepted; Stay limit: 14 days; Open Oct-Apr; Tent & RV camping: $15; Elev: 97ft/30m; Nearest town: Altoona. GPS: 28.985894, -81.784419

3 • Big Scrub

Total sites: 48; RV sites: 48; Elec sites: 2; Central water; Flush toilets; Showers; No RV dump; Reservations accepted; Stay limit: 14 days; Open all year; Tents: $20/RVs: $20-30; Elev: 171ft/52m; Tel: 352-625-2520; Nearest town: Umatilla. GPS: 29.050537, -81.755615

4 • Camel Lake

Total sites: 10; RV sites: 3; Elec sites: 5; Water at site; Flush toilets; Showers; No RV dump; Reservations accepted; Open all year; Tents: $20/RVs: $20-30; Elev: 102ft/31m; Tel: 850-643-2282; Nearest town: Bristol. GPS: 30.276629, -84.987302

5 • Clearwater Lake

Total sites: 25; RV sites: 25; Central water; Flush toilets; Showers; RV dump; Reservations accepted; Open all year; Tent & RV camping: $23; Elev: 131ft/40m; Tel: 352-669-0078; Nearest town: Paisley. GPS: 28.979611, -81.553523

6 • Davenport Landing

Total sites: 3; No water; No toilets; Stay limit: 14 days; Open all year; Tents only: Free; Elev: 62ft/19m; Nearest town: Possum Bluff. GPS: 29.472265, -81.773457

7 • Delancey East

Total sites: 29; RV sites: 29; Central water; Vault toilets; No showers; No RV dump; Reservations not accepted; Stay limit: 14 days; Open Oct-Jun; Tent & RV camping: $15; Elev: 33ft/10m; Nearest town: Salt Springs. GPS: 29.430317, -81.786039

8 • Delancey West

Total sites: 30; RV sites: 30; No water; Vault toilets; Reservations not accepted; Stay limit: 14 days; Open all year; Tent & RV camping: $5; Elev: 29ft/9m; Nearest town: Salt Springs. GPS: 29.428051, -81.788953

9 • East Tower Hunt Camp

Total sites: 15; Central water; Vault toilets; No showers; No RV dump; Open all year; Tents only: Free; Elev: 112ft/34m; Tel: 386-752-2577; Nearest town: Sanderson. GPS: 30.382955, -82.330369

10 • Fore Lake

Total sites: 30; RV sites: 30; Central water; Flush toilets; Showers; RV dump; Stay limit: 14 days; Open all year; Tent & RV camping: $20; Elev: 105ft/32m; Nearest town: Ocala. GPS: 29.270508, -81.917969

11 • Hickory Landing Hunt Camp

Total sites: 10; RV sites: 10; Central water; Vault toilets; No showers; No RV dump; Reservations not accepted; Generator hours: 0600-2200; Open all year; Tent & RV camping: $10; Elev: 30ft/9m; Nearest town: Sumatra. GPS: 29.988825, -85.012969

12 • Hog Pen Landing

Total sites: 8; RV sites: 8; No water; Vault toilets; Reservations not accepted; Max length: 24ft; Open all year; Tent & RV camping: $10; Elev: 131ft/40m; Tel: 386-752-2577; Nearest town: Olustee. GPS: 30.237888, -82.449417

13 • Holton Creek - FT

Total sites: 12; No water; No toilets; Reservations not accepted; Open all year; Tents only: Free; Elev: 61ft/19m; Tel: 352-378-8823; Nearest town: Live Oak. GPS: 30.437202, -83.055779

14 • Hopkins Prairie

Total sites: 21; RV sites: 21; Central water; Vault toilets; No showers; No RV dump; Reservations not accepted; Stay limit: 14 days; Open Oct-May; Tent & RV camping: $15; Elev: 56ft/17m; Nearest town: Ocala. GPS: 29.275500, -81.693700

15 • Juniper Springs

Total sites: 78; RV sites: 59; Central water; Flush toilets; Showers; RV dump; Reservations accepted; Generator hours: 0600-2200; Open all year; Tent & RV camping: $25; Elev: 69ft/21m; Tel: 352-625-3147; Nearest town: Salt Springs. GPS: 29.182373, -81.712402

16 • Lake Dorr

Total sites: 34; RV sites: 32; Central water; Flush toilets; Showers; No RV dump; Reservations not accepted; Stay limit: 14 days; Open all year; Tent & RV camping: $20; Elev: 62ft/19m; Nearest town: Umatilla. GPS: 29.012927, -81.635559

17 • Lake Eaton

Total sites: 14; RV sites: 14; No water; Vault toilets; Reservations not accepted; Stay limit: 14 days; Open Oct-May; Tent & RV camping: $10; Elev: 43ft/13m; Nearest town: Ocala. GPS: 29.254187, -81.865303

18 • Little Lake Bryant

Total sites: 6; No water; No toilets; Open all year; Tents only: Free; Elev: 62ft/19m; Nearest town: Silver Springs. GPS: 29.143658, -81.898461

19 • Ocean Pond

Total sites: 67; RV sites: 67; Elec sites: 19; Water at site; Flush toilets; Showers; Laundry; RV dump; Reservations not accepted; Open all year; Tents: $8/RVs: $18-20; Elev: 131ft/40m; Nearest town: Lake City. GPS: 30.239326, -82.433856

20 • Salt Springs RV Area

Total sites: 98; RV sites: 98; Elec sites: 98; Water at site; Flush toilets; Showers; RV dump; Reservations accepted; Open all year; No tents/RVs: $34; Elev: 69ft/21m; Tel: 352-685-2048; Nearest town: Ocala; Notes: 98 FHU. GPS: 29.357342, -81.732211

21 • Salt Springs Tent Area

Total sites: 52; Reservations accepted; Open all year; Tents only: $23; Elev: 15ft/5m; Tel: 352-685-2048; Nearest town: Ocala. GPS: 29.354063, -81.731572

22 • Trout Pond

Total sites: 2; No water; No toilets; Stay limit: 14 days; Tents only: Free; Elev: 65ft/20m; Tel: 352-236-0288; Nearest town: Altoona. GPS: 29.051768, -81.828456

23 • Wright Lake

Total sites: 19; RV sites: 19; Elec sites: 1; Central water; Flush toilets; Showers; RV dump; Stay limit: 14 days; Open all year; Tents: $20/RVs: $20-30; Elev: 33ft/10m; Nearest town: Bristol. GPS: 30.000359, -85.002318

Georgia

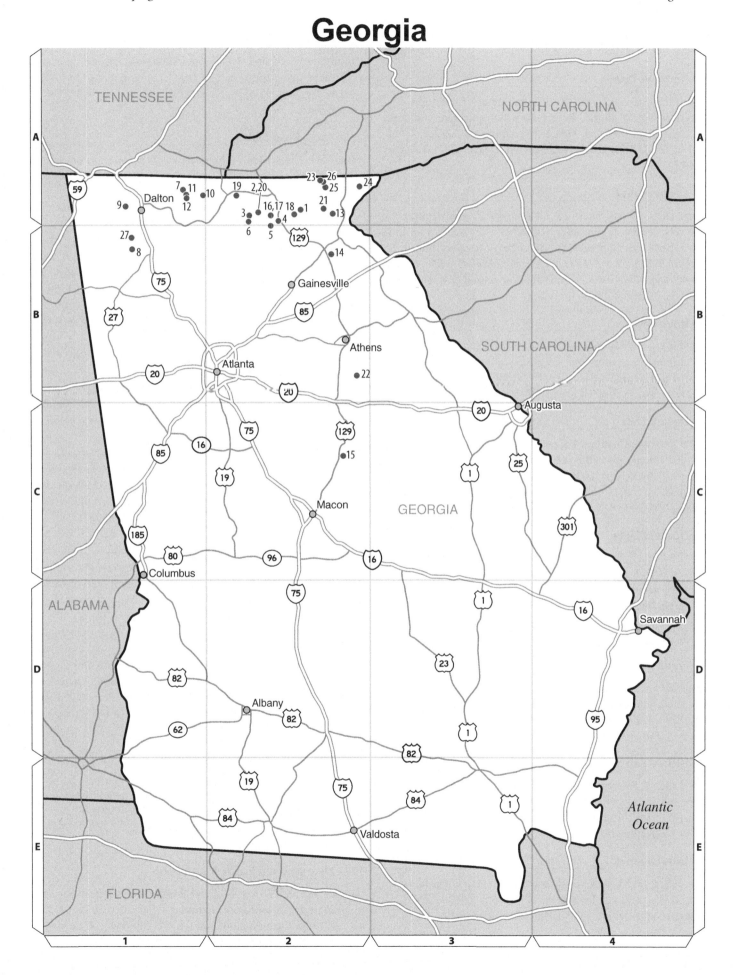

Georgia Camping Areas

1 • Andrews Cove

Total sites: 10; RV sites: 10; Central water; Vault toilets; No showers; No RV dump; Reservations not accepted; Stay limit: 14 days; Open Mar-Oct; Tent & RV camping: $12; Elev: 2136ft/651m; Tel: 770-297-3000; Nearest town: Helen. GPS: 34.777993, -83.737357

2 • Cooper Creek

Total sites: 15; RV sites: 15; Central water; Vault toilets; No showers; No RV dump; Reservations not accepted; Stay limit: 14 days; Generator hours: 0600-2200; Open Mar-Dec; Tent & RV camping: $15; Elev: 2171ft/662m; Tel: 706-745-6928; Nearest town: Blairsville; Notes: 1/2 off mid-Nov to mid-Mar - no water. GPS: 34.762852, -84.068016

3 • Deep Hole

Total sites: 8; RV sites: 8; No water; Vault toilets; No showers; No RV dump; Reservations not accepted; Stay limit: 14 days; Open all year; Tents: $15/RVs: $16; Elev: 1996ft/608m; Tel: 706-745-6928; Nearest town: Suches. GPS: 34.739741, -84.140595

4 • Desoto Falls

Total sites: 24; RV sites: 24; Central water; Flush toilets; Showers; No RV dump; Stay limit: 14 days; Open all year; Tent & RV camping: $20; Elev: 2083ft/635m; Tel: 706-745-6928; Nearest town: Cleveland; Notes: 1/2 off mid-Nov to mid-Mar - no water. GPS: 34.707266, -83.915153

5 • Dockery Lake

Total sites: 11; RV sites: 11; Central water; Flush toilets; No showers; No RV dump; Reservations not accepted; Stay limit: 14 days; Generator hours: 0600-2200; Open Mar-Dec; Tent & RV camping: $8; Elev: 2461ft/750m; Tel: 706-745-6928; Nearest town: Dahlonega; Notes: 1/2 off mid-Nov through Dec - no water. GPS: 34.675224, -83.974102

6 • Frank Gross

Total sites: 9; RV sites: 9; No water; Vault toilets; Reservations not accepted; Stay limit: 14 days; Open Mar-Nov; Tent & RV camping: $8; Elev: 2248ft/685m; Tel: 706-745-6928; Nearest town: Blue Ridge. GPS: 34.701251, -84.149148

7 • Hickey Gap

Total sites: 5; RV sites: 5; No water; Vault toilets; Reservations not accepted; Max length: 24ft; Generator hours: 0600-2200; Open all year; Tent & RV camping: Free; Elev: 1919ft/585m; Tel: 706-695-6736; Nearest town: Chatsworth. GPS: 34.894086, -84.672397

8 • Hidden Creek

Total sites: 15; RV sites: 15; No water; No toilets; Open May-Oct; Tent & RV camping: Free; Elev: 938ft/286m; Tel: 706-397-2265; Nearest town: Calhoun. GPS: 34.514997, -85.074019

9 • Houston Valley OHV

Total sites: 3; RV sites: 3; No water; Vault toilets; Reservations not accepted; Open Apr-Dec; Tent & RV camping: Free; Elev: 988ft/301m; Tel: 706-695-6736; Nearest town: Dalton. GPS: 34.788855, -85.129528

10 • Jacks River Fields

Total sites: 7; RV sites: 7; No water; Vault toilets; Reservations not accepted; Max length: 24ft; Generator hours: 0600-2200; Open all year; Tent & RV camping: $5; Elev: 2756ft/840m; Tel: 706-695-6736; Nearest town: Blue Ridge; Notes: Jan-Mar accessible only from Blue Ridge GA. GPS: 34.863374, -84.519984

11 • Lake Conasauga

Total sites: 31; RV sites: 31; Central water; Flush toilets; No showers; No RV dump; Reservations not accepted; Stay limit: 14 days; Open Apr-Oct; Tent & RV camping: $15; Elev: 3205ft/977m; Tel: 706-695-6736; Nearest town: Crandall. GPS: 34.860644, -84.649885

12 • Lake Conasauga Overflow

Total sites: 6; No water; Vault toilets; Reservations not accepted; Open Mar-Dec; Tents only: $8; Elev: 3266ft/995m; Tel: 706-695-6736; Nearest town: Chatsworth. GPS: 34.853937, -84.649466

13 • Lake Rabun Beach

Total sites: 80; RV sites: 80; Elec sites: 21; Water at site; Flush toilets; Showers; RV dump; Reservations accepted; Open Apr-Oct; Tents: $18/RVs: $29; Elev: 1775ft/541m; Tel: 706-754-6221; Nearest town: Clarkesville. GPS: 34.755182, -83.480393

14 • Lake Russell

Total sites: 40; RV sites: 40; Central water; Flush toilets; Showers; RV dump; Max length: 26ft; Open Apr-Oct; Tent & RV camping: $18; Elev: 1109ft/338m; Tel: 706-754-6221; Nearest town: Mount Airy. GPS: 34.493261, -83.495074

15 • Lake Sinclair

Total sites: 44; RV sites: 44; Elec sites: 6; Water at site; Flush toilets; Showers; RV dump; Reservations not accepted; Generators prohibited; Open all year; Tents: $9/RVs: $9-15; Elev: 407ft/124m; Tel: 706-485-7110; Nearest town: Eatonton; Notes: Group site: $80. GPS: 33.206635, -83.398261

16 • Lake Winfield Scott - North Loop

Total sites: 17; RV sites: 17; Central water; Flush toilets; Showers; No RV dump; Reservations not accepted; Open all year; Tents: $18/RVs: $18-25; Elev: 2995ft/913m; Tel: 706-455-0342; Nearest town: Suches; Notes: Cabin(s), Group site: $45. GPS: 34.742490, -83.968310

17 • Lake Winfield Scott - South Loop

Total sites: 14; RV sites: 14; Central water; Flush toilets; Showers; No RV dump; Reservation required; Open all year; Tents: $18/RVs: $18-25; Elev: 2905ft/885m; Tel: 706-455-0342; Nearest town: Suches; Notes: Cabin(s). GPS: 34.734549, -83.972994

18 • Low Gap

Total sites: 13; RV sites: 13; Central water; Vault toilets; No showers; No RV dump; Reservations not accepted; Max length: 28ft; Stay limit: 14 days; Generator hours: 0700-2200; Open Mar-Oct; Tent & RV camping: $12; Elev: 1815ft/553m; Tel: 706-754-6221; Nearest town: Helen; Notes: Narrow steep winding access road. GPS: 34.752102, -83.785691

19 • Morganton Point

Total sites: 42; RV sites: 36; Central water; Flush toilets; Showers; No RV dump; Reservations accepted; Open Apr-Nov; Tents: $18/RVs: $18-27; Elev: 1758ft/536m; Tel: 706-455-0342; Nearest town: Morganton; Notes: Outdoor showers. GPS: 34.869214, -84.248256

20 • Mulky

Total sites: 11; RV sites: 11; Central water; Vault toilets; No showers; No RV dump; Reservations not accepted; Stay limit: 14 days; Open all year; Tent & RV camping: $15; Elev: 2160ft/658m; Tel: 706-745-6928; Nearest town: Morganton; Notes: Half price mid-Nov to mid-Mar when water is off. GPS: 34.761802, -84.073087

21 • Oakey Mountain

Total sites: 6; RV sites: 6; Central water; Vault toilets; No showers; No RV dump; Reservations not accepted; Open Mar-Dec; Tent & RV camping: $10; Elev: 2320ft/707m; Tel: 770-297-3000; Nearest town: Clayton; Notes: Steep narrow road - no large RVs. GPS: 34.784117, -83.554331

22 • Oconee River

Total sites: 5; No water; Vault toilets; Reservations not accepted; Generators prohibited; Open all year; Tents only: $5; Elev: 452ft/138m; Tel: 706-485-7110; Nearest town: Greensboro. GPS: 33.721501, -83.290675

23 • Sandy Bottoms

Total sites: 14; RV sites: 14; Central water; Vault toilets; No showers; No RV dump; Reservations not accepted; Stay limit: 14 days; Generator hours: 0700-2200; Open Mar-Oct; Tent & RV camping: $15; Elev: 2480ft/756m; Tel: 706-754-6221; Nearest town: Clayton. GPS: 34.960809, -83.557585

24 • Sarahs Creek

Total sites: 26; RV sites: 26; No water; Vault toilets; Reservations not accepted; Stay limit: 14 days; Generator hours: 0700-2200; Open all year; Tent & RV camping: $10; Elev: 2093ft/638m; Tel: 706-754-6221; Nearest town: Clayton. GPS: 34.925877, -83.262862

25 • Tallulah River

Total sites: 17; RV sites: 17; Central water; Vault toilets; No showers; No RV dump; Reservations not accepted; Stay limit: 14 days; Open all year; Tent & RV camping: $15; Elev: 2119ft/646m; Tel: 770-297-3000; Nearest town: Clayton. GPS: 34.927395, -83.544111

26 • Tate Branch

Total sites: 19; RV sites: 19; Central water; Vault toilets; No showers; No RV dump; Reservations not accepted; Stay limit: 14 days; Open Mar-Oct; Tent & RV camping: $15; Elev: 2385ft/727m; Tel: 706-754-6221; Nearest town: Clayton. GPS: 34.955176, -83.552405

27 • The Pocket

Total sites: 26; RV sites: 26; Central water; No toilets; No showers; No RV dump; Reservations not accepted; Stay limit: 14 days; Open Apr-Oct; Tent & RV camping: $15; Elev: 935ft/285m; Tel: 706-695-6736; Nearest town: Dalton. GPS: 34.585532, -85.083369

Idaho

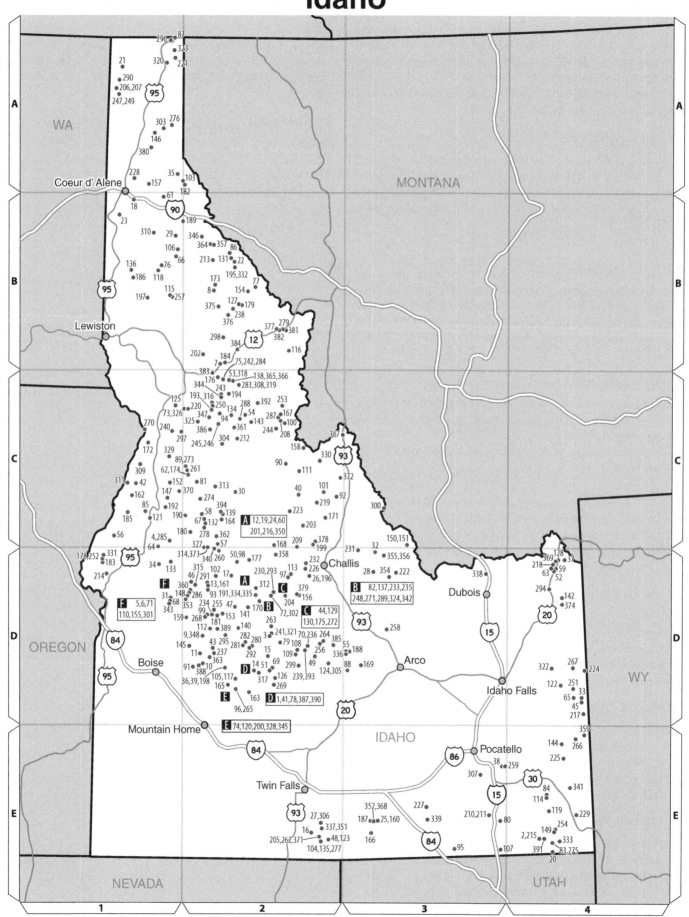

Idaho Camping Areas

1 • Abbott

Total sites: 7; RV sites: 7; No water; Vault toilets; Reservations not accepted; Open May-Oct; Tent & RV camping: $6; Elev: 4701ft/ 1433m; Tel: 208-764-3202; Nearest town: Featherville. GPS: 43.607925, -115.217813

2 • Albert Moser

Total sites: 9; RV sites: 9; Central water; Vault toilets; No showers; No RV dump; Reservations accepted; Max length: 20ft; Open May-Sep; Tent & RV camping: $14; Elev: 5328ft/1624m; Tel: 208-847-0375; Nearest town: Preston. GPS: 42.138463, -111.694053

3 • Alturas Inlet

Total sites: 28; RV sites: 28; Central water; Vault toilets; No showers; No RV dump; Reservations accepted; Max length: 32ft; Stay limit: 10 days; Open Jun-Sep; Tent & RV camping: $15; Elev: 7050ft/2149m; Tel: 208-727-5000; Nearest town: Obsidian. GPS: 43.905057, -114.880569

4 • Amanita

Total sites: 10; RV sites: 10; Central water; Vault toilets; No showers; No RV dump; Reservations accepted; Open May-Sep; Tent & RV camping: $15; Elev: 4836ft/1474m; Tel: 208-382-7400; Nearest town: Donnelly. GPS: 44.701811, -116.131199

5 • Antelope

Total sites: 20; RV sites: 20; Central water; Vault toilets; No showers; No RV dump; Reservations accepted; Open May-Oct; Tent & RV camping: $15; Elev: 5082ft/1549m; Tel: 208-365-7000; Nearest town: Cascade; Notes: Group site $64. GPS: 44.335232, -116.186181

6 • Antelope Annex

Total sites: 8; RV sites: 8; No water; Vault toilets; Reservations not accepted; Max length: 20ft; Open May-Sep; Tent & RV camping: $15; Elev: 5001ft/1524m; Tel: 208-365-7000; Nearest town: Emmett. GPS: 44.337534, -116.188409

7 • Apgar

Total sites: 7; RV sites: 7; Central water; Vault toilets; No showers; No RV dump; Reservations not accepted; Max length: 24ft; Open May-Sep; Tent & RV camping: $14; Elev: 1618ft/493m; Tel: 208-926-4274; Nearest town: Lowell. GPS: 46.213729, -115.536871

8 • Aquarius

Total sites: 7; RV sites: 7; No water; Vault toilets; Reservations not accepted; Max length: 22ft; Open May-Oct; Tent & RV camping: $10; Elev: 1850ft/564m; Tel: 208-476-4541; Nearest town: Headquarters; Notes: 2 group sites (Purple Beach). GPS: 46.840911, -115.617109

9 • Bad Bear

Total sites: 6; RV sites: 6; Central water; Vault toilets; No showers; No RV dump; Reservations accepted; Open May-Sep; Tent & RV camping: $15; Elev: 5076ft/1547m; Tel: 208-392-6681; Nearest town: Idaho City. GPS: 43.901323, -115.708278

10 • Badger Creek

Total sites: 5; RV sites: 5; No water; Vault toilets; Reservations not accepted; Open May-Sep; Tent & RV camping: Free; Elev: 3346ft/ 1020m; Tel: 208-587-7961; Nearest town: Boise; Notes: Narrow rough road. GPS: 43.661985, -115.711797

11 • Bald Mountain

Total sites: 4; RV sites: 4; No water; Vault toilets; Reservations not accepted; Open Jul-Sep; Tent & RV camping: Free; Elev: 6794ft/2071m; Tel: 208-392-6681; Nearest town: Idaho City. GPS: 43.749168, -115.737703

12 • Banner Creek

Total sites: 5; RV sites: 5; No water; Vault toilets; Reservations not accepted; Max length: 16ft; Open Jun-Oct; Tent & RV camping: $5; Elev: 6690ft/2039m; Tel: 208-879-4101; Nearest town: Stanley. GPS: 44.353385, -115.214278

13 • Barney's

Total sites: 8; RV sites: 8; Central water; Vault toilets; No showers; No RV dump; Reservations accepted; Max length: 22ft; Open Jun-Oct; Tent & RV camping: $12; Elev: 5354ft/1632m; Tel: 208-259-3361; Nearest town: Lowman. GPS: 44.326147, -115.649221

14 • Baumgartner

Total sites: 39; RV sites: 39; Central water; Vault toilets; No showers; No RV dump; Reservations accepted; Open May-Sep; Tent & RV camping: $10; Elev: 4931ft/1503m; Tel: 208-764-3202; Nearest town: Featherville; Notes: Group site $40-$100. GPS: 43.605734, -115.076137

15 • Bear Creek Transfer Camp

Total sites: 6; RV sites: 6; No water; Vault toilets; Reservations not accepted; Open May-Oct; Tent & RV camping: Free; Elev: 6083ft/ 1854m; Nearest town: Fairfield. GPS: 43.726289, -114.904914

16 • Bear Gulch (Hopper Gulch)

Total sites: 8; RV sites: 8; No water; Vault toilets; Reservations not accepted; Stay limit: 14 days; Open May-Oct; Tent & RV camping: Free; Elev: 6017ft/1834m; Tel: 208-678-0439; Nearest town: Burley. GPS: 42.227454, -114.378672

17 • Bear Valley

Total sites: 6; RV sites: 6; No water; Vault toilets; Reservations not accepted; Open Jun-Sep; Tent & RV camping: Free; Elev: 6414ft/1955m; Tel: 208-259-3361; Nearest town: Stanley. GPS: 44.410971, -115.369787

18 • Beauty Creek

Total sites: 19; RV sites: 11; Central water; Vault toilets; No showers; No RV dump; Reservations accepted; Open May-Sep; Tent & RV camping: $23; Elev: 2398ft/731m; Tel: 208-664-2318; Nearest town: Coeur d'Alene. GPS: 47.606364, -116.667582

19 • Beaver Creek (Cape Horn)

Total sites: 8; RV sites: 8; Central water; Vault toilets; No showers; No RV dump; Reservations not accepted; Max length: 32ft; Open

Jun-Sep; Tent & RV camping: $10; Elev: 6568ft/2002m; Tel: 208-879-4101; Nearest town: Stanley. GPS: 44.414254, -115.146931

20 • Beaver Creek (Egan Basin)

Total sites: 5; RV sites: 5; No water; Vault toilets; Reservations not accepted; Open Jun-Sep; Tent & RV camping: $8; Elev: 7812ft/2381m; Tel: 208-847-0375; Nearest town: St Charles. GPS: 42.020719, -111.529289

21 • Beaver Creek (Priest Lake)

Total sites: 42; RV sites: 42; Central water; Vault toilets; No showers; No RV dump; Reservations accepted; Open May-Sep; Tent & RV camping: $23; Elev: 2507ft/764m; Tel: 208-443-1801; Nearest town: Priest Lake; Notes: Group site: $75. GPS: 48.734845, -116.860511

22 • Beaver Creek (Red Ives)

Total sites: 2; RV sites: 2; No water; Vault toilets; Tent & RV camping: Fee unknown; Elev: 3635ft/1108m. GPS: 47.083039, -115.355303

23 • Bell Bay

Total sites: 26; RV sites: 26; Central water; Vault toilets; No showers; No RV dump; Reservations accepted; Stay limit: 14 days; Open May-Sep; Tent & RV camping: $21; Elev: 2369ft/722m; Tel: 208-689-9636; Nearest town: Coeur D'Alene; Notes: Group site $98. GPS: 47.474067, -116.845317

24 • Bench Creek

Total sites: 5; RV sites: 5; No water; Vault toilets; Reservations not accepted; Max length: 16ft; Open Jun-Sep; Tent & RV camping: $5; Elev: 6965ft/2123m; Tel: 208-879-4101; Nearest town: Stanley. GPS: 44.319549, -115.235385

25 • Bennett Springs

Total sites: 6; RV sites: 6; No water; Vault toilets; Reservations not accepted; Stay limit: 14 days; Open Jun-Oct; Tent & RV camping: Free; Elev: 7421ft/2262m; Tel: 208-678-0439; Nearest town: Burley. GPS: 42.326496, -113.601639

26 • Big Bayhorse

Total sites: 10; RV sites: 10; No water; Vault toilets; Reservations not accepted; Max length: 32ft; Open Jul-Oct; Tent & RV camping: Free; Elev: 8665ft/2641m; Tel: 208-879-4100; Nearest town: Stanley; Notes: Narrow steep dirt road. GPS: 44.410177, -114.398127

27 • Big Bluff

Total sites: 3; No water; No toilets; Reservations not accepted; Stay limit: 14 days; Tents only: Free; Elev: 4921ft/1500m; Tel: 208-678-0430; Nearest town: Steer Basin. GPS: 42.310438, -114.260199

28 • Big Creek (Big Creek Peak)

Total sites: 3; RV sites: 3; No water; Vault toilets; Reservations not accepted; Max length: 16ft; Open May-Sep; Tent & RV camping: Free; Elev: 6657ft/2029m; Tel: 208-879-4100; Nearest town: Challis. GPS: 44.441716, -113.598972

29 • Big Creek (Marble Creek)

Total sites: 9; RV sites: 9; Central water; Vault toilets; No showers; No RV dump; Reservations not accepted; Open May-Sep; Tent & RV camping: Free; Elev: 2444ft/745m; Nearest town: St. Maries. GPS: 47.303456, -116.120193

30 • Big Creek Airstrip

Total sites: 4; RV sites: 4; No water; Vault toilets; Reservations not accepted; Tent & RV camping: $10; Elev: 5718ft/1743m; Tel: 208-634-0600; Nearest town: Yellow Pine. GPS: 45.127987, -115.322785

31 • Big Eddy

Total sites: 4; RV sites: 4; No water; Vault toilets; Reservations not accepted; Max length: 30ft; Open May-Oct; Tent & RV camping: $15; Elev: 4134ft/1260m; Tel: 208-365-7000; Nearest town: Banks. GPS: 44.220378, -116.106772

32 • Big Eightmile

Total sites: 10; RV sites: 10; Central water; Vault toilets; No showers; No RV dump; Reservations not accepted; Open May-Sep; Tent & RV camping: Free; Elev: 7546ft/2300m; Tel: 208-768-2500; Nearest town: Leadore. GPS: 44.608583, -113.577099

33 • Big Elk

Total sites: 15; RV sites: 15; Central water; Vault toilets; No showers; No RV dump; Reservations not accepted; Open May-Sep; Tent & RV camping: $12; Elev: 5676ft/1730m; Tel: 208-523-1412; Nearest town: Irwin; Notes: Reservable group site $50. GPS: 43.322344, -111.117521

34 • Big Flat

Total sites: 12; RV sites: 12; Central water; Vault toilets; No showers; No RV dump; Reservations not accepted; Tent & RV camping: $10; Elev: 4154ft/1266m; Tel: 208 253-0100; Nearest town: Cambridge; Notes: Windy narrow gravel road. GPS: 44.500841, -116.259733

35 • Big Hank

Total sites: 30; RV sites: 30; Central water; Vault toilets; No showers; No RV dump; Reservations accepted; Stay limit: 14 days; Open May-Sep; Tent & RV camping: $21; Elev: 2759ft/841m; Tel: 208-664-2318; Nearest town: Kingston. GPS: 47.824038, -116.101334

36 • Big Roaring River Lake

Total sites: 12; RV sites: 12; Central water; Vault toilets; No showers; No RV dump; Reservations not accepted; Tent & RV camping: $10; Elev: 8107ft/2471m; Tel: 208-587-7961; Nearest town: Pine. GPS: 43.620629, -115.444039

37 • Big Springs

Total sites: 15; RV sites: 15; Potable water; Vault toilets; No showers; No RV dump; Reservations not accepted; Open Jun-Sep; Tent & RV camping: $15; Elev: 6430ft/1960m; Tel: 208-558-7658; Nearest town: Island Park; Notes: Reservable group site $50-$100. GPS: 44.497446, -111.254743

38 • Big Springs (Caribou)

Total sites: 15; RV sites: 15; Central water; Vault toilets; No showers; No RV dump; Reservations accepted; Open May-Sep; Tent & RV camping: $12; Elev: 6358ft/1938m; Tel: 208-652-7442; Nearest town: Lava Hot Springs; Notes: Group site: $50-$60. GPS: 42.765636, -112.095479

39 • Big Trinity Lake

Total sites: 17; RV sites: 17; Central water; Vault toilets; No showers; No RV dump; Reservations not accepted; Max length: 22ft; Open Jul-Sep; Tent & RV camping: $10; Elev: 7848ft/2392m; Tel: 208-587-7961; Nearest town: Mountain Home. GPS: 43.624188, -115.432192

40 • Bighorn Crags

Total sites: 14; RV sites: 14; Central water; Vault toilets; No showers; No RV dump; Reservations not accepted; Open Jul-Oct; Tent & RV camping: $4; Elev: 8474ft/2583m; Tel: 208-756-5200; Nearest town: Cobalt. GPS: 45.103516, -114.522831

41 • Bird Creek

Total sites: 5; RV sites: 5; No water; Vault toilets; Reservations not accepted; Open May-Oct; Tent & RV camping: $6; Elev: 4754ft/1449m; Tel: 208-764-3202; Nearest town: Featherville; Notes: Free with no services in winter. GPS: 43.620832, -115.175204

42 • Black Lake

Total sites: 4; No water; Vault toilets; Reservations not accepted; Open Jun-Sep; Tents only: Free; Elev: 7228ft/2203m; Tel: 541-426-5546; Nearest town: Council. GPS: 45.189535, -116.561543

43 • Black Rock

Total sites: 11; RV sites: 11; Central water; Vault toilets; No showers; No RV dump; Reservations accepted; Open May-Sep; Tent & RV camping: $15; Elev: 4045ft/1233m; Tel: 208-392-6681; Nearest town: Idaho City. GPS: 43.795769, -115.588883

44 • Blind Creek

Total sites: 5; RV sites: 5; No water; Vault toilets; Reservations not accepted; Max length: 32ft; Open May-Sep; Tent & RV camping: $5; Elev: 6037ft/1840m; Tel: 208-879-4100; Nearest town: Stanley. GPS: 44.280646, -114.732802

45 • Blowout

Total sites: 15; RV sites: 15; Central water; Vault toilets; No showers; No RV dump; Reservations not accepted; Open May-Sep; Tent & RV camping: $12; Elev: 5718ft/1743m; Tel: 208-523-1412; Nearest town: Alpine WY. GPS: 43.284948, -111.122132

46 • Boiling Springs

Total sites: 9; RV sites: 9; Central water; Vault toilets; No showers; No RV dump; Reservations not accepted; Max length: 30ft; Open May-Oct; Tent & RV camping: $15; Elev: 4091ft/1247m; Tel: 208-365-7000; Nearest town: Smiths Ferry. GPS: 44.359874, -115.858043

47 • Bonneville

Total sites: 22; RV sites: 18; Central water; Vault toilets; No showers; No RV dump; Reservations accepted; Open Apr-Oct; Tent & RV camping: $15; Elev: 4767ft/1453m; Tel: 208-259-3361; Nearest town: Lowman. GPS: 44.150962, -115.310909

48 • Bostetter

Total sites: 10; RV sites: 10; Central water; Vault toilets; No showers; No RV dump; Reservations not accepted; Stay limit: 14 days; Tent & RV camping: Fee unknown; Elev: 7188ft/2191m; Tel: 208-678-0430; Nearest town: Oakley; Notes: Group site. GPS: 42.165771, -114.168945

49 • Boundary (Sun Valley)

Total sites: 9; RV sites: 9; Central water; Vault toilets; No showers; No RV dump; Reservations not accepted; Stay limit: 7 days; Open May-Sep; Tent & RV camping: $10; Elev: 6070ft/1850m; Tel: 208-622-5371; Nearest town: Sun Valley. GPS: 43.721863, -114.326665

50 • Boundary Creek

Total sites: 15; RV sites: 15; Central water; Vault toilets; No showers; No RV dump; Reservations accepted; Open Jun-Aug; Tent & RV camping: $10; Elev: 5732ft/1747m; Tel: 208-879-4101; Nearest town: Stanley; Notes: Narrow rough road. GPS: 44.529396, -115.293015

51 • Bowns

Total sites: 12; RV sites: 12; No toilets; No showers; No RV dump; Reservations not accepted; Open Jun-Oct; Tent & RV camping: $6; Elev: 5568ft/1697m; Tel: 208-764-3202; Nearest town: Fairfield; Notes: Free with no services in winter. GPS: 43.607122, -114.880934

52 • Box Canyon

Total sites: 18; RV sites: 18; Central water; Vault toilets; No showers; No RV dump; Reservations not accepted; Open May-Sep; Tent & RV camping: $15; Elev: 6297ft/1919m; Tel: 208-558-7301; Nearest town: Island Park. GPS: 44.409805, -111.396596

53 • Boyd Creek

Total sites: 6; RV sites: 6; No water; Vault toilets; Reservations not accepted; Open all year; Tent & RV camping: $8; Elev: 1716ft/523m; Tel: 208-926-4258; Nearest town: Lowell; Notes: Limited winter access. GPS: 46.080953, -115.442696

54 • Bridge Creek

Total sites: 5; RV sites: 5; No water; Vault toilets; Reservations not accepted; Max length: 20ft; Open all year; Tent & RV camping: Free; Elev: 4847ft/1477m; Tel: 208-842-2245; Nearest town: Elk City; Notes: Limited winter access. GPS: 45.783055, -115.206529

55 • Broad Canyon

Total sites: 8; RV sites: 8; No water; Vault toilets; Reservations not accepted; Max length: 35ft; Open Jul-Sep; Tent & RV camping: Free; Elev: 7825ft/2385m; Nearest town: Mackay. GPS: 43.768363, -113.943128

56 • Brownlee

Total sites: 11; RV sites: 11; Central water; Vault toilets; No showers; No RV dump; Reservations not accepted; Max length: 16ft; Tent & RV camping: $10; Elev: 4282ft/1305m; Tel: 208-549-4200; Nearest town: Cambridge. GPS: 44.738605, -116.819723

57 • Buck Mountain

Total sites: 4; RV sites: 4; No water; Vault toilets; Reservations not accepted; Open May-Sep; Tent & RV camping: Free; Elev: 6686ft/2038m; Tel: 208-382-7400; Nearest town: Landmark. GPS: 44.681788, -115.539819

58 • Buckhorn Bar

Total sites: 13; RV sites: 5; Central water; Vault toilets; No showers; No RV dump; Reservations not accepted; Tent & RV camping: $10; Elev: 3888ft/1185m; Tel: 208-634-0600; Nearest town: Cascade; Notes: Also walk-to sites, 4 walk-to sites. GPS: 44.937161, -115.739133

59 • Buffalo

Total sites: 121; RV sites: 121; Elec sites: 19; Flush toilets; No showers; No RV dump; Reservations accepted; Max length: 32ft; Open Jun-Sep; Tents: $15/RVs: $15-20; Elev: 6306ft/1922m; Tel: 208-558-7112; Nearest town: Island Park; Notes: Group site $80-$160. GPS: 44.426264, -111.368546

60 • Bull Trout Lake

Total sites: 38; RV sites: 38; No water; Vault toilets; Reservations accepted; Open Jun-Oct; Tent & RV camping: $15; Elev: 6962ft/2122m; Tel: 208-259-3361; Nearest town: Stanley; Notes: Group site: $75. GPS: 44.302801, -115.258827

61 • Bumblebee

Total sites: 25; RV sites: 25; Central water; Vault toilets; No showers; No RV dump; Reservations accepted; Stay limit: 14 days; Open May-Sep; Tent & RV camping: $21; Elev: 2246ft/685m; Tel: 208-664-2318; Nearest town: Pinehurst; Notes: Group site: $167. GPS: 47.634394, -116.277392

62 • Burgdorf

Total sites: 5; RV sites: 5; Central water; Vault toilets; No showers; No RV dump; Reservations not accepted; Tent & RV camping: $10; Elev: 6083ft/1854m; Tel: 208-634-0400; Nearest town: McCall. GPS: 45.269086, -115.914251

63 • Buttermilk

Total sites: 53; RV sites: 53; Elec sites: 1; Central water; Vault toilets; No showers; No RV dump; Reservations accepted; Max length: 32ft; Open May-Sep; Tent & RV camping: $15; Elev: 6329ft/1929m; Tel: 208-558-7301; Nearest town: Island Park. GPS: 44.432125, -111.425953

64 • Cabin Creek

Total sites: 12; RV sites: 12; Central water; Vault toilets; No showers; No RV dump; Reservations not accepted; Tent & RV camping: $10; Elev: 4226ft/1288m; Tel: 208-253-0100; Nearest town: Council. GPS: 44.655152, -116.272523

65 • Calamity

Total sites: 41; RV sites: 35; Central water; Vault toilets; No showers; No RV dump; Reservations accepted; Max length: 32ft; Open May-Sep; Tent & RV camping: $12; Elev: 5646ft/1721m; Tel: 208-523-1412; Nearest town: Irwin. GPS: 43.326332, -111.214626

66 • Camp 3

Total sites: 4; RV sites: 4; No water; Vault toilets; Reservations not accepted; Open May-Sep; Tent & RV camping: Free; Elev: 3222ft/982m; Nearest town: St. Maries. GPS: 47.129986, -116.103074

67 • Camp Creek

Total sites: 4; RV sites: 4; No water; Vault toilets; Reservations not accepted; Tent & RV camping: $10; Elev: 4144ft/1263m; Tel: 208-634-0600; Nearest town: Yellow Pine. GPS: 44.890565, -115.707389

68 • Canyon

Total sites: 6; RV sites: 6; Central water; Vault toilets; No showers; No RV dump; Reservations not accepted; Max length: 13ft; Open May-Sep; Tent & RV camping: $12; Elev: 3855ft/1175m; Tel: 208-365-7000; Nearest town: Banks. GPS: 44.187871, -116.115344

69 • Canyon Transfer

Total sites: 6; RV sites: 6; Central water; Vault toilets; No showers; No RV dump; Reservations not accepted; Open May-Oct; Tent & RV camping: $6; Elev: 5599ft/1707m; Tel: 208-764-3202; Nearest town: Fairfield; Notes: Free with no services in winter. GPS: 43.628264, -114.858755

70 • Caribou

Total sites: 7; Central water; Vault toilets; No showers; No RV dump; Reservations not accepted; Stay limit: 10 days; Open May-Sep; Tents only: $16; Elev: 6478ft/1974m; Tel: 208-678-0439; Nearest town: Ketchum; Notes: RVs and trailers not recommended because of the inability to turn around once you enter. GPS: 43.814678, -114.424957

71 • Cartwright Ridge

Total sites: 6; RV sites: 6; No water; Vault toilets; Reservations not accepted; Max length: 10ft; Open May-Sep; Tent & RV camping: $15; Elev: 5092ft/1552m; Tel: 208-365-7000; Nearest town: Emmett. GPS: 44.333952, -116.191647

72 • Casino Creek

Total sites: 19; RV sites: 17; Central water; Vault toilets; No showers; No RV dump; Reservations not accepted; Stay limit: 10 days; Open Mar-Nov; Tent & RV camping: $16; Elev: 6171ft/1881m; Tel: 208-678-0439; Nearest town: Stanley. GPS: 44.256592, -114.855228

73 • Castle Creek

Total sites: 8; RV sites: 8; Central water; Vault toilets; No showers; No RV dump; Reservations not accepted; Open all year; Tent & RV camping: $12; Elev: 2336ft/712m; Tel: 208-839-2211; Nearest town: Grangeville; Notes: Winter access may be limited. GPS: 45.828155, -115.968432

74 • Castle Creek

Total sites: 2; RV sites: 2; No water; Vault toilets; Reservations not accepted; Max length: 25ft; Open May-Sep; Tent & RV camping: Free; Elev: 4268ft/1301m; Tel: 208-587-7961; Nearest town: Mountain Home. GPS: 43.410805, -115.395014

75 • CCC

Total sites: 3; RV sites: 1; No water; Vault toilets; Reservations not accepted; Open all year; Tent & RV camping: Free; Elev: 1576ft/480m; Tel: 208-926-4258; Nearest town: Kooskia; Notes: Limited winter access. GPS: 46.090691, -115.520092

76 • Cedar Creek

Total sites: 3; RV sites: 3; No water; Vault toilets; Reservations not accepted; Open May-Sep; Tent & RV camping: $10; Elev: 2779ft/847m; Nearest town: Clarkia. GPS: 47.050956, -116.289101

77 • Cedars

Total sites: 5; No water; Vault toilets; Reservations not accepted; Open all year; Tents only: Free; Elev: 3707ft/1130m; Tel: 208-476-4541; Nearest town: Pierce; Notes: Limited winter access. GPS: 46.869589, -115.080037

78 • Chaparral

Total sites: 9; RV sites: 9; No water; Vault toilets; Reservations not accepted; Open all year; Tent & RV camping: $6; Elev: 4633ft/1412m; Tel: 208-764-3202; Nearest town: Featherville; Notes: Free with no services in winter. GPS: 43.613417, -115.201751

79 • Chemeketan

Total sites: 13; RV sites: 13; Central water; Vault toilets; No showers; No RV dump; Reservations not accepted; Stay limit: 10 days; Open Jun-Sep; Tent & RV camping: $10; Elev: 7559ft/2304m; Tel: 928-537-8888; Nearest town: Stanley; Notes: Reservable group site ($50-$150) available as single sites when not reserved. GPS: 43.847764, -114.753942

80 • Cherry Creek

Total sites: 5; RV sites: 5; No water; No toilets; Reservations not accepted; Tent & RV camping: Free; Elev: 5839ft/1780m; Nearest town: Downey. GPS: 42.304463, -112.135386

81 • Chinook

Total sites: 11; RV sites: 11; Central water; Vault toilets; No showers; No RV dump; Reservations not accepted; Open May-Oct; Tent & RV camping: $10; Elev: 5709ft/1740m; Tel: 208-634-0400; Nearest town: McCall. GPS: 45.212235, -115.809857

82 • Chinook Bay

Total sites: 13; Central water; Flush toilets; No showers; No RV dump; Reservations not accepted; Stay limit: 10 days; Open May-Sep; Tents only: $20; Elev: 6519ft/1987m; Tel: 208-727-5000; Nearest town: Stanley. GPS: 44.163991, -114.905512

83 • Cloverleaf

Total sites: 19; RV sites: 19; Central water; Flush toilets; No showers; No RV dump; Reservations accepted; Open May-Sep; Tent & RV camping: $16; Elev: 6923ft/2110m; Tel: 208-847-0375; Nearest town: St. Charles; Notes: Group site: $57-$115. GPS: 42.094418, -111.531587

84 • Cold Springs (Banks)

Total sites: 6; RV sites: 6; No water; Vault toilets; Reservations not accepted; Open May-Sep; Tent & RV camping: Free; Elev: 6371ft/1942m; Tel: 208-847-0375; Nearest town: Soda Springs. GPS: 42.510625, -111.582985

85 • Cold Springs (New Meadows)

Total sites: 30; RV sites: 30; Central water; Vault toilets; No showers; RV dump; Reservations accepted; Max length: 22ft; Open May-Sep; Tent & RV camping: $10-15; Elev: 4829ft/1472m; Tel: 208-347-0300; Nearest town: New Meadows. GPS: 44.949228, -116.440353

86 • Conrad Crossing

Total sites: 8; RV sites: 8; Central water; Vault toilets; No showers; No RV dump; Reservations not accepted; Open May-Sep; Tent & RV camping: $15; Elev: 3432ft/1046m; Nearest town: Avery; Notes: $12 when water turned off. GPS: 47.158448, -115.416833

87 • Copper Creek

Total sites: 16; RV sites: 16; Central water; Vault toilets; No showers; No RV dump; Reservations not accepted; Max length: 30ft; Open all year; Tent & RV camping: $15; Elev: 2664ft/812m; Nearest town: Bonners Ferry; Notes: No fee Sep-May - no water. GPS: 48.985577, -116.167975

88 • Copper Creek

Total sites: 8; RV sites: 8; No water; Vault toilets; Reservations not accepted; Open May-Oct; Tent & RV camping: Free; Elev: 6604ft/2013m; Tel: 208-622-5371; Nearest town: Bellevue. GPS: 43.607146, -113.929486

89 • Corduroy Meadows

Total sites: 1; RV sites: 1; No water; No toilets; Reservations not accepted; Tent & RV camping: Free; Elev: 6406ft/1953m; Nearest town: Burgdorf. GPS: 45.343204, -115.946772

90 • Corn Creek

Total sites: 10; RV sites: 10; Central water; Vault toilets; No showers; No RV dump; Reservations not accepted; Open Mar-Oct; Tent & RV camping: $10; Elev: 3094ft/943m; Tel: 208-865-2700; Nearest town: North Fork. GPS: 45.369929, -114.685717

91 • Cottonwood

Total sites: 3; RV sites: 3; No water; Vault toilets; Reservations not accepted; Open May-Sep; Tent & RV camping: Free; Elev: 3300ft/1006m; Tel: 208-587-7961; Nearest town: Boise. GPS: 43.632278, -115.825072

92 • Cougar Point

Total sites: 18; RV sites: 18; No water; Vault toilets; Reservations not accepted; Open May-Oct; Tent & RV camping: Free; Elev: 6581ft/2006m; Tel: 208-756-5200; Nearest town: Salmon. GPS: 45.082567, -114.054335

93 • Cozy Cove

Total sites: 16; RV sites: 16; Central water; Vault toilets; No showers; No RV dump; Reservations accepted; Open Jun-Oct; Tent & RV camping: $12; Elev: 5351ft/1631m; Tel: 208-259-3361; Nearest town: Garden Valley. GPS: 44.290644, -115.653193

94 • Crooked River #4

Total sites: 1; Vault toilets; Open all year; Tents only: Free; Elev: 3958ft/1206m; Tel: 208-842-2245; Nearest town: Elk City. GPS: 45.793615, -115.530946

95 • Curlew

Total sites: 9; RV sites: 9; Central water; Vault toilets; No showers; No RV dump; Reservations accepted; Open all year; Tent & RV camping: $10; Elev: 4619ft/1408m; Tel: 208-236-7500; Nearest town: Holbrook; Notes: Group site: $50-$60. GPS: 42.070646, -112.691329

96 • Curlew Creek

Total sites: 9; RV sites: 9; Central water; Vault toilets; No showers; No RV dump; Reservations not accepted; Open May-Sep; Tent & RV camping: $5; Elev: 4232ft/1290m; Tel: 208-587-7961; Nearest town: Mountain Home. GPS: 43.436209, -115.288575

97 • Custer #1

Total sites: 6; RV sites: 6; No water; Vault toilets; Reservations not accepted; Max length: 32ft; Open Jun-Sep; Tent & RV camping: $5; Elev: 6726ft/2050m; Tel: 208-879-4100; Nearest town: Stanley. GPS: 44.399295, -114.663673

98 • Dagger Falls

Total sites: 8; RV sites: 8; Central water; Vault toilets; No showers; No RV dump; Reservations not accepted; Max length: 16ft; Open Jun-Oct; Tent & RV camping: $10; Elev: 5843ft/1781m; Tel: 208-879-4101; Nearest town: Stanley; Notes: Narrow rough road. GPS: 44.529063, -115.285744

99 • Deadwood

Total sites: 6; RV sites: 6; Central water; Vault toilets; No showers; No RV dump; Reservations not accepted; Max length: 15ft; Open May-Sep; Tent & RV camping: $15; Elev: 3724ft/1135m; Tel: 208-259-3361; Nearest town: Boise. GPS: 44.080895, -115.658707

100 • Deep Creek

Total sites: 3; RV sites: 3; No water; Vault toilets; Reservations not accepted; Max length: 30ft; Stay limit: 16 days; Tent & RV camping: Free; Elev: 4337ft/1322m; Tel: 406-821-3269; Nearest town: Darby (MT); Notes: Horses allowed. GPS: 45.714061, -114.709281

101 • Deep Creek (Beaver Jack)

Total sites: 3; RV sites: 3; No water; Vault toilets; Reservations not accepted; Open Jun-Oct; Tent & RV camping: Fee unknown; Elev: 5039ft/1536m; Tel: 208-756-5200; Nearest town: North Fork. GPS: 45.126023, -114.215059

102 • Deer Flat

Total sites: 5; RV sites: 5; No water; Vault toilets; Reservations not accepted; Max length: 22ft; Open Jun-Sep; Tent & RV camping: Free; Elev: 6283ft/1915m; Tel: 208-259-3361; Nearest town: Boise. GPS: 44.408713, -115.553703

103 • Devils Elbow

Total sites: 20; RV sites: 20; Central water; Vault toilets; No showers; No RV dump; Reservations accepted; Open May-Sep; Tent & RV camping: $21; Elev: 2621ft/799m; Tel: 208-664-2318; Nearest town: Kingston; Notes: Group site: $80. GPS: 47.770996, -116.032471

104 • Diamondfield Jack

Total sites: 12; RV sites: 12; Central water; Vault toilets; No showers; No RV dump; Reservations not accepted; Stay limit: 14 days; Open all year; Tent & RV camping: Fee unknown; Elev: 7001ft/2134m; Tel: 208-678-0439; Nearest town: Oakley. GPS: 42.171875, -114.279565

105 • Dog Creek

Total sites: 13; RV sites: 13; Central water; Vault toilets; No showers; No RV dump; Reservations accepted; Open all year; Tent & RV camping: $10; Elev: 4446ft/1355m; Tel: 208-587-7961; Nearest town: Pine; Notes: 2 group sites: $20. GPS: 43.527344, -115.306641

106 • Donkey Creek

Total sites: 5; RV sites: 4; No water; No toilets; Tent & RV camping: Free; Elev: 2930ft/893m; Nearest town: St Maries. GPS: 47.185119, -116.080703

107 • Dry Canyon

Total sites: 3; RV sites: 3; No water; Vault toilets; Reservations not accepted; Open Jun-Sep; Tent & RV camping: Free; Elev: 6355ft/1937m; Tel: 208-236-7500; Nearest town: Weston. GPS: 42.057849, -112.143917

108 • Easley

Total sites: 10; RV sites: 10; Vault toilets; Reservations accepted; Open May-Sep; Tent & RV camping: $14; Elev: 6627ft/2020m; Tel: 208-678-0439; Nearest town: Ketchum. GPS: 43.781264, -114.538375

109 • East Fork Baker Creek

Total sites: 7; RV sites: 7; No water; Vault toilets; Reservations not accepted; Open Jun-Nov; Tent & RV camping: Free; Elev: 6926ft/2111m; Tel: 208-622-5371; Nearest town: Ketchum. GPS: 43.744618, -114.565129

110 • Eastside Group

Total sites: 6; RV sites: 6; Central water; Vault toilets; No showers; No RV dump; Reservations not accepted; Open Apr-Oct; Tent & RV camping: $16; Elev: 5000ft/1524m; Tel: 208-365-7000; Nearest town: Ola; Notes: Reservable group site: $93. GPS: 44.332123, -116.175187

111 • Ebenezer

Total sites: 11; RV sites: 11; Central water; Vault toilets; No showers; No RV dump; Reservations not accepted; Open May-Oct; Tent & RV camping: $5; Elev: 3110ft/948m; Tel: 208-865-2700; Nearest town: North Fork. GPS: 45.304896, -114.515601

112 • Edna Creek

Total sites: 9; RV sites: 9; Central water; Vault toilets; No showers; No RV dump; Reservations accepted; Open May-Sep; Tent & RV camping: $15; Elev: 5249ft/1600m; Tel: 208-392-6681; Nearest town: Idaho City. GPS: 43.962552, -115.622362

113 • Eightmile

Total sites: 4; RV sites: 4; No water; Vault toilets; Reservations not accepted; Max length: 16ft; Open May-Sep; Tent & RV camping: Free; Elev: 6850ft/2088m; Tel: 208-879-4100; Nearest town: Stanley; Notes: Meadow across the road can accommodate larger camp trailers. GPS: 44.426304, -114.621188

114 • Eightmile

Total sites: 5; RV sites: 5; No water; Vault toilets; Reservations not accepted; Open May Sep; Tent & RV camping: Free, Elev: 6749ft/2057m; Tel: 208-847-0375; Nearest town: Soda Springs. GPS: 42.487631, -111.584482

115 • Elk Creek

Total sites: 14; RV sites: 14; Elec sites: 14; Central water; Vault toilets; No showers; No RV dump; Reservations accepted; Max length: 40ft; Open May-Oct; Tent & RV camping: $20; Elev: 2843ft/867m; Tel: 208-875-1131; Nearest town: Elk River. GPS: 46.793569, -116.171648

116 • Elk Summit

Total sites: 15; RV sites: 15; No water; Vault toilets; Reservations not accepted; Stay limit: 14 days; Open all year; Tent & RV camping: Free; Elev: 5781ft/1762m; Tel: 208-942-3113; Nearest town: Lowell; Notes: Stock facilities, Limited winter access. GPS: 46.327986, -114.647344

117 • Elks Flat

Total sites: 36; RV sites: 36; Central water; Vault toilets; No showers; No RV dump; Reservations not accepted; Open May-Sep; Tent & RV camping: $10; Elev: 4339ft/1323m; Tel: 208-587-7961; Nearest town: Mountain Home; Notes: Reservable group site $100. GPS: 43.537894, -115.294592

118 • Emerald Creek

Total sites: 18; RV sites: 18; Central water; Vault toilets; No showers; No RV dump; Reservations not accepted; Open May-Sep; Tent & RV camping: $10; Elev: 2900ft/884m; Nearest town: Fernwood. GPS: 47.006973, -116.326698

119 • Emigration

Total sites: 23; RV sites: 23; Central water; Flush toilets; No showers; No RV dump; Reservations accepted; Max length: 40ft; Open Jun-Sep; Tent & RV camping: $17; Elev: 7234ft/2205m; Tel: 208-847-0375; Nearest town: Montpelier; Notes: 2 group sites: $67. GPS: 42.369629, -111.556885

120 • Evans Creek

Total sites: 10; RV sites: 10; No water; Vault toilets; Reservations not accepted; Stay limit: 14 days; Generator hours: 0600-2200; Open May-Sep; Tent & RV camping: Free; Elev: 4222ft/1287m; Tel: 208-587-7961; Nearest town: Mountain Home; Notes: Hairpin turns may be difficult for longer rigs. GPS: 43.400146, -115.414244

121 • Evergreen

Total sites: 12; RV sites: 12; Central water; Vault toilets; No showers; No RV dump; Reservations not accepted; Tent & RV camping: $10; Elev: 3947ft/1203m; Tel: 208-253-0100; Nearest town: New Meadows. GPS: 44.893184, -116.388566

122 • Falls

Total sites: 22; RV sites: 22; Central water; Vault toilets; No showers; No RV dump; Reservations accepted; Open May-Sep; Tent & RV camping: $12; Elev: 5289ft/1612m; Tel: 208-523-1412; Nearest town: Swan Valley; Notes: Group site: $50. GPS: 43.432802, -111.361261

123 • Father And Sons

Total sites: 12; RV sites: 12; Central water; Vault toilets; No showers; No RV dump; Reservations not accepted; Stay limit: 14 days; Open Jun-Sep; Tent & RV camping: Fee unknown; Elev: 7284ft/2220m; Tel: 208-678-0430; Nearest town: Oakley; Notes: Group site available. GPS: 42.163086, -114.185547

124 • Federal Gulch

Total sites: 3; RV sites: 3; No water; Vault toilets; Reservations not accepted; Max length: 18ft; Stay limit: 16 days; Open Jun-Sep; Tent & RV camping: Free; Elev: 6801ft/2073m; Tel: 208-622-5371; Nearest town: Hailey. GPS: 43.668589, -114.153456

125 • Fish Creek

Total sites: 10; RV sites: 10; Central water; Vault toilets; No showers; No RV dump; Reservations not accepted; Open all year; Tent & RV camping: $12; Elev: 5115ft/1559m; Tel: 208-839-2211; Nearest town: Grangeville; Notes: Limited winter access. GPS: 45.857666, -116.082275

126 • Five Points

Total sites: 5; RV sites: 5; No water; Vault toilets; Reservations not accepted; Tent & RV camping: Free; Elev: 5892ft/1796m; Tel: 208-764-3202; Nearest town: Fairfield. GPS: 43.542478, -114.818662

127 • Flat Creek

Total sites: 11; RV sites: 11; No water; Vault toilets; Reservations not accepted; Tent & RV camping: Free; Elev: 2708ft/825m; Nearest town: Pierce. GPS: 46.721051, -115.292398

128 • Flat Rock (Island Park)

Total sites: 38; RV sites: 38; Elec sites: 8; Central water; Vault toilets; No showers; No RV dump; Reservations accepted; Open May-

Sep; Tents: $15/RVs: $15-22; Elev: 6388ft/1947m; Tel: 208-652-7442; Nearest town: Island Park. GPS: 44.498796, -111.340193

129 • Flat Rock (Stanley)

Total sites: 6; RV sites: 6; Central water; Vault toilets; No showers; No RV dump; Reservations not accepted; Max length: 32ft; Open May-Sep; Tent & RV camping: $10; Elev: 6119ft/1865m; Tel: 208-879-4100; Nearest town: Stanley. GPS: 44.290607, -114.718274

130 • Flat Rock Extension

Total sites: 3; RV sites: 3; No water; Vault toilets; Reservations not accepted; Max length: 16ft; Open May-Sep; Tent & RV camping: $5; Elev: 6227ft/1898m; Tel: 208-879-4100; Nearest town: Stanley. GPS: 44.293341, -114.715837

131 • Fly Flat

Total sites: 14; RV sites: 14; Central water; Vault toilets; No showers; No RV dump; Reservations not accepted; Open May-Oct; Tent & RV camping: $15; Elev: 3507ft/1069m; Nearest town: Avery; Notes: $12 when water turned off. GPS: 47.112793, -115.390869

132 • Four Mile (White Rock Peak)

Total sites: 4; RV sites: 4; No water; Vault toilets; Reservations not accepted; Tent & RV camping: $10; Elev: 4183ft/1275m; Tel: 208-634-0600; Nearest town: Cascade. GPS: 44.862835, -115.692063

133 • French Creek

Total sites: 21; RV sites: 21; Central water; Vault toilets; No RV dump; Reservations accepted; Open May-Oct; Tent & RV camping: $15; Elev: 4879ft/1487m; Tel: 208-382-7400; Nearest town: Cascade. GPS: 44.527566, -116.107995

134 • French Gulch

Total sites: 2; RV sites: 2; No water; Vault toilets; Reservations not accepted; Open all year; Tent & RV camping: Free; Elev: 4199ft/1280m; Tel: 208-842-2245; Nearest town: Elk City; Notes: Limited winter access. GPS: 45.779331, -115.385365

135 • FS Flats

Total sites: 19; RV sites: 19; No water; Vault toilets; Reservations not accepted; Stay limit: 14 days; Tent & RV camping: Free; Elev: 6971ft/2125m; Tel: 208-678-0430; Nearest town: Hansen; Notes: 2 group sites. GPS: 42.154118, -114.258898

136 • Giant White Pine

Total sites: 14; RV sites: 14; Central water; Vault toilets; No showers; No RV dump; Reservations not accepted; Max length: 30ft; Open May-Sep; Tent & RV camping: $12; Elev: 2910ft/887m; Tel: 208-875-1131; Nearest town: Princeton. GPS: 47.008875, -116.676841

137 • Glacier View

Total sites: 63; RV sites: 63; Central water; Flush toilets; No showers; RV dump; Reservations accepted; Stay limit: 10 days; Open May-Sep; Tent & RV camping: $20; Elev: 6571ft/2003m; Tel: 208-678-0439; Nearest town: Stanley. GPS: 44.146452, -114.915103

138 • Glover

Total sites: 7; RV sites: 7; No water; Vault toilets; Reservations not accepted; Tent & RV camping: $8; Elev: 1808ft/551m; Tel: 208-926-4258; Nearest town: Lowell; Notes: Winter access may be limited, Free Oct-Apr. GPS: 46.068971, -115.363253

139 • Golden Gate

Total sites: 9; RV sites: 9; No water; Vault toilets; Reservations not accepted; Open May-Sep; Tent & RV camping: Free; Elev: 4875ft/1486m; Tel: 208-382-7400; Nearest town: Yellow Pine; Notes: Non-potable water. GPS: 44.935345, -115.485407

140 • Graham Bridge

Total sites: 3; RV sites: 3; No water; Vault toilets; Reservations not accepted; Tent & RV camping: Free; Elev: 5695ft/1736m; Tel: 208-392-6681; Nearest town: Idaho City. GPS: 43.963886, -115.274778

141 • Grandjean

Total sites: 34; RV sites: 34; Central water; Vault toilets; No showers; No RV dump; Reservations not accepted; Max length: 22ft; Tent & RV camping: $16; Elev: 5203ft/1586m; Tel: 208-774-3000; Nearest town: Lowman; Notes: 10 equestrian sites. GPS: 44.148291, -115.151975

142 • Grandview

Total sites: 8; RV sites: 8; Elec sites: 8; Central water; Vault toilets; No showers; No RV dump; Reservations not accepted; Open May-Sep; Tent & RV camping: $20; Elev: 5928ft/1807m; Tel: 208-652-7442; Nearest town: Ashton. GPS: 44.175298, -111.313552

143 • Granite Springs

Total sites: 4; RV sites: 4; Central water; Vault toilets; No showers; No RV dump; Reservations not accepted; Open all year; Tent & RV camping: Free; Elev: 6683ft/2037m; Tel: 208-842-2245; Nearest town: Dixie; Notes: Spring water, Not recommended for low-clearance vehicles or motor homes, Horse facilities, Limited winter access. GPS: 45.725046, -115.129192

144 • Gravel Creek

Total sites: 12; RV sites: 12; No water; Vault toilets; Reservations not accepted; Open May-Sep; Tent & RV camping: Fee unknown; Elev: 6667ft/2032m; Tel: 208-547-4356; Nearest town: Soda Springs. GPS: 42.936574, -111.379461

145 • Grayback

Total sites: 20; RV sites: 20; Central water; Vault toilets; No showers; No RV dump; Reservations accepted; Open May-Sep; Tent & RV camping: $15; Elev: 3893ft/1187m; Tel: 208-392-6681; Nearest town: Idaho City. GPS: 43.807042, -115.866452

146 • Green Bay

Total sites: 11; Central water; Vault toilets; Reservations not accepted; Open May-Oct; Tents only: Free; Elev: 2274ft/693m; Tel: 208-765-7223; Nearest town: Sandpoint. GPS: 48.178068, -116.408008

147 • Grouse

Total sites: 22; RV sites: 22; Central water; Vault toilets; No showers; No RV dump; Reservations accepted; Open Jul-Sep; Tent & RV camping: $10-15; Elev: 6381ft/1945m; Tel: 208-347-0300; Nearest town: McCall. GPS: 45.068183, -116.167956

148 • Hardscrabble

Total sites: 6; RV sites: 6; No water; Vault toilets; Reservations not accepted; Max length: 30ft; Open May-Sep; Tent & RV camping: $12; Elev: 3284ft/1001m; Tel: 208-365-7000; Nearest town: Garden Valley. GPS: 44.239013, -115.899204

149 • Harrys Hollow

Total sites: 3; RV sites: 3; No water; Vault toilets; Reservations not accepted; Tent & RV camping: Free; Elev: 6742ft/2055m; Nearest town: Bloomington. GPS: 42.190296, -111.508191

150 • Hawley Creek (Lower)

Total sites: 4; RV sites: 4; No water; Vault toilets; Reservations not accepted; Open May-Sep; Tent & RV camping: Free; Elev: 6722ft/2049m; Tel: 208-768-2500; Nearest town: Leadore. GPS: 44.667474, -113.190627

151 • Hawley Creek (Upper)

Total sites: 6; RV sites: 6; No water; Vault toilets; Reservations not accepted; Open May-Sep; Tent & RV camping: Free; Elev: 6791ft/2070m; Tel: 208-768-2500; Nearest town: Leadore. GPS: 44.671810, -113.181507

152 • Hazard Lake

Total sites: 13; RV sites: 13; Central water; Vault toilets; No showers; No RV dump; Reservations not accepted; Open Jul-Sep; Tent & RV camping: $10; Elev: 7067ft/2154m; Tel: 208-347-0300; Nearest town: McCall. GPS: 45.201492, -116.143287

153 • Helende

Total sites: 15; RV sites: 15; Central water; Vault toilets; No showers; No RV dump; Reservations accepted; Open Apr-Oct; Tent & RV camping: $12; Elev: 4185ft/1276m; Tel: 208-259-3361; Nearest town: Boise. GPS: 44.092938, -115.475806

154 • Hidden Creek

Total sites: 13; RV sites: 13; Central water; Vault toilets; No showers; No RV dump; Reservations not accepted; Open May-Sep; Tent & RV camping: $10; Elev: 3333ft/1016m; Tel: 208-476-4541; Nearest town: Pierce. GPS: 46.831719, -115.178566

155 • Hollywood

Total sites: 6; RV sites: 6; Central water; Vault toilets; No showers; No RV dump; Reservations not accepted; Max length: 22ft; Open May-Sep; Tent & RV camping: $16; Elev: 4993ft/1522m; Tel: 208-365-7000; Nearest town: Emmett. GPS: 44.326954, -116.179038

156 • Holman Creek

Total sites: 10; Central water; Vault toilets; No showers; No RV dump; Reservations not accepted; Stay limit: 10 days; Tents only: $10; Elev: 5636ft/1718m; Tel: 208-774-3000; Nearest town: Clayton. GPS: 44.249023, -114.529785

157 • Honeysuckle

Total sites: 7; RV sites: 7; Central water; Vault toilets; No showers; No RV dump; Reservations not accepted; Open May-Sep; Tent & RV camping: $16; Elev: 2776ft/846m; Nearest town: Coeur d'Alene. GPS: 47.739245, -116.474743

158 • Horse Creek Hot Springs

Total sites: 9; RV sites: 7; No water; Vault toilets; Reservations not accepted; Open Jun-Oct; Tent & RV camping: Free; Elev: 6072ft/1851m; Tel: 208-865-2700; Nearest town: Shoup. GPS: 45.504021, -114.459792

159 • Hot Springs

Total sites: 8; RV sites: 8; Central water; Vault toilets; No showers; No RV dump; Reservations not accepted; Max length: 35ft; Open May-Oct; Tent & RV camping: $16; Elev: 3186ft/971m; Tel: 208-365-7000; Nearest town: Emmett; Notes: Reservable group site $115-$230. GPS: 44.055508, -115.908447

160 • Howell Canyon Sno-Park

Total sites: 2; RV sites: 2; No water; Vault toilets; Tent & RV camping: Free; Elev: 7614ft/2321m; Nearest town: Malta. GPS: 42.327564, -113.608842

161 • Howers

Total sites: 10; RV sites: 10; Central water; Vault toilets; No showers; No RV dump; Reservations accepted; Max length: 22ft; Open Jun-Oct; Tent & RV camping: $12; Elev: 5364ft/1635m; Tel: 208-259-3361; Nearest town: Garden Valley. GPS: 44.322303, -115.648745

162 • Huckleberry

Total sites: 8; RV sites: 8; Central water; Vault toilets; No showers; No RV dump; Reservations not accepted; Tent & RV camping: $10; Elev: 4911ft/1497m; Tel: 208-253-0100; Nearest town: Council. GPS: 45.084022, -116.614705

163 • Hunter Creek Transfer Camp

Total sites: 4; RV sites: 4; No water; Vault toilets; Reservations not accepted; Open May-Oct; Tent & RV camping: Free; Elev: 5455ft/1663m; Tel: 208-764-3202; Nearest town: Fairfield; Notes: No services in winter. GPS: 43.424222, -115.132442

164 • Ice Hole

Total sites: 10; RV sites: 10; Central water; Vault toilets; No showers; No RV dump; Reservations not accepted; Open May-Oct; Tent & RV camping: Free; Elev: 5092ft/1552m; Tel: 208-382-7400; Nearest town: Cascade. GPS: 44.887939, -115.499512

165 • Ice Springs

Total sites: 4; RV sites: 4; No water; Vault toilets; Reservations not accepted; Open May-Sep; Tent & RV camping: Free; Elev: 4993ft/1522m; Tel: 208-587-7961; Nearest town: Mountain Home. GPS: 43.482909, -115.396997

166 • Independence Lakes

Total sites: 9; RV sites: 9; No water; Vault toilets; Reservations not accepted; Stay limit: 14 days; Open Jul-Oct; Tent & RV camping: Free; Elev: 7707ft/2349m; Tel: 208-678-0439; Nearest town: Oakley. GPS: 42.218924, -113.673615

167 • Indian Creek (Spot Mt)

Total sites: 2; RV sites: 2; No water; Vault toilets; Reservations not accepted; Max length: 25ft; Tent & RV camping: Free; Elev: 3406ft/1038m; Tel: 406-821-3269; Nearest town: Darby MT. GPS: 45.789032, -114.763769

168 • Indian Springs

Total sites: 2; No water; Vault toilets; Reservations not accepted; Open Jul-Oct; Tents only: Free; Elev: 7703ft/2348m; Tel: 208-879-4101; Nearest town: Stanley; Notes: High clearance vehicles recommended. GPS: 44.675211, -114.837718

169 • Iron Bog

Total sites: 21; RV sites: 21; Central water; Vault toilets; No showers; No RV dump; Reservations not accepted; Max length: 35ft; Tent & RV camping: $10; Elev: 7162ft/2183m; Tel: 208-588-3400; Nearest town: Mackay. GPS: 43.649892, -113.765254

170 • Iron Creek

Total sites: 9; Central water; Vault toilets; No showers; No RV dump; Reservations not accepted; Stay limit: 10 days; Tents only: $16; Elev: 6719ft/2048m; Tel: 208-727-5000; Nearest town: Stanley. GPS: 44.198730, -115.009766

171 • Iron Lake

Total sites: 8; Central water; Vault toilets; No showers; No RV dump; Reservations not accepted; Max length: 16ft; Open Jul-Oct; Tents only: $4; Elev: 8865ft/2702m; Tel: 208-756-5200; Nearest town: Salmon; Notes: Narrow rough mountain road requiring slow and careful driving. GPS: 44.905786, -114.193567

172 • Iron Phone Junction

Total sites: 4; RV sites: 4; No water; Vault toilets; Reservations not accepted; Open all year; Tent & RV camping: Free; Elev: 5340ft/1628m; Tel: 208-839-2211; Nearest town: Riggins; Notes: Limited winter access. GPS: 45.533566, -116.420873

173 • Isabella Point

Total sites: 2; No water; Vault toilets; Reservations not accepted; Open Jun-Oct; Tents only: Free; Elev: 2421ft/738m; Tel: 208-476-4541; Nearest town: Headquarters. GPS: 46.892041, -115.597432

174 • Jeanette

Total sites: 6; RV sites: 6; No water; Vault toilets; Reservations not accepted; Tent & RV camping: $10; Elev: 6247ft/1904m; Tel: 208-634-0400; Nearest town: McCall. GPS: 45.279643, -115.913952

175 • Jerrys Creek

Total sites: 3; No water; Vault toilets; Reservations not accepted; Tents only: Free; Elev: 6230ft/1899m; Notes: Rough road - high clearance vehicle recommended. GPS: 44.329313, -114.719986

176 • Johnson Bar

Total sites: 9; RV sites: 3; Central water; Vault toilets; No showers; No RV dump; Reservations not accepted; Open all year; Tent & RV camping: $8; Elev: 1637ft/499m; Tel: 208-926-4258; Nearest town: Lowell; Notes: Reservable group site $40, Limited winter access. GPS: 46.102551, -115.558696

177 • Josephus Lake

Total sites: 3; RV sites: 3; No water; Vault toilets; Reservations not accepted; Open Jul-Oct; Tent & RV camping: Free; Elev: 7072ft/2156m; Tel: 208-879-4101; Nearest town: Stanley. GPS: 44.548894, -115.143553

178 • Justrite

Total sites: 4; RV sites: 4; No water; Vault toilets; Reservations not accepted; Tent & RV camping: Free; Elev: 4341ft/1323m; Tel: 208-549-4200; Nearest town: Weiser. GPS: 44.540918, -116.953046

179 • Kelly Forks

Total sites: 13; RV sites: 13; Central water; Vault toilets; No showers; No RV dump; Reservations not accepted; Open May-Oct; Tent & RV camping: $10; Elev: 2802ft/854m; Tel: 208-476-4541; Nearest town: Pierce. GPS: 46.717041, -115.255859

180 • Kennally Creek

Total sites: 11; RV sites: 9; Central water; Vault toilets; No showers; No RV dump; Reservations not accepted; Tent & RV camping: $10; Elev: 5709ft/1740m; Tel: 208-634-0400; Nearest town: Donnelly. GPS: 44.781957, -115.875404

181 • Kirkham

Total sites: 16; RV sites: 16; Central water; Vault toilets; No showers; No RV dump; Reservations accepted; Open Apr-Oct; Tent & RV camping: $15; Elev: 3973ft/1211m; Tel: 208-259-3361; Nearest town: Lowman; Notes: Hot springs. GPS: 44.072021, -115.542969

182 • Kit Price

Total sites: 53; RV sites: 53; Central water; Vault toilets; No showers; No RV dump; Reservations accepted; Stay limit: 14 days; Open May-Sep; Tent & RV camping: $18; Elev: 2602ft/793m; Tel: 208-664-2318; Nearest town: Prichard. GPS: 47.739990, -116.006592

183 • Kiwanis

Total sites: 1; RV sites: 1; No water; Vault toilets; Reservations not accepted; Tent & RV camping: Free; Elev: 3881ft/1183m; Tel: 208-549-4200; Nearest town: Weiser; Notes: Can be dusty and noisy. GPS: 44.512715, -116.953094

184 • Knife Edge

Total sites: 5; RV sites: 5; No water; Vault toilets; Reservations not accepted; Open all year; Tent & RV camping: Free; Elev: 1788ft/545m; Tel: 208-926-4274; Nearest town: Lowell; Notes: Limited winter access. GPS: 46.227242, -115.474474

185 • Lafferty

Total sites: 8; RV sites: 8; No water; Vault toilets; Reservations not accepted; Tent & RV camping: $10; Elev: 4311ft/1314m; Tel: 208-253-0100; Nearest town: McCall. GPS: 44.939851, -116.655186

186 • Laird Park

Total sites: 35; RV sites: 31; Central water; Vault toilets; No showers; No RV dump; Reservations not accepted; Max length: 30ft; Open May-Sep; Tent & RV camping: $12; Elev: 2713ft/827m; Tel: 208-875-1131; Nearest town: Harvard. GPS: 46.942871, -116.649902

187 • Lake Cleveland - East

Total sites: 17; RV sites: 17; Central water; Vault toilets; No showers; No RV dump; Reservations accepted; Stay limit: 14 days; Open Jul-Sep; Tent & RV camping: $10; Elev: 8235ft/2510m; Tel: 208-678-0430; Nearest town: Albion. GPS: 42.324146, -113.646827

188 • Lake Creek

Total sites: 4; RV sites: 4; Central water; Vault toilets; No showers; No RV dump; Reservations not accepted; Max length: 35ft; Open May-Sep; Tent & RV camping: $5; Elev: 8080ft/2463m. GPS: 43.765196, -113.897029

189 • Lake Elsie

Total sites: 7; RV sites: 3; No water; Vault toilets; Reservations not accepted; Tent & RV camping: Free; Elev: 5138ft/1566m; Tel: 208-783-2363; Nearest town: Osburn. GPS: 47.428208, -116.022835

190 • Lake Fork

Total sites: 9; RV sites: 9; Central water; Vault toilets; No showers; No RV dump; Reservations not accepted; Tent & RV camping: $10; Elev: 5394ft/1644m; Tel: 208-634-0400; Nearest town: McCall. GPS: 44.922953, -115.945956

191 • Lake View

Total sites: 6; RV sites: 6; Central water; Vault toilets; No showers; No RV dump; Reservations not accepted; Stay limit: 10 days; Tent & RV camping: $18; Elev: 6545ft/1995m; Tel: 208-727-5000; Nearest town: Stanley. GPS: 44.248209, -115.057813

192 • Last Chance

Total sites: 23; RV sites: 23; Central water; Vault toilets; No showers; No RV dump; Reservations not accepted; Open May-Sep; Tent & RV camping: $10; Elev: 4767ft/1453m; Tel: 208-347-0300; Nearest town: McCall. GPS: 44.989258, -116.190674

193 • Leggett Creek

Total sites: 5; RV sites: 5; No water; Vault toilets; Reservations not accepted; Open all year; Tent & RV camping: Free; Elev: 3730ft/1137m; Tel: 208-842-2245; Nearest town: Grangeville; Notes: Limited winter access. GPS: 45.827803, -115.628908

194 • Limber Luke

Total sites: 5; RV sites: 5; No water; Vault toilets; Reservations not accepted; Tent & RV camping: Free; Elev: 5389ft/1643m; Tel: 208-842-2245; Nearest town: Elk City. GPS: 45.963589, -115.424007

195 • Line Creek Stock Camp

Total sites: 9; RV sites: 9; No water; Vault toilets; Reservations not accepted; Open May-Nov; Tent & RV camping: Free; Elev: 3743ft/1141m; Nearest town: Avery. GPS: 47.043923, -115.349783

196 • Little Bayhorse Lake

Total sites: 3; RV sites: 3; No water; Vault toilets; Reservations not accepted; Open Jul-Sep; Tent & RV camping: Free; Elev: 8399ft/2560m; Tel: 208-879-4100; Nearest town: Stanley; Notes: Steep narrow road extremely hazardous when wet - RVs/trailers not recommended. GPS: 44.413088, -114.386868

197 • Little Boulder

Total sites: 16; RV sites: 16; Central water; Vault toilets; No showers; No RV dump; Reservations not accepted; Max length: 30ft; Open May-Oct; Tent & RV camping: $12; Elev: 2620ft/799m; Tel: 208-875-1131; Nearest town: Deary; Notes: No water in Oct. GPS: 46.772561, -116.457662

198 • Little Roaring River Lake

Total sites: 4; RV sites: 4; No water; Vault toilets; Reservations not accepted; Open Jul-Sep; Tent & RV camping: Free; Elev: 7858ft/2395m; Tel: 208-587-7961; Nearest town: Mountain Home. GPS: 43.629575, -115.443523

199 • Little West Fork

Total sites: 1; RV sites: 1; No water; No toilets; Reservations not accepted; Tent & RV camping: Free; Elev: 7592ft/2314m; Tel: 208-879-4100; Nearest town: Challis. GPS: 44.684726, -114.342465

200 • Little Wilson Creek

Total sites: 2; RV sites: 2; No water; Vault toilets; Reservations not accepted; Open May-Oct; Tent & RV camping: Free; Elev: 4255ft/1297m; Tel: 208-587-7961; Nearest town: Mountain Home. GPS: 43.377474, -115.434413

201 • Lola Creek

Total sites: 21; RV sites: 21; Central water; Vault toilets; No showers; No RV dump; Reservations not accepted; Max length: 35ft; Open May-Oct; Tent & RV camping: $10; Elev: 6482ft/1976m; Tel: 208-879-4101; Nearest town: Stanley. GPS: 44.407908, -115.178069

202 • Lolo Creek

Total sites: 8; RV sites: 6; No toilets; Reservations not accepted; Open May-Oct; Tent & RV camping: Free; Elev: 2878ft/877m; Tel: 208-926-4274; Nearest town: Kamiah. GPS: 46.293437, -115.752283

203 • Lost Spring

Total sites: 6; RV sites: 6; No water; Vault toilets; Reservations not accepted; Open Jul-Oct; Tent & RV camping: Free; Elev: 5344ft/1629m; Tel: 208-756-5200; Nearest town: Cobalt. GPS: 44.842999, -114.466441

204 • Lower O'Brien

Total sites: 10; RV sites: 10; Central water; Vault toilets; No showers; No RV dump; Reservations not accepted; Stay limit: 10 days; Open

Jun-Sep; Tent & RV camping: $16; Elev: 5899ft/1798m; Tel: 208-774-3000; Nearest town: Clayton. GPS: 44.257404, -114.695143

205 • Lower Penstemon

Total sites: 5; RV sites: 5; Central water; Vault toilets; No showers; No RV dump; Reservations accepted; Stay limit: 14 days; Open May-Sep; Tent & RV camping: $8; Elev: 6637ft/2023m; Tel: 208-678-0439; Nearest town: Burley. GPS: 42.196553, -114.283356

206 • Luby Bay Lower

Total sites: 25; RV sites: 25; Central water; Flush toilets; No showers; RV dump; Reservations accepted; Max length: 60ft; Open May-Sep; Tent & RV camping: $23; Elev: 2530ft/771m; Tel: 208-443-1801; Nearest town: Nordman. GPS: 48.549561, -116.924561

207 • Luby Bay Upper

Total sites: 33; RV sites: 33; Central water; Flush toilets; No showers; RV dump; Reservations accepted; Open May-Sep; Tent & RV camping: $23; Elev: 2577ft/785m; Tel: 208-443-1801; Nearest town: Nordman. GPS: 48.550954, -116.927976

208 • Magruder Crossing

Total sites: 6; RV sites: 6; No water; Vault toilets; Reservations not accepted; Max length: 30ft; Stay limit: 16 days; Tent & RV camping: Free; Elev: 3832ft/1168m; Tel: 406-821-3269; Nearest town: Darby MT; Notes: Horses accommodated. GPS: 45.736291, -114.759174

209 • Mahoney Springs

Total sites: 6; No water; Vault toilets; Reservations not accepted; Open Jul-Oct; Tents only: Free; Elev: 8448ft/2575m; Nearest town: Challis. GPS: 44.660398, -114.542309

210 • Malad Summit

Total sites: 11; RV sites: 11; Central water; Vault toilets; No showers; No RV dump; Reservations accepted; Open May-Sep; Tent & RV camping: $12; Elev: 6207ft/1892m; Tel: 208-236-7500; Nearest town: Malad; Notes: Group site: $60. GPS: 42.350137, -112.275445

211 • Malad Summit Guard Station

Total sites: 3; RV sites: 3; Central water; Vault toilets; No showers; No RV dump; Reservations accepted; Tent & RV camping: Fee unknown; Elev: 6010ft/1832m; Tel: 208-236-7500; Nearest town: Malad; Notes: Cabin(s), Cabin $50. GPS: 42.351100, -112.264400

212 • Mallad Creek

Total sites: 5; RV sites: 5; No water; Vault toilets; Reservations not accepted; Open all year; Tent & RV camping: Free; Elev: 5108ft/1557m; Tel: 208-842-2245; Nearest town: Elk City; Notes: Limited winter access. GPS: 45.579256, -115.308627

213 • Mammoth Springs

Total sites: 8; RV sites: 8; Central water; Vault toilets; No showers; No RV dump; Reservations not accepted; Open Jun-Oct; Tent

& RV camping: $15; Elev: 5633ft/1717m; Nearest town: Avery; Notes: $12 when water turned off. GPS: 47.103929, -115.629608

214 • Mann Creek

Total sites: 13; RV sites: 13; Central water; Vault toilets; No showers; No RV dump; Reservations accepted; Open Apr-Sep; Tent & RV camping: $10; Elev: 2943ft/897m; Tel: 208-549-4200; Nearest town: Weiser. GPS: 44.412354, -116.906738

215 • Marijuana Flat

Total sites: 10; RV sites: 10; No water; Vault toilets; Reservations not accepted; Open May-Sep; Tent & RV camping: Fee unknown; Elev: 5487ft/1672m; Tel: 208-524-7500; Nearest town: Preston. GPS: 42.138678, -111.670233

216 • Marsh Creek

Total sites: 3; RV sites: 3; No water; Vault toilets; Reservations not accepted; Tent & RV camping: Free; Elev: 6486ft/1977m; Nearest town: Stanley. GPS: 44.410575, -115.184298

217 • McCoy Creek

Total sites: 17; RV sites: 17; Central water; Vault toilets; No showers; No RV dump; Reservations not accepted; Tent & RV camping: $10; Elev: 5617ft/1712m; Tel: 208-523-1412; Nearest town: Alpine. GPS: 43.183793, -111.100767

218 • McCrea's Bridge

Total sites: 23; RV sites: 23; Potable water; Vault toilets; No showers; No RV dump; Reservations accepted; Max length: 32ft; Open May-Sep; Tent & RV camping: $15; Elev: 6348ft/1935m; Tel: 208-652-7442; Nearest town: Island Park. GPS: 44.462402, -111.399902

219 • McDonald Flat

Total sites: 6; RV sites: 6; Central water; Vault toilets; No showers; No RV dump; Max length: 20ft; Open May-Oct; Tent & RV camping: Fee unknown; Elev: 5420ft/1652m; Tel: 208-756-5200; Nearest town: Salmon. GPS: 45.034704, -114.296561

220 • Meadow Creek (Hungry Ridge)

Total sites: 3; RV sites: 3; No water; Vault toilets; Reservations not accepted; Open all year; Tent & RV camping: Free; Elev: 2464ft/751m; Tel: 208-839-2211; Nearest town: Harpster; Notes: Limited winter access, Not for larger RVs. GPS: 45.828974, -115.928205

221 • Meadow Creek (Meadow Creek)

Total sites: 22; RV sites: 22; Central water; Vault toilets; No showers; No RV dump; Reservations not accepted; Open May-Sep; Tent & RV camping: Fee unknown; Elev: 2323ft/708m; Nearest town: Bonners Ferry. GPS: 48.819276, -116.148063

222 • Meadow Lake

Total sites: 18; RV sites: 18; No water; Vault toilets; No showers; No RV dump; Reservations accepted; Open Jul-Sep; Tent & RV camping: $10; Elev: 9163ft/2793m; Tel: 208-768-2500; Nearest town: Leadore. GPS: 44.432715, -113.317259

223 • Middle Fork Peak

Total sites: 3; RV sites: 3; No water; Vault toilets; Reservations not accepted; Open Jul-Oct; Tent & RV camping: Free; Elev: 7812ft/2381m; Tel: 208-756-5200; Nearest town: Cobalt. GPS: 44.961855, -114.643602

224 • Mike Harris

Total sites: 12; RV sites: 12; Central water; Vault toilets; No showers; No RV dump; Reservations accepted; Open May-Sep; Tent & RV camping: $12; Elev: 6529ft/1990m; Tel: 208-354-2312; Nearest town: Victor. GPS: 43.556399, -111.069352

225 • Mill Canyon

Total sites: 10; RV sites: 10; No water; Vault toilets; Reservations not accepted; Open May-Sep; Tent & RV camping: Fee unknown; Elev: 6519ft/1987m; Tel: 208-547-4356; Nearest town: Soda Springs. GPS: 42.810565, -111.360043

226 • Mill Creek (Bayhorse)

Total sites: 8; RV sites: 8; Central water; Vault toilets; No showers; No RV dump; Reservations not accepted; Open Jun-Sep; Tent & RV camping: $10; Elev: 7546ft/2300m; Tel: 208-879-4100; Nearest town: Challis. GPS: 44.472412, -114.441162

227 • Mill Flat

Total sites: 7; RV sites: 7; No water; Vault toilets; Reservations not accepted; Stay limit: 14 days; Open Jun-Oct; Tent & RV camping: Free; Elev: 5938ft/1810m; Tel: 208-678-0439; Nearest town: Rockland. GPS: 42.432009, -113.015975

228 • Mokins Bay

Total sites: 15; RV sites: 15; Central water; Vault toilets; No showers; No RV dump; Reservations accepted; Open May-Sep; Tent & RV camping: $21; Elev: 2346ft/715m; Tel: 208-762-7444; Nearest town: Coeur d'Alene. GPS: 47.784424, -116.665527

229 • Montpelier Canyon

Total sites: 15; RV sites: 13; No water; Vault toilets; Reservations accepted; Max length: 30ft; Open May-Sep; Tent & RV camping: $10; Elev: 6250ft/1905m; Tel: 208-847-0375; Nearest town: Montpelier; Notes: Larger RVs and trailers may have difficulty maneuvering through the campground. GPS: 42.331216, -111.232747

230 • Mormon Bend

Total sites: 15; RV sites: 15; Central water; Vault toilets; No showers; No RV dump; Reservations not accepted; Stay limit: 10 days; Tent & RV camping: $16; Elev: 6142ft/1872m; Tel: 208-774-3000; Nearest town: Stanley. GPS: 44.261475, -114.842041

231 • Morse Creek

Total sites: 3; RV sites: 3; No water; Vault toilets; Reservations not accepted; Max length: 16ft; Open May-Sep; Tent & RV camping: Free; Elev: 6332ft/1930m; Tel: 208-879-4100; Nearest town: Ellis. GPS: 44.630867, -113.790528

232 • Mosquito Flat

Total sites: 11; RV sites: 11; Central water; Vault toilets; No showers; No RV dump; Reservations not accepted; Max length: 32ft; Open Jun-Oct; Tent & RV camping: Free; Elev: 7024ft/2141m; Tel: 208-879-4100; Nearest town: Challis. GPS: 44.519616, -114.433212

233 • Mount Heyburn

Total sites: 20; RV sites: 20; Central water; Vault toilets; No showers; RV dump; Reservations not accepted; Stay limit: 10 days; Open May-Sep; Tent & RV camping: $18; Elev: 6581ft/2006m; Tel: 208-727-5000; Nearest town: Stanley; Notes: Dump station nearby. GPS: 44.135010, -114.915527

234 • Mountain View (Lowman)

Total sites: 14; RV sites: 14; Central water; Vault toilets; No showers; No RV dump; Reservations accepted; Open Apr-Oct; Tent & RV camping: $15; Elev: 3921ft/1195m; Tel: 208-259-3361; Nearest town: Lowman. GPS: 44.078857, -115.604004

235 • Mountain View (Stanley)

Total sites: 6; RV sites: 6; Central water; No toilets; No showers; No RV dump; Reservations not accepted; Stay limit: 10 days; Tent & RV camping: $18; Elev: 6526ft/1989m; Tel: 208-737-3200; Nearest town: Stanley. GPS: 44.161874, -114.904244

236 • Murdock

Total sites: 11; RV sites: 11; Central water; Vault toilets; No showers; No RV dump; Reservations not accepted; Stay limit: 10 days; Tent & RV camping: $16; Elev: 6388ft/1947m; Tel: 208-727-5000; Nearest town: Ketchum. GPS: 43.803467, -114.420410

237 • Ninemeyer

Total sites: 8; RV sites: 8; No water; Vault toilets; Reservations not accepted; Open Jun-Oct; Tent & RV camping: Free; Elev: 3855ft/1175m; Tel: 208-392-6681; Nearest town: Atlanta. GPS: 43.755774, -115.567925

238 • Noe Creek

Total sites: 6; RV sites: 6; Central water; Vault toilets; No showers; No RV dump; Reservations not accepted; Max length: 22ft; Open May-Oct; Tent & RV camping: $10; Elev: 2533ft/772m; Tel: 208-476-4541; Nearest town: Pierce. GPS: 46.684376, -115.366523

239 • North Fork (Ketchum)

Total sites: 29; RV sites: 29; Central water; Vault toilets; No showers; No RV dump; Reservations accepted; Max length: 16ft; Open May-Sep; Tent & RV camping: $16; Elev: 6250ft/1905m; Tel: 208-727-5000; Nearest town: Ketchum. GPS: 43.787598, -114.425537

240 • North Fork (Slate Creek)

Total sites: 5; RV sites: 5; No water; Vault toilets; Reservations not accepted; Max length: 22ft; Open all year; Tent & RV camping: Free; Elev: 2986ft/910m; Tel: 208-839-2211; Nearest town: White Bird; Notes: Limited winter access. GPS: 45.639956, -116.119606

241 • North Shore

Total sites: 14; RV sites: 14; Central water; Vault toilets; No showers; No RV dump; Reservations not accepted; Stay limit: 10 days; Open Jun-Sep; Tent & RV camping: $18; Elev: 7064ft/2153m; Tel: 208-774-3000; Nearest town: Stanley. GPS: 43.918701, -114.866699

242 • O'hara Bar

Total sites: 32; RV sites: 32; Central water; Vault toilets; No showers; No RV dump; Reservations accepted; Open May-Sep; Tent & RV camping: $14; Elev: 1552ft/473m; Tel: 208-926-4258; Nearest town: Lowell. GPS: 46.085523, -115.513397

243 • O'Hara Saddle

Total sites: 2; RV sites: 2; No water; No toilets; Reservations not accepted; Open all year; Tent & RV camping: Free; Elev: 5184ft/1580m; Tel: 208-842-2245; Nearest town: Elk City; Notes: Limited winter access. GPS: 45.952271, -115.517223

244 • Observation Point

Total sites: 4; RV sites: 4; No water; Vault toilets; Reservations not accepted; Tent & RV camping: Free; Elev: 7598ft/2316m; Tel: 406-821-3269; Nearest town: Darby. GPS: 45.665376, -114.809505

245 • Orogrande #1 and #2

Total sites: 3; RV sites: 3; No water; Vault toilets; Reservations not accepted; Open all year; Tent & RV camping: Free; Elev: 4603ft/1403m; Tel: 208-842-2245; Nearest town: Boise; Notes: Limited winter access. GPS: 45.702093, -115.544483

246 • Orogrande #3 and #4

Total sites: 6; RV sites: 6; No water; Vault toilets; Reservations not accepted; Open all year; Tent & RV camping: Free; Elev: 4646ft/1416m; Tel: 208-842-2245; Nearest town: Boise; Notes: Limited winter access. GPS: 45.698336, -115.546177

247 • Osprey

Total sites: 16; RV sites: 16; Central water; Flush toilets; No showers; No RV dump; Reservations accepted; Open May-Sep; Tent & RV camping: $21-23; Elev: 2503ft/763m; Tel: 208-443-1801; Nearest town: Priest River. GPS: 48.506104, -116.888672

248 • Outlet

Total sites: 18; RV sites: 18; Central water; Vault toilets; No showers; No RV dump; Reservations accepted; Stay limit: 10 days; Open May-Sep; Tent & RV camping: $20; Elev: 6585ft/2007m; Tel: 928-537-8888; Nearest town: Stanley. GPS: 44.141087, -114.911644

249 • Outlet (Priest Lake)

Total sites: 27; RV sites: 27; Central water; Flush toilets; No showers; No RV dump; Reservations accepted; Open May-Sep; Tent & RV camping: $21-23; Elev: 2549ft/777m; Tel: 208-443-8053; Nearest town: Lamb Creek. GPS: 48.498779, -116.893311

250 • Oxbow

Total sites: 1; RV sites: 1; No water; Vault toilets; Reservations not accepted; Open all year; Tent & RV camping: Free; Elev: 3878ft/1182m; Tel: 208-842-2245; Nearest town: Elk City; Notes: Limited winter access. GPS: 45.856541, -115.618058

251 • Palisades Creek

Total sites: 7; RV sites: 7; Central water; Vault toilets; No showers; No RV dump; Reservations not accepted; Max length: 22ft; Open May-Sep; Tent & RV camping: $12; Elev: 5555ft/1693m; Tel: 208-523-1412; Nearest town: Swan Valley. GPS: 43.396866, -111.214193

252 • Paradise

Total sites: 2; Central water; Vault toilets; No showers; No RV dump; Reservations not accepted; Tents only: Free; Elev: 4282ft/1305m; Tel: 208-549-4200; Nearest town: Weiser. GPS: 44.544188, -116.952183

253 • Paradise (Burnt Strip Mt)

Total sites: 11; RV sites: 11; Central water; Vault toilets; No showers; No RV dump; Reservations not accepted; Max length: 25ft; Tent & RV camping: Fee unknown; Elev: 3120ft/951m; Tel: 406-821-3269; Nearest town: Darby,MT. GPS: 45.860959, -114.738000

254 • Paris Springs

Total sites: 9; RV sites: 9; Central water; Vault toilets; No showers; No RV dump; Reservations accepted; Max length: 20ft; Open May-Sep; Tent & RV camping: $14; Elev: 6578ft/2005m; Tel: 208-847-0375; Nearest town: Paris; Notes: 3 group sites $67-$87. GPS: 42.207322, -111.494793

255 • Park Creek (Lowman)

Total sites: 24; RV sites: 24; Central water; Vault toilets; No showers; No RV dump; Reservations accepted; Max length: 32ft; Open May-Oct; Tent & RV camping: $12; Elev: 4383ft/1336m; Tel: 208-259-3361; Nearest town: Lowman; Notes: 2 group sites: $100, Individual sites available FC/FS when no group use. GPS: 44.116943, -115.581299

256 • Park Creek (Sun Valley)

Total sites: 12; RV sites: 12; Central water; Vault toilets; No showers; No RV dump; Reservations not accepted; Open Jun-Sep; Tent & RV camping: $10; Elev: 7674ft/2339m; Tel: 208-588-3400; Nearest town: Ketchum; Notes: 1 group site. GPS: 43.835938, -114.258789

257 • Partridge Creek

Total sites: 10; RV sites: 10; No water; Vault toilets; Reservations not accepted; Open May-Oct; Tent & RV camping: Free; Elev: 3022ft/921m; Tel: 208-875-1131; Nearest town: Elk River. GPS: 46.784317, -116.148461

258 • Pass Creek Narrows

Total sites: 7; RV sites: 7; No water; Vault toilets; Reservations not accepted; Open May-Sep; Tent & RV camping: Free; Elev: 6376ft/1943m; Tel: 208-842-2245; Nearest town: Mackay. GPS: 43.950649, -113.444765

259 • Pebble Guard Station

Total sites: 4; RV sites: 4; Central water; Vault toilets; No showers; No RV dump; Tent & RV camping: Fee unknown; Elev: 6283ft/1915m; Tel: 208-236-7500; Nearest town: Bancroft. GPS: 42.763422, -112.087737

260 • Penn Basin

Total sites: 6; RV sites: 6; No water; Vault toilets; Reservations not accepted; Open May-Sep; Tent & RV camping: Free; Elev: 6683ft/2037m; Tel: 208-382-7400; Nearest town: Landmark. GPS: 44.624417, -115.524476

261 • Pete Creek

Total sites: 11; RV sites: 11; No water; Vault toilets; Reservations not accepted; Tent & RV camping: Free; Elev: 6288ft/1917m; Nearest town: Burgdorf. GPS: 45.305872, -115.931774

262 • Pettit

Total sites: 8; RV sites: 8; Central water; Vault toilets; No showers; No RV dump; Reservations not accepted; Stay limit: 14 days; Open Jun-Sep; Tent & RV camping: Fee unknown; Elev: 6834ft/2083m; Tel: 208 678 0439; Nearest town: Hansen. GPS: 42.183774, -114.283264

263 • Pettit Lake

Total sites: 12; RV sites: 12; Central water; Vault toilets; No showers; No RV dump; Reservations not accepted; Max length: 22ft; Stay limit: 14 days; Open Jun-Nov; Tent & RV camping: $16; Elev: 7050ft/2149m; Tel: 208-678-0439; Nearest town: Stanley. GPS: 43.984648, -114.869254

264 • Phi Kappa

Total sites: 21; RV sites: 21; Central water; Vault toilets; No showers; No RV dump; Reservations not accepted; Max length: 32ft; Open May-Sep; Tent & RV camping: $10; Elev: 7467ft/2276m; Tel: 208-588-3400; Nearest town: Ketchum. GPS: 43.858643, -114.218994

265 • Pine

Total sites: 7; RV sites: 7; No water; Vault toilets; Reservations not accepted; Open May-Sep; Tent & RV camping: $10; Elev: 4200ft/1280m; Tel: 208-587-7961; Nearest town: Mountain Home. GPS: 43.458002, -115.312239

266 • Pine Bar

Total sites: 5; RV sites: 5; No water; Vault toilets; Reservations not accepted; Tent & RV camping: Free; Elev: 6424ft/1958m; Tel: 208-547-4356; Nearest town: Freedom. GPS: 42.972455, -111.210285

267 • Pine Creek (Fourth of July Peak)

Total sites: 10; RV sites: 10; No water; Vault toilets; Reservations not accepted; Max length: 30ft; Open May-Sep; Tent & RV camping: $10; Elev: 6627ft/2020m; Tel: 208-354-2312; Nearest town: Swan Valley. GPS: 43.573132, -111.207142

268 • Pine Flats

Total sites: 26; RV sites: 26; Central water; Vault toilets; No showers; No RV dump; Reservations accepted; Max length: 32ft; Open May-Sep; Tent & RV camping: $15; Elev: 3695ft/1126m; Tel: 208-259-3361; Nearest town: Lowman. GPS: 44.063286, -115.682234

269 • Pioneer

Total sites: 5; RV sites: 5; Central water; Vault toilets; No showers; No RV dump; Reservations not accepted; Open May-Sep; Tent & RV camping: Free; Elev: 5846ft/1782m; Tel: 208-764-3202; Nearest town: Fairfield; Notes: No services in winter. GPS: 43.489571, -114.831383

270 • Pittsburgh Landing

Total sites: 28; RV sites: 28; Central water; Vault toilets; No showers; No RV dump; Reservations not accepted; Open all year; Tent & RV camping: $8; Elev: 1250ft/381m; Nearest town: White Bird. GPS: 45.635727, -116.478202

271 • Point

Total sites: 17; RV sites: 9; Central water; Flush toilets; No showers; No RV dump; Reservations accepted; Stay limit: 10 days; Open May-Sep; Tent & RV camping: $20; Elev: 6581ft/2006m; Tel: 208-678-0439; Nearest town: Stanley; Notes: Nothing larger than van/truck camper. GPS: 44.138971, -114.925496

272 • Pole Flat

Total sites: 10; RV sites: 10; Central water; Vault toilets; No showers; No RV dump; Reservations not accepted; Max length: 32ft; Open May-Sep; Tent & RV camping: $10; Elev: 6171ft/1881m; Tel: 208-879-4100; Nearest town: Stanley; Notes: 1 group site. GPS: 44.303467, -114.719727

273 • Pond Camp

Total sites: 9; RV sites: 9; No water; Vault toilets; Tent & RV camping: Free; Elev: 6423ft/1958m; Nearest town: Burgdorf. GPS: 45.339552, -115.945335

274 • Ponderosa

Total sites: 10; RV sites: 10; Central water; Vault toilets; No showers; No RV dump; Reservations not accepted; Max length: 20ft; Tent & RV camping: $10; Elev: 4114ft/1254m; Tel: 208-634-0600; Nearest town: Cascade. GPS: 45.062012, -115.759521

275 • Porcupine

Total sites: 13; RV sites: 13; Central water; No toilets; No showers; No RV dump; Reservations accepted; Open May-Sep; Tent & RV camping: $16; Elev: 6804ft/2074m; Tel: 208-847-0375; Nearest town: Bear Lake; Notes: Group site: $32. GPS: 42.095459, -111.518311

276 • Porcupine Lake

Total sites: 5; RV sites: 5; Central water; Vault toilets; No showers; No RV dump; Reservations not accepted; Open May-Sep; Tent & RV camping: Free; Elev: 4774ft/1455m; Tel: 208-263-5111; Nearest town: Clark Fork; Notes: Rough road. GPS: 48.243986, -116.184989

277 • Porcupine Springs

Total sites: 18; RV sites: 18; Potable water; Vault toilets; No showers; No RV dump; Reservations accepted; Max length: 32ft; Stay limit: 14 days; Open Jun-Sep; Tent & RV camping: $10; Elev: 6926ft/2111m; Tel: 208-678-0439; Nearest town: Burley; Notes: 3 reservable group sites $75. GPS: 42.167462, -114.261091

278 • Poverty Flat

Total sites: 10; RV sites: 6; Central water; Vault toilets; No showers; No RV dump; Reservations not accepted; Tent & RV camping: $10; Elev: 4278ft/1304m; Tel: 208-634-0600; Nearest town: Cascade. GPS: 44.822897, -115.703721

279 • Powell

Total sites: 34; RV sites: 34; Elec sites: 22; Central water; No toilets; No showers; No RV dump; Reservations accepted; Open May-Oct; Tents: $14/RVs: $14-20; Elev: 3478ft/1060m; Tel: 208-942-3113; Nearest town: Powell. GPS: 46.512207, -114.722656

280 • Power Plant

Total sites: 24; RV sites: 24; Central water; Vault toilets; No showers; No RV dump; Reservations not accepted; Open May-Sep; Tent & RV camping: $15; Elev: 5443ft/1659m; Tel: 208-392-6681; Nearest town: Lowman; Notes: Narrow rough road. GPS: 43.813988, -115.104677

281 • Queen's River

Total sites: 4; RV sites: 4; No water; Vault toilets; Reservations not accepted; Open Jun-Sep; Tent & RV camping: Free; Elev: 4987ft/1520m; Tel: 208-392-6681; Nearest town: Atlanta; Notes: Narrow rough road. GPS: 43.820994, -115.210097

282 • Queens River Transfer Camp

Total sites: 6; RV sites: 6; No water; Vault toilets; Reservations not accepted; Tent & RV camping: Free; Elev: 5250ft/1600m; Tel: 208-392-6681; Nearest town: Atlanta. GPS: 43.843162, -115.183984

283 • Race Creek

Total sites: 3; RV sites: 3; No water; Vault toilets; Reservations not accepted; Open all year; Tent & RV camping: Free; Elev: 1893ft/577m; Tel: 208-926-4258; Nearest town: Lowell; Notes: Limited winter access. GPS: 46.044038, -115.284032

284 • Rackliff

Total sites: 6; RV sites: 6; No water; Vault toilets; Reservations not accepted; Open all year; Tent & RV camping: $8; Elev: 1696ft/517m; Tel: 208-926-4258; Nearest town: Lowell; Notes: Limited winter access - free Oct-Apr. GPS: 46.085081, -115.494346

285 • Rainbow Point

Total sites: 12; RV sites: 12; Central water; Vault toilets; No showers; No RV dump; Reservations accepted; Max length: 22ft; Open May-Sep; Tent & RV camping: $15; Elev: 4846ft/1477m; Tel: 208-382-7400; Nearest town: Donnelly. GPS: 44.703388, -116.131643

286 • Rattlesnake (Sixmile Point)

Total sites: 11; RV sites: 11; Central water; Vault toilets; Reservations not accepted; Open May-Oct; Tent & RV camping: $15; Elev: 3674ft/1120m; Tel: 435-245-6521; Nearest town: Crouch; Notes: Reservable group site $125. GPS: 44.266865, -115.880157

287 • Raven Creek

Total sites: 2; RV sites: 2; No water; Vault toilets; Reservations not accepted; Max length: 25ft; Tent & RV camping: Free; Elev: 3711ft/1131m; Tel: 406-821-3269; Nearest town: Red River Hot Springs. GPS: 45.761995, -114.783556

288 • Red River

Total sites: 40; RV sites: 31; No water; Vault toilets; Reservations not accepted; Open all year; Tent & RV camping: $12; Elev: 4665ft/1422m; Tel: 208-842-2245; Nearest town: Elk City; Notes: Limited access for large RVs, Limited winter access. GPS: 45.750366, -115.269932

289 • Redfish Outlet

Total sites: 5; RV sites: 5; No water; Vault toilets; Reservations not accepted; Max length: 22ft; Tent & RV camping: Fee unknown; Elev: 6611ft/2015m; Nearest town: Stanley. GPS: 44.145256, -114.911093

290 • Reeder Bay

Total sites: 24; RV sites: 24; Central water; Vault toilets; No showers; No RV dump; Reservations accepted; Open May-Sep; Tent & RV camping: $23-25; Elev: 2490ft/759m; Tel: 208-443-1801; Nearest town: Priest River. GPS: 48.625244, -116.891846

291 • River Side (Deadwood Reservoir)

Total sites: 8; RV sites: 8; Central water; Vault toilets; No showers; No RV dump; Reservations accepted; Open Jun-Oct; Tent & RV camping: $12; Elev: 5377ft/1639m; Tel: 208-259-3361; Nearest town: Lowman. GPS: 44.341236, -115.657573

292 • Riverside (Idaho City)

Total sites: 11; RV sites: 11; Central water; Vault toilets; No showers; No RV dump; Reservations not accepted; Open May-Sep; Tent & RV camping: $15; Elev: 5325ft/1623m; Tel: 208-392-6681; Nearest town: Lowman; Notes: Narrow rough road. GPS: 43.808789, -115.130637

293 • Riverside (Stanley))

Total sites: 17; RV sites: 17; Central water; Vault toilets; No showers; No RV dump; Reservations not accepted; Stay limit: 10 days; Tent & RV camping: $14; Elev: 6126ft/1867m; Tel: 208-774-3000; Nearest town: Stanley. GPS: 44.265922, -114.850719

294 • Riverside Park

Total sites: 56; RV sites: 56; Central water; Vault toilets; No showers; No RV dump; Reservations accepted; Max length: 22ft; Open May-Sep; Tent & RV camping: $20; Elev: 6088ft/1856m; Tel: 208-523-1412; Nearest town: Ashton; Notes: Group site: $50. GPS: 44.265744, -111.456602

295 • Robert E Lee

Total sites: 8; RV sites: 4; No water; No toilets; Reservations not accepted; Tent & RV camping: Free; Elev: 4705ft/1434m; Nearest town: Boise; Notes: No large RVs. GPS: 43.905798, -115.434609

296 • Robinson Lake

Total sites: 10; RV sites: 10; Central water; Vault toilets; No showers; No RV dump; Reservations not accepted; Max length: 27ft; Open all year; Tent & RV camping: $15; Elev: 2667ft/813m; Tel: 208-267-5561; Nearest town: Eastport; Notes: No fee in off-season with no water. GPS: 48.970074, -116.217665

297 • Rocky Bluff

Total sites: 5; RV sites: 3; No water; No toilets; Reservations not accepted; Max length: 15ft; Open all year; Tent & RV camping: Free; Elev: 5253ft/1601m; Tel: 208-839-2211; Nearest town: White Bird; Notes: Limited winter access. GPS: 45.632316, -116.010984

298 • Rocky Ridge Lake

Total sites: 6; RV sites: 6; No water; No toilets; Reservations not accepted; Open Jun-Sep; Tent & RV camping: Free; Elev: 5671ft/1729m; Tel: 208-926-4274; Nearest town: Pierce. GPS: 46.441078, -115.491879

299 • Rooks Creek

Total sites: 5; RV sites: 5; No water; Vault toilets; Reservations not accepted; Tent & RV camping: Free; Elev: 6460ft/1969m; Nearest town: Ketchum. GPS: 43.649749, -114.522937

300 • Sacajawea Memorial

Total sites: 6; RV sites: 2; No water; Vault toilets; Reservations not accepted; Max length: 18ft; Open Jun-Oct; Tent & RV camping: Free; Elev: 7279ft/2219m. GPS: 44.969891, -113.443482

301 • Sagehen Creek

Total sites: 15; RV sites: 15; Central water; Vault toilets; No showers; No RV dump; Reservations accepted; Open May-Sep; Tent & RV camping: $15; Elev: 5049ft/1539m; Tel: 208-365-7000; Nearest town: Cascade. GPS: 44.334859, -116.174724

302 • Salmon River

Total sites: 30; RV sites: 30; Central water; Vault toilets; No showers; No RV dump; Reservations not accepted; Stay limit: 10 days; Open all year; Tent & RV camping: $16; Elev: 6148ft/1874m; Tel: 208-727-5000; Nearest town: Stanley. GPS: 44.248535, -114.870117

303 • Sam Owen

Total sites: 80; RV sites: 59; Central water; Vault toilets; No showers; RV dump; Reservations accepted; Max length: 50ft; Open May-Sep; Tent & RV camping: $23-25; Elev: 2165ft/660m; Tel: 208-264-0209; Nearest town: Hope; Notes: Dump fee - $7. GPS: 48.218994, -116.287842

304 • Sam's Creek

Total sites: 3; RV sites: 3; No water; Vault toilets; Reservations not accepted; Max length: 22ft; Open all year; Tent & RV camping: Free; Elev: 5423ft/1653m; Tel: 208-842-2245; Nearest town: Dixie; Notes: Limited winter access. GPS: 45.536287, -115.495845

305 • Sawmill

Total sites: 3; RV sites: 3; No water; Vault toilets; Reservations not accepted; Max length: 16ft; Stay limit: 16 days; Open May-Sep; Tent & RV camping: Free; Elev: 6762ft/2061m; Tel: 208-622-5371; Nearest town: Sun Valley. GPS: 43.666556, -114.163628

306 • Schipper

Total sites: 5; RV sites: 5; No water; Vault toilets; Reservations not accepted; Stay limit: 14 days; Open May-Oct; Tent & RV camping: $5; Elev: 4698ft/1432m; Tel: 208-678-0439; Nearest town: Hansen. GPS: 42.322495, -114.268247

307 • Scout Mountain

Total sites: 28; RV sites: 28; Central water; Vault toilets; No showers; No RV dump; Reservations accepted; Max length: 16ft; Open May-Sep; Tent & RV camping: $12; Elev: 6529ft/1990m; Tel: 208-236-7500; Nearest town: Pocatello; Notes: Group site: $60. GPS: 42.693604, -112.358887

308 • Selway Falls

Total sites: 7; RV sites: 7; No water; Vault toilets; Reservations not accepted; Tent & RV camping: $6; Elev: 1770ft/539m; Tel: 208-926-4258; Nearest town: Lowell; Notes: Limited winter access - free Oct-Apr. GPS: 46.040224, -115.295183

309 • Seven Devils

Total sites: 10; No water; Vault toilets; Reservations not accepted; Open Jun-Oct; Tents only: Free; Elev: 7559ft/2304m; Tel: 541-426-5546; Nearest town: Riggins; Notes: Very steep and narrow road - low clearance vehicles/RVs/trailers are not recommended. GPS: 45.347062, -116.517467

310 • Shadowy St. Joe

Total sites: 14; RV sites: 14; Central water; Vault toilets; No showers; No RV dump; Reservations not accepted; Open May-Nov; Tent & RV camping: $20; Elev: 2316ft/706m; Nearest town: St. Maries. GPS: 47.325668, -116.393254

311 • Sheep Rock

Total sites: 2; No water; Vault toilets; Reservations not accepted; Tent & RV camping: Free; Elev: 6598ft/2011m; Tel: 208-253-0100; Nearest town: Council. GPS: 45.191573, -116.669156

312 • Sheep Trail

Total sites: 3; RV sites: 3; Central water; Vault toilets; No showers; No RV dump; Reservations not accepted; Open May-Sep; Tent & RV camping: $14; Elev: 6588ft/2008m; Tel: 208-678-0439; Nearest town: Stanley; Notes: Group site: $47, Single sites available if not in use as group site. GPS: 44.305658, -115.056445

313 • Shiefer

Total sites: 5; RV sites: 5; No water; Vault toilets; Reservations not accepted; Tent & RV camping: Free; Elev: 2979ft/908m; Tel: 208-634-0400; Nearest town: Warren. GPS: 45.173472, -115.579919

314 • Shoreline

Total sites: 30; RV sites: 30; Central water; Vault toilets; No showers; No RV dump; Reservations accepted; Max length: 30ft; Open May-Sep; Tent & RV camping: $15; Elev: 5312ft/1619m; Tel: 208-382-7400; Nearest town: Cascade; Notes: Group site $100. GPS: 44.654768, -115.665227

315 • Silver Creek

Total sites: 55; RV sites: 51; Central water; Vault toilets; No showers; No RV dump; Reservations accepted; Open May-Oct; Tent & RV camping: $15; Elev: 4941ft/1506m; Tel: 208-739-3400; Nearest town: Garden Valley; Notes: Group site $150. GPS: 44.332218, -115.803352

316 • Sing Lee

Total sites: 4; RV sites: 4; Central water; Vault toilets; No showers; No RV dump; Reservations not accepted; Open all year; Tent & RV camping: Free; Elev: 3996ft/1218m; Tel: 208-842-2245; Nearest town: Elk City; Notes: Limited winter access. GPS: 45.885108, -115.625228

317 • Skeleton

Total sites: 5; RV sites: 5; No water; Vault toilets; Reservations not accepted; Tent & RV camping: Free; Elev: 5095ft/1553m; Nearest town: Fairfield. GPS: 43.590082, -115.018428

318 • Slide Creek

Total sites: 3; RV sites: 3; No water; Vault toilets; Reservations not accepted; Open all year; Tent & RV camping: Free; Elev: 1906ft/581m; Tel: 208-926-4258; Nearest town: Lowell; Notes: Limited winter access. GPS: 46.084831, -115.452568

319 • Slims Camp

Total sites: 2; RV sites: 2; No water; Vault toilets; Reservations not accepted; Open all year; Tent & RV camping: Free; Elev: 1796ft/547m; Tel: 208-926-4258; Nearest town: Lowell. GPS: 46.030311, -115.289988

320 • Smith Lake

Total sites: 7; RV sites: 7; Central water; Vault toilets; No showers; No RV dump; Reservations not accepted; Max length: 16ft; Open May-Sep; Tent & RV camping: Free; Elev: 3032ft/924m; Nearest town: Bonners Ferry. GPS: 48.778823, -116.263806

321 • Smokey Bear

Total sites: 12; RV sites: 12; Central water; Vault toilets; No showers; No RV dump; Reservations not accepted; Stay limit: 10 days; Tent & RV camping: $16; Elev: 7044ft/2147m; Tel: 208-774-3000; Nearest town: Stanley. GPS: 43.920166, -114.862061

322 • Snake River - Lufkin Bottoms

Total sites: 7; RV sites: 7; No water; No toilets; Tent & RV camping: Free; Elev: 5139ft/1566m; Nearest town: Idaho Falls; Notes: Also hike-in sites. GPS: 43.581197, -111.464968

323 • Snyder Guard Station

Total sites: 16; RV sites: 6; Central water; No toilets; No showers; No RV dump; Tent & RV camping: Fee unknown; Elev: 2488ft/758m; Tel: 208-267-5561; Nearest town: Bonners Ferry; Notes: Cabin(s), Campsites available only with cabin rental, $50-$110. GPS: 48.885534, -116.169215

324 • Sockeye

Total sites: 23; RV sites: 23; Central water; Vault toilets; No showers; RV dump; Reservations not accepted; Stay limit: 10 days; Open May-Sep; Tent & RV camping: $20; Elev: 6601ft/2012m; Tel: 208-678-0439; Nearest town: Stanley; Notes: Dump station nearby. GPS: 44.132519, -114.917355

325 • Sourdough Saddle

Total sites: 4; RV sites: 4; No water; Vault toilets; Reservations not accepted; Tent & RV camping: Free; Elev: 6095ft/1858m; Tel: 208-842-2245; Nearest town: Grangeville; Notes: Corrals & hitching rails. GPS: 45.722563, -115.805756

326 • South Fork (Hungry Ridge)

Total sites: 9; RV sites: 9; Central water; Vault toilets; No showers; No RV dump; Reservations not accepted; Max length: 30ft; Open all year; Tent & RV camping: $12; Elev: 2284ft/696m; Tel: 208-983-1950; Nearest town: Grangeville; Notes: Limited winter access. GPS: 45.826228, -115.961588

327 • South Fork Salmon River

Total sites: 11; RV sites: 11; Central water; Vault toilets; No showers; No RV dump; Reservations not accepted; Open May-Sep; Tent & RV camping: $15; Elev: 5128ft/1563m; Tel: 208-382-7400; Nearest town: Cascade. GPS: 44.653021, -115.702094

328 • Spillway

Total sites: 3; RV sites: 3; No water; Vault toilets; Reservations not accepted; Open May-Sep; Tent & RV camping: Free; Elev: 4203ft/1281m; Tel: 208-587-7961; Nearest town: Mountain Home. GPS: 43.357214, -115.447505

329 • Spring Bar

Total sites: 18; Central water; Vault toilets; No showers; No RV dump; Reservations not accepted; Max length: 20ft; Open all year; Tents only: $12; Elev: 1942ft/592m; Tel: 208-839-2211; Nearest town: Riggins; Notes: Limited winter access. GPS: 45.426514, -116.153076

330 • Spring Creek (North Fork)

Total sites: 5; RV sites: 5; Central water; Vault toilets; No showers; No RV dump; Reservations not accepted; Open May-Oct; Tent & RV camping: $10; Elev: 3409ft/1039m; Tel: 208-865-2700; Nearest town: North Fork. GPS: 45.390991, -114.254967

331 • Spring Creek (Weiser)

Total sites: 14; RV sites: 14; Central water; Vault toilets; No showers; No RV dump; Reservations accepted; Tent & RV camping: $10-15; Elev: 4928ft/1502m; Tel: 208-549-4200; Nearest town: Weiser. GPS: 44.569824, -116.946533

332 • Spruce Tree

Total sites: 9; RV sites: 9; Central water; Vault toilets; No showers; No RV dump; Reservations not accepted; Open May-Oct; Tent & RV camping: $15; Elev: 3786ft/1154m; Nearest town: Avery; Notes: $12 when no water. GPS: 47.037994, -115.347921

333 • St Charles

Total sites: 6; RV sites: 6; Central water; No toilets; No showers; No RV dump; Reservations not accepted; Open May-Sep; Tent & RV camping: $5; Elev: 6125ft/1867m; Tel: 435-245-6521; Nearest town: St. Charles; Notes: Reservable group site $37. GPS: 42.113041, -111.446759

334 • Stanley Lake

Total sites: 19; RV sites: 19; Central water; Vault toilets; No showers; No RV dump; Reservations accepted; Open May-Sep; Tent & RV camping: $18; Elev: 6555ft/1998m; Tel: 208-678-0439; Nearest town: Stanley. GPS: 44.248747, -115.054425

335 • Stanley Lake Inlet

Total sites: 14; Central water; Vault toilets; No showers; No RV dump; Stay limit: 10 days; Tents only: $18; Elev: 6530ft/1990m; Tel: 208-727-5000; Nearest town: Stanley. GPS: 44.246405, -115.064801

336 • Star Hope

Total sites: 21; RV sites: 21; Central water; Vault toilets; No showers; No RV dump; Reservations not accepted; Open May-Sep; Tent & RV camping: $10; Elev: 7913ft/2412m; Tel: 208-588-3400; Nearest town: Mackay. GPS: 43.743645, -113.942588

337 • Steer Basin

Total sites: 4; RV sites: 4; No water; No toilets; Reservations not accepted; Max length: 20ft; Open May-Oct; Tent & RV camping: $5; Elev: 5256ft/1602m; Nearest town: Burley. GPS: 42.279611, -114.260306

338 • Stoddard Creek

Total sites: 20; RV sites: 20; Central water; Vault toilets; No showers; No RV dump; Reservations accepted; Max length: 32ft; Open May-Sep; Tent & RV camping: $10; Elev: 6263ft/1909m; Tel: 208-374-5422; Nearest town: Dubois; Notes: Group site $75-$150. GPS: 44.417969, -112.216797

339 • Sublett

Total sites: 9; RV sites: 9; No water; Vault toilets; Reservations not accepted; Stay limit: 14 days; Open Jun-Nov; Tent & RV camping: Free; Elev: 5430ft/1655m; Tel: 208-678-0439; Nearest town: Burley. GPS: 42.327704, -113.003233

340 • Summit Lake

Total sites: 3; RV sites: 3; No water; Vault toilets; Reservations not accepted; Open May-Sep; Tent & RV camping: Free; Elev: 7313ft/2229m; Tel: 208-382-7400; Nearest town: Cascade. GPS: 44.644943, -115.585514

341 • Summit View (Georgetown)

Total sites: 18; RV sites: 18; Central water; Vault toilets; No showers; No RV dump; Reservations accepted; Open Jun-Sep; Tent & RV camping: $14; Elev: 7238ft/2206m; Tel: 208-847-0375; Nearest town: Montpelier; Notes: 3 group sites $56-$67. GPS: 42.558601, -111.296052

342 • Sunny Gulch

Total sites: 19; RV sites: 19; Central water; Vault toilets; No showers; No RV dump; Reservations accepted; Stay limit: 10 days; Open Jun-Sep; Tent & RV camping: $18; Elev: 6453ft/1967m; Tel: 208-678-0439; Nearest town: Stanley. GPS: 44.175045, -114.909738

343 • Swinging Bridge

Total sites: 11; RV sites: 11; Central water; Vault toilets; No showers; No RV dump; Reservations accepted; Open May-Sep; Tent & RV camping: $14; Elev: 3681ft/1122m; Tel: 208-365-7000; Nearest town: Horseshoe Bend. GPS: 44.171598, -116.120888

344 • Table Meadows

Total sites: 6; RV sites: 6; No water; Vault toilets; Reservations not accepted; Open all year; Tent & RV camping: Free; Elev: 4895ft/1492m; Tel: 208-842-2245; Nearest town: Elk City; Notes: Limited winter access. GPS: 45.934253, -115.511608

345 • Tailwaters

Total sites: 3; RV sites: 3; No water; Vault toilets; Reservations not accepted; Tent & RV camping: Free; Elev: 3983ft/1214m; Tel: 208-587-7961; Nearest town: Mountain Home. GPS: 43.355917, -115.455304

346 • Telichpah

Total sites: 5; RV sites: 5; No water; Vault toilets; Reservations not accepted; Open May-Sep; Tent & RV camping: Free; Elev: 2762ft/842m; Nearest town: Avery; Notes: Nothing bigger than truck campers. GPS: 47.295484, -115.774753

347 • Ten Mile

Total sites: 2; RV sites: 2; No water; No toilets; Reservations not accepted; Open all year; Tent & RV camping: Free; Elev: 4094ft/1248m; Tel: 208-842-2245; Nearest town: Elk City; Notes: Limited winter access. GPS: 45.761216, -115.658993

348 • Ten Mile

Total sites: 16; RV sites: 16; Central water; Vault toilets; No showers; No RV dump; Reservations not accepted; Open May-Sep; Tent & RV camping: $15; Elev: 4875ft/1486m; Tel: 208-392-6681; Nearest town: Idaho City. GPS: 43.898566, -115.712541

349 • Teton Canyon

Total sites: 22; RV sites: 22; Central water; No toilets; No showers; No RV dump; Reservations accepted; Open May-Sep; Tent & RV camping: $12; Elev: 6995ft/2132m; Tel: 208-354-2312; Nearest town: Driggs. GPS: 43.756710, -110.918950

350 • Thatcher

Total sites: 5; RV sites: 5; Central water; Vault toilets; No showers; No RV dump; Reservations not accepted; Max length: 32ft; Open May-Oct; Tent & RV camping: $10; Elev: 6601ft/2012m; Tel: 208-879-4101; Nearest town: Stanley. GPS: 44.367658, -115.145382

351 • Third Fork

Total sites: 5; RV sites: 5; No water; Vault toilets; Reservations not accepted; Stay limit: 14 days; Open May-Sep; Tent & RV camping: Free; Elev: 5197ft/1584m; Tel: 208-678-0439; Nearest town: Twin Falls. GPS: 42.252024, -114.248199

352 • Thompson Flat

Total sites: 20; RV sites: 20; Vault toilets; Reservations not accepted; Stay limit: 14 days; Open Jul-Oct; Tent & RV camping: $8; Elev: 8051ft/2454m; Tel: 208-678-0439; Nearest town: Albion; Notes: Reservable group site $50. GPS: 42.324951, -113.623779

353 • Tie Creek

Total sites: 8; RV sites: 8; Central water; Vault toilets; No showers; No RV dump; Reservations not accepted; Open May-Oct; Tent & RV camping: $15; Elev: 3120ft/951m; Tel: 208-365-7000; Nearest town: Crouch. GPS: 44.208281, -115.925726

354 • Timber Creek

Total sites: 12; RV sites: 12; Central water; Vault toilets; No showers; No RV dump; Reservations not accepted; Open May-Sep; Tent & RV camping: $5; Elev: 7274ft/2217m; Tel: 208-588-3400; Nearest town: Howe. GPS: 44.395793, -113.409203

355 • Timber Creek Reservoir (Lower)

Total sites: 2; RV sites: 2; No water; Vault toilets; Reservations not accepted; Open May-Sep; Tent & RV camping: Free; Elev: 7589ft/2313m; Tel: 208-768-2500; Nearest town: Leadore. GPS: 44.581076, -113.466366

356 • Timber Creek Reservoir (Upper)

Total sites: 5; RV sites: 5; No water; Vault toilets; Reservations not accepted; Open May-Sep; Tent & RV camping: Free; Elev: 7592ft/2314m; Tel: 208-768-2500; Nearest town: Mackay. GPS: 44.576867, -113.470996

357 • Tin Can Flat

Total sites: 11; RV sites: 11; Central water; Vault toilets; No showers; No RV dump; Reservations not accepted; Open May-Oct; Tent & RV camping: Fee unknown; Elev: 2910ft/887m; Nearest town: Avery. GPS: 47.229980, -115.621094

358 • Tin Cup

Total sites: 13; RV sites: 13; No water; Vault toilets; Reservations not accepted; Open Jul-Oct; Tent & RV camping: Free; Elev: 5466ft/1666m; Tel: 208-879-4101; Nearest town: Challis; Notes: High clearance vehicles recommended. GPS: 44.597168, -114.813477

359 • Tin Cup

Total sites: 5; RV sites: 5; No water; Vault toilets; Reservations not accepted; Open May-Sep; Tent & RV camping: Free; Elev: 5863ft/1787m; Tel: 208-547-4356; Nearest town: Freedom. GPS: 43.004643, -111.102652

360 • Trail Creek (Garden Valley)

Total sites: 11; RV sites: 11; Central water; Vault toilets; No showers; No RV dump; Reservations not accepted; Max length: 35ft; Open May-Sep; Tent & RV camping: $12; Elev: 3766ft/1148m; Tel: 208-365-7000; Nearest town: Garden Valley. GPS: 44.276552, -115.875152

361 • Trapper Creek

Total sites: 1; RV sites: 1; No water; Vault toilets; Reservations not accepted; Open all year; Tent & RV camping: Free; Elev: 4680ft/1426m; Tel: 208-842-2245; Nearest town: Elk City; Notes: Limited winter access. GPS: 45.674178, -115.344016

362 • Trout Creek

Total sites: 8; RV sites: 8; No water; Vault toilets; Reservations not accepted; Open May-Sep; Tent & RV camping: Free; Elev: 6348ft/1935m; Tel: 208-382-7400; Nearest town: Landmark. GPS: 44.747081, -115.555146

363 • Troutdale

Total sites: 5; RV sites: 5; No water; Vault toilets; Reservations not accepted; Open Apr-Oct; Tent & RV camping: Free; Elev: 3566ft/1087m; Tel: 208-587-7961; Nearest town: Boise. GPS: 43.716272, -115.625111

364 • Turner Flat

Total sites: 10; RV sites: 10; Central water; Vault toilets; No showers; No RV dump; Reservations not accepted; Open May-Nov; Tent & RV camping: $12-15; Elev: 2822ft/860m; Nearest town: Avery. GPS: 47.236816, -115.654297

365 • Twenty Mile Bar

Total sites: 2; RV sites: 2; No water; Vault toilets; Reservations not accepted; Open all year; Tent & RV camping: Free; Elev: 1886ft/575m; Tel: 208-926-4258; Nearest town: Elk City; Notes: Limited winter access. GPS: 46.073011, -115.376516

366 • Twenty-five Mile Bar

Total sites: 3; RV sites: 3; No water; Vault toilets; Reservations not accepted; Open all year; Tent & RV camping: Free; Elev: 1745ft/532m; Tel: 208-926-4258; Nearest town: Elk city. GPS: 46.076114, -115.412178

367 • Twin Creek (Gibbonsville)

Total sites: 40; RV sites: 40; Central water; Vault toilets; No showers; No RV dump; Reservations not accepted; Max length: 22ft; Open Jun-Sep; Tent & RV camping: $10; Elev: 5299ft/1615m; Tel: 208-865-2700; Nearest town: Gibbonsville. GPS: 45.608238, -113.969836

368 • Twin Lakes

Total sites: 12; RV sites: 12; No water; Vault toilets; Reservations not accepted; Stay limit: 14 days; Open Jul-Oct; Tent & RV camping: Fee unknown; Elev: 8205ft/2501m; Tel: 208-678-0430. GPS: 42.317651, -113.625334

369 • Upper Coffee Pot

Total sites: 14; RV sites: 14; Elec sites: 5; Central water; Vault toilets; No showers; No RV dump; Reservations accepted; Open Jun-Sep; Tents: $15/RVs: $15-21; Elev: 6394ft/1949m; Tel: 208-652-7442; Nearest town: Island Park. GPS: 44.490913, -111.366123

370 • Upper Payette Lake

Total sites: 24; RV sites: 24; Central water; Vault toilets; No showers; No RV dump; Reservations accepted; Open Jun-Sep; Tent & RV camping: $10-15; Elev: 5584ft/1702m; Tel: 208-634-0400; Nearest town: McCall; Notes: Group site $20-$30. GPS: 45.125844, -116.027232

371 • Upper Penstemon

Total sites: 8; RV sites: 8; Central water; Vault toilets; No showers; No RV dump; Reservations not accepted; Stay limit: 14 days; Open Jun-Sep; Tent & RV camping: $8; Elev: 6660ft/2030m; Tel: 208-678-0439; Nearest town: Burley. GPS: 42.194331, -114.285882

372 • Wallace Lake

Total sites: 12; Central water; Vault toilets; No showers; No RV dump; Reservations not accepted; Open Jul-Oct; Tents only: $4; Elev: 8159ft/2487m; Tel: 208-756-5200; Nearest town: Salmon; Notes: RVs/trailers not recommended. GPS: 45.247037, -114.003965

373 • Warm Lake

Total sites: 12; RV sites: 12; Central water; Vault toilets; No showers; No RV dump; Reservations accepted; Open May-Sep; Tent & RV camping: $15; Elev: 5377ft/1639m; Tel: 208-382-7400; Nearest town: Cascade. GPS: 44.651674, -115.656918

374 • Warm River

Total sites: 28; RV sites: 17; Water at site; Vault toilets; No showers; No RV dump; Reservations accepted; Open May-Sep; Tents: $15/RVs: $15-21; Elev: 5315ft/1620m; Tel: 208-652-7442; Nearest town: Ashton; Notes: Group site $75-$150. GPS: 44.120154, -111.311145

375 • Washington Creek

Total sites: 23; RV sites: 23; Central water; Vault toilets; No showers; No RV dump; Reservations not accepted; Open May-Oct; Tent & RV camping: $10; Elev: 2139ft/652m; Tel: 208-476-4541; Nearest town: Pierce. GPS: 46.703984, -115.555859

376 • Weitas Creek

Total sites: 6; Vault toilets; Reservations not accepted; Open all year; Tents only: Free; Elev: 2371ft/723m; Tel: 208-476-4541; Nearest town: Orofino; Notes: Limited winter access. GPS: 46.637658, -115.433586

377 • Wendover

Total sites: 26; RV sites: 26; Central water; Vault toilets; No showers; No RV dump; Reservations not accepted; Max length: 40ft; Open May-Sep; Tent & RV camping: $14; Elev: 3343ft/1019m; Tel: 208-942-3113; Nearest town: Lowell. GPS: 46.510010, -114.784668

378 • West Fork Morgan Creek

Total sites: 1; RV sites: 1; No water; Vault toilets; Reservations not accepted; Open Jul-Oct; Tent & RV camping: Free; Elev: 6453ft/1967m; Tel: 208-879-4100; Nearest town: Challis. GPS: 44.702738, -114.315662

379 • Whiskey Flat

Total sites: 6; RV sites: 4; Central water; Vault toilets; No showers; No RV dump; Reservations not accepted; Stay limit: 10 days; Tent & RV camping: $10; Elev: 5659ft/1725m; Tel: 208-774-3000; Nearest town: Clayton. GPS: 44.254864, -114.552384

380 • Whiskey Rock Bay

Total sites: 9; RV sites: 9; Central water; Vault toilets; No showers; No RV dump; Reservations not accepted; Open May-Sep; Tent & RV camping: Free; Elev: 2123ft/647m; Nearest town: Clark Fork. GPS: 48.050677, -116.452781

381 • White Sand

Total sites: 7; RV sites: 7; Central water; Vault toilets; No showers; No RV dump; Reservations not accepted; Max length: 30ft; Open May-Oct; Tent & RV camping: $14; Elev: 3439ft/1048m; Tel: 208-942-3113; Nearest town: Powell. GPS: 46.507291, -114.686584

382 • Whitehouse

Total sites: 11; RV sites: 11; Central water; Vault toilets; No showers; No RV dump; Reservations not accepted; Max length: 30ft; Open May-Sep; Tent & RV camping: $14; Elev: 3327ft/1014m; Tel: 208-942-3113; Nearest town: Lowell. GPS: 46.506838, -114.774632

383 • Wild Goose

Total sites: 8; RV sites: 8; Central water; Vault toilets; No showers; No RV dump; Reservations not accepted; Max length: 24ft; Open May-Sep; Tent & RV camping: $14; Elev: 1604ft/489m; Tel: 208-926-4274; Nearest town: Lowell. GPS: 46.135726, -115.626239

384 • Wilderness Gateway

Total sites: 85; RV sites: 85; Central water; Vault toilets; No showers; RV dump; Reservations accepted; Max length: 32ft; Open Apr-Oct; Tent & RV camping: $14; Elev: 2116ft/645m; Tel:

208-926-4274; Nearest town: Lowell; Notes: Group site: $280. GPS: 46.340129, -115.309191

385 • Wildhorse

Total sites: 13; RV sites: 13; Central water; Vault toilets; No showers; No RV dump; Reservations not accepted; Open Jun-Sep; Tent & RV camping: $10; Elev: 7356ft/2242m; Tel: 208-588-3400; Nearest town: Mackay; Notes: Limited winter access. GPS: 43.822510, -114.095947

386 • Wildhorse Lake

Total sites: 8; No water; Vault toilets; Reservations not accepted; Tents only: Free; Elev: 7552ft/2302m; Tel: 208-842-2245; Nearest town: Elk City; Notes: Primitive road. GPS: 45.655736, -115.650964

387 • Willow Creek

Total sites: 3; RV sites: 3; No water; Vault toilets; Reservations not accepted; Open May-Oct; Tent & RV camping: $6; Elev: 4813ft/1467m; Tel: 208-764-3202; Nearest town: Featherville. GPS: 43.606105, -115.142189

388 • Willow Creek (Arrowrock)

Total sites: 9; RV sites: 9; Central water; Vault toilets; No showers; No RV dump; Reservations not accepted; Open Apr-Oct; Tent & RV camping: Free; Elev: 3307ft/1008m; Tel: 208-587-7961; Nearest town: Boise. GPS: 43.644043, -115.752686

389 • Willow Creek (Idaho City)

Total sites: 4; RV sites: 4; No water; Vault toilets; Reservations not accepted; Tent & RV camping: Free; Elev: 5426ft/1654m; Tel: 208-392-6681; Nearest town: Idaho City. GPS: 43.959142, -115.532166

390 • Willow Creek Transfer Camp

Total sites: 3; RV sites: 3; No water; Vault toilets; Reservations not accepted; Open May-Oct; Tent & RV camping: Donation; Elev: 5118ft/1560m; Tel: 208-764-3202; Nearest town: Featherville; Notes: Corrals. GPS: 43.626408, -115.134416

391 • Willow Flat

Total sites: 55; RV sites: 45; Central water; No toilets; No showers; No RV dump; Reservations accepted; Max length: 22ft; Open May-Sep; Tent & RV camping: $17; Elev: 6119ft/1865m; Tel: 208-847-0375; Nearest town: Preston; Notes: 6 group sites: $28-$87. GPS: 42.138677, -111.625128

392 • Windy Saddle

Total sites: 6; RV sites: 3; No water; Vault toilets; Reservations not accepted; Tent & RV camping: Free; Elev: 6549ft/1996m; Nearest town: Elk City. GPS: 45.882187, -115.042773

393 • Wood River

Total sites: 30; RV sites: 30; Central water; Flush toilets; No showers; No RV dump; Reservations not accepted; Max length: 22ft; Open May-Sep; Tent & RV camping: $16; Elev: 6368ft/1941m; Tel: 208-

678-0439; Nearest town: Ketchum; Notes: Reservable group site: $42-$116. GPS: 43.792969, -114.459473

394 • Yellow Pine

Total sites: 14; RV sites: 14; Central water; Vault toilets; No showers; No RV dump; Reservations not accepted; Open May-Sep; Tent & RV camping: Free; Elev: 4734ft/1443m; Tel: 208-382-7400; Nearest town: Cascade. GPS: 44.954590, -115.496582

Illinois

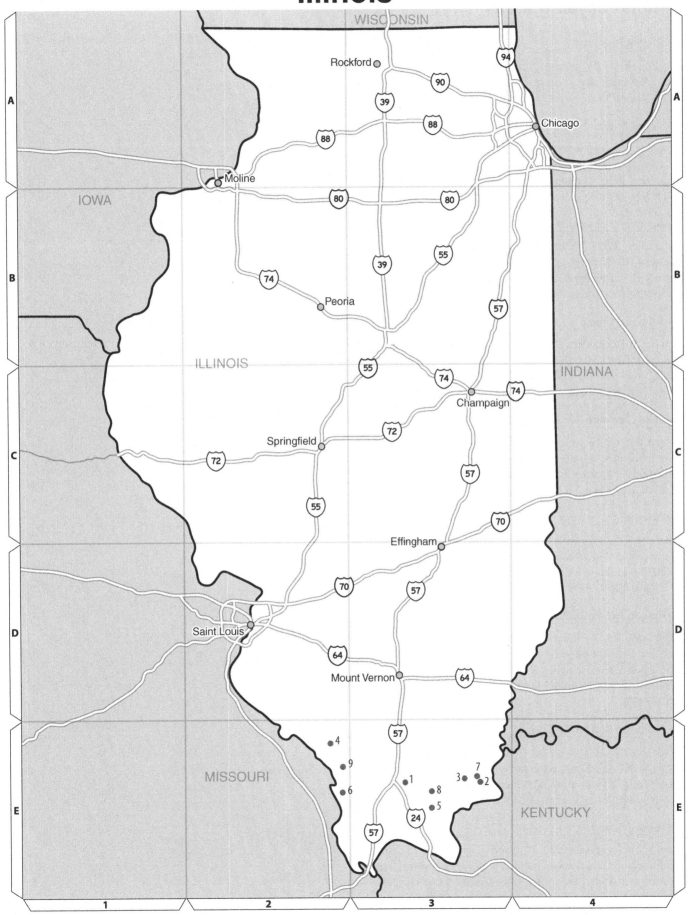

Illinois Camping Areas

1 • Buck Ridge

Total sites: 37; RV sites: 37; Central water; Vault toilets; Open Mar-Dec; Tent & RV camping: $5; Elev: 574ft/175m; Tel: 618-253-7114; Nearest town: Creal Springs. GPS: 37.579346, -88.883057

2 • Camp Cadiz

Total sites: 8; RV sites: 8; No water; Vault toilets; Reservations not accepted; Max length: 18ft; Generator hours: 0600-2200; Open all year; Tent & RV camping: $10; Elev: 591ft/180m; Tel: 618-658-2111; Nearest town: Karber's Ridge. GPS: 37.578296, -88.244672

3 • Garden of the Gods

Total sites: 12; RV sites: 12; Central water; Vault toilets; No showers; No RV dump; Reservations not accepted; Open all year; Tent & RV camping: $10; Elev: 817ft/249m; Tel: 618-253-7114; Nearest town: Karbers Ridge. GPS: 37.602539, -88.380615

4 • Johnson Creek

Total sites: 20; RV sites: 20; No water; No toilets; Reservations not accepted; Open Mar-Dec; Tent & RV camping: $10; Elev: 617ft/188m; Tel: 618-833-8576; Nearest town: Murphysboro. GPS: 37.834581, -89.520042

5 • Lake Glendale Rec Area - Oak Point

Total sites: 59; RV sites: 59; Elec sites: 34; Central water; Flush toilets; Showers; RV dump; Reservations not accepted; Open all year; Tent & RV camping: $12-22; Elev: 459ft/140m; Tel: 618-638-3246; Nearest town: Vienna. GPS: 37.409379, -88.662301

6 • Pine Hills

Total sites: 13; RV sites: 13; No water; Vault toilets; Reservations not accepted; Open Mar-Dec; Tent & RV camping: $10; Elev: 456ft/139m; Tel: 618-833-8576; Nearest town: Jonesboro. GPS: 37.514893, -89.423096

7 • Pine Ridge-Pounds Hollow

Total sites: 35; RV sites: 35; Central water; Vault toilets; No showers; No RV dump; Reservations not accepted; Max length: 40ft; Open Mar-Dec; Tent & RV camping: $10; Elev: 636ft/194m; Tel: 618-658-2111; Nearest town: Karber's Ridge. GPS: 37.615511, -88.268439

8 • Redbud - Bell Smith Springs

Total sites: 21; RV sites: 21; Central water; Vault toilets; No showers; No RV dump; Reservations not accepted; Open Mar-Dec; Tent & RV camping: $10; Elev: 673ft/205m; Tel: 618-253-7114; Nearest town: Vienna. GPS: 37.523142, -88.656819

9 • Turkey Bayou

Total sites: 16; RV sites: 16; No water; No toilets; No showers; No RV dump; Reservations not accepted; Open all year; Tent & RV camping: Free; Elev: 371ft/113m; Tel: 618-833-8576; Nearest town: Murphysboro. GPS: 37.684798, -89.411678

Indiana

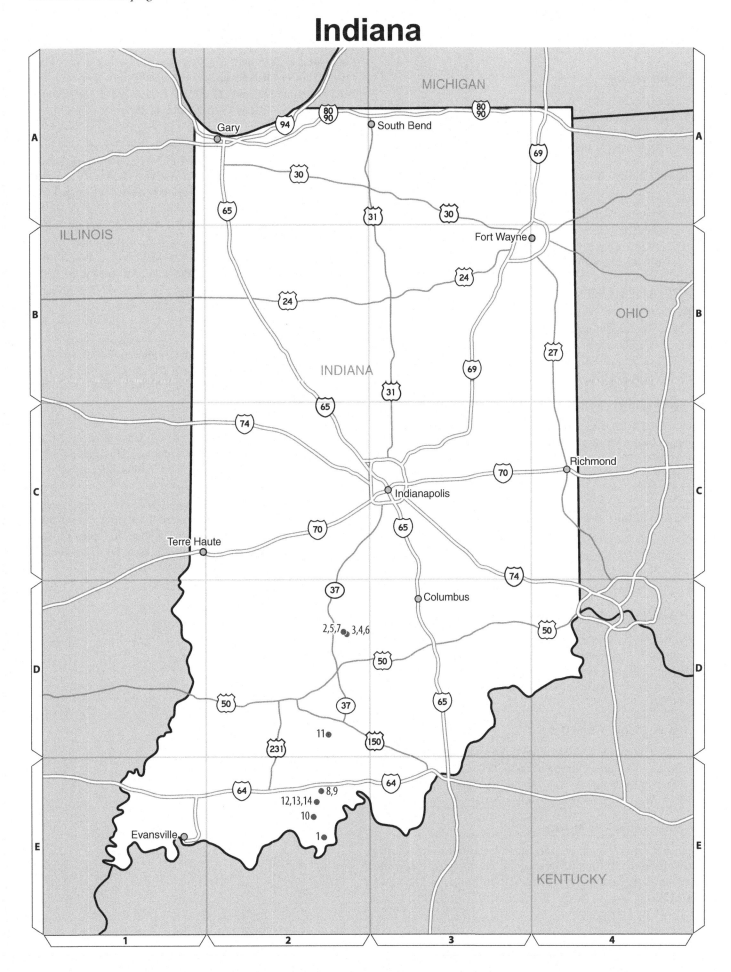

Indiana Camping Areas

1 • German Ridge

Total sites: 20; RV sites: 20; No water; Vault toilets; Reservations not accepted; Open all year; Tent & RV camping: $8; Elev: 745ft/227m; Tel: 812-547-7051; Nearest town: Cannelton; Notes: Non-potable stock water available. GPS: 37.951525, -86.588828

2 • Hardin Ridge - Blue Gill

Total sites: 51; RV sites: 35; Elec sites: 17; Water at site; Flush toilets; Showers; RV dump; Reservations not accepted; Generator hours: 0600-2200; Open May-Sep; Tent & RV camping: $20-27; Elev: 745ft/227m; Tel: 812-837-9453; Nearest town: Bloomington. GPS: 39.022143, -86.440976

3 • Hardin Ridge - Eads

Total sites: 23; RV sites: 23; Central water; Vault toilets; No showers; No RV dump; Reservations not accepted; Generator hours: 0600-2200; Open Apr-Sep; Tent & RV camping: $20; Elev: 728ft/222m; Tel: 812-837-9453; Nearest town: Bloomington. GPS: 39.014715, -86.431189

4 • Hardin Ridge - Holland

Total sites: 13; RV sites: 13; Elec sites: 13; Central water; Flush toilets; Showers; RV dump; Reservations not accepted; Generator hours: 0600-2200; Tent & RV camping: $27; Elev: 784ft/239m; Tel: 812-837-9453; Nearest town: Bloomington. GPS: 39.017743, -86.436279

5 • Hardin Ridge - Pine

Total sites: 40; RV sites: 40; Elec sites: 20; Central water; RV dump; Reservations not accepted; Generator hours: 0600-2200; Tent & RV camping: $20-27; Elev: 696ft/212m; Tel: 812-837-9453; Nearest town: Bloomington. GPS: 39.026558, -86.451816

6 • Hardin Ridge - Southern Point

Total sites: 60; RV sites: 46; Central water; No toilets; No showers; RV dump; Reservations not accepted; Generator hours: 0600-2200; Open all year; Tent & RV camping: $20; Elev: 774ft/236m; Tel: 812-837-9453; Nearest town: Bloomington. GPS: 39.014525, -86.445091

7 • Hardin Ridge - White Oak

Total sites: 17; RV sites: 17; Elec sites: 17; Central water; No toilets; No showers; RV dump; Generator hours: 0600-2200; Open May-Sep; Tent & RV camping: $30; Elev: 771ft/235m; Tel: 812-837-9453; Nearest town: Bloomington. GPS: 39.021584, -86.444933

8 • Indian-Celina - North Face

Total sites: 36; RV sites: 36; Elec sites: 3; Central water; Flush toilets; Showers; RV dump; Reservations not accepted; Open all year; Tent & RV camping: $20-27; Elev: 732ft/223m; Tel: 812-843-4880; Nearest town: St Croix. GPS: 38.197192, -86.605512

9 • Indian-Celina - South Slope

Total sites: 27; RV sites: 27; Elec sites: 27; Central water; Flush toilets; Showers; Reservations not accepted; Open Apr-Nov; Tent & RV camping: $27; Elev: 755ft/230m; Tel: 812-843-4880; Nearest town: St Croix. GPS: 38.192722, -86.608235

10 • Saddle Lake

Total sites: 13; RV sites: 13; No water; Vault toilets; Reservations not accepted; Max length: 21ft; Open all year; Tent & RV camping: $5; Elev: 656ft/200m; Tel: 812-547-7051; Nearest town: Tell City. GPS: 38.060245, -86.657067

11 • Springs Valley

Total sites: 6; RV sites: 6; No water; Vault toilets; Reservations not accepted; Generator hours: 0600-2200; Open all year; Tent & RV camping: Free; Elev: 653ft/199m; Tel: 812-547-7051; Nearest town: Paoli. GPS: 38.488384, -86.560126

12 • Tipsaw Lake - Catbrier

Total sites: 10; RV sites: 10; Elec sites: 5; Flush toilets; Showers; No RV dump; Max length: 65ft; Tent & RV camping: $20-27; Elev: 617ft/188m; Nearest town: Tell City. GPS: 38.135497, -86.636889

13 • Tipsaw Lake - Dogwood

Total sites: 14; RV sites: 12; Elec sites: 4; Central water; No RV dump; Open Apr-Oct; Tent & RV camping: $20-27; Elev: 597ft/182m; Nearest town: Tell City. GPS: 38.133608, -86.642724

14 • Tipsaw Lake - Jackpine

Total sites: 21; RV sites: 21; Elec sites: 8; Central water; No RV dump; Reservations accepted; Max length: 55ft; Open Apr-Oct; Tent & RV camping: $20-27; Elev: 614ft/187m; Tel: 812-843-4890; Nearest town: Tell City. GPS: 38.135136, -86.642415

Kansas

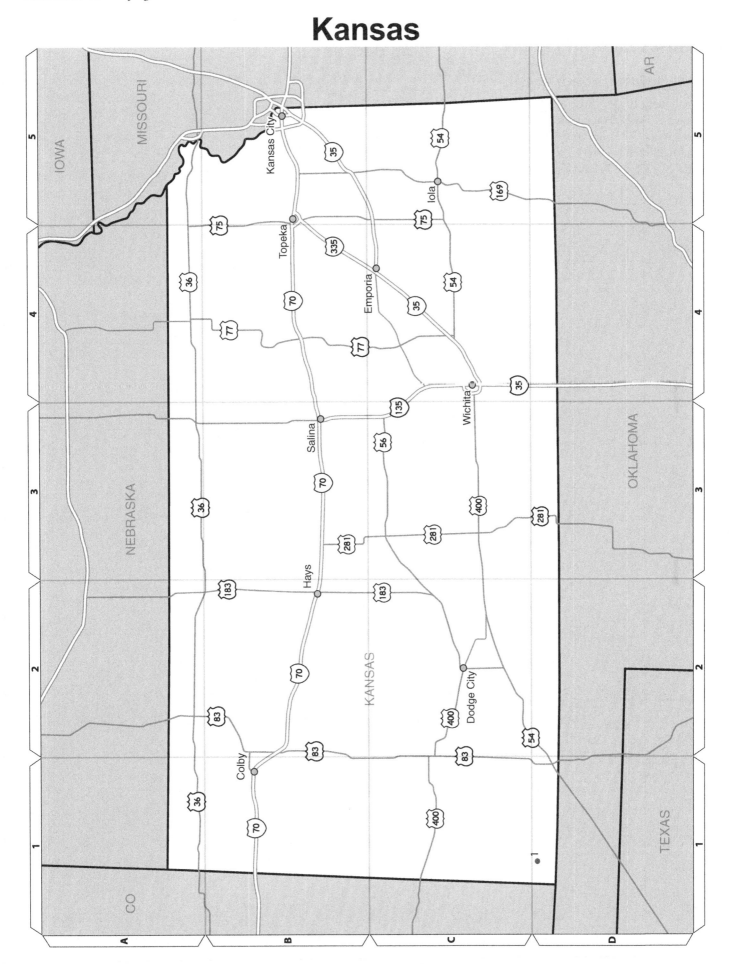

Kansas Camping Areas

1 • Cimarron Recreation Area

Total sites: 12; RV sites: 12; Central water; Vault toilets; No showers; No RV dump; Reservations not accepted; Open all year; Tent & RV camping: $7; Elev: 3345ft/1020m; Nearest town: Elkhart; Notes: No water Dec-Mar, No open fires, Group site $38. GPS: 37.135591, -101.824756

Kentucky

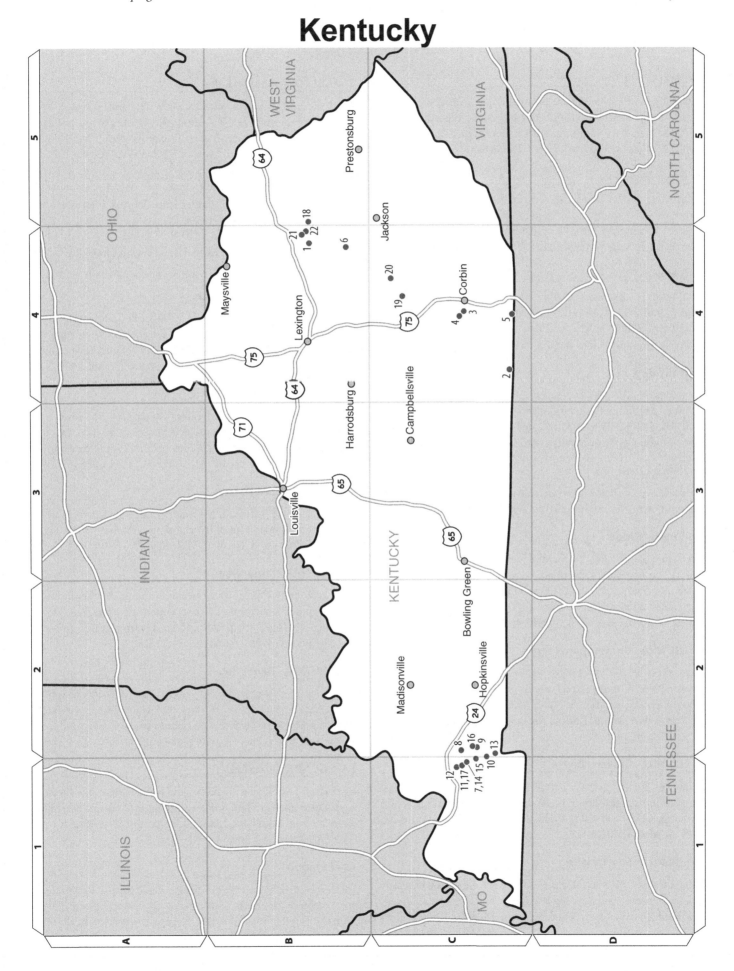

Kentucky Camping Areas

1 • Clear Creek

Total sites: 21; RV sites: 21; Central water; Vault toilets; No showers; No RV dump; Reservations not accepted; Max length: 30ft; Open Apr-Dec; Tent & RV camping: $10-15; Elev: 817ft/249m; Tel: 606-768-2722; Nearest town: Salt Lick. GPS: 38.044316, -83.585544

2 • Great Meadow

Total sites: 18; RV sites: 18; Central water; Vault toilets; No showers; No RV dump; Reservations not accepted; Open all year; Tent & RV camping: Free; Elev: 1020ft/311m; Tel: 606-376-5323; Nearest town: Stearns. GPS: 36.628971, -84.725843

3 • Grove

Total sites: 56; RV sites: 52; Elec sites: 52; Central water; Flush toilets; Showers; RV dump; Reservations accepted; Open Apr-Oct; Tents: $18/RVs: $29-35; Elev: 1171ft/357m; Tel: 606-528-6156; Nearest town: Corbin. GPS: 36.943604, -84.215332

4 • Holly Bay

Total sites: 94; RV sites: 75; Elec sites: 29; Water at site; Flush toilets; Showers; RV dump; Reservations accepted; Open Apr-Oct; Tents: $18/RVs: $29-35; Elev: 1073ft/327m; Tel: 606-528-6156; Nearest town: London. GPS: 36.981201, -84.261230

5 • Jellico Creek

Total sites: 2; RV sites: 2; No water; No toilets; Tent & RV camping: Fee unknown; Elev: 1086ft/331m. GPS: 36.601145, -84.248238

6 • Koomer Ridge

Total sites: 54; RV sites: 19; Central water; Flush toilets; Showers; No RV dump; Reservations not accepted; Stay limit: 14 days; Generator hours: 0600-2200; Open all year; Tents: $20/RVs: $25; Elev: 1299ft/396m; Tel: 606-663-8100; Nearest town: Stanton; Notes: Nov-Mar: $10. GPS: 37.784264, -83.633136

7 • LBL NRA - Birmingham Ferry

Total sites: 26; RV sites: 16; Central water; Vault toilets; No showers; No RV dump; Reservations not accepted; Stay limit: 14 days; Open all year; Tent & RV camping: $10; Elev: 433ft/132m; Nearest town: Grand Rivers; Notes: 3-day permit: $10. GPS: 36.923038, -88.162656

8 • LBL NRA - Cravens Bay

Total sites: 30; RV sites: 27; Central water; No toilets; No showers; No RV dump; Stay limit: 14 days; Open all year; Tent & RV camping: $12; Elev: 446ft/136m; Nearest town: Grand Rivers. GPS: 36.960641, -88.053177

9 • LBL NRA - Energy lake

Total sites: 48; RV sites: 43; Elec sites: 35; Central water; Flush toilets; Showers; Laundry; No RV dump; Reservations accepted; Stay limit: 14 days; Open Mar-Nov; Tents: $12/RVs: $22-24; Elev: 423ft/129m; Tel: 270-924-2270; Nearest town: Canton. GPS: 36.855645, -88.020201

10 • LBL NRA - Fenton Lake

Total sites: 12; RV sites: 12; Elec sites: 12; Central water; Vault toilets; No showers; No RV dump; Reservations not accepted; Stay limit: 14 days; Open all year; Tent & RV camping: $22; Elev: 407ft/124m; Nearest town: Aurora. GPS: 36.775703, -88.103585

11 • LBL NRA - Hillman Ferry

Total sites: 302; RV sites: 238; Elec sites: 267; Water at site; Flush toilets; Showers; RV dump; Reservations accepted; Stay limit: 14 days; Open Mar-Nov; Tents: $12/RVs: $22-40; Elev: 404ft/123m; Tel: 270-924-2181; Nearest town: Grand Rivers; Notes: FHU sites. GPS: 36.947287, -88.178188

12 • LBL NRA - Nickell Branch

Total sites: 13; RV sites: 4; No water; Vault toilets; Reservations not accepted; Stay limit: 14 days; Open all year; Tent & RV camping: $10; Elev: 351ft/107m; Tel: 270-924-2000; Nearest town: Grand Rivers; Notes: 3-day permit: $10. GPS: 36.988025, -88.199979

13 • LBL NRA - Redd Hollow

Total sites: 39; RV sites: 33; No water; Vault toilets; No showers; No RV dump; Reservations not accepted; Stay limit: 14 days; Open all year; Tent & RV camping: $10; Elev: 423ft/129m; Nearest town: Canton; Notes: 3-day permit: $10. GPS: 36.713419, -88.073739

14 • LBL NRA - Smith Bay

Total sites: 16; RV sites: 14; No water; Vault toilets; Stay limit: 14 days; Open all year; Tent & RV camping: $10; Elev: 364ft/111m; Nearest town: Grand Rivers. GPS: 36.909075, -88.147868

15 • LBL NRA - Sugar Bay

Total sites: 16; RV sites: 10; No water; Vault toilets; Reservations not accepted; Stay limit: 14 days; Open all year; Tent & RV camping: $10; Elev: 407ft/124m; Nearest town: Aurora; Notes: 3-day permit: $10. GPS: 36.856339, -88.126283

16 • LBL NRA - Taylor Bay

Total sites: 35; RV sites: 35; No water; Vault toilets; Reservations not accepted; Stay limit: 14 days; Open all year; Tent & RV camping: $10; Elev: 407ft/124m; Nearest town: Canton; Notes: 3-day permit: $10. GPS: 36.883902, -88.020205

17 • LBL NRA - Twin Lakes

Total sites: 14; RV sites: 7; No water; Vault toilets; Stay limit: 14 days; Open all year; Tent & RV camping: $10; Elev: 450ft/137m; Nearest town: Eddyville; Notes: 3-day permit: $10, Rough road. GPS: 36.964951, -88.198443

18 • Paragon

Total sites: 7; RV sites: 7; No water; Vault toilets; Reservations not accepted; Open all year; Tent & RV camping: Free; Elev: 722ft/220m; Tel: 606-784-6428; Nearest town: Morehead. GPS: 38.048095, -83.394986

19 • S-Tree

Total sites: 20; RV sites: 20; No water; Vault toilets; Reservations not accepted; Max length: 25ft; Open all year; Tent & RV camping: Free; Elev: 1426ft/435m; Tel: 606-864-4163; Nearest town: McKee. GPS: 37.386719, -84.074219

20 • Turkey Foot

Total sites: 20; RV sites: 20; No water; Vault toilets; Reservations not accepted; Open all year; Tent & RV camping: Free; Elev: 879ft/268m; Tel: 606-864-4163; Nearest town: McKee; Notes: Steep road. GPS: 37.466496, -83.917419

21 • Twin Knobs

Total sites: 216; RV sites: 216; Elec sites: 116; Central water; Flush toilets; Showers; RV dump; Reservations accepted; Open Mar-Oct; Tent & RV camping: $25-55; Elev: 879ft/268m; Tel: 606-784-8816; Nearest town: Lexington; Notes: Group sites: $95-$115, Dump fee: $6. GPS: 38.091735, -83.508153

22 • Zilpo

Total sites: 172; RV sites: 172; Elec sites: 40; Central water; Flush toilets; Showers; RV dump; Reservations accepted; Open Mar-Oct; Tents: $22/RVs: $22-30; Elev: 761ft/232m; Tel: 606-768-2722; Nearest town: Salt Lick; Notes: Cabin(s), $5 elec fee. GPS: 38.070557, -83.484375

Louisiana

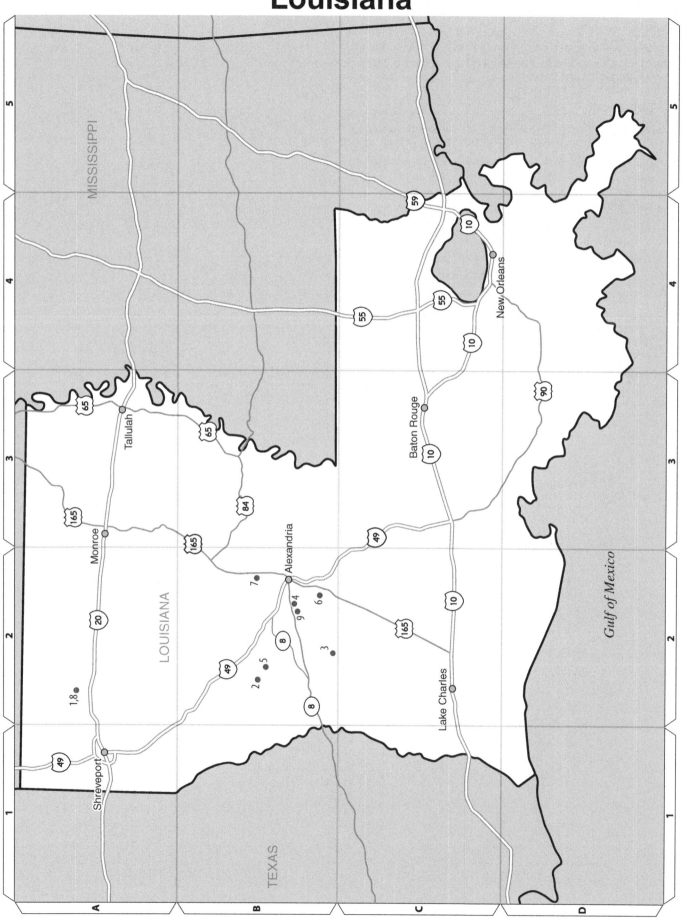

Louisiana Camping Areas

1 • Beaver Dam

Total sites: 29; RV sites: 29; Elec sites: 29; Water at site; Flush toilets; Showers; RV dump; Reservations accepted; Tent & RV camping: $25; Elev: 236ft/72m; Tel: 318-473-7160; Nearest town: Minden. GPS: 32.673392, -93.292061

2 • Dogwood

Total sites: 16; RV sites: 16; Central water; Flush toilets; No showers; No RV dump; Reservations not accepted; Max length: 20ft; Open all year; Tent & RV camping: Free; Elev: 213ft/65m; Tel: 318-473-7160; Nearest town: Natchitoches. GPS: 31.493239, -93.193046

3 • Fullerton Lake

Total sites: 15; RV sites: 15; Central water; Flush toilets; No showers; No RV dump; Reservations not accepted; Open all year; Tent & RV camping: $15; Elev: 236ft/72m; Tel: 318-473-7160; Nearest town: Cravens. GPS: 31.010628, -92.986239

4 • Kincaid Lake

Total sites: 41; RV sites: 41; Elec sites: 41; Water at site; Flush toilets; Showers; RV dump; Reservations not accepted; Tents: $10/RVs: $25; Elev: 121ft/37m; Tel: 318-743-7160; Nearest town: Gardner. GPS: 31.262939, -92.633301

5 • Kisatchie Bayou

Total sites: 18; No water; Vault toilets; Reservations not accepted; Open all year; Tents only: $2; Elev: 223ft/68m; Tel: 318-473-7160; Nearest town: Provencal; Notes: Also walk-to sites. GPS: 31.445071, -93.093061

6 • Loran/Claiborne Camp

Total sites: 39; RV sites: 39; No water; Vault toilets; Reservations not accepted; Tent & RV camping: $10; Elev: 249ft/76m; Tel: 318-473-7160; Nearest town: Woodworth. GPS: 31.097801, -92.566609

7 • Stuart Lake

Total sites: 8; RV sites: 8; Central water; No toilets; No showers; No RV dump; Reservations not accepted; Open all year; Tent & RV camping: $15; Elev: 230ft/70m; Tel: 318-473-7160; Nearest town: Alexandria; Notes: Reservable group site: $35-$75. GPS: 31.508578, -92.444018

8 • Turtle Slide

Total sites: 20; RV sites: 20; Central water; Flush toilets; No showers; RV dump; Reservations not accepted; Tent & RV camping: $10; Elev: 220ft/67m; Tel: 318-473-7160; Nearest town: Minden. GPS: 32.672852, -93.297678

9 • Valentine Lake Northshore

Total sites: 14; RV sites: 14; Central water; Vault toilets; No showers; No RV dump; Reservations not accepted; Tent & RV camping: $10; Elev: 220ft/67m; Tel: 318-473-7160; Nearest town: Gardner. GPS: 31.243408, -92.681396

Maine

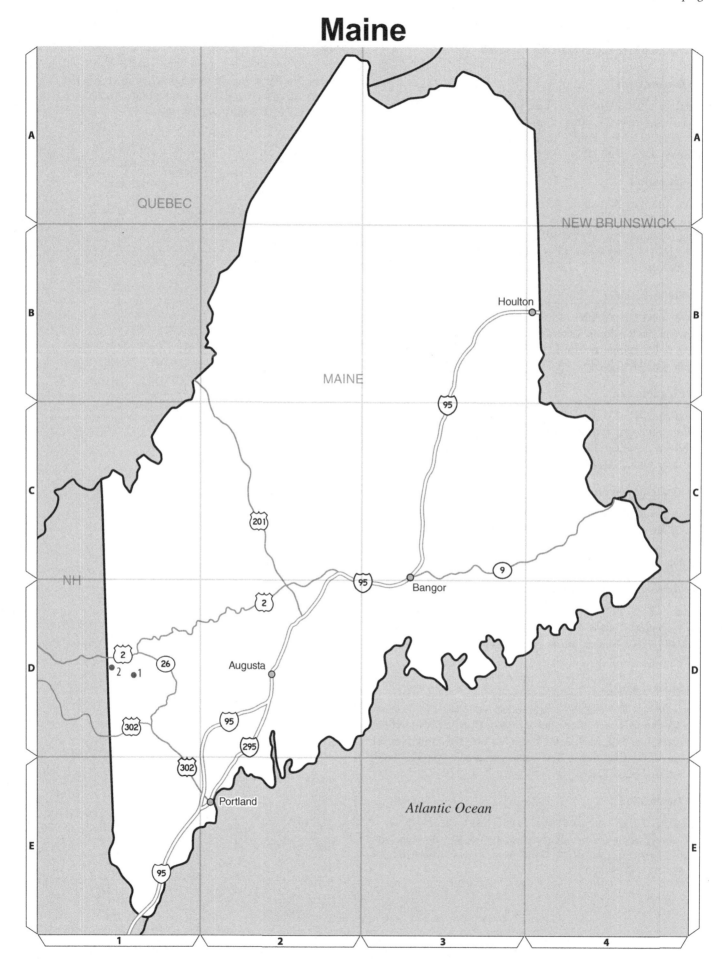

Maine Camping Areas

1 • Crocker Pond

Total sites: 7; RV sites: 7; Central water; Vault toilets; No showers; No RV dump; Reservations not accepted; Open May-Oct; Tent & RV camping: $18; Elev: 879ft/268m; Nearest town: Bethel. GPS: 44.310000, -70.824000

2 • Hastings

Total sites: 24; RV sites: 23; Central water; Vault toilets; No showers; No RV dump; Reservations accepted; Open May-Oct; Tent & RV camping: $20; Elev: 863ft/263m; Tel: 603-466-2713; Nearest town: Gilead. GPS: 44.352328, -70.983656

Michigan

Michigan Camping Areas

1 • Au Sable Loop

Total sites: 5; RV sites: 5; Central water; Vault toilets; No showers; No RV dump; Reservations not accepted; Max length: 25ft; Open all year; Tent & RV camping: $10; Elev: 938ft/286m; Tel: 989-826-3252; Nearest town: Mio. GPS: 44.651868, -84.099871

2 • Au Train Lake

Total sites: 37; RV sites: 37; Central water; Vault toilets; No showers; No RV dump; Reservations accepted; Open May-Sep; Tent & RV camping: $20; Elev: 617ft/188m; Tel: 906-387-2512; Nearest town: AuTrain. GPS: 46.393126, -86.836706

3 • Bay Furnace

Total sites: 50; RV sites: 50; Central water; Vault toilets; No showers; RV dump; Reservations accepted; Open May-Oct; Tent & RV camping: $20; Elev: 614ft/187m; Tel: 906-387-2512; Nearest town: Munising. GPS: 46.441406, -86.708252

4 • Bay View

Total sites: 24; RV sites: 24; Central water; Vault toilets; No showers; No RV dump; Reservations accepted; Open May-Oct; Tent & RV camping: $18; Elev: 594ft/181m; Tel: 906-203-9872; Nearest town: Raco. GPS: 46.449661, -84.781185

5 • Bear Track

Total sites: 20; RV sites: 15; Central water; Vault toilets; No showers; No RV dump; Reservations not accepted; Open May-Sep; Tent & RV camping: $18; Elev: 751ft/229m; Tel: 231-723-2211; Nearest town: Irons. GPS: 44.147657, -86.031859

6 • Benton Lake

Total sites: 25; RV sites: 25; Central water; Vault toilets; No showers; No RV dump; Reservations not accepted; Open May-Sep; Tent & RV camping: $18; Elev: 804ft/245m; Tel: 231-745-4631; Nearest town: Brohman. GPS: 43.669678, -85.890381

7 • Black River Harbor

Total sites: 40; RV sites: 40; Central water; Vault toilets; No showers; No RV dump; Reservations accepted; Stay limit: 14 days; Open May-Sep; Tent & RV camping: $16; Elev: 722ft/220m; Tel: 218-310-1954; Nearest town: Bessemer. GPS: 46.664382, -90.051884

8 • Blacksmith Bayou Access

Total sites: 6; RV sites: 6; No water; Vault toilets; Reservations not accepted; Open Apr-Nov; Tent & RV camping: $5; Elev: 614ft/187m; Tel: 231-723-2211; Nearest town: Brethren. GPS: 44.261574, -86.034838

9 • Blockhouse

Total sites: 4; RV sites: 4; No water; No toilets; Reservations not accepted; Open all year; Tent & RV camping: Free; Elev: 1493ft/455m; Tel: 906-932-1330; Nearest town: Iron River. GPS: 46.242096, -88.633329

10 • Bob Lake

Total sites: 17; RV sites: 17; Central water; Vault toilets; No showers; No RV dump; Reservations not accepted; Open May-Oct; Tent & RV camping: $14; Elev: 1191ft/363m; Tel: 906-852-3232; Nearest town: Ontonagon. GPS: 46.661865, -88.914551

11 • Bobcat Lake

Total sites: 11; RV sites: 11; Central water; Vault toilets; No showers; No RV dump; Reservations not accepted; Stay limit: 14 days; Open May-Sep; Tent & RV camping: $13; Elev: 1591ft/485m; Tel: 218-310-1954; Nearest town: Bessemer. GPS: 46.359131, -89.673096

12 • Bowman Bridge

Total sites: 20; RV sites: 16; Central water; Vault toilets; No showers; No RV dump; Reservations accepted; Open May-Oct; Tent & RV camping: $18; Elev: 758ft/231m; Tel: 231-745-4631; Nearest town: Baldwin; Notes: Group site: $66. GPS: 43.888228, -85.941584

13 • Brevoort Lake

Total sites: 70; RV sites: 70; Central water; Flush toilets; No showers; RV dump; Reservations accepted; Open May-Oct; Tents: $20/RVs: $29; Elev: 633ft/193m; Tel: 906-203-9872; Nearest town: Brevort; Notes: Dump fee. GPS: 46.007719, -84.972433

14 • Brush Lake

Total sites: 7; RV sites: 7; No water; Vault toilets; Reservations not accepted; Max length: 35ft; Open all year; Tent & RV camping: $10; Elev: 1014ft/309m; Tel: 231-745-4631; Nearest town: Woodville. GPS: 43.639086, -85.689831

15 • Buttercup

Total sites: 3; RV sites: 3; No water; Vault toilets; Reservations not accepted; Open all year; Tent & RV camping: Free; Elev: 899ft/274m; Tel: 989-826-3252; Nearest town: Mio; Notes: Not plowed in winter. GPS: 44.641338, -83.913507

16 • Camp Cook

Total sites: 4; RV sites: 3; Central water; Vault toilets; No showers; No RV dump; Reservation required; Open May-Oct; Tent & RV camping: $8; Elev: 771ft/235m; Tel: 906-387-2512; Nearest town: Rapid River. GPS: 46.038867, -86.581558

17 • Camp Seven Lake

Total sites: 41; RV sites: 41; Elec sites: 10; Central water; Vault toilets; No showers; No RV dump; Reservations accepted; Max length: 39ft; Open May-Oct; Tent & RV camping: $24; Elev: 778ft/237m; Tel: 906-428-5800; Nearest town: Rapid River. GPS: 46.057112, -86.548643

18 • Carp River

Total sites: 38; RV sites: 38; Potable water; Vault toilets; No showers; No RV dump; Reservations accepted; Open May-Oct; Tent & RV camping: $18; Elev: 646ft/197m; Tel: 906-203-9872; Nearest town: St. Ignace. GPS: 46.031941, -84.721499

19 • Claybanks

Total sites: 9; RV sites: 9; Central water; Vault toilets; No showers; No RV dump; Reservations not accepted; Max length: 25ft; Open May-Sep; Tent & RV camping: $10; Elev: 843ft/257m; Tel: 231-745-4631; Nearest town: Baldwin. GPS: 43.868354, -85.881645

20 • Colwell Lake

Total sites: 39; RV sites: 37; Elec sites: 7; Potable water; Vault toilets; No showers; RV dump; Reservations accepted; Open May-Oct; Tents: $18/RVs: $20-24; Elev: 774ft/236m; Tel: 906-428-5800; Nearest town: Munising; Notes: Dump Fee $4, Group site $55. GPS: 46.222168, -86.436279

21 • Condon Lake

Total sites: 6; RV sites: 6; No water; Vault toilets; No showers; No RV dump; Reservations not accepted; Open all year; Tent & RV camping: Free; Elev: 879ft/268m; Tel: 231-745-4631; Nearest town: Baldwin. GPS: 43.738838, -85.890756

22 • Cookson Lake

Total sites: 5; RV sites: 5; No water; Vault toilets; Reservations accepted; Open May-Oct; Tent & RV camping: $8; Elev: 764ft/233m; Tel: 906-387-3700; Nearest town: Munising. GPS: 46.195305, -86.561425

23 • Corner Lake

Total sites: 9; RV sites: 9; Potable water; Vault toilets; No showers; No RV dump; Reservations not accepted; Open May-Sep; Tent & RV camping: $20; Elev: 758ft/231m; Tel: 906-428-5800; Nearest town: Munising. GPS: 46.152975, -86.609299

24 • Courtney Lake

Total sites: 21; RV sites: 19; Central water; Vault toilets; No showers; No RV dump; Reservations not accepted; Open May-Oct; Tent & RV camping: $14; Elev: 1161ft/354m; Tel: 906-884-2085; Nearest town: Ontonagon; Notes: Also walk-to sites, 2 walk-to sites. GPS: 46.753662, -88.940674

25 • Diamond Point

Total sites: 2; RV sites: 2; No water; Vault toilets; Reservations not accepted; Max length: 20ft; Open May-Nov; Tent & RV camping: $10; Elev: 617ft/188m; Tel: 231-745-4631; Nearest town: Muskegon. GPS: 43.474614, -86.212343

26 • Flowing Well

Total sites: 10; RV sites: 10; Central water; Vault toilets; No showers; No RV dump; Reservations accepted; Open May-Oct; Tent & RV camping: $20; Elev: 630ft/192m; Tel: 906-341-5666; Nearest town: Rapid River; Notes: The well water has a heavy iron and sulfur content but is safe to consume. GPS: 45.936827, -86.706979

27 • Gabions

Total sites: 4; RV sites: 4; No water; Vault toilets; Reservations not accepted; Max length: 25ft; Open all year; Tent & RV camping: $10; Elev: 846ft/258m; Tel: 989-826-3252; Nearest town: Glennie; Notes: Not plowed in winter. GPS: 44.620952, -83.846278

28 • Golden Lake

Total sites: 22; RV sites: 22; Central water; Vault toilets; No showers; No RV dump; Reservations not accepted; Stay limit: 14 days; Open May-Sep; Tent & RV camping: $16; Elev: 1660ft/506m; Tel: 906-358-4724; Nearest town: Iron River. GPS: 46.171201, -88.883485

29 • Government Landing

Total sites: 3; No water; Vault toilets; Reservations not accepted; Open Apr-Nov; Tents only: Free; Elev: 745ft/227m; Tel: 231-723-2211; Nearest town: Brethren. GPS: 44.264847, -85.936138

30 • Hemlock

Total sites: 18; RV sites: 18; Central water; Vault toilets; No showers; No RV dump; Reservations not accepted; Open May-Sep; Tent & RV camping: $18; Elev: 1326ft/404m; Tel: 231-723-2211; Nearest town: Cadillac. GPS: 44.231464, -85.503312

31 • Henry Lake

Total sites: 11; RV sites: 11; Central water; Vault toilets; No showers; No RV dump; Reservations not accepted; Stay limit: 14 days; Open May-Sep; Tent & RV camping: $13; Elev: 1611ft/491m; Tel: 218-310-1954; Nearest town: Marenisco. GPS: 46.330465, -89.792184

32 • Highbank Lake

Total sites: 9; RV sites: 9; Central water; Vault toilets; No showers; No RV dump; Reservations not accepted; Max length: 20ft; Open May-Sep; Tent & RV camping: $18; Elev: 928ft/283m; Tel: 231-745-4631; Nearest town: Bitely. GPS: 43.770904, -85.888797

33 • Horseshoe Lake

Total sites: 9; RV sites: 9; Central water; Vault toilets; No showers; No RV dump; Reservations not accepted; Max length: 25ft; Open May-Nov; Tent & RV camping: $10; Elev: 984ft/300m; Tel: 989-739-0728; Nearest town: Curran. GPS: 44.600795, -83.765459

34 • Hungerford Lake

Total sites: 2; RV sites: 2; No water; Vault toilets; No showers; No RV dump; Reservations not accepted; Open May-Oct; Tent & RV camping: Free; Elev: 1087ft/331m; Tel: 231-745-4631; Nearest town: Big Rapids. GPS: 43.695657, -85.618769

35 • Hungerford Trail Camp

Total sites: 48; RV sites: 48; Central water; Vault toilets; Reservations not accepted; Open May-Oct; Tent & RV camping: $15; Elev: 1131ft/345m; Tel: 231-745-4631; Nearest town: Big Rapids; Notes: Group site: $75. GPS: 43.701425, -85.621094

36 • Imp Lake

Total sites: 22; RV sites: 22; Central water; Vault toilets; No showers; No RV dump; Reservations not accepted; Stay limit: 14 days; Open May-Sep; Tent & RV camping: $16; Elev: 1706ft/520m; Tel: 906-265-5420; Nearest town: Watersmeet. GPS: 46.217899, -89.070991

37 • Indian Lake

Total sites: 6; RV sites: 6; No water; Vault toilets; Reservations not accepted; Open all year; Tent & RV camping: $10; Elev: 974ft/297m; Tel: 231-745-4631; Nearest town: Brohman. GPS: 43.670189, -85.829379

38 • Indian River

Total sites: 5; RV sites: 5; Potable water; Vault toilets; No showers; No RV dump; Reservations not accepted; Open May-Oct; Tent & RV camping: $20; Elev: 718ft/219m; Tel: 906-428-5800; Nearest town: Manistique. GPS: 46.154755, -86.403878

39 • Ironjaw Lake

Total sites: 1; RV sites: 1; No water; Vault toilets; No showers; No RV dump; Reservation required; Stay limit: 14 days; Open May-Oct; Tent & RV camping: $8; Elev: 791ft/241m; Nearest town: Rapid River; Notes: Tent or small RV, Horses OK. GPS: 46.171497, -86.548521

40 • Island Lake

Total sites: 23; RV sites: 23; Central water; Vault toilets; No showers; No RV dump; Reservations accepted; Open May-Sep; Tent & RV camping: $20; Elev: 860ft/262m; Tel: 906-387-2512; Nearest town: Munising; Notes: Group site: $45. GPS: 46.270020, -86.650635

41 • Island Lake

Total sites: 17; RV sites: 17; Potable water; Vault toilets; No showers; No RV dump; Reservations not accepted; Max length: 25ft; Open May-Sep; Tent & RV camping: $15; Elev: 1310ft/399m; Tel: 989-826-3252; Nearest town: Mio. GPS: 44.508723, -84.141476

42 • Jewell Lake

Total sites: 32; RV sites: 32; Central water; Vault toilets; No showers; No RV dump; Reservations not accepted; Max length: 25ft; Open May-Oct; Tent & RV camping: $15; Elev: 846ft/258m; Tel: 989-739-0728; Nearest town: Harrisville. GPS: 44.677979, -83.599121

43 • Kneff Lake

Total sites: 27; RV sites: 27; Central water; Vault toilets; No showers; No RV dump; Reservations not accepted; Max length: 25ft; Open May-Sep; Tent & RV camping: $15; Elev: 1201ft/366m; Tel: 989-826-3252; Nearest town: Grayling. GPS: 44.636963, -84.579102

44 • Lake Michigan (Manistee)

Total sites: 99; RV sites: 99; Central water; Vault toilets; No showers; No RV dump; Reservations accepted; Open May-Oct; Tent & RV camping: $25-29; Elev: 659ft/201m; Tel: 231-723-2211; Nearest town: Manistee; Notes: Group sites: $50-$65. GPS: 44.115537, -86.423471

45 • Lake Michigan (St Ignace)

Total sites: 34; RV sites: 34; Central water; Flush toilets; No showers; No RV dump; Reservations accepted; Open May-Oct; Tent & RV camping: $20; Elev: 606ft/185m; Tel: 906-203-9872; Nearest town: St. Ignace. GPS: 45.985685, -84.971857

46 • Lake Ottawa

Total sites: 32; RV sites: 32; Central water; No toilets; No showers; RV dump; Reservations not accepted; Open May-Sep; Tent & RV camping: $18; Elev: 1608ft/490m; Tel: 906-396-5428; Nearest town: Iron River. GPS: 46.078445, -88.761411

47 • Lake Sainte Kathryn

Total sites: 24; RV sites: 24; Central water; Vault toilets; No showers; No RV dump; Reservations not accepted; Stay limit: 14 days; Open May-Oct; Tent & RV camping: $14; Elev: 1601ft/488m; Tel: 906-852-3232; Nearest town: Sidnaw. GPS: 46.393078, -88.722501

48 • Langford Lake

Total sites: 11; RV sites: 11; Central water; Vault toilets; No showers; No RV dump; Reservations not accepted; Stay limit: 14 days; Tent & RV camping: $13; Elev: 1686ft/514m; Tel: 218-310-1954; Nearest town: Marenisco. GPS: 46.272686, -89.492335

49 • Leg Lake Site #1

Total sites: 1; RV sites: 1; No water; Vault toilets; Reservation required; Stay limit: 14 days; Open May-Oct; Tent & RV camping: $8; Elev: 702ft/214m; Tel: 906-387-2512; Nearest town: Manistique. GPS: 46.128326, -86.485941

50 • Leg Lake Site #2

Total sites: 1; No water; Vault toilets; Reservation required; Stay limit: 14 days; Open May-Oct; Tents only: $8; Elev: 718ft/219m; Tel: 906-387-2512; Nearest town: Manistique. GPS: 46.130153, -86.481258

51 • Little Bass Lake

Total sites: 12; RV sites: 12; Central water; Vault toilets; No showers; No RV dump; Reservation required; Stay limit: 14 days; Open May-Oct; Tent & RV camping: $8; Elev: 794ft/242m; Tel: 906-428-5800; Nearest town: Manistique. GPS: 46.162973, -86.449885

52 • Little Bay de Noc - Maywood Loop

Total sites: 14; RV sites: 14; Central water; Vault toilets; No showers; No RV dump; Reservations accepted; Open May-Oct; Tent & RV camping: $20-21; Elev: 597ft/182m; Tel: 906-428-5800; Nearest town: Rapid River. GPS: 45.841134, -86.984074

53 • Little Bay de Noc - Twin Springs/Oaks Loops

Total sites: 22; RV sites: 22; Central water; Vault toilets; No showers; No RV dump; Reservations accepted; Open May-Oct; Tent & RV camping: $20-21; Elev: 594ft/181m; Tel: 906-428-5800; Nearest town: Rapid River; Notes: 2 group sites: $55. GPS: 45.833336, -86.992321

54 • Mack Lake ORV

Total sites: 42; RV sites: 42; Central water; Vault toilets; No showers; No RV dump; Reservations not accepted; Max length: 50ft; Open May-Nov; Tent & RV camping: $15; Elev: 1184ft/361m; Tel: 989-826-3252; Nearest town: Mio. GPS: 44.577637, -84.064453

55 • Marion Lake East

Total sites: 40; RV sites: 40; Central water; Vault toilets; No showers; No RV dump; Reservations not accepted; Open all year; Tent & RV camping: $16; Elev: 1670ft/509m; Tel: 906-396-5428; Nearest town: Watersmeet. GPS: 46.267477, -89.083501

56 • Marion Lake West

Total sites: 15; RV sites: 15; Central water; Vault toilets; No showers; No RV dump; Reservations not accepted; Open all year; Tent & RV camping: $16; Elev: 1641ft/500m; Tel: 906-396-5428; Nearest town: Watersmeet. GPS: 46.269505, -89.093077

57 • Meadows ORV

Total sites: 16; RV sites: 16; Central water; Vault toilets; No showers; No RV dump; Reservations not accepted; Max length: 25ft; Open all year; Tent & RV camping: $10; Elev: 1161ft/354m; Tel: 989-826-3252; Nearest town: Luzerne; Notes: Not plowed in winter. GPS: 44.559948, -84.311133

58 • Minnie Pond

Total sites: 11; RV sites: 11; No water; Vault toilets; Reservations not accepted; Max length: 25ft; Open all year; Tent & RV camping: $10; Elev: 830ft/253m; Tel: 231-745-4631; Nearest town: White Cloud. GPS: 43.627076, -85.898939

59 • Monocle Lake

Total sites: 39; RV sites: 39; Central water; Vault toilets; No showers; No RV dump; Reservations accepted; Open May-Sep; Tent & RV camping: $18; Elev: 666ft/203m; Tel: 906-203-9872; Nearest town: Bay Mills. GPS: 46.472168, -84.639404

60 • Monument

Total sites: 19; RV sites: 19; Central water; Vault toilets; No showers; No RV dump; Reservations accepted; Open May-Oct; Tent & RV camping: $15; Elev: 846ft/258m; Tel: 989-739-0728; Nearest town: Oscoda. GPS: 44.434149, -83.620150

61 • Moosehead Lake

Total sites: 13; RV sites: 13; Central water; Vault toilets; No showers; No RV dump; Reservations not accepted; Stay limit: 14 days; Open May-Sep; Tent & RV camping: $13; Elev: 1693ft/516m; Tel: 906-265-5420; Nearest town: Marenisco. GPS: 46.240479, -89.605469

62 • Norway Lake

Total sites: 27; RV sites: 27; Central water; Vault toilets; No showers; No RV dump; Reservations not accepted; Stay limit: 14 days; Open May-Oct; Tent & RV camping: $14; Elev: 1552ft/473m; Tel: 906-852-3232; Nearest town: Sidnaw. GPS: 46.417480, -88.684326

63 • Old Grade

Total sites: 20; RV sites: 20; Central water; Vault toilets; No showers; No RV dump; Reservations not accepted; Open Apr-Sep; Tent & RV camping: $18; Elev: 882ft/269m; Tel: 231-745-4631; Nearest town: Baldwin. GPS: 44.060791, -85.849365

64 • Paint River Forks

Total sites: 4; RV sites: 4; No water; Vault toilets; Reservations not accepted; Open May-Sep; Tent & RV camping: Free; Elev: 1466ft/447m; Tel: 906-932-1330; Nearest town: Iron River. GPS: 46.232722, -88.718654

65 • Perch Lake

Total sites: 20; RV sites: 20; Central water; Vault toilets; No showers; No RV dump; Reservations not accepted; Stay limit: 14 days; Open May-Oct; Tent & RV camping: $14; Elev: 1539ft/469m; Tel: 906-852-3232; Nearest town: Sidnaw. GPS: 46.364746, -88.674561

66 • Pete's Lake

Total sites: 46; RV sites: 46; Central water; Vault toilets; No showers; No RV dump; Reservations accepted; Open May-Sep; Tent & RV camping: $20-22; Elev: 837ft/255m; Tel: 906-387-2512; Nearest town: Munising. GPS: 46.229511, -86.598265

67 • Peterson Bridge

Total sites: 30; RV sites: 17; Central water; Vault toilets; No showers; No RV dump; Reservations accepted; Open Apr-Sep; Tent & RV camping: $21-25; Elev: 817ft/249m; Tel: 231-745-4631; Nearest town: Baldwin. GPS: 44.201917, -85.798837

68 • Pine Lake

Total sites: 12; RV sites: 12; Central water; Vault toilets; No showers; No RV dump; Reservations not accepted; Open May-Sep; Tent & RV camping: $18; Elev: 755ft/230m; Tel: 231-723-2211; Nearest town: Wellston. GPS: 44.195567, -86.009457

69 • Pine River

Total sites: 11; RV sites: 11; Central water; Vault toilets; No showers; No RV dump; Reservations not accepted; Max length: 25ft; Open May-Nov; Tent & RV camping: $15; Elev: 761ft/232m; Tel: 989-739-0728; Nearest town: Mikado. GPS: 44.563721, -83.599609

70 • Pines Point

Total sites: 29; RV sites: 29; Central water; Vault toilets; No showers; No RV dump; Reservations not accepted; Max length: 40ft; Open May-Oct; Tent & RV camping: $18; Elev: 663ft/202m; Tel: 231-745-4631; Nearest town: Hesperia; Notes: Reservable group site $66. GPS: 43.527786, -86.119390

71 • Pomeroy Lake

Total sites: 17; RV sites: 17; Central water; Vault toilets; No showers; No RV dump; Reservations not accepted; Stay limit: 14 days; Open May-Sep; Tent & RV camping: $13; Elev: 1663ft/507m; Tel: 218-310-1954; Nearest town: Marenisco. GPS: 46.282022, -89.573775

72 • Red Bridge Access

Total sites: 4; RV sites: 4; Central water; Vault toilets; No showers; No RV dump; Reservations not accepted; Open all year; Tent & RV camping: Free; Elev: 709ft/216m; Tel: 231-723-2211; Nearest town: Brethren. GPS: 44.283925, -85.861524

73 • Robbins Pond

Total sites: 3; RV sites: 3; No water; Vault toilets; No showers; No RV dump; Reservations not accepted; Open May-Sep; Tent & RV camping: Free; Elev: 1307ft/398m; Tel: 906-358-4551; Nearest town: Watersmeet. GPS: 46.381058, -89.228336

74 • Rollways

Total sites: 19; RV sites: 19; Central water; Vault toilets; No showers; No RV dump; Reservations accepted; Max length: 50ft; Open May-Sep; Tent & RV camping: $15; Elev: 864ft/263m; Tel: 989-739-0728; Nearest town: Hale. GPS: 44.459557, -83.773463

75 • Round Lake

Total sites: 33; RV sites: 33; Central water; Vault toilets; No showers; No RV dump; Reservations accepted; Max length: 25ft; Open May-Sep; Tent & RV camping: $15; Elev: 800ft/244m; Tel: 989-739-0728; Nearest town: Hale. GPS: 44.341029, -83.663457

76 • Sand Lake

Total sites: 47; RV sites: 47; Central water; Flush toilets; Showers; No RV dump; Reservations accepted; Open May-Sep; Tent & RV camping: $25; Elev: 863ft/263m; Tel: 231-723-2211; Nearest town: Wellston; Notes: Group site: $61. GPS: 44.165814, -85.936383

77 • Sawdust Hole Access

Total sites: 8; RV sites: 8; No water; Vault toilets; Reservations not accepted; Open Apr-Nov; Tent & RV camping: $5; Elev: 696ft/212m; Tel: 231-723-2211; Nearest town: Brethren. GPS: 44.268511, -85.952483

78 • Seaton Creek

Total sites: 17; RV sites: 17; Central water; Vault toilets; No showers; No RV dump; Reservations accepted; Open May-Sep; Tent & RV camping: $18-22; Elev: 873ft/266m; Tel: 231-723-2211; Nearest town: Mesick; Notes: Group site $44. GPS: 44.358046, -85.809591

79 • Shelley Lake

Total sites: 8; RV sites: 8; No water; Vault toilets; Reservations not accepted; Open all year; Tent & RV camping: $10; Elev: 975ft/297m; Tel: 231-745-4631; Nearest town: Brohman. GPS: 43.711566, -85.816976

80 • Soldier Lake

Total sites: 43; RV sites: 43; Central water; Vault toilets; No showers; No RV dump; Reservations accepted; Open May-Sep; Tent & RV camping: $18; Elev: 902ft/275m; Tel: 906-203-9872; Nearest town: Raco. GPS: 46.348674, -84.864005

81 • South Branch Trail Camp

Total sites: 21; RV sites: 21; Central water; Vault toilets; No showers; No RV dump; Reservations not accepted; Open May-Nov; Tent & RV camping: $15; Elev: 863ft/263m; Tel: 989-739-0728; Nearest town: Hale; Notes: Reservable group site - free. GPS: 44.485438, -83.796343

82 • South Nichols Lake

Total sites: 30; RV sites: 30; Central water; No toilets; No showers; No RV dump; Reservations accepted; Open May-Oct; Tent & RV camping: $18-22; Elev: 824ft/251m; Tel: 231-745-4631; Nearest town: Brohman. GPS: 43.723877, -85.903564

83 • Sparrow Rapids

Total sites: 6; RV sites: 6; No water; Vault toilets; Reservations not accepted; Open May-Sep; Tent & RV camping: Free; Elev: 1158ft/353m; Tel: 906-932-1330; Nearest town: Kenton. GPS: 46.504416, -88.947039

84 • Sturgeon River

Total sites: 9; RV sites: 9; No water; Vault toilets; Reservations not accepted; Open May-Sep; Tent & RV camping: Free; Elev: 1089ft/332m; Tel: 906-932-1330; Nearest town: Baraga. GPS: 46.570499, -88.656194

85 • Sulak

Total sites: 12; RV sites: 12; No water; Vault toilets; Reservations not accepted; Max length: 25ft; Open May-Oct; Tent & RV camping: Free; Elev: 791ft/241m; Tel: 231-745-4631; Nearest town: Baldwin. GPS: 43.924342, -86.011379

86 • Sylvania (Clark Lake)

Total sites: 48; RV sites: 48; Central water; Flush toilets; Showers; RV dump; Reservations not accepted; Open all year; Tents: $18/RVs: $18-23; Elev: 1844ft/562m; Tel: 906-396-5428; Nearest town: Watersmeet. GPS: 46.240682, -89.321216

87 • Taylor Lake

Total sites: 10; RV sites: 10; Central water; Vault toilets; No showers; No RV dump; Stay limit: 14 days; Open May-Nov; Tent & RV camping: Fee unknown; Elev: 1687ft/514m; Tel: 906-358-4724; Nearest town: Watersmeet. GPS: 46.248146, -89.049122

88 • Tepee Lake

Total sites: 17; RV sites: 17; Central water; Vault toilets; No showers; No RV dump; Max length: 60ft; Stay limit: 14 days; Open May-Nov; Tent & RV camping: Fee unknown; Elev: 1657ft/505m; Tel: 906-932-1330; Nearest town: Sidnaw. GPS: 46.388606, -88.881607

89 • Three Lakes

Total sites: 28; RV sites: 28; Potable water; Vault toilets; No showers; No RV dump; Reservations accepted; Open May-Oct; Tent & RV camping: $16; Elev: 879ft/268m; Tel: 906-643-7900; Nearest town: Sault Ste Marie. GPS: 46.319824, -84.981689

90 • Timber Creek

Total sites: 9; RV sites: 9; Central water; Vault toilets; No showers; No RV dump; Reservations not accepted; Max length: 50ft; Open all year; Tent & RV camping: $10; Elev: 830ft/253m; Tel: 231-745-4631; Nearest town: Branch. GPS: 43.948292, -85.995896

91 • Twinwood Lake

Total sites: 5; RV sites: 5; No water; Vault toilets; Reservations not accepted; Open all year; Tent & RV camping: $10; Elev: 755ft/230m; Tel: 231-745-4631; Nearest town: White Cloud; Notes: Not plowed in winter. GPS: 43.476112, -85.767567

92 • Wagner Lake

Total sites: 12; RV sites: 12; Central water; Vault toilets; No showers; No RV dump; Reservations not accepted; Max length: 50ft; Open May-Sep; Tent & RV camping: $15; Elev: 1158ft/353m; Tel: 989-826-3252; Nearest town: Mio; Notes: 3 group sites. GPS: 44.553223, -84.147217

93 • Wakeley Lake

Total sites: 5; RV sites: 5; No water; Vault toilets; Reservations not accepted; Open all year; Tent & RV camping: $10; Elev: 1116ft/340m; Tel: 989-826-3252; Nearest town: Grayling; Notes: Parking lot plowed in winter. GPS: 44.633281, -84.508971

94 • Walkup Lake

Total sites: 12; RV sites: 12; Central water; Vault toilets; No showers; No RV dump; Reservations not accepted; Max length: 35ft; Open all year; Tent & RV camping: $10; Elev: 863ft/263m; Tel: 231-745-4631; Nearest town: Bitely; Notes: Not plowed in winter. GPS: 43.733822, -85.904996

95 • Whelan Lake

Total sites: 6; No water; No toilets; Reservations not accepted; Open all year; Tents only: Free; Elev: 650ft/198m; Tel: 231-745-4631; Nearest town: Walhalla; Notes: Not plowed in winter. GPS: 43.910743, -86.152935

96 • Widewaters

Total sites: 34; RV sites: 34; Potable water; Vault toilets; No showers; No RV dump; Reservations accepted; Open May-Sep; Tent & RV camping: $20; Elev: 804ft/245m; Tel: 906-387-2512; Nearest town: Munising. GPS: 46.217285, -86.627197

Minnesota

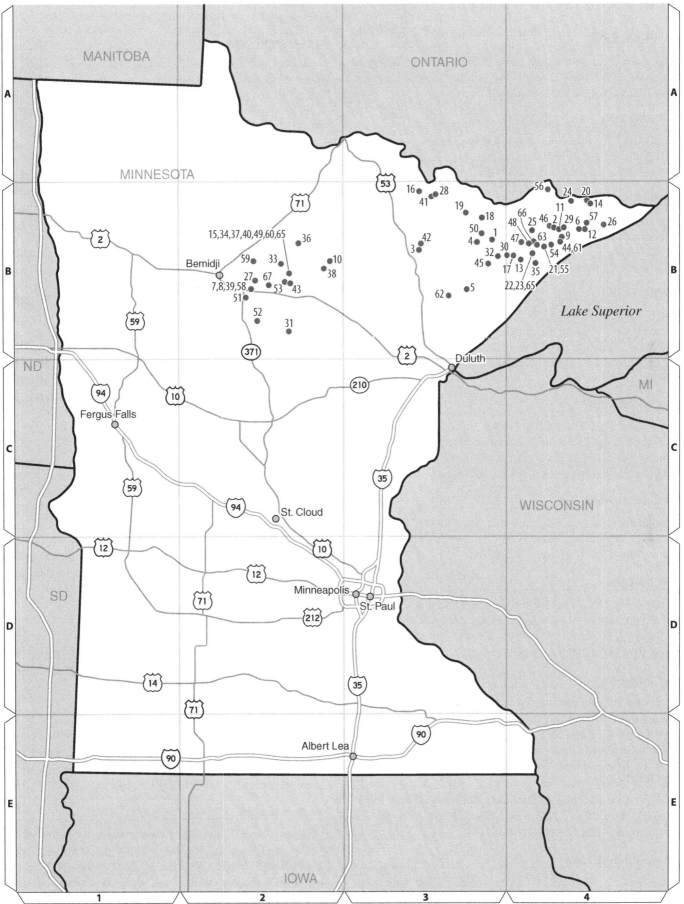

Minnesota Camping Areas

1 • August Lake

Total sites: 1; No water; Vault toilets; Reservations not accepted; Tents only: Free; Elev: 1565ft/477m; Tel: 218-365-7600; Nearest town: Ely. GPS: 47.768502, -91.606948

2 • Baker Lake

Total sites: 5; RV sites: 5; Central water; Vault toilets; No showers; No RV dump; Tent & RV camping: Free; Elev: 1749ft/533m; Tel: 218-663-8060; Nearest town: Tofte. GPS: 47.844528, -90.817046

3 • Big Rice Lake

Total sites: 3; RV sites: 3; No water; Vault toilets; Reservations not accepted; Max length: 20ft; Tent & RV camping: Free; Elev: 1466ft/447m; Tel: 218-229-8800; Nearest town: Virginia. GPS: 47.704199, -92.498842

4 • Birch Lake

Total sites: 30; RV sites: 30; Central water; Vault toilets; No showers; No RV dump; Reservations accepted; Open May-Oct; Tent & RV camping: $15; Elev: 1460ft/445m; Tel: 218-365-7600; Nearest town: Ely; Notes: Group site: $50. GPS: 47.758632, -91.785303

5 • Cadotte Lake

Total sites: 27; RV sites: 27; Central water; Vault toilets; No showers; No RV dump; Reservations accepted; Open May-Oct; Tent & RV camping: $20-22; Elev: 1637ft/499m; Tel: 218-229-8800; Nearest town: Hoyt Lakes. GPS: 47.380410, -91.917040

6 • Cascade River

Total sites: 4; RV sites: 1; No water; Vault toilets; Tent & RV camping: Free; Elev: 1631ft/497m; Tel: 218-387-1750; Nearest town: Tofte. GPS: 47.833646, -90.530676

7 • Cass Lake

Total sites: 23; RV sites: 23; Central water; Flush toilets; Showers; RV dump; Reservations accepted; Open May-Sep; Tent & RV camping: $21; Elev: 1289ft/393m; Tel: 218-335-8600; Nearest town: Cass Lake. GPS: 47.379944, -94.529361

8 • Chippewa

Total sites: 46; RV sites: 46; Elec sites: 46; Central water; Flush toilets; Showers; RV dump; Reservations accepted; Open May-Sep; Tent & RV camping: $26; Elev: 1358ft/414m; Tel: 218-335-8600; Nearest town: Bemidji. GPS: 47.382888, -94.510472

9 • Clara Lake

Total sites: 3; RV sites: 1; No water; Vault toilets; Tent & RV camping: Free; Elev: 1726ft/526m; Tel: 218-663-8060; Nearest town: Lutsen. GPS: 47.774354, -90.752134

10 • Clubhouse Lake

Total sites: 47; RV sites: 47; Central water; Vault toilets; No showers; No RV dump; Reservations not accepted; Open May-Nov; Tent & RV camping: $16; Elev: 1411ft/430m; Tel: 218-335-8600; Nearest town: Marcell. GPS: 47.610350, -93.577150

11 • Crescent Lake

Total sites: 32; RV sites: 32; Central water; Vault toilets; No showers; No RV dump; Reservations accepted; Open May-Oct; Tent & RV camping: $18; Elev: 1788ft/545m; Tel: 218-663-8060; Nearest town: Tofte; Notes: No services in winter. GPS: 47.834562, -90.771574

12 • Devil Track Lake

Total sites: 16; RV sites: 8; Central water; Vault toilets; No showers; No RV dump; Tent & RV camping: $16-18; Elev: 1670ft/509m; Tel: 218-387-1750; Nearest town: Grand Marais. GPS: 47.830197, -90.466931

13 • Divide Lake

Total sites: 3; RV sites: 3; Central water; Vault toilets; No showers; No RV dump; Reservations not accepted; Tent & RV camping: $15; Elev: 1949ft/594m; Tel: 218-323-7722; Nearest town: Isabella. GPS: 47.609981, -91.256365

14 • East Bearskin Lake

Total sites: 29; RV sites: 27; Central water; Vault toilets; No showers; No RV dump; Reservations accepted; Open May-Oct; Tent & RV camping: $20; Elev: 1729ft/527m; Tel: 218-387-1750; Nearest town: Grand Marais. GPS: 48.037109, -90.394043

15 • East Seelye Bay

Total sites: 13; RV sites: 13; Central water; Vault toilets; No showers; No RV dump; Reservations not accepted; Open May-Oct; Tent & RV camping: $16; Elev: 1316ft/401m; Tel: 218-335-8600; Nearest town: Deer River. GPS: 47.524227, -94.095952

16 • Echo Lake

Total sites: 24; RV sites: 24; Central water; Vault toilets; No showers; No RV dump; Reservations accepted; Open May-Oct; Tent & RV camping: $12; Elev: 1214ft/370m; Tel: 218-666-0020; Nearest town: Orr. GPS: 48.170698, -92.490649

17 • Eighteen Lake

Total sites: 3; RV sites: 3; No water; Vault toilets; Tent & RV camping: Free; Elev: 1926ft/587m; Tel: 218-323-7722; Nearest town: Isabella. GPS: 47.643759, -91.344178

18 • Fall Lake

Total sites: 62; RV sites: 53; Elec sites: 53; Central water; Flush toilets; Showers; No RV dump; Open May-Oct; Tent & RV camping: $22; Elev: 1339ft/408m; Tel: 218-365-7600; Nearest town: Ely; Notes: Group site: $85-$105. GPS: 47.951828, -91.719153

19 • Fenske Lake

Total sites: 15; RV sites: 10; Central water; Vault toilets; No showers; No RV dump; Max length: 20ft; Open May-Sep; Tent & RV camping: $15; Elev: 1486ft/453m; Tel: 218-365-7600; Nearest town: Ely; Notes: Also walk-to and group sites, Group site: $50. GPS: 47.994873, -91.915527

20 • Flour Lake

Total sites: 37; RV sites: 30; Central water; Vault toilets; No showers; No RV dump; Reservations accepted; Open May-Oct; Tent & RV camping: $20; Elev: 1775ft/541m; Tel: 218-387-1750; Nearest town: Grand Marais. GPS: 48.052490, -90.408447

21 • Fourmile Lake

Total sites: 4; RV sites: 2; No water; Vault toilets; Reservations not accepted; Tent & RV camping: Free; Elev: 1670ft/509m; Tel: 218-663-8060; Nearest town: Tofte. GPS: 47.702262, -90.963536

22 • Harriet Lake

Total sites: 4; RV sites: 2; No water; Vault toilets; Tent & RV camping: Free; Elev: 1772ft/540m; Tel: 218-663-8060; Nearest town: Tofte. GPS: 47.656881, -91.115144

23 • Hogback Lake

Total sites: 3; RV sites: 3; No water; Vault toilets; Reservations not accepted; Tent & RV camping: Free; Elev: 1775ft/541m; Tel: 218-323-7722; Nearest town: Isabella; Notes: access to 5 back-country sites. GPS: 47.644385, -91.136046

24 • Iron Lake

Total sites: 7; RV sites: 7; Central water; Vault toilets; No showers; No RV dump; Reservations accepted; Open Apr-Oct; Tent & RV camping: $22; Elev: 1886ft/575m; Tel: 218-387-1750; Nearest town: Grand Marais. GPS: 48.067485, -90.615216

25 • Kawishiwi Lake Rustic

Total sites: 5; RV sites: 5; No water; Vault toilets; No showers; No RV dump; Reservations not accepted; Max length: 25ft; Tent & RV camping: Free; Elev: 1656ft/505m; Tel: 218-663-8060; Nearest town: Tofte. GPS: 47.838663, -91.102413

26 • Kimble Lake

Total sites: 10; RV sites: 10; Central water; Vault toilets; No showers; No RV dump; Tent & RV camping: $16-18; Elev: 1709ft/521m; Tel: 218-387-1750; Nearest town: Grand Marais. GPS: 47.863994, -90.227176

27 • Knutson Dam

Total sites: 14; RV sites: 14; Central water; Vault toilets; No showers; No RV dump; Reservations not accepted; Open May-Sep; Tent & RV camping: $16; Elev: 1293ft/394m; Tel: 218-835-4291; Nearest town: Cass Lake. GPS: 47.450684, -94.483154

28 • Lake Jeanette

Total sites: 12; RV sites: 10; Central water; Vault toilets; No showers; No RV dump; Reservations accepted; Open May-Oct; Tent & RV camping: $12; Elev: 1352ft/412m; Tel: 218-666-0020; Nearest town: Orr. GPS: 48.131517, -92.296745

29 • Lichen Lake Canoe Camp

Total sites: 1; RV sites: 1; No water; Vault toilets; Open Apr-Sep; Tent & RV camping: Free; Elev: 1808ft/551m; Tel: 218-663-8060; Nearest town: Tofte. GPS: 47.850391, -90.712627

30 • Little Isabella River

Total sites: 11; RV sites: 11; Central water; Vault toilets; No showers; No RV dump; Reservations not accepted; Open May-Sep; Tent & RV camping: $15; Elev: 1821ft/555m; Tel: 218-323-7722; Nearest town: Isabella. GPS: 47.647217, -91.423828

31 • Mabel Lake

Total sites: 22; RV sites: 22; Central water; Vault toilets; No showers; No RV dump; Open May-Sep; Tent & RV camping: $14; Elev: 1348ft/411m; Tel: 218-335-8600; Nearest town: Remer. GPS: 47.049686, -94.072044

32 • McDougal Lake

Total sites: 21; RV sites: 21; Central water; Vault toilets; No showers; No RV dump; Reservations not accepted; Open May-Sep; Tent & RV camping: $15; Elev: 1798ft/548m; Tel: 218-323-7722; Nearest town: Isabella. GPS: 47.639160, -91.534912

33 • Middle Pigeon Lake

Total sites: 4; Central water; Vault toilets; No showers; No RV dump; Tents only: Free; Elev: 1355ft/413m; Tel: 218-246-2123; Nearest town: Squaw Lake. GPS: 47.586730, -94.166130

34 • Mosomo Point

Total sites: 23; RV sites: 23; Central water; Vault toilets; No showers; No RV dump; Reservations accepted; Open May-Sep; Tent & RV camping: $16; Elev: 1335ft/407m; Tel: 218-335-8600; Nearest town: Deer River. GPS: 47.517817, -94.048071

35 • Ninemile Lake

Total sites: 24; RV sites: 18; Central water; Vault toilets; No showers; No RV dump; Reservations not accepted; Tent & RV camping: $15; Elev: 1624ft/495m; Tel: 218-663-8060; Nearest town: Schroeder. GPS: 47.579031, -91.073808

36 • Noma Lake

Total sites: 14; RV sites: 14; Central water; Vault toilets; No showers; No RV dump; Reservations not accepted; Open May-Sep; Tent & RV camping: $14; Elev: 1332ft/406m; Tel: 218-335-8600; Nearest town: Wirt. GPS: 47.756274, -93.966107

37 • North Deer Lake

Total sites: 17; RV sites: 17; Central water; Vault toilets; No showers; No RV dump; Reservations accepted; Open May-Nov; Tent & RV camping: $16; Elev: 1365ft/416m; Tel: 218-335-8600; Nearest town: Deer River. GPS: 47.517761, -94.101456

38 • North Star

Total sites: 38; RV sites: 38; Central water; Vault toilets; No showers; No RV dump; Reservations not accepted; Open May-Oct; Tent & RV camping: $14; Elev: 1398ft/426m; Tel: 218-335-8600; Nearest town: Marcell. GPS: 47.556925, -93.652379

39 • Norway Beach

Total sites: 55; RV sites: 55; Central water; Flush toilets; Showers; No RV dump; Reservations accepted; Open May-Sep; Tent &

RV camping: $21; Elev: 1329ft/405m; Tel: 218-335-8600; Nearest town: Cass Lake. GPS: 47.379662, -94.517959

40 • O-Ne-Gum-E

Total sites: 48; RV sites: 48; Central water; Vault toilets; No showers; No RV dump; Reservations accepted; Open May-Nov; Tents: $16/RVs: $23; Elev: 1312ft/400m; Tel: 218-335-8600; Nearest town: Deer River; Notes: Electric fee additional. GPS: 47.510964, -94.043215

41 • Pauline Lake

Total sites: 1; No water; Vault toilets; Tents only: Free; Elev: 1411ft/430m; Tel: 218-666-0020; Nearest town: Orr. GPS: 48.127621, -92.332795

42 • Pfeiffer Lake

Total sites: 16; RV sites: 16; Central water; Vault toilets; No showers; No RV dump; Reservations accepted; Max length: 45ft; Open May-Sep; Tent & RV camping: $12; Elev: 1470ft/448m; Tel: 218-229-8800; Nearest town: Tower. GPS: 47.751293, -92.473474

43 • Plug Hat Point

Total sites: 13; RV sites: 13; Vault toilets; Tent & RV camping: Fee unknown; Elev: 1345ft/410m; Nearest town: Deer River. GPS: 47.437062, -94.054675

44 • Poplar River

Total sites: 4; RV sites: 2; No water; Vault toilets; Max length: 20ft; Tent & RV camping: Free; Elev: 1572ft/479m; Tel: 218-663-8060; Nearest town: Lutsen. GPS: 47.738693, -90.777797

45 • Sand Lake

Total sites: 2; No water; Vault toilets; Reservations not accepted; Tents only: Free; Elev: 1693ft/516m; Tel: 218-323-7722; Nearest town: Isabella. GPS: 47.581409, -91.663755

46 • Sawbill Lake

Total sites: 51; RV sites: 51; Central water; Vault toilets; No showers; Laundry; RV dump; Reservations accepted; Open May-Oct; Tent & RV camping: $18; Elev: 1842ft/561m; Tel: 218-663-8060; Nearest town: Tofte. GPS: 47.863561, -90.886004

47 • Section 29 Lake

Total sites: 3; RV sites: 3; No water; Vault toilets; Reservations not accepted; Tent & RV camping: Free; Elev: 1627ft/496m; Tel: 218-323-7722; Nearest town: Isabella. GPS: 47.741338, -91.241822

48 • Silver Island Lake

Total sites: 8; RV sites: 8; No water; Vault toilets; Tent & RV camping: Free; Elev: 1640ft/500m; Tel: 218-323-7722; Nearest town: Isabella. GPS: 47.727398, -91.149167

49 • South Deer Lake

Total sites: 31; RV sites: 31; Central water; Vault toilets; No showers; No RV dump; Reservations accepted; Open May-Sep; Tent & RV camping: $16; Elev: 1326ft/404m; Tel: 218-335-8600; Nearest town: Deer River. GPS: 47.514730, -94.105550

50 • South Kawishiwi River

Total sites: 31; RV sites: 31; Elec sites: 23; Central water; Vault toilets; No showers; No RV dump; Open May-Sep; Tents: $15/RVs: $19-21; Elev: 1470ft/448m; Tel: 218-365-7600; Nearest town: Ely. GPS: 47.815844, -91.731616

51 • South Pike Bay

Total sites: 24; RV sites: 24; No water; Vault toilets; Reservations not accepted; Open May-Sep; Tent & RV camping: $16; Elev: 1302ft/397m; Tel: 218-335-8600; Nearest town: Cass Lake. GPS: 47.328806, -94.582578

52 • Stony Point

Total sites: 44; RV sites: 44; Elec sites: 44; Central water; Flush toilets; Showers; RV dump; Reservations accepted; Open May-Sep; Tent & RV camping: $26; Elev: 1312ft/400m; Tel: 218-335-8600; Nearest town: Walker; Notes: Electric fee additional. GPS: 47.136891, -94.455805

53 • Tamarack Point

Total sites: 32; RV sites: 32; Central water; Vault toilets; No showers; No RV dump; Reservations not accepted; Open May-Jul; Tent & RV camping: $14; Elev: 1319ft/402m; Tel: 218-335-8600; Nearest town: Bena. GPS: 47.444092, -94.120605

54 • Temperance River

Total sites: 9; RV sites: 9; Central water; Vault toilets; No showers; No RV dump; Reservations not accepted; Tent & RV camping: $18; Elev: 1532ft/467m; Tel: 218-663-8060; Nearest town: Tofte. GPS: 47.718279, -90.879572

55 • Toohey Lake

Total sites: 5; RV sites: 3; No water; Vault toilets; Tent & RV camping: Free; Elev: 1690ft/515m; Tel: 218-663-8060; Nearest town: Tofte. GPS: 47.712827, -90.953511

56 • Trails End

Total sites: 32; RV sites: 18; Central water; Vault toilets; No showers; No RV dump; Reservations accepted; Open Apr-Oct; Tent & RV camping: $22-24; Elev: 1466ft/447m; Tel: 218-387-1750; Nearest town: Grand Marais. GPS: 48.158975, -90.893034

57 • Two Island Lake

Total sites: 30; RV sites: 25; Central water; Vault toilets; No showers; No RV dump; Tent & RV camping: $16-18; Elev: 1785ft/544m; Tel: 218-387-1750; Nearest town: Grand Marais. GPS: 47.879347, -90.445628

58 • Wanaki Loop

Total sites: 46; RV sites: 46; Central water; Flush toilets; Showers; RV dump; Open May-Sep; Tent & RV camping: $21; Elev: 1319ft/402m; Tel: 218-335-8600; Nearest town: Bemidji. GPS: 47.386963, -94.507568

59 • Webster Lake

Total sites: 15; RV sites: 15; Central water; Vault toilets; No showers; No RV dump; Reservations not accepted; Open May-Oct; Tent & RV camping: $14; Elev: 1388ft/423m; Tel: 218-335-8600; Nearest town: Blackduck. GPS: 47.604980, -94.506836

60 • West Seelye Bay

Total sites: 22; RV sites: 22; Central water; Vault toilets; No showers; No RV dump; Reservations not accepted; Open May-Jul; Tent & RV camping: $14; Elev: 1329ft/405m; Tel: 218-335-8600; Nearest town: Deer River. GPS: 47.524108, -94.101543

61 • White Pine Lake

Total sites: 3; RV sites: 2; No water; Vault toilets; Max length: 20ft; Tent & RV camping: Free; Elev: 1618ft/493m; Tel: 218-663-8060; Nearest town: Lutsen. GPS: 47.738251, -90.752428

62 • Whiteface Reservoir

Total sites: 52; RV sites: 52; Elec sites: 32; Central water; Vault toilets; No showers; No RV dump; Reservations accepted; Open May-Nov; Tent & RV camping: $21-23; Elev: 1483ft/452m; Tel: 218-229-8800; Nearest town: Hoyt Lakes; Notes: Group Site: $125. GPS: 47.334557, -92.145631

63 • Whitefish Lake

Total sites: 3; RV sites: 2; No water; Vault toilets; Tent & RV camping: Free; Elev: 1700ft/518m; Tel: 218-663-8060; Nearest town: Tofte. GPS: 47.719106, -91.045364

64 • Williams Narrows

Total sites: 17; RV sites: 17; Central water; Vault toilets; No showers; No RV dump; Reservations accepted; Open May-Sep; Tent & RV camping: $16; Elev: 1309ft/399m; Tel: 218-335-8600; Nearest town: Bena. GPS: 47.503882, -94.063261

65 • Wilson Lake

Total sites: 4; RV sites: 3; No water; Vault toilets; Tent & RV camping: Free; Elev: 1713ft/522m; Tel: 218-663-8060; Nearest town: Tofte. GPS: 47.660068, -91.062459

66 • Windy Lake

Total sites: 1; RV sites: 1; No water; Vault toilets; Tent & RV camping: Free; Elev: 1680ft/512m; Tel: 218-663-8060; Nearest town: Tofte. GPS: 47.743903, -91.087007

67 • Winnie

Total sites: 35; RV sites: 35; Central water; Vault toilets; No showers; No RV dump; Reservations accepted; Open May-Sep; Tent & RV camping: $16; Elev: 1358ft/414m; Tel: 218-335-8600; Nearest town: Cass Lake. GPS: 47.425322, -94.320031

Mississippi

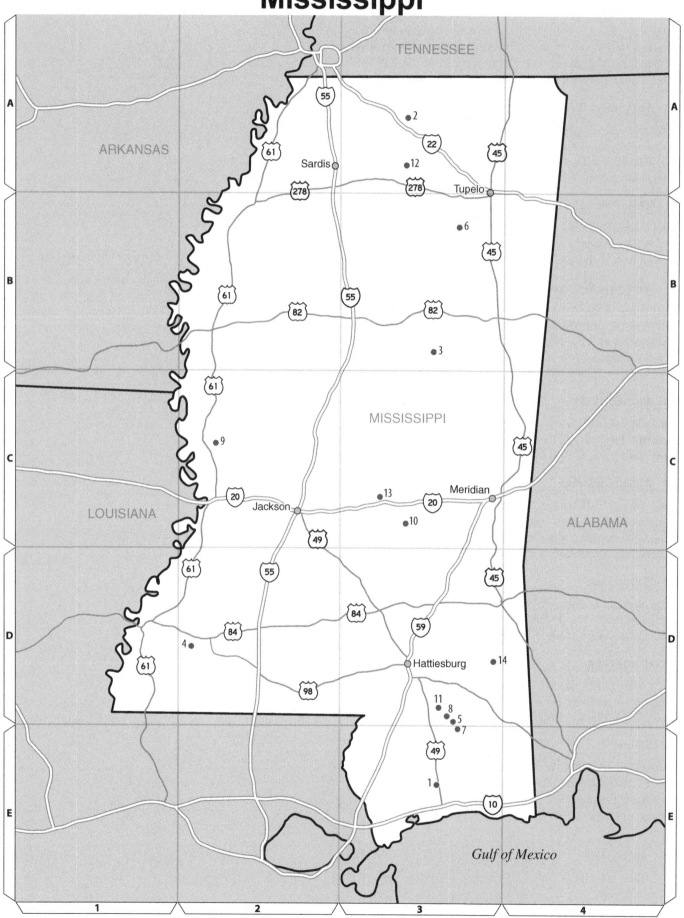

Mississippi Camping Areas

1 • Big Biloxi

Total sites: 25; RV sites: 25; Elec sites: 25; Water at site; Flush toilets; Showers; RV dump; Reservations not accepted; Stay limit: 14-30 days; Generator hours: 0600-2200; Open all year; Tent & RV camping: $20; Elev: 82ft/25m; Nearest town: Saucier; Notes: $13 w/Golden Age Pass. GPS: 30.568873, -89.129295

2 • Chewalla Lake

Total sites: 36; RV sites: 36; Elec sites: 9; Central water; Flush toilets; Showers; RV dump; Reservations accepted; Open Mar-Nov; Tents: $7/RVs: $20; Elev: 381ft/116m; Tel: 662-236-6550; Nearest town: Holly Springs. GPS: 34.735132, -89.338918

3 • Choctaw Lake

Total sites: 18; RV sites: 18; Elec sites: 18; Water at site; Flush toilets; Showers; RV dump; Reservations accepted; Open Mar-Nov; Tent & RV camping: $20; Elev: 499ft/152m; Tel: 662-285-3264; Nearest town: Ackerman. GPS: 33.272949, -89.145508

4 • Clear Springs

Total sites: 44; RV sites: 44; Elec sites: 22; Central water; Flush toilets; Showers; RV dump; Reservations not accepted; Open all year; Tents: $7/RVs: $20; Elev: 348ft/106m; Tel: 601-384-5876; Nearest town: Meadville. GPS: 31.425326, -90.988256

5 • Cypress Creek Landing

Total sites: 14; RV sites: 14; Central water; Flush toilets; Showers; No RV dump; Reservations not accepted; Stay limit: 14 days; Open all year; Tents only: $7; Elev: 164ft/50m; Tel: 601-965-1791; Nearest town: Wiggins. GPS: 30.965954, -89.004636

6 • Davis Lake

Total sites: 26; RV sites: 26; Elec sites: 26; Water at site; Flush toilets; Showers; RV dump; Reservations accepted; Open all year; Tent & RV camping: $20; Elev: 400ft/122m; Tel: 662-285-3264; Nearest town: Ackerman. GPS: 34.046802, -88.940141

7 • Fairley Bridge Landing

Total sites: 3; RV sites: 3; No water; Vault toilets; Reservations not accepted; Stay limit: 14 days; Open all year; Tent & RV camping: Free; Elev: 108ft/33m; Tel: 601-965-1600; Nearest town: Wiggins. GPS: 30.918153, -88.966392

8 • Janice Landing

Total sites: 5; Central water; Vault toilets; No showers; No RV dump; Stay limit: 14 days; Tents only: Free; Elev: 158ft/48m; Tel: 601-965-1791; Nearest town: Brooklyn. GPS: 30.995052, -89.050385

9 • Little Sunflower River

Total sites: 3; RV sites: 3; No water; Vault toilets; Reservation required; Open all year; Tent & RV camping: $7; Elev: 125ft/38m; Tel: 662-873-6256; Nearest town: Onward; Notes: Call district office for reservations. GPS: 32.695336, -90.817248

10 • Marathon Lake

Total sites: 34; RV sites: 34; Elec sites: 34; Water at site; Flush toilets; Showers; RV dump; Reservations not accepted; Stay limit: 14 days; Open Mar-Dec; Tent & RV camping: $20; Elev: 450ft/137m; Tel: 601-965-1600; Nearest town: Forest. GPS: 32.200928, -89.360352

11 • Moody's Landing

Total sites: 4; Central water; Vault toilets; No showers; No RV dump; Reservations not accepted; Stay limit: 14 days; Open all year; Tents only: Free; Elev: 125ft/38m; Nearest town: Brooklyn; Notes: Also boat-in sites. GPS: 31.051328, -89.116989

12 • Puskus Lake

Total sites: 19; RV sites: 19; Vault toilets; Reservations not accepted; Open all year; Tent & RV camping: $7; Elev: 371ft/113m; Tel: 601-965-1600; Nearest town: Oxford. GPS: 34.438141, -89.351275

13 • Shockaloe Base Camp I

Total sites: 10; RV sites: 10; Central water; Vault toilets; No showers; No RV dump; Reservations not accepted; Stay limit: 14 days; Open Mar-Dec; Tent & RV camping: $7; Elev: 564ft/172m; Nearest town: Forest. GPS: 32.366612, -89.562469

14 • Turkey Fork

Total sites: 28; RV sites: 20; Elec sites: 20; Water at site; Flush toilets; Showers; RV dump; Generator hours: 0600-2200; Open all year; Tents: $7/RVs: $20; Elev: 230ft/70m; Tel: 601-428-0594; Nearest town: Richton. GPS: 31.339407, -88.703506

Missouri

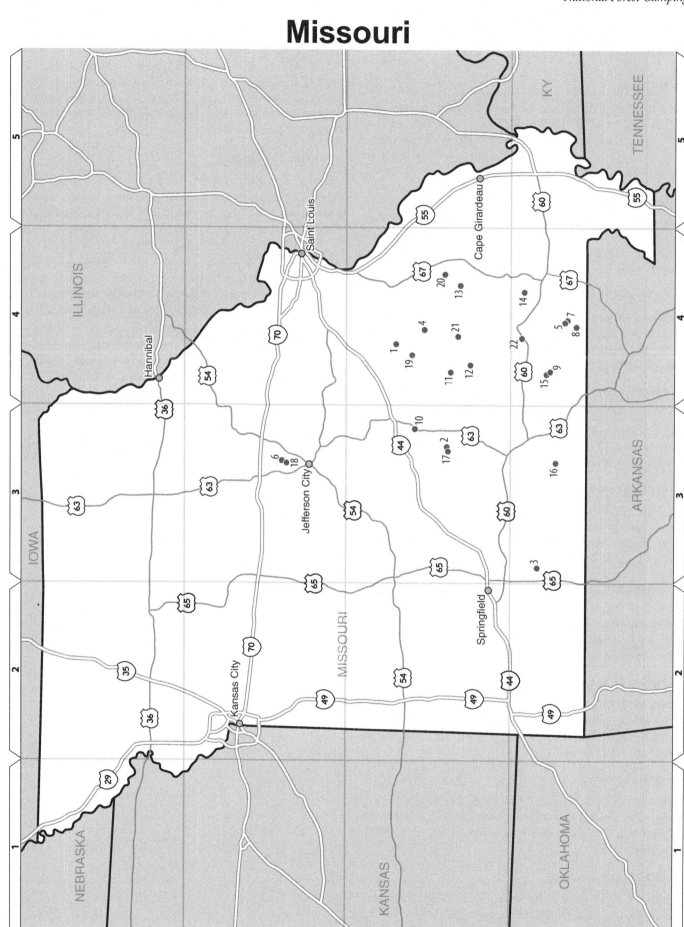

Missouri Camping Areas

1 • Berryman

Total sites: 8; RV sites: 8; No water; Vault toilets; Max length: 34ft; Tent & RV camping: Free; Elev: 1053ft/321m; Nearest town: Potosi. GPS: 37.929903, -91.062986

2 • Big Piney Trail Camp

Total sites: 2; RV sites: 2; No water; Vault toilets; Tent & RV camping: Free; Elev: 1130ft/344m; Nearest town: Licking. GPS: 37.560908, -92.012028

3 • Cobb Ridge

Total sites: 43; RV sites: 38; Elec sites: 25; Central water; Flush toilets; Showers; No RV dump; Max length: 34ft; Open all year; Tents: $10/RVs: $10-15; Elev: 1342ft/409m; Tel: 417-683-4428; Nearest town: Chadwick. GPS: 36.889901, -93.100946

4 • Council Bluff RA - Wild Boar CG

Total sites: 51; RV sites: 43; Central water; Vault toilets; No showers; No RV dump; Reservations accepted; Max length: 40ft; Open all year; Tent & RV camping: $11; Elev: 1312ft/400m; Tel: 573-766-5765; Nearest town: Belgrade; Notes: Group site: $25-$100. GPS: 37.722634, -90.937009

5 • Deer Leap

Total sites: 10; RV sites: 10; Central water; Vault toilets; No showers; No RV dump; Reservations not accepted; Max length: 34ft; Open May-Sep; Tent & RV camping: $12; Elev: 374ft/114m; Nearest town: Doniphan. GPS: 36.676399, -90.885546

6 • Dry Fork

Total sites: 8; RV sites: 8; Central water; Vault toilets; No showers; No RV dump; Reservations not accepted; Max length: 30ft; Open Apr-Nov; Tent & RV camping: Donation; Elev: 781ft/238m; Tel: 573-364-4621; Nearest town: Fulton. GPS: 38.783924, -92.125471

7 • Float Camp

Total sites: 20; RV sites: 20; Elec sites: 8; Central water; Vault toilets; No showers; No RV dump; Open May-Sep; Tents: $12/RVs: $12-20; Elev: 413ft/126m; Nearest town: Doniphan. GPS: 36.665362, -90.871496

8 • Fourche Lake RA

Total sites: 6; RV sites: 6; Central water; Vault toilets; No showers; No RV dump; Tent & RV camping: Free; Elev: 568ft/173m; Nearest town: Doniphan. GPS: 36.599501, -90.930136

9 • Greer Crossing

Total sites: 19; RV sites: 19; Central water; Vault toilets; No showers; No RV dump; Reservations not accepted; Open all year; Tent & RV camping: $10; Elev: 600ft/183m; Nearest town: Alton; Notes: No water/services in winter. GPS: 36.795410, -91.329834

10 • Lane Spring

Total sites: 18; RV sites: 18; Elec sites: 6; Central water; Vault toilets; No showers; No RV dump; Max length: 34ft; Open Apr-Oct; Tents: $8/RVs: $8-15; Elev: 863ft/263m; Nearest town: Vida. GPS: 37.797258, -91.836485

11 • Little Scotia Pond

Total sites: 14; RV sites: 14; Central water; Vault toilets; No showers; No RV dump; Reservations not accepted; Tent & RV camping: Free; Elev: 1371ft/418m; Nearest town: Bunker. GPS: 37.529541, -91.330078

12 • Loggers Lake

Total sites: 14; RV sites: 14; Central water; Vault toilets; No showers; No RV dump; Max length: 34ft; Open all year; Tent & RV camping: $10; Elev: 1073ft/327m; Nearest town: Bunker; Notes: Also walk-to sites, Walk-in in winter. GPS: 37.388184, -91.260498

13 • Marble Creek

Total sites: 26; RV sites: 26; No water; Vault toilets; Reservations not accepted; Open Apr-Nov; Tent & RV camping: $10; Elev: 682ft/208m; Tel: 573-783-3769; Nearest town: Arcadia. GPS: 37.451172, -90.540771

14 • Markham Spring

Total sites: 12; RV sites: 12; Elec sites: 12; Central water; Flush toilets; Showers; No RV dump; Reservations accepted; Max length: 34ft; Open May-Sep; Tents: $10/RVs: $17; Elev: 420ft/128m; Tel: 573-785-1475; Nearest town: Williamsville. GPS: 36.981434, -90.604934

15 • McCormack Lake RA

Total sites: 8; RV sites: 8; Central water; Vault toilets; No showers; No RV dump; Reservations not accepted; Tent & RV camping: Free; Elev: 607ft/185m; Nearest town: Alton. GPS: 36.821904, -91.352333

16 • North Fork

Total sites: 20; RV sites: 20; Elec sites: 2; Central water; Vault toilets; No showers; No RV dump; Reservations not accepted; Max length: 34ft; Generator hours: 0600-2200; Open May-Nov; Tents: $10/RVs: $10-15; Elev: 814ft/248m; Tel: 417-683-4428; Nearest town: Dora; GPS: 36.755217, -92.151948

17 • Paddy Creek

Total sites: 23; RV sites: 23; No water; Vault toilets; Reservations not accepted; Max length: 34ft; Tent & RV camping: Donation; Elev: 890ft/271m; Nearest town: Licking. GPS: 37.555656, -92.042308

18 • Pine Ridge Rec. Area

Total sites: 8; RV sites: 8; Central water; Vault toilets; No showers; No RV dump; Max length: 34ft; Tent & RV camping: Free; Elev: 787ft/240m; Nearest town: Ashland. GPS: 38.758900, -92.144390

19 • Red Bluff

Total sites: 48; RV sites: 48; Elec sites: 6; Central water; Vault toilets; No showers; No RV dump; Reservations accepted; Max length: 45ft; Tents: $11/RVs: $18; Elev: 827ft/252m; Tel: 573-743-6042; Nearest town: Viburnum. GPS: 37.812988, -91.169189

20 • Silver Mines

Total sites: 75; RV sites: 75; Elec sites: 11; Central water; Vault toilets; No showers; No RV dump; Reservations accepted; Max length: 50ft; Tents: $11/RVs: $11-18; Elev: 764ft/233m; Tel: 573-783-3769; Nearest town: Fredericktown; Notes: Group site: $25-$100. GPS: 37.560716, -90.438814

21 • Sutton Bluff

Total sites: 33; RV sites: 33; Elec sites: 12; Central water; Flush toilets; Showers; No RV dump; Reservations accepted; Max length: 60ft; Open Mar-Nov; Tents: $10/RVs: $20; Elev: 860ft/262m; Tel: 573-729-6656; Nearest town: Centerville; Notes: Group site: $40. GPS: 37.475586, -91.006592

22 • Watercress Spring

Total sites: 17; RV sites: 17; Central water; Vault toilets; No showers; No RV dump; Reservations not accepted; Open May-Sep; Tent & RV camping: $10; Elev: 515ft/157m; Tel: 573-996-2153; Nearest town: Van Buren. GPS: 36.999512, -91.018799

Montana

ND

SD

SASKATCHEWAN

ALBERTA

BRITISH COLUMBIA

IDAHO

WYOMING

MONTANA

Glendive

Miles City

Malta

Billings

Bozeman

Great Falls

Shelby

Kalispell

Missoula

Butte

Dillon

C 63,75,123 127,139,140 163,201

B 32,69,79 133,178,182 224,229,250

A 27,80,134 177,259

Montana Camping Areas

1 • Alta

Total sites: 9; RV sites: 9; Central water; Vault toilets; No showers; No RV dump; Reservations accepted; Max length: 30ft; Open May-Sep; Tent & RV camping: $8; Elev: 4970ft/1515m; Tel: 406-821-3269; Nearest town: Darby. GPS: 45.624432, -114.302107

2 • Ashley Lake North

Total sites: 5; RV sites: 5; No water; Vault toilets; Reservations not accepted; Max length: 12ft; Stay limit: 5 days; Generator hours: 0600-2200; Open May-Sep; Tent & RV camping: Free; Elev: 4032ft/1229m; Tel: 406-758-5208; Nearest town: Whitefish. GPS: 48.213724, -114.616946

3 • Aspen (Belt Park Butte)

Total sites: 6; RV sites: 6; Central water; Vault toilets; No showers; No RV dump; Reservations not accepted; Open May-Sep; Tent & RV camping: $10; Elev: 5141ft/1567m; Tel: 406-236-5100; Nearest town: Neihart. GPS: 46.992981, -110.768313

4 • Aspen (Chrome Mt)

Total sites: 8; RV sites: 8; Central water; Vault toilets; No showers; No RV dump; Reservations not accepted; Open all year; Tent & RV camping: $5; Elev: 5433ft/1656m; Tel: 406-932-5155; Nearest town: Big Timber; Notes: Limited access/no water in winter. GPS: 45.456575, -110.197144

5 • Aspen Grove

Total sites: 19; RV sites: 19; Central water; Vault toilets; No showers; No RV dump; Reservations not accepted; Max length: 20ft; Stay limit: 14 days; Open May-Oct; Tent & RV camping: $8; Elev: 4787ft/1459m; Tel: 406-362-7000; Nearest town: Lincoln. GPS: 46.978516, -112.531494

6 • Bad Medicine

Total sites: 18; RV sites: 18; Central water; Vault toilets; No showers; No RV dump; Reservations not accepted; Max length: 32ft; Stay limit: 16 days; Open all year; Tent & RV camping: $10; Elev: 2395ft/730m; Tel: 406-295-4693; Nearest town: Troy; Notes: Limited winter access. GPS: 48.221005, -115.856651

7 • Baker's Hole

Total sites: 73; RV sites: 73; Elec sites: 33; Central water; Vault toilets; No showers; No RV dump; Reservations not accepted; Max length: 32ft; Open May-Sep; Tents: $16/RVs: $16-22; Elev: 6578ft/2005m; Tel: 406-823-6961; Nearest town: West Yellowstone. GPS: 44.704102, -111.101563

8 • Barron Creek

Total sites: 7; RV sites: 7; No water; Vault toilets; Reservations not accepted; Max length: 40ft; Stay limit: 14 days; Open May-Oct; Tent & RV camping: Free; Elev: 2549ft/777m; Tel: 406-293-7773; Nearest town: Libby; Notes: Winter access may be limited. GPS: 48.516000, -115.291000

9 • Basin

Total sites: 30; RV sites: 30; No water; Vault toilets; Reservations accepted; Max length: 30ft; Open May-Sep; Tent & RV camping: $18; Elev: 6923ft/2110m; Tel: 406-446-2103; Nearest town: Red Lodge. GPS: 45.163014, -109.392697

10 • Basin Canyon

Total sites: 2; RV sites: 2; No water; Vault toilets; Reservations not accepted; Max length: 16ft; Tent & RV camping: Free; Elev: 5828ft/1776m; Tel: 406-287-3223; Nearest town: Butte. GPS: 45.855608, -112.546106

11 • Basin Creek

Total sites: 4; RV sites: 4; No water; Vault toilets; Reservations not accepted; Tent & RV camping: Free; Elev: 5669ft/1728m; Nearest town: Checkerboard. GPS: 46.642202, -110.430243

12 • Battle Ridge

Total sites: 13; RV sites: 13; Central water; Vault toilets; No showers; No RV dump; Open May-Sep; Tent & RV camping: Free; Elev: 6390ft/1948m; Tel: 406-522-2520; Nearest town: Bozeman. GPS: 45.882487, -110.879923

13 • Bear Creek

Total sites: 12; RV sites: 12; Central water; Vault toilets; No showers; No RV dump; Reservations not accepted; Max length: 28ft; Stay limit: 16 days; Open Jun-Oct; Tent & RV camping: Free; Elev: 6365ft/1940m; Tel: 406-682-4253; Nearest town: Cameron. GPS: 45.156557, -111.553688

14 • Beaver Creek

Total sites: 4; RV sites: 4; No water; Vault toilets; Reservations not accepted; Max length: 32ft; Stay limit: 14 days; Open May-Nov; Tent & RV camping: Free; Elev: 4150ft/1265m; Tel: 406-758-5376; Nearest town: Hungry Horse. GPS: 47.923596, -113.373361

15 • Beaver Creek

Total sites: 65; RV sites: 65; Central water; Vault toilets; No showers; No RV dump; Reservations accepted; Max length: 50ft; Open May-Sep; Tent & RV camping: $20; Elev: 6575ft/2004m; Tel: 406-823-6961; Nearest town: West Yellowstone. GPS: 44.855733, -111.373557

16 • Beaver Dam

Total sites: 15; RV sites: 15; Central water; Vault toilets; No showers; No RV dump; Max length: 50ft; Stay limit: 16 days; Open May-Sep; Tent & RV camping: $5; Elev: 6490ft/1978m; Tel: 406-494-2147; Nearest town: Butte. GPS: 45.884332, -112.782974

17 • Benchmark

Total sites: 25; RV sites: 25; Central water; Vault toilets; No showers; Reservations not accepted; Max length: 22ft; Open Jun-Sep; Tent & RV camping: $6; Elev: 5318ft/1621m; Nearest town: Augusta. GPS: 47.486572, -112.881104

18 • Big Beaver

Total sites: 5; RV sites: 5; No water; Vault toilets; Reservations not accepted; Max length: 32ft; Open all year; Tent & RV camping: Free; Elev: 5348ft/1630m; Tel: 406-932-5155; Nearest town: Big Timber; Notes: Limited winter access. GPS: 45.463875, -110.199043

19 • Big Creek

Total sites: 22; RV sites: 22; Central water; Vault toilets; No showers; No RV dump; Reservations accepted; Stay limit: 14 days; Open May-Sep; Tent & RV camping: $16; Elev: 3330ft/1015m; Tel: 406-387-3800; Nearest town: Columbia Falls; Notes: Group site: $50-$200. GPS: 48.600586, -114.163086

20 • Big Eddy

Total sites: 5; RV sites: 5; No water; Vault toilets; Reservations not accepted; Max length: 30ft; Stay limit: 16 days; Open all year; Tent & RV camping: Free; Elev: 2297ft/700m; Tel: 406-827-3533; Nearest town: Heron; Notes: Limited winter access. GPS: 48.067000, -115.923000

21 • Big Larch

Total sites: 48; RV sites: 48; Central water; Vault toilets; No showers; No RV dump; Reservations not accepted; Max length: 32ft; Open all year; Tent & RV camping: $10; Elev: 4065ft/1239m; Tel: 406-677-2233; Nearest town: Seeley Lake; Notes: Reservable group sites $35. GPS: 47.184326, -113.492676

22 • Big Therriault Lake

Total sites: 10; RV sites: 10; Central water; Vault toilets; No showers; No RV dump; Reservations not accepted; Max length: 32ft; Stay limit: 14 days; Open all year; Tent & RV camping: $5; Elev: 5548ft/1691m; Tel: 406-882-4451; Nearest town: Eureka; Notes: Access may be limited in winter. GPS: 48.936523, -114.878906

23 • Bitterroot Flat

Total sites: 15; Central water; Vault toilets; No showers; No RV dump; Reservations not accepted; Open all year; Tents only: $6; Elev: 4429ft/1350m; Tel: 406-329-3814; Nearest town: Clinton; Notes: Rough road, Limited services and no fees Sep-Apr. GPS: 46.467568, -113.777049

24 • Black Bear

Total sites: 6; RV sites: 6; No water; Vault toilets; Reservations not accepted; Max length: 50ft; Stay limit: 16 days; Generator hours: 0600-2200; Open Jun-Sep; Tent & RV camping: Free; Elev: 4626ft/1410m; Tel: 406-821-3913; Nearest town: Hamilton. GPS: 46.166026, -113.924677

25 • Blacks Pond

Total sites: 2; RV sites: 2; No water; No toilets; Reservations not accepted; Open all year; Tent & RV camping: Free; Elev: 3678ft/1121m; Tel: 406-784-2344; Nearest town: Ashland. GPS: 45.346975, -106.286373

26 • Blodgett

Total sites: 6; RV sites: 5; Central water; Vault toilets; No showers; No RV dump; Reservations not accepted; Max length: 45ft; Open May-Sep; Tent & RV camping: Fee unknown; Elev: 4304ft/1312m; Tel: 406-777-5461; Nearest town: Hamilton. GPS: 46.269529, -114.243869

27 • Boulder Creek

Total sites: 13; RV sites: 13; Central water; Vault toilets; No showers; No RV dump; Reservations not accepted; Max length: 30ft; Open Jun-Sep; Tent & RV camping: Fee unknown; Elev: 6457ft/1968m; Tel: 406-832-3178; Nearest town: Wise River. GPS: 45.651812, -113.066888

28 • Branham Lakes

Total sites: 6; No water; Vault toilets; Reservations not accepted; Stay limit: 16 days; Open Jul-Sep; Tents only: Free; Elev: 8884ft/2708m; Tel: 406-682-4253; Nearest town: West Yellowstone. GPS: 45.516491, -111.989771

29 • Bull River

Total sites: 26; RV sites: 26; Central water; Vault toilets; No showers; No RV dump; Reservations not accepted; Max length: 40ft; Stay limit: 16 days; Open May-Nov; Tent & RV camping: $10; Elev: 2313ft/705m; Tel: 406-827-3533; Nearest town: Noxon; Notes: Reservable group site $30. GPS: 48.030233, -115.842666

30 • Cabin City

Total sites: 24; RV sites: 24; Central water; Vault toilets; No showers; No RV dump; Reservations not accepted; Open May-Sep; Tent & RV camping: $7; Elev: 3165ft/965m; Tel: 406-822-4233; Nearest town: De Borgia. GPS: 47.374415, -115.262408

31 • Cabin Creek

Total sites: 15; RV sites: 15; Central water; Vault toilets; No showers; No RV dump; Reservations accepted; Open May-Sep; Tent & RV camping: $20; Elev: 6532ft/1991m; Tel: 406-823-6961; Nearest town: West Yellowstone. GPS: 44.871571, -111.343822

32 • Cable Mountain

Total sites: 11; RV sites: 11; Central water; Vault toilets; No showers; No RV dump; Reservations not accepted; Max length: 22ft; Open May-Sep; Tent & RV camping: $13; Elev: 6627ft/2020m; Tel: 406-859-3211; Nearest town: Philipsburg. GPS: 46.221436, -113.246826

33 • Camp 32

Total sites: 8; RV sites: 8; Central water; Vault toilets; No showers; No RV dump; Max length: 20ft; Stay limit: 14 days; Open all year; Tent & RV camping: Free; Elev: 2779ft/847m; Tel: 406-296-2536; Nearest town: Rexford. GPS: 48.837000, -115.190000

34 • Canyon

Total sites: 17; RV sites: 17; No water; Vault toilets; Reservations not accepted; Max length: 48ft; Open all year; Tent & RV camping: $7; Elev: 5112ft/1558m; Tel: 406-848-7375; Nearest town: Gardiner. GPS: 45.182857, -110.887965

35 • Canyon Creek (Vipond Park)

Total sites: 3; RV sites: 3; No water; Vault toilets; Max length: 18ft; Tent & RV camping: Free; Elev: 7323ft/2232m; Tel: 406-832-3178; Nearest town: Melrose. GPS: 45.626110, -112.941390

36 • Caribou

Total sites: 3; RV sites: 3; No water; Vault toilets; Reservations not accepted; Max length: 32ft; Stay limit: 14 days; Open all year; Tent & RV camping: Free; Elev: 3770ft/1149m; Tel: 406-295-4693; Nearest town: Troy. GPS: 48.948806, -115.503202

37 • Cascade

Total sites: 30; RV sites: 30; Central water; Vault toilets; No showers; No RV dump; Reservations accepted; Max length: 30ft; Stay limit: 16 days; Open Jun-Sep; Tent & RV camping: $15; Elev: 7602ft/2317m; Tel: 406-446-2103; Nearest town: Red Lodge. GPS: 45.173096, -109.450928

38 • Cascade

Total sites: 10; RV sites: 10; Central water; Vault toilets; No showers; No RV dump; Reservations not accepted; Open May-Oct; Tent & RV camping: $10; Elev: 2516ft/767m; Tel: 406-826-3821; Nearest town: Plains. GPS: 47.306644, -114.825312

39 • Cave Mountain

Total sites: 14; RV sites: 14; Central water; Vault toilets; No showers; No RV dump; Reservations not accepted; Max length: 30ft; Open May-Sep; Tent & RV camping: $6; Elev: 5131ft/1564m; Tel: 406-466-5341; Nearest town: Choteau. GPS: 47.890137, -112.726563

40 • Charles Waters

Total sites: 27; RV sites: 27; Central water; Vault toilets; No showers; No RV dump; Reservations not accepted; Max length: 70ft; Open May-Sep; Tent & RV camping: $10; Elev: 3740ft/1140m; Tel: 406-777-5461; Nearest town: Stevensville. GPS: 46.575439, -114.140625

41 • Cherry Creek

Total sites: 7; RV sites: 7; No water; Vault toilets; Reservations not accepted; Open May-Oct; Tent & RV camping: Free; Elev: 6545ft/1995m; Tel: 406-823-6961; Nearest town: West Yellowstone. GPS: 44.751044, -111.263946

42 • Chippy Park

Total sites: 7; RV sites: 7; Central water; Vault toilets; No showers; No RV dump; Reservations not accepted; Open all year; Tent & RV camping: $5; Elev: 5607ft/1709m; Tel: 406-932-5155; Nearest town: Big Timber; Notes: Limited winter access. GPS: 45.437377, -110.189457

43 • Chisholm

Total sites: 10; RV sites: 10; Central water; Vault toilets; No showers; No RV dump; Reservations accepted; Max length: 35ft; Open May-Sep; Tent & RV camping: $20; Elev: 6778ft/2066m; Tel: 406-522-2520; Nearest town: Bozeman. GPS: 45.474644, -110.956458

44 • Clark Memorial

Total sites: 5; No water; Vault toilets; Reservations not accepted; Tents only: Free; Elev: 2585ft/788m; Tel: 406-826-3821; Nearest town: Thompson Falls. GPS: 47.631795, -115.174211

45 • Clearwater Crossing

Total sites: 3; RV sites: 3; Central water; Vault toilets; No showers; No RV dump; Reservations not accepted; Tent & RV camping: Free; Elev: 3493ft/1065m; Tel: 406-626-5201; Nearest town: Alberton. GPS: 46.908889, -114.803115

46 • Cliff Point

Total sites: 6; RV sites: 6; Central water; Vault toilets; No showers; No RV dump; Reservations not accepted; Max length: 16ft; Stay limit: 16 days; Open May-Sep; Tent & RV camping: $15; Elev: 6345ft/1934m; Tel: 406-682-4253; Nearest town: West Yellowstone. GPS: 44.792000, -111.562000

47 • Colter

Total sites: 23; RV sites: 23; Central water; Vault toilets; No showers; No RV dump; Reservations not accepted; Max length: 32ft; Open Jul-Sep; Tent & RV camping: $8; Elev: 8044ft/2452m; Tel: 406-848-7375; Nearest town: Cooke City. GPS: 45.028033, -109.894038

48 • Copper Creek (Moose Lake)

Total sites: 7; RV sites: 7; Central water; Vault toilets; No showers; No RV dump; Reservations not accepted; Stay limit: 16 days; Open May-Nov; Tent & RV camping: Free; Elev: 5981ft/1823m; Tel: 406-859-3211; Nearest town: Philipsburg. GPS: 46.066272, -113.543706

49 • Copper Creek (Silver King Mt)

Total sites: 17; RV sites: 17; Central water; Vault toilets; No showers; No RV dump; Reservations not accepted; Stay limit: 14 days; Open May-Aug; Tent & RV camping: $8; Elev: 5322ft/1622m; Tel: 406-362-7000; Nearest town: Lincoln. GPS: 47.078369, -112.619385

50 • Copper King

Total sites: 4; No water; Vault toilets; Reservations not accepted; Open Jun-Oct; Tents only: Free; Elev: 2556ft/779m; Tel: 406-826-3821; Nearest town: Thompson Falls. GPS: 47.619478, -115.188245

51 • Cottonwood

Total sites: 10; RV sites: 10; No toilets; Reservations not accepted; Max length: 28ft; Stay limit: 16 days; Tent & RV camping: Free; Elev: 6335ft/1931m; Tel: 406-682-4253; Nearest town: Sheridan. GPS: 44.973933, -111.976399

52 • Cow Creek

Total sites: 4; RV sites: 4; No water; Vault toilets; Reservations not accepted; Max length: 32ft; Stay limit: 10 days; Open all year; Tent & RV camping: Free; Elev: 3888ft/1185m; Tel: 406-784-2344; Nearest town: Ashland. GPS: 45.310201, -106.244534

53 • Crazy Creek

Total sites: 7; RV sites: 7; Central water; Vault toilets; No showers; No RV dump; Reservations not accepted; Max length: 26ft; Generator hours: 0600-2200; Open Jun-Nov; Tent & RV camping: $8; Elev: 4901ft/1494m; Tel: 406-821-3201; Nearest town: Sula. GPS: 45.810633, -114.068597

54 • Cromwell-Dixon

Total sites: 15; RV sites: 15; Central water; Vault toilets; No showers; No RV dump; Reservations not accepted; Open Jun-Sep; Tent & RV camping: $8; Elev: 6250ft/1905m; Tel: 406-449-5490; Nearest town: Helena. GPS: 46.556303, -112.315633

55 • Crystal Creek

Total sites: 3; RV sites: 3; No water; Vault toilets; Reservations not accepted; Max length: 16ft; Open Jul-Sep; Tent & RV camping: Free; Elev: 6972ft/2125m; Tel: 406-859-3211; Nearest town: Philipsburg. GPS: 46.232615, -113.745901

56 • Crystal Lake

Total sites: 23; RV sites: 23; Central water; Vault toilets; No showers; No RV dump; Reservations not accepted; Max length: 22ft; Stay limit: 16 days; Open Jun-Sep; Tent & RV camping: $10; Elev: 6056ft/1846m; Tel: 406-566-2292; Nearest town: Lewistown. GPS: 46.794678, -109.511475

57 • Daisy Dean

Total sites: 10; RV sites: 10; No water; Vault toilets; Reservations not accepted; Tent & RV camping: Free; Elev: 6099ft/1859m; Nearest town: Martinsdale. GPS: 46.623207, -110.358729

58 • Dalles

Total sites: 10; Central water; Vault toilets; No showers; No RV dump; Reservations not accepted; Open May-Oct; Tents only: $6; Elev: 4058ft/1237m; Tel: 406-329-3814; Nearest town: Clinton; Notes: Limited services and no fees Sep - Apr. GPS: 46.557257, -113.710092

59 • Delmoe Lake

Total sites: 25; RV sites: 25; Central water; Vault toilets; No showers; No RV dump; Reservations not accepted; Max length: 32ft; Stay limit: 16 days; Open May-Sep; Tent & RV camping: $8; Elev: 6102ft/1860m; Tel: 406-287-3223; Nearest town: Butte. GPS: 45.986047, -112.353668

60 • Devil Creek

Total sites: 14; RV sites: 14; Central water; Vault toilets; No showers; No RV dump; Reservations accepted; Open May-Sep; Tent & RV camping: $14; Elev: 4459ft/1359m; Tel: 406-387-3800; Nearest town: East Glacier Park. GPS: 48.251141, -113.463589

61 • Devils Corkscrew

Total sites: 4; RV sites: 4; No water; Vault toilets; Reservations not accepted; Max length: 32ft; Stay limit: 16 days; Tent & RV camping: Free; Elev: 3648ft/1112m; Tel: 406-387-3800; Nearest town: Martin City. GPS: 48.110029, -113.696335

62 • Dinner Station

Total sites: 8; RV sites: 8; Central water; Vault toilets; No showers; No RV dump; Reservations not accepted; Max length: 16ft; Stay limit: 16 days; Open May-Sep; Tent & RV camping: Fee unknown; Elev: 7142ft/2177m; Tel: 406-683-3900; Nearest town: Dillon. GPS: 45.428976, -112.903551

63 • Doris Creek

Total sites: 10; RV sites: 10; No water; Vault toilets; Reservations accepted; Open May-Sep; Tent & RV camping: $14; Elev: 3579ft/1091m; Tel: 406-387-3800; Nearest town: Columbia Falls. GPS: 48.305000, -113.981000

64 • Dorr Skeels

Total sites: 8; RV sites: 2; Central water; Vault toilets; No showers; No RV dump; Reservations not accepted; Max length: 32ft; Stay limit: 16 days; Open all year; Tent & RV camping: $7; Elev: 2339ft/713m; Tel: 406-295-4693; Nearest town: Troy; Notes: Limited winter access. GPS: 48.267648, -115.854925

65 • Double Falls

Total sites: 4; RV sites: 4; No water; Vault toilets; Reservations not accepted; Tent & RV camping: Free; Elev: 5282ft/1610m; Tel: 406-466-5341; Nearest town: Augusta; Notes: Mandatory food storage. GPS: 47.407334, -112.722084

66 • Dry Wolf

Total sites: 25; RV sites: 25; Central water; Vault toilets; No showers; No RV dump; Reservations not accepted; Max length: 32ft; Tent & RV camping: $5; Elev: 5915ft/1803m; Nearest town: Stanford; Notes: Mandatory food storage. GPS: 46.979004, -110.518311

67 • Eagle Creek

Total sites: 16; RV sites: 16; No water; Vault toilets; Reservations not accepted; Max length: 40ft; Open all year; Tent & RV camping: $7; Elev: 6145ft/1873m; Tel: 406-848-7375; Nearest town: Gardiner. GPS: 45.045609, -110.679758

68 • East Creek

Total sites: 4; RV sites: 4; Central water; Vault toilets; No showers; No RV dump; Reservations not accepted; Max length: 16ft; Stay limit: 16 days; Open May-Sep; Tent & RV camping: Free; Elev: 7031ft/2143m; Tel: 406-683-3900; Nearest town: Dillon. GPS: 44.564000, -112.661000

69 • East Fork

Total sites: 7; RV sites: 7; Central water; Vault toilets; No showers; No RV dump; Reservations not accepted; Max length: 22ft; Stay limit: 16 days; Open May-Nov; Tent & RV camping: Free; Elev: 6096ft/1858m; Tel: 406-859-3211; Nearest town: Butte. GPS: 46.134885, -113.387323

70 • East Rosebud Lake

Total sites: 14; RV sites: 14; Central water; Vault toilets; No showers; No RV dump; Reservations not accepted; Max length: 20ft; Open all year; Tent & RV camping: $9; Elev: 6375ft/1943m;

Tel: 406-446-2103; Nearest town: Absarokee; Notes: No services in winter. GPS: 45.198973, -109.634409

71 • Ekalaka Park

Total sites: 8; RV sites: 8; Central water; Vault toilets; No showers; No RV dump; Reservations not accepted; Max length: 30ft; Stay limit: 14 days; Open May-Nov; Tent & RV camping: Free; Elev: 3780ft/1152m; Tel: 605-797-4432; Nearest town: Ekalaka. GPS: 45.798633, -104.511426

72 • Elk Lake

Total sites: 2; No water; Vault toilets; Reservations not accepted; Stay limit: 16 days; Tents only: Free; Elev: 6686ft/2038m; Tel: 406-682-4253; Nearest town: Monida (ID). GPS: 44.669922, -111.631286

73 • Elko

Total sites: 3; RV sites: 3; No water; Vault toilets; Reservations not accepted; Tent & RV camping: Free; Elev: 5349ft/1630m; Tel: 406-466-5341; Nearest town: Choteau; Notes: Mandatory food storage. GPS: 47.924348, -112.763595

74 • Emerald Lake

Total sites: 32; RV sites: 32; Central water; Vault toilets; No showers; No RV dump; Reservations not accepted; Max length: 30ft; Open all year; Tent & RV camping: $9; Elev: 6342ft/1933m; Tel: 406-446-2103; Nearest town: Fishtail; Notes: No services in winter. GPS: 45.254883, -109.699707

75 • Emery Bay

Total sites: 22; RV sites: 22; Central water; Vault toilets; No showers; No RV dump; Reservations accepted; Open May-Sep; Tent & RV camping: $16; Elev: 3596ft/1096m; Tel: 406-387-3800; Nearest town: Hungry Horse; Notes: Group site: $90-$200. GPS: 48.334147, -113.950346

76 • Fairy Lake

Total sites: 9; Central water; Vault toilets; No showers; No RV dump; Reservations not accepted; Open Jul-Sep; Tents only: Free; Elev: 7658ft/2334m; Tel: 406-522-2520; Nearest town: Bozeman; Notes: High clearance vehicle recommended, Steep gravel road, slippery when wet - not suitable for RV or towed unit travel. GPS: 45.906741, -110.961021

77 • Falls Creek

Total sites: 8; Central water; Vault toilets; No showers; No RV dump; Reservations not accepted; Open all year; Tents only: Free; Elev: 5254ft/1601m; Tel: 406-932-5155; Nearest town: Big Timber. GPS: 45.490236, -110.219095

78 • Fishtrap Lake

Total sites: 13; RV sites: 4; Central water; Vault toilets; No showers; No RV dump; Reservations not accepted; Max length: 28ft; Open all year; Tent & RV camping: Free; Elev: 4131ft/1259m; Tel: 406-329-3750; Nearest town: Thompson Falls; Notes: No water Oct-May. GPS: 47.861395, -115.202918

79 • Flint Creek

Total sites: 16; RV sites: 16; No water; Vault toilets; Reservations not accepted; Max length: 22ft; Open May-Oct; Tent & RV camping: Free; Elev: 5620ft/1713m; Tel: 406-859-3211; Nearest town: Philipsburg. GPS: 46.233448, -113.300439

80 • Fourth of July

Total sites: 5; RV sites: 5; Central water; Vault toilets; No showers; No RV dump; Max length: 30ft; Stay limit: 16 days; Open Jun-Sep; Tent & RV camping: $8; Elev: 6401ft/1951m; Tel: 406-832-3178; Nearest town: Wise River. GPS: 45.662372, -113.064284

81 • Gipsy Lake

Total sites: 5; RV sites: 5; No water; Vault toilets; Reservations not accepted; Max length: 16ft; Stay limit: 14 days; Open Jun-Sep; Tent & RV camping: $10; Elev: 6398ft/1950m; Tel: 406-266-3425; Nearest town: Townsend. GPS: 46.499952, -111.209615

82 • Gold Creek

Total sites: 4; RV sites: 4; No water; Vault toilets; Reservations not accepted; Max length: 25ft; Tent & RV camping: Free; Elev: 4951ft/1509m; Tel: 406-777-5461; Nearest town: Stevensville; Notes: Rough road. GPS: 46.397539, -113.902325

83 • Gold Rush

Total sites: 7; RV sites: 7; Central water; Vault toilets; No showers; No RV dump; Reservations not accepted; Open Jun-Oct; Tent & RV camping: Free; Elev: 3573ft/1089m; Tel: 406-826-3821; Nearest town: Thompson Falls; Notes: No water Oct-May. GPS: 47.522820, -115.311470

84 • Grasshopper (Elkhorn Hot Springs)

Total sites: 24; RV sites: 24; Central water; Vault toilets; No showers; No RV dump; Max length: 30ft; Stay limit: 16 days; Open Jun-Sep; Tent & RV camping: $8; Elev: 7050ft/2149m; Tel: 406-683-3900; Nearest town: Dillon. GPS: 45.452542, -113.120816

85 • Grasshopper (Fourmile Spring) Creek

Total sites: 12; RV sites: 12; Central water; Vault toilets; No showers; No RV dump; Reservations not accepted; Open Jun-Sep; Tent & RV camping: $10; Elev: 5833ft/1778m; Nearest town: White Sulphur Springs. GPS: 46.544149, -110.747806

86 • Grave Creek

Total sites: 4; RV sites: 4; No water; Vault toilets; Reservations not accepted; Max length: 20ft; Stay limit: 14 days; Open all year; Tent & RV camping: Free; Elev: 3030ft/924m; Tel: 406-882-4451; Nearest town: Fortine; Notes: Access may be limited in winter. GPS: 48.819282, -114.886547

87 • Graves Bay

Total sites: 10; RV sites: 10; Tent & RV camping: Free; Elev: 3547ft/1081m; Nearest town: Hungry Horse. GPS: 48.126689, -113.809421

88 • Greek Creek

Total sites: 15; RV sites: 15; Central water; Vault toilets; No showers; No RV dump; Reservations accepted; Max length: 60ft; Open May-Sep; Tent & RV camping: $20; Elev: 5768ft/1758m; Tel: 406-522-2520; Nearest town: Big Sky. GPS: 45.380606, -111.181799

89 • Greenough Lake

Total sites: 18; RV sites: 18; Central water; Vault toilets; No showers; No RV dump; Reservations accepted; Max length: 45ft; Open May-Sep; Tent & RV camping: $18; Elev: 7201ft/2195m; Tel: 406-446-2103; Nearest town: Red Lodge. GPS: 45.056111, -109.412967

90 • Grizzly

Total sites: 9; Central water; Vault toilets; No showers; No RV dump; Reservations not accepted; Open May-Sep; Tents only: $6; Elev: 4056ft/1236m; Tel: 406-329-3814; Nearest town: Clinton; Notes: RVs not recommended due to narrow and rough road. GPS: 46.574239, -113.660637

91 • Half Moon

Total sites: 12; RV sites: 12; Central water; Vault toilets; No showers; No RV dump; Reservations not accepted; Max length: 32ft; Open all year; Tent & RV camping: $5; Elev: 6486ft/1977m; Tel: 406-932-5155; Nearest town: Big Timber; Notes: Limited winter access. GPS: 46.041437, -110.239562

92 • Harry's Flat

Total sites: 15; Central water; Vault toilets; No showers; No RV dump; Reservations not accepted; Open all year; Tents only: $6; Elev: 4110ft/1253m; Tel: 406-329-3814; Nearest town: Clinton; Notes: Limited services and no fees Oct - Apr. GPS: 46.535255, -113.752288

93 • Hay Canyon

Total sites: 9; RV sites: 9; No water; Vault toilets; Reservations not accepted; Max length: 30ft; Tent & RV camping: Free; Elev: 5178ft/1578m; Nearest town: Utica; Notes: Mandatory food storage. GPS: 46.798738, -110.300043

94 • Hells Canyon

Total sites: 11; RV sites: 11; No water; Vault toilets; Reservations not accepted; Max length: 20ft; Open all year; Tent & RV camping: Free; Elev: 6132ft/1869m; Tel: 406-932-5155; Nearest town: Big Timber; Notes: Limited winter access. GPS: 45.361892, -110.215052

95 • Hicks Park

Total sites: 16; RV sites: 16; Central water; Vault toilets; No showers; No RV dump; Reservations not accepted; Max length: 32ft; Open all year; Tent & RV camping: $5; Elev: 6430ft/1960m; Tel: 406-932-5155; Nearest town: Big Timber; Notes: Limited winter access. GPS: 45.297993, -110.239914

96 • Hilltop

Total sites: 18; RV sites: 18; Central water; Vault toilets; No showers; No RV dump; Reservations not accepted; Max length: 22ft; Stay limit: 16 days; Open Jun-Sep; Tent & RV camping: Fee unknown; Elev: 6588ft/2008m; Tel: 4060682-4253; Nearest town: West Yellowstone. GPS: 44.796657, -111.561075

97 • Holiday Spring

Total sites: 6; RV sites: 6; No water; Vault toilets; Reservations not accepted; Stay limit: 10 days; Open Apr-Nov; Tent & RV camping: Free; Elev: 4009ft/1222m; Tel: 406-784-2344; Nearest town: Ashland. GPS: 45.638499, -105.974276

98 • Holland Lake - Bay Loop

Total sites: 22; RV sites: 22; Central water; Flush toilets; No showers; RV dump; Reservations accepted; Open May-Sep; Tent & RV camping: $18; Elev: 4078ft/1243m; Tel: 406-837-7500; Nearest town: Seeley Lake; Notes: Dump fee. GPS: 47.451098, -113.607858

99 • Holland Lake - Larch Loop

Total sites: 15; RV sites: 15; Central water; Flush toilets; No showers; RV dump; Reservations accepted; Open May-Sep; Tent & RV camping: $18; Elev: 4065ft/1239m; Tel: 406-837-7500; Nearest town: Seeley Lake; Notes: Dump fee, Group site $100-$325. GPS: 47.445358, -113.616815

100 • Home Gulch

Total sites: 15; RV sites: 15; Central water; Vault toilets; No showers; No RV dump; Reservations not accepted; Open Jun-Sep; Tent & RV camping: $6; Elev: 4488ft/1368m; Tel: 406-466-5341; Nearest town: Augusta; Notes: May be reserved for larger groups. GPS: 47.616012, -112.726167

101 • Hood Creek

Total sites: 25; RV sites: 25; Central water; Vault toilets; No showers; No RV dump; Reservations accepted; Open May-Sep; Tent & RV camping: $20; Elev: 6827ft/2081m; Tel: 406-522-2520; Nearest town: Bozeman. GPS: 45.484152, -110.967554

102 • Howard Lake

Total sites: 10; RV sites: 10; Central water; Vault toilets; No showers; No RV dump; Reservations not accepted; Stay limit: 14 days; Open May-Nov; Tent & RV camping: $8; Elev: 4154ft/1266m; Tel: 406-293-7773; Nearest town: Libby. GPS: 48.101318, -115.530518

103 • Hyalite Below Dam

Total sites: 11; RV sites: 11; No water; Vault toilets; No showers; No RV dump; Reservations not accepted; Tent & RV camping: Free; Elev: 6670ft/2033m; Nearest town: Bozeman; Notes: Water at nearby day-use area. GPS: 45.488645, -110.981294

104 • Indian Hill

Total sites: 7; RV sites: 7; Central water; Vault toilets; No showers; No RV dump; Reservations not accepted; Max length: 20ft; Stay limit: 16 days; Open May-Sep; Tent & RV camping: Fee unknown; Elev: 5131ft/1564m; Nearest town: Utica; Notes: Mandatory food storage. GPS: 46.814059, -110.286281

105 • Indian Trees

Total sites: 15; RV sites: 14; Central water; Vault toilets; No showers; No RV dump; Reservations accepted; Max length: 50ft; Generator hours: 0600-2200; Open May-Sep; Tent & RV camping:

$10; Elev: 5144ft/1568m; Tel: 406-821-3201; Nearest town: Sula. GPS: 45.755859, -113.954346

106 • Initial Creek

Total sites: 6; RV sites: 6; No water; No toilets; Reservations not accepted; Max length: 20ft; Stay limit: 16 days; Open all year; Tent & RV camping: Free; Elev: 6214ft/1894m; Tel: 406-446-2103; Nearest town: Nye; Notes: No services in winter. GPS: 45.404000, -109.954000

107 • Jellison Place

Total sites: 10; RV sites: 10; No water; Vault toilets; Reservations not accepted; Tent & RV camping: Free; Elev: 5853ft/1784m; Tel: 406-632-4391; Nearest town: Harlowton; Notes: Mandatory food storage. GPS: 46.673281, -110.072132

108 • Jennings Camp

Total sites: 4; RV sites: 4; No water; Vault toilets; Reservations not accepted; Max length: 20ft; Generator hours: 0600-2200; Open May-Nov; Tent & RV camping: Free; Elev: 4895ft/1492m; Tel: 406-821-3201; Nearest town: Sula. GPS: 45.896241, -113.819515

109 • Jimmy Joe

Total sites: 12; RV sites: 12; No water; Vault toilets; Reservations not accepted; Max length: 30ft; Stay limit: 16 days; Open May-Sep; Tent & RV camping: Free; Elev: 5597ft/1706m; Tel: 406-446-2103; Nearest town: Roscoe. GPS: 45.232034, -109.603149

110 • Judith Station

Total sites: 3; RV sites: 3; Central water; Vault toilets; No showers; No RV dump; Reservations not accepted; Max length: 30ft; Stay limit: 16 days; Tent & RV camping: Fee unknown; Elev: 5072ft/1546m; Nearest town: Utica. GPS: 46.848313, -110.289512

111 • Jumping Creek

Total sites: 10; RV sites: 10; Central water; Vault toilets; No showers; No RV dump; Reservations not accepted; Open Jun-Sep; Tent & RV camping: $10; Elev: 5922ft/1805m; Tel: 406-547-3361; Nearest town: Neihart. GPS: 46.763916, -110.785400

112 • Kading

Total sites: 11; RV sites: 11; Central water; Vault toilets; No showers; No RV dump; Reservations not accepted; Max length: 16ft; Open Jun-Sep; Tent & RV camping: $8; Elev: 6125ft/1867m; Tel: 406-449-5490; Nearest town: Elliston. GPS: 46.428069, -112.482357

113 • Kamloops Terrace

Total sites: 20; RV sites: 20; Central water; Flush toilets; No showers; RV dump; Reservations not accepted; Max length: 32ft; Stay limit: 14 days; Open May-Sep; Tent & RV camping: $9; Elev: 2500ft/762m; Tel: 406-296-2536; Nearest town: Rexford; Notes: Dump station: $5. GPS: 48.902836, -115.159892

114 • Kilbrennan Lake

Total sites: 7; RV sites: 7; No water; Vault toilets; Reservations not accepted; Max length: 24ft; Stay limit: 14 days; Open all year; Tent & RV camping: Free; Elev: 2946ft/898m; Nearest town: Troy. GPS: 48.596611, -115.888234

115 • Kings Hill

Total sites: 18; RV sites: 18; Central water; Vault toilets; No showers; No RV dump; Reservations not accepted; Open May-Sep; Tent & RV camping: $10; Elev: 7444ft/2269m; Nearest town: Neihart. GPS: 46.841628, -110.696879

116 • Kreis Pond

Total sites: 7; RV sites: 7; No water; Vault toilets; Reservations not accepted; Tent & RV camping: Free; Elev: 3711ft/1131m; Tel: 406-626-5201; Nearest town: Alberton. GPS: 47.099820, -114.426330

117 • Ladysmith

Total sites: 6; No water; Vault toilets; Open May-Sep; Tents only: Free; Elev: 5797ft/1767m; Tel: 406-287-3223; Nearest town: Butte. GPS: 46.251268, -112.403687

118 • Lake Alva

Total sites: 39; RV sites: 39; Central water; Vault toilets; No showers; No RV dump; Reservations not accepted; Max length: 27ft; Open all year; Tent & RV camping: $10; Elev: 4127ft/1258m; Tel: 406-677-2233; Nearest town: Seeley Lake; Notes: 2 reservable group sites $25-$35, No winter fee. GPS: 47.324754, -113.583819

119 • Lake Como

Total sites: 10; RV sites: 10; Elec sites: 10; Water at site; Vault toilets; No showers; No RV dump; Reservations not accepted; Stay limit: 7 days; Open Jun-Sep; Tent & RV camping: $16; Elev: 4285ft/1306m; Tel: 406-821-3913; Nearest town: Darby. GPS: 46.068276, -114.235772

120 • Lake Creek

Total sites: 4; RV sites: 4; Central water; Vault toilets; No showers; No RV dump; Reservations not accepted; Max length: 32ft; Stay limit: 14 days; Open all year; Tent & RV camping: Free; Elev: 3412ft/1040m; Tel: 406-293-7773; Nearest town: Libby; Notes: Limited winter access. GPS: 48.038909, -115.489955

121 • Lake Inez

Total sites: 5; RV sites: 5; No water; Vault toilets; Reservations not accepted; Open all year; Tent & RV camping: Free; Elev: 4209ft/1283m; Tel: 406-677-2233; Nearest town: Seeley Lake; Notes: Group site: $14. GPS: 47.294099, -113.567813

122 • Lakeside (Old Alva)

Total sites: 4; RV sites: 4; No water; Vault toilets; Reservations not accepted; Open May-Sep; Tent & RV camping: $14; Elev: 4176ft/1273m; Tel: 406-677-2233; Nearest town: Seeley Lake; Notes: Reservable group site $14-$28. GPS: 47.307000, -113.576000

123 • Lakeview

Total sites: 5; RV sites: 5; No water; Vault toilets; Reservations not accepted; Tent & RV camping: Free; Elev: 3530ft/1076m; Tel: 406-387-3800; Nearest town: Hungry Horse. GPS: 48.219127, -113.805384

124 • Langohr

Total sites: 19; RV sites: 19; Central water; Vault toilets; No showers; No RV dump; Reservations accepted; Max length: 32ft; Open May-Sep; Tent & RV camping: $20; Elev: 6174ft/1882m; Tel: 406-522-2520; Nearest town: Bozeman. GPS: 45.532853, -111.015097

125 • Lantis Spring

Total sites: 4; RV sites: 4; Central water; Vault toilets; No showers; No RV dump; Reservations not accepted; Max length: 16ft; Stay limit: 14 days; Open May-Nov; Tent & RV camping: Free; Elev: 3914ft/1193m; Tel: 605-797-4432; Nearest town: Camp Crook (SD). GPS: 45.630606, -104.177136

126 • Lee Creek

Total sites: 22; RV sites: 22; Central water; Vault toilets; No showers; No RV dump; Reservations not accepted; Open May-Sep; Tent & RV camping: $10; Elev: 4245ft/1294m; Tel: 406-329-3814; Nearest town: Lolo. GPS: 46.705233, -114.537089

127 • Lid Creek

Total sites: 23; RV sites: 23; No water; Vault toilets; Reservations accepted; Stay limit: 16 days; Open May-Sep; Tent & RV camping: $14; Elev: 3596ft/1096m; Tel: 406-387-3800; Nearest town: Hungry Horse. GPS: 48.286516, -113.910682

128 • Limber Pine

Total sites: 13; RV sites: 13; Central water; Vault toilets; No showers; No RV dump; Reservations accepted; Max length: 45ft; Open May-Sep; Tent & RV camping: $18; Elev: 7164ft/2184m; Tel: 406-446-2103; Nearest town: Red Lodge. GPS: 45.059695, -109.408583

129 • Lindberg Lake

Total sites: 11; RV sites: 11; No water; Vault toilets; Reservations not accepted; Max length: 20ft; Stay limit: 16 days; Generator hours: 0600-2200; Tent & RV camping: Free; Elev: 4393ft/1339m; Tel: 406-837-7500; Nearest town: Seeley Lake. GPS: 47.407645, -113.721879

130 • Lion Creek Lower

Total sites: 1; RV sites: 1; No water; Vault toilets; Reservations not accepted; Tent & RV camping: Free; Elev: 5869ft/1789m; Nearest town: White Sulphur Springs; Notes: Mandatory food storage. GPS: 46.665849, -110.573302

131 • Little Joe

Total sites: 5; RV sites: 5; Central water; Vault toilets; No showers; No RV dump; Reservations not accepted; Max length: 28ft; Open May-Sep; Tent & RV camping: $8; Elev: 6821ft/2079m; Tel: 406-832-3178; Nearest town: Wise River. GPS: 45.554635, -113.091505

132 • Little Therriault Lake

Total sites: 6; RV sites: 6; Central water; Vault toilets; No showers; No RV dump; Reservations not accepted; Max length: 32ft; Stay limit: 14 days; Open all year; Tent & RV camping: $5; Elev: 5554ft/1693m; Tel: 406-882-4451; Nearest town: Eureka. GPS: 48.943399, -114.890434

133 • Lodgepole (Georgetown Lake)

Total sites: 31; RV sites: 31; Central water; Vault toilets; No showers; No RV dump; Reservations accepted; Max length: 32ft; Open May-Sep; Tent & RV camping: $15; Elev: 6457ft/1968m; Tel: 406-859-3211; Nearest town: Philipsburg. GPS: 46.211654, -113.273937

134 • Lodgepole (Stine Mt)

Total sites: 10; RV sites: 10; Central water; Vault toilets; No showers; No RV dump; Reservations not accepted; Max length: 30ft; Open May-Sep; Tent & RV camping: $8; Elev: 6450ft/1966m; Tel: 406-832-3178; Nearest town: Wise River. GPS: 45.648696, -113.070888

135 • Logging Creek

Total sites: 25; RV sites: 25; Central water; Vault toilets; No showers; No RV dump; Reservations not accepted; Open May-Sep; Tent & RV camping: $10; Elev: 4610ft/1405m; Nearest town: Monarch. GPS: 47.100359, -111.010023

136 • Lolo Creek

Total sites: 17; RV sites: 17; Central water; Vault toilets; No showers; No RV dump; Reservations not accepted; Open May-Sep; Tent & RV camping: $10; Elev: 3783ft/1153m; Tel: 406-329-3814; Nearest town: Lolo. GPS: 46.775829, -114.383892

137 • Lonesomehurst

Total sites: 27; RV sites: 27; Elec sites: 5; Central water; Vault toilets; No showers; No RV dump; Reservations accepted; Max length: 32ft; Open May-Sep; Tents: $20/RVs: $20-28; Elev: 6545ft/1995m; Tel: 406-823-6961; Nearest town: West Yellowstone. GPS: 44.735481, -111.231338

138 • Loon Lake

Total sites: 4; RV sites: 4; No water; Vault toilets; Reservations not accepted; Max length: 20ft; Stay limit: 14 days; Open all year; Tent & RV camping: Free; Elev: 3698ft/1127m; Tel: 406-293-7773; Nearest town: Libby. GPS: 48.597851, -115.671557

139 • Lost Johnny

Total sites: 5; RV sites: 5; Central water; Vault toilets; No showers; No RV dump; Reservations not accepted; Max length: 24ft; Stay limit: 16 days; Open May-Sep; Tent & RV camping: $14; Elev: 3566ft/1087m; Tel: 406-387-3800; Nearest town: Hungry Horse. GPS: 48.306125, -113.969631

140 • Lost Johnny Point

Total sites: 21; RV sites: 21; Central water; Vault toilets; No showers; No RV dump; Reservations accepted; Open May-Sep; Tent & RV camping: $16; Elev: 3592ft/1095m; Tel: 406-387-3800; Nearest town: Hungry Horse. GPS: 48.310241, -113.963725

141 • Lowland

Total sites: 11; RV sites: 11; Central water; Vault toilets; No showers; No RV dump; Reservations not accepted; Max length: 22ft; Stay limit: 16 days; Open May-Sep; Tent & RV camping: $5; Elev: 6562ft/2000m; Tel: 406-494-2147; Nearest town: Butte. GPS: 46.139188, -112.504444

142 • M-K Campground

Total sites: 10; RV sites: 7; No water; Vault toilets; Reservations not accepted; Max length: 20ft; Stay limit: 16 days; Open May-Sep; Tent & RV camping: Free; Elev: 7408ft/2258m; Tel: 406-446-2103; Nearest town: Red Lodge; Notes: No services in winter. GPS: 45.038323, -109.429648

143 • Macnab Pond

Total sites: 2; RV sites: 2; No water; Vault toilets; Reservations not accepted; Max length: 30ft; Open May-Nov; Tent & RV camping: Free; Elev: 3474ft/1059m; Tel: 605-797-4432; Nearest town: Ekalaka. GPS: 45.835842, -104.432014

144 • Madison River

Total sites: 10; RV sites: 10; Central water; Vault toilets; No showers; No RV dump; Reservations not accepted; Max length: 30ft; Stay limit: 16 days; Open Jun-Sep; Tent & RV camping: $15; Elev: 5899ft/1798m; Tel: 406-682-4253; Nearest town: Ennis. GPS: 44.878722, -111.572474

145 • Many Pines

Total sites: 22; RV sites: 22; Central water; Vault toilets; No showers; No RV dump; Reservations not accepted; Open May-Sep; Tent & RV camping: $10; Elev: 6050ft/1844m; Nearest town: Neihart. GPS: 46.898665, -110.690765

146 • Marten Creek

Total sites: 6; RV sites: 6; No water; Vault toilets; Reservations not accepted; Max length: 32ft; Stay limit: 14 days; Open all year; Tent & RV camping: Free; Elev: 2418ft/737m; Tel: 406-827-3533; Nearest town: Trout Creek; Notes: 1 group site. GPS: 47.882121, -115.747711

147 • Martin Creek

Total sites: 7; RV sites: 7; Central water; Vault toilets; No showers; No RV dump; Reservations not accepted; Max length: 50ft; Generator hours: 0600-2200; Open May-Nov; Tent & RV camping: $10; Elev: 5315ft/1620m; Tel: 406-821-3201; Nearest town: Sula. GPS: 45.931801, -113.722608

148 • May Creek

Total sites: 21; RV sites: 21; Central water; Vault toilets; No showers; No RV dump; Reservations not accepted; Max length: 30ft; Stay limit: 16 days; Open Jun-Sep; Tent & RV camping: $7; Elev: 6384ft/1946m; Tel: 406-689-3243; Nearest town: Wisdom. GPS: 45.651556, -113.781353

149 • McGillivray

Total sites: 33; RV sites: 33; Central water; Vault toilets; No showers; No RV dump; Reservations not accepted; Max length: 40ft; Stay limit: 14 days; Open May-Oct; Tent & RV camping: $10; Elev: 2592ft/790m; Tel: 406-293-7773; Nearest town: Libby; Notes: 2 reservable group sites: $30-$60. GPS: 48.487943, -115.300718

150 • McGregor Lake

Total sites: 27; RV sites: 27; Central water; Vault toilets; No showers; No RV dump; Reservations not accepted; Max length: 32ft; Stay limit: 14 days; Open May-Sep; Tent & RV camping: $12; Elev: 3909ft/1191m; Tel: 406-293-7773; Nearest town: Libby; Notes: Reservable group site: $30. GPS: 48.032139, -114.902378

151 • Mill Creek (Copper Mt)

Total sites: 10; RV sites: 10; Central water; Vault toilets; No showers; No RV dump; Reservations not accepted; Max length: 22ft; Open Jun-Oct; Tent & RV camping: Free; Elev: 6539ft/1993m; Tel: 406-682-4253; Nearest town: Sheridan. GPS: 45.477391, -112.069183

152 • Mill Falls

Total sites: 4; RV sites: 4; No water; Vault toilets; Reservations not accepted; Tent & RV camping: Free; Elev: 5682ft/1732m; Nearest town: Choteau; Notes: Mandatory food storage. GPS: 47.859049, -112.772458

153 • Miner Lake

Total sites: 18; RV sites: 18; Central water; Vault toilets; No showers; No RV dump; Reservations not accepted; Max length: 20ft; Open Jun-Sep; Tent & RV camping: $7; Elev: 7034ft/2144m; Tel: 406-689-3243; Nearest town: Jackson. GPS: 45.322943, -113.578941

154 • Missoula Lake

Total sites: 5; RV sites: 5; No water; Vault toilets; Reservations not accepted; Tent & RV camping: Free; Elev: 6319ft/1926m; Nearest town: Superior. GPS: 47.060302, -115.116204

155 • Mono Creek

Total sites: 5; RV sites: 5; Central water; Vault toilets; No showers; No RV dump; Reservations not accepted; Max length: 18ft; Open Jun-Sep; Tent & RV camping: $8; Elev: 7001ft/2134m; Tel: 406-832-3178; Nearest town: Wise River. GPS: 45.534977, -113.078945

156 • Monture Creek

Total sites: 5; RV sites: 5; No water; Vault toilets; Reservations not accepted; Open May-Sep; Tent & RV camping: Free; Elev: 4203ft/1281m; Tel: 406-677-2233; Nearest town: Ovando. GPS: 47.123893, -113.145456

157 • Moose Creek (MacDonald Pass)

Total sites: 9; RV sites: 9; Central water; Vault toilets; No showers; No RV dump; Reservations not accepted; Open Jun-Sep; Tent & RV camping: $5; Elev: 4859ft/1481m; Tel: 406-449-5490; Nearest town: Helena. GPS: 46.525061, -112.256927

158 • Moose Creek (Moose Mt)

Total sites: 6; RV sites: 6; Central water; Vault toilets; No showers; No RV dump; Open Jun-Sep; Tent & RV camping: $10; Elev: 5879ft/1792m; Nearest town: White Sulphur Springs. GPS: 46.835789, -110.874981

159 • Moose Creek Flat

Total sites: 13; RV sites: 13; Central water; Vault toilets; No showers; No RV dump; Reservations accepted; Open May-Sep; Tent & RV camping: $20; Elev: 5699ft/1737m; Tel: 406-522-2520; Nearest town: Big Sky. GPS: 45.355545, -111.172396

160 • Moose Lake

Total sites: 3; RV sites: 3; No water; Vault toilets; Reservations not accepted; Stay limit: 14 days; Tent & RV camping: Free; Elev: 5728ft/1746m; Tel: 406-387-3800; Nearest town: Columbia Falls. GPS: 48.628775, -114.388784

161 • Mormon Gulch

Total sites: 16; RV sites: 16; No water; Vault toilets; Reservations not accepted; Max length: 16ft; Open May-Nov; Tent & RV camping: Free; Elev: 5824ft/1775m; Tel: 406-287-3223; Nearest town: Butte. GPS: 46.256792, -112.362653

162 • Mortimer Gulch

Total sites: 26; RV sites: 26; Central water; Vault toilets; No showers; No RV dump; Reservations not accepted; Max length: 22ft; Open Jun-Sep; Tent & RV camping: $8; Elev: 4993ft/1522m; Tel: 406-466-5341; Nearest town: Augusta; Notes: Reservable group site. GPS: 47.609583, -112.770733

163 • Murray Bay (Complex III)

Total sites: 20; RV sites: 20; Central water; Vault toilets; No showers; No RV dump; Reservations accepted; Max length: 32ft; Open May-Sep; Tent & RV camping: $16; Elev: 3632ft/1107m; Tel: 406-387-3800; Nearest town: Martin City. GPS: 48.265434, -113.813581

164 • Mussigbrod

Total sites: 10; RV sites: 10; Central water; Vault toilets; No showers; No RV dump; Reservations not accepted; Max length: 30ft; Open Jun-Sep; Tent & RV camping: $7; Elev: 6549ft/1996m; Tel: 406-689-3243; Nearest town: Wisdom. GPS: 45.789696, -113.609238

165 • North Dickey Lake

Total sites: 25; RV sites: 25; Central water; Vault toilets; No showers; No RV dump; Reservations accepted; Max length: 32ft; Stay limit: 14 days; Open May-Sep; Tent & RV camping: $10; Elev: 3163ft/964m; Tel: 406-882-4451; Nearest town: Eureka. GPS: 48.718506, -114.833496

166 • North Shore

Total sites: 16; RV sites: 16; Central water; Vault toilets; No showers; No RV dump; Reservations not accepted; Max length: 40ft; Stay limit: 14 days; Open May-Nov; Tent & RV camping: $10; Elev: 2361ft/720m; Tel: 406-827-3533; Nearest town: Trout Creek. GPS: 47.861806, -115.631149

167 • North Van Houten

Total sites: 3; RV sites: 3; Central water; Vault toilets; No showers; No RV dump; Reservations not accepted; Max length: 20ft; Stay limit: 16 days; Open Jun-Sep; Tent & RV camping: Free; Elev: 7057ft/2151m; Tel: 406-689-3243; Nearest town: Jackson. GPS: 45.246561, -113.478182

168 • Norton

Total sites: 13; Central water; Vault toilets; No showers; No RV dump; Reservations not accepted; Open Apr-Sep; Tents only: $6; Elev: 3947ft/1203m; Tel: 406-329-3814; Nearest town: Clinton. GPS: 46.587703, -113.668702

169 • Orofino

Total sites: 10; RV sites: 10; Central water; Vault toilets; No showers; No RV dump; Reservations not accepted; Max length: 22ft; Stay limit: 16 days; Open May-Sep; Tent & RV camping: Free; Elev: 6463ft/1970m; Tel: 406-859-3211; Nearest town: Deer Lodge. GPS: 46.259372, -112.608902

170 • Owl Creek Packer Camp

Total sites: 8; RV sites: 8; Central water; Vault toilets; Reservations not accepted; Open all year; Tent & RV camping: Fee unknown; Elev: 4069ft/1240m; Tel: 406-309-2018; Nearest town: Seeley Lake. GPS: 47.440315, -113.607721

171 • Palisades

Total sites: 6; RV sites: 6; No water; Vault toilets; Reservations not accepted; Max length: 16ft; Open May-Sep; Tent & RV camping: Free; Elev: 6378ft/1944m; Tel: 406-446-2103; Nearest town: Red Lodge. GPS: 45.171578, -109.308995

172 • Park Lake

Total sites: 22; RV sites: 22; Central water; Vault toilets; No showers; No RV dump; Reservations not accepted; Open Jun-Sep; Tent & RV camping: $8; Elev: 6384ft/1946m; Tel: 406-449-5490; Nearest town: Clancy. GPS: 46.442273, -112.169016

173 • Parkside

Total sites: 28; RV sites: 28; Central water; Vault toilets; No showers; No RV dump; Reservations accepted; Max length: 45ft; Stay limit: 16 days; Open May-Sep; Tent & RV camping: $18; Elev: 7132ft/2174m; Tel: 406-446-2103; Nearest town: Red Lodge; Notes: Group sites $75-$95. GPS: 45.060652, -109.405341

174 • Peck Gulch

Total sites: 22; RV sites: 22; Central water; Vault toilets; No showers; No RV dump; Reservations not accepted; Max length: 32ft; Stay limit: 14 days; Open all year; Tent & RV camping: $9; Elev: 2513ft/766m; Tel: 406-296-2536; Nearest town: Eureka; Notes: Narrow, steep access road. GPS: 48.724062, -115.307511

175 • Pete Creek

Total sites: 13; RV sites: 13; Central water; Vault toilets; No showers; No RV dump; Reservations not accepted; Stay limit: 14 days; Open all year; Tent & RV camping: $7; Elev: 2972ft/906m; Tel: 406-295-4693; Nearest town: Yaak. GPS: 48.830811, -115.766602

176 • Peters Creek

Total sites: 6; RV sites: 6; No water; Vault toilets; Reservations not accepted; Max length: 30ft; Stay limit: 14 days; Open May-Sep; Tent & RV camping: Free; Elev: 3691ft/1125m; Tel: 406-758-5376; Nearest town: Hungry Horse; Notes: Mandatory food storage. GPS: 48.057377, -113.644569

177 • Pettengill

Total sites: 3; RV sites: 3; No water; Vault toilets; Reservations not accepted; Max length: 24ft; Tent & RV camping: $6; Elev: 6286ft/1916m; Tel: 406-832-3178; Nearest town: Wise River. GPS: 45.681421, -113.060971

178 • Philipsburg Bay

Total sites: 69; RV sites: 69; Central water; Vault toilets; No showers; No RV dump; Reservations accepted; Max length: 32ft; Open May-Sep; Tent & RV camping: $15; Elev: 6401ft/1951m; Tel: 406-859-3211; Nearest town: Philipsburg. GPS: 46.206778, -113.290954

179 • Pigeon Creek

Total sites: 6; Central water; Vault toilets; No showers; No RV dump; Reservations not accepted; Stay limit: 16 days; Open May-Sep; Tents only: Free; Elev: 6155ft/1876m; Tel: 406-287-3223; Nearest town: Butte; Notes: Narrow access road with sharp turns, Mandatory food storage. GPS: 45.800717, -112.399795

180 • Pine Creek

Total sites: 25; RV sites: 25; Central water; Vault toilets; No showers; No RV dump; Reservations accepted; Max length: 50ft; Open May-Sep; Tent & RV camping: $20; Elev: 5653ft/1723m; Tel: 406-222-1892; Nearest town: Livingston; Notes: Group site: $35-$75, Narrow winding road. GPS: 45.498534, -110.522397

181 • Pine Grove

Total sites: 46; RV sites: 46; Central water; Vault toilets; No showers; No RV dump; Reservations not accepted; Max length: 30ft; Stay limit: 16 days; Open May-Sep; Tent & RV camping: $9; Elev: 5892ft/1796m; Tel: 406-446-2103; Nearest town: Fishtail. GPS: 45.275661, -109.643163

182 • Piney

Total sites: 48; RV sites: 32; Central water; Vault toilets; No showers; No RV dump; Reservations accepted; Max length: 32ft; Stay limit: 16 days; Open May-Sep; Tent & RV camping: $15; Elev: 6394ft/1949m; Tel: 406-859-3211; Nearest town: Philipsburg. GPS: 46.196045, -113.302246

183 • Pintler

Total sites: 2; RV sites: 2; Central water; Vault toilets; No showers; No RV dump; Reservations not accepted; Max length: 18ft; Stay limit: 16 days; Tent & RV camping: Free; Elev: 6365ft/1940m; Tel: 406-832-3178; Nearest town: Wise River. GPS: 45.838743, -113.436441

184 • Pleasant Valley

Total sites: 7; RV sites: 7; No water; Vault toilets; No showers; No RV dump; Reservations not accepted; Max length: 32ft; Stay limit: 14 days; Open all year; Tent & RV camping: Free; Elev: 3067ft/935m; Nearest town: Libby; Notes: Limited winter access. GPS: 48.042314, -115.290626

185 • Potosi

Total sites: 15; RV sites: 15; Central water; Vault toilets; No showers; No RV dump; Reservations not accepted; Max length: 22ft; Open Jun-Sep; Tent & RV camping: Free; Elev: 6240ft/1902m; Tel: 406-682-4253; Nearest town: Harrison. GPS: 45.572359, -111.913602

186 • Price Creek

Total sites: 28; RV sites: 28; Central water; Vault toilets; No showers; No RV dump; Reservations not accepted; Max length: 30ft; Open Jun-Nov; Tent & RV camping: Fee unknown; Elev: 7877ft/2401m; Tel: 406-683-3900; Nearest town: Dillon. GPS: 45.480019, -113.083201

187 • Quartz Flat

Total sites: 77; RV sites: 35; Central water; Flush toilets; No showers; RV dump; Reservations not accepted; Open May-Sep; Tent & RV camping: $10; Elev: 2868ft/874m; Tel: 406-822-4233; Nearest town: Superior. GPS: 47.075819, -114.767481

188 • Racetrack

Total sites: 13; RV sites: 13; Central water; Vault toilets; No showers; No RV dump; Reservations not accepted; Max length: 22ft; Open May-Sep; Tent & RV camping: Free; Elev: 5381ft/1640m; Tel: 406-859-3211; Nearest town: Butte. GPS: 46.280272, -112.938662

189 • Rainbow Point

Total sites: 85; RV sites: 85; Elec sites: 26; Central water; Vault toilets; No showers; No RV dump; Reservations accepted; Max length: 32ft; Open May-Sep; Tents: $20/RVs: $20-28; Elev: 6558ft/1999m; Tel: 406-823-6961; Nearest town: West Yellowstone. GPS: 44.778682, -111.177063

190 • Rainy Lake

Total sites: 5; RV sites: 2; No water; Vault toilets; Reservations not accepted; Tent & RV camping: Free; Elev: 4157ft/1267m; Tel: 406-677-2233; Nearest town: Seeley Lake. GPS: 47.336831, -113.593337

191 • Rattin

Total sites: 6; RV sites: 6; Central water; Vault toilets; No showers; No RV dump; Reservations accepted; Max length: 20ft; Stay limit: 16 days; Open May-Sep; Tent & RV camping: $17; Elev: 6371ft/1942m; Tel: 406-446-2103; Nearest town: Red Lodge. GPS: 45.087717, -109.322796

192 • Red Cliff

Total sites: 65; RV sites: 65; Elec sites: 27; Central water; Vault toilets; No showers; No RV dump; Reservations accepted; Open May-Sep; Tents: $20/RVs: $20-28; Elev: 6289ft/1917m; Tel: 406-522-2520; Nearest town: Big Sky. GPS: 45.174115, -111.241582

193 • Red Meadow Lake

Total sites: 6; RV sites: 6; No water; Vault toilets; Reservations not accepted; Stay limit: 14 days; Tent & RV camping: Free; Elev: 5562ft/1695m; Tel: 406-387-3800; Nearest town: Columbia Falls. GPS: 48.753736, -114.563547

194 • Red Shale

Total sites: 14; RV sites: 14; No water; Vault toilets; Reservations not accepted; Max length: 32ft; Stay limit: 10 days; Open Apr-Dec; Tent & RV camping: Free; Elev: 3209ft/978m; Tel: 406-784-2344; Nearest town: Ashland. GPS: 45.568933, -106.146433

195 • Red Top

Total sites: 3; RV sites: 3; No water; Vault toilets; Stay limit: 14 days; Open all year; Tent & RV camping: Free; Elev: 2825ft/861m;

Tel: 406-295-4693; Nearest town: Troy; Notes: Limited winter access. GPS: 48.760935, -115.918299

196 • Reservoir Lake

Total sites: 16; RV sites: 16; Central water; Vault toilets; No showers; No RV dump; Max length: 16ft; Stay limit: 16 days; Open Jun-Sep; Tent & RV camping: $8; Elev: 7070ft/2155m; Tel: 406-683-3900; Nearest town: Dillon; Notes: Group site: $25. GPS: 45.121849, -113.453644

197 • Rexford Bench

Total sites: 54; RV sites: 54; Central water; Flush toilets; No showers; RV dump; Reservations accepted; Max length: 40ft; Stay limit: 14 days; Open Apr-Sep; Tent & RV camping: $12; Elev: 2562ft/781m; Tel: 406-296-2536; Nearest town: Eureka; Notes: Dump station: $5. GPS: 48.899702, -115.157247

198 • Rexford Bench - Boat Site

Total sites: 30; RV sites: 30; Central water; Vault toilets; No showers; No RV dump; Stay limit: 14 days; Open all year; No tents/RVs: $8; Elev: 2462ft/750m; Tel: 406-296-2536; Nearest town: Rexford. GPS: 48.903949, -115.162726

199 • Richardson Creek

Total sites: 3; RV sites: 3; No water; Vault toilets; Reservations not accepted; Max length: 16ft; Stay limit: 16 days; Open Jun-Sep; Tent & RV camping: Fee unknown; Elev: 5902ft/1799m; Nearest town: White Sulphur Springs; Notes: Mandatory food storage. GPS: 46.540448, -110.730859

200 • River Point

Total sites: 26; RV sites: 26; Central water; Vault toilets; No showers; No RV dump; Reservations not accepted; Max length: 22ft; Open Jun-Sep; Tent & RV camping: $10; Elev: 3996ft/1218m; Tel: 406-677-2233; Nearest town: Seeley Lake. GPS: 47.187256, -113.514404

201 • Riverside Boating Site

Total sites: 3; RV sites: 3; No water; Vault toilets; No showers; No RV dump; Reservations not accepted; Max length: 50ft; Open May-Sep; Tent & RV camping: $14; Elev: 3578ft/1091m; Tel: 406-646-1012; Nearest town: Hungry Horse; Notes: 2 sites are double - $28. GPS: 48.272008, -113.816511

202 • Riverview

Total sites: 24; RV sites: 24; Central water; Vault toilets; No showers; No RV dump; Reservations not accepted; Max length: 30ft; Stay limit: 16 days; Tent & RV camping: $15; Elev: 5945ft/1812m; Tel: 406-682-4253; Nearest town: Ennis. GPS: 44.882035, -111.577385

203 • Rock Lake

Total sites: 5; RV sites: 5; No water; Vault toilets; Max length: 20ft; Stay limit: 14 days; Tent & RV camping: Free; Elev: 2890ft/881m; Tel: 406-882-4451; Nearest town: Eureka. GPS: 48.823787, -115.010269

204 • Rocky Gorge

Total sites: 60; RV sites: 60; Central water; Vault toilets; No showers; No RV dump; Reservations not accepted; Max length: 32ft; Stay limit: 14 days; Open all year; Tent & RV camping: $9; Elev: 2502ft/763m; Nearest town: Eureka. GPS: 48.652234, -115.311173

205 • Rombo

Total sites: 15; RV sites: 15; Central water; Vault toilets; No showers; No RV dump; Reservations accepted; Open May-Oct; Tent & RV camping: $8; Elev: 4521ft/1378m; Tel: 406-821-3269; Nearest town: Darby; Notes: Camping is permitted during the off-season but water is not available. GPS: 45.763896, -114.281992

206 • Russian Flat

Total sites: 2; RV sites: 2; No water; Vault toilets; Reservations not accepted; Tent & RV camping: Free; Elev: 6346ft/1934m; Nearest town: Checkerboard; Notes: Mandatory food storage. GPS: 46.725368, -110.423697

207 • Sage Creek

Total sites: 12; RV sites: 12; Central water; Vault toilets; No showers; No RV dump; Reservations not accepted; Max length: 30ft; Stay limit: 16 days; Open May-Sep; Tent & RV camping: $5; Elev: 5564ft/1696m; Tel: 406-446-2103; Nearest town: Bridger; Notes: RVs/trailers should access from the south via the Crooked Creek Road, No services in winter - free. GPS: 45.213479, -108.554408

208 • Sam Billings Memorial

Total sites: 11; RV sites: 11; No water; Vault toilets; Reservations not accepted; Max length: 30ft; Open May-Nov; Tent & RV camping: Free; Elev: 4524ft/1379m; Tel: 406-821-3269; Nearest town: Darby. GPS: 45.825741, -114.250667

209 • Schumaker

Total sites: 14; RV sites: 14; No water; Vault toilets; Reservations not accepted; Stay limit: 16 days; Generator hours: 0600-2200; Open Jul-Sep; Tent & RV camping: Free; Elev: 6549ft/1996m; Tel: 406-821-3913; Nearest town: Darby. GPS: 46.151268, -114.496812

210 • Seeley Lake

Total sites: 29; RV sites: 29; Central water; Vault toilets; No showers; No RV dump; Reservations not accepted; Max length: 32ft; Open May-Sep; Tent & RV camping: $10; Elev: 4042ft/1232m; Tel: 406-677-2233; Nearest town: Seeley Lake. GPS: 47.191650, -113.518555

211 • Seymour Creek

Total sites: 17; RV sites: 17; Central water; Vault toilets; No showers; No RV dump; Reservations not accepted; Max length: 18ft; Stay limit: 16 days; Open May-Sep; Tent & RV camping: Free; Elev: 6824ft/2080m; Tel: 406-832-3178; Nearest town: Wise River. GPS: 45.988162, -113.184851

212 • Sheridan

Total sites: 9; RV sites: 9; Central water; Vault toilets; No showers; No RV dump; Reservations accepted; Max length: 30ft; Stay limit: 16 days; Open May-Sep; Tent & RV camping: $17; Elev: 6299ft/1920m; Tel: 406-446-2103; Nearest town: Red Lodge. GPS: 45.100831, -109.307426

213 • Shields River

Total sites: 6; RV sites: 6; No water; Vault toilets; Reservations not accepted; Max length: 22ft; Open Jun-Nov; Tent & RV camping: Free; Elev: 6417ft/1956m; Tel: 406-222-1892; Nearest town: Livingston. GPS: 46.184327, -110.405053

214 • Siria

Total sites: 4; No water; Vault toilets; Open all year; Tents only: Free; Elev: 4477ft/1365m; Tel: 406-329-3814; Nearest town: Philipsburg. GPS: 46.422936, -113.719738

215 • Skidway

Total sites: 14; RV sites: 14; Central water; Vault toilets; No showers; No RV dump; Reservations not accepted; Max length: 16ft; Stay limit: 14 days; Open May-Sep; Tent & RV camping: $15; Elev: 5804ft/1769m; Tel: 406-266-3425; Nearest town: Townsend. GPS: 46.354492, -111.097168

216 • Slate Creek

Total sites: 4; RV sites: 4; No water; Vault toilets; Reservations not accepted; Max length: 25ft; Open May-Nov; Tent & RV camping: Free; Elev: 4820ft/1469m; Tel: 406-821-3269; Nearest town: Darby. GPS: 45.697908, -114.281373

217 • Slowey

Total sites: 27; RV sites: 27; Central water; Vault toilets; No showers; No RV dump; Reservations not accepted; Open May-Sep; Tent & RV camping: $10; Elev: 2671ft/814m; Tel: 406-822-4233; Nearest town: Superior. GPS: 47.232718, -115.021814

218 • Snowbank

Total sites: 10; RV sites: 10; Central water; Vault toilets; No showers; No RV dump; Reservations accepted; Open May-Sep; Tent & RV camping: $20; Elev: 5774ft/1760m; Tel: 406-222-1892; Nearest town: Livingston; Notes: Group site: $35-$75, Narrow winding road. GPS: 45.288273, -110.544128

219 • Soda Butte

Total sites: 27; RV sites: 27; Central water; Vault toilets; No showers; No RV dump; Reservations not accepted; Max length: 48ft; Open Jul-Sep; No tents/RVs: $9; Elev: 7874ft/2400m; Tel: 406-848-7375; Nearest town: Cooke City; Notes: Hard-side units only. GPS: 45.024126, -109.912052

220 • South Fork

Total sites: 7; RV sites: 7; Central water; Vault toilets; No showers; No RV dump; Reservations not accepted; Open Jun-Sep; Tent & RV camping: $8; Elev: 5325ft/1623m; Tel: 406-466-5341; Nearest town: Augusta. GPS: 47.501821, -112.887862

221 • South Van Houten

Total sites: 3; RV sites: 3; Central water; Vault toilets; No showers; No RV dump; Reservations not accepted; Max length: 30ft; Stay limit: 16 days; Open Jun-Sep; Tent & RV camping: Free; Elev: 7024ft/2141m; Tel: 406-689-3243; Nearest town: Jackson. GPS: 45.243839, -113.478157

222 • Spanish Creek

Total sites: 5; Central water; Vault toilets; No showers; No RV dump; Open May-Sep; Tent & RV camping: Free; Elev: 6109ft/1862m; Nearest town: Big Sky. GPS: 45.447388, -111.377289

223 • Spar Lake

Total sites: 13; RV sites: 13; Central water; Vault toilets; No showers; No RV dump; Reservations not accepted; Max length: 28ft; Stay limit: 16 days; Open all year; Tent & RV camping: $8; Elev: 3356ft/1023m; Tel: 406-295-4693; Nearest town: Troy; Notes: Limited access and services in winter. GPS: 48.269662, -115.953219

224 • Spillway

Total sites: 13; RV sites: 13; Central water; Vault toilets; No showers; No RV dump; Max length: 22ft; Open May-Nov; Tent & RV camping: Free; Elev: 6056ft/1846m; Tel: 406-859-3211; Nearest town: Philipsburg. GPS: 46.127441, -113.383301

225 • Spire Rock

Total sites: 19; RV sites: 19; No water; Vault toilets; Reservations accepted; Open May-Sep; Tent & RV camping: $16; Elev: 5663ft/1726m; Tel: 406-522-2520; Nearest town: Big Sky; Notes: Group site: $30-$60. GPS: 45.439546, -111.192903

226 • Spotted Bear

Total sites: 13; RV sites: 13; Central water; Vault toilets; No showers; No RV dump; Reservations not accepted; Max length: 32ft; Stay limit: 14 days; Open all year; Tent & RV camping: $10; Elev: 3747ft/1142m; Tel: 406-758-5376; Nearest town: Hungry Horse; Notes: No fee 9/30 - 5/15. GPS: 47.926321, -113.527434

227 • Spring Creek (Mount Howe)

Total sites: 10; RV sites: 10; Central water; Vault toilets; No showers; No RV dump; Reservations not accepted; Open May-Sep; Tent & RV camping: $7; Elev: 5305ft/1617m; Nearest town: White Sulphur Springs. GPS: 46.586426, -110.467529

228 • Spring Gulch

Total sites: 9; RV sites: 8; Central water; Vault toilets; No showers; No RV dump; Reservations accepted; Open Jul-Sep; Tent & RV camping: $12; Elev: 4386ft/1337m; Tel: 406-821-3201; Nearest town: Sula. GPS: 45.858467, -114.022254

229 • Spring Hill

Total sites: 15; RV sites: 15; Central water; Vault toilets; No showers; No RV dump; Reservations accepted; Max length: 22ft; Open May-Sep; Tent & RV camping: $13; Elev: 6178ft/1883m; Tel: 406-859-3211; Nearest town: Anaconda. GPS: 46.171631, -113.164795

230 • Steel Creek

Total sites: 9; RV sites: 9; Central water; Vault toilets; No showers; No RV dump; Reservations not accepted; Max length: 22ft; Open Jun-Sep; Tent & RV camping: $7; Elev: 6378ft/1944m; Tel: 406-689-3243; Nearest town: Dillon. GPS: 45.600845, -113.343496

231 • Stony

Total sites: 10; RV sites: 10; Central water; Vault toilets; No showers; No RV dump; Reservations not accepted; Max length: 32ft; Open Apr-Oct; Tent & RV camping: Free; Elev: 4806ft/1465m; Tel: 406-859-3211; Nearest town: Philipsburg. GPS: 46.348739, -113.607499

232 • Summit

Total sites: 17; RV sites: 17; Central water; Vault toilets; No showers; No RV dump; Reservations not accepted; Tent & RV camping: $10; Elev: 5249ft/1600m; Tel: 406-466-5341; Nearest town: East Glacier Park; Notes: May be reserved as group site, Near RR, Mandatory food storage. GPS: 48.318978, -113.351053

233 • Swan Creek

Total sites: 13; RV sites: 13; Central water; Vault toilets; No showers; No RV dump; Reservations accepted; Open May-Sep; Tent & RV camping: $20; Elev: 5892ft/1796m; Tel: 406-522-2520; Nearest town: Big Sky. GPS: 45.372464, -111.163764

234 • Swan Lake

Total sites: 33; RV sites: 33; Central water; Vault toilets; No showers; No RV dump; Reservations accepted; Open May-Sep; Tent & RV camping: $18; Elev: 3173ft/967m; Tel: 406-837-7500; Nearest town: Swan Lake; Notes: Group site $100-$325. GPS: 47.936559, -113.847533

235 • Sylvan Lake

Total sites: 5; RV sites: 5; No water; Vault toilets; Reservations not accepted; Stay limit: 16 days; Open all year; Tent & RV camping: Free; Elev: 3627ft/1106m; Tel: 406-293-7773; Nearest town: Kalispell; Notes: Limited winter access. GPS: 47.916343, -115.278677

236 • Sylvia Lake

Total sites: 3; RV sites: 3; No water; Vault toilets; Reservations not accepted; Max length: 12ft; Generator hours: 0600-2200; Open May-Nov; Tent & RV camping: Free; Elev: 5056ft/1541m; Tel: 406-758-5208; Nearest town: Kalispell. GPS: 48.344423, -114.818601

237 • Tally Lake

Total sites: 40; RV sites: 40; Central water; Vault toilets; No showers; RV dump; Reservations accepted; Max length: 27ft; Generator hours: 0600-2200; Open May-Sep; Tent & RV camping: $18; Elev: 3366ft/1026m; Tel: 406-758-5208; Nearest town: Whitefish. GPS: 48.413818, -114.584473

238 • Thain Creek

Total sites: 16; RV sites: 16; Central water; Vault toilets; Reservations not accepted; Tent & RV camping: $5; Elev: 4596ft/1401m; Tel: 406-566-2292; Nearest town: Great Falls. GPS: 47.475586, -110.584229

239 • Three Frogs

Total sites: 20; RV sites: 16; Central water; Vault toilets; No showers; No RV dump; Reservations not accepted; Max length: 30ft; Stay limit: 16 days; Generator hours: 0600-2200; Open May-Sep; Tent & RV camping: $8; Elev: 4383ft/1336m; Tel: 406-821-3913; Nearest town: Darby. GPS: 46.066601, -114.244992

240 • Tobacco River

Total sites: 6; RV sites: 6; No water; Vault toilets; Reservations not accepted; Max length: 20ft; Stay limit: 14 days; Open all year; Tent & RV camping: Free; Elev: 2457ft/749m; Tel: 406-296-2536; Nearest town: Eureka. GPS: 48.894411, -115.134981

241 • Toll Mountain

Total sites: 5; RV sites: 5; No water; Vault toilets; Reservations not accepted; Max length: 22ft; Stay limit: 16 days; Open May-Sep; Tent & RV camping: Free; Elev: 5909ft/1801m; Tel: 406-287-3223; Nearest town: Whitehall. GPS: 45.847955, -112.366663

242 • Tom Miner

Total sites: 16; RV sites: 16; Central water; Vault toilets; No showers; No RV dump; Reservations not accepted; Open Jun-Oct; Tent & RV camping: $7; Elev: 7244ft/2208m; Tel: 406-848-7375; Nearest town: Gardiner. GPS: 45.129705, -111.063281

243 • Trout Creek (Lozeau)

Total sites: 12; RV sites: 12; Central water; Vault toilets; No showers; No RV dump; Reservations not accepted; Max length: 18ft; Open all year; Tent & RV camping: $6; Elev: 2923ft/891m; Tel: 406-822-4233; Nearest town: Superior. GPS: 47.116943, -114.868652

244 • Tuchuck

Total sites: 7; RV sites: 7; No water; Vault toilets; Reservations not accepted; Max length: 22ft; Stay limit: 14 days; Open Jun-Sep; Tent & RV camping: Free; Elev: 4629ft/1411m; Tel: 406-387-3800; Nearest town: Columbia Falls; Notes: Horse facilities. GPS: 48.922626, -114.599057

245 • Twin Lakes Camp

Total sites: 21; RV sites: 21; Central water; Vault toilets; No showers; No RV dump; Reservations not accepted; Max length: 25ft; Open Jun-Sep; Tent & RV camping: $7; Elev: 7287ft/2221m; Tel: 406-689-3243; Nearest town: Wisdom. GPS: 45.411133, -113.688721

246 • Upper Stillwater Lake

Total sites: 5; RV sites: 5; No water; Vault toilets; Reservations not accepted; Generator hours: 0600-2200; Open May-Nov; Tent & RV camping: Free; Elev: 3205ft/977m; Tel: 406-758-5208; Nearest town: Whitefish. GPS: 48.603516, -114.656307

247 • Vigilante

Total sites: 14; RV sites: 14; Central water; Vault toilets; No showers; No RV dump; Reservations not accepted; Max length: 16ft; Open May-Sep; Tent & RV camping: $8; Elev: 4485ft/1367m; Tel: 406-449-5490; Nearest town: Helena. GPS: 46.766846, -111.650635

248 • Wade Lake

Total sites: 30; RV sites: 30; Central water; Vault toilets; No showers; No RV dump; Reservations not accepted; Max length: 32ft; Stay limit: 16 days; Open Jun-Sep; Tent & RV camping: $15; Elev: 6224ft/1897m; Tel: 406-682-4253; Nearest town: West Yellowstone. GPS: 44.807682, -111.566885

249 • Warm Springs

Total sites: 13; RV sites: 13; Central water; Vault toilets; No showers; No RV dump; Reservations not accepted; Generator hours: 0600-2200; Open May-Sep; Tent & RV camping: $8; Elev: 4495ft/1370m; Tel: 406-821-3201; Nearest town: Sula. GPS: 45.843018, -114.040039

250 • Warm Springs

Total sites: 6; Central water; Vault toilets; No showers; No RV dump; Reservations not accepted; Tents only: Free; Elev: 6381ft/1945m; Tel: 406-859-3211; Nearest town: Anaconda. GPS: 46.199399, -113.166814

251 • West Boulder

Total sites: 10; RV sites: 10; Central water; Vault toilets; No showers; No RV dump; Reservations not accepted; Max length: 20ft; Open all year; Tent & RV camping: $5; Elev: 5538ft/1688m; Tel: 406-932-5155; Nearest town: Big Timber; Notes: Limited winter access - no fee. GPS: 45.548901, -110.307702

252 • West Fork Fishtrap Creek

Total sites: 4; RV sites: 4; Central water; Vault toilets; No showers; No RV dump; Reservations not accepted; Open all year; Tent & RV camping: Free; Elev: 3596ft/1096m; Tel: 406-826-3821; Nearest town: Thompson Falls; Notes: No water Oct-May. GPS: 47.816600, -115.149220

253 • West Fork Madison

Total sites: 7; Central water; Vault toilets; No showers; No RV dump; Reservations not accepted; Stay limit: 16 days; Open Jun-Sep; Tents only: $12; Elev: 5886ft/1794m; Tel: 406-682-4253; Nearest town: Ennis. GPS: 44.886906, -111.582661

254 • West Fork Teton

Total sites: 6; Central water; Vault toilets; No showers; No RV dump; Reservations not accepted; Tents only: $6; Elev: 5640ft/1719m; Tel: 406-466-5341; Nearest town: Choteau; Notes: Mandatory food storage. GPS: 47.961182, -112.806931

255 • Whitehouse

Total sites: 5; RV sites: 5; Central water; Vault toilets; No showers; No RV dump; Reservations not accepted; Max length: 22ft; Stay limit: 16 days; Open May-Nov; Tent & RV camping: Free; Elev: 6086ft/1855m; Tel: 406-494-2147; Nearest town: Butte. GPS: 46.258166, -112.478539

256 • Whitetail

Total sites: 12; RV sites: 12; Central water; Vault toilets; No showers; No RV dump; Reservations not accepted; Stay limit: 14 days; Open all year; Tent & RV camping: $7; Elev: 2976ft/907m; Tel: 406-295-4693; Nearest town: Troy; Notes: Limited access and services in winter. GPS: 48.827637, -115.814453

257 • Whitetail Camp

Total sites: 12; RV sites: 12; No water; Vault toilets; Reservations not accepted; Tent & RV camping: Free; Elev: 6375ft/1943m; Nearest town: Checkerboard; Notes: Mandatory food storage. GPS: 46.682363, -110.502753

258 • Wickham Gulch

Total sites: 2; RV sites: 2; Central water; Vault toilets; No showers; No RV dump; Reservations not accepted; Max length: 16ft; Stay limit: 14 days; Open all year; Tent & RV camping: Free; Elev: 3520ft/1073m; Tel: 605-797-4432; Nearest town: Camp Crook (SD). GPS: 45.580109, -104.070973

259 • Willow

Total sites: 5; RV sites: 5; Central water; Vault toilets; No showers; No RV dump; Reservations not accepted; Max length: 26ft; Open Jun-Sep; Tent & RV camping: $8; Elev: 6532ft/1991m; Tel: 406-832-3178; Nearest town: Dillon. GPS: 45.636246, -113.076866

260 • Wood Lake

Total sites: 9; RV sites: 9; Central water; Vault toilets; No showers; No RV dump; Reservations not accepted; Max length: 22ft; Stay limit: 14 days; Open Jun-Sep; Tent & RV camping: $6; Elev: 5896ft/1797m; Nearest town: Augusta. GPS: 47.427762, -112.793671

261 • Woodbine

Total sites: 44; RV sites: 44; Central water; Vault toilets; No showers; No RV dump; Reservations accepted; Max length: 40ft; Stay limit: 16 days; Open May-Sep; Tent & RV camping: $19; Elev: 5223ft/1592m; Tel: 406-446-2103; Nearest town: Nye. GPS: 45.352701, -109.896774

262 • Yaak Falls

Total sites: 7; RV sites: 7; No water; Vault toilets; Reservations not accepted; Max length: 24ft; Stay limit: 14 days; Open all year; Tent & RV camping: Free; Elev: 2444ft/745m; Tel: 406-295-4693; Nearest town: Troy; Notes: Limited winter access. GPS: 48.645021, -115.885458

263 • Yaak River

Total sites: 44; RV sites: 44; Central water; Vault toilets; No showers; No RV dump; Reservations not accepted; Max length: 32ft; Stay limit: 14 days; Open all year; Tent & RV camping: $10; Elev: 1855ft/565m; Tel: 406-295-4693; Nearest town: Troy; Notes: Limited access and services in winter. GPS: 48.561822, -115.972106

Nebraska

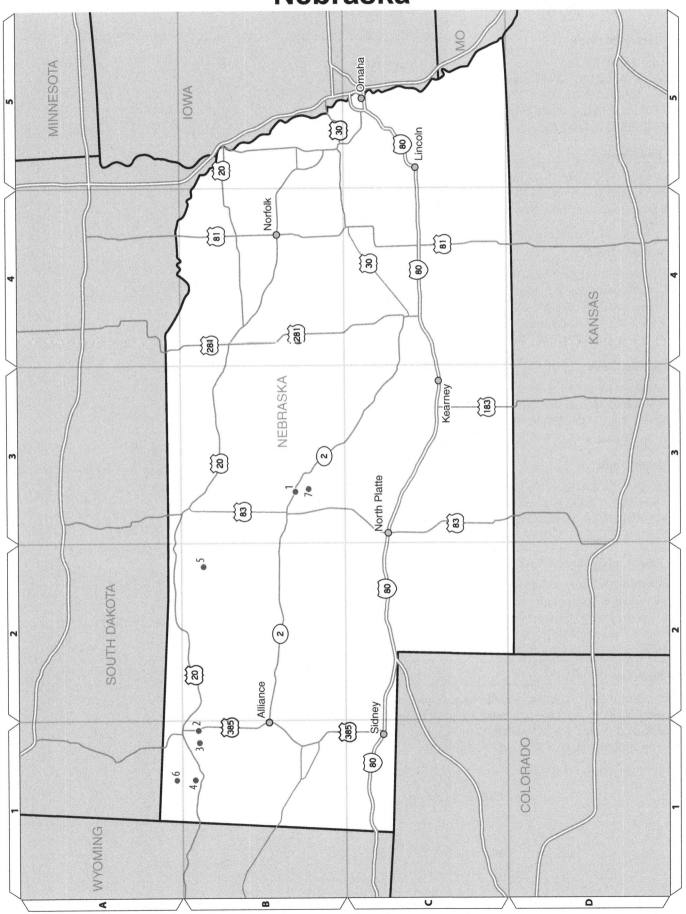

Nebraska Camping Areas

1 • Bessey Rec Area

Total sites: 40; RV sites: 40; Elec sites: 18; Central water; Flush toilets; Showers; RV dump; Reservations accepted; Open all year; Tents: $8/RVs: $8-11; Elev: 2743ft/836m; Tel: 308-533-2257; Nearest town: Halsey; Notes: Group site: $75, No water in winter. GPS: 41.898881, -100.297357

2 • Red Cloud

Total sites: 13; No water; Vault toilets; Reservations not accepted; Open all year; Tents only: $5; Elev: 3884ft/1184m; Nearest town: Chadron; Notes: Free mid-Nov to mid-Apr. GPS: 42.696774, -103.005046

3 • Roberts Tract

Total sites: 4; RV sites: 1; No toilets; No showers; No RV dump; Reservations not accepted; Open all year; Tent & RV camping: $8; Elev: 3960ft/1207m; Tel: 308-432-0300; Nearest town: Chadron; Notes: Stock water available mid-May to mid-Oct, Free mid-Nov to early May. GPS: 42.678746, -103.151260

4 • Soldier Creek

Total sites: 4; RV sites: 4; Central water; Vault toilets; No showers; No RV dump; Open all year; Tent & RV camping: $8; Elev: 4104ft/1251m; Tel: 308-432-0300; Nearest town: Crawford; Notes: Free mid-Nov to mid-May. GPS: 42.697811, -103.570514

5 • Steer Creek

Total sites: 23; RV sites: 23; Central water; Vault toilets; No showers; No RV dump; Reservations not accepted; Open all year; Tent & RV camping: $5; Elev: 3064ft/934m; Nearest town: Nenzel. GPS: 42.688524, -101.152975

6 • Toadstool Geological Park

Total sites: 6; RV sites: 6; Central water; Vault toilets; No showers; No RV dump; Reservations not accepted; Open all year; Tent & RV camping: $5; Elev: 3780ft/1152m; Tel: 308-432-0300; Nearest town: Crawford; Notes: Free in winter. GPS: 42.857956, -103.584193

7 • Whitetail

Total sites: 10; RV sites: 10; Central water; Vault toilets; No showers; No RV dump; Reservations not accepted; Open all year; Tent & RV camping: $8; Elev: 2703ft/824m; Tel: 308-533-2257; Nearest town: Halsey. GPS: 41.796088, -100.264495

Nevada

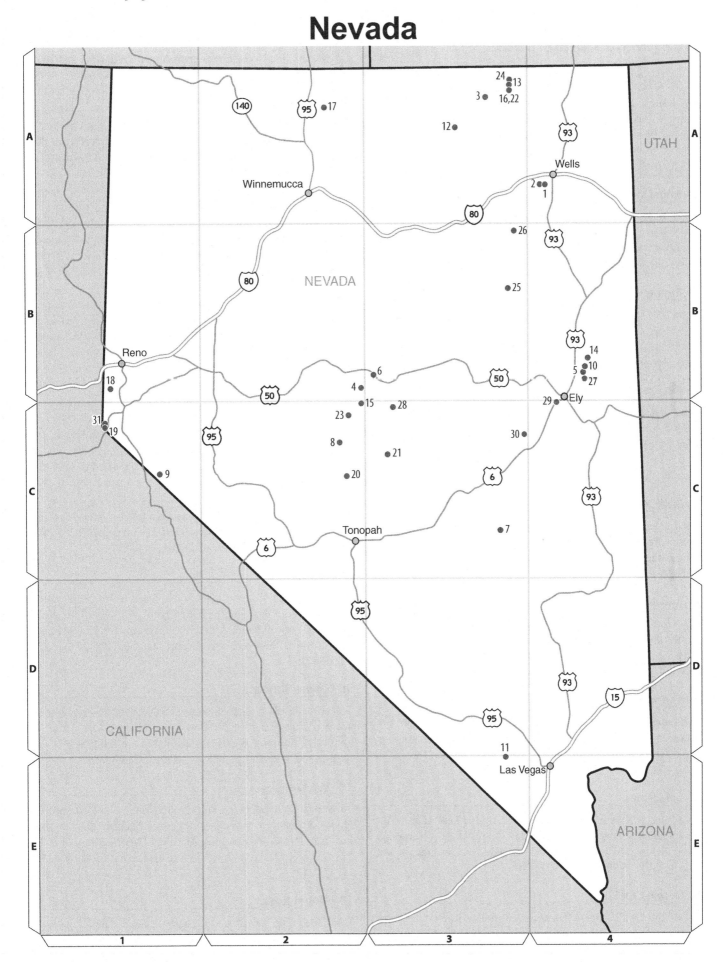

Nevada Camping Areas

1 • Angel Creek

Total sites: 12; RV sites: 12; Central water; Vault toilets; No showers; No RV dump; Reservations accepted; Open May-Sep; Tent & RV camping: $16; Elev: 6621ft/2018m; Tel: 775-752-3357; Nearest town: Wells; Notes: Group site: $60. GPS: 41.027344, -115.050293

2 • Angel Lake

Total sites: 26; RV sites: 26; Central water; Vault toilets; No showers; No RV dump; Reservations accepted; Open Jun-Sep; Tent & RV camping: $17; Elev: 8379ft/2554m; Tel: 775-752-3357; Nearest town: Wells. GPS: 41.026988, -115.083439

3 • Big Bend

Total sites: 19; RV sites: 19; No water; Vault toilets; Reservations not accepted; Max length: 25ft; Open May-Nov; Tent & RV camping: $8; Elev: 6978ft/2127m; Tel: 775-738-5171; Nearest town: Mountain City. GPS: 41.765869, -115.700195

4 • Big Creek

Total sites: 5; RV sites: 5; Central water; Vault toilets; No showers; No RV dump; Reservations not accepted; Max length: 35ft; Open May-Oct; Tent & RV camping: Free; Elev: 6942ft/2116m; Tel: 775-964-2671; Nearest town: Austin; Notes: Trailers prohibited from crossing the top of FSR 002. GPS: 39.345493, -117.136112

5 • Bird Creek

Total sites: 4; Central water; Vault toilets; No showers; No RV dump; Reservations accepted; Open May-Oct; Tents only: $8; Elev: 7426ft/2263m; Tel: 775-289-3031; Nearest town: McGill. GPS: 39.463316, -114.652932

6 • Bob Scott

Total sites: 9; RV sites: 9; Central water; Vault toilets; No showers; No RV dump; Reservations not accepted; Max length: 35ft; Open May-Oct; Tent & RV camping: $10; Elev: 7260ft/2213m; Tel: 775-964-2671; Nearest town: Austin. GPS: 39.457631, -116.995003

7 • Cherry Creek

Total sites: 4; RV sites: 4; No water; Vault toilets; Reservations not accepted; Max length: 20ft; Open May-Sep; Tent & RV camping: Free; Elev: 6932ft/2113m; Tel: 775-289-3031; Nearest town: Ely. GPS: 38.153799, -115.624325

8 • Columbine

Total sites: 5; RV sites: 5; No water; Vault toilets; Reservations not accepted; Max length: 35ft; Open May-Oct; Tent & RV camping: Free; Elev: 8661ft/2640m; Tel: 775-964-2671; Nearest town: Austin. GPS: 38.900342, -117.376796

9 • Desert Creek

Total sites: 19; RV sites: 6; No water; No toilets; Reservations not accepted; Max length: 18ft; Open all year; Tent & RV camping: Free; Elev: 6398ft/1950m; Tel: 760-932-7070; Nearest town: Bridgeport CA; Notes: Creek crossing required. GPS: 38.620677, -119.340101

10 • East Creek

Total sites: 6; RV sites: 6; No water; Vault toilets; Reservations not accepted; Max length: 20ft; Open May-Sep; Tent & RV camping: $4; Elev: 7625ft/2324m; Tel: 775-289-3031; Nearest town: McGill. GPS: 39.497021, -114.639096

11 • Fletcher View

Total sites: 11; RV sites: 11; Elec sites: 11; Central water; Flush toilets; Showers; No RV dump; Reservations accepted; Open all year; Tent & RV camping: $33; Elev: 7054ft/2150m; Tel: 702-515-5400; Nearest town: Las Vegas. GPS: 36.262442, -115.617812

12 • Jack Creek

Total sites: 3; RV sites: 3; No water; Vault toilets; Reservations not accepted; Max length: 30ft; Open all year; Tent & RV camping: Free; Elev: 6519ft/1987m; Tel: 775-738-5171; Nearest town: Mountain City; Notes: May be inaccessible in winter. GPS: 41.513491, -116.063984

13 • Jarbridge

Total sites: 5; RV sites: 5; No water; No toilets; Max length: 16ft; Open May-Sep; Tent & RV camping: Fee unknown; Elev: 6470ft/1972m; Nearest town: Jarbridge. GPS: 41.863348, -115.429145

14 • Kalamazoo

Total sites: 5; RV sites: 5; No water; No toilets; Open May-Nov; Tent & RV camping: Free; Elev: 7032ft/2143m; Tel: 775-289-3031; Nearest town: Ely. GPS: 39.565337, -114.597821

15 • Kingston

Total sites: 11; RV sites: 11; No water; Vault toilets; Reservations not accepted; Max length: 35ft; Open May-Oct; Tent & RV camping: Fee unknown; Elev: 7195ft/2193m; Tel: 775-964-2671; Nearest town: Austin; Notes: Group site also. GPS: 39.225185, -117.139586

16 • Lower Bluster

Total sites: 2; RV sites: 2; No water; Vault toilets; Reservations not accepted; Max length: 25ft; Stay limit: 14 days; Open Jun-Sep; Tent & RV camping: Free; Elev: 6696ft/2041m; Tel: 775-331-6444; Nearest town: Jarbridge. GPS: 41.838215, -115.426697

17 • Lye Creek

Total sites: 18; RV sites: 5; Central water; Vault toilets; No showers; No RV dump; Reservations not accepted; Max length: 24ft; Open Jun-Oct; Tent & RV camping: $8; Elev: 7309ft/2228m; Tel: 775-623-5025 x4; Nearest town: Winnemucca. GPS: 41.685415, -117.557312

18 • Mount Rose

Total sites: 26; RV sites: 26; Central water; Vault toilets; No showers; No RV dump; Reservations accepted; Open Jun-Sep;

Tent & RV camping: $22; Elev: 8966ft/2733m; Tel: 775-882-2766; Nearest town: Reno. GPS: 39.313232, -119.892334

19 • Nevada Beach

Total sites: 54; RV sites: 54; Central water; Flush toilets; No showers; No RV dump; Reservations accepted; Max length: 35ft; Stay limit: 14 days; Open May-Oct; Tent & RV camping: $36-42; Elev: 6296ft/1919m; Tel: 530-543-2600; Nearest town: Stateline. GPS: 38.980957, -119.952637

20 • Peavine

Total sites: 15; RV sites: 15; No water; Vault toilets; Reservations not accepted; Max length: 35ft; Open May-Oct; Tent & RV camping: Free; Elev: 6391ft/1948m; Tel: 775-482-6286; Nearest town: Austin. GPS: 38.616291, -117.302569

21 • Pine Creek

Total sites: 21; RV sites: 21; No water; Vault toilets; Reservations not accepted; Open May-Oct; Tent & RV camping: Free; Elev: 7493ft/2284m; Tel: 775-482-6286; Nearest town: Tonopah; Notes: Group site available. GPS: 38.795619, -116.850387

22 • Pine Creek (Jarbridge)

Total sites: 5; RV sites: 5; No water; Vault toilets; Reservations not accepted; Max length: 25ft; Stay limit: 14 days; Open all year; Tent & RV camping: Free; Elev: 6782ft/2067m; Tel: 775-331-6444; Nearest town: Jarbridge; Notes: May be inaccessible in winter. GPS: 41.835688, -115.426141

23 • San Juan Creek

Total sites: 10; RV sites: 10; No water; Vault toilets; Reservations not accepted; Open May-Oct; Tent & RV camping: Free; Elev: 7282ft/2220m; Tel: 775-964-2671; Nearest town: Austin. GPS: 39.121823, -117.275517

24 • Sawmill

Total sites: 5; RV sites: 5; No water; Vault toilets; Reservations not accepted; Open all year; Tent & RV camping: Free; Elev: 6116ft/1864m; Tel: 775-752-3357; Nearest town: Jarbridge; Notes: May be inaccessible in winter. GPS: 41.885462, -115.429515

25 • South Ruby

Total sites: 35; RV sites: 35; Central water; Vault toilets; No showers; No RV dump; Reservations accepted; Open May-Sep; Tent & RV camping: $16; Elev: 6092ft/1857m; Tel: 775-752-3357; Nearest town: Elko. GPS: 40.175929, -115.494557

26 • Thomas Canyon

Total sites: 40; RV sites: 40; Central water; Vault toilets; No showers; No RV dump; Reservations accepted; Open May-Oct; Tent & RV camping: $18; Elev: 7634ft/2327m; Tel: 775-752-3357; Nearest town: Spring Creek. GPS: 40.649902, -115.404541

27 • Timber Creek

Total sites: 5; RV sites: 5; Central water; Vault toilets; No showers; No RV dump; Reservations accepted; Max length: 30ft; Open May-Oct; Tent & RV camping: $8; Elev: 8472ft/2582m; Tel: 775-289-3031; Nearest town: Ely; Notes: 6 group sites: $10-$35. GPS: 39.401944, -114.638452

28 • Toquima Caves

Total sites: 5; RV sites: 1; No water; Vault toilets; Reservations not accepted; Max length: 25ft; Open May-Oct; Tent & RV camping: Free; Elev: 7972ft/2430m; Tel: 775-482-6286; Nearest town: Tonopah; Notes: Available group site. GPS: 39.187411, -116.787364

29 • Ward Mountain

Total sites: 29; RV sites: 29; Central water; Vault toilets; No showers; No RV dump; Reservations accepted; Max length: 16ft; Open Apr-Nov; Tent & RV camping: $8; Elev: 7356ft/2242m; Tel: 775-289-3031; Nearest town: Ely. GPS: 39.211914, -114.968018

30 • White River

Total sites: 10; RV sites: 10; No toilets; Reservations not accepted; Open May-Nov; Tent & RV camping: $4; Elev: 6986ft/2129m; Tel: 775-289-3031; Nearest town: Ely. GPS: 38.943647, -115.341326

31 • Zephyr Cove

Total sites: 150; RV sites: 93; Elec sites: 93; Water at site; Flush toilets; Showers; Laundry; RV dump; Max length: 45ft; Open all year; Tents: $30/RVs: $30-40; Elev: 6270ft/1911m; Tel: 775-589-4906; Nearest town: Lake Tahoe; Notes: Also walk-to sites, Cabin(s), 93 FHU, Concessionaire. GPS: 39.006444, -119.946467

New Hampshire

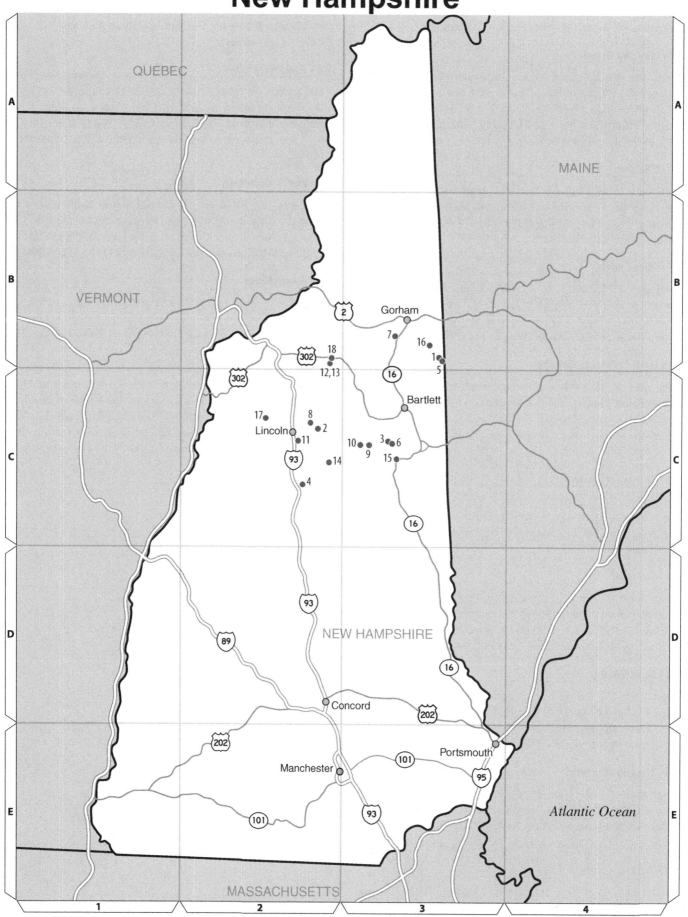

New Hampshire Camping Areas

1 • Basin Pond

Total sites: 21; RV sites: 14; Central water; Vault toilets; No showers; No RV dump; Reservations accepted; Open May-Oct; Tent & RV camping: $20; Elev: 712ft/217m; Tel: 603-447-5448; Nearest town: Gilead ME. GPS: 44.267900, -71.022000

2 • Big Rock

Total sites: 28; RV sites: 20; Central water; Vault toilets; No showers; No RV dump; Reservations not accepted; Open May-Oct; Tent & RV camping: $22; Elev: 1637ft/499m; Tel: 603-536-6100; Nearest town: Lincoln. GPS: 44.048340, -71.559570

3 • Blackberry Crossing

Total sites: 26; RV sites: 26; Central water; Vault toilets; No showers; No RV dump; Reservations not accepted; Open Apr-Oct; Tent & RV camping: $22; Elev: 909ft/277m; Tel: 603-447-5448; Nearest town: Conway. GPS: 44.006967, -71.244546

4 • Campton

Total sites: 58; RV sites: 58; Central water; Flush toilets; Pay showers; No RV dump; Reservations accepted; Open May-Oct; Tent & RV camping: $22; Elev: 718ft/219m; Tel: 603-536-6100; Nearest town: Campton. GPS: 43.873779, -71.626953

5 • Cold River

Total sites: 14; RV sites: 12; Central water; Vault toilets; No showers; No RV dump; Reservations accepted; Open May-Oct; Tent & RV camping: $18; Elev: 627ft/191m; Tel: 603-447-5448; Nearest town: North Chatham. GPS: 44.265194, -71.012469

6 • Covered Bridge

Total sites: 49; RV sites: 41; Central water; Vault toilets; No showers; No RV dump; Reservations accepted; Open May-Oct; Tent & RV camping: $22; Elev: 899ft/274m; Tel: 603-447-5448; Nearest town: Conway; Notes: 7' 9" height limit from west. GPS: 44.004024, -71.233154

7 • Dolly Copp - Big Meadow

Total sites: 177; RV sites: 177; Central water; No toilets; No showers; No RV dump; Reservations not accepted; Open May-Oct; Tent & RV camping: $22; Elev: 1273ft/388m; Tel: 603-466-2713; Nearest town: Gorham. GPS: 44.332648, -71.218862

8 • Hancock

Total sites: 56; RV sites: 35; Central water; Vault toilets; No showers; No RV dump; Reservations not accepted; Open all year; Tent & RV camping: $24; Elev: 1198ft/365m; Tel: 603-536-6100; Nearest town: Lincoln. GPS: 44.064453, -71.593750

9 • Jigger Johnson

Total sites: 74; RV sites: 50; Central water; Flush toilets; Pay showers; No RV dump; Reservations not accepted; Open May-Oct; Tent & RV camping: $24; Elev: 1257ft/383m; Tel: 603-447-5448; Nearest town: Conway. GPS: 43.996094, -71.333496

10 • Passaconway

Total sites: 33; RV sites: 33; Central water; Vault toilets; No showers; No RV dump; Reservations not accepted; Open May-Oct; Tent & RV camping: $22; Elev: 1263ft/385m; Tel: 603-447-5448; Nearest town: Conway. GPS: 43.997094, -71.369482

11 • Russell Pond

Total sites: 84; RV sites: 15; Central water; Flush toilets; Pay showers; No RV dump; Reservations not accepted; Open May-Oct; Tent & RV camping: $24; Elev: 1732ft/528m; Tel: 603-536-6100; Nearest town: Lincoln. GPS: 44.011963, -71.650635

12 • Sugarloaf Area I

Total sites: 29; RV sites: 29; Central water; Vault toilets; No showers; No RV dump; Reservations accepted; Open May-Oct; Tent & RV camping: $20; Elev: 1657ft/505m; Tel: 603-536-6100; Nearest town: Twin Mountain. GPS: 44.258057, -71.503662

13 • Sugarloaf Area II

Total sites: 32; RV sites: 32; Central water; Vault toilets; No showers; No RV dump; Reservations accepted; Open May-Oct; Tent & RV camping: $18; Elev: 1631ft/497m; Tel: 603-536-6100; Nearest town: Twin Mountain. GPS: 44.260742, -71.504150

14 • Waterville Valley

Total sites: 26; RV sites: 19; Central water; Vault toilets; No showers; No RV dump; Reservations accepted; Open May-Oct; Tent & RV camping: $18; Elev: 1466ft/447m; Tel: 603-536-6100; Nearest town: Waterville Valley. GPS: 43.942954, -71.509827

15 • White Ledge

Total sites: 28; RV sites: 28; Central water; Vault toilets; No showers; No RV dump; Reservations accepted; Generator hours: 0800--1000/1700-1900; Open May-Oct; Tent & RV camping: $18; Elev: 761ft/232m; Tel: 603-447-5448; Nearest town: Conway. GPS: 43.954327, -71.214093

16 • Wild River

Total sites: 12; RV sites: 3; Central water; Vault toilets; No showers; No RV dump; Reservations not accepted; Open May-Sep; Tent & RV camping: $18; Elev: 1178ft/359m; Tel: 603-466-2713; Nearest town: Gilead. GPS: 44.305000, -71.065000

17 • Wildwood

Total sites: 26; RV sites: 26; Central water; Vault toilets; No showers; No RV dump; Reservations not accepted; Open May-Oct; Tent & RV camping: $18; Elev: 1375ft/419m; Tel: 603-536-6100; Nearest town: North Woodstock. GPS: 44.076172, -71.793457

18 • Zealand

Total sites: 11; RV sites: 11; Central water; Vault toilets; No showers; No RV dump; Reservations not accepted; Open May-Oct; Tent & RV camping: $18; Elev: 1506ft/459m; Tel: 603-536-1310; Nearest town: Twin Mountain. GPS: 44.264925, -71.499242

New Mexico

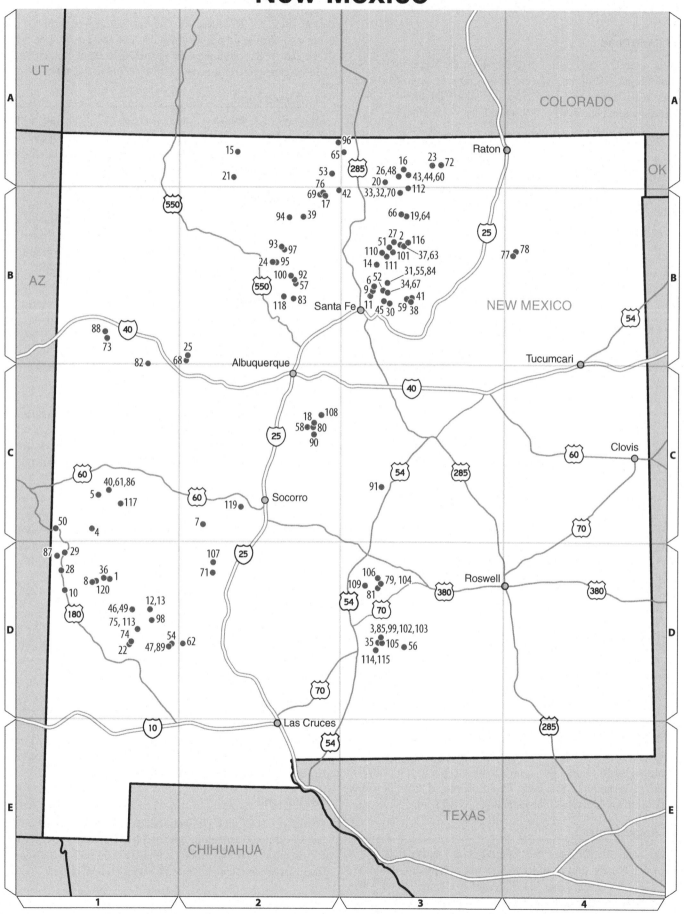

New Mexico Camping Areas

1 • Aeroplane Mesa

Total sites: 6; RV sites: 6; No water; Vault toilets; Open all year; Tent & RV camping: Free; Elev: 8022ft/2445m; Tel: 575-533-6231; Nearest town: Reserve. GPS: 33.417495, -108.441222

2 • Agua Piedra

Total sites: 44; RV sites: 44; Central water; Vault toilets; No showers; No RV dump; Reservations accepted; Open May-Oct; Tent & RV camping: $17; Elev: 8415ft/2565m; Nearest town: Penasco; Notes: Horse Corral, Group sites $65-$115, Water in lower loop has strong sulphur smell - but is potable, Loops A and B have no water. GPS: 36.135254, -105.529053

3 • Apache

Total sites: 25; RV sites: 25; Central water; Vault toilets; No showers; No RV dump; Reservations not accepted; Max length: 32ft; Stay limit: 14 days; Open May-Sep; Tent & RV camping: $22; Elev: 8917ft/2718m; Tel: 575-682-2551; Nearest town: Cloudcroft; Notes: Water: $0.25 per gallon after 1st free 5 gallons. GPS: 32.966797, -105.728760

4 • Apache Creek

Total sites: 20; RV sites: 20; No water; Vault toilets; Stay limit: 14 days; Open May-Nov; Tent & RV camping: Free; Elev: 6460ft/1969m; Tel: 575-533-6231; Nearest town: Reserve. GPS: 33.828564, -108.627903

5 • Armijo Springs

Total sites: 5; RV sites: 5; No water; Vault toilets; Reservations not accepted; Max length: 40ft; Stay limit: 14 days; Open all year; Tent & RV camping: Free; Elev: 7959ft/2426m; Tel: 575-773-4678; Nearest town: Quemado. GPS: 34.096528, -108.569956

6 • Aspen Basin

Total sites: 10; RV sites: 10; No water; Vault toilets; Reservations not accepted; Open all year; Tent & RV camping: Free; Elev: 10358ft/3157m; Tel: 505-753-7331; Nearest town: Santa Fe; Notes: Severe winter conditions. GPS: 35.795966, -105.805287

7 • Bear Trap

Total sites: 4; RV sites: 4; No water; Vault toilets; Max length: 20ft; Open May-Sep; Tent & RV camping: Free; Elev: 8606ft/2623m; Tel: 505-854-2281; Nearest town: Magdalena. GPS: 33.883174, -107.514862

8 • Ben Lilly

Total sites: 7; No water; Vault toilets; Reservations not accepted; Max length: 17ft; Stay limit: 14 days; Open May-Nov; Tents only: Free; Elev: 8087ft/2465m; Tel: 575-533-6231; Nearest town: Reserve. GPS: 33.397586, -108.593641

9 • Big Tesuque

Total sites: 10; No water; Vault toilets; Reservations not accepted; Open all year; Tents only: Free; Elev: 9767ft/2977m; Tel: 505-753-7331; Nearest town: Santa Fe. GPS: 35.769396, -105.809089

10 • Bighorn

Total sites: 6; RV sites: 6; No water; Vault toilets; Reservations not accepted; Max length: 30ft; Stay limit: 14 days; Open all year; Tent & RV camping: Free; Elev: 4833ft/1473m; Tel: 575-539-2481; Nearest town: Glenwood; Notes: Can walk to town. GPS: 33.324129, -108.882746

11 • Black Canyon

Total sites: 42; RV sites: 36; Central water; Vault toilets; No showers; No RV dump; Reservations accepted; Max length: 32ft; Open May-Oct; Tent & RV camping: $10; Elev: 8448ft/2575m; Tel: 575-536-2250; Nearest town: Santa Fe; Notes: Some walk-to sites. GPS: 35.725889, -105.836607

12 • Black Canyon Lower

Total sites: 3; RV sites: 3; No water; Vault toilets; Reservations not accepted; Stay limit: 14 days; Open Apr-Nov; Tent & RV camping: Free; Elev: 6765ft/2062m; Tel: 575-536-2250; Nearest town: Mimbres,. GPS: 33.184064, -108.035107

13 • Black Canyon Upper

Total sites: 2; No water; Vault toilets; Reservations not accepted; Max length: 17ft; Stay limit: 14 days; Open Apr-Nov; Tents only: Free; Elev: 6772ft/2064m; Tel: 575-536-2250; Nearest town: Mimbres,. GPS: 33.185325, -108.033076

14 • Borrego Mesa

Total sites: 8; RV sites: 8; No water; No toilets; Reservations not accepted; Max length: 14ft; Open all year; Tent & RV camping: Free; Elev: 8802ft/2683m; Tel: 505-753-7331; Nearest town: Espanola; Notes: Small horse corrals at each site, Vault toilets vandalized. GPS: 35.979192, -105.772525

15 • Buzzard Park

Total sites: 4; RV sites: 4; No water; Vault toilets; Reservations not accepted; Open May-Nov; Tent & RV camping: Free; Elev: 6975ft/2126m; Tel: 505-632-2956; Nearest town: Dulce; Notes: No large RVs. GPS: 36.881061, -107.216887

16 • Cabresto Lake

Total sites: 9; No water; Vault toilets; Reservations not accepted; Open May-Sep; Tent & RV camping: Free; Elev: 9160ft/2792m; Tel: 575-586-0520; Nearest town: Questa; Notes: Nothing larger than van/pickup. GPS: 36.746685, -105.499292

17 • Canjilon Creek

Total sites: 4; RV sites: 4; No water; Vault toilets; Reservations not accepted; Max length: 16ft; Open Jun-Sep; Tent & RV camping: Free; Elev: 9452ft/2881m; Nearest town: Canjilon. GPS: 36.543352, -106.317422

18 • Capilla Peak

Total sites: 8; RV sites: 8; No water; Vault toilets; Reservations not accepted; Max length: 16ft; Open May-Sep; Tents only: $5; Elev: 9304ft/2836m; Nearest town: Manzano. GPS: 34.699729, -106.402676

19 • Capulin

Total sites: 11; RV sites: 11; No water; Vault toilets; Reservations not accepted; Max length: 16ft; Open May-Oct; Tent & RV camping: $10; Elev: 7868ft/2398m; Tel: 575-587-2255; Nearest town: Taos. GPS: 36.370707, -105.483165

20 • Cebolla Mesa

Total sites: 5; RV sites: 5; No water; Vault toilets; Reservations not accepted; Max length: 32ft; Open May-Sep; Tent & RV camping: Fee unknown; Elev: 7375ft/2248m; Tel: 575-586-0520; Nearest town: Questa; Notes: Road is dirt/gravel and hazardous in muddy conditions. GPS: 36.640308, -105.689195

21 • Cedar Springs

Total sites: 4; No water; No toilets; Reservations not accepted; Open May-Nov; Tents only: Free; Elev: 7461ft/2274m; Tel: 505-632-2956; Nearest town: Gobernador. GPS: 36.671958, -107.253189

22 • Cherry Creek

Total sites: 12; RV sites: 12; No water; Vault toilets; Reservations not accepted; Max length: 17ft; Stay limit: 14 days; Open all year; Tent & RV camping: Free; Elev: 6864ft/2092m; Tel: 575-388-8201; Nearest town: Silver City. GPS: 32.914239, -108.224214

23 • Cimarron

Total sites: 36; RV sites: 36; No water; Vault toilets; Reservations accepted; Max length: 32ft; Open May-Oct; Tent & RV camping: $18; Elev: 9485ft/2891m; Tel: 505-586-0520; Nearest town: Costilla; Notes: Horse facilities. GPS: 36.769433, -105.204977

24 • Clear Creek

Total sites: 15; RV sites: 15; Central water; Vault toilets; Reservations accepted; Max length: RV-30ft-Tlr-16ft; Generator hours: 0600-2200; Open May-Sep; Tent & RV camping: $10; Elev: 8428ft/2569m; Tel: 505-289-3265; Nearest town: Cuba; Notes: Group area $35. GPS: 35.996835, -106.826928

25 • Coal Mine

Total sites: 15; RV sites: 15; No water; Vault toilets; Reservations accepted; Max length: 22ft; Open May-Sep; Tent & RV camping: $5; Elev: 7484ft/2281m; Tel: 505-287-8833; Nearest town: Grants. GPS: 35.234371, -107.701862

26 • Columbine

Total sites: 27; RV sites: 27; Central water; Vault toilets; No showers; No RV dump; Reservations accepted; Max length: 32ft; Open Mar-Sep; Tent & RV camping: $18; Elev: 7900ft/2408m; Tel: 505-586-0520; Nearest town: Questa. GPS: 36.679199, -105.515625

27 • Comales

Total sites: 10; RV sites: 10; No water; Vault toilets; Reservations not accepted; Max length: 36ft; Open May-Sep; Tent & RV camping: $10; Elev: 7936ft/2419m; Tel: 575-587-2255; Nearest town: Penasco. GPS: 36.160028, -105.596415

28 • Cosmic

Total sites: 6; RV sites: 6; No water; Vault toilets; Reservations not accepted; Max length: 36ft; Generator hours: 0600-2200; Open all year; Tent & RV camping: Free; Elev: 5363ft/1635m; Tel: 575-539-2481; Nearest town: Alma; Notes: First International Dark Sky Sanctuary in North America. GPS: 33.480066, -108.922918

29 • Cottonwood

Total sites: 4; RV sites: 4; No water; Vault toilets; Reservations not accepted; Max length: 22ft; Stay limit: 14 days; Open Apr-Nov; Tent & RV camping: Free; Elev: 5813ft/1772m; Tel: 575-539-2481; Nearest town: Glenwood. GPS: 33.618849, -108.894143

30 • Cow Creek

Total sites: 5; No water; No toilets; Reservations not accepted; Open Apr-Nov; Tents only: Free; Elev: 8540ft/2603m; Tel: 505-757-6121; Nearest town: Pecos. GPS: 35.671000, -105.640000

31 • Cowles

Total sites: 9; No water; Vault toilets; Reservations not accepted; Open Apr-Nov; Tents only: $6; Elev: 8360ft/2548m; Tel: 505-757-6121; Nearest town: Pecos. GPS: 35.812344, -105.663428

32 • Cuchilla

Total sites: 3; RV sites: 3; No water; Vault toilets; Reservations not accepted; Max length: 22ft; Open May-Sep; Tent & RV camping: Free; Elev: 8240ft/2512m; Nearest town: Taos. GPS: 36.569361, -105.518488

33 • Cuchilla del Medio

Total sites: 3; RV sites: 3; No water; Vault toilets; Reservations not accepted; Max length: 16ft; Open May-Sep; Tent & RV camping: Free; Elev: 8064ft/2458m; Tel: 575-586-0520; Nearest town: Taos. GPS: 36.559253, -105.535424

34 • Davis Willow

Total sites: 15; RV sites: 15; No water; Vault toilets; Reservations not accepted; Open Apr-Nov; Tent & RV camping: Free; Elev: 8114ft/2473m; Tel: 505-757-6121; Nearest town: Pecos. GPS: 35.757409, -105.663266

35 • Deerhead

Total sites: 20; RV sites: 20; Central water; Vault toilets; No showers; No RV dump; Reservations not accepted; Max length: 30ft; Open May-Sep; Tent & RV camping: $22; Elev: 8770ft/2673m; Tel: 575-682-2551; Nearest town: Cloudcroft. GPS: 32.943604, -105.746338

36 • Dipping Vat

Total sites: 40; RV sites: 40; Central water; Vault toilets; No showers; No RV dump; Reservations not accepted; Max length: 19ft; Open Apr-Sep; Tent & RV camping: $6; Elev: 7379ft/2249m; Tel: 575-533-6231; Nearest town: Reserve. GPS: 33.423045, -108.500849

37 • Duran Canyon

Total sites: 12; RV sites: 12; No water; Vault toilets; Reservations not accepted; Stay limit: 14 days; Open May-Oct; Tent & RV camping: $11; Elev: 8842ft/2695m; Tel: 575-587-2255; Nearest town: Penasco. GPS: 36.134033, -105.477295

38 • E.V. Long

Total sites: 14; RV sites: 14; No water; Vault toilets; No showers; No RV dump; Reservations not accepted; Max length: 16ft; Generator hours: 0700-2200; Open Apr-Nov; Tent & RV camping: $8; Elev: 7493ft/2284m; Tel: 505-757-6121; Nearest town: Las Vegas. GPS: 35.698386, -105.422791

39 • Echo Amphitheater

Total sites: 9; RV sites: 9; Central water; Flush toilets; No showers; No RV dump; Open all year; Tent & RV camping: $10; Elev: 6624ft/2019m; Tel: 505-684-2486; Nearest town: Abiquiu; Notes: No water in winter. GPS: 36.359703, -106.523562

40 • El Caso

Total sites: 22; RV sites: 22; No water; Vault toilets; Max length: 20ft; Stay limit: 14 days; Open May-Sep; Tent & RV camping: Free; Elev: 7695ft/2345m; Tel: 505-773-4678; Nearest town: Quemado. GPS: 34.137404, -108.471583

41 • El Porvenir

Total sites: 13; RV sites: 13; Central water; Vault toilets; No showers; No RV dump; Reservations not accepted; Max length: 32ft; Open Apr-Nov; Tent & RV camping: $8; Elev: 7556ft/2303m; Tel: 505-757-6121; Nearest town: Las Vegas. GPS: 35.710205, -105.412109

42 • El Rito Creek

Total sites: 9; RV sites: 9; No water; Vault toilets; Reservations not accepted; Open Apr-Nov; Tent & RV camping: Free; Elev: 8091ft/2466m; Tel: 575-581-4554; Nearest town: El Rito. GPS: 36.579414, -106.168605

43 • Elephant Rock

Total sites: 22; RV sites: 22; Central water; Vault toilets; No showers; No RV dump; Reservations accepted; Max length: 36ft; Open May-Sep; Tent & RV camping: $20; Elev: 8556ft/2608m; Tel: 505-586-0520; Nearest town: Red River. GPS: 36.707333, -105.448790

44 • Fawn Lakes

Total sites: 22; RV sites: 22; Central water; Vault toilets; No showers; No RV dump; Reservations accepted; Max length: 32ft; Open May-Oct; Tent & RV camping: $20; Elev: 8488ft/2587m; Tel: 505-586-0520; Nearest town: Red River. GPS: 36.705811, -105.456543

45 • Field Tract

Total sites: 15; RV sites: 15; Central water; Flush toilets; No showers; No RV dump; Reservations accepted; Max length: 22ft; Open Apr-Nov; Tent & RV camping: $8; Elev: 7382ft/2250m; Tel: 505-757-6121; Nearest town: Pecos; Notes: 6 sites have shelters. GPS: 35.686768, -105.693115

46 • Forks

Total sites: 7; RV sites: 7; No water; Vault toilets; Reservations not accepted; Open all year; Tent & RV camping: Free; Elev: 5571ft/1698m; Tel: 575-536-2250; Nearest town: Mimbres,. GPS: 33.183819, -108.205823

47 • Gallinas Upper

Total sites: 10; RV sites: 10; No water; Vault toilets; Reservations not accepted; Stay limit: 14 days; Open all year; Tent & RV camping: Free; Elev: 7024ft/2141m; Tel: 575-388-8201; Nearest town: Mimbres,. GPS: 32.898743, -107.823695

48 • Goat Hill

Total sites: 6; RV sites: 6; No water; Vault toilets; Reservations not accepted; Max length: 32ft; Open May-Oct; Tent & RV camping: $8; Elev: 7716ft/2352m; Tel: 575-586-0520; Nearest town: Questa. GPS: 36.688141, -105.540516

49 • Grapevine

Total sites: 20; No water; Vault toilets; No showers; No RV dump; Open all year; Tents only: Free; Elev: 5584ft/1702m; Tel: 575-536-2250; Nearest town: Silver City. GPS: 33.179336, -108.204978

50 • Head Of the Ditch

Total sites: 12; RV sites: 4; No water; Vault toilets; Reservations not accepted; Max length: 40ft; Open all year; Tent & RV camping: Free; Elev: 7244ft/2208m; Tel: 505-547-2612; Nearest town: Alpine AZ. GPS: 33.818745, -108.990777

51 • Hodges

Total sites: 8; RV sites: 8; No water; Vault toilets; Open May-Oct; Tent & RV camping: Free; Elev: 8478ft/2584m; Tel: 575-587-2255; Nearest town: Rodarte. GPS: 36.114022, -105.639376

52 • Holy Ghost

Total sites: 23; No water; Vault toilets; No showers; No RV dump; Reservations not accepted; Max length: 32ft; Generator hours: 0700-2200; Open Apr-Nov; Tents only: $8; Elev: 8379ft/2554m; Tel: 505-757-6121; Nearest town: Santa Fe. GPS: 35.773000, -105.701000

53 • Hopewell Lake

Total sites: 21; RV sites: 21; Central water; Vault toilets; No showers; No RV dump; Reservations accepted; Open May-Sep; Tent & RV camping: $20; Elev: 9754ft/2973m; Tel: 505-758-8678; Nearest town: Tres Piedras. GPS: 36.704448, -106.235506

54 • Iron Creek

Total sites: 15; RV sites: 15; No water; Vault toilets; Reservations not accepted; Max length: 17ft; Stay limit: 14 days; Open Mar-Oct; Tent & RV camping: Free; Elev: 7260ft/2213m; Tel: 505-536-2250; Nearest town: Mimbres. GPS: 32.909123, -107.805018

55 • Jacks Creek

Total sites: 39; RV sites: 39; Central water; Vault toilets; No showers; No RV dump; Reservations not accepted; Max length: 32ft; Open Apr-Nov; Tent & RV camping: $10; Elev: 9006ft/2745m; Tel: 505-757-6121; Nearest town: Pecos. GPS: 35.841372, -105.654891

56 • James Canyon

Total sites: 5; RV sites: 5; No water; Vault toilets; Reservations not accepted; Max length: 16ft; Open all year; Tent & RV camping: Free; Elev: 6801ft/2073m; Nearest town: Tularosa. GPS: 32.904536, -105.504667

57 • Jemez Falls

Total sites: 52; RV sites: 52; Central water; Vault toilets; No showers; No RV dump; Reservation required; Max length: 40ft; Open May-Sep; Tent & RV camping: $10; Elev: 8008ft/2441m; Tel: 505-829-3535; Nearest town: Jemez Springs. GPS: 35.824173, -106.606912

58 • John F Kennedy

Total sites: 14; RV sites: 14; No water; No toilets; Reservations not accepted; Stay limit: 14 days; Open all year; Tent & RV camping: Fee unknown; Elev: 6201ft/1890m; Tel: 505-847-2990; Nearest town: Belen. GPS: 34.671448, -106.468076

59 • Johnson Mesa

Total sites: 17; RV sites: 17; No water; Vault toilets; Reservations not accepted; Max length: 30ft; Open Apr-Nov; Tent & RV camping: Free; Elev: 9465ft/2885m; Tel: 505-757-6121; Nearest town: Las Vegas. GPS: 35.703394, -105.468662

60 • Junebug

Total sites: 20; RV sites: 20; Central water; Vault toilets; No showers; No RV dump; Reservations not accepted; Max length: 22ft; Open May-Sep; Tent & RV camping: $18; Elev: 8606ft/2623m; Tel: 505-586-0520; Nearest town: Red River. GPS: 36.707764, -105.434814

61 • Juniper

Total sites: 34; RV sites: 17; Elec sites: 17; Central water; Vault toilets; No showers; No RV dump; Reservations not accepted; Max length: 30ft; Stay limit: 14 days; Open May-Sep; Tents: $10/RVs: $15; Elev: 7720ft/2353m; Tel: 575-773-4678; Nearest town: Quemado. GPS: 34.137674, -108.488936

62 • Kingston

Total sites: 2; No water; Vault toilets; Reservations not accepted; Max length: 20ft; Stay limit: 14 days; Open Sep-Jun; Tents only: Free; Elev: 6184ft/1885m; Tel: 575-388-8201; Nearest town: Kingston. GPS: 32.918414, -107.700616

63 • La Junta Canyon

Total sites: 30; RV sites: 30; Central water; Vault toilets; No showers; No RV dump; Reservations not accepted; Max length: 16ft; Tent & RV camping: $6; Elev: 8707ft/2654m; Tel: 575-587-2255; Nearest town: Taos. GPS: 36.127856, -105.497767

64 • La Sombra

Total sites: 13; No water; Vault toilets; Reservations not accepted; Max length: 16ft; Open May-Oct; Tents only: $6; Elev: 8008ft/2441m; Tel: 575-587-2255; Nearest town: Taos. GPS: 36.369141, -105.473389

65 • Laguna Larga

Total sites: 4; RV sites: 4; No water; No toilets; Reservations not accepted; Open May-Oct; Tent & RV camping: Free; Elev: 9003ft/2744m; Tel: 575-758-8678; Nearest town: Tres Piedras. GPS: 36.884181, -106.108633

66 • Las Petacas

Total sites: 9; RV sites: 9; No water; Vault toilets; Reservations not accepted; Max length: 16ft; Open May-Oct; Tent & RV camping: $10; Elev: 7438ft/2267m; Tel: 575-587-2255; Nearest town: Taos. GPS: 36.381683, -105.521949

67 • Links Tract

Total sites: 12; RV sites: 12; No water; Vault toilets; Reservations not accepted; Max length: 32ft; Generator hours: 0700-2200; Tent & RV camping: Free; Elev: 8176ft/2492m; Nearest town: Pecos. GPS: 35.757152, -105.662069

68 • Lobo Canyon

Total sites: 9; No water; Vault toilets; Reservations not accepted; Stay limit: 14 days; Open May-Sep; Tents only: Free; Elev: 7487ft/2282m; Tel: 505-287-8833; Nearest town: Grants. GPS: 35.203738, -107.715035

69 • Lower Canjilon Lake

Total sites: 48; RV sites: 48; No water; Vault toilets; Reservations not accepted; Max length: 22ft; Stay limit: 14 days; Tent & RV camping: $5; Elev: 9859ft/3005m; Tel: 575-684-2489; Nearest town: Cebolla. GPS: 36.549461, -106.344159

70 • Lower Hondo

Total sites: 5; RV sites: 4; No water; Vault toilets; Reservations not accepted; Max length: 16ft; Open May-Oct; Tent & RV camping: Free; Elev: 7861ft/2396m; Tel: 575-586-0520; Nearest town: Taos. GPS: 36.548528, -105.549558

71 • Luna Park

Total sites: 3; RV sites: 3; No water; Vault toilets; Reservations not accepted; Max length: 20ft; Stay limit: 14 days; Open Mar-Nov; Tent & RV camping: Free; Elev: 6842ft/2085m; Tel: 575-854-2281; Nearest town: Monticello. GPS: 33.496266, -107.416005

72 • McCrystal Creek

Total sites: 60; RV sites: 60; No water; Vault toilets; Reservations not accepted; Max length: 32ft; Open May-Sep; Tent & RV camping: $13; Elev: 8140ft/2481m; Tel: 505-586-0520; Nearest town: Costilla; Notes: 6 sites for horse campers. GPS: 36.776981, -105.113884

73 • McGaffey

Total sites: 29; RV sites: 29; Central water; No toilets; No showers; No RV dump; Reservations not accepted; Max length: 22ft; Stay limit: 14 days; Open May-Sep; Tents: $10/RVs: $10-15; Elev: 7813ft/2381m; Tel: 505-287-8833; Nearest town: Fort Wingate. GPS: 35.368302, -108.522008

74 • McMillan

Total sites: 3; RV sites: 3; No water; Vault toilets; Reservations not accepted; Max length: 17ft; Stay limit: 14 days; Open Apr-Oct; Tent & RV camping: Free; Elev: 7034ft/2144m; Tel: 575-388-8201; Nearest town: Silver City. GPS: 32.924001, -108.213686

75 • Mesa

Total sites: 36; RV sites: 12; Elec sites: 12; Water at site; No toilets; No showers; RV dump; Reservations not accepted; Stay limit: 14 days; Open all year; Tents: $10/RVs: $15; Elev: 6151ft/1875m; Tel: 505-536-2250; Nearest town: Mimbres. GPS: 33.032886, -108.155379

76 • Middle Canjilon Lake

Total sites: 22; RV sites: 22; Vault toilets; Reservations not accepted; Stay limit: 14 days; Tent & RV camping: $5; Elev: 10023ft/3055m; Tel: 575-684-2489; Nearest town: Cebolla. GPS: 36.554733, -106.332348

77 • Mills Canyon

Total sites: 12; No water; Vault toilets; Reservations not accepted; Stay limit: 14 days; Open all year; Tents only: Free; Elev: 5154ft/1571m; Tel: 505-374-9652; Nearest town: Roy; Notes: High clearance vehicles recommended. GPS: 36.048109, -104.377551

78 • Mills Canyon Rim

Total sites: 6; RV sites: 6; No water; Vault toilets; Reservations not accepted; Stay limit: 14 days; Tent & RV camping: Free; Elev: 5738ft/1749m; Tel: 505-374-9652; Nearest town: Roy. GPS: 36.071977, -104.350478

79 • Monjeau

Total sites: 4; No water; Vault toilets; Stay limit: 14 days; Open May-Sep; Tents only: Free; Elev: 9258ft/2822m; Tel: 575-257-4095; Nearest town: Tularosa. GPS: 33.432111, -105.730042

80 • New Canyon

Total sites: 3; RV sites: 3; No water; Vault toilets; Reservations not accepted; Max length: 18ft; Stay limit: 14 days; Open all year; Tent & RV camping: Free; Elev: 7904ft/2409m; Nearest town: Tajique. GPS: 34.671133, -106.410193

81 • Oak Grove

Total sites: 30; RV sites: 30; No water; Vault toilets; Reservations not accepted; Max length: 18ft; Stay limit: 14 days; Open May-Sep; Tent & RV camping: $6; Elev: 8379ft/2554m; Tel: 575-257-4095; Nearest town: Ruidoso. GPS: 33.396176, -105.747131

82 • Ojo Redondo

Total sites: 15; RV sites: 15; No water; Vault toilets; Reservations not accepted; Max length: 22ft; Stay limit: 14 days; Open May-Sep; Tent & RV camping: Free; Elev: 8835ft/2693m; Tel: 505-287-8833; Nearest town: Thoreau. GPS: 35.158849, -108.107332

83 • Paliza

Total sites: 30; RV sites: 30; No water; Vault toilets; Reservations not accepted; Max length: 16ft; Stay limit: 14 days; Open May-Oct; Tent & RV camping: $8; Elev: 6860ft/2091m; Tel: 575-829-3535; Nearest town: San Ysidra; Notes: High clearance vehicle recommended. GPS: 35.704385, -106.627059

84 • Panchuela

Total sites: 5; Central water; Vault toilets; No showers; No RV dump; Reservations not accepted; Generator hours: 0700-2200; Open Apr-Nov; Tents only: $5; Elev: 8432ft/2570m; Tel: 505-757-6121; Nearest town: Pecos. GPS: 35.831094, -105.665007

85 • Pines

Total sites: 24; RV sites: 24; Central water; Vault toilets; No showers; No RV dump; Reservations not accepted; Max length: 40ft; Open May-Sep; Tent & RV camping: $22; Elev: 8691ft/2649m; Tel: 575-682-2551; Nearest town: Cloudcroft. GPS: 32.966309, -105.737305

86 • Pinon

Total sites: 23; Central water; Vault toilets; No showers; RV dump; Reservations not accepted; Stay limit: 14 days; Open May-Sep; Tents only: $10; Elev: 7877ft/2401m; Tel: 575-773-4678; Nearest town: Quemado; Notes: 2 reservable group sites: $35-$55, Dump fee: $5. GPS: 34.137918, -108.483035

87 • Pueblo Park

Total sites: 10; No water; Vault toilets; Reservations not accepted; Open Apr-Nov; Tents only: Free; Elev: 6217ft/1895m; Tel: 505-539-2481; Nearest town: Reserve. GPS: 33.595066, -108.962161

88 • Quaking Aspen

Total sites: 20; RV sites: 20; No water; Vault toilets; Reservations not accepted; Max length: 22ft; Stay limit: 14 days; Open May-Sep; Tent & RV camping: $5; Elev: 7579ft/2310m; Tel: 505-287-8833; Nearest town: Wingate. GPS: 35.407179, -108.539472

89 • Railroad Canyon

Total sites: 6; RV sites: 6; No water; Vault toilets; Reservations not accepted; Open all year; Tent & RV camping: Free; Elev: 7149ft/2179m; Tel: 575-388-8201; Nearest town: Mimbres,. GPS: 32.908974, -107.816725

90 • Red Canyon Lower

Total sites: 38; RV sites: 38; No water; Vault toilets; Reservations not accepted; Max length: 22ft; Stay limit: 14 days; Open Apr-Oct; Tent & RV camping: $7; Elev: 7723ft/2354m; Nearest town: Tajique. GPS: 34.616876, -106.403317

91 • Red Cloud

Total sites: 5; RV sites: 5; No water; Vault toilets; Reservations not accepted; Stay limit: 14 days; Tent & RV camping: Free; Elev: 7264ft/2214m; Nearest town: Corona. GPS: 34.190267, -105.725883

92 • Redondo

Total sites: 60; RV sites: 60; No water; Vault toilets; Reservations not accepted; Max length: 30ft; Open May-Oct; Tent & RV camping: $10; Elev: 8140ft/2481m; Tel: 505-829-3535; Nearest town: Jemez Springs. GPS: 35.861606, -106.626933

93 • Resumidero

Total sites: 15; RV sites: 6; No water; Vault toilets; Reservations not accepted; Max length: 16ft; Open May-Sep; Tent & RV camping: Free; Elev: 8976ft/2736m; Tel: 575-638-5526; Nearest town: Coyote. GPS: 36.113076, -106.745846

94 • Rio Chama

Total sites: 18; RV sites: 18; No water; Vault toilets; Reservations not accepted; Max length: 20ft; Open Apr-Oct; Tent & RV camping: Free; Elev: 6427ft/1959m; Tel: 575-638-5526; Nearest town: Abiquiu. GPS: 36.355248, -106.673673

95 • Rio de Las Vacas

Total sites: 15; RV sites: 15; Central water; Vault toilets; No showers; No RV dump; Reservations accepted; Max length: 30ft; Open May-Sep; Tent & RV camping: $10; Elev: 8353ft/2546m; Tel: 505-289-3265; Nearest town: Cuba. GPS: 35.997017, -106.806788

96 • Rio de Los Pinos

Total sites: 4; RV sites: 4; No water; Vault toilets; Reservations not accepted; Max length: 16ft; Open Jun-Sep; Tent & RV camping: Free; Elev: 8290ft/2527m; Tel: 575-758-8678; Nearest town: Tres Piedras. GPS: 36.955753, -106.178232

97 • Rio Puerco

Total sites: 5; RV sites: 5; No water; Vault toilets; Reservations not accepted; Max length: 20ft; Open May-Sep; Tent & RV camping: Free; Elev: 8271ft/2521m; Tel: 575-638-5526; Nearest town: Coyote; Notes: Very tight turn around loop. GPS: 36.100641, -106.723683

98 • Rocky Canyon

Total sites: 2; RV sites: 2; No water; Vault toilets; Max length: 17ft; Open Apr-Nov; Tent & RV camping: Free; Elev: 7484ft/2281m; Tel: 575-536-2250; Nearest town: Mimbres,. GPS: 33.100174, -108.013248

99 • Saddle

Total sites: 16; RV sites: 16; Central water; Flush toilets; Showers; RV dump; Reservations not accepted; Max length: 32ft; Open May-Sep; Tent & RV camping: $20; Elev: 8983ft/2738m; Tel: 575-682-2551; Nearest town: Cloudcroft; Notes: Fee showers and RV dump available at nearby Silver CG. GPS: 32.970459, -105.725586

100 • San Antonio

Total sites: 21; RV sites: 21; Elec sites: 6; Water at site; Vault toilets; No showers; No RV dump; Reservations accepted; Max length: 35ft; Open May-Sep; Tents: $10/RVs: $10-15; Elev: 7812ft/2381m; Tel: 575-829-3535; Nearest town: Jemez Springs; Notes: Group area with 9 sites. GPS: 35.886613, -106.646995

101 • Santa Barbara

Total sites: 22; RV sites: 22; Central water; Vault toilets; No showers; No RV dump; Reservations accepted; Open May-Sep; Tent & RV camping: $20; Elev: 8921ft/2719m; Tel: 505-587-2255; Nearest town: Penasco. GPS: 36.086576, -105.609551

102 • Silver

Total sites: 30; RV sites: 30; Central water; Flush toilets; Pay showers; RV dump; Reservations not accepted; Max length: 32ft; Open Apr-Oct; Tent & RV camping: $22; Elev: 9003ft/2744m; Tel: 505-682-2551; Nearest town: Cloudcroft; Notes: $5 dump fee. GPS: 32.973389, -105.725342

103 • Silver Overflow

Total sites: 52; RV sites: 52; Central water; Vault toilets; Showers; No RV dump; Reservations not accepted; Open Apr-Oct; Tent & RV camping: $18; Elev: 8990ft/2740m; Tel: 575-682-2551; Nearest town: Cloudcroft; Notes: Fee showers and RV available at nearby Silver CG. GPS: 32.975605, -105.723941

104 • Skyline

Total sites: 17; No water; Vault toilets; Reservations not accepted; Stay limit: 14 days; Open all year; Tents only: Free; Elev: 8953ft/2729m; Tel: 575-257-4095; Nearest town: Ruidoso; Notes: Rough road. GPS: 33.419281, -105.733444

105 • Sleepy Grass

Total sites: 15; RV sites: 15; Central water; Vault toilets; No showers; No RV dump; Reservations not accepted; Max length: 16ft; Open May-Sep; Tent & RV camping: $16; Elev: 8855ft/2699m; Tel: 575-682-2551; Nearest town: Cloudcroft; Notes: 2 double and 3 triple sites. GPS: 32.943902, -105.725759

106 • South Fork

Total sites: 60; RV sites: 60; Central water; Vault toilets; No showers; No RV dump; Reservations not accepted; Max length: 35ft; Stay limit: 14 days; Open May-Sep; Tent & RV camping: $10; Elev: 7612ft/2320m; Tel: 505-257-4095; Nearest town: Ruidoso. GPS: 33.449525, -105.753432

107 • Springtime

Total sites: 6; No water; Vault toilets; Reservations not accepted; Stay limit: 14 days; Open Mar-Nov; Tents only: Free; Elev: 7385ft/2251m; Tel: 575-854-2281; Nearest town: Monticello; Notes: Log shelters - trailers must park by entrance. GPS: 33.575401, -107.404515

108 • Tajique

Total sites: 6; No water; Vault toilets; Reservations not accepted; Stay limit: 14 days; Open all year; Tents only: Free; Elev: 7018ft/2139m; Nearest town: Tajique. GPS: 34.765894, -106.327772

109 • Three Rivers

Total sites: 12; RV sites: 12; Central water; Vault toilets; No showers; No RV dump; Reservations not accepted; Max length: 25ft; Stay limit: 14 days; Open all year; Tent & RV camping: $6; Elev: 6408ft/1953m; Tel: 575-257-4095; Nearest town: Tularosa. GPS: 33.401275, -105.884961

110 • Trampas Diamante

Total sites: 5; RV sites: 5; No water; Vault toilets; Max length: 16ft; Open May-Sep; Tent & RV camping: Fee unknown; Elev: 8491ft/2588m; Nearest town: Penasco. GPS: 36.067077, -105.708816

111 • Trampas Trailhead

Total sites: 4; RV sites: 4; No water; Vault toilets; Open all year; Tent & RV camping: Free; Elev: 9035ft/2754m; Nearest town: Penasco. GPS: 36.044556, -105.673089

112 • Twining

Total sites: 4; RV sites: 4; No water; Vault toilets; Max length: 22ft; Open May-Oct; Tent & RV camping: Free; Elev: 9426ft/2873m; Tel: 575-586-0520; Nearest town: Taos; Notes: Self-contained units only. GPS: 36.596690, -105.449619

113 • Upper End

Total sites: 12; RV sites: 12; Central water; Vault toilets; No showers; No RV dump; Reservations not accepted; Max length: 32ft; Stay limit: 14 days; Open all year; Tent & RV camping: $10; Elev: 6070ft/1850m; Tel: 505-536-2250; Nearest town: Mimbres. GPS: 33.027458, -108.152117

114 • Upper Karr

Total sites: 6; RV sites: 6; No water; Vault toilets; Max length: 16ft; Stay limit: 14 days; Open all year; Tent & RV camping: Free; Elev: 9341ft/2847m; Tel: 575-682-2551; Nearest town: Cloudcroft. GPS: 32.880363, -105.780001

115 • Upper Karr Canyon

Total sites: 6; RV sites: 6; No water; Vault toilets; Reservations not accepted; Max length: 16ft; Stay limit: 14 days; Open all year; Tent & RV camping: Free; Elev: 9400ft/2865m; Tel: 575-434-7200; Nearest town: Cloudcroft. GPS: 32.880557, -105.780365

116 • Upper La Junta

Total sites: 8; RV sites: 8; Central water; Vault toilets; No showers; No RV dump; Reservations not accepted; Open Jun-Oct; Tent & RV camping: $11; Elev: 9203ft/2805m; Tel: 575-587-2255; Nearest town: Penasco. GPS: 36.147822, -105.455297

117 • Valle Tio Vinces

Total sites: 4; RV sites: 4; No water; Vault toilets; Reservations not accepted; Max length: 40ft; Stay limit: 14 days; Open all year; Tent & RV camping: Free; Elev: 8120ft/2475m; Tel: 575-773-4678; Nearest town: Aragon. GPS: 34.029903, -108.350778

118 • Vista Linda

Total sites: 13; RV sites: 13; Central water; Vault toilets; No showers; No RV dump; Reservations not accepted; Max length: 40ft; Stay limit: 14 days; Generator hours: 0700-2100; Open Mar-Oct; Tent & RV camping: $10; Elev: 5860ft/1786m; Tel: 575-829-3535; Nearest town: San Ysidro. GPS: 35.717363, -106.721290

119 • Water Canyon

Total sites: 16; RV sites: 16; No water; Vault toilets; Reservations not accepted; Max length: 20ft; Stay limit: 14 days; Open Mar-Nov; Tent & RV camping: Free; Elev: 6870ft/2094m; Tel: 505-854-2381; Nearest town: Magdalena; Notes: Rough twisting road. GPS: 34.024619, -107.133125

120 • Willow Creek

Total sites: 9; RV sites: 9; No water; Vault toilets; Reservations not accepted; Max length: 17ft; Open Apr-Nov; Tent & RV camping: Fee unknown; Elev: 7956ft/2425m; Tel: 505-773-4678; Nearest town: Reserve. GPS: 33.402367, -108.579565

New York

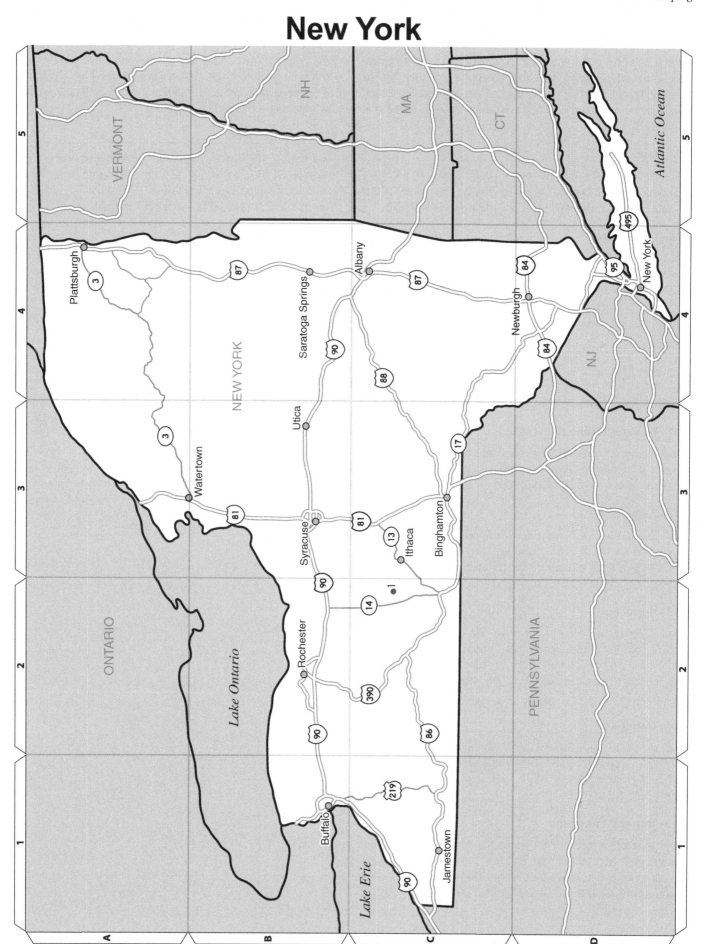

New York Camping Areas

1 • Blueberry Patch

Total sites: 9; RV sites: 9; No water; Vault toilets; No showers; No RV dump; Reservations not accepted; Max length: 24ft; Open May-Oct; Tent & RV camping: $15; Elev: 1831ft/558m; Tel: 607-546-4470; Nearest town: Logan. GPS: 42.483471, -76.799511

North Carolina

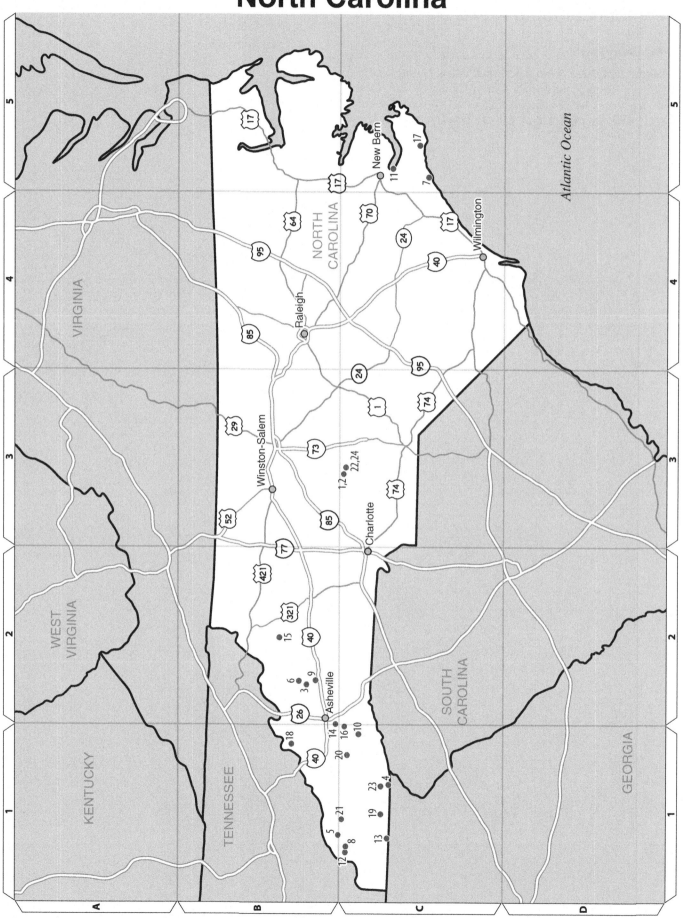

North Carolina Camping Areas

1 • Arrowhead

Total sites: 48; RV sites: 44; Elec sites: 33; Central water; Flush toilets; Showers; RV dump; Reservations accepted; Open all year; Tent & RV camping: $20-27; Elev: 584ft/178m; Tel: 910-576-6391; Nearest town: Uwharrie. GPS: 35.438468, -80.070593

2 • Badin Lake

Total sites: 34; RV sites: 33; Central water; Flush toilets; Showers; No RV dump; Reservations accepted; Open all year; Tent & RV camping: $20; Elev: 561ft/171m; Tel: 910-576-6391; Nearest town: Troy. GPS: 35.448126, -80.078354

3 • Black Mountain

Total sites: 37; RV sites: 37; Elec sites: 3; Central water; Flush toilets; Showers; RV dump; Reservations not accepted; Open Apr-Oct; Tents: $22/RVs: $22-29; Elev: 3036ft/925m; Tel: 828-675-5616; Nearest town: Asheville. GPS: 35.748351, -82.225523

4 • Blue Valley

Total sites: 22; RV sites: 22; No water; Vault toilets; Reservations not accepted; Open all year; Tent & RV camping: Free; Elev: 2621ft/799m; Tel: 828-524-6441; Nearest town: Highlands. GPS: 35.009317, -83.227345

5 • Cable Cove

Total sites: 26; RV sites: 26; Central water; Vault toilets; No showers; No RV dump; Reservations not accepted; Open Apr-Oct; Tent & RV camping: $15; Elev: 1804ft/550m; Tel: 828-479-6431; Nearest town: Fontana Village. GPS: 35.432332, -83.751514

6 • Carolina Hemlocks

Total sites: 37; RV sites: 34; Central water; Flush toilets; Pay showers; No RV dump; Reservations accepted; Open Apr-Oct; Tent & RV camping: $22; Elev: 2772ft/845m; Tel: 828-675-5509; Nearest town: Burnsville. GPS: 35.804596, -82.203406

7 • Cedar Point

Total sites: 40; RV sites: 40; Elec sites: 40; Central water; Flush toilets; Showers; RV dump; Reservations accepted; Max length: 50ft; Open all year; Tent & RV camping: $27; Elev: 23ft/7m; Tel: 252-393-7642; Nearest town: Cape Carteret. GPS: 34.692527, -77.083597

8 • Cheoah Point

Total sites: 26; RV sites: 26; Elec sites: 6; Central water; Flush toilets; Showers; No RV dump; Reservations accepted; Open Apr-Oct; Tent & RV camping: $20-25; Elev: 1982ft/604m; Tel: 828-479-6431; Nearest town: Robbinsville. GPS: 35.370605, -83.871338

9 • Curtis Creek

Total sites: 14; RV sites: 8; Central water; Vault toilets; No showers; No RV dump; Reservations accepted; Generator hours: 0600-2200; Open Apr-Dec; Tent & RV camping: $10; Elev: 1690ft/515m; Nearest town: Old Fort. GPS: 35.671691, -82.192913

10 • Davidson River

Total sites: 163; RV sites: 163; Elec sites: 3; Central water; Flush toilets; Showers; No RV dump; Reservations accepted; Open all year; Tents: $22/RVs: $22-28; Elev: 2201ft/671m; Tel: 828-862-5960; Nearest town: Brevard; Notes: FHU sites. GPS: 35.282898, -82.726105

11 • Fishers Landing

Total sites: 9; Central water; Vault toilets; No showers; No RV dump; Reservations not accepted; Open all year; Tents only: Free; Elev: 10ft/3m; Tel: 252-638-5628; Nearest town: New Bern. GPS: 35.000782, -76.976317

12 • Horse Cove

Total sites: 18; RV sites: 11; Central water; No toilets; No showers; No RV dump; Reservations not accepted; Open all year; Tent & RV camping: $15; Elev: 2076ft/633m; Tel: 828-479-6431; Nearest town: Robbinsville; Notes: No water in winter. GPS: 35.365251, -83.921242

13 • Jackrabbit Mountain

Total sites: 100; RV sites: 90; Central water; Flush toilets; Showers; RV dump; Reservations accepted; Open May-Sep; Tent & RV camping: $20; Elev: 1946ft/593m; Tel: 828-837-5152; Nearest town: Hayesville. GPS: 35.011230, -83.772705

14 • Lake Powhatan

Total sites: 85; RV sites: 54; Elec sites: 24; Water at site; Flush toilets; Showers; RV dump; Reservations accepted; Open Apr-Oct; Tents: $22/RVs: $22-31; Elev: 2182ft/665m; Tel: 828-670-5627; Nearest town: Asheville; Notes: 21 FHU. GPS: 35.482503, -82.627823

15 • Mortimer

Total sites: 21; RV sites: 16; Central water; Flush toilets; Showers; No RV dump; Reservations not accepted; Generator hours: 0600-2200; Open Apr-Nov; Tent & RV camping: $15; Elev: 1631ft/497m; Tel: 828-652-2144; Nearest town: Lenoir. GPS: 35.991595, -81.761015

16 • North Mills River

Total sites: 31; RV sites: 31; Central water; Flush toilets; Showers; No RV dump; Reservations accepted; Open all year; Tent & RV camping: $22; Elev: 2274ft/693m; Tel: 828-890-3284; Nearest town: Mills River; Notes: 1 FHU, $11 in winter - no water. GPS: 35.406250, -82.646240

17 • Oyster Point

Total sites: 15; RV sites: 15; Central water; Vault toilets; No showers; No RV dump; Reservations not accepted; Open all year; Tent & RV camping: $8; Elev: 43ft/13m; Tel: 252-638-5628; Nearest town: Morehead City. GPS: 34.760951, -76.761564

18 • Rocky Bluff

Total sites: 15; RV sites: 15; Central water; No toilets; No showers; No RV dump; Reservations not accepted; Stay limit: 14 days; Open May-Sep; Tent & RV camping: $15; Elev: 1798ft/548m;

Tel: 828-689-9694; Nearest town: Hot Springs. GPS: 35.861542, -82.846535

19 • Standing Indian

Total sites: 81; RV sites: 81; Central water; Flush toilets; Showers; RV dump; Reservations accepted; Open Apr-Nov; Tent & RV camping: $20; Elev: 3576ft/1090m; Nearest town: Franklin; Notes: Group site: $75. GPS: 35.076542, -83.528542

20 • Sunburst

Total sites: 9; RV sites: 9; Central water; Flush toilets; No showers; No RV dump; Reservations not accepted; Open May-Oct; Tent & RV camping: $15; Elev: 3163ft/964m; Tel: 828-648-7841; Nearest town: Canton. GPS: 35.373863, -82.940325

21 • Tsali

Total sites: 42; RV sites: 29; Central water; Flush toilets; Showers; No RV dump; Reservations not accepted; Open Apr-Oct; Tent & RV camping: $20; Elev: 1801ft/549m; Nearest town: Bryson City. GPS: 35.407471, -83.587402

22 • Uwharrie Hunt Camp

Total sites: 8; Central water; Vault toilets; No showers; No RV dump; Reservations not accepted; Open all year; Tents only: $5; Elev: 423ft/129m; Tel: 910-576-6391; Nearest town: Troy. GPS: 35.428983, -80.020376

23 • Vanhook Glade

Total sites: 18; RV sites: 14; Central water; Flush toilets; Showers; No RV dump; Reservations accepted; Max length: 34ft; Open Apr-Oct; Tent & RV camping: $24; Elev: 3340ft/1018m; Tel: 828-526-5918; Nearest town: Highlands. GPS: 35.077285, -83.248173

24 • West Morris Mountain

Total sites: 14; RV sites: 14; No water; Vault toilets; Open all year; Tent & RV camping: $5; Elev: 482ft/147m; Tel: 910-576-6391; Nearest town: Troy; Notes: 2 group sites - $10. GPS: 35.428352, -79.993708

North Dakota

MINNESOTA

MANITOBA

SASKATCHEWAN

MT

NORTH DAKOTA

SOUTH DAKOTA

Grand Forks

Fargo

Jamestown

Bismarck

Minot

Williston

6

7

4

12

1

8

85

5

13

2

3

85

9,10,11

5

29

29

29

94

5

2

52

281

281

281

52

2

5

52

83

83

94

83

281

94

85

12

85

12

52

2

5

85

2

North Dakota Camping Areas

1 • Bennett Camp

Total sites: 13; RV sites: 13; Central water; Vault toilets; No showers; Stay limit: 14 days; Tent & RV camping: $6; Elev: 2188ft/667m; Tel: 701-842-2393; Nearest town: Watford City; Notes: Steep road. GPS: 47.490129, -103.349335

2 • Buffalo Gap

Total sites: 37; RV sites: 37; Central water; Flush toilets; Pay showers; No RV dump; Reservations not accepted; Stay limit: 1 day; Open all year; Tent & RV camping: $6; Elev: 2579ft/786m; Tel: 701-227-7800; Nearest town: Medora; Notes: Limited services in winter. GPS: 46.954550, -103.674660

3 • Burning Coal Vein

Total sites: 5; RV sites: 5; Central water; Vault toilets; No showers; No RV dump; Reservations not accepted; Stay limit: 14 days; Tent & RV camping: $10; Elev: 2526ft/770m; Tel: 701-227-7800; Nearest town: Belfield. GPS: 46.597091, -103.443322

4 • CCC

Total sites: 38; RV sites: 38; Central water; Vault toilets; No showers; No RV dump; Tent & RV camping: $6; Elev: 1968ft/600m; Tel: 701-842-2393; Nearest town: Watford City. GPS: 47.587159, -103.276698

5 • Elkhorn

Total sites: 9; RV sites: 9; Central water; Vault toilets; No showers; No RV dump; Reservations not accepted; Stay limit: 14 days; Tent & RV camping: $6; Elev: 2310ft/704m; Tel: 701-227-7800; Nearest town: Beach. GPS: 47.228665, -103.669126

6 • Hankinson Hills

Total sites: 15; RV sites: 15; Central water; Vault toilets; No showers; No RV dump; Reservations not accepted; Tent & RV camping: $6; Elev: 1063ft/324m; Tel: 701-683-4342; Nearest town: Hankinson; Notes: 6 equestrian sites. GPS: 46.118907, -96.967129

7 • Jorgen's Hollow

Total sites: 14; RV sites: 14; Central water; Vault toilets; No showers; No RV dump; Reservations not accepted; Tent & RV camping: Fee unknown; Elev: 1049ft/320m; Nearest town: Leonard; Notes: 7 horse sites. GPS: 46.524089, -97.202116

8 • Magpie Camp

Total sites: 11; RV sites: 11; Central water; Vault toilets; No showers; No RV dump; Reservations not accepted; Stay limit: 14 days; Tent & RV camping: $6; Elev: 2229ft/679m; Tel: 701-227-7800; Nearest town: Watford City. GPS: 47.308468, -103.473431

9 • Sather Lake - Bass Loop

Total sites: 6; RV sites: 6; No water; Vault toilets; Reservations not accepted; Stay limit: 14 days; Open all year; Tent & RV camping: $10; Elev: 2284ft/696m; Tel: 701-842-8500; Nearest town: Watford City. GPS: 47.672721, -103.805279

10 • Sather Lake - Perch Loop

Total sites: 6; RV sites: 6; No water; Vault toilets; Reservations not accepted; Stay limit: 14 days; Open all year; Tent & RV camping: $10; Elev: 2274ft/693m; Tel: 701-842-8500; Nearest town: Watford City. GPS: 47.665648, -103.810448

11 • Sather Lake - Trout Loop

Total sites: 5; RV sites: 5; No water; Vault toilets; Reservations not accepted; Stay limit: 14 days; Open all year; Tent & RV camping: $10; Elev: 2260ft/689m; Tel: 701-842-8500; Nearest town: Watford City. GPS: 47.669241, -103.811099

12 • Summit

Total sites: 5; RV sites: 3; No water; Vault toilets; Reservations not accepted; Tent & RV camping: Free; Elev: 2518ft/767m; Tel: 701-842-8500; Nearest town: Watford City. GPS: 47.539945, -103.241835

13 • Wannagan

Total sites: 10; RV sites: 10; Central water; Vault toilets; No showers; No RV dump; Reservations not accepted; Tent & RV camping: $6; Elev: 2434ft/742m; Tel: 701-227-7800; Nearest town: Beach. GPS: 47.055293, -103.587699

Ohio

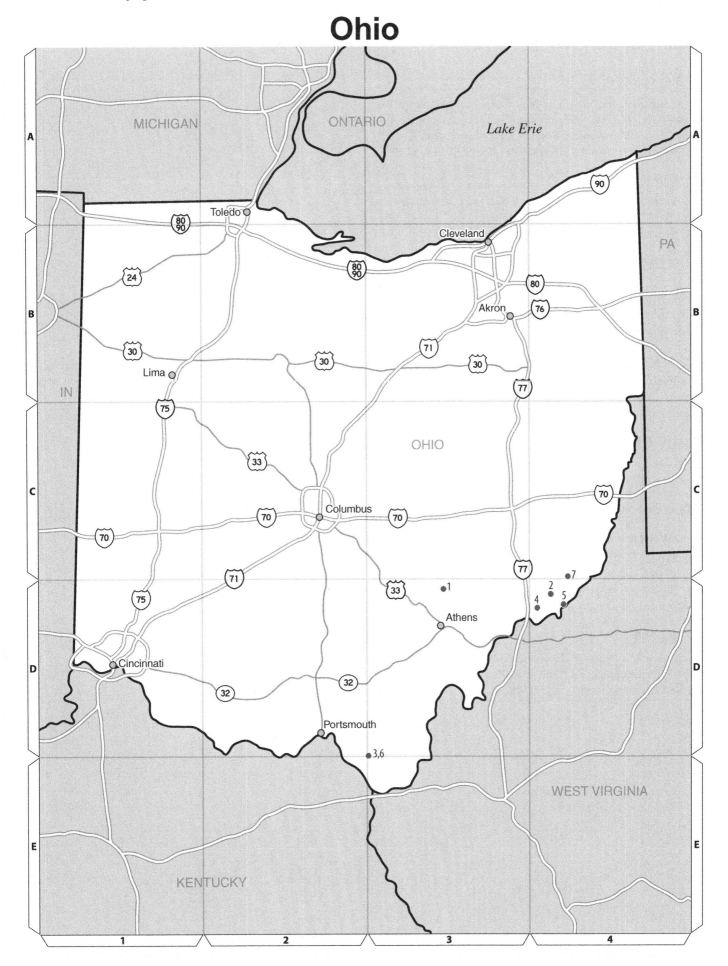

Ohio Camping Areas

1 • Burr Oak Cove

Total sites: 19; RV sites: 15; Central water; Vault toilets; No showers; No RV dump; Reservations not accepted; Open Apr-Dec; Tent & RV camping: $44119; Elev: 853ft/260m; Tel: 740-753-0101; Nearest town: Glouster. GPS: 39.549566, -82.060194

2 • Hune Bridge

Total sites: 3; RV sites: 3; No water; Vault toilets; Open all year; Tent & RV camping: Free; Elev: 643ft/196m; Tel: 740-373-9055; Nearest town: Marietta. GPS: 39.509969, -81.250889

3 • Iron Ridge at Lake Vesuvius

Total sites: 41; RV sites: 19; Elec sites: 22; Central water; Vault toilets; No showers; No RV dump; Open Apr-Oct; Tent & RV camping: $13-18; Elev: 748ft/228m; Tel: 740-534-6500; Nearest town: Ironton. GPS: 38.612635, -82.619392

4 • Lane Farm

Total sites: 4; RV sites: 4; No water; Vault toilets; Open all year; Tent & RV camping: Free; Elev: 610ft/186m; Tel: 740-373-9055; Nearest town: Marietta. GPS: 39.435556, -81.358611

5 • Leith Run

Total sites: 21; RV sites: 18; Elec sites: 18; Central water; Flush toilets; Showers; RV dump; Open Apr-Oct; Tents: $15/RVs: $21; Elev: 607ft/185m; Tel: 740-373-9055; Nearest town: Newport. GPS: 39.445474, -81.151795

6 • Oak Hill (Lake Vesuvius)

Total sites: 32; RV sites: 32; Elec sites: 32; Water at site; Flush toilets; Showers; RV dump; Open Apr-Oct; Tent & RV camping: $21; Elev: 820ft/250m; Tel: 740-534-6500; Nearest town: Ironton. GPS: 38.614414, -82.633615

7 • Ring Mill

Total sites: 3; RV sites: 3; No water; Vault toilets; Open all year; Tent & RV camping: Free; Elev: 702ft/214m; Tel: 740-373-9055; Nearest town: Sistersville. GPS: 39.608231, -81.122444

Oklahoma

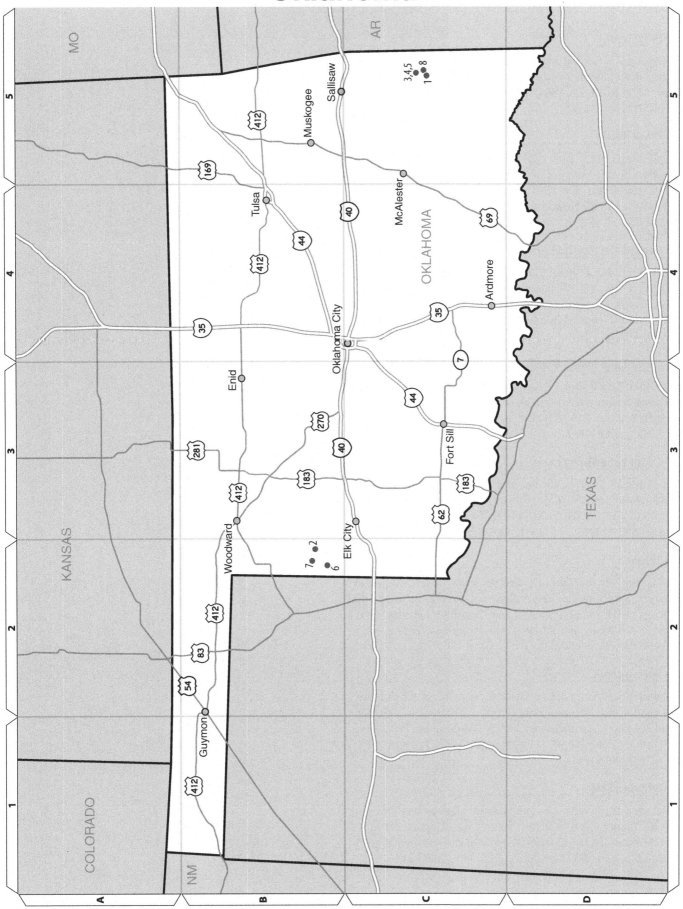

Oklahoma Camping Areas

1 • Billy Creek

Total sites: 12; Central water; Vault toilets; No showers; No RV dump; Reservations not accepted; Open all year; Tents only: Free; Elev: 877ft/267m; Tel: 580-494-6402; Nearest town: Muse. GPS: 34.690822, -94.731482

2 • Black Kettle

Total sites: 12; RV sites: 12; Central water; Vault toilets; No showers; No RV dump; Reservations not accepted; Max length: 27ft; Open all year; Tent & RV camping: Free; Elev: 2100ft/640m; Tel: 580-497-2143; Nearest town: Cheyenne. GPS: 35.745318, -99.714557

3 • Cedar Lake North Shore

Total sites: 24; RV sites: 24; Elec sites: 24; Central water; Vault toilets; No showers; RV dump; Reservations accepted; Open all year; Tent & RV camping: $21; Elev: 830ft/253m; Tel: 918-653-2991; Nearest town: Heavener; Notes: 24 FHU. GPS: 34.779858, -94.693582

4 • Cedar Lake Sandy Beach

Total sites: 22; RV sites: 22; Elec sites: 18; Water at site; RV dump; Reservations accepted; Open all year; Tents: $10/RVs: $17; Elev: 715ft/218m; Tel: 918-653-2991; Nearest town: Heavener. GPS: 34.778082, -94.697967

5 • Cedar Lake Shady Lane

Total sites: 25; RV sites: 25; Elec sites: 25; Water at site; RV dump; Reservations accepted; Open all year; Tent & RV camping: $21; Elev: 758ft/231m; Tel: 918-653-2991; Nearest town: Heavener; Notes: 25 FHU. GPS: 34.774981, -94.695581

6 • Skipout

Total sites: 12; RV sites: 12; Central water; Vault toilets; No showers; No RV dump; Reservations not accepted; Max length: 27ft; Stay limit: 14 days; Open all year; Tent & RV camping: Free; Elev: 2313ft/705m; Tel: 580-497-2143; Nearest town: Cheyenne. GPS: 35.635595, -99.880054

7 • Spring Creek

Total sites: 5; RV sites: 5; Central water; Vault toilets; No showers; No RV dump; Reservations not accepted; Max length: 22ft; Stay limit: 14 days; Open all year; Tent & RV camping: Free; Elev: 2198ft/670m; Tel: 580-497-2143; Nearest town: Cheyenne. GPS: 35.772811, -99.839531

8 • Winding Stair

Total sites: 28; RV sites: 23; Central water; Flush toilets; Showers; No RV dump; Open Mar-Dec; Tent & RV camping: $8; Elev: 1942ft/592m; Tel: 918-653-2991; Nearest town: Heavener; Notes: 5 backpacker sites ($3) open all year. GPS: 34.714508, -94.675571

Oregon

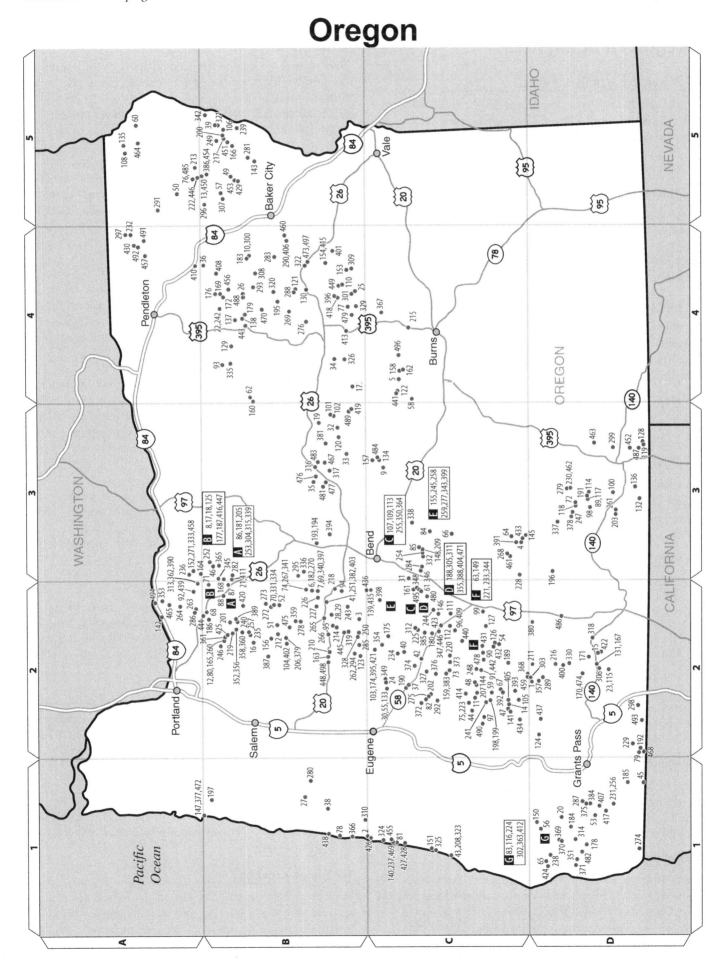

Oregon Camping Areas

1 • Abbott Creek (Abbott Butte)

Total sites: 25; RV sites: 25; Central water; Vault toilets; No showers; No RV dump; Reservations not accepted; Max length: 20ft; Stay limit: 14 days; Generator hours: 0600-2200; Open May-Oct; Tent & RV camping: $14; Elev: 3084ft/940m; Tel: 541-865-2795; Nearest town: Prospect. GPS: 42.881095, -122.506241

2 • Alder Dune

Total sites: 39; RV sites: 39; Central water; Flush toilets; No showers; No RV dump; Reservations accepted; Max length: 60ft; Stay limit: 14 days; Open all year; Tent & RV camping: $24; Elev: 187ft/57m; Tel: 541-997-2526; Nearest town: Florence. GPS: 44.068894, -124.101891

3 • Alder Springs

Total sites: 6; No water; Vault toilets; Reservations not accepted; Stay limit: 14 days; Open Jun-Oct; Tents only: Free; Elev: 3724ft/1135m; Tel: 541-822-3381; Nearest town: Silver Lake. GPS: 44.177649, -121.913313

4 • Alder Springs

Total sites: 3; No water; Vault toilets; Open Jun-Nov; Tents only: Free; Elev: 5233ft/1595m. GPS: 42.969152, -121.132492

5 • Alder Springs Camp

Total sites: 3; RV sites: 3; No water; Vault toilets; Reservations not accepted; Stay limit: 14 days; Open May-Sep; Tent & RV camping: Free; Elev: 5489ft/1673m; Tel: 541-575-3000; Nearest town: Burns. GPS: 43.877429, -119.505422

6 • Allen Springs

Total sites: 16; RV sites: 7; No water; Vault toilets; Reservations accepted; Max length: 30ft; Open Apr-Oct; Tent & RV camping: $16; Elev: 2746ft/837m; Tel: 541-338-7869; Nearest town: Sisters; Notes: $12 winter rate. GPS: 44.528672, -121.629017

7 • Allingham

Total sites: 10; RV sites: 10; Central water; Vault toilets; No showers; No RV dump; Reservations accepted; Max length: 50ft; Open May-Sep; Tent & RV camping: $16-18; Elev: 3005ft/916m; Tel: 541-338-7869; Nearest town: Sisters. GPS: 44.472772, -121.637072

8 • Alpine

Total sites: 16; Central water; Vault toilets; No showers; No RV dump; Reservations not accepted; Max length: 16ft; Open Jun-Sep; Tents only: $21; Elev: 5476ft/1669m; Tel: 503-668 1700; Nearest town: Government Camp. GPS: 45.319761, -121.706135

9 • Antelope Flat Reservoir

Total sites: 24; RV sites: 24; Central water; Vault toilets; No showers; No RV dump; Reservations not accepted; Stay limit: 14 days; Open May-Sep; Tent & RV camping: $8; Elev: 5036ft/1535m; Tel: 541-416-6500; Nearest town: Prineville. GPS: 44.001692, -120.392416

10 • Anthony Lake

Total sites: 37; RV sites: 16; Central water; Vault toilets; No showers; No RV dump; Reservations not accepted; Max length: 22ft; Stay limit: 14 days; Open Jul-Sep; Tents: $10/RVs: $14; Elev: 7198ft/2194m; Tel: 541-523-6391; Nearest town: Haines. GPS: 44.961514, -118.228125

11 • Apple Creek

Total sites: 8; RV sites: 8; No water; Vault toilets; Reservations not accepted; Max length: 22ft; Stay limit: 14 days; Generator hours: 0600-2200; Open May-Sep; Tent & RV camping: $10; Elev: 1457ft/444m; Tel: 541-957-3200; Nearest town: North Umpqua. GPS: 43.305406, -122.676727

12 • Armstrong

Total sites: 12; RV sites: 12; Central water; Vault toilets; No showers; No RV dump; Reservations accepted; Max length: 16ft; Generator hours: 0600-2200; Open Apr-Sep; Tent & RV camping: $19-21; Elev: 896ft/273m; Tel: 503-630-5721; Nearest town: Estacada. GPS: 45.161993, -122.152311

13 • Arrow Forest Camp

Total sites: 3; No water; Vault toilets; Reservations not accepted; Stay limit: 14 days; Open Jun-Sep; Tents only: $5; Elev: 5469ft/1667m; Tel: 541-523-6391; Nearest town: Enterprise. GPS: 45.265666, -117.385674

14 • Ash Flat Forest Camp

Total sites: 4; RV sites: 4; No water; Vault toilets; Reservations not accepted; Max length: 35ft; Stay limit: 14 days; Generator hours: 0600-2200; Open all year; Tent & RV camping: $10; Elev: 1654ft/504m; Tel: 541-825-3100; Nearest town: Tiller. GPS: 43.045037, -122.732246

15 • Aspen Point

Total sites: 49; RV sites: 43; Central water; Flush toilets; No showers; RV dump; Reservations accepted; Open May-Sep; Tent & RV camping: $23; Elev: 5020ft/1530m; Tel: 541-885-3400; Nearest town: Klamath Falls; Notes: Group site: $90-$95. GPS: 42.384521, -122.213623

16 • Bagby

Total sites: 15; No water; Vault toilets; Reservations not accepted; Open Apr-Sep; Tents only: $18; Elev: 2091ft/637m; Tel: 503-668 1700; Nearest town: Estacada. GPS: 44.954369, -122.169159

17 • Barlow Creek

Total sites: 3; RV sites: 3; No water; Vault toilets; Reservations not accepted; Open Jun-Sep; Tent & RV camping: $12; Elev: 3084ft/940m; Tel: 503-668 1700; Nearest town: Government Creek. GPS: 45.235156, -121.626947

18 • Barlow Crossing

Total sites: 6; RV sites: 6; No water; Vault toilets; Reservations not accepted; Open Jun-Sep; Tent & RV camping: $12; Elev: 3061ft/933m; Tel: 503-668 1700; Nearest town: Parkdale. GPS: 45.216759, -121.614176

19 • Barnhouse

Total sites: 6; RV sites: 6; No water; Vault toilets; Reservations not accepted; Max length: 25ft; Stay limit: 14 days; Open all year; Tent & RV camping: Free; Elev: 5076ft/1547m; Tel: 541-416-6500; Nearest town: Paulina. GPS: 44.473809, -119.934569

20 • Bear Camp Pasture

Total sites: 1; RV sites: 1; No water; Vault toilets; Reservations not accepted; Stay limit: 14 days; Generator hours: 0600-2200; Open May-Sep; Tent & RV camping: Free; Elev: 4806ft/1465m; Tel: 541-471 6514; Nearest town: Grants Pass. GPS: 42.627158, -123.830147

21 • Bear Springs

Total sites: 21; RV sites: 21; Central water; Vault toilets; No showers; No RV dump; Reservations not accepted; Max length: 32ft; Open May-Sep; Tent & RV camping: $17; Elev: 3146ft/959m; Tel: 541-467-2291; Nearest town: Government Camp; Notes: Reservable group sites $51-$76. GPS: 45.116748, -121.531466

22 • Bear Wallow Creek

Total sites: 8; RV sites: 8; No water; Vault toilets; Reservations not accepted; Max length: 25ft; Stay limit: 14 days; Open all year; Tent & RV camping: $8; Elev: 3921ft/1195m; Tel: 541-278-3716; Nearest town: Ukiah; Notes: Free Nov-May - no services. GPS: 45.184082, -118.752197

23 • Beaver Dam

Total sites: 4; RV sites: 2; No water; Vault toilets; Reservations not accepted; Max length: 16ft; Stay limit: 14 days; Generator hours: 0600-2200; Open May-Nov; Tent & RV camping: $8; Elev: 4550ft/1387m; Tel: 541-560-3400; Nearest town: Butte Falls. GPS: 42.304182, -122.367211

24 • Bedrock

Total sites: 15; RV sites: 9; No water; Vault toilets; Reservations not accepted; Max length: 30ft; Stay limit: 14 days; Generator hours: 0600-2200; Open Apr-Sep; Tent & RV camping: $17; Elev: 1263ft/385m; Tel: 541-782-2283; Nearest town: Lowell. GPS: 43.973251, -122.546771

25 • Big Creek

Total sites: 15; RV sites: 15; No water; Vault toilets; Reservations not accepted; Stay limit: 14 days; Open May-Sep; Tent & RV camping: $8; Elev: 5125ft/1562m; Tel: 541-575-3000; Nearest town: Seneca. GPS: 44.183105, -118.615723

26 • Big Creek Meadows

Total sites: 3; RV sites: 3; No water; Vault toilets; Reservations not accepted; Stay limit: 14 days; Open all year; Tent & RV camping: Free; Elev: 5066ft/1544m; Tel: 541-278-3716; Nearest town: Ukiah; Notes: Rough road. GPS: 45.009755, -118.617112

27 • Big Elk

Total sites: 8; RV sites: 8; Central water; No toilets; No showers; No RV dump; Reservations not accepted; Stay limit: 14 days; Open all year; Tent & RV camping: $10; Elev: 459ft/140m; Tel: 541-563-8400; Nearest town: Newport. GPS: 44.543847, -123.722922

28 • Big Lake

Total sites: 49; RV sites: 49; Central water; No toilets; No showers; No RV dump; Reservations accepted; Max length: 30ft; Stay limit: 14 days; Open May-Oct; Tent & RV camping: $24; Elev: 4669ft/1423m; Tel: 801-226-3564; Nearest town: Sisters. GPS: 44.379639, -121.870117

29 • Big Lake West

Total sites: 11; RV sites: 1; Central water; Vault toilets; Reservations accepted; Max length: 20ft; Stay limit: 14 days; Open May-Oct; Tent & RV camping: $24; Elev: 4682ft/1427m; Tel: 801-226-3564; Nearest town: Sisters. GPS: 44.375395, -121.881832

30 • Big Pool

Total sites: 5; RV sites: 1; No water; Vault toilets; Reservations not accepted; Max length: 14ft; Stay limit: 14 days; Generator hours: 0600-2200; Open Apr-Sep; Tent & RV camping: $14; Elev: 1001ft/305m; Nearest town: Lowell. GPS: 43.966481, -122.598404

31 • Big River

Total sites: 10; RV sites: 10; No water; Vault toilets; Reservations accepted; Max length: 26ft; Open May-Oct; Tent & RV camping: $12; Elev: 4180ft/1274m; Tel: 541-383-4000; Nearest town: La Pine; Notes: 3 reservable group sites: $30. GPS: 43.816895, -121.497803

32 • Big Spring

Total sites: 5; RV sites: 5; No water; Vault toilets; Reservations not accepted; Stay limit: 14 days; Open all year; Tent & RV camping: Free; Elev: 5052ft/1540m; Tel: 541-416-6500; Nearest town: Paulina. GPS: 44.331874, -119.991419

33 • Biggs Springs

Total sites: 3; RV sites: 3; No water; Vault toilets; Reservations not accepted; Stay limit: 14 days; Open all year; Tent & RV camping: Free; Elev: 4898ft/1493m; Tel: 541-416-6500; Nearest town: Post. GPS: 44.272121, -120.259769

34 • Billy Fields Forest Camp

Total sites: 4; RV sites: 3; No water; Vault toilets; Reservations not accepted; Stay limit: 14 days; Open Jun-Oct; Tent & RV camping: Free; Elev: 4190ft/1277m; Tel: 541-575-3000; Nearest town: Mount Vernon. GPS: 44.346585, -119.299542

35 • Bingham Spring

Total sites: 4; RV sites: 1; No water; Vault toilets; Reservations not accepted; Max length: 18ft; Stay limit: 14 days; Open all year; Tent & RV camping: Free; Elev: 5495ft/1675m; Tel: 541-416-6500; Nearest town: Paulina. GPS: 44.514082, -120.529316

36 • Birdtrack Springs

Total sites: 22; RV sites: 22; No water; Vault toilets; Reservations not accepted; Stay limit: 14 days; Open May-Sep; Tent & RV camping: $5; Elev: 3120ft/951m; Tel: 541-523-6391; Nearest town: La Grande. GPS: 45.300000, -118.306000

37 • Black Canyon

Total sites: 72; RV sites: 59; Central water; Vault toilets; No showers; No RV dump; Reservations accepted; Max length: 38ft; Stay limit: 14 days; Generator hours: 0600-2200; Open May-Oct; Tent & RV camping: $20; Elev: 1017ft/310m; Tel: 541-782-2283; Nearest town: Oakridge. GPS: 43.806396, -122.566650

38 • Blackberry

Total sites: 32; RV sites: 32; Central water; Vault toilets; No showers; No RV dump; Reservations accepted; Max length: 32ft; Stay limit: 14 days; Open all year; Tent & RV camping: $24; Elev: 112ft/34m; Tel: 541-563-8400; Nearest town: Waldport. GPS: 44.373346, -123.835367

39 • Blackhorse

Total sites: 16; RV sites: 16; No water; Vault toilets; Reservations not accepted; Stay limit: 14 days; Open Jun-Sep; Tent & RV camping: $8; Elev: 3980ft/1213m; Tel: 541-426-5546; Nearest town: Joseph. GPS: 45.158753, -116.874729

40 • Blair Lake

Total sites: 7; Central water; Vault toilets; No showers; No RV dump; Reservations not accepted; Stay limit: 14 days; Generator hours: 0600-2200; Open Jun-Sep; Tents only: $8; Elev: 4787ft/1459m; Tel: 541-782-2283; Nearest town: Oakridge; Notes: Also walk-to sites, 4 walk-to sites. GPS: 43.836113, -122.241594

41 • Blue Bay

Total sites: 25; RV sites: 25; Central water; Vault toilets; No showers; No RV dump; Reservations accepted; Max length: 50ft; Open May-Sep; Tent & RV camping: $18; Elev: 3510ft/1070m; Tel: 541-338-7869; Nearest town: Sisters. GPS: 44.419926, -121.732334

42 • Blue Pool

Total sites: 24; RV sites: 17; Central water; No toilets; No showers; No RV dump; Reservations not accepted; Max length: 20ft; Stay limit: 14 days; Generator hours: 0600-2200; Open May-Sep; Tent & RV camping: $19; Elev: 2031ft/619m; Tel: 541-782-2283; Nearest town: Oakridge; Notes: Also walk-to sites, 7 walk-to sites. GPS: 43.708984, -122.298584

43 • Bluebill Lake

Total sites: 18; RV sites: 18; Central water; Vault toilets; No showers; No RV dump; Reservations accepted; Max length: 45ft; Stay limit: 14 days; Open May-Sep; Tent & RV camping: $22; Elev: 36ft/11m; Tel: 541-271-6000; Nearest town: North Bend. GPS: 43.450463, -124.261922

44 • Bogus Creek

Total sites: 15; RV sites: 15; Central water; No toilets; No showers; No RV dump; Reservations accepted; Max length: 35ft; Stay limit: 14 days; Generator hours: 0600-2200; Open May-Oct; Tent & RV camping: $15; Elev: 1266ft/386m; Tel: 541-496-3534; Nearest town: Idleyld Park. GPS: 43.324755, -122.800278

45 • Bolan Lake

Total sites: 12; RV sites: 12; No water; Vault toilets; Reservations not accepted; Stay limit: 14 days; Generator hours: 0800-2000; Tent & RV camping: $10; Elev: 5558ft/1694m; Tel: 541-592-4000; Nearest town: Cave Junction. GPS: 42.023625, -123.458695

46 • Bonney Crossing

Total sites: 8; RV sites: 8; No water; Vault toilets; Reservations not accepted; Max length: 16ft; Open May-Sep; Tent & RV camping: $12; Elev: 2195ft/669m; Tel: 541-467-2291; Nearest town: Dufur. GPS: 45.255917, -121.390567

47 • Boulder Creek

Total sites: 7; RV sites: 7; Central water; Vault toilets; No showers; No RV dump; Reservations not accepted; Max length: 22ft; Stay limit: 14 days; Generator hours: 0600-2200; Open May-Oct; Tent & RV camping: $10; Elev: 1522ft/464m; Tel: 541-825-3100; Nearest town: Tiller. GPS: 43.053971, -122.777537

48 • Boulder Flat

Total sites: 9; RV sites: 9; No water; Vault toilets; No showers; No RV dump; Reservations accepted; Max length: 24ft; Stay limit: 14 days; Generator hours: 0600-2200; Open all year; Tent & RV camping: $10; Elev: 1791ft/546m; Tel: 541-498-2515; Nearest town: Idleyld Park. GPS: 43.303947, -122.526648

49 • Boulder Park

Total sites: 7; RV sites: 7; No water; Vault toilets; Stay limit: 14 days; Open May-Sep; Tent & RV camping: Free; Elev: 4954ft/1510m; Tel: 541-523-6391; Nearest town: Medical Springs. GPS: 45.068311, -117.406406

50 • Boundary

Total sites: 8; No water; Vault toilets; Stay limit: 14 days; Open Jun-Sep; Tents only: Free; Elev: 3776ft/1151m; Tel: 541-523-6391; Nearest town: Enterprise. GPS: 45.472012, -117.559108

51 • Breitenbush

Total sites: 29; RV sites: 29; Central water; Vault toilets; No showers; No RV dump; Reservations accepted; Max length: 24ft; Stay limit: 14 days; Open May-Sep; Tent & RV camping: $18; Elev: 2270ft/692m; Tel: 503-854-3366; Nearest town: Detroit. GPS: 44.780583, -121.991033

52 • Breitenbush Lake

Total sites: 20; RV sites: 20; No water; Vault toilets; Tent & RV camping: Free; Elev: 5541ft/1689m; Tel: 541-553-2001; Nearest town: Detroit. GPS: 44.765107, -121.785687

53 • Briggs Creek

Total sites: 3; RV sites: 3; No water; Vault toilets; Reservations not accepted; Stay limit: 14 days; Generator hours: 0600-2200; Open May-Oct; Tent & RV camping: Free; Elev: 891ft/272m; Tel: 541-471-6500; Nearest town: Selma. GPS: 42.377761, -123.804198

54 • Broken Arrow

Total sites: 128; RV sites: 128; Central water; Flush toilets; Showers; RV dump; Reservations accepted; Max length: 32ft; Stay limit: 14 days; Generator hours: 0600-2200; Open May-Sep; Tent & RV camping: $15; Elev: 5220ft/1591m; Tel: 541-498-2531; Nearest town: Diamond Lake; Notes: 4 group sites $70-$165. GPS: 43.133347, -122.143579

55 • Broken Bowl

Total sites: 16; RV sites: 6; Central water; Flush toilets; No showers; No RV dump; Reservations not accepted; Max length: 20ft; Stay limit: 14 days; Generator hours: 0600-2200; Open Apr-Sep; Tent & RV camping: $19; Elev: 1089ft/332m; Tel: 541-782-2283; Nearest town: Lowell; Notes: Also walk-to sites, 3 walk-to sites. GPS: 43.962058, -122.610583

56 • Buck Creek

Total sites: 2; RV sites: 2; No water; Vault toilets; Reservations not accepted; Stay limit: 14 days; Generator hours: 0600-2200; Open all year; Tent & RV camping: Free; Elev: 2277ft/694m; Tel: 541-439-6200; Nearest town: Powers. GPS: 42.774739, -123.952364

57 • Buck Creek Forest Camp

Total sites: 4; RV sites: 4; No water; Vault toilets; Reservations not accepted; Stay limit: 14 days; Open May-Oct; Tent & RV camping: $5; Elev: 5558ft/1694m; Tel: 541-426-5546; Nearest town: Union. GPS: 45.148123, -117.572106

58 • Buck Spring

Total sites: 7; RV sites: 7; No water; Vault toilets; Reservations not accepted; Max length: 20ft; Stay limit: 14 days; Open May-Sep; Tent & RV camping: $6; Elev: 5033ft/1534m; Tel: 541-575-3000; Nearest town: Burns. GPS: 43.789005, -119.708701

59 • Buckhead Mt

Total sites: 3; RV sites: 3; Vault toilets; Max length: 18ft; Stay limit: 14 days; Tent & RV camping: Free; Elev: 5075ft/1547m; Tel: 541-825-3100; Nearest town: North Umpqua. GPS: 43.177256, -122.625617

60 • Buckhorn

Total sites: 5; No water; Vault toilets; Reservations not accepted; Stay limit: 14 days; Open Jun-Sep; Tents only: Free; Elev: 5240ft/1597m; Tel: 541-523-6391; Nearest town: Enterprise. GPS: 45.755214, -116.837007

61 • Bull Bend

Total sites: 12; RV sites: 12; No water; Vault toilets; Reservations not accepted; Max length: 30ft; Open May-Oct; Tent & RV camping: $12; Elev: 4275ft/1303m; Tel: 541-383-4000; Nearest town: La Pine. GPS: 43.725398, -121.628082

62 • Bull Prairie Lake

Total sites: 59; RV sites: 58; Central water; Vault toilets; No showers; RV dump; Reservations not accepted; Stay limit: 14 days; Open all year; Tent & RV camping: $14; Elev: 4058ft/1237m; Tel: 541-278-3716; Nearest town: Heppner; Notes: Group site: $28, Free - no services Nov-May. GPS: 44.972912, -119.663944

63 • Bunker Hill

Total sites: 5; RV sites: 5; No water; Vault toilets; No showers; No RV dump; Reservations accepted; Max length: 22ft; Stay limit: 14 days; Generator hours: 0600-2200; Open Jun-Oct; Tent & RV camping: $10; Elev: 4278ft/1304m; Tel: 541-498-2531; Nearest town: Diamond Lake. GPS: 43.319346, -122.187985

64 • Bunyard Crossing

Total sites: 3; RV sites: 3; No water; Vault toilets; Reservations not accepted; Open May-Nov; Tent & RV camping: Free; Elev: 4530ft/1381m; Tel: 541-576-2107; Nearest town: Silver Lake. GPS: 43.043797, -121.081691

65 • Butler Bar

Total sites: 7; RV sites: 7; Central water; Vault toilets; No showers; No RV dump; Reservations not accepted; Stay limit: 14 days; Generator hours: 0600-2200; Open all year; Tent & RV camping: Free; Elev: 626ft/191m; Tel: 541-439-6200; Nearest town: Powers. GPS: 42.725667, -124.270727

66 • Cabin Lake

Total sites: 14; RV sites: 14; No water; No toilets; Tent & RV camping: Free; Elev: 4554ft/1388m; Nearest town: Bend. GPS: 43.495064, -121.057634

67 • Camp Comfort

Total sites: 5; RV sites: 5; No water; Vault toilets; Reservations not accepted; Max length: 22ft; Stay limit: 14 days; Generator hours: 0600-2200; Open all year; Tent & RV camping: $10; Elev: 2156ft/657m; Tel: 541-825-3100; Nearest town: Tiller. GPS: 43.105919, -122.593664

68 • Camp Creek

Total sites: 25; RV sites: 25; Central water; Vault toilets; No showers; No RV dump; Reservations accepted; Max length: 22ft; Open May-Sep; Tent & RV camping: $19-21; Elev: 2228ft/679m; Tel: 541-328-0909; Nearest town: Zigzag. GPS: 45.302979, -121.865967

69 • Camp Sherman

Total sites: 15; RV sites: 15; Central water; Vault toilets; No showers; No RV dump; Reservations accepted; Max length: 50ft; Open May-Sep; Tent & RV camping: $16-18; Elev: 2979ft/908m; Tel: 541-338-7869; Nearest town: Sisters; Notes: $14 in winter, no water. GPS: 44.463135, -121.639893

70 • Camp Ten

Total sites: 10; RV sites: 10; No water; Vault toilets; Reservations not accepted; Max length: 16ft; Open May-Nov; Tent & RV camping: $15-20; Elev: 4948ft/1508m; Tel: 503-668 1700; Nearest town: Detroit. GPS: 44.803152, -121.788898

71 • Camp Windy

Total sites: 3; No water; Vault toilets; Reservations not accepted; Open May-Sep; Tents only: Free; Elev: 5407ft/1648m; Tel: 503-668 1700; Nearest town: Dufur. GPS: 45.288707, -121.583394

72 • Campbell Lake

Total sites: 16; RV sites: 16; Central water; Vault toilets; No showers; No RV dump; Open all year; Tent & RV camping: $6; Elev: 7257ft/2212m; Tel: 541-943-3114; Nearest town: Paisley; Notes: Reduced services 10/15-5/14. GPS: 42.560547, -120.753174

73 • Campers Flat

Total sites: 5; RV sites: 5; Central water; Vault toilets; No showers; No RV dump; Reservations not accepted; Max length: 18ft; Stay limit: 14 days; Generator hours: 0600-2200; Open May-Sep; Tent & RV camping: $14; Elev: 2087ft/636m; Tel: 541-782-2283; Nearest town: Oakridge. GPS: 43.500845, -122.413367

74 • Candle Creek

Total sites: 10; No water; Vault toilets; Reservations not accepted; Open May-Sep; Tents only: $12-14; Elev: 2700ft/823m; Tel: 541-338-7869; Nearest town: Sisters. GPS: 44.574981, -121.620231

75 • Canton Creek

Total sites: 5; RV sites: 5; Central water; No toilets; No showers; No RV dump; Reservations accepted; Max length: 24ft; Stay limit: 14 days; Generator hours: 0600-2200; Open May-Sep; Tent & RV camping: $10; Elev: 1201ft/366m; Tel: 541-496-3532; Nearest town: North Umpqua. GPS: 43.348321, -122.729937

76 • Canyon Forest

Total sites: 4; No water; Vault toilets; Reservations not accepted; Stay limit: 14 days; Open May-Sep; Tents only: Free; Elev: 4931ft/1503m; Tel: 541-523-6391; Nearest town: Lostine. GPS: 45.351447, -117.414866

77 • Canyon Meadows

Total sites: 5; RV sites: 5; No water; Vault toilets; Reservations not accepted; Stay limit: 14 days; Open May-Sep; Tent & RV camping: Free; Elev: 5197ft/1584m; Tel: 541-575-3000; Nearest town: Canyon City. GPS: 44.238525, -118.771973

78 • Cape Perpetua

Total sites: 38; RV sites: 38; Central water; Flush toilets; No showers; No RV dump; Reservations accepted; Stay limit: 14 days; Open Mar-Sep; Tent & RV camping: $24; Elev: 158ft/48m; Tel: 541-547-4580; Nearest town: Yachats. GPS: 44.281064, -124.104979

79 • Carberry

Total sites: 10; No water; Vault toilets; Reservations not accepted; Stay limit: 14 days; Generator hours: 0600-2200; Open all year; Tents only: $15; Elev: 2293ft/699m; Tel: 541-899-3800; Nearest town: Applegate; Notes: No fees in winter. GPS: 42.058943, -123.163844

80 • Carter Bridge

Total sites: 15; RV sites: 15; No water; Vault toilets; Reservations not accepted; Max length: 28ft; Open May-Sep; Tent & RV camping: $17; Elev: 1217ft/371m; Tel: 503-668 1700; Nearest town: Estacada. GPS: 45.168006, -122.156662

81 • Carter Lake

Total sites: 23; RV sites: 23; Central water; Flush toilets; No showers; No RV dump; Reservations accepted; Max length: 20ft; Stay limit: 14 days; Open May-Sep; Tent & RV camping: $22; Elev: 89ft/27m; Tel: 541-271-6000; Nearest town: Florence. GPS: 43.857229, -124.145963

82 • Cedar Creek

Total sites: 10; RV sites: 10; No water; Vault toilets; Reservations not accepted; Max length: 16ft; Stay limit: 14 days; Generator hours: 0600-2200; Open May-Sep; Tent & RV camping: $8; Elev: 1693ft/516m; Tel: 541-767-5000; Nearest town: Cottage Grove. GPS: 43.669812, -122.705852

83 • China Flat

Total sites: 15; RV sites: 15; No water; Vault toilets; Reservations not accepted; Stay limit: 14 days; Generator hours: 0600-2200; Tent & RV camping: Free; Elev: 725ft/221m; Tel: 541-439-6200; Nearest town: Powers. GPS: 42.778692, -124.065509

84 • China Hat

Total sites: 13; RV sites: 13; No water; Vault toilets; Max length: 30ft; Open Apr-Oct; Tent & RV camping: Free; Elev: 5079ft/1548m; Tel: 541-383-5300; Nearest town: La Pine. GPS: 43.657625, -121.036915

85 • Cinder Hill

Total sites: 108; RV sites: 108; Central water; Vault toilets; No showers; No RV dump; Reservations accepted; Max length: 30ft; Open Jun-Oct; Tent & RV camping: $18; Elev: 6394ft/1949m; Tel: 541-338-7869; Nearest town: La Pine. GPS: 43.736683, -121.199299

86 • Clackamas Lake

Total sites: 46; RV sites: 46; Central water; Vault toilets; No showers; No RV dump; Reservations accepted; Max length: 32ft; Open May-Sep; Tent & RV camping: $21-23; Elev: 3369ft/1027m; Tel: 541-328-0909; Nearest town: Government Camp; Notes: 11 reservable equestrian sites. GPS: 45.095642, -121.747536

87 • Clear Creek Crossing

Total sites: 7; RV sites: 7; No water; Vault toilets; Reservations not accepted; Max length: 16ft; Open May-Sep; Tent & RV camping: $12; Elev: 3061ft/933m; Tel: 503-668 1700; Nearest town: Dufur. GPS: 45.144834, -121.578996

88 • Clear Lake

Total sites: 32; RV sites: 32; Central water; Vault toilets; No showers; No RV dump; Reservations accepted; Max length: 32ft; Open May-Sep; Tent & RV camping: $23-25; Elev: 3645ft/1111m; Tel: 541-328-0909; Nearest town: Government Camp. GPS: 45.180893, -121.697515

89 • Clear Springs

Total sites: 2; RV sites: 2; Central water; Vault toilets; No showers; No RV dump; Open all year; Tent & RV camping: Free; Elev:

5466ft/1666m; Tel: 541-943-3114; Nearest town: Paisley; Notes: Reduced services 10/15-5/14. GPS: 42.471846, -120.711657

90 • Clearwater Falls

Total sites: 12; RV sites: 12; No water; Vault toilets; Reservations not accepted; Max length: 25ft; Stay limit: 14 days; Generator hours: 0600-2200; Open Jun-Oct; Tent & RV camping: $10; Elev: 4318ft/1316m; Tel: 541-957-3200; Nearest town: Diamond Lake. GPS: 43.248356, -122.230595

91 • Clearwater Forebay

Total sites: 5; RV sites: 5; No water; Vault toilets; Reservations not accepted; Stay limit: 14 days; Tent & RV camping: Free; Elev: 3185ft/971m; Tel: 541-498-2531; Nearest town: Toketee Falls. GPS: 43.261991, -122.404545

92 • Cloud Cap Saddle

Total sites: 3; RV sites: 3; Central water; Vault toilets; No showers; No RV dump; Reservations not accepted; Tent & RV camping: $21; Elev: 5879ft/1792m; Tel: 503-668 1700; Nearest town: Parkdale. GPS: 45.402195, -121.655298

93 • Coalmine Hill

Total sites: 10; RV sites: 10; No water; Vault toilets; Reservations not accepted; Stay limit: 14 days; Open all year; Tent & RV camping: $8; Elev: 4856ft/1480m; Tel: 541-278-3716; Nearest town: Heppner; Notes: Free Nov-May - no services. GPS: 45.167000, -119.332000

94 • Cold Spring (Black Crater)

Total sites: 23; RV sites: 23; Central water; Vault toilets; No showers; No RV dump; Reservations accepted; Max length: 50ft; Open May-Oct; Tent & RV camping: $15-17; Elev: 3399ft/1036m; Tel: 541-338-7869; Nearest town: Sisters. GPS: 44.309706, -121.630268

95 • Cold Water Cove

Total sites: 35; RV sites: 35; Central water; Vault toilets; No showers; No RV dump; Reservations accepted; Max length: 30ft; Stay limit: 14 days; Open May-Oct; Tent & RV camping: $22; Elev: 3258ft/993m; Tel: 801-226-3564; Nearest town: McKenzie Bridge. GPS: 44.366281, -121.987521

96 • Contorta Flat

Total sites: 19; RV sites: 13; No water; Vault toilets; Reservations accepted; Max length: 35ft; Open May-Oct; Tent & RV camping: $11-13; Elev: 4855ft/1480m; Tel: 541-338-7869; Nearest town: Crescent. GPS: 43.461356, -122.006782

97 • Coolwater

Total sites: 7; RV sites: 7; Central water; Vault toilets; No showers; No RV dump; Reservations not accepted; Max length: 24ft; Stay limit: 14 days; Generator hours: 0600-2200; Open Jun-Oct; Tent & RV camping: $10; Elev: 1512ft/461m; Tel: 541-496-3534; Nearest town: North Umpqua. GPS: 43.232301, -122.872557

98 • Corral Creek

Total sites: 6; RV sites: 6; No water; Vault toilets; Open all year; Tent & RV camping: Free; Elev: 5955ft/1815m; Tel: 541-943-3114; Nearest town: Bly; Notes: Reduced services 10/15-5/14. GPS: 42.457116, -120.784746

99 • Corral Springs

Total sites: 5; RV sites: 5; No water; Vault toilets; Reservations not accepted; Max length: 50ft; Open all year; Tent & RV camping: Free; Elev: 4878ft/1487m; Tel: 541-365-7001; Nearest town: Chemult; Notes: Reduced services 10/15-5/14. GPS: 43.252518, -121.822121

100 • Cottonwood

Total sites: 27; RV sites: 23; Central water; Vault toilets; No showers; No RV dump; Reservations not accepted; Open all year; Tent & RV camping: $6; Elev: 6204ft/1891m; Tel: 541-943-3114; Nearest town: Lakeview; Notes: Reduced services 10/15-5/14. GPS: 42.285360, -120.639240

101 • Cottonwood (Antone)

Total sites: 6; RV sites: 5; No water; Vault toilets; Reservations not accepted; Stay limit: 14 days; Open all year; Tent & RV camping: Free; Elev: 5745ft/1751m; Tel: 541-416-6500; Nearest town: Paulina. GPS: 44.387618, -119.854969

102 • Cottonwood Pit

Total sites: 3; RV sites: 3; No water; Vault toilets; Stay limit: 14 days; Open May-Sep; Tent & RV camping: Free; Elev: 5630ft/1716m; Tel: 541-416-6500; Nearest town: Paulina. GPS: 44.368809, -119.869979

103 • Cougar Crossing

Total sites: 11; RV sites: 11; No water; Vault toilets; Reservations accepted; Stay limit: 14 days; Open all year; Tent & RV camping: $14; Elev: 1795ft/547m; Tel: 541-603-8564; Nearest town: Blue River. GPS: 44.057667, -122.219946

104 • Cove Creek

Total sites: 65; RV sites: 65; Central water; Flush toilets; Pay showers; No RV dump; Reservations accepted; Stay limit: 14 days; Open May-Sep; Tent & RV camping: $24; Elev: 1696ft/517m; Tel: 801-226-3564; Nearest town: Detroit; Notes: Group site: $217. GPS: 44.711978, -122.159347

105 • Cover

Total sites: 7; RV sites: 7; Central water; Vault toilets; No showers; No RV dump; Reservations not accepted; Max length: 22ft; Stay limit: 14 days; Generator hours: 0600-2200; Open May-Oct; Tent & RV camping: $10; Elev: 1795ft/547m; Tel: 541-825-3100; Nearest town: Tiller. GPS: 42.975924, -122.687963

106 • Coverdale

Total sites: 7; RV sites: 2; No water; Vault toilets; Reservations not accepted; Stay limit: 14 days; Open Jun-Sep; Tent & RV camping: $6; Elev: 4318ft/1316m; Tel: 541-523-6391; Nearest town: Enterprise. GPS: 45.108154, -116.923340

107 • Cow Meadow

Total sites: 18; RV sites: 18; No water; Vault toilets; Reservations accepted; Max length: 26ft; Open May-Sep; Tent & RV camping: $12; Elev: 4472ft/1363m; Tel: 541-338-7869; Nearest town: Crescent. GPS: 43.812988, -121.776367

108 • Coyote

Total sites: 29; RV sites: 8; No water; Vault toilets; Reservations not accepted; Stay limit: 14 days; Generator hours: 0600-2200; Open Jun-Sep; Tent & RV camping: Free; Elev: 5085ft/1550m; Tel: 541-523-6391; Nearest town: Enterprise. GPS: 45.842285, -117.113281

109 • Crane Prairie

Total sites: 146; RV sites: 140; Central water; No toilets; No showers; No RV dump; Reservations accepted; Open Apr-Oct; Tent & RV camping: $16-18; Elev: 4478ft/1365m; Tel: 541-338-7869; Nearest town: Sunriver. GPS: 43.797852, -121.758545

110 • Crescent

Total sites: 4; RV sites: 4; No water; Vault toilets; Reservations not accepted; Stay limit: 14 days; Open May-Sep; Tent & RV camping: Free; Elev: 5236ft/1596m; Tel: 541-820-3800; Nearest town: Prairie City. GPS: 44.281779, -118.545261

111 • Crescent Creek

Total sites: 9; RV sites: 9; Central water; Vault toilets; No showers; No RV dump; Reservations accepted; Open May-Sep; Tent & RV camping: $14-16; Elev: 4544ft/1385m; Tel: 541-338-7869; Nearest town: Crescent. GPS: 43.498949, -121.848129

112 • Crescent Lake

Total sites: 46; RV sites: 46; Central water; Vault toilets; No showers; No RV dump; Reservations accepted; Max length: 50ft; Open all year; Tent & RV camping: $14-18; Elev: 4866ft/1483m; Tel: 541-338-7869; Nearest town: Crescent Lake. GPS: 43.502346, -121.974723

113 • Cultus Lake

Total sites: 55; RV sites: 55; Central water; Vault toilets; No showers; No RV dump; Reservations accepted; Max length: 30ft; Open May-Sep; Tent & RV camping: $18-22; Elev: 4747ft/1447m; Tel: 541-338-7869; Nearest town: Bend. GPS: 43.836776, -121.834062

114 • Dairy Point

Total sites: 5; RV sites: 5; Central water; Vault toilets; No showers; No RV dump; Reservations not accepted; Open all year; Tent & RV camping: Free; Elev: 5201ft/1585m; Tel: 541-943-3114; Nearest town: Lakeview; Notes: Reduced services 10/15-5/14. GPS: 42.467041, -120.640637

115 • Daley Creek

Total sites: 6; RV sites: 3; No water; Vault toilets; Reservations not accepted; Stay limit: 14 days; Generator hours: 0800-2200; Open May-Nov; Tent & RV camping: $8; Elev: 4583ft/1397m; Tel: 541-865-2700; Nearest town: Butte Falls. GPS: 42.306475, -122.367068

116 • Daphne Grove

Total sites: 14; RV sites: 14; Central water; Vault toilets; No showers; No RV dump; Reservations not accepted; Max length: 30ft; Stay limit: 14 days; Generator hours: 0600-2200; Open all year; Tent & RV camping: $10; Elev: 1224ft/373m; Tel: 541-439-6200; Nearest town: Powers. GPS: 42.736328, -124.053955

117 • Dead Horse Creek

Total sites: 4; RV sites: 4; No water; Vault toilets; Open Apr-Oct; Tent & RV camping: Free; Elev: 5390ft/1643m; Nearest town: Paisley. GPS: 42.474167, -120.703889

118 • Dead Horse Lake

Total sites: 9; RV sites: 9; Central water; No toilets; No showers; No RV dump; Reservations not accepted; Open all year; Tent & RV camping: $6; Elev: 7429ft/2264m; Tel: 541-943-3114; Nearest town: Paisley; Notes: Reduced services Oct-May. GPS: 42.559752, -120.775017

119 • Deep Creek

Total sites: 4; RV sites: 4; No water; Vault toilets; Reservations not accepted; Open all year; Tent & RV camping: Free; Elev: 5876ft/1791m; Tel: 541-947-6300; Nearest town: Lakeview; Notes: Reduced services 10/15-5/14. GPS: 42.057583, -120.174339

120 • Deep Creek

Total sites: 14; RV sites: 14; Central water; Vault toilets; No showers; No RV dump; Reservations not accepted; Stay limit: 14 days; Open May-Oct; Tent & RV camping: $8; Elev: 4373ft/1333m; Tel: 541-416-6500; Nearest town: Prineville. GPS: 44.327862, -120.077131

121 • Deerhorn Forest Camp

Total sites: 5; RV sites: 5; No water; Vault toilets; Reservations not accepted; Stay limit: 14 days; Open May-Sep; Tent & RV camping: $8; Elev: 3993ft/1217m; Tel: 541-575-3000; Nearest town: Austin Junction. GPS: 44.622625, -118.581575

122 • Delintment Lake

Total sites: 35; RV sites: 29; Central water; Vault toilets; No showers; No RV dump; Reservations not accepted; Max length: 20ft; Stay limit: 14 days; Open May-Sep; Tent & RV camping: $10; Elev: 5598ft/1706m; Nearest town: Hines. GPS: 43.889639, -119.626504

123 • Delta

Total sites: 38; RV sites: 38; Central water; Vault toilets; No showers; No RV dump; Reservations accepted; Max length: 36ft; Stay limit: 14 days; Open Apr-Oct; Tent & RV camping: $19; Elev: 1138ft/347m; Tel: 801-226-3564; Nearest town: Blue River. GPS: 44.163755, -122.281539

124 • Devil's Flat

Total sites: 3; RV sites: 3; No water; Vault toilets; Reservations not accepted; Max length: 22ft; Stay limit: 14 days; Generator hours: 0600-2200; Open May-Oct; Tent & RV camping: $10; Elev: 2503ft/763m; Tel: 541-825-3100; Nearest town: Tiller. GPS: 42.817701, -123.026486

125 • Devils Half Acre

Total sites: 2; RV sites: 2; No water; Vault toilets; Reservations not accepted; Open May-Oct; Tent & RV camping: Free; Elev: 3881ft/1183m; Tel: 541-352-6002; Nearest town: Parkdale. GPS: 45.273948, -121.679715

126 • Diamond Lake

Total sites: 238; RV sites: 238; Central water; Flush toilets; Showers; RV dump; Reservations accepted; Max length: T-30ft/RV-35'; Stay limit: 14 days; Open May-Oct; Tent & RV camping: $16-22; Elev: 5256ft/1602m; Tel: 541-498-2531; Nearest town: Diamond Lake. GPS: 43.159481, -122.134086

127 • Digit Point

Total sites: 65; RV sites: 64; Central water; Flush toilets; RV dump; Reservations not accepted; Max length: 33ft; Open Jun-Oct; Tent & RV camping: $12; Elev: 5699ft/1737m; Tel: 541-365-7001; Nearest town: Chemult; Notes: Reduced services 10/15-5/14. GPS: 43.228271, -121.965576

128 • Dismal Creek

Total sites: 3; RV sites: 3; No water; Vault toilets; Reservations not accepted; Open Jun-Oct; Tent & RV camping: Free; Elev: 5760ft/1756m; Nearest town: Lakeview. GPS: 42.062389, -120.152574

129 • Divide Well

Total sites: 11; RV sites: 11; No water; Vault toilets; Reservations not accepted; Stay limit: 14 days; Open all year; Tent & RV camping: Free; Elev: 4747ft/1447m; Tel: 541-278-3716; Nearest town: Ukiah; Notes: Snow-mobile access only Nov-May - no services. GPS: 45.102637, -119.142102

130 • Dixie

Total sites: 10; RV sites: 10; No water; Vault toilets; Reservations not accepted; Stay limit: 14 days; Open May-Sep; Tent & RV camping: $8; Elev: 5181ft/1579m; Tel: 541-820-3800; Nearest town: Prairie City. GPS: 44.538809, -118.589757

131 • Doe Point

Total sites: 29; RV sites: 24; Central water; Flush toilets; No showers; RV dump; Reservations accepted; Stay limit: 14 days; Open May-Oct; Tents: $13/RVs: $25; Elev: 4744ft/1446m; Tel: 541-560-3900; Nearest town: White City. GPS: 42.392634, -122.323913

132 • Dog Lake

Total sites: 15; RV sites: 15; No water; Vault toilets; Reservations not accepted; Open all year; Tent & RV camping: $6; Elev: 5257ft/1602m; Tel: 541-947-3334; Nearest town: Lakeview; Notes: Reduced services 10/15-5/14. GPS: 42.085179, -120.706878

133 • Dolly Varden

Total sites: 5; No water; Vault toilets; Reservations not accepted; Stay limit: 14 days; Generator hours: 0600-2200; Open Apr-Sep; Tents only: $15; Elev: 1142ft/348m; Tel: 541-782-2283; Nearest town: Lowell. GPS: 43.963706, -122.616735

134 • Double Cabin

Total sites: 5; RV sites: 5; No water; Vault toilets; Reservations not accepted; Stay limit: 14 days; Open all year; Tent & RV camping: Free; Elev: 5246ft/1599m; Tel: 541-416-6500; Nearest town: Prineville. GPS: 44.029298, -120.320336

135 • Dougherty Springs

Total sites: 12; RV sites: 4; No water; Vault toilets; Reservations not accepted; Stay limit: 14 days; Open Jun-Sep; Tent & RV camping: Free; Elev: 5154ft/1571m; Tel: 541-523-6391; Nearest town: Enterprise. GPS: 45.852295, -117.033203

136 • Drews Creek

Total sites: 3; RV sites: 3; Central water; Vault toilets; No showers; No RV dump; Reservations not accepted; Open all year; Tent & RV camping: Free; Elev: 4842ft/1476m; Tel: 541-947-3334; Nearest town: Lakeview; Notes: 2 group sites, Reduced services 10/15-5/14. GPS: 42.119277, -120.581392

137 • Drift Fence

Total sites: 6; RV sites: 4; No water; Vault toilets; Reservations not accepted; Stay limit: 14 days; Open May-Nov; Tent & RV camping: Free; Elev: 4626ft/1410m; Tel: 541-278-3716; Nearest town: Ukiah; Notes: Nov-May - no services. GPS: 45.071777, -118.875732

138 • Driftwood

Total sites: 6; RV sites: 6; No water; Vault toilets; Reservations not accepted; Stay limit: 14 days; Open all year; Tent & RV camping: $8; Elev: 3054ft/931m; Tel: 541-278-3716; Nearest town: Dale; Notes: Free Nov-May - no services. GPS: 45.018687, -118.858867

139 • Driftwood (Broken Top)

Total sites: 18; RV sites: 18; No water; Vault toilets; Reservations accepted; Open Jun-Oct; Tent & RV camping: $14-16; Elev: 6551ft/1997m; Tel: 541-338-7869; Nearest town: Sisters. GPS: 44.102904, -121.626101

140 • Driftwood II OHV

Total sites: 59; RV sites: 59; Central water; Flush toilets; Pay showers; No RV dump; Reservations accepted; Max length: 30ft; Stay limit: 14 days; Open all year; Tent & RV camping: $25; Elev: 33ft/10m; Tel: 541-271-3611; Nearest town: Florence. GPS: 43.881121, -124.148414

141 • Dumont Creek

Total sites: 3; No water; Vault toilets; Reservations not accepted; Stay limit: 14 days; Generator hours: 0600-2200; Open May-Oct; Tents only: $10; Elev: 1457ft/444m; Tel: 541-825-3100; Nearest town: Tiller; Notes: Trailers not recommended. GPS: 43.035911, -122.809475

142 • Eagle Creek (Bonneville Dam)

Total sites: 20; RV sites: 20; Central water; Vault toilets; No showers; No RV dump; Reservations accepted; Max length: 20ft; Stay limit: 14 days; Open May-Sep; Tent & RV camping: $15; Elev: 417ft/127m; Tel: 541-386-2333; Nearest town: Cascade Locks. GPS: 45.640625, -121.924072

143 • Eagle Forks

Total sites: 8; RV sites: 8; Central water; Vault toilets; No showers; No RV dump; Reservations not accepted; Stay limit: 14 days; Open May-Sep; Tent & RV camping: $5; Elev: 3058ft/932m; Tel: 541-523-6391; Nearest town: Richland. GPS: 44.891494, -117.262072

144 • Eagle Rock

Total sites: 25; RV sites: 25; No water; Vault toilets; Reservations accepted; Max length: 30ft; Stay limit: 14 days; Open May-Sep; Tent & RV camping: $10; Elev: 1627ft/496m; Tel: 541-496-3532; Nearest town: Steamboat. GPS: 43.295654, -122.553916

145 • East Bay

Total sites: 17; RV sites: 17; Central water; Vault toilets; No showers; No RV dump; Reservations not accepted; Open all year; Tent & RV camping: $10; Elev: 4993ft/1522m; Tel: 541-576-2107; Nearest town: Silver Lake; Notes: Reduced services 10/15-5/14. GPS: 42.942947, -121.065849

146 • East Davis

Total sites: 20; RV sites: 20; Central water; Vault toilets; No showers; No RV dump; Reservations accepted; Max length: 50ft; Open Apr-Sep; Tent & RV camping: $13-15; Elev: 4419ft/1347m; Tel: 541-338-7869; Nearest town: Crescent. GPS: 43.588379, -121.853027

147 • East Dune

Total sites: 61; RV sites: 61; Central water; Vault toilets; No showers; No RV dump; Reservations not accepted; Max length: 40ft; Stay limit: 14 days; Open all year; No tents/RVs: $25; Elev: 33ft/10m; Tel: 503-392-3161; Nearest town: Pacific City. GPS: 45.287307, -123.957833

148 • East Lake

Total sites: 29; RV sites: 29; Central water; Flush toilets; No showers; No RV dump; Reservations accepted; Max length: 26ft; Open May-Oct; Tent & RV camping: $18; Elev: 6434ft/1961m; Tel: 541-338-7869; Nearest town: La Pine. GPS: 43.717529, -121.210693

149 • East Lemolo

Total sites: 15; RV sites: 15; Central water; Vault toilets; No showers; No RV dump; Reservations accepted; Max length: 22ft; Stay limit: 14 days; Open May-Oct; Tent & RV camping: $10; Elev: 4232ft/1290m; Tel: 541-498-2531; Nearest town: Chemult. GPS: 43.312831, -122.166357

150 • Eden Valley

Total sites: 11; RV sites: 11; No water; Vault toilets; Reservations not accepted; Stay limit: 14 days; Generator hours: 0600-2200; Open all year; Tent & RV camping: Free; Elev: 2441ft/744m; Tel: 541-439-6200; Nearest town: Powers. GPS: 42.809014, -123.890941

151 • Eel Creek

Total sites: 53; RV sites: 53; Central water; Flush toilets; No showers; No RV dump; Reservations accepted; Max length: 20ft; Stay limit: 14 days; Open all year; Tent & RV camping: $22; Elev: 95ft/29m; Tel: 541-271-6000; Nearest town: Reedsport. GPS: 43.588447, -124.186566

152 • Eight Mile Crossing

Total sites: 21; RV sites: 21; No water; Vault toilets; Reservations not accepted; Max length: 30ft; Open May-Oct; Tent & RV camping: $21; Elev: 3934ft/1199m; Tel: 503-668 1700; Nearest town: Hood River. GPS: 45.406250, -121.456787

153 • Elk Creek

Total sites: 5; RV sites: 5; No water; Vault toilets; Reservations not accepted; Stay limit: 14 days; Open May-Sep; Tent & RV camping: Free; Elev: 5062ft/1543m; Tel: 541-820-3800; Nearest town: Prairie City. GPS: 44.245921, -118.398393

154 • Elk Creek (Rail Gulch)

Total sites: 10; RV sites: 6; No water; Vault toilets; Reservations not accepted; Stay limit: 14 days; Open May-Oct; Tent & RV camping: $5; Elev: 4518ft/1377m; Tel: 541-523-6391; Nearest town: Unity. GPS: 44.400649, -118.329041

155 • Elk Lake

Total sites: 26; RV sites: 22; Central water; Vault toilets; No showers; No RV dump; Reservations accepted; Max length: 26ft; Open May-Sep; Tent & RV camping: $14-16; Elev: 4948ft/1508m; Tel: 541-338-7869; Nearest town: Bend. GPS: 43.978994, -121.808823

156 • Elk Lake (Battle Ax)

Total sites: 17; No water; Vault toilets; Reservations not accepted; Stay limit: 14 days; Open Jul-Oct; Tents only: $10; Elev: 3776ft/1151m; Tel: 503-854-3366; Nearest town: Detroit. GPS: 44.821965, -122.127506

157 • Elkhorn

Total sites: 4; RV sites: 4; No water; Vault toilets; Reservations not accepted; Stay limit: 14 days; Open all year; Tent & RV camping: Free; Elev: 4452ft/1357m; Tel: 541-416-6500; Nearest town: Prineville. GPS: 44.080509, -120.319147

158 • Emigrant

Total sites: 6; RV sites: 6; No water; Vault toilets; Reservations not accepted; Max length: 20ft; Stay limit: 14 days; Open May-Sep; Tent & RV camping: $8; Elev: 4905ft/1495m; Tel: 541-575-3000; Nearest town: Burns. GPS: 43.864739, -119.418362

159 • Everage Flat

Total sites: 8; RV sites: 6; No water; No toilets; Reservations not accepted; Stay limit: 14 days; Tent & RV camping: Free; Elev: 1942ft/592m; Nearest town: Oakridge. GPS: 43.524096, -122.447401

160 • Fairview

Total sites: 5; RV sites: 5; Central water; Vault toilets; No showers; No RV dump; Reservations not accepted; Stay limit: 14 days; Open all year; Tent & RV camping: Free; Elev: 4324ft/1318m; Tel: 541-278-3716; Nearest town: Heppner; Notes: No services Nov-May. GPS: 44.955151, -119.712474

161 • Fall River

Total sites: 12; RV sites: 12; No water; Vault toilets; Reservations accepted; Max length: 30ft; Open May-Sep; Tent & RV camping: $12-14; Elev: 4275ft/1303m; Tel: 541-383-4000; Nearest town: La Pine. GPS: 43.772705, -121.620117

162 • Falls

Total sites: 6; RV sites: 6; Central water; Vault toilets; No showers; No RV dump; Reservations not accepted; Stay limit: 14 days; Open May-Sep; Tent & RV camping: $8; Elev: 4823ft/1470m; Tel: 541-575-3000; Nearest town: Burns. GPS: 43.849786, -119.410735

163 • Fernview

Total sites: 11; RV sites: 9; Central water; Vault toilets; No showers; No RV dump; Reservations not accepted; Max length: 22ft; Stay limit: 14 days; Open May-Sep; Tent & RV camping: $18; Elev: 1411ft/430m; Tel: 541-967-3917; Nearest town: Sweet Home; Notes: Reservable group site $150. GPS: 44.402344, -122.299805

164 • Fifteenmile

Total sites: 3; RV sites: 3; No water; Vault toilets; Reservations not accepted; Max length: 16ft; Open Jun-Sep; Tent & RV camping: Free; Elev: 4610ft/1405m; Tel: 503-668 1700; Nearest town: Dufur. GPS: 45.350278, -121.472778

165 • Fish Creek

Total sites: 24; RV sites: 24; Central water; Vault toilets; No showers; No RV dump; Reservations accepted; Max length: 16ft; Open May-Sep; Tent & RV camping: $22-24; Elev: 951ft/290m; Tel: 503-630-6861; Nearest town: Estacada. GPS: 45.159444, -122.152222

166 • Fish Lake (Deadman Point)

Total sites: 21; RV sites: 21; Central water; Vault toilets; No showers; No RV dump; Reservations not accepted; Max length: 30ft; Stay limit: 14 days; Open Jun-Oct; Tent & RV camping: $6; Elev: 6722ft/2049m; Tel: 541-523-6391; Nearest town: Halfway. GPS: 45.050381, -117.095487

167 • Fish Lake (Mt McLoughlin)

Total sites: 20; RV sites: 17; Central water; No toilets; No showers; No RV dump; Reservations accepted; Stay limit: 14 days; Open May-Sep; Tents: $12/RVs: $25; Elev: 4816ft/1468m; Tel: 541-560-3900; Nearest town: Klamath Falls; Notes: Also walk-to sites. GPS: 42.395055, -122.321433

168 • Forest Creek

Total sites: 8; RV sites: 8; No water; Vault toilets; Reservations not accepted; Max length: 16ft; Open May-Sep; Tent & RV camping: $12; Elev: 3176ft/968m; Tel: 503-668 1700; Nearest town: Dufur. GPS: 45.179976, -121.524673

169 • Four Corners Sno-Park

Total sites: 2; RV sites: 2; No water; Vault toilets; Stay limit: 14 days; Tent & RV camping: Free; Elev: 4442ft/1354m; Tel: 541-278-3716; Nearest town: Ukiah. GPS: 45.178511, -118.606898

170 • Fourbit Ford

Total sites: 7; RV sites: 7; Central water; Vault toilets; No showers; No RV dump; Reservations not accepted; Stay limit: 14 days; Generator hours: 0600-2200; Open May-Sep; Tent & RV camping: $14; Elev: 3264ft/995m; Tel: 541-560-3400; Nearest town: Butte Falls. GPS: 42.501214, -122.404295

171 • Fourmile Lake

Total sites: 29; RV sites: 29; No water; Vault toilets; Reservations accepted; Max length: 36ft; Generator hours: 0700-2200; Open Jun-Sep; Tent & RV camping: $18; Elev: 5758ft/1755m; Tel: 541-885-3400; Nearest town: Klamath Falls. GPS: 42.455322, -122.248291

172 • Frazier

Total sites: 20; RV sites: 20; Central water; Vault toilets; No showers; No RV dump; Reservations not accepted; Max length: 40ft; Stay limit: 14 days; Open all year; Tent & RV camping: $10; Elev: 4334ft/1321m; Tel: 541-278-3716; Nearest town: Ukiah; Notes: Group site: $25, Free Nov-May - no services. GPS: 45.159668, -118.639893

173 • Frazier

Total sites: 10; RV sites: 9; No water; Vault toilets; Reservations not accepted; Stay limit: 14 days; Open May-Sep; Tent & RV camping: Free; Elev: 4603ft/1403m; Tel: 541-416-6500; Nearest town: Prineville; Notes: No services in winter. GPS: 44.220865, -119.576757

174 • French Pete

Total sites: 17; RV sites: 17; Central water; Vault toilets; No showers; No RV dump; Reservations accepted; Max length: 30ft; Stay limit: 14 days; Open May-Sep; Tent & RV camping: $17; Elev: 1883ft/574m; Tel: 801-226-3564; Nearest town: Blue River. GPS: 44.041758, -122.208482

175 • Frissell Crossing

Total sites: 12; RV sites: 12; Central water; Vault toilets; No showers; No RV dump; Reservations accepted; Max length: 36ft; Stay limit: 14 days; Open May-Sep; Tent & RV camping: $14; Elev: 2607ft/795m; Tel: 801-226-3564; Nearest town: Blue River. GPS: 43.958733, -122.085201

176 • Frog Heaven Forest Camp

Total sites: 6; RV sites: 6; No water; No toilets; Reservations not accepted; Stay limit: 14 days; Open May-Sep; Tent & RV camping: Free; Elev: 4797ft/1462m; Tel: 541-523-6391; Nearest town: La Grande. GPS: 45.212624, -118.601921

177 • Frog Lake

Total sites: 33; RV sites: 33; Central water; Vault toilets; No showers; No RV dump; Reservations accepted; Max length: 22ft; Open May-Sep; Tent & RV camping: $22-24; Elev: 3927ft/1197m; Tel: 541-328-0909; Nearest town: Government Camp. GPS: 45.222244, -121.693725

178 • Game Lake

Total sites: 3; RV sites: 3; No water; Vault toilets; Reservations not accepted; Stay limit: 14 days; Generator hours: 0600-2200;

Open May-Nov; Tent & RV camping: Free; Elev: 3983ft/1214m; Tel: 541-247-3600; Nearest town: Gold Beach. GPS: 42.432765, -124.087062

179 • Gold Dredge

Total sites: 7; RV sites: 7; No water; Vault toilets; Reservations not accepted; Max length: 40ft; Stay limit: 14 days; Open May-Nov; Tent & RV camping: $8; Elev: 3110ft/948m; Tel: 541-278-3716; Nearest town: Dale; Notes: Free Nov-May - no services. GPS: 45.001816, -118.819135

180 • Gold Lake

Total sites: 21; RV sites: 21; Central water; Vault toilets; No showers; No RV dump; Reservations not accepted; Max length: 24ft; Stay limit: 14 days; Open May-Oct; Tent & RV camping: $21; Elev: 4885ft/1489m; Tel: 541-782-2283; Nearest town: Oakridge. GPS: 43.631162, -122.050106

181 • Gone Creek

Total sites: 50; RV sites: 50; Central water; Vault toilets; No showers; No RV dump; Reservations accepted; Max length: 32ft; Open Jul-Sep; Tent & RV camping: $20; Elev: 3284ft/1001m; Tel: 503-622-3191; Nearest town: Government Camp. GPS: 45.112872, -121.777546

182 • Gorge

Total sites: 18; RV sites: 18; No water; Vault toilets; Reservations accepted; Max length: 50ft; Stay limit: 14 days; Open May-Sep; Tent & RV camping: $16-18; Elev: 2953ft/900m; Tel: 541-338-7869; Nearest town: Sisters. GPS: 44.485840, -121.640137

183 • Grande Ronde Lake

Total sites: 8; RV sites: 8; Central water; Vault toilets; No showers; No RV dump; Reservations not accepted; Stay limit: 14 days; Open Jul-Oct; Tent & RV camping: $10; Elev: 7172ft/2186m; Tel: 541-523-6391; Nearest town: Baker City. GPS: 44.975441, -118.243155

184 • Grassy Flats

Total sites: 5; RV sites: 5; No water; No toilets; Stay limit: 14 days; Generator hours: 0600-2200; Open May-Oct; Tent & RV camping: Free; Elev: 4429ft/1350m; Tel: 541-471 6514; Nearest town: Agness. GPS: 42.553000, -123.919000

185 • Grayback

Total sites: 39; Central water; Vault toilets; No showers; No RV dump; Reservations not accepted; Max length: 35ft; Stay limit: 14 days; Generator hours: 0600-2200; Open May-Oct; Tents only: $15; Elev: 1909ft/582m; Tel: 541-592-4000; Nearest town: Cave Junction. GPS: 42.141628, -123.462913

186 • Green Canyon

Total sites: 15; RV sites: 15; No water; Vault toilets; Reservations not accepted; Max length: 22ft; Open May-Sep; Tent & RV camping: $21; Elev: 1680ft/512m; Tel: 503-668 1700; Nearest town: Zigzag. GPS: 45.283203, -121.942871

187 • Grindstone

Total sites: 3; RV sites: 3; No water; Vault toilets; Reservations not accepted; Tent & RV camping: Free; Elev: 3402ft/1037m; Tel: 503-668 1700; Nearest town: Parkdale. GPS: 45.247319, -121.658907

188 • Gull Point

Total sites: 79; RV sites: 79; Central water; No toilets; No showers; RV dump; Reservations accepted; Max length: 30ft; Open Apr-Oct; Tent & RV camping: $18-20; Elev: 4364ft/1330m; Tel: 541-338-7869; Nearest town: Bend; Notes: $10 dump fee. GPS: 43.704466, -121.762789

189 • Hamaker

Total sites: 10; RV sites: 10; No water; Vault toilets; Reservations not accepted; Stay limit: 14 days; Open May-Sep; Tent & RV camping: $12; Elev: 4131ft/1259m; Nearest town: Prospect. GPS: 43.056792, -122.328718

190 • Hampton

Total sites: 4; RV sites: 4; Central water; Vault toilets; No showers; No RV dump; Reservations not accepted; Stay limit: 14 days; Open Apr-Sep; Tent & RV camping: $5; Elev: 919ft/280m; Tel: 541-782-2283; Nearest town: Oakridge. GPS: 43.816011, -122.589591

191 • Happy Camp

Total sites: 9; RV sites: 9; Central water; Vault toilets; Reservations not accepted; Open all year; Tent & RV camping: Free; Elev: 5325ft/1623m; Tel: 541-943-3114; Nearest town: Paisley; Notes: Reduced services 10/15-5/14. GPS: 42.476078, -120.684258

192 • Hart-tish Park

Total sites: 15; RV sites: 8; Central water; Flush toilets; Reservations accepted; Stay limit: 14 days; Open Apr-Sep; Tent & RV camping: $20; Elev: 2090ft/637m; Tel: 541-899-9220; Nearest town: Jacksonville; Notes: Group site $40. GPS: 42.052041, -123.128651

193 • Haystack Reservoir

Total sites: 24; RV sites: 24; Central water; Vault toilets; No showers; No RV dump; Reservations accepted; Max length: 32ft; Open Apr-Oct; Tent & RV camping: $15; Elev: 2923ft/891m; Tel: 208-270-0094; Nearest town: Madras. GPS: 44.493478, -121.140846

194 • Haystack Reservoir - West Shore

Total sites: 14; RV sites: 14; No water; Vault toilets; Reservations not accepted; Max length: 32ft; Stay limit: 14 days; Open Apr-Nov; Tent & RV camping: $12; Elev: 2838ft/865m; Tel: 208-270-0094; Nearest town: Culver. GPS: 44.493743, -121.159938

195 • Head O Boulder Forest Camp

Total sites: 3; RV sites: 3; No water; Vault toilets; Reservations not accepted; Stay limit: 14 days; Tent & RV camping: Free; Elev: 7182ft/2189m; Tel: 541-575-3000; Nearest town: Austin Junction. GPS: 44.755000, -118.692000

196 • Head of the River

Total sites: 5; No water; Vault toilets; Reservations not accepted; Open all year; Tents only: Free; Elev: 4636ft/1413m; Tel: 541-783-

4001; Nearest town: Chiloquin; Notes: Reduced services 10/15-5/14. GPS: 42.731532, -121.420563

197 • Hebo Lake

Total sites: 12; RV sites: 12; No water; Vault toilets; Reservations accepted; Stay limit: 14 days; Open Apr-Oct; Tent & RV camping: $18; Elev: 1685ft/514m; Tel: 503-392-5100; Nearest town: Beaver. GPS: 45.231466, -123.794595

198 • Hemlock Lake (Quartz Mt)

Total sites: 13; RV sites: 10; No water; Vault toilets; Reservations not accepted; Max length: 35ft; Stay limit: 14 days; Generator hours: 0600-2200; Open May-Nov; Tent & RV camping: $10; Elev: 4550ft/1387m; Tel: 541-496-3534; Nearest town: Glide. GPS: 43.191439, -122.703961

199 • Hemlock Meadows

Total sites: 4; RV sites: 4; No water; Vault toilets; Reservations not accepted; Max length: 35ft; Stay limit: 14 days; Generator hours: 0600-2200; Open Jun-Oct; Tent & RV camping: $10; Elev: 4541ft/1384m; Tel: 541-496-3534; Nearest town: North Umpqua. GPS: 43.188629, -122.696646

200 • Hidden

Total sites: 10; RV sites: 10; No water; Vault toilets; Reservations not accepted; Stay limit: 14 days; Open Jun-Sep; Tent & RV camping: $6; Elev: 4537ft/1383m; Tel: 541-523-6391; Nearest town: Joseph. GPS: 45.113770, -116.980225

201 • Hideaway Lake

Total sites: 9; RV sites: 9; No water; Vault toilets; Reservations not accepted; Max length: 16ft; Open Jun-Sep; Tent & RV camping: $19; Elev: 4163ft/1269m; Tel: 503-668 1700; Nearest town: Estacada. GPS: 45.123321, -121.967825

202 • Hobo Forest Camp

Total sites: 4; RV sites: 4; No water; Vault toilets; Reservations not accepted; Max length: 16ft; Stay limit: 14 days; Generator hours: 0600-2200; Open all year; Tent & RV camping: Free; Elev: 2113ft/644m; Tel: 541-957-3200; Nearest town: Cottage Grove; Notes: No services in winter. GPS: 43.647035, -122.667811

203 • Holbrook Reservoir

Total sites: 1; RV sites: 1; No water; Vault toilets; Reservations not accepted; Open all year; Tent & RV camping: Free; Elev: 5439ft/1658m; Tel: 541-353-2427; Nearest town: Bly; Notes: Reduced services 10/15-5/14. GPS: 42.265477, -120.853135

204 • Hood River Meadows

Total sites: 5; RV sites: 5; No water; No toilets; Max length: 21ft; Tent & RV camping: Free; Elev: 4520ft/1378m; Tel: 503-668 1700; Nearest town: Mt Hood. GPS: 45.320637, -121.634325

205 • Hoodview

Total sites: 43; RV sites: 43; Central water; Vault toilets; No showers; No RV dump; Reservations accepted; Max length: 32ft; Open May-Sep; Tent & RV camping: $20; Elev: 3249ft/990m; Tel: 503-622-3191; Nearest town: Government Camp. GPS: 45.107911, -121.791844

206 • Hoover

Total sites: 37; RV sites: 37; Central water; Vault toilets; No showers; No RV dump; Reservations accepted; Max length: 30ft; Stay limit: 14 days; Open May-Sep; Tent & RV camping: $24; Elev: 1591ft/485m; Tel: 801-226-3564; Nearest town: Detroit. GPS: 44.713264, -122.124048

207 • Horseshoe Bend (Steamboat)

Total sites: 25; RV sites: 25; Central water; Flush toilets; No showers; No RV dump; Reservations accepted; Max length: 35ft; Stay limit: 14 days; Open May-Sep; Tent & RV camping: $15; Elev: 1424ft/434m; Tel: 541-496-3534; Nearest town: Idleyld Park. GPS: 43.288704, -122.627577

208 • Horsfall Beach

Total sites: 34; RV sites: 34; Central water; Flush toilets; No showers; No RV dump; Reservations accepted; Max length: 57ft; Stay limit: 14 days; Open all year; Tent & RV camping: $25; Elev: 13ft/4m; Tel: 541-271-3611; Nearest town: North Bend. GPS: 43.453695, -124.276075

209 • Hot Springs

Total sites: 26; RV sites: 26; No toilets; Reservations not accepted; Max length: 26ft; Tent & RV camping: $10; Elev: 6421ft/1957m; Nearest town: La Pine. GPS: 43.717435, -121.200735

210 • House Rock

Total sites: 17; RV sites: 12; Central water; Vault toilets; No showers; No RV dump; Reservations accepted; Max length: 22ft; Stay limit: 14 days; Open May-Sep; Tent & RV camping: $18; Elev: 1768ft/539m; Tel: 541-967-3917; Nearest town: Sweet Home. GPS: 44.392773, -122.245205

211 • Huckleberry Mountain

Total sites: 25; RV sites: 25; No water; Vault toilets; Reservations not accepted; Max length: 16ft; Stay limit: 14 days; Generator hours: 0600-2200; Open May-Oct; Tent & RV camping: Free; Elev: 5467ft/1666m; Tel: 541-560-3400; Nearest town: Prospect. GPS: 42.876344, -122.338061

212 • Humbug

Total sites: 21; RV sites: 21; Central water; Vault toilets; No showers; No RV dump; Reservations accepted; Max length: 30ft; Stay limit: 14 days; Open May-Sep; Tent & RV camping: $18; Elev: 1913ft/583m; Tel: 503-854-3366; Nearest town: Detroit. GPS: 44.771973, -122.077881

213 • Hurricane Creek

Total sites: 8; RV sites: 3; No water; Vault toilets; Reservations not accepted; Stay limit: 14 days; Open Jun-Sep; Tent & RV camping: $6; Elev: 4655ft/1419m; Tel: 541-523-6391; Nearest town: Enterprise. GPS: 45.332183, -117.298794

214 • Ice Cap Creek

Total sites: 22; RV sites: 14; No water; Vault toilets; Reservations accepted; Max length: 30ft; Stay limit: 14 days; Open May-Sep; Tent & RV camping: $18; Elev: 2815ft/858m; Tel: 801-226-3564; Nearest town: Blue River. GPS: 44.341309, -122.001953

215 • Idlewild

Total sites: 22; RV sites: 22; Central water; Vault toilets; No showers; No RV dump; Reservations not accepted; Stay limit: 14 days; Open May-Sep; Tent & RV camping: $10; Elev: 5348ft/1630m; Tel: 541-575-3000; Nearest town: Burns. GPS: 43.799561, -118.989990

216 • Imnaha

Total sites: 5; RV sites: 5; Central water; Vault toilets; No showers; No RV dump; Reservations not accepted; Stay limit: 14 days; Open May-Oct; Tent & RV camping: $10; Elev: 3852ft/1174m; Tel: 541-865-2700; Nearest town: Butte Falls. GPS: 42.702528, -122.334408

217 • Indian Crossing

Total sites: 14; RV sites: 14; No water; Vault toilets; Reservations not accepted; Stay limit: 14 days; Open Jun-Oct; Tent & RV camping: $6; Elev: 4606ft/1404m; Tel: 541-523-6391; Nearest town: Joseph. GPS: 45.113214, -117.013494

218 • Indian Ford

Total sites: 25; RV sites: 25; No water; Vault toilets; Reservations accepted; Max length: 50ft; Open May-Oct; Tent & RV camping: $12-14; Elev: 3287ft/1002m; Tel: 541-338-7869; Nearest town: Sisters. GPS: 44.357432, -121.610434

219 • Indian Henry

Total sites: 86; RV sites: 86; Central water; Flush toilets; No showers; RV dump; Reservations accepted; Max length: 36ft; Open May-Sep; Tent & RV camping: $22-24; Elev: 1348ft/411m; Tel: 503-630-6861; Nearest town: Estacada. GPS: 45.108177, -122.075636

220 • Indigo Springs

Total sites: 3; No water; Vault toilets; Reservations not accepted; Stay limit: 14 days; Generator hours: 0600-2200; Open all year; Tents only: Free; Elev: 2946ft/898m; Tel: 541-782-2283; Nearest town: Oakridge. GPS: 43.497564, -122.264448

221 • Inlet

Total sites: 14; RV sites: 14; No water; Vault toilets; Reservations accepted; Max length: 25ft; Stay limit: 14 days; Open Jun-Oct; Tent & RV camping: $10; Elev: 4213ft/1284m; Tel: 541-498-2531; Nearest town: Chemult; Notes: 1 group site. GPS: 43.311751, -122.150246

222 • Irondyke Forest Camp

Total sites: 5; No water; Vault toilets; Reservations not accepted; Stay limit: 14 days; Open Jun-Sep; Tents only: $5; Elev: 5213ft/1589m; Tel: 541-523-6391; Nearest town: Lostine. GPS: 45.297648, -117.396855

223 • Island (Steamboat)

Total sites: 7; RV sites: 7; No water; Vault toilets; Reservations not accepted; Max length: 24ft; Stay limit: 14 days; Generator hours: 0600-2200; Open all year; Tent & RV camping: $10; Elev: 1381ft/421m; Tel: 541-957-3200; Nearest town: Powers. GPS: 43.339539, -122.722845

224 • Island Camp (Illahe)

Total sites: 5; RV sites: 5; No water; Vault toilets; Reservations not accepted; Stay limit: 14 days; Open all year; Tent & RV camping: $10; Elev: 1099ft/335m; Tel: 541-439-6200; Nearest town: Powers. GPS: 42.722243, -124.042249

225 • Islet

Total sites: 55; RV sites: 55; Central water; Vault toilets; No showers; No RV dump; Reservations accepted; Max length: 30ft; Stay limit: 14 days; Open Jun-Sep; Tent & RV camping: $22; Elev: 5502ft/1677m; Tel: 801-226-3564; Nearest town: Oakridge. GPS: 43.748732, -122.006976

226 • Jack Creek

Total sites: 19; RV sites: 19; No water; Vault toilets; Reservations accepted; Max length: 50ft; Open May-Oct; Tent & RV camping: $12-14; Elev: 3110ft/948m; Tel: 541-338-7869; Nearest town: Sisters. GPS: 44.484351, -121.700815

227 • Jack Lake

Total sites: 2; No water; Vault toilets; Open May-Oct; Tents only: Free; Elev: 5161ft/1573m; Tel: 541-549-7700; Nearest town: Sisters; Notes: Wilderness Permits required May-Oct. GPS: 44.491898, -121.794484

228 • Jackson Creek

Total sites: 12; No water; Vault toilets; Reservations not accepted; Open all year; Tents only: Free; Elev: 4744ft/1446m; Tel: 541-365-7001; Nearest town: Chemult; Notes: Reduced services 10/16-5/14. GPS: 42.983092, -121.457146

229 • Jackson on Applegate

Total sites: 12; RV sites: 8; Central water; Flush toilets; No showers; No RV dump; Reservations not accepted; Max length: 18ft; Stay limit: 14 days; Open all year; Tent & RV camping: $20; Elev: 1673ft/510m; Tel: 541-899-3800; Nearest town: Ruch; Notes: Tents/small RVs only - no trailers. GPS: 42.114108, -123.087455

230 • Jones Crossing Forest Camp

Total sites: 8; RV sites: 8; No water; Vault toilets; Reservations not accepted; Open all year; Tent & RV camping: Free; Elev: 4829ft/1472m; Tel: 541-943-3114; Nearest town: Paisley; Notes: Reduced services 10/15-5/14. GPS: 42.605851, -120.598874

231 • Josephine

Total sites: 6; RV sites: 6; No water; Vault toilets; Reservations not accepted; Stay limit: 14 days; Generator hours: 0600-2200; Open all year; Tent & RV camping: Free; Elev: 1204ft/367m; Tel: 541-592-4000; Nearest town: Cave Junction. GPS: 42.242434, -123.686041

232 • Jubilee Lake

Total sites: 53; RV sites: 48; Central water; No toilets; No showers; No RV dump; Reservations not accepted; Max length: 32ft; Stay limit: 14 days; Open Jul-Oct; Tent & RV camping: $17; Elev: 4724ft/1440m; Tel: 541-278-3716; Nearest town: Walla Walla. GPS: 45.829332, -117.966029

233 • Kelsay Valley Forest Camp

Total sites: 15; RV sites: 15; No water; Vault toilets; Reservations accepted; Max length: 20ft; Stay limit: 14 days; Open Jun-Oct; Tent & RV camping: $10; Elev: 4360ft/1329m; Tel: 541-498-2531; Nearest town: Chemult; Notes: 11 sites with corral. GPS: 43.312316, -122.112586

234 • Kiahanie

Total sites: 19; RV sites: 19; Central water; Vault toilets; No showers; No RV dump; Reservations not accepted; Max length: 24ft; Stay limit: 14 days; Open May-Oct; Tent & RV camping: $10; Elev: 2270ft/692m; Tel: 541-782-2283; Nearest town: Oakridge. GPS: 43.885010, -122.257813

235 • Kingfisher Camp

Total sites: 23; RV sites: 23; Central water; Vault toilets; No showers; No RV dump; Reservations accepted; Max length: 36ft; Open May-Sep; Tent & RV camping: $22-24; Elev: 1864ft/568m; Tel: 503-630-5721; Nearest town: Estacada. GPS: 44.976189, -122.092852

236 • Knebal Springs

Total sites: 8; RV sites: 8; No water; Vault toilets; Reservations not accepted; Max length: 22ft; Open May-Sep; Tent & RV camping: $19; Elev: 3809ft/1161m; Tel: 503-668 1700; Nearest town: Dufur. GPS: 45.434195, -121.478651

237 • Lagoon

Total sites: 39; RV sites: 39; Central water; Flush toilets; No showers; No RV dump; Reservations accepted; Max length: 35ft; Stay limit: 14 days; Open all year; Tent & RV camping: $22; Elev: 30ft/9m; Tel: 541-271-3611; Nearest town: Florence. GPS: 43.879944, -124.142074

238 • Laird Lake

Total sites: 4; RV sites: 4; No water; Vault toilets; Reservations not accepted; Stay limit: 14 days; Generator hours: 0600-2200; Open all year; Tent & RV camping: Free; Elev: 1893ft/577m; Tel: 541-439-6200; Nearest town: Powers; Notes: Winter access limited. GPS: 42.699259, -124.203098

239 • Lake Fork

Total sites: 10; RV sites: 10; No water; Vault toilets; Reservations not accepted; Stay limit: 14 days; Open May-Oct; Tent & RV camping: $6; Elev: 3242ft/988m; Nearest town: Joseph. GPS: 45.008392, -116.912068

240 • Lake Harriet

Total sites: 8; RV sites: 8; Central water; Vault toilets; No showers; No RV dump; Reservations accepted; Max length: 30ft; Open May-Sep; Tent & RV camping: $18; Elev: 2198ft/670m; Tel: 503-630-6861; Nearest town: Estacada; Notes: Managed by PGE. GPS: 45.073291, -121.958426

241 • Lake in the Woods

Total sites: 11; RV sites: 10; Central water; No toilets; No showers; No RV dump; Reservations not accepted; Max length: 35ft; Stay limit: 14 days; Open May-Oct; Tent & RV camping: $10; Elev: 3032ft/924m; Tel: 541-496-3534; Nearest town: Glide. GPS: 43.216958, -122.722065

242 • Lane Creek

Total sites: 7; RV sites: 7; No water; Vault toilets; Reservations not accepted; Max length: 20ft; Stay limit: 14 days; Open all year; Tent & RV camping: $8; Elev: 3908ft/1191m; Tel: 541-278-3716; Nearest town: Ukiah; Notes: 1 group site $25, Free - no services Nov-May. GPS: 45.189595, -118.766126

243 • Lava Camp Lake

Total sites: 12; RV sites: 12; No water; Vault toilets; Reservations not accepted; Max length: 35ft; Open Jun-Oct; Tent & RV camping: Free; Elev: 5312ft/1619m; Tel: 541-549-7700; Nearest town: Sisters. GPS: 44.261227, -121.785608

244 • Lava Flow

Total sites: 6; RV sites: 6; No water; Vault toilets; Max length: 60ft; Open Apr-Oct; Tent & RV camping: Free; Elev: 4475ft/1364m; Nearest town: Crescent. GPS: 43.622943, -121.820543

245 • Lava Lake

Total sites: 44; RV sites: 38; Central water; Vault toilets; No showers; No RV dump; Reservations accepted; Max length: 30ft; Open May-Sep; Tent & RV camping: $16; Elev: 4751ft/1448m; Tel: 541-338-7869; Nearest town: Bend. GPS: 43.913964, -121.767884

246 • Lazy Bend

Total sites: 21; RV sites: 21; Central water; Flush toilets; No showers; No RV dump; Reservations accepted; Max length: 24ft; Open Apr-Oct; Tent & RV camping: $22-24; Elev: 814ft/248m; Tel: 503-630-4156; Nearest town: Estacada. GPS: 45.190891, -122.207558

247 • Lee Thomas

Total sites: 7; RV sites: 7; Central water; No RV dump; Reservations not accepted; Open all year; Tent & RV camping: Free; Elev: 6253ft/1906m; Tel: 541-943-3114; Nearest town: Paisley; Notes: Reduced services 10/15-5/14. GPS: 42.590151, -120.838902

248 • Lemolo Two Forebay

Total sites: 3; No water; Vault toilets; Reservations not accepted; Stay limit: 14 days; Open May-Oct; Tents only: Free; Elev: 3264ft/995m; Tel: 541-498-2531; Nearest town: Roseburg. GPS: 43.293946, -122.402288

249 • Lick Creek

Total sites: 12; RV sites: 5; No water; Vault toilets; Reservations not accepted; Stay limit: 14 days; Open Jun-Sep; Tent & RV camping: $6; Elev: 5472ft/1668m; Tel: 541-523-6391; Nearest town: Joseph. GPS: 45.158159, -117.034239

250 • Limberlost

Total sites: 12; RV sites: 10; No water; Vault toilets; Reservations accepted; Max length: 16ft; Stay limit: 14 days; Open May-Sep; Tent & RV camping: $13; Elev: 1762ft/537m; Tel: 801-226-3564; Nearest town: Blue River. GPS: 44.174316, -122.053223

251 • Link Creek

Total sites: 33; RV sites: 33; Central water; Vault toilets; No showers; No RV dump; Reservations accepted; Max length: 50ft; Open Apr-Nov; Tent & RV camping: $16-18; Elev: 3481ft/1061m; Tel: 541-338-7869; Nearest town: Sisters. GPS: 44.416260, -121.755615

252 • Little Badger

Total sites: 3; RV sites: 3; No water; Vault toilets; Reservations not accepted; Max length: 16ft; Open May-Sep; Tent & RV camping: Free; Elev: 2077ft/633m; Tel: 503-668 1700; Nearest town: Dufur. GPS: 45.281799, -121.348385

253 • Little Crater Lake

Total sites: 16; RV sites: 8; Central water; Vault toilets; No showers; No RV dump; Reservations accepted; Max length: 22ft; Open May-Sep; Tent & RV camping: $21-23; Elev: 3327ft/1014m; Tel: 541-328-0909; Nearest town: Government Camp. GPS: 45.148453, -121.745648

254 • Little Crater Lake

Total sites: 49; RV sites: 49; Central water; Vault toilets; No showers; No RV dump; Reservations accepted; Max length: 30ft; Open May-Oct; Tent & RV camping: $18; Elev: 6371ft/1942m; Tel: 541-338-7869; Nearest town: Bend. GPS: 43.713538, -121.242541

255 • Little Cultus Lake

Total sites: 31; RV sites: 31; Central water; Vault toilets; No showers; No RV dump; Reservations accepted; Max length: 30ft; Open May-Sep; Tent & RV camping: $16-18; Elev: 4777ft/1456m; Tel: 541-338-7869; Nearest town: Crescent. GPS: 43.799887, -121.867789

256 • Little Falls

Total sites: 3; RV sites: 3; No water; Vault toilets; Reservations not accepted; Stay limit: 14 days; Generator hours: 0600-2200; Open May-Sep; Tent & RV camping: $10; Elev: 1368ft/417m; Tel: 541-592-4000; Nearest town: Cave Junction. GPS: 42.240779, -123.676284

257 • Little Fan Creek

Total sites: 4; RV sites: 4; Vault toilets; Reservations not accepted; Tent & RV camping: $14; Elev: 1686ft/514m; Tel: 503-668 1700; Nearest town: Estacada. GPS: 44.991726, -122.063976

258 • Little Fawn

Total sites: 20; RV sites: 20; No water; Vault toilets; No showers; No RV dump; Reservations accepted; Max length: 30ft; Open May-Sep; Tent & RV camping: $16-18; Elev: 4905ft/1495m; Tel: 541-338-7869; Nearest town: Bend; Notes: Group site: $100-$225. GPS: 43.962662, -121.796447

259 • Little Lava Lake

Total sites: 13; RV sites: 13; Central water; Flush toilets; No showers; No RV dump; Reservations accepted; Max length: 40ft; Open May-Oct; Tent & RV camping: $14-16; Elev: 4751ft/1448m; Tel: 541-338-7869; Nearest town: Bend; Notes: Group site: $50-$90. GPS: 43.910325, -121.762277

260 • Lockaby

Total sites: 30; RV sites: 4; Central water; Vault toilets; No showers; No RV dump; Reservations accepted; Max length: 16ft; Open May-Sep; Tent & RV camping: $22-24; Elev: 945ft/288m; Tel: 503-630-6861; Nearest town: Estacada. GPS: 45.165676, -122.153137

261 • Lofton Reservoir

Total sites: 26; RV sites: 26; No water; Vault toilets; Reservations not accepted; Open May-Oct; Tent & RV camping: $6; Elev: 6174ft/1882m; Tel: 541-353-2750; Nearest town: Bly; Notes: Reduced services 10/15-5/14. GPS: 42.262939, -120.816895

262 • Lookout

Total sites: 20; RV sites: 20; Central water; Vault toilets; No showers; No RV dump; Reservations accepted; Max length: 40ft; Stay limit: 14 days; Open all year; Tent & RV camping: $14; Elev: 1357ft/414m; Tel: 541-822-3381; Nearest town: Blue River. GPS: 44.202493, -122.260586

263 • Lost Creek

Total sites: 16; RV sites: 8; Central water; Vault toilets; No showers; No RV dump; Reservations accepted; Max length: 22ft; Open May-Sep; Tent & RV camping: $21-23; Elev: 2467ft/752m; Tel: 541-328-0909; Nearest town: Zigzag. GPS: 45.381697, -121.836174

264 • Lost Lake

Total sites: 129; RV sites: 129; Central water; Vault toilets; No showers; RV dump; Reservations accepted; Max length: 40ft; Open May-Sep; Tents: $30-40/RVs: $36-43; Elev: 3261ft/994m; Tel: 503-668 1700; Nearest town: Parkdale; Notes: Group sites $67-$80. GPS: 45.497501, -121.816337

265 • Lost Lake

Total sites: 15; RV sites: 15; No water; Vault toilets; Reservations not accepted; Stay limit: 14 days; Open May-Oct; Tent & RV camping: $8; Elev: 4039ft/1231m; Tel: 541-822-3381; Nearest town: McKenzie Bridge; Notes: Trailers not recommended. GPS: 44.433216, -121.909772

266 • Lost Prairie

Total sites: 10; RV sites: 2; Central water; Vault toilets; No showers; No RV dump; Reservations not accepted; Max length: 24ft; Stay limit: 14 days; Open May-Oct; Tent & RV camping: $18; Elev: 3389ft/1033m; Tel: 541-967-3917; Nearest town: Sweet Home; Notes: Can reserve whole park - $125. GPS: 44.402588, -122.076172

267 • Lower Bridge

Total sites: 12; RV sites: 12; Central water; Vault toilets; No showers; No RV dump; Reservations accepted; Max length: 40ft; Open May-Dec; Tent & RV camping: $16-18; Elev: 2802ft/854m; Tel: 541-338-7869; Nearest town: Sisters. GPS: 44.557461, -121.619857

268 • Lower Buck Creek Forest Camp

Total sites: 5; RV sites: 5; No water; Vault toilets; Reservations not accepted; Open all year; Tent & RV camping: Free; Elev: 4917ft/ 1499m; Tel: 541-576-2107; Nearest town: Silver Lake; Notes: Reduced services 10/15-5/14. GPS: 43.068544, -121.246333

269 • Lower Camp Creek

Total sites: 6; RV sites: 6; No water; Vault toilets; Reservations not accepted; Stay limit: 14 days; Open Jun-Sep; Tent & RV camping: $6; Elev: 3622ft/1104m; Tel: 541-820-3800; Nearest town: Prairie City. GPS: 44.673000, -118.799000

270 • Lower Canyon Creek

Total sites: 7; RV sites: 7; No water; Vault toilets; Reservations accepted; Max length: 20ft; Open May-Sep; Tent & RV camping: $12-14; Elev: 2877ft/877m; Tel: 541-338-7869; Nearest town: Sisters. GPS: 44.501341, -121.641506

271 • Lower Eightmile Crossing

Total sites: 3; RV sites: 3; No water; Vault toilets; Reservations not accepted; Max length: 16ft; Open May-Oct; Tent & RV camping: $21; Elev: 3737ft/1139m; Tel: 503-668 1700; Nearest town: Dufur. GPS: 45.413592, -121.442771

272 • Lower Lake

Total sites: 8; RV sites: 8; No water; No toilets; Reservations not accepted; Max length: 16ft; Open Jun-Sep; Tent & RV camping: $15-20; Elev: 4875ft/1486m; Tel: 503-668 1700; Nearest town: Estacada. GPS: 44.822873, -121.797541

273 • Lower Olallie Meadow

Total sites: 7; RV sites: 7; No water; Vault toilets; Reservations not accepted; Open Jun-Sep; Tent & RV camping: $15-20; Elev: 4492ft/1369m; Tel: 503-668 1700; Nearest town: Estacada. GPS: 44.859666, -121.773714

274 • Ludlum

Total sites: 7; RV sites: 7; Central water; No toilets; No showers; No RV dump; Reservations not accepted; Stay limit: 14 days; Generator hours: 0600-2200; Open Apr-Nov; Tent & RV camping: $10; Elev: 233ft/71m; Tel: 541-412-6000; Nearest town: Chetco. GPS: 42.035683, -124.109192

275 • Lund Park

Total sites: 10; RV sites: 10; No water; Vault toilets; Reservations not accepted; Max length: 16ft; Stay limit: 14 days; Generator hours: 0600-2200; Open May-Nov; Tent & RV camping: $8; Elev: 2057ft/ 627m; Tel: 541-767-5000; Nearest town: Cottage Grove; Notes: 3 spaces outside gate open year round. GPS: 43.650908, -122.676731

276 • Magone Lake

Total sites: 22; RV sites: 19; Central water; Vault toilets; No showers; No RV dump; Reservations not accepted; Max length: 16ft; Stay limit: 14 days; Open May-Sep; Tent & RV camping: $13; Elev: 5052ft/1540m; Tel: 541-820-3800; Nearest town: Mount Vernon; Notes: Reservable group site: $25-$60. GPS: 44.552464, -118.911023

277 • Mallard Marsh

Total sites: 15; RV sites: 15; No water; Flush toilets; Reservations accepted; Max length: 26ft; Open May-Sep; Tent & RV camping: $10-14; Elev: 4974ft/1516m; Tel: 541-338-7869; Nearest town: Bend. GPS: 43.963379, -121.782715

278 • Marion Forks

Total sites: 15; RV sites: 15; No water; Vault toilets; Reservations not accepted; Max length: 24ft; Stay limit: 14 days; Open all year; Tent & RV camping: $10; Elev: 2566ft/782m; Tel: 503-854-3366; Nearest town: Detroit. GPS: 44.609474, -121.946124

279 • Marster Spring

Total sites: 10; RV sites: 10; Central water; Vault toilets; No showers; No RV dump; Reservations not accepted; Open May-Oct; Tent & RV camping: $6; Elev: 4767ft/1453m; Tel: 541-943-4479; Nearest town: Paisley; Notes: Reduced services 10/15-5/14. GPS: 42.623337, -120.605521

280 • Marys Peak

Total sites: 6; RV sites: 6; No water; Vault toilets; Reservations not accepted; Stay limit: 14 days; Open May-Sep; Tent & RV camping: $12; Elev: 3570ft/1088m; Tel: 541-563-8400; Nearest town: Corvallis; Notes: Permit required. GPS: 44.509323, -123.561007

281 • McBride

Total sites: 7; RV sites: 7; No water; Vault toilets; Reservations not accepted; Max length: 30ft; Stay limit: 14 days; Open Jul-Sep; Tent & RV camping: Free; Elev: 4774ft/1455m; Tel: 541-523-6391; Nearest town: Halfway. GPS: 44.934672, -117.222522

282 • McCubbins Gulch

Total sites: 15; RV sites: 15; No water; Vault toilets; Reservations not accepted; Max length: 25ft; Open May-Sep; Tent & RV camping: $12; Elev: 3025ft/922m; Tel: 503-668 1700; Nearest town: Government Camp. GPS: 45.115286, -121.483065

283 • McCully Forks

Total sites: 7; RV sites: 7; No water; Vault toilets; Reservations not accepted; Stay limit: 14 days; Open Jun-Sep; Tent & RV camping: $6; Elev: 4632ft/1412m; Tel: 541-523-6391; Nearest town: Baker City. GPS: 44.767061, -118.247249

284 • McKay Crossing

Total sites: 16; RV sites: 16; No water; Vault toilets; Reservations accepted; Max length: 26ft; Open May-Oct; Tent & RV camping: $10; Elev: 4758ft/1450m; Tel: 541-383-4000; Nearest town: Bend. GPS: 43.716825, -121.377324

285 • McKenzie Bridge

Total sites: 20; RV sites: 20; Central water; Vault toilets; No showers; No RV dump; Reservations accepted; Max length: 35ft; Stay limit: 14 days; Open Apr-Sep; Tent & RV camping: $19; Elev: 1394ft/425m; Tel: 801-226-3564; Nearest town: McKenzie Bridge. GPS: 44.174805, -122.176270

286 • McNeil

Total sites: 34; RV sites: 34; No water; Vault toilets; Reservations not accepted; Max length: 22ft; Open May-Sep; Tent & RV camping: $17-19; Elev: 2100ft/640m; Tel: 503-668 1700; Nearest town: Welches. GPS: 45.385453, -121.866818

287 • Meyers Camp

Total sites: 2; RV sites: 2; No water; Vault toilets; Reservations not accepted; Stay limit: 14 days; Generator hours: 0600-2200; Open May-Sep; Tent & RV camping: Free; Elev: 2497ft/761m; Tel: 541-592-4000; Nearest town: Grants Pass. GPS: 42.472516, -123.670827

288 • Middle Fork

Total sites: 10; RV sites: 10; No water; Vault toilets; Reservations not accepted; Max length: 30ft; Stay limit: 14 days; Open May-Sep; Tent & RV camping: $8; Elev: 3917ft/1194m; Tel: 541-575-3000; Nearest town: Austin. GPS: 44.630019, -118.605254

289 • Mill Creek

Total sites: 10; RV sites: 10; No water; Vault toilets; Reservations not accepted; Stay limit: 14 days; Generator hours: 0800-2200; Open May-Oct; Tent & RV camping: $8; Elev: 2813ft/857m; Tel: 541-865-2700; Nearest town: Prospect. GPS: 42.795382, -122.467727

290 • Millers Lane

Total sites: 8; RV sites: 4; No water; Vault toilets; Reservations not accepted; Stay limit: 14 days; Open May-Sep; Tent & RV camping: $10; Elev: 4065ft/1239m; Tel: 541-523-6391; Nearest town: Baker City; Notes: Small RVs only. GPS: 44.673317, -118.068025

291 • Minam SRA

Total sites: 12; RV sites: 12; Central water; Vault toilets; No showers; No RV dump; Reservations not accepted; Open all year; Tent & RV camping: $10; Elev: 2520ft/768m; Tel: 800-551-6949; Nearest town: Elgin. GPS: 45.621823, -117.722912

292 • Mineral Forest Camp

Total sites: 3; RV sites: 3; No water; Vault toilets; Reservations not accepted; Stay limit: 14 days; Open all year; Tent & RV camping: Free; Elev: 1913ft/583m; Tel: 541-957-3200; Nearest town: Cottage Grove; Notes: Reduced services Sep-May. GPS: 43.582621, -122.713668

293 • Misery Spring

Total sites: 5; RV sites: 5; No water; Vault toilets; Reservations not accepted; Stay limit: 14 days; Open all year; Tent & RV camping: Fee unknown; Elev: 5922ft/1805m; Tel: 541-278-3716; Nearest town: Pomeroy; Notes: No services Nov-May. GPS: 44.935000, -118.547000

294 • Mona

Total sites: 23; RV sites: 23; Central water; No toilets; No showers; No RV dump; Reservations accepted; Max length: 36ft; Stay limit: 14 days; Open May-Sep; Tent & RV camping: $19; Elev: 1413ft/431m; Tel: 541-822-3381; Nearest town: Blue River. GPS: 44.203187, -122.263298

295 • Monty

Total sites: 34; RV sites: 34; No water; Vault toilets; Reservations accepted; Max length: 18ft; Open Jun-Sep; Tent & RV camping: $16; Elev: 2014ft/614m; Tel: 541-338-7869; Nearest town: Culver; Notes: Rough access road, Managed by PGE. GPS: 44.625488, -121.483154

296 • Moss Springs

Total sites: 8; RV sites: 8; No water; Vault toilets; Reservations not accepted; Max length: 18ft; Stay limit: 14 days; Open Jun-Sep; Tent & RV camping: $5; Elev: 5896ft/1797m; Tel: 541-523-6391; Nearest town: Cove. GPS: 45.275204, -117.679141

297 • Mottet

Total sites: 6; RV sites: 5; Central water; Vault toilets; No showers; No RV dump; Reservations not accepted; Stay limit: 14 days; Open Jul-Nov; Tent & RV camping: $8; Elev: 5164ft/1574m; Tel: 541-278-3716; Nearest town: Walla Walla. GPS: 45.867916, -117.961325

298 • Mt Ashland

Total sites: 9; RV sites: 9; No water; Vault toilets; Reservations not accepted; Open May-Oct; Tent & RV camping: Free; Elev: 6795ft/2071m; Tel: 530-493-2243; Nearest town: Ashland. GPS: 42.075548, -122.714284

299 • Mud Creek

Total sites: 7; RV sites: 7; No water; Vault toilets; Reservations not accepted; Open all year; Tent & RV camping: Free; Elev: 6486ft/1977m; Tel: 541-947-6300; Nearest town: Lakeview; Notes: Reduced services 10/15-5/14. GPS: 42.281714, -120.204986

300 • Mud Lake

Total sites: 7; RV sites: 7; No water; Vault toilets; Reservations not accepted; Max length: 18ft; Stay limit: 14 days; Open Jul-Oct; Tent & RV camping: $10; Elev: 7134ft/2174m; Tel: 541-894-2393; Nearest town: Baker City; Notes: Reservable group site: $50. GPS: 44.964459, -118.232954

301 • Murray

Total sites: 5; RV sites: 5; No water; Vault toilets; Reservations not accepted; Stay limit: 14 days; Open May-Sep; Tent & RV camping: $8; Elev: 5299ft/1615m; Tel: 541-575-3000; Nearest town: Seneca. GPS: 44.212369, -118.638214

302 • Myrtle Grove

Total sites: 5; RV sites: 5; No water; Vault toilets; Reservations not accepted; Stay limit: 14 days; Generator hours: 0600-2200; Open all year; Tent & RV camping: Free; Elev: 699ft/213m; Tel: 541-439-6200; Nearest town: Powers. GPS: 42.785651, -124.024461

303 • Natural Bridge

Total sites: 17; RV sites: 17; No water; Vault toilets; Reservations not accepted; Max length: 30ft; Stay limit: 14 days; Generator hours: 0600-2200; Open May-Oct; Tent & RV camping: $15; Elev: 3268ft/996m; Tel: 541-560-3400; Nearest town: Prospect. GPS: 42.889648, -122.463867

304 • North Arm

Total sites: 19; RV sites: 15; No water; Vault toilets; Reservations not accepted; Max length: 16ft; Open May-Sep; Tents: $16/RVs: $20; Elev: 3284ft/1001m; Tel: 503-668 1700; Nearest town: Sandy; Notes: Also walk-to sites. GPS: 45.144315, -121.771605

305 • North Davis Creek

Total sites: 14; RV sites: 14; Central water; Vault toilets; No showers; No RV dump; Reservations accepted; Max length: 26ft; Open May-Sep; Tent & RV camping: $10-12; Elev: 4350ft/1326m; Tel: 541-338-7869; Nearest town: Crescent. GPS: 43.675655, -121.822956

306 • North Fork (Mt McLoughlin)

Total sites: 6; RV sites: 3; Central water; Vault toilets; No showers; No RV dump; Reservations accepted; Max length: 24ft; Stay limit: 14 days; Generator hours: 0600-2200; Open May-Oct; Tent & RV camping: $16; Elev: 4675ft/1425m; Tel: 541-865-2700; Nearest town: Butte Falls. GPS: 42.378131, -122.360263

307 • North Fork Catherine Creek

Total sites: 7; RV sites: 7; No water; No toilets; Reservations not accepted; Max length: 18ft; Stay limit: 14 days; Open Jun-Sep; Tent & RV camping: Free; Elev: 3937ft/1200m; Tel: 541-523-6391; Nearest town: La Grande; Notes: Campsites are composed of pull-off parking areas and several small campsites along the road. GPS: 45.131867, -117.629586

308 • North Fork John Day

Total sites: 20; RV sites: 15; No water; Vault toilets; Reservations not accepted; Stay limit: 14 days; Open all year; Tent & RV camping: $8; Elev: 5236ft/1596m; Tel: 541-278-3716; Nearest town: Granite; Notes: Free Nov-May - no services. GPS: 44.913985, -118.401882

309 • North Fork Malheur

Total sites: 5; RV sites: 5; No water; Vault toilets; Reservations not accepted; Stay limit: 14 days; Open May-Sep; Tent & RV camping: Free; Elev: 4780ft/1457m; Tel: 541-820-3800; Nearest town: Prairie City. GPS: 44.208885, -118.382434

310 • North Fork Siuslaw

Total sites: 7; RV sites: 7; No water; Vault toilets; Reservations not accepted; Stay limit: 14 days; Open May-Sep; Tent & RV camping: Free; Elev: 240ft/73m; Tel: 541-563-8400; Nearest town: Florence. GPS: 44.101526, -123.936956

311 • North Twin Lake

Total sites: 20; RV sites: 20; No water; Vault toilets; Reservations accepted; Max length: 30ft; Open May-Oct; Tent & RV camping: $13-15; Elev: 4383ft/1336m; Tel: 541-338-7869; Nearest town: Crescent. GPS: 43.732569, -121.764971

312 • North Waldo

Total sites: 58; RV sites: 58; Central water; Vault toilets; No showers; No RV dump; Reservations accepted; Max length: 30ft; Stay limit: 14 days; Open Jun-Oct; Tent & RV camping: $22; Elev: 5495ft/1675m; Tel: 541-782-2283; Nearest town: Oakridge; Notes: RV dump nearby. GPS: 43.758176, -122.003921

313 • Nottingham

Total sites: 23; RV sites: 23; No water; No toilets; Reservations accepted; Max length: 32ft; Open May-Sep; Tent & RV camping: $21; Elev: 3303ft/1007m; Tel: 503-668 1700; Nearest town: Hood River. GPS: 45.367668, -121.569518

314 • Oak Flat/Gravel Bar

Total sites: 15; RV sites: 15; No water; Vault toilets; Reservations not accepted; Max length: 18ft; Stay limit: 14 days; Generator hours: 0600-2200; Open all year; Tent & RV camping: Free; Elev: 364ft/111m; Tel: 541-247-3600; Nearest town: Agness. GPS: 42.517147, -124.039712

315 • Oak Fork (Timothy Lake)

Total sites: 44; RV sites: 36; Central water; Vault toilets; No showers; No RV dump; Reservations accepted; Max length: 32ft; Open May-Sep; Tents: $16/RVs: $20; Elev: 3268ft/996m; Tel: 503-668-1700; Nearest town: Government Camp; Notes: Also walk-to sites, Cabin(s). GPS: 45.115058, -121.770519

316 • Ochoco Divide

Total sites: 28; RV sites: 28; No water; Vault toilets; Reservations not accepted; Stay limit: 14 days; Open May-Oct; Tent & RV camping: $13; Elev: 4823ft/1470m; Tel: 208-270-0094; Nearest town: Prineville. GPS: 44.500244, -120.385742

317 • Ochoco Forest Camp

Total sites: 5; RV sites: 5; Central water; Vault toilets; No showers; No RV dump; Reservations accepted; Stay limit: 14 days; Open May-Oct; Tent & RV camping: $15; Elev: 4029ft/1228m; Tel: 541-416-3689; Nearest town: Prineville. GPS: 44.395999, -120.422446

318 • Odessa

Total sites: 6; RV sites: 6; No water; No toilets; Reservations not accepted; Open all year; Tent & RV camping: Free; Elev: 4190ft/1277m; Tel: 541-885-3400; Nearest town: Odessa. GPS: 42.429045, -122.061419

319 • Olallie (Willamette)

Total sites: 17; RV sites: 17; Central water; Vault toilets; No showers; No RV dump; Reservations accepted; Max length: 35ft; Stay limit: 14 days; Open Apr-Oct; Tent & RV camping: $19; Elev: 2100ft/640m; Tel: 801-226-3564; Nearest town: Estacada. GPS: 44.256974, -122.039976

320 • Olive Lake

Total sites: 23; RV sites: 23; No water; Vault toilets; Reservations not accepted; Max length: 40ft; Stay limit: 14 days; Open all year; Tent & RV camping: $12; Elev: 6061ft/1847m; Tel: 541-278-3716; Nearest town: Granite; Notes: Free Nov-May - no services. GPS: 44.784424, -118.598292

321 • Ollokot

Total sites: 12; RV sites: 12; Central water; Vault toilets; No showers; No RV dump; Reservations not accepted; Stay limit: 14 days; Open Jun-Oct; Tent & RV camping: $8; Elev: 4042ft/1232m; Tel: 541-523-6391; Nearest town: Enterprise. GPS: 45.151436, -116.876775

322 • Oregon

Total sites: 8; RV sites: 8; Central water; Vault toilets; No showers; No RV dump; Reservations not accepted; Max length: 16ft; Stay limit: 14 days; Open Jun-Sep; Tent & RV camping: $5; Elev: 5016ft/1529m; Tel: 541-523-6391; Nearest town: Unity. GPS: 44.546231, -118.341067

323 • Oregon Dunes NRA - Horsfall OHV

Total sites: 70; RV sites: 70; Central water; Flush toilets; Showers; No RV dump; Reservations accepted; Max length: 50ft; Stay limit: 14 days; Open all year; Tent & RV camping: $25; Elev: 43ft/13m; Tel: 541-271-3611; Nearest town: North Bend. GPS: 43.441576, -124.246016

324 • Oregon Dunes NRA - South Jetty Sand Camps

Total sites: 13; No water; No toilets; Reservations accepted; Open all year; Tents only: $10; Elev: 46ft/14m; Tel: 541-271-6000; Nearest town: Florence; Notes: Group site: $20. GPS: 43.954263, -124.130618

325 • Oregon Dunes NRA - Spinreel OHV

Total sites: 36; RV sites: 36; Water at site; Flush toilets; No showers; No RV dump; Reservations accepted; Max length: 40ft; Stay limit: 14 days; Open all year; Tent & RV camping: $25; Elev: 22ft/7m; Tel: 541-271-3611; Nearest town: Reedsport; Notes: OHV campground. GPS: 43.568766, -124.203247

326 • Oregon Mine

Total sites: 1; RV sites: 1; No water; Vault toilets; Reservations not accepted; Stay limit: 14 days; Open all year; Tent & RV camping: Free; Elev: 4409ft/1344m; Tel: 541-575-3000; Nearest town: Mt Vernon. GPS: 44.276935, -119.296968

327 • Packard Creek

Total sites: 35; RV sites: 35; Central water; Vault toilets; No showers; No RV dump; Reservations accepted; Max length: 28ft; Stay limit: 14 days; Open May-Sep; Tent & RV camping: $19; Elev: 1634ft/498m; Tel: 541-523-6391; Nearest town: Oakridge. GPS: 43.669481, -122.431955

328 • Paradise

Total sites: 64; RV sites: 64; Central water; Flush toilets; No showers; No RV dump; Reservations accepted; Max length: 40ft; Stay limit: 14 days; Open May-Oct; Tent & RV camping: $22; Elev: 1533ft/467m; Tel: 541-822-3381; Nearest town: McKenzie Bridge. GPS: 44.185093, -122.091239

329 • Parish Cabin

Total sites: 18; RV sites: 18; No water; Vault toilets; Reservations not accepted; Stay limit: 14 days; Open May-Sep; Tent & RV camping: $8; Elev: 4980ft/1518m; Tel: 541-575-3000; Nearest town: Seneca. GPS: 44.179932, -118.765381

330 • Parker Meadows

Total sites: 8; RV sites: 5; Central water; Vault toilets; No showers; No RV dump; Reservations not accepted; Stay limit: 14 days; Generator hours: 0600-2200; Open Jul-Oct; Tent & RV camping: $10; Elev: 5007ft/1526m; Tel: 541-560-3400; Nearest town: Butte Falls. GPS: 42.600143, -122.323304

331 • Paul Dennis (Olallie Lake)

Total sites: 17; RV sites: 17; No water; Vault toilets; Reservations not accepted; Max length: 16ft; Open Jun-Sep; Tent & RV camping: $15-20; Elev: 4968ft/1514m; Tel: 503-668 1700; Nearest town: Estacada. GPS: 44.811387, -121.786948

332 • Paulina Lake

Total sites: 69; RV sites: 69; Central water; Flush toilets; No showers; RV dump; Reservations accepted; Max length: 30ft; Open May-Sep; Tent & RV camping: $18; Elev: 6329ft/1929m; Tel: 541-338-7869; Nearest town: La Pine; Notes: Dump fee $10. GPS: 43.711914, -121.274902

333 • Pebble Ford

Total sites: 3; RV sites: 3; No water; Vault toilets; Reservations not accepted; Max length: 16ft; Open May-Sep; Tent & RV camping: $19; Elev: 4209ft/1283m; Tel: 503-668 1700; Nearest town: Dufur. GPS: 45.400081, -121.463902

334 • Peninsula (Olallie Lake)

Total sites: 36; RV sites: 36; No water; Vault toilets; Reservations not accepted; Tent & RV camping: $15-20; Elev: 4984ft/1519m; Tel: 503-630-6861; Nearest town: Detroit. GPS: 44.802547, -121.783142

335 • Penland Lake

Total sites: 12; RV sites: 10; No water; Vault toilets; Reservations not accepted; Stay limit: 14 days; Open all year; Tent & RV camping: $8; Elev: 4951ft/1509m; Tel: 541-278-3716; Nearest town: Heppner; Notes: Free Nov-May - no services, Rough road. GPS: 45.118641, -119.315989

336 • Perry South

Total sites: 64; RV sites: 75; Central water; Flush toilets; No showers; No RV dump; Reservations accepted; Max length: 50ft; Open May-Sep; Tent & RV camping: $20; Elev: 1998ft/609m; Tel: 541-338-7869; Nearest town: Culver. GPS: 44.584621, -121.448015

337 • Pike's Crossing

Total sites: 6; RV sites: 6; No water; Vault toilets; Reservations not accepted; Open May-Oct; Tent & RV camping: Free; Elev: 5712ft/1741m; Tel: 541-943-4479; Nearest town: Paisley. GPS: 42.697896, -120.933069

338 • Pine Mountain

Total sites: 6; RV sites: 6; No water; Vault toilets; Reservations not accepted; Max length: 30ft; Open May-Sep; Tent & RV camping: Fee unknown; Elev: 6234ft/1900m; Tel: 541-383-5300; Nearest town: Bend; Notes: Near observatory. GPS: 43.790879, -120.942974

339 • Pine Point

Total sites: 13; RV sites: 13; Central water; Vault toilets; No showers; No RV dump; Reservations accepted; Max length: 32ft; Open May-Sep; Tent & RV camping: $20; Elev: 3254ft/992m; Tel:

503-622-3191; Nearest town: Government Camp; Notes: Group site: $60-$120. GPS: 45.113432, -121.801335

340 • Pine Rest

Total sites: 7; No water; Vault toilets; Reservations not accepted; Open Apr-Dec; Tents only: $18-20; Elev: 2982ft/909m; Tel: 541-338-7869; Nearest town: Sisters. GPS: 44.481736, -121.638038

341 • Pioneer Ford

Total sites: 20; RV sites: 18; Central water; Vault toilets; No showers; No RV dump; Reservations accepted; Max length: 50ft; Open May-Sep; Tent & RV camping: $18-20; Elev: 2805ft/855m; Tel: 541-338-7869; Nearest town: Sisters. GPS: 44.552156, -121.620839

342 • PO Saddle Trailhead

Total sites: 10; No water; Vault toilets; Reservations not accepted; Stay limit: 14 days; Tents only: $5; Elev: 5827ft/1776m; Tel: 541-523-6391; Nearest town: Halfway. GPS: 45.236091, -116.766372

343 • Point

Total sites: 9; RV sites: 9; No water; Vault toilets; Reservations accepted; Max length: 26ft; Open May-Sep; Tent & RV camping: $14-16; Elev: 4892ft/1491m; Tel: 541-323-1746; Nearest town: Bend. GPS: 43.966718, -121.808304

344 • Poole Creek

Total sites: 60; RV sites: 60; Central water; Vault toilets; No showers; No RV dump; Reservations accepted; Max length: T-30ft/RV-35'; Stay limit: 14 days; Generator hours: 0600-2200; Open May-Oct; Tent & RV camping: $15-20; Elev: 4173ft/1272m; Tel: 541-498-2531; Nearest town: Diamond Lake; Notes: Group site: $72-$85. GPS: 43.310928, -122.196128

345 • Post Camp

Total sites: 4; RV sites: 4; No water; Vault toilets; Reservations not accepted; Max length: 16ft; Open May-Sep; Tent & RV camping: Free; Elev: 4045ft/1233m; Tel: 541-467-2291; Nearest town: Dufur. GPS: 45.216371, -121.520079

346 • Prairie

Total sites: 17; RV sites: 17; Central water; Vault toilets; No showers; RV dump; Reservations accepted; Max length: 30ft; Open May-Oct; Tent & RV camping: $14; Elev: 4318ft/1316m; Tel: 541-383-4000; Nearest town: La Pine; Notes: $10 dump fee. GPS: 43.725071, -121.424191

347 • Princess Creek

Total sites: 32; RV sites: 32; No water; Vault toilets; Reservations accepted; Max length: 26ft; Open May-Sep; Tent & RV camping: $14-16; Elev: 4931ft/1503m; Tel: 541-338-7869; Nearest town: Crescent Lake. GPS: 43.586426, -122.010498

348 • Pringle Falls

Total sites: 7; RV sites: 7; Central water; Vault toilets; No showers; No RV dump; Reservations accepted; Max length: 26ft; Open May-Oct; Tent & RV camping: $11-13; Elev: 4236ft/1291m; Tel: 541-383-4000; Nearest town: La Pine. GPS: 43.747831, -121.603025

349 • Puma

Total sites: 11; RV sites: 8; Central water; Vault toilets; No showers; No RV dump; Reservations not accepted; Max length: 25ft; Stay limit: 14 days; Open Apr-Sep; Tent & RV camping: $15; Elev: 1220ft/372m; Tel: 541-782-2283; Nearest town: Lowell. GPS: 43.978516, -122.515381

350 • Quinn River

Total sites: 41; RV sites: 41; Central water; Vault toilets; No showers; No RV dump; Reservations accepted; Max length: 30ft; Open May-Sep; Tent & RV camping: $16-18; Elev: 4475ft/1364m; Tel: 541-338-7869; Nearest town: Bend. GPS: 43.785156, -121.836426

351 • Quosatana

Total sites: 43; RV sites: 43; Central water; Flush toilets; No showers; RV dump; Reservations not accepted; Max length: 30ft; Stay limit: 14 days; Generator hours: 0600-2200; Open all year; Tent & RV camping: $20; Elev: 216ft/66m; Tel: 541-479-3735; Nearest town: Gold Beach. GPS: 42.497751, -124.232023

352 • Rainbow (Fish Creek Mt)

Total sites: 19; RV sites: 19; Central water; Vault toilets; Reservations accepted; Max length: 24ft; Open May-Sep; Tent & RV camping: $19-21; Elev: 1654ft/504m; Tel: 503-834-2322; Nearest town: Estacada. GPS: 45.076172, -122.044189

353 • Rainy Lake

Total sites: 4; No water; Vault toilets; Reservations not accepted; Open Jun-Oct; Tents only: $19; Elev: 4068ft/1240m; Tel: 503-668-1700; Nearest town: Parkdale. GPS: 45.626757, -121.758763

354 • Red Diamond

Total sites: 6; RV sites: 6; Vault toilets; Reservations not accepted; Max length: 36ft; Stay limit: 14 days; Open May-Sep; Tent & RV camping: $18; Elev: 2047ft/624m; Tel: 541-822-3381; Nearest town: Coburg; Notes: Reservable as group site: $44. GPS: 44.002842, -122.172244

355 • Reservoir

Total sites: 24; RV sites: 24; No water; Vault toilets; Reservations accepted; Max length: 30ft; Open May-Sep; Tent & RV camping: $11-13; Elev: 4341ft/1323m; Tel: 541-338-7869; Nearest town: La Pine. GPS: 43.672119, -121.770508

356 • Ripplebrook

Total sites: 13; RV sites: 13; No water; Vault toilets; No showers; No RV dump; Reservations accepted; Max length: 16ft; Open Apr-Sep; Tent & RV camping: $19-21; Elev: 1578ft/481m; Tel: 503-834-2322; Nearest town: Estacada. GPS: 45.080197, -122.042118

357 • River Bridge

Total sites: 11; RV sites: 11; No water; Vault toilets; Reservations not accepted; Max length: 25ft; Stay limit: 14 days; Generator hours: 0600-2200; Open May-Oct; Tent & RV camping: $8; Elev: 2930ft/893m; Tel: 541-560-3400; Nearest town: Prospect. GPS: 42.822012, -122.493674

358 • Riverford

Total sites: 10; RV sites: 10; No water; Vault toilets; Reservations not accepted; Max length: 16ft; Open May-Sep; Tent & RV camping: $19; Elev: 1490ft/454m; Tel: 503-668 1700; Nearest town: Estacada. GPS: 45.032567, -122.058574

359 • Riverside

Total sites: 38; RV sites: 38; No water; Vault toilets; Reservations accepted; Max length: 24ft; Stay limit: 14 days; Open May-Sep; Tent & RV camping: $18; Elev: 2398ft/731m; Tel: 503-854-3366; Nearest town: Detroit. GPS: 44.641824, -121.945452

360 • Riverside

Total sites: 16; RV sites: 16; Central water; Vault toilets; No showers; No RV dump; Reservations accepted; Max length: 24ft; Open May-Sep; Tent & RV camping: $18; Elev: 1624ft/495m; Tel: 503-630-6861; Nearest town: Estacada. GPS: 45.044619, -122.062532

361 • Roaring River

Total sites: 14; RV sites: 14; Central water; Vault toilets; No showers; No RV dump; Reservations accepted; Max length: 16ft; Open May-Sep; Tent & RV camping: $19-21; Elev: 1253ft/382m; Tel: 503-630-6861; Nearest town: Estacada. GPS: 45.158203, -122.114258

362 • Robinhood

Total sites: 24; No water; Vault toilets; Reservations not accepted; Tents only: Free; Elev: 3572ft/1089m; Tel: 541-352-6002; Nearest town: Mount Hood Parkdale. GPS: 45.338012, -121.572062

363 • Rock Creek (Coquille)

Total sites: 7; No water; Vault toilets; Reservations not accepted; Max length: 16ft; Stay limit: 14 days; Generator hours: 0600-2200; Open all year; Tents only: $10; Elev: 1227ft/374m; Tel: 541-439-6200; Nearest town: Powers; Notes: No fee Nov-May. GPS: 42.707905, -124.059248

364 • Rock Creek (Crane Prairie)

Total sites: 30; RV sites: 30; Central water; Vault toilets; No showers; No RV dump; Reservations accepted; Max length: 30ft; Open May-Sep; Tent & RV camping: $16-18; Elev: 4472ft/1363m; Tel: 541-338-7869; Nearest town: Crescent. GPS: 43.768197, -121.834184

365 • Rock Creek (Mt Hood)

Total sites: 33; RV sites: 33; Central water; Vault toilets; No showers; No RV dump; Reservations not accepted; Max length: 35ft; Open Apr-Oct; Tent & RV camping: $21-22; Elev: 2213ft/675m; Tel: 503-668 1700; Nearest town: Dufur. GPS: 45.216783, -121.385783

366 • Rock Creek (Siuslaw)

Total sites: 15; RV sites: 15; Central water; Vault toilets; No showers; No RV dump; Reservations accepted; Stay limit: 14 days; Open May-Sep; Tent & RV camping: $24; Elev: 269ft/82m; Tel: 541-563-8400; Nearest town: Yachats. GPS: 44.185644, -124.110748

367 • Rock Springs

Total sites: 12; RV sites: 12; No water; Vault toilets; Reservations not accepted; Stay limit: 14 days; Open May-Sep; Tent & RV camping: $6; Elev: 5144ft/1568m; Tel: 541-575-3000; Nearest town: John Day. GPS: 43.998989, -118.838203

368 • Rogue River - Farewell Bend

Total sites: 61; RV sites: 61; Central water; Flush toilets; No showers; No RV dump; Reservations accepted; Max length: 40ft; Stay limit: 14 days; Generator hours: 0600-2200; Open May-Oct; Tent & RV camping: $25; Elev: 3433ft/1046m; Tel: 541-479-3735; Nearest town: Prospect; Notes: Use of fire pans mandatory. GPS: 42.916234, -122.435059

369 • Rogue River - Foster Bar

Total sites: 8; RV sites: 4; Central water; Flush toilets; No showers; No RV dump; Reservations not accepted; Stay limit: 14 days; Generator hours: 0600-2200; Open all year; Tent & RV camping: $15; Elev: 207ft/63m; Tel: 541-479-3735; Nearest town: Illahe; Notes: Also boat-in sites, Use of fire pans mandatory. GPS: 42.634255, -124.051978

370 • Rogue River - Illahe

Total sites: 14; RV sites: 9; Central water; Flush toilets; No showers; No RV dump; Reservations not accepted; Stay limit: 14 days; Generator hours: 0600-2200; Open May-Sep; Tent & RV camping: Free; Elev: 341ft/104m; Tel: 541-479-3735; Nearest town: Illahe; Notes: Also boat-in sites. GPS: 42.626199, -124.057353

371 • Rogue River - Lobster Creek

Total sites: 7; RV sites: 4; Central water; Flush toilets; No showers; No RV dump; Reservations not accepted; Stay limit: 14 days; Generator hours: 0600-2200; Open all year; Tent & RV camping: $15; Elev: 49ft/15m; Tel: 541-479-3735; Nearest town: Gold Beach. GPS: 42.502564, -124.295414

372 • Rujada

Total sites: 15; RV sites: 15; Central water; Flush toilets; No showers; No RV dump; Reservations accepted; Max length: 22ft; Stay limit: 14 days; Generator hours: 0600-2200; Open May-Sep; Tent & RV camping: $12; Elev: 1273ft/388m; Tel: 541-767-5000; Nearest town: Cottage Grove. GPS: 43.705924, -122.744463

373 • Sacandaga

Total sites: 17; RV sites: 17; Central water; Vault toilets; No showers; No RV dump; Reservations not accepted; Max length: 24ft; Stay limit: 14 days; Open Jun-Oct; Tent & RV camping: $8; Elev: 2566ft/782m; Tel: 541-782-2283; Nearest town: Oakridge. GPS: 43.496094, -122.329834

374 • Salmon Creek Falls

Total sites: 15; RV sites: 15; Central water; Vault toilets; No showers; No RV dump; Reservations not accepted; Max length: 20ft; Stay limit: 14 days; Generator hours: 0600-2200; Open Apr-Sep; Tent & RV camping: $17; Elev: 1558ft/475m; Tel: 541-782-2283; Nearest town: Oakridge. GPS: 43.762623, -122.374212

375 • Sam Brown

Total sites: 19; RV sites: 19; No water; Vault toilets; Reservations not accepted; Max length: 24ft; Stay limit: 14 days; Generator hours: 0600-2200; Open May-Oct; Tent & RV camping: $10; Elev:

2041ft/622m; Tel: 541-592-4000; Nearest town: Merlin. GPS: 42.441902, -123.686355

376 • Sand Prairie

Total sites: 21; RV sites: 21; No water; Vault toilets; Reservations not accepted; Max length: 28ft; Stay limit: 14 days; Open May-Sep; Tent & RV camping: $14; Elev: 1634ft/498m; Tel: 541-782-2283; Nearest town: Oakridge. GPS: 43.601318, -122.452637

377 • Sandbeach

Total sites: 80; RV sites: 80; Central water; Flush toilets; No showers; RV dump; Reservations accepted; Max length: 30ft; Stay limit: 14 days; Open Apr-Sep; Tent & RV camping: $25; Elev: 13ft/4m; Tel: 503-392-5100; Nearest town: Pacific City. GPS: 45.283203, -123.956787

378 • Sandhill Crossing

Total sites: 5; RV sites: 5; Central water; Vault toilets; No showers; No RV dump; Reservations not accepted; Open all year; Tent & RV camping: Free; Elev: 6119ft/1865m; Tel: 541-943-4479; Nearest town: Paisley; Notes: Reduced services 10/15-5/14. GPS: 42.594055, -120.879944

379 • Santiam Flats

Total sites: 32; RV sites: 32; Central water; Vault toilets; No showers; No RV dump; Reservations accepted; Stay limit: 14 days; Open May-Sep; Tent & RV camping: $18; Elev: 1624ft/495m; Tel: 503-854-3366; Nearest town: Detroit. GPS: 44.711526, -122.115679

380 • Scott Creek

Total sites: 6; RV sites: 6; No water; Vault toilets; Reservations not accepted; Open all year; Tent & RV camping: Free; Elev: 4710ft/1436m; Tel: 541-365-7001; Nearest town: Chemult; Notes: Reduced services 10/15-5/14. GPS: 42.885341, -121.924226

381 • Scotts Camp

Total sites: 3; RV sites: 3; No water; Vault toilets; Reservations not accepted; Stay limit: 14 days; Open all year; Tent & RV camping: Free; Elev: 5423ft/1653m; Tel: 541-416-6500; Nearest town: Big Summit Prairie. GPS: 44.424523, -120.145264

382 • Scout Lake

Total sites: 10; RV sites: 1; Central water; Vault toilets; No showers; No RV dump; Reservations accepted; Open May-Sep; Tent & RV camping: $18-20; Elev: 3681ft/1122m; Tel: 541-338-7869; Nearest town: Sisters; Notes: Group sites: $34-$60, 1 single site/6 doubles/3 triples, No dogs at beach. GPS: 44.411713, -121.749652

383 • Secret

Total sites: 6; RV sites: 6; No water; Vault toilets; Reservations not accepted; Max length: 24ft; Stay limit: 14 days; Generator hours: 0600-2200; Open May-Sep; Tent & RV camping: $14; Elev: 1965ft/599m; Tel: 541-782-2283; Nearest town: Oakridge. GPS: 43.514232, -122.441477

384 • Secret Creek

Total sites: 4; RV sites: 4; No water; Vault toilets; Reservations not accepted; Stay limit: 14 days; Generator hours: 0600-2200; Open

May-Sep; Tent & RV camping: Free; Elev: 2070ft/631m; Tel: 541-592-4000; Nearest town: Galice. GPS: 42.421799, -123.688916

385 • Shadow Bay

Total sites: 92; RV sites: 92; Central water; Vault toilets; No showers; No RV dump; Reservations accepted; Max length: 32ft; Stay limit: 14 days; Open Jun-Sep; Tent & RV camping: $22; Elev: 5489ft/1673m; Tel: 541-782-2283; Nearest town: Oakridge; Notes: Group site: $92-$350. GPS: 43.692871, -122.042725

386 • Shady

Total sites: 11; RV sites: 7; No water; Vault toilets; Reservations not accepted; Stay limit: 14 days; Open Jun-Sep; Tent & RV camping: $5; Elev: 5528ft/1685m; Tel: 541-523-6391; Nearest town: Enterprise. GPS: 45.257324, -117.383789

387 • Shady Cove

Total sites: 13; RV sites: 13; No water; Vault toilets; Reservations not accepted; Max length: 16ft; Stay limit: 14 days; Open all year; Tent & RV camping: $8; Elev: 1565ft/477m; Tel: 503-854-3366; Nearest town: Mill City. GPS: 44.844886, -122.301194

388 • Sheep Bridge

Total sites: 20; RV sites: 20; Central water; Vault toilets; No showers; No RV dump; Reservations accepted; Max length: 30ft; Open May-Oct; Tent & RV camping: $11-13; Elev: 4354ft/1327m; Tel: 541-338-7869; Nearest town: Crescent; Notes: 3 group sites: $30. GPS: 43.732005, -121.785076

389 • Shellrock Creek

Total sites: 8; RV sites: 8; No water; Vault toilets; Reservations not accepted; Max length: 16ft; Open Jun-Sep; Tent & RV camping: $19; Elev: 2411ft/735m; Tel: 503-668 1700; Nearest town: Estacada. GPS: 45.084558, -121.923683

390 • Sherwood

Total sites: 14; RV sites: 14; No water; Vault toilets; Reservations not accepted; Max length: 16ft; Open May-Sep; Tent & RV camping: $15; Elev: 3143ft/958m; Tel: 503-668 1700; Nearest town: Hood River. GPS: 45.394531, -121.571289

391 • Silver Creek Marsh

Total sites: 17; RV sites: 17; Central water; No toilets; No showers; No RV dump; Reservations not accepted; Stay limit: 14 days; Open all year; Tent & RV camping: $6; Elev: 4824ft/1470m; Tel: 541-576-2107; Nearest town: Silver Lake; Notes: Horse corrals, Reduced services 10/15-5/14. GPS: 43.006236, -121.134888

392 • Skillet Creek

Total sites: 4; RV sites: 4; Vault toilets; Reservations not accepted; Stay limit: 14 days; Tent & RV camping: Fee unknown; Elev: 1982ft/604m; Tel: 541-825-3100; Nearest town: Tiller. GPS: 43.091843, -122.620226

393 • Skookum Pond

Total sites: 3; No water; No toilets; Reservations not accepted; Stay limit: 14 days; Tents only: Free; Elev: 3502ft/1067m; Tel: 541-825-3100; Nearest town: Tiller. GPS: 43.008725, -122.599581

394 • Skull Hollow Camp

Total sites: 28; RV sites: 28; No water; Vault toilets; Reservations not accepted; Open May-Nov; Tent & RV camping: $10; Elev: 3002ft/915m; Tel: 541-416-6640; Nearest town: Terrebonne. GPS: 44.397404, -121.062925

395 • Slide Creek

Total sites: 16; RV sites: 16; No water; Vault toilets; Reservations accepted; Max length: 40ft; Stay limit: 14 days; Open Apr-Sep; Tent & RV camping: $17; Elev: 1923ft/586m; Tel: 541-822-3381; Nearest town: Blue River. GPS: 44.076644, -122.224531

396 • Slide Creek

Total sites: 3; RV sites: 3; No water; Vault toilets; Reservations not accepted; Stay limit: 14 days; Open May-Sep; Tent & RV camping: Free; Elev: 4934ft/1504m; Tel: 541-820-3800; Nearest town: Prairie City. GPS: 44.342302, -118.657366

397 • Smiling River

Total sites: 36; RV sites: 36; Central water; Flush toilets; No showers; No RV dump; Reservations accepted; Max length: 50ft; Open May-Sep; Tent & RV camping: $18-20; Elev: 2972ft/906m; Tel: 541-338-7869; Nearest town: Camp Sherman. GPS: 44.474558, -121.636496

398 • Soda Creek

Total sites: 10; RV sites: 10; No water; Vault toilets; No showers; No RV dump; Reservations accepted; Max length: 30ft; Open May-Sep; Tent & RV camping: $14-16; Elev: 5463ft/1665m; Tel: 541-338-7869; Nearest town: Bend. GPS: 44.024619, -121.726901

399 • South

Total sites: 23; RV sites: 23; No water; Vault toilets; Reservations accepted; Max length: 26ft; Open May-Sep; Tent & RV camping: $12-16; Elev: 5000ft/1524m; Tel: 541-338-7869; Nearest town: Bend. GPS: 43.960361, -121.788116

400 • South Fork (Rogue River)

Total sites: 6; RV sites: 6; No water; Vault toilets; Reservations not accepted; Stay limit: 14 days; Generator hours: 0600-2200; Open May-Oct; Tent & RV camping: $15; Elev: 4058ft/1237m; Tel: 541-865-2700; Nearest town: Prospect. GPS: 42.645000, -122.334000

401 • South Fork Camp Creek

Total sites: 14; RV sites: 12; Vault toilets; Reservations not accepted; Stay limit: 14 days; Open May-Oct; Tent & RV camping: $5; Elev: 4829ft/1472m; Tel: 541-523-6391; Nearest town: Unity. GPS: 44.343018, -118.201416

402 • South Shore (Detroit)

Total sites: 32; RV sites: 32; Central water; Vault toilets; No showers; No RV dump; Reservations accepted; Max length: 30ft; Stay limit: 14 days; Open May-Sep; Tent & RV camping: $22; Elev: 1644ft/501m; Tel: 503-854-3366; Nearest town: Detroit. GPS: 44.705817, -122.176186

403 • South Shore (Suttle Lake)

Total sites: 38; RV sites: 38; Central water; Vault toilets; No showers; No RV dump; Reservations accepted; Max length: 50ft; Open May-Sep; Tent & RV camping: $18-20; Elev: 3461ft/1055m; Tel: 541-338-7869; Nearest town: Sisters. GPS: 44.417969, -121.741455

404 • South Twin Lake

Total sites: 21; RV sites: 21; Central water; Flush toilets; No showers; No RV dump; Reservations accepted; Max length: 26ft; Open May-Oct; Tent & RV camping: $19-22; Elev: 4373ft/1333m; Tel: 541-338-7869; Nearest town: Bend. GPS: 43.717059, -121.770587

405 • South Umpqua Falls

Total sites: 19; RV sites: 19; No water; Vault toilets; Reservations not accepted; Max length: 35ft; Stay limit: 14 days; Open all year; Tent & RV camping: $10; Elev: 1722ft/525m; Tel: 541-825-3100; Nearest town: Tiller. GPS: 43.055401, -122.689745

406 • Southwest Shore

Total sites: 16; RV sites: 16; No water; Vault toilets; Reservations not accepted; Stay limit: 14 days; Open May-Sep; Tent & RV camping: $10; Elev: 4098ft/1249m; Tel: 541-523-6391; Nearest town: Baker City. GPS: 44.675308, -118.082142

407 • Spalding Pond

Total sites: 4; RV sites: 4; No water; No toilets; Reservations not accepted; Stay limit: 14 days; Generator hours: 0600-2200; Open May-Oct; Tent & RV camping: Free; Elev: 3402ft/1037m; Tel: 541-592-4000; Nearest town: Galice. GPS: 42.346501, -123.703682

408 • Spool Cart

Total sites: 12; RV sites: 12; No water; Vault toilets; Reservations not accepted; Max length: 45ft; Stay limit: 14 days; Open May-Sep; Tent & RV camping: $5; Elev: 3550ft/1082m; Tel: 541-523-6391; Nearest town: La Grande. GPS: 45.202634, -118.394946

409 • Spring

Total sites: 73; RV sites: 68; Central water; Vault toilets; No showers; No RV dump; Reservations accepted; Open May-Sep; Tent & RV camping: $18-20; Elev: 4875ft/1486m; Tel: 541-338-7869; Nearest town: Crescent; Notes: Group site: $125. GPS: 43.461595, -122.016413

410 • Spring Creek

Total sites: 4; No water; Vault toilets; Reservations not accepted; Stay limit: 14 days; Open May-Sep; Tents only: Free; Elev: 3382ft/1031m; Tel: 541-383-5300; Nearest town: La Grande. GPS: 45.357359, -118.312294

411 • Spring Drive RV Park

Total sites: 8; RV sites: 8; Elec sites: 8; Water at site; No toilets; No showers; RV dump; Reservations accepted; Open May-Oct; No tents/RVs: $30-32; Elev: 3281ft/1000m; Tel: 541-328-0909; Nearest town: Maupin. GPS: 45.115316, -121.517711

412 • Sru Lake

Total sites: 6; RV sites: 6; No water; Vault toilets; Reservations not accepted; Stay limit: 14 days; Generator hours: 0600-2200; Open all year; Tent & RV camping: Free; Elev: 2362ft/720m; Tel: 541-439-6200; Nearest town: Powers. GPS: 42.730834, -124.006088

413 • Starr

Total sites: 9; RV sites: 9; No water; Vault toilets; Reservations not accepted; Stay limit: 14 days; Open May-Sep; Tent & RV camping: $6; Elev: 5148ft/1569m; Tel: 541-575-3000; Nearest town: John Day. GPS: 44.259033, -119.018066

414 • Steamboat Falls

Total sites: 10; RV sites: 7; No water; Vault toilets; Reservations not accepted; Max length: 20ft; Stay limit: 14 days; Generator hours: 0600-2200; Open all year; Tent & RV camping: $10; Elev: 1736ft/529m; Tel: 541-957-3200; Nearest town: Steamboat. GPS: 43.374852, -122.642835

415 • Stevens Creek

Total sites: 7; No water; Vault toilets; Reservations not accepted; Stay limit: 14 days; Open May-Sep; Tents only: $5; Elev: 4524ft/1379m; Tel: 541-523-6391; Nearest town: Unity. GPS: 44.400181, -118.320831

416 • Still Creek

Total sites: 27; RV sites: 27; Central water; Vault toilets; No showers; No RV dump; Reservations accepted; Max length: 16ft; Open Jun-Sep; Tent & RV camping: $22-24; Elev: 3852ft/1174m; Tel: 541-328-0909; Nearest town: Government Camp. GPS: 45.295410, -121.737305

417 • Store Gulch

Total sites: 6; RV sites: 4; No water; Vault toilets; Reservations not accepted; Stay limit: 14 days; Generator hours: 0600-2200; Open May-Sep; Tent & RV camping: $10; Elev: 1178ft/359m; Tel: 541-592-4000; Nearest town: Galice; Notes: Also walk-to sites, 2 walk-to sites. GPS: 42.295385, -123.754264

418 • Strawberry

Total sites: 10; RV sites: 10; Central water; Vault toilets; Reservations not accepted; Stay limit: 14 days; Open May-Sep; Tent & RV camping: $8; Elev: 5761ft/1756m; Tel: 541-820-3311; Nearest town: Prairie City. GPS: 44.319241, -118.674645

419 • Sugar Creek

Total sites: 3; RV sites: 3; Central water; Vault toilets; No showers; No RV dump; Reservations not accepted; Stay limit: 14 days; Open May-Oct; Tent & RV camping: $8; Elev: 4042ft/1232m; Tel: 541-416-6500; Nearest town: Paulina. GPS: 44.233944, -119.805076

420 • Summit Lake

Total sites: 8; RV sites: 8; No water; Vault toilets; Reservations not accepted; Max length: 16ft; Open Jun-Sep; Tent & RV camping: $17-19; Elev: 4213ft/1284m; Tel: 503-668 1700; Nearest town: Sand. GPS: 45.031808, -121.789967

421 • Sunnyside

Total sites: 13; No water; Vault toilets; Reservations accepted; Stay limit: 14 days; Open May-Sep; Tents only: $14; Elev: 1715ft/523m; Tel: 541-822-3381; Nearest town: Blue River. GPS: 44.061697, -122.220903

422 • Sunset

Total sites: 64; RV sites: 64; Central water; Flush toilets; Reservations accepted; Open May-Sep; Tent & RV camping: $23; Elev: 5059ft/1542m; Tel: 866-201-4194; Nearest town: Klamath Falls. GPS: 42.370648, -122.205256

423 • Sunset Cove

Total sites: 21; RV sites: 21; Central water; Vault toilets; No showers; No RV dump; Reservations accepted; Max length: 50ft; Open May-Oct; Tent & RV camping: $16-18; Elev: 4885ft/1489m; Tel: 541-338-7869; Nearest town: Crescent. GPS: 43.562500, -121.964111

424 • Sunshine Bar

Total sites: 6; RV sites: 6; No water; Vault toilets; Reservations not accepted; Stay limit: 14 days; Generator hours: 0600-2200; Open all year; Tent & RV camping: Free; Elev: 594ft/181m; Tel: 541-439-6200; Nearest town: Powers. GPS: 42.712405, -124.311761

425 • Sunstrip

Total sites: 8; No water; Vault toilets; Reservations accepted; Max length: 18ft; Open Apr-Sep; Tents only: $21-23; Elev: 1168ft/356m; Tel: 503-630-4156; Nearest town: Estacada. GPS: 45.150593, -122.106215

426 • Sutton

Total sites: 77; RV sites: 77; Elec sites: 22; Central water; Flush toilets; No showers; No RV dump; Reservations accepted; Stay limit: 14 days; Open all year; Tents: $22/RVs: $22-27; Elev: 44ft/13m; Tel: 541-563-8400; Nearest town: Florence; Notes: Group sites: $85-$148. GPS: 44.053989, -124.106445

427 • Takhenitch

Total sites: 34; RV sites: 34; Central water; Flush toilets; No showers; No RV dump; Reservations accepted; Max length: 30ft; Stay limit: 14 days; Open May-Sep; Tent & RV camping: $22; Elev: 49ft/15m; Tel: 541-271-6000; Nearest town: Reedsport. GPS: 43.795898, -124.148682

428 • Takhenitch Landing

Total sites: 27; RV sites: 27; No water; Vault toilets; No showers; No RV dump; Reservations accepted; Max length: 30ft; Stay limit: 14 days; Open all year; Tent & RV camping: $22; Elev: 92ft/28m; Tel: 541-271-6000; Nearest town: Florence. GPS: 43.800369, -124.145994

429 • Tamarack

Total sites: 12; RV sites: 12; Central water; Vault toilets; No showers; No RV dump; Reservations not accepted; Stay limit: 14 days; Open Jun-Sep; Tent & RV camping: $6; Elev: 4531ft/1381m; Tel: 541-523-6391; Nearest town: Baker City. GPS: 45.019804, -117.453801

430 • Target Meadows

Total sites: 18; RV sites: 16; Central water; Vault toilets; No showers; No RV dump; Reservations not accepted; Stay limit: 14 days; Open Jul-Nov; Tent & RV camping: $12; Elev: 4839ft/1475m; Tel: 541-278-3716; Nearest town: Weston; Notes: Usable in winter - no services. GPS: 45.806038, -118.076837

431 • Thielsen Forest Camp

Total sites: 4; RV sites: 4; No water; Vault toilets; Reservations not accepted; Max length: 20ft; Stay limit: 14 days; Open all year; Tent & RV camping: Free; Elev: 4531ft/1381m; Tel: 541-498-2531; Nearest town: Diamond Lake. GPS: 43.256028, -122.164725

432 • Thielsen View

Total sites: 60; RV sites: 60; Central water; Vault toilets; No showers; No RV dump; Reservations accepted; Max length: 35ft; Stay limit: 14 days; Open Jun-Oct; Tents: $15/RVs: $17; Elev: 5216ft/1590m; Tel: 541-498-2531; Nearest town: Diamond Lake. GPS: 43.166612, -122.166518

433 • Thompson Reservoir

Total sites: 19; RV sites: 19; Central water; Vault toilets; No showers; No RV dump; Reservations not accepted; Open all year; Tent & RV camping: $6; Elev: 4987ft/1520m; Tel: 541-576-2107; Nearest town: Silver Lake; Notes: Reduced services 10/15-5/14. GPS: 42.959473, -121.091309

434 • Three C Rock

Total sites: 5; RV sites: 5; No water; Vault toilets; Reservations not accepted; Max length: 35ft; Stay limit: 14 days; Generator hours: 0600-2200; Open all year; Tent & RV camping: $10; Elev: 1113ft/339m; Tel: 541-825-3100; Nearest town: Tiller. GPS: 42.964847, -122.887799

435 • Three Creek Lake

Total sites: 11; RV sites: 11; No water; Vault toilets; Reservations accepted; Max length: 20ft; Open Jul-Oct; Tent & RV camping: $14-16; Elev: 6539ft/1993m; Tel: 541-338-7869; Nearest town: Sisters. GPS: 44.095703, -121.624756

436 • Three Creek Meadow

Total sites: 20; RV sites: 20; No water; Vault toilets; Reservations not accepted; Open Jun-Sep; Tent & RV camping: $16-20; Elev: 6332ft/1930m; Tel: 541-338-7869; Nearest town: Sisters; Notes: 9 horse sites. GPS: 44.115048, -121.625248

437 • Threehorn

Total sites: 5; RV sites: 5; No water; Vault toilets; Reservations not accepted; Max length: 22ft; Stay limit: 14 days; Generator hours: 0600-2200; Open all year; Tent & RV camping: $10; Elev: 2743ft/836m; Tel: 541-825-3100; Nearest town: Tiller. GPS: 42.802909, -122.867552

438 • Tillicum Beach

Total sites: 59; RV sites: 59; Elec sites: 7; Central water; Flush toilets; No showers; No RV dump; Reservations accepted; Stay limit: 14 days; Open all year; Tents: $26/RVs: $26-33; Elev: 72ft/22m; Tel: 541-563-8400; Nearest town: Waldport. GPS: 44.366314, -124.091484

439 • Tilly Jane

Total sites: 14; No water; Vault toilets; Reservations not accepted; Open Jun-Sep; Tents only: $21; Elev: 5718ft/1743m; Tel: 541-352-6002; Nearest town: Parkdale; Notes: Narrow winding and may require high-clearance or 4X4. GPS: 45.399902, -121.647705

440 • Timpanogas Lake

Total sites: 10; RV sites: 10; Central water; Vault toilets; No showers; No RV dump; Reservations not accepted; Max length: 24ft; Stay limit: 14 days; Open Jun-Oct; Tent & RV camping: $8; Elev: 5279ft/1609m; Tel: 541-782-2283; Nearest town: Oakridge. GPS: 43.410238, -122.114467

441 • Tip Top

Total sites: 4; RV sites: 4; No water; Vault toilets; Reservations not accepted; Stay limit: 14 days; Open May-Sep; Tent & RV camping: $6; Elev: 5527ft/1685m; Tel: 541-575-3000; Nearest town: Burns. GPS: 43.896612, -119.642755

442 • Toketee Lake

Total sites: 33; RV sites: 33; No water; Vault toilets; Reservations accepted; Max length: 30ft; Stay limit: 14 days; Generator hours: 0600-2200; Open all year; Tent & RV camping: $10; Elev: 2461ft/750m; Tel: 541-498-2531; Nearest town: Idleyld Park; Notes: Group site: $50. GPS: 43.273594, -122.406351

443 • Toll Bridge

Total sites: 5; RV sites: 5; No water; Vault toilets; Reservations not accepted; Stay limit: 14 days; Open May-Oct; Tent & RV camping: $8; Elev: 2831ft/863m; Tel: 541-278-3716; Nearest town: Mt Hood; Notes: Free Nov-May - no services, Rough road. GPS: 44.997539, -118.935124

444 • Toll Gate

Total sites: 15; RV sites: 15; Central water; Vault toilets; No showers; No RV dump; Reservations accepted; Max length: 16ft; Open May-Sep; Tent & RV camping: $22-24; Elev: 1791ft/546m; Tel: 541-328-0909; Nearest town: Zigzag. GPS: 45.322118, -121.905628

445 • Trail Bridge

Total sites: 46; RV sites: 19; Central water; No toilets; No showers; No RV dump; Reservations not accepted; Max length: 45ft; Stay limit: 14 days; Open May-Oct; Tent & RV camping: $10; Elev: 2111ft/643m; Tel: 541-822-3381; Nearest town: McKenzie Bridge. GPS: 44.279675, -122.048815

446 • Trapper Creek

Total sites: 29; RV sites: 29; Central water; Vault toilets; No showers; No RV dump; Reservations accepted; Max length: 40ft; Open May-Oct; Tent & RV camping: $16-18; Elev: 4879ft/1487m; Tel: 541-338-7869; Nearest town: Crescent Lake. GPS: 43.582001, -122.043818

447 • Trillium Lake

Total sites: 57; RV sites: 57; Central water; Vault toilets; No showers; No RV dump; Reservations accepted; Max length: 40ft; Open May-Sep; Tent & RV camping: $22-24; Elev: 3658ft/1115m; Tel: 503-272-3220; Nearest town: Government Camp; Notes: Group site: $86. GPS: 45.270508, -121.735596

448 • Trout Creek

Total sites: 23; RV sites: 19; Central water; Vault toilets; No showers; No RV dump; Reservations accepted; Max length: 32ft; Stay limit: 14 days; Open May-Sep; Tent & RV camping: $18; Elev: 1339ft/408m; Tel: 541-367-5168; Nearest town: Sweet Home. GPS: 44.397606, -122.348613

449 • Trout Farm

Total sites: 6; RV sites: 6; Central water; Vault toilets; No showers; No RV dump; Reservations not accepted; Stay limit: 14 days; Open May-Sep; Tent & RV camping: $8; Elev: 4980ft/1518m; Tel: 541-820-3800; Nearest town: Prairie City. GPS: 44.305178, -118.551941

450 • Turkey Flat Forest Camp

Total sites: 4; RV sites: 4; No water; Vault toilets; Reservations not accepted; Max length: 18ft; Stay limit: 14 days; Open Jun-Sep; Tent & RV camping: $5; Elev: 5440ft/1658m; Tel: 541-523-6391; Nearest town: Lostine. GPS: 45.279683, -117.390693

451 • Twin Lakes

Total sites: 8; No water; Vault toilets; Reservations not accepted; Stay limit: 14 days; Open Jun-Sep; Tents only: Free; Elev: 6427ft/1959m; Tel: 541-523-6391; Nearest town: Halfway. GPS: 45.079846, -117.055333

452 • Twin Springs

Total sites: 3; Central water; Vault toilets; No showers; No RV dump; Reservations not accepted; Open May-Sep; Tents only: Free; Elev: 6457ft/1968m; Tel: 541-947-6300; Nearest town: Lakeview. GPS: 42.156855, -120.212942

453 • Two Color

Total sites: 11; RV sites: 11; No water; Vault toilets; Reservations not accepted; Stay limit: 14 days; Open Jun-Sep; Tent & RV camping: Free; Elev: 4806ft/1465m; Tel: 541-523-6391; Nearest town: Baker City. GPS: 45.037354, -117.445557

454 • Two Pan

Total sites: 5; RV sites: 5; No water; Vault toilets; Reservations not accepted; Max length: 18ft; Stay limit: 14 days; Open Jun-Sep; Tent & RV camping: $5; Elev: 5732ft/1747m; Tel: 541-523-6391; Nearest town: Enterprise. GPS: 45.250459, -117.376091

455 • Tyee

Total sites: 9; RV sites: 9; Central water; Vault toilets; No showers; No RV dump; Reservations accepted; Stay limit: 14 days; Open all year; Tent & RV camping: $22; Elev: 72ft/22m; Tel: 541-271-6000; Nearest town: Florence. GPS: 43.883461, -124.122236

456 • Umapine

Total sites: 5; RV sites: 5; No water; Vault toilets; Reservations not accepted; Stay limit: 14 days; Open May-Sep; Tent & RV camping: Free; Elev: 5079ft/1548m; Tel: 541-523-6391; Nearest town: Ukiah. GPS: 45.114075, -118.562078

457 • Umatilla Forks

Total sites: 12; RV sites: 6; Central water; Vault toilets; No showers; No RV dump; Reservations not accepted; Stay limit: 14 days; Open Jun-Sep; Tent & RV camping: $10; Elev: 2526ft/770m; Tel: 541-278-3716; Nearest town: Athena. GPS: 45.726311, -118.187534

458 • Underhill Site

Total sites: 2; RV sites: 2; No water; Vault toilets; Reservations not accepted; Max length: 18ft; Open May-Sep; Tent & RV camping: $5; Elev: 3556ft/1084m; Tel: 503-668 1700; Nearest town: Dufur. GPS: 45.396911, -121.415751

459 • Union Creek

Total sites: 74; RV sites: 74; Elec sites: 3; Central water; Vault toilets, No showers; No RV dump; Reservations accepted; Max length: 30ft; Stay limit: 14 days; Generator hours: 0600-2200; Open May-Oct; Tents: $22/RVs: $22-35; Elev: 3386ft/1032m; Tel: 541-560-3400; Nearest town: Prospect; Notes: 3 FHU. GPS: 42.909011, -122.450656

460 • Union Creek (Wallowa)

Total sites: 78; RV sites: 60; Elec sites: 38; Water at site; Flush toilets; No showers; No RV dump; Reservations accepted; Stay limit: 14 days; Open May-Sep; Tents: $20/RVs: $34; Elev: 4144ft/1263m; Tel: 541-523-6391; Nearest town: Baker City; Notes: 22 FHU, Group sites: $60. GPS: 44.687861, -118.027186

461 • Upper Buck Creek

Total sites: 6; RV sites: 6; No water; Vault toilets; Reservations not accepted; Open all year; Tent & RV camping: Free; Elev: 5066ft/1544m; Tel: 541-576-2107; Nearest town: Silver Lake; Notes: Reduced services 10/15-5/14. GPS: 43.053408, -121.266372

462 • Upper Jones

Total sites: 2; RV sites: 2; No water; No toilets; Reservations not accepted; Open Apr-Oct; Tent & RV camping: Free; Elev: 4879ft/1487m; Nearest town: Paisley. GPS: 42.598642, -120.599055

463 • Vee Lake

Total sites: 2; RV sites: 2; No water; Vault toilets; Reservations not accepted; Open all year; Tent & RV camping: Free; Elev: 6132ft/1869m; Tel: 541-947-6300; Nearest town: Lakeview; Notes: Reduced services 10/15-5/14. GPS: 42.422085, -120.161946

464 • Vigne

Total sites: 6; RV sites: 6; Central water; Vault toilets; No showers; No RV dump; Reservations not accepted; Max length: 16ft; Stay limit: 14 days; Open Jun-Oct; Tent & RV camping: $6; Elev: 3806ft/1160m; Tel: 541-523-6391; Nearest town: Enterprise. GPS: 45.745381, -117.021862

465 • Wahtum Lake

Total sites: 5; RV sites: 5; No water; Vault toilets; Reservations not accepted; Open Jun-Oct; Tent & RV camping: $21; Elev: 4012ft/1223m; Tel: 503-668 1700; Nearest town: Hood River. GPS: 45.577413, -121.792704

466 • Walla Walla Forest Camp

Total sites: 4; RV sites: 4; No water; Vault toilets; Reservations not accepted; Max length: 18ft; Stay limit: 14 days; Open Jun-Sep; Tent & RV camping: $5; Elev: 5010ft/1527m; Tel: 541-523-6391; Nearest town: Lostine. GPS: 45.316277, -117.402473

467 • Walton Lake

Total sites: 27; RV sites: 21; Central water; Vault toilets; No showers; No RV dump; Reservations accepted; Stay limit: 14 days; Open May-Oct; Tent & RV camping: $15; Elev: 5194ft/1583m; Tel: 541-416-6500; Nearest town: Prineville; Notes: 2 group sites $60-$100. GPS: 44.433535, -120.336334

468 • Watkins

Total sites: 14; No water; Vault toilets; Reservations not accepted; Stay limit: 14 days; Generator hours: 0600-2200; Open all year; Tents only: $15; Elev: 2165ft/660m; Tel: 541-899-3800; Nearest town: Applegate; Notes: Group site. GPS: 42.023943, -123.156515

469 • Waxmyrtle

Total sites: 55; RV sites: 55; Central water; Flush toilets; No showers; No RV dump; Reservations accepted; Max length: 30ft; Stay limit: 14 days; Open May-Sep; Tent & RV camping: $22; Elev: 33ft/10m; Tel: 541-271-3611; Nearest town: Florence. GPS: 43.876487, -124.143307

470 • Welch Creek

Total sites: 7; RV sites: 7; No water; Vault toilets; Reservations not accepted; Stay limit: 14 days; Open May-Nov; Tent & RV camping: $8; Elev: 4646ft/1416m; Tel: 541-278-3716; Nearest town: Dale; Notes: Free Nov-May - no services. GPS: 44.877000, -118.777000

471 • West South Twin

Total sites: 24; RV sites: 24; Central water; Flush toilets; No showers; No RV dump; Reservations accepted; Max length: 30ft; Open May-Sep; Tent & RV camping: $15-19; Elev: 4347ft/1325m; Tel: 541-338-7869; Nearest town: La Pine. GPS: 43.714772, -121.772355

472 • West Winds

Total sites: 20; RV sites: 20; Central water; Vault toilets; No showers; No RV dump; Reservations not accepted; Max length: 40ft; Stay limit: 14 days; Open all year; No tents/RVs: $25; Elev: 56ft/17m; Tel: 503-392-3161; Nearest town: Pacific City. GPS: 45.286855, -123.955851

473 • Wetmore

Total sites: 12; RV sites: 12; Central water; Vault toilets; No showers; No RV dump; Reservations not accepted; Stay limit: 14 days; Open May-Sep; Tent & RV camping: $5; Elev: 4370ft/1332m; Tel: 541-523-6391; Nearest town: Unity. GPS: 44.523835, -118.303948

474 • Whiskey Springs

Total sites: 34; RV sites: 34; Central water; Vault toilets; No showers; No RV dump; Reservations accepted; Max length: 30ft; Stay limit: 14 days; Generator hours: 0600-2200; Open May-Oct; Tent & RV camping: $18; Elev: 3182ft/970m; Tel: 541-865-2700; Nearest town: Butte Falls. GPS: 42.496811, -122.419475

475 • Whispering Falls

Total sites: 16; RV sites: 16; Central water; Vault toilets; No showers; No RV dump; Reservations accepted; Max length: 30ft; Stay limit: 14 days; Open May-Sep; Tent & RV camping: $18; Elev: 2060ft/628m; Tel: 503-854-3366; Nearest town: Detroit. GPS: 44.687744, -122.009521

476 • Whistler

Total sites: 4; RV sites: 4; No water; Vault toilets; Reservations not accepted; Stay limit: 14 days; Open all year; Tent & RV camping: Free; Elev: 5745ft/1751m; Nearest town: Paulina; Notes: Very rough road. GPS: 44.497803, -120.482553

477 • White Rock

Total sites: 3; RV sites: 1; No water; Vault toilets; Reservations not accepted; Stay limit: 14 days; Open all year; Tent & RV camping: Free; Elev: 5479ft/1670m; Tel: 541-416-6500; Nearest town: Prineville. GPS: 44.423165, -120.543703

478 • Whitehorse Falls

Total sites: 5; RV sites: 5; No water; Vault toilets; Reservations not accepted; Max length: 25ft; Stay limit: 14 days; Open May-Oct; Tent & RV camping: $10; Elev: 3773ft/1150m; Tel: 541-957-3200; Nearest town: Diamond Lake. GPS: 43.246698, -122.304341

479 • Wickiup

Total sites: 6; RV sites: 6; No water; Vault toilets; Reservations not accepted; Stay limit: 14 days; Open May-Sep; Tent & RV camping: $6; Elev: 4364ft/1330m; Tel: 541-575-3000; Nearest town: John Day. GPS: 44.216537, -118.852416

480 • Wickiup Butte

Total sites: 8; RV sites: 8; No water; Vault toilets; Reservations not accepted; Open Apr-Sep; Tent & RV camping: Free; Elev: 4356ft/1328m; Tel: 541-383-4000; Nearest town: La Pine. GPS: 43.673562, -121.685304

481 • Wildcat

Total sites: 17; RV sites: 17; Central water; Vault toilets; No showers; No RV dump; Reservations not accepted; Stay limit: 14 days; Open May-Sep; Tent & RV camping: $15; Elev: 3802ft/1159m; Tel: 541-416-6500; Nearest town: Prineville. GPS: 44.440303, -120.578431

482 • Wildhorse

Total sites: 3; RV sites: 3; No water; Vault toilets; Reservations not accepted; Stay limit: 14 days; Generator hours: 0600-2200; Open May-Nov; Tent & RV camping: Free; Elev: 3556ft/1084m; Tel: 541-247-3600; Nearest town: Gold Beach. GPS: 42.460766, -124.162819

483 • Wildwood

Total sites: 5; RV sites: 5; No water; Vault toilets; Reservations not accepted; Stay limit: 14 days; Open all year; Tent & RV camping: Free; Elev: 4869ft/1484m; Tel: 541-416-6500; Nearest town: Prineville. GPS: 44.485000, -120.335000

484 • Wiley Flat

Total sites: 5; RV sites: 5; No water; Vault toilets; Reservations not accepted; Stay limit: 14 days; Open all year; Tent & RV camping: Free; Elev: 5364ft/1635m; Tel: 541-416-6500; Nearest town: Prineville. GPS: 44.042271, -120.297644

485 • Williamson

Total sites: 13; RV sites: 8; No water; Vault toilets; Reservations not accepted; Max length: 18ft; Stay limit: 14 days; Open Jun-Sep; Tent & RV camping: $6; Elev: 5003ft/1525m; Tel: 541-523-6391; Nearest town: Enterprise. GPS: 45.342432, -117.411691

486 • Williamson River

Total sites: 20; RV sites: 20; Central water; Vault toilets; No showers; No RV dump; Reservations not accepted; Open all year; Tent & RV camping: $15; Elev: 4236ft/1291m; Tel: 541-783-4009; Nearest town: Chiloquin; Notes: Reduced services 10/15-5/14. GPS: 42.659001, -121.854485

487 • Willow Creek

Total sites: 8; RV sites: 8; No water; Vault toilets; Reservations not accepted; Open all year; Tent & RV camping: Free; Elev: 6129ft/1868m; Tel: 541-947-6300; Nearest town: Lakeview; Notes: Reduced services 10/15-5/14. GPS: 42.093062, -120.201818

488 • Winom Creek

Total sites: 7; RV sites: 7; No water; Vault toilets; Reservations not accepted; Stay limit: 14 days; Open May-Nov; Tent & RV camping: $10; Elev: 4944ft/1507m; Tel: 541-278-3716; Nearest town: Ukiah; Notes: Free Nov-May - no services. GPS: 45.012236, -118.641641

489 • Wolf Creek

Total sites: 16; RV sites: 16; No water; Vault toilets; Reservations not accepted; Max length: 20ft; Stay limit: 14 days; Open all year; Tent & RV camping: $6; Elev: 4003ft/1220m; Tel: 541-416-6500; Nearest town: Paulina; Notes: No services in winter, Narrow CG roads with sharp turns. GPS: 44.252930, -119.825928

490 • Wolf Creek

Total sites: 8; RV sites: 5; Central water; No toilets; No showers; No RV dump; Reservations not accepted; Max length: 30ft; Stay limit: 14 days; Open May-Sep; Tent & RV camping: $15; Elev: 1145ft/349m; Tel: 541-496-3534; Nearest town: Glide. GPS: 43.240235, -122.933447

491 • Woodland

Total sites: 6; RV sites: 6; No water; Vault toilets; Reservations not accepted; Stay limit: 14 days; Open Jun-Nov; Tent & RV camping: $8; Elev: 5220ft/1591m; Tel: 541-278-3716; Nearest town: Toll Gate. GPS: 45.734000, -118.030000

492 • Woodward

Total sites: 15; RV sites: 15; Central water; Vault toilets; No showers; No RV dump; Reservations not accepted; Stay limit: 14 days; Open Jul-Sep; Tent & RV camping: $12; Elev: 4948ft/1508m; Tel: 541-278-3716; Nearest town: Weston. GPS: 45.779053, -118.098389

493 • Wrangle

Total sites: 5; No water; Vault toilets; Reservations not accepted; Stay limit: 14 days; Generator hours: 0600-2200; Open Jun-Oct; Tents only: Free; Elev: 6283ft/1915m; Tel: 541-899-3800; Nearest town: Ashland. GPS: 42.050203, -122.856392

494 • Wyeth

Total sites: 14; RV sites: 14; Central water; No toilets; No showers; No RV dump; Reservations not accepted; Max length: 30ft; Stay limit: 14 days; Open May-Sep; Tent & RV camping: $20; Elev: 138ft/42m; Tel: 541-308-1700; Nearest town: Cascade Locks. GPS: 45.690024, -121.771425

495 • Wyeth

Total sites: 5; RV sites: 5; No water; Vault toilets; Reservations accepted; Max length: 26ft; Open Apr-Oct; Tent & RV camping: $12-14; Elev: 4278ft/1304m; Tel: 541-383-4000; Nearest town: Hood River. GPS: 43.738888, -121.614573

496 • Yellow Jacket

Total sites: 20; RV sites: 20; Central water; Vault toilets; No showers; No RV dump; Reservations not accepted; Stay limit: 14 days; Open May-Sep; Tent & RV camping: $10; Elev: 4810ft/1466m; Tel: 541-575-3000; Nearest town: Hines. GPS: 43.876221, -119.272544

497 • Yellow Pine

Total sites: 20; RV sites: 20; Central water; Vault toilets; No showers; No RV dump; Reservations not accepted; Stay limit: 14 days; Open May-Sep; Tent & RV camping: $5; Elev: 4478ft/1365m; Tel: 541-523-6391; Nearest town: Unity. GPS: 44.530272, -118.310439

498 • Yukwah

Total sites: 19; RV sites: 19; Central water; Vault toilets; No showers; No RV dump; Reservations accepted; Max length: 32ft; Stay limit: 14 days; Open May-Sep; Tent & RV camping: $18; Elev: 1348ft/411m; Tel: 541-367-5168; Nearest town: Sweet Home. GPS: 44.399248, -122.338179

Pennsylvania

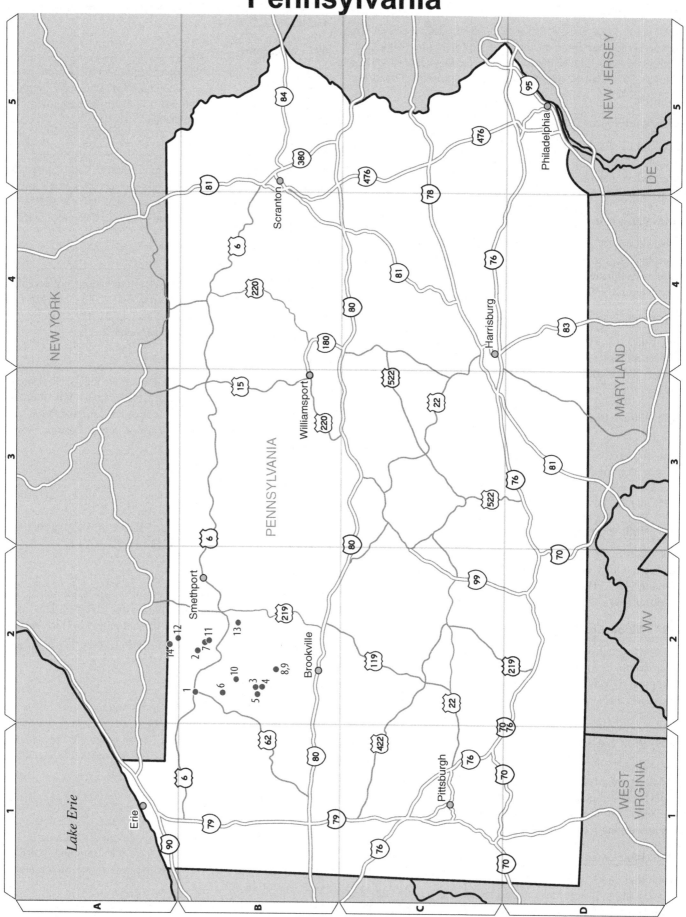

Pennsylvania Camping Areas

1 • Buckaloons

Total sites: 51; RV sites: 51; Elec sites: 43; Central water; Flush toilets; Showers; RV dump; Reservations accepted; Stay limit: 14 days; Generator hours: 0600-2200; Open May-Oct; Tents: $20/RVs: $20-25; Elev: 1164ft/355m; Tel: 814-362-4613; Nearest town: Warren; Notes: Group site: $20-$60. GPS: 41.838855, -79.257367

2 • Dewdrop

Total sites: 74; RV sites: 56; Central water; Flush toilets; Showers; RV dump; Reservations accepted; Stay limit: 14 days; Generator hours: 0600-2200; Open May-Sep; Tent & RV camping: $20-24; Elev: 1437ft/438m; Tel: 814-945-6511; Nearest town: Warren. GPS: 41.832031, -78.959229

3 • FR 145 Site 17

Total sites: 2; RV sites: 1; No water; No toilets; Stay limit: 14 days; Tent & RV camping: Free; Elev: 1273ft/388m; Tel: 814-728-6100; Nearest town: Marienville. GPS: 41.507126, -79.210917

4 • FR 145 Site 24

Total sites: 2; RV sites: 1; No water; No toilets; Stay limit: 14 days; Tent & RV camping: Free; Elev: 1353ft/412m; Tel: 814-728-6100; Nearest town: Marienville. GPS: 41.475287, -79.209062

5 • FR 210 Site 3

Total sites: 3; RV sites: 1; No water; No toilets; Stay limit: 14 days; Tent & RV camping: Free; Elev: 1751ft/534m; Tel: 814-728-6100; Nearest town: Marienville. GPS: 41.499857, -79.256063

6 • Hearts Content

Total sites: 26; RV sites: 26; Central water; Vault toilets; No showers; RV dump; Reservations accepted; Open May-Oct; Tent & RV camping: $12-14; Elev: 1925ft/587m; Tel: 814-368-4158; Nearest town: Warren; Notes: Group site: $20-$60, 2 sites with lean-to shelters. GPS: 41.691282, -79.257121

7 • Kiasutha

Total sites: 93; RV sites: 92; Elec sites: 17; Water at site; Flush toilets; Showers; RV dump; Reservations accepted; Stay limit: 14 days; Generator hours: 0600-2200; Open May-Sep; Tents: $20/RVs: $20-35; Elev: 1348ft/411m; Tel: 814-945-6511; Nearest town: Kane; Notes: 12 FHU. GPS: 41.785156, -78.902344

8 • Loleta Basic

Total sites: 18; RV sites: 18; Central water; Vault toilets; No showers; No RV dump; Reservations accepted; Max length: 20ft; Stay limit: 14 days; Generator hours: 0600-2200; Open Apr-Oct; Tent & RV camping: $16; Elev: 1501ft/458m; Nearest town: Marienville; Notes: Showers at beach bathhouse. GPS: 41.404424, -79.079684

9 • Loleta RV

Total sites: 20; RV sites: 20; Elec sites: 20; Central water; Vault toilets; No showers; No RV dump; Reservations accepted; Max length: 50ft; Stay limit: 14 days; Generator hours: 0600-2200; Open Apr-Sep; Tent & RV camping: $16-25; Elev: 1344ft/410m; Nearest town: Marienville; Notes: Showers at beach bathhouse. GPS: 41.400006, -79.082301

10 • Minister Creek

Total sites: 6; RV sites: 6; Central water; Vault toilets; No showers; No RV dump; Reservations not accepted; Stay limit: 14 days; Generator hours: 0600-2200; Open Apr-Dec; Tent & RV camping: $12; Elev: 1371ft/418m; Tel: 814-362-4613; Nearest town: Sheffield. GPS: 41.621406, -79.154023

11 • Red Bridge

Total sites: 65; RV sites: 55; Elec sites: 23; Central water; Flush toilets; Showers; RV dump; Reservations accepted; Stay limit: 14 days; Open Apr-Oct; Tents: $20-24/RVs: $20-39; Elev: 1430ft/436m; Tel: 814-945-6511; Nearest town: Kane; Notes: 12 FHU. GPS: 41.776367, -78.887207

12 • Tracy Ridge

Total sites: 173; RV sites: 173; Central water; Vault toilets; No showers; RV dump; Reservations accepted; Stay limit: 14 days; Open May-Dec; Tent & RV camping: $12; Elev: 2257ft/688m; Tel: 814-368-4158; Nearest town: Bradford; Notes: Group site: $75. GPS: 41.943003, -78.876615

13 • Twin Lakes

Total sites: 50; RV sites: 49; Elec sites: 19; Central water; Flush toilets; Showers; RV dump; Reservations accepted; Max length: 28ft; Stay limit: 14 days; Open May-Dec; Tents: $16/RVs: $16-23; Elev: 1814ft/553m; Tel: 814-368-4158; Nearest town: Wilcox; Notes: 10' height limit - low bridge. GPS: 41.613178, -78.759647

14 • Willow Bay

Total sites: 101; RV sites: 58; Elec sites: 38; Central water; Flush toilets; Showers; RV dump; Reservations accepted; Stay limit: 14 days; Open May-Oct; Tents: $18-20/RVs: $23-25; Elev: 1332ft/406m; Tel: 814-362-4613; Nearest town: Bradford; Notes: Cabin(s). GPS: 41.988770, -78.917236

South Carolina

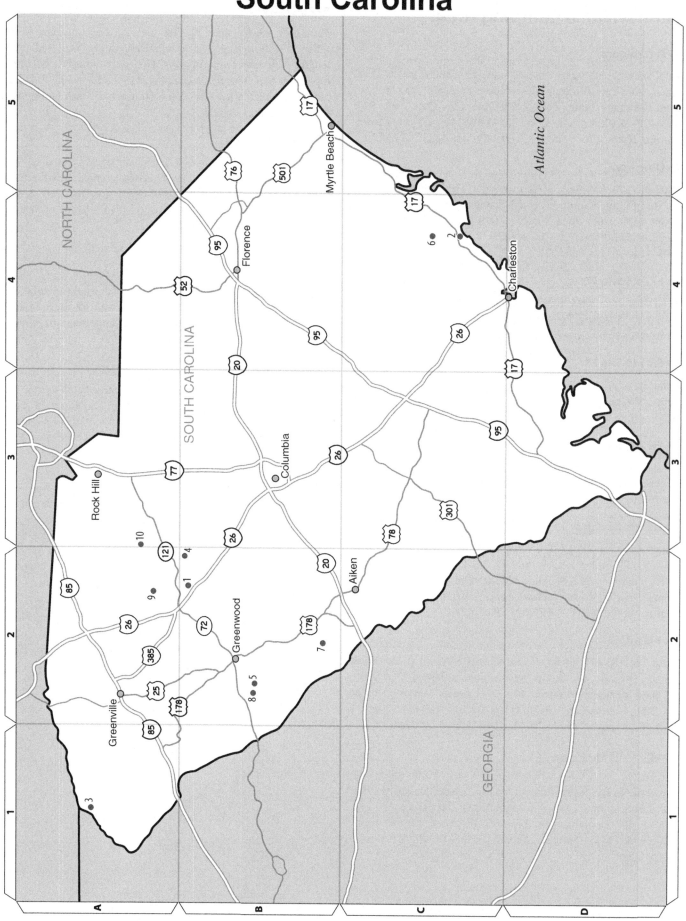

South Carolina Camping Areas

1 • Brick House

Total sites: 23; RV sites: 23; Central water; Vault toilets; No showers; No RV dump; Reservations not accepted; Open all year; Tent & RV camping: $5; Elev: 581ft/177m; Tel: 803-276-4810; Nearest town: Whitmire; Notes: 8 extended-stay sites. GPS: 34.447991, -81.706659

2 • Buck Hall

Total sites: 19; RV sites: 14; Elec sites: 14; Central water; Flush toilets; Showers; RV dump; Reservations accepted; Open all year; Tents: $20/RVs: $28; Elev: 7ft/2m; Tel: 843-336-3248; Nearest town: McClellanville. GPS: 33.038086, -79.562256

3 • Cherry Hill

Total sites: 29; RV sites: 12; Central water; Flush toilets; Showers; RV dump; Reservations accepted; Open Apr-Oct; Tent & RV camping: $15; Elev: 2267ft/691m; Tel: 864-638-9568; Nearest town: Mountain Rest. GPS: 34.941573, -83.087634

4 • Collins Creek Seasonal Camp

Total sites: 43; Central water; Vault toilets; Showers; No RV dump; Reservations not accepted; Open all year; Tent & RV camping: $5; Elev: 472ft/144m; Tel: 803-276-4810; Nearest town: Long Branch; Notes: Check for open dates, Hot outdoor showers. GPS: 34.471974, -81.524344

5 • Fell Camp

Total sites: 66; RV sites: 66; Central water; Vault toilets; Reservations not accepted; Open all year; Tent & RV camping: $5; Elev: 545ft/166m; Tel: 803-637-5396; Nearest town: Greenwood. GPS: 34.093158, -82.292014

6 • Honey Hill

Total sites: 10; Central water; Vault toilets; No showers; No RV dump; Reservations not accepted; Open all year; Tents only: Free; Elev: 49ft/15m; Tel: 843-336-3248; Nearest town: McClellanville. GPS: 33.174365, -79.561842

7 • Lick Fork Lake

Total sites: 9; RV sites: 9; Central water; Vault toilets; No showers; No RV dump; Reservations not accepted; Stay limit: 14 days; Open May-Nov; Tent & RV camping: $7; Elev: 469ft/143m; Tel: 803-637-5396; Nearest town: Edgefield. GPS: 33.729736, -82.039795

8 • Parsons Mountain Lake

Total sites: 23; RV sites: 23; Central water; No toilets; No showers; No RV dump; Reservations not accepted; Stay limit: 14 days; Open May-Nov; Tent & RV camping: $7; Elev: 532ft/162m; Tel: 803-637-5396; Nearest town: Anderson. GPS: 34.099795, -82.354187

9 • Sedalia

Total sites: 4; RV sites: 4; Central water; Vault toilets; No showers; No RV dump; Reservations not accepted; Stay limit: 14 days; Open all year; Tent & RV camping: $5; Elev: 614ft/187m; Tel: 803-276-4810; Nearest town: Union; Notes: Some seasonal hunting sites. GPS: 34.630848, -81.738211

10 • Woods Ferry

Total sites: 28; RV sites: 28; Central water; Vault toilets; No showers; No RV dump; Reservations not accepted; Stay limit: 14 days; Open Apr-Oct; Tent & RV camping: $7; Elev: 436ft/133m; Tel: 803-276-4810; Nearest town: Union; Notes: 2 group sites: $14, Corrals. GPS: 34.700684, -81.450684

South Dakota

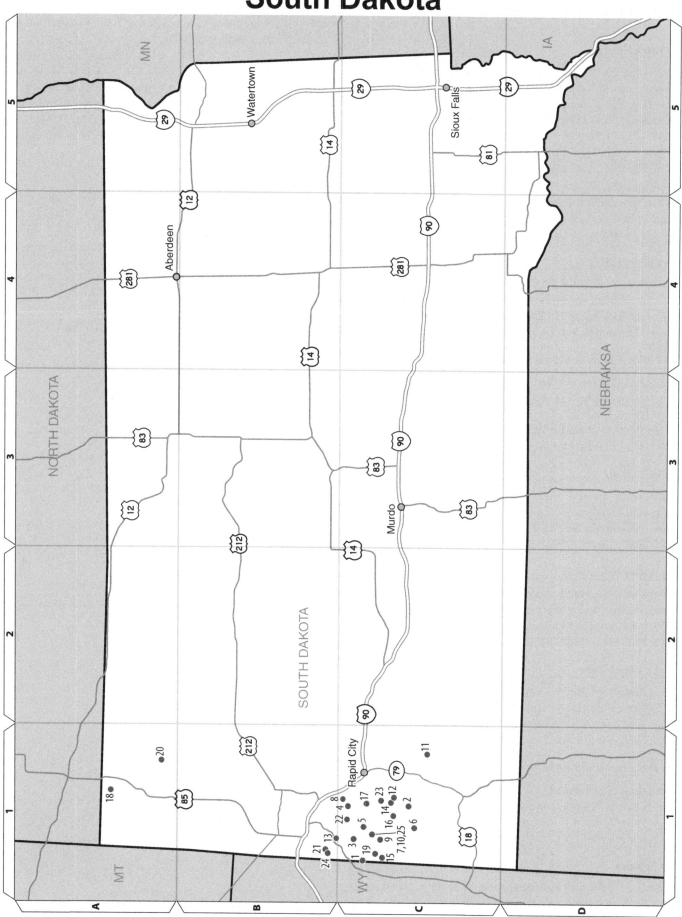

South Dakota Camping Areas

1 • Beaver Creek

Total sites: 8; RV sites: 8; Central water; Vault toilets; No showers; No RV dump; Reservations not accepted; Max length: 45ft; Tent & RV camping: $16; Elev: 6207ft/1892m; Nearest town: Newcastle. GPS: 44.075334, -104.051017

2 • Bismarck Lake

Total sites: 23; RV sites: 23; Central water; Flush toilets; No showers; No RV dump; Reservations not accepted; Open May-Sep; Tent & RV camping: $26; Elev: 5266ft/1605m; Tel: 605-574-4402; Nearest town: Custer. GPS: 43.774976, -103.510969

3 • Black Fox

Total sites: 9; RV sites: 9; No water; Vault toilets; Reservations not accepted; Open all year; Tent & RV camping: $16; Elev: 5892ft/1796m; Nearest town: Rochford. GPS: 44.144884, -103.845871

4 • Boxelder Forks

Total sites: 14; RV sites: 14; Central water; No toilets; No showers; No RV dump; Reservations not accepted; Tent & RV camping: $18; Elev: 4852ft/1479m; Nearest town: Nemo. GPS: 44.198011, -103.535601

5 • Castle Peak

Total sites: 9; RV sites: 9; No water; Vault toilets; Reservations not accepted; Open all year; Tent & RV camping: $16; Elev: 5420ft/1652m; Nearest town: Hill City. GPS: 44.080118, -103.727335

6 • Comanche Park

Total sites: 34; RV sites: 34; Central water; Vault toilets; No showers; No RV dump; Reservations not accepted; Open May-Oct; Tent & RV camping: $16; Elev: 5528ft/1685m; Tel: 605-574-4402; Nearest town: Custer. GPS: 43.733831, -103.714427

7 • Custer Trail

Total sites: 16; RV sites: 16; Central water; Vault toilets; No showers; No RV dump; Reservations not accepted; Tent & RV camping: $16; Elev: 5955ft/1815m; Nearest town: Hill City. GPS: 44.025428, -103.798437

8 • Dalton Lake

Total sites: 11; RV sites: 11; Central water; Vault toilets; No showers; No RV dump; Reservations not accepted; Tent & RV camping: $18; Elev: 4406ft/1343m; Nearest town: Nemo. GPS: 44.230169, -103.476212

9 • Ditch Creek

Total sites: 13; RV sites: 13; Central water; Vault toilets; No showers; No RV dump; Reservations not accepted; Tent & RV camping: $20; Elev: 6243ft/1903m; Nearest town: Hill City. GPS: 43.960709, -103.841905

10 • Dutchman

Total sites: 44; RV sites: 44; Potable water; Vault toilets; No showers; No RV dump; Reservations accepted; Open all year; Tent & RV camping: $20; Elev: 6079ft/1853m; Nearest town: Hill City. GPS: 44.022019, -103.781002

11 • French Creek

Total sites: 3; RV sites: 3; No water; Vault toilets; Reservations not accepted; Tent & RV camping: Fee unknown; Elev: 2897ft/883m; Tel: 605-745-4107; Nearest town: Fairburn. GPS: 43.662331, -103.022473

12 • Grizzly Creek

Total sites: 20; RV sites: 20; Central water; Vault toilets; No showers; No RV dump; Reservations not accepted; Max length: 28ft; Tent & RV camping: $20; Elev: 4544ft/1385m; Nearest town: Keystone; Notes: Large trailers not recommended. GPS: 43.876898, -103.439542

13 • Hanna

Total sites: 13; RV sites: 6; Central water; Vault toilets; No showers; No RV dump; Reservations not accepted; Open all year; Tent & RV camping: $18; Elev: 5653ft/1723m; Tel: 605-673-9200; Nearest town: Lead; Notes: Walk-to tent sites open year round. GPS: 44.274805, -103.851459

14 • Horsethief Lake

Total sites: 36; RV sites: 36; Potable water; No toilets; No showers; No RV dump; Reservations not accepted; Open May-Sep; Tent & RV camping: $26; Elev: 5013ft/1528m; Tel: 605-574-4402; Nearest town: Keystone. GPS: 43.895020, -103.483643

15 • Moon

Total sites: 3; RV sites: 3; No water; Vault toilets; Max length: 30ft; Open Jun-Nov; Tent & RV camping: Free; Elev: 6440ft/1963m; Nearest town: Newcastle WY. GPS: 43.946136, -104.009197

16 • Oreville

Total sites: 24; RV sites: 24; Potable water; Vault toilets; No showers; No RV dump; Reservations accepted; Open May-Sep; Tent & RV camping: $20; Elev: 5377ft/1639m; Tel: 605-574-4402; Nearest town: Hill City. GPS: 43.877383, -103.611668

17 • Pactola

Total sites: 77; RV sites: 77; Central water; Vault toilets; No showers; No RV dump; Reservations accepted; Open May-Sep; Tent & RV camping: $26; Elev: 4665ft/1422m; Tel: 605-574-4402; Nearest town: Hill City. GPS: 44.068095, -103.506349

18 • Picnic Spring

Total sites: 8; RV sites: 8; Central water; Vault toilets; No showers; No RV dump; Reservations not accepted; Max length: 30ft; Open May-Sep; Tent & RV camping: Free; Elev: 3245ft/989m; Tel: 605-797-4432; Nearest town: Camp Crook. GPS: 45.874398, -103.485574

19 • Redbank Spring

Total sites: 4; RV sites: 4; No water; Vault toilets; Reservations not accepted; Open all year; Tent & RV camping: $16; Elev: 6614ft/2016m; Nearest town: Newcastle. GPS: 43.990745, -103.981186

20 • Reva Gap

Total sites: 8; RV sites: 8; Central water; Vault toilets; No showers; No RV dump; Reservations not accepted; Max length: 30ft; Tent & RV camping: Free; Elev: 3284ft/1001m; Tel: 605-797-4432; Nearest town: Camp Crook. GPS: 45.525763, -103.177222

21 • Rod and Gun

Total sites: 7; RV sites: 7; Central water; No toilets; No showers; No RV dump; Reservations not accepted; Tent & RV camping: $18; Elev: 5518ft/1682m; Tel: 605-673-9200; Nearest town: Spearfish. GPS: 44.338543, -103.963657

22 • Roubaix Lake

Total sites: 56; RV sites: 56; Potable water; No toilets; No showers; No RV dump; Reservations not accepted; Open all year; Tent & RV camping: $24; Elev: 5548ft/1691m; Tel: 605-574-4402; Nearest town: Deadwood. GPS: 44.198245, -103.664012

23 • Sheridan Lake South Shore

Total sites: 129; RV sites: 129; Potable water; Vault toilets; No showers; No RV dump; Reservations not accepted; Open May-Sep; Tent & RV camping: $26; Elev: 4678ft/1426m; Tel: 605-574-4402; Nearest town: Hill City. GPS: 43.970604, -103.474207

24 • Timon

Total sites: 7; RV sites: 7; Central water; Vault toilets; No showers; No RV dump; Reservations not accepted; Tent & RV camping: $18; Elev: 5699ft/1737m; Tel: 605-673-9200; Nearest town: Spearfish. GPS: 44.328046, -103.988151

25 • Whitetail

Total sites: 17; RV sites: 17; Central water; Vault toilets; No showers; No RV dump; Reservations not accepted; Open May-Sep; Tent & RV camping: $20; Elev: 5938ft/1810m; Tel: 605-673-9200; Nearest town: Hill City; Notes: Several sites remain open off-season - free. GPS: 44.013049, -103.803456

Tennessee

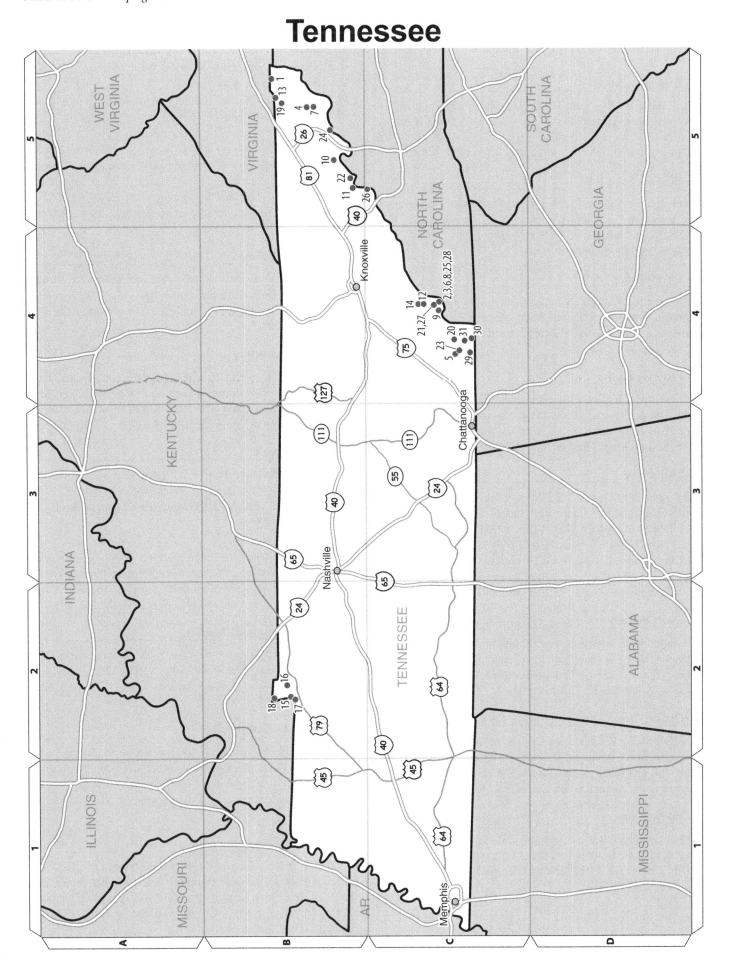

Tennessee Camping Areas

1 • Backbone Rock

Total sites: 11; RV sites: 11; Central water; Flush toilets; No showers; No RV dump; Reservations accepted; Open May-Dec; Tent & RV camping: $10; Elev: 2313ft/705m; Tel: 423-735-1500; Nearest town: Bristol. GPS: 36.594493, -81.814255

2 • Big Oak Cove

Total sites: 11; RV sites: 11; No water; Vault toilets; Reservations not accepted; Open Mar-Dec; Tent & RV camping: $10; Elev: 2602ft/793m; Tel: 423-253-8400; Nearest town: Tellico Plains. GPS: 35.264355, -84.086709

3 • Birch Branch

Total sites: 5; RV sites: 5; No water; Vault toilets; Reservations not accepted; Open all year; Tent & RV camping: $10; Elev: 2234ft/681m; Tel: 423-253-8400; Nearest town: Tellico Plains. GPS: 35.282325, -84.097144

4 • Cardens Bluff

Total sites: 41; RV sites: 3; Central water; Flush toilets; Showers; No RV dump; Reservations accepted; Max length: 30ft; Open Apr-Nov; Tent & RV camping: $12; Elev: 2028ft/618m; Tel: 423-735-1500; Nearest town: Elizabethton. GPS: 36.312744, -82.117432

5 • Chilhowee

Total sites: 78; RV sites: 71; Elec sites: 36; Central water; Flush toilets; Showers; RV dump; Reservations accepted; Open Apr-Oct; Tents: $12-15/RVs: $12-20; Elev: 1926ft/587m; Tel: 423-338-3300; Nearest town: Benton; Notes: 16 sites open through winter with limited services, Be Aware: Do not use GPS directions - GPS will direct you up Benton Springs Road (narrow and winding) - recommend use of FSR 77. GPS: 35.149642, -84.612428

6 • Davis Branch

Total sites: 6; RV sites: 6; No water; Vault toilets; Reservations not accepted; Open all year; Tent & RV camping: $10; Elev: 2424ft/739m; Tel: 423-253-8400; Nearest town: Tellico Plains. GPS: 35.279077, -84.096412

7 • Dennis Cove

Total sites: 15; RV sites: 15; Central water; Flush toilets; No showers; No RV dump; Reservations accepted; Max length: 30ft; Open Jul-Oct; Tent & RV camping: $10; Elev: 2703ft/824m; Nearest town: Hampton. GPS: 36.257568, -82.110352

8 • Holder Cove

Total sites: 7; RV sites: 7; No water; Vault toilets; Reservations not accepted; Open all year; Tent & RV camping: $10; Elev: 2516ft/767m; Tel: 423-253-8400; Nearest town: Tellico Plains. GPS: 35.271096, -84.086348

9 • Holly Flats

Total sites: 16; RV sites: 16; No water; Vault toilets; Reservations not accepted; Open May-Nov; Tent & RV camping: $6; Elev: 1939ft/591m; Tel: 423-253-8400; Nearest town: Tellico Plains. GPS: 35.285400, -84.177734

10 • Horse Creek

Total sites: 15; RV sites: 9; Central water; Flush toilets; Showers; No RV dump; Reservations not accepted; Max length: 24ft; Open Apr-Nov; Tent & RV camping: $10; Elev: 1883ft/574m; Tel: 423-638-4109; Nearest town: Greeneville. GPS: 36.108629, -82.656702

11 • Houston Valley

Total sites: 8; RV sites: 8; Central water; Vault toilets; No showers; No RV dump; Reservations accepted; Open May-Oct; Tent & RV camping: $7; Elev: 1834ft/559m; Nearest town: Greeneville. GPS: 35.964807, -82.942937

12 • Indian Boundary

Total sites: 87; RV sites: 87; Elec sites: 87; Central water; Flush toilets; Showers; RV dump; Reservations accepted; Open May-Oct; Tent & RV camping: $20; Elev: 1880ft/573m; Tel: 423-253-8400; Nearest town: Knoxville. GPS: 35.402100, -84.105957

13 • Jacobs Creek

Total sites: 27; RV sites: 27; Central water; Flush toilets; Showers; RV dump; Reservations not accepted; Open May-Oct; Tent & RV camping: $12; Elev: 1726ft/526m; Nearest town: Bristol. GPS: 36.568115, -82.011963

14 • Jake Best

Total sites: 7; RV sites: 7; No water; Vault toilets; Reservations not accepted; Open Mar-Nov; Tent & RV camping: $6; Elev: 1079ft/329m; Nearest town: Vonore. GPS: 35.445937, -84.109288

15 • LBL NRA - Boswell Landing

Total sites: 19; RV sites: 16; No water; Vault toilets; Stay limit: 14 days; Open all year; Tent & RV camping: $10; Elev: 364ft/111m; Nearest town: Dover; Notes: 3-day permit: $10. GPS: 36.519217, -88.024924

16 • LBL NRA - Gatlin Point

Total sites: 19; RV sites: 17; Central water; Vault toilets; No showers; No RV dump; Reservations not accepted; Stay limit: 14 days; Open all year; Tent & RV camping: $10; Elev: 374ft/114m; Nearest town: Dover; Notes: 3-day permit: $10. GPS: 36.556641, -87.903809

17 • LBL NRA - Piney

Total sites: 384; RV sites: 394; Elec sites: 327; Central water; Flush toilets; Showers; Laundry; RV dump; Reservations accepted; Stay limit: 14 days; Open all year; Tents: $12/RVs: $34-40; Elev: 397ft/121m; Tel: 931-232-5331; Nearest town: Dover; Notes: Cabin(s), 44 FHU. GPS: 36.486026, -88.038251

18 • LBL NRA - Rushing Creek

Total sites: 40; RV sites: 40; Central water; Flush toilets; Showers; No RV dump; Reservations not accepted; Stay limit: 14 days; Open all year; Tent & RV camping: $10; Elev: 358ft/109m; Tel: 270-924-2000; Nearest town: Canton; Notes: 3-day permit: $10. GPS: 36.658654, -88.037148

19 • Little Oak

Total sites: 68; RV sites: 68; Central water; Flush toilets; Showers; RV dump; Reservations accepted; Open Apr-Nov; Tent & RV camping: $12; Elev: 1788ft/545m; Tel: 423-735-1500; Nearest town: Bristol; Notes: $10 during shoulder seasons with limited facilities, no water. GPS: 36.520264, -82.061279

20 • Lost Creek

Total sites: 15; RV sites: 15; No water; Vault toilets; Reservations not accepted; Max length: 24ft; Open all year; Tent & RV camping: Free; Elev: 994ft/303m; Nearest town: Benton. GPS: 35.160291, -84.468434

21 • North River

Total sites: 11; RV sites: 11; No water; Vault toilets; Reservations not accepted; Open May-Nov; Tent & RV camping: $8; Elev: 1982ft/604m; Tel: 423-253-8400; Nearest town: Tellico Plains. GPS: 35.318634, -84.125181

22 • Paint Creek

Total sites: 20; RV sites: 20; Central water; Vault toilets; No showers; No RV dump; Reservations not accepted; Open May-Oct; Tent & RV camping: $10; Elev: 1883ft/574m; Nearest town: Greeneville. GPS: 35.978027, -82.844482

23 • Parksville Lake

Total sites: 41; RV sites: 17; Elec sites: 17; Central water; Flush toilets; Showers; RV dump; Reservations accepted; Open Apr-Oct; Tent & RV camping: $20; Elev: 899ft/274m; Nearest town: Benton. GPS: 35.117385, -84.575472

24 • Rock Creek

Total sites: 37; RV sites: 32; Elec sites: 32; Central water; Flush toilets; Showers; RV dump; Reservations accepted; Open May-Oct; Tent & RV camping: $20; Elev: 2316ft/706m; Tel: 423-638-4109; Nearest town: Erwin. GPS: 36.137647, -82.352559

25 • Rough Ridge

Total sites: 5; RV sites: 5; No water; Vault toilets; Reservations not accepted; Max length: 26ft; Open all year; Tent & RV camping: $10-20; Elev: 2674ft/815m; Tel: 423-253-8400; Nearest town: Tellico Plains. GPS: 35.261107, -84.084183

26 • Round Mountain

Total sites: 14; RV sites: 12; No water; Vault toilets; Reservations not accepted; Open May-Oct; Tent & RV camping: $7; Elev: 3163ft/964m; Nearest town: Greeneville. GPS: 35.838575, -82.955323

27 • Spivey Cove

Total sites: 16; RV sites: 16; No water; Vault toilets; Reservations not accepted; Open May-Nov; Tent & RV camping: $6; Elev: 1995ft/608m; Tel: 423-253-8400; Nearest town: Tellico Plains. GPS: 35.303759, -84.113611

28 • State Line

Total sites: 7; RV sites: 7; No water; Vault toilets; Reservations not accepted; Max length: 26ft; Tent & RV camping: $10-20; Elev: 2703ft/824m; Tel: 423-253-8400; Nearest town: Tellico Plains; Notes: Group site. GPS: 35.261567, -84.081259

29 • Sylco

Total sites: 12; RV sites: 12; No water; No toilets; Reservations not accepted; Open all year; Tent & RV camping: Free; Elev: 1151ft/351m; Nearest town: Ducktown. GPS: 35.028096, -84.602215

30 • Thunder Rock

Total sites: 38; RV sites: 38; Elec sites: 1; Central water; Flush toilets; Showers; No RV dump; Reservations not accepted; Open Apr-Nov; Tents: $12/RVs: $12-20; Elev: 1148ft/350m; Tel: 423-338-3300; Nearest town: Ducktown; Notes: 3 sites open all winter. GPS: 35.076357, -84.486237

31 • Tumbling Creek

Total sites: 8; RV sites: 8; No water; No toilets; Reservations not accepted; Open all year; Tent & RV camping: Free; Elev: 1512ft/461m; Nearest town: Ducktown. GPS: 35.016771, -84.466506

Texas

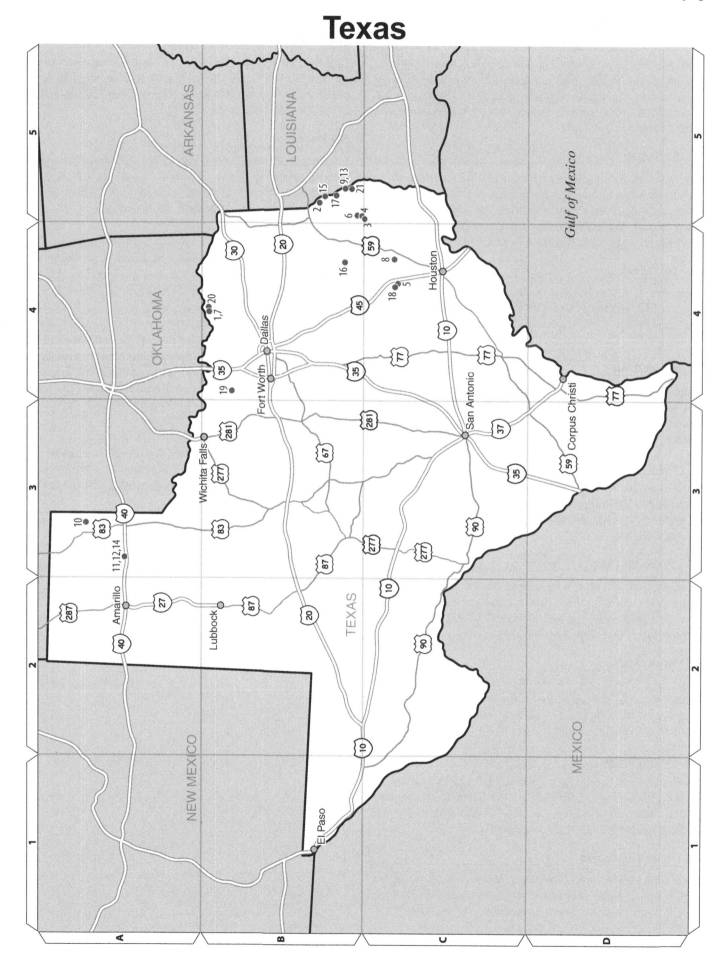

Texas Camping Areas

1 • Bois D' Arc

Total sites: 20; RV sites: 20; Central water; Vault toilets; Reservations not accepted; Tent & RV camping: $6; Elev: 584ft/178m; Tel: 940-627-5475; Nearest town: Bonham. GPS: 33.745427, -95.990136

2 • Boles Field

Total sites: 20; RV sites: 20; Elec sites: 20; Water at site; Flush toilets; Showers; No RV dump; Reservations not accepted; Max length: 24ft; Open all year; Tent & RV camping: $6; Elev: 374ft/114m; Tel: 409-625-1940; Nearest town: Shelbyville. GPS: 31.772612, -93.968167

3 • Bouton Lake Recreation Area

Total sites: 7; No water; Vault toilets; Reservations not accepted; Tents only: Free; Elev: 151ft/46m; Tel: 936-897-1068; Nearest town: Zavalla. GPS: 31.027309, -94.316954

4 • Boykin Springs

Total sites: 24; RV sites: 21; Central water; Flush toilets; Showers; No RV dump; Reservations not accepted; Max length: 24ft; Open all year; Tent & RV camping: $6; Elev: 210ft/64m; Tel: 936-897-1068; Nearest town: Zavalla. GPS: 31.059117, -94.274294

5 • Cagle

Total sites: 47; RV sites: 47; Elec sites: 47; Water at site; Flush toilets; Showers; RV dump; Reservations accepted; Open all year; Tent & RV camping: $27; Elev: 295ft/90m; Tel: 936-344-6205; Nearest town: New Waverly; Notes: 47 FHU. GPS: 30.523001, -95.589109

6 • Caney Creek

Total sites: 26; RV sites: 26; No water; Vault toilets; No showers; No RV dump; Reservations not accepted; Max length: 24ft; Tent & RV camping: $6; Elev: 226ft/69m; Tel: 936-897-2073; Nearest town: Zavalla. GPS: 31.134033, -94.256104

7 • Coffee Mill Lake

Total sites: 8; RV sites: 4; Central water; Vault toilets; No showers; No RV dump; Reservations not accepted; Tent & RV camping: $4; Elev: 541ft/165m; Tel: 940-627-5475; Nearest town: Honey Grove. GPS: 33.737091, -95.972987

8 • Double Lake

Total sites: 74; RV sites: 73; Elec sites: 41; Water at site; Flush toilets; Showers; No RV dump; Reservations accepted; Open all year; Tents: $20/RVs: $20-32; Elev: 331ft/101m; Tel: 936-653-3448; Nearest town: Coldspring; Notes: Group site: $85. GPS: 30.550631, -95.132224

9 • Indian Mounds

Total sites: 52; RV sites: 37; Central water; Vault toilets; No showers; No RV dump; Reservations not accepted; Max length: 24ft; Open all year; Tent & RV camping: $4; Elev: 200ft/61m; Tel: 409-625-1940; Nearest town: Hemphill. GPS: 31.309326, -93.695801

10 • Lake Marvin

Total sites: 12; RV sites: 4; Elec sites: 4; Central water; Vault toilets; No showers; No RV dump; Reservations not accepted; Stay limit: 14 days; Open all year; Tents: Free/RVs: $20; Elev: 2297ft/700m; Tel: 580-497-2143; Nearest town: Canadian. GPS: 35.886063, -100.180689

11 • Lake McClellan

Total sites: 23; RV sites: 18; Elec sites: 13; Central water; Vault toilets; No showers; No RV dump; Reservations not accepted; Open all year; Tents: $10/RVs: $10-15; Elev: 2940ft/896m; Tel: 580-497-2143; Nearest town: Groom. GPS: 35.212139, -100.873703

12 • Lake McClellan - East Bluff #1

Total sites: 7; No water; Vault toilets; Reservations not accepted; Open all year; Tents only: $10; Elev: 2930ft/893m; Tel: 580-497-2143; Nearest town: McLean. GPS: 35.212403, -100.865032

13 • Lakeview

Total sites: 10; RV sites: 10; Central water; Vault toilets; No showers; No RV dump; Reservations not accepted; Max length: 24ft; Stay limit: 28 days; Tent & RV camping: $3; Elev: 220ft/67m; Tel: 409-565-2273; Nearest town: Pineland. GPS: 31.261462, -93.679696

14 • McDowell

Total sites: 9; RV sites: 9; Elec sites: 6; Central water; Vault toilets; No showers; No RV dump; Reservations not accepted; Open all year; Tents: $10/RVs: $15; Elev: 2928ft/892m; Tel: 580-497-2143; Nearest town: Groom. GPS: 35.215517, -100.866309

15 • Ragtown

Total sites: 25; RV sites: 25; Central water; Flush toilets; Showers; RV dump; Reservations not accepted; Max length: 24ft; Tent & RV camping: $5; Elev: 292ft/89m; Tel: 409-625-1940; Nearest town: Shelbyville. GPS: 31.682129, -93.825684

16 • Ratcliff Lake

Total sites: 72; RV sites: 72; Elec sites: 17; Central water; Flush toilets; Showers; RV dump; Reservations accepted; Max length: 50ft; Open all year; Tent & RV camping: $15-20; Elev: 394ft/120m; Tel: 936-655-2299; Nearest town: Ratcliff. GPS: 31.391956, -95.154438

17 • Red Hills Lake

Total sites: 26; RV sites: 9; Elec sites: 9; Central water; Vault toilets; No showers; RV dump; Reservations not accepted; Max length: 35ft; Open May-Sep; Tents: $6/RVs: $6-10; Elev: 381ft/116m; Tel: 409-625-1940; Nearest town: Hemphill; Notes: Outside showers. GPS: 31.473877, -93.832764

18 • Stubblefield Lake

Total sites: 30; RV sites: 30; Central water; Flush toilets; Showers; No RV dump; Reservations not accepted; Max length: 28ft; Tent & RV camping: $15; Elev: 230ft/70m; Tel: 936-344-6205; Nearest town: New Waverly. GPS: 30.561132, -95.637576

19 • Tadra Point Trailhead Camp

Total sites: 26; RV sites: 26; No water; Vault toilets; Reservations not accepted; Tent & RV camping: $4; Elev: 909ft/277m; Tel: 940-627-5475; Nearest town: Decatur. GPS: 33.381740, -97.571530

20 • West Lake Davy Crockett

Total sites: 10; RV sites: 10; Central water; Vault toilets; No showers; No RV dump; Reservations not accepted; Tent & RV camping: $4; Elev: 551ft/168m; Tel: 940-627-5475; Nearest town: Caddo. GPS: 33.736987, -95.928651

21 • Willow Oak

Total sites: 15; RV sites: 15; Central water; Vault toilets; No showers; No RV dump; Reservations not accepted; Stay limit: 28 days; Tent & RV camping: $4; Elev: 177ft/54m; Tel: 409-565-2273; Nearest town: Fairmount. GPS: 31.210117, -93.733339

Utah

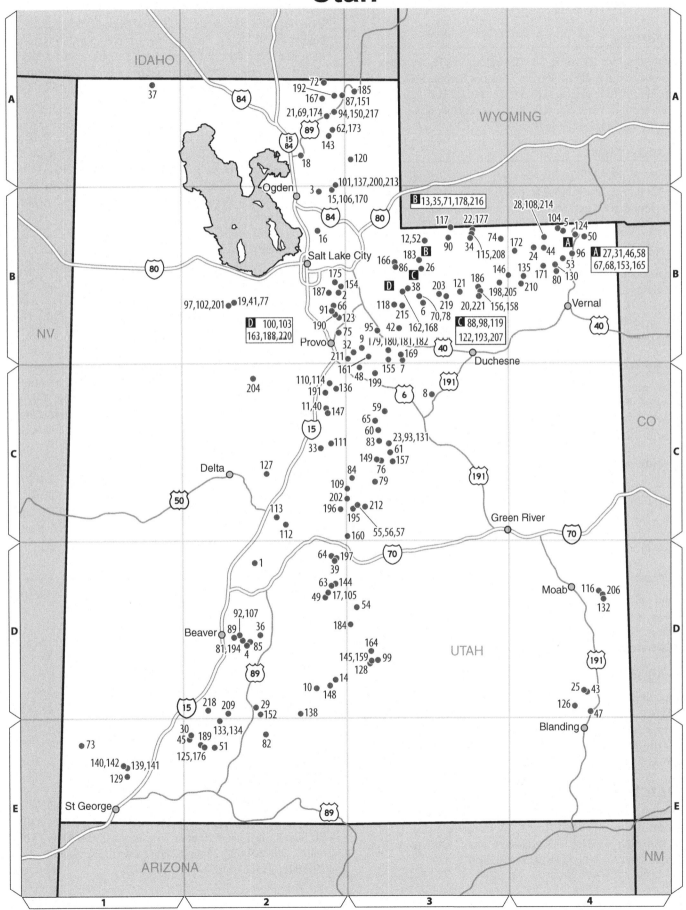

Utah Camping Areas

1 • Adelaide

Total sites: 10; RV sites: 10; Central water; Flush toilets; No showers; No RV dump; Reservations not accepted; Open May-Sep; Tent & RV camping: $12; Elev: 5591ft/1704m; Tel: 435-743-5721; Nearest town: Kanosh; Notes: Reservable group site: $50. GPS: 38.753946, -112.364498

2 • Albion Basin

Total sites: 19; RV sites: 19; No water; Vault toilets; No showers; No RV dump; Reservations accepted; Stay limit: 7 days; Open Jul-Sep; Tent & RV camping: $25; Elev: 9442ft/2878m; Tel: 801-733-2660; Nearest town: Alta . GPS: 40.577881, -111.613525

3 • Anderson Cove

Total sites: 67; RV sites: 67; Central water; Vault toilets; No showers; RV dump; Reservations accepted; Stay limit: 7 days; Generator hours: 0600-2200; Open May-Oct; Tent & RV camping: $28; Elev: 4931ft/1503m; Tel: 801-745-3215; Nearest town: Ogden; Notes: Group site: $255. GPS: 41.250184, -111.787519

4 • Anderson Meadow

Total sites: 10; RV sites: 10; Central water; Vault toilets; No showers; No RV dump; Reservations accepted; Open Jun-Sep; Tent & RV camping: $14; Elev: 9593ft/2924m; Tel: 435-438-2436; Nearest town: Beaver. GPS: 38.210649, -112.431714

5 • Antelope Flat

Total sites: 46; RV sites: 46; Potable water; No toilets; No showers; RV dump; Reservations accepted; Max length: 45ft; Open May-Sep; Tent & RV camping: $18; Elev: 6083ft/1854m; Tel: 435-889-3000; Nearest town: Dutch John; Notes: Group sites: $105-$120. GPS: 40.965164, -109.550618

6 • Aspen

Total sites: 29; RV sites: 29; Central water; Vault toilets; No showers; No RV dump; Reservations accepted; Open May-Sep; Tent & RV camping: $10; Elev: 7169ft/2185m; Tel: 435-738-2482; Nearest town: Hanna. GPS: 40.497070, -110.846436

7 • Aspen Grove

Total sites: 53; RV sites: 53; Elec sites: 1; Central water; Flush toilets; No showers; No RV dump; Reservations accepted; Stay limit: 7 days; Open Jun-Oct; Tents: $23/RVs: $23-36; Elev: 7779ft/2371m; Tel: 801-226-3564; Nearest town: Hanna; Notes: 1 FHU: $36. GPS: 40.120767, -111.036691

8 • Avintaquin

Total sites: 17; RV sites: 17; No water; Vault toilets; Reservations accepted; Open Jun-Sep; Tent & RV camping: $5; Elev: 8983ft/2738m; Tel: 435-738-2482; Nearest town: Duchesne; Notes: Group site $20. GPS: 39.884033, -110.775879

9 • Balsam

Total sites: 25; RV sites: 12; Central water; Vault toilets; No showers; No RV dump; Reservations accepted; Stay limit: 16 days; Open May-Sep; Tent & RV camping: $23; Elev: 6020ft/1835m; Tel: 801-226-3564; Nearest town: Springville; Notes: Group site: $65-$220. GPS: 40.198486, -111.402100

10 • Barker Reservoir

Total sites: 13; RV sites: 13; Central water; Vault toilets; No showers; No RV dump; Reservations accepted; Max length: 35ft; Open May-Sep; Tent & RV camping: $14; Elev: 9305ft/2836m; Tel: 435-826-5499; Nearest town: Escalante; Notes: FSR 149 is steep single-lane with switchbacks and turnouts. GPS: 37.920443, -111.816583

11 • Bear Canyon

Total sites: 6; RV sites: 6; Central water; Flush toilets; Reservations not accepted; Stay limit: 16 days; Open May-Oct; Tent & RV camping: $21; Elev: 6700ft/2042m; Tel: 801-798-3571; Nearest town: Payson; Notes: Reservable group sites: $75-$105, Non-potable water. GPS: 39.787699, -111.731098

12 • Bear River

Total sites: 4; RV sites: 4; Central water; Vault toilets; No showers; No RV dump; Reservations not accepted; Stay limit: 14 days; Open all year; Tent & RV camping: $18; Elev: 8360ft/2548m; Tel: 307-789-3194; Nearest town: Evanston; Notes: No water in winter. GPS: 40.910239, -110.830246

13 • Beaver View

Total sites: 17; RV sites: 17; Central water; Vault toilets; No showers; No RV dump; Reservations not accepted; Tent & RV camping: $21; Elev: 8990ft/2740m; Tel: 307-789-3194; Nearest town: Evanston. GPS: 40.823828, -110.863135

14 • Blue Spruce

Total sites: 6; RV sites: 4; Central water; Vault toilets; No showers; No RV dump; Reservations not accepted; Stay limit: 14 days; Open all year; Tent & RV camping: $9; Elev: 7979ft/2432m; Tel: 435-826-5499; Nearest town: Escalante. GPS: 37.972745, -111.651841

15 • Botts

Total sites: 8; RV sites: 8; Central water; Vault toilets; No showers; No RV dump; Reservations not accepted; Generator hours: 0800-2200; Open May-Dec; Tent & RV camping: $23; Elev: 5282ft/1610m; Tel: 801-226-3564; Nearest town: Ogden. GPS: 41.278549, -111.657137

16 • Bountiful Peak

Total sites: 43; RV sites: 43; Potable water; Vault toilets; No showers; No RV dump; Reservations not accepted; Max length: 24ft; Stay limit: 7 days; Tent & RV camping: $16; Elev: 7526ft/2294m; Tel: 801-733-2660; Nearest town: Farmington. GPS: 40.979801, -111.804612

17 • Bowery Creek

Total sites: 44; RV sites: 44; Central water; Flush toilets; No showers; RV dump; Reservations accepted; Stay limit: 10 days; Generator hours: 0600-2200; Open May-Sep; Tent & RV camping: $15; Elev: 8924ft/2720m; Tel: 435-638-1069; Nearest town: Loa; Notes: Group sites: $45. GPS: 38.560547, -111.709961

18 • Box Elder

Total sites: 25; RV sites: 20; Central water; Flush toilets; No showers; No RV dump; Reservations accepted; Stay limit: 7 days; Open May-Oct; Tent & RV camping: $22; Elev: 5158ft/1572m; Tel: 435-755-3620; Nearest town: Brigham City; Notes: 4 group sites $70-$180. GPS: 41.494325, -111.950222

19 • Boy Scout

Total sites: 8; RV sites: 8; No water; No toilets; Reservations not accepted; Stay limit: 7 days; Open May-Oct; Tent & RV camping: $14; Elev: 6532ft/1991m; Tel: 801-733-2660; Nearest town: Salt Lake City; Notes: 1 group site: $45. GPS: 40.494091, -112.578581

20 • Bridge

Total sites: 5; RV sites: 5; Potable water; Vault toilets; No showers; No RV dump; Max length: 15ft; Open May-Sep; Tent & RV camping: $8; Elev: 7680ft/2341m; Nearest town: Altamont. GPS: 40.545594, -110.334169

21 • Bridger

Total sites: 10; RV sites: 10; Potable water; No toilets; No showers; No RV dump; Reservations not accepted; Stay limit: 7 days; Open May-Sep; Tent & RV camping: $20; Elev: 5158ft/1572m; Tel: 435-755-3620; Nearest town: Logan. GPS: 41.748047, -111.735352

22 • Bridger Lake

Total sites: 30; RV sites: 30; No water; Vault toilets; Reservations accepted; Stay limit: 14 days; Open Jun-Oct; Tent & RV camping: $21; Elev: 9403ft/2866m; Tel: 307-789-3194; Nearest town: Mountain View. GPS: 40.964701, -110.387964

23 • Bridges

Total sites: 4; RV sites: 4; No water; Vault toilets; Open Jun-Sep; Tent & RV camping: $5; Elev: 8251ft/2515m; Tel: 435-637-2817; Nearest town: Huntington; Notes: 2 group sites: $40-$50. GPS: 39.561755, -111.174854

24 • Browne Lake

Total sites: 20; RV sites: 20; No water; Vault toilets; Reservations not accepted; Open May-Sep; Tent & RV camping: $14; Elev: 8363ft/2549m; Tel: 435-784-3483; Nearest town: Flaming Gorge; Notes: Reservable group site: $60. GPS: 40.861164, -109.816312

25 • Buckboard

Total sites: 8; RV sites: 8; Central water; Vault toilets; No showers; No RV dump; Reservations accepted; Open May-Sep; Tent & RV camping: $10; Elev: 8724ft/2659m; Tel: 435-637-2817; Nearest town: Monticello; Notes: Group site: $50. GPS: 37.880649, -109.449293

26 • Butterfly Lake

Total sites: 20; RV sites: 20; Potable water; Vault toilets; No showers; No RV dump; Reservations not accepted; Stay limit: 7 days; Open Jul-Sep; Tent & RV camping: $21; Elev: 10354ft/3156m; Tel: 435-654-0470; Nearest town: Kamas. GPS: 40.721436, -110.869141

27 • Canyon Rim

Total sites: 15; RV sites: 7; Potable water; Vault toilets; No showers; No RV dump; Max length: 45ft; Open May-Sep; Tent & RV camping: $20; Elev: 7431ft/2265m; Tel: 435-784-3445; Nearest town: Dutch John; Notes: 7 sites open for pack-in until snow closes. GPS: 40.884521, -109.546875

28 • Carmel

Total sites: 15; RV sites: 15; No water; Vault toilets; Reservations not accepted; Max length: 25ft; Open May-Sep; Tent & RV camping: $12; Elev: 6293ft/1918m; Nearest town: Manila. GPS: 40.931043, -109.731705

29 • Casto Canyon

Total sites: 5; RV sites: 5; No water; Vault toilets; Max length: 35ft; Tent & RV camping: Free; Elev: 7028ft/2142m; Tel: 435-676-2676; Nearest town: Panguitch. GPS: 37.785266, -112.339231

30 • Cedar Canyon

Total sites: 18; RV sites: 18; Central water; Flush toilets; No showers; No RV dump; Reservations accepted; Open May-Sep; Tent & RV camping: $19; Elev: 8547ft/2605m; Tel: 435-865-3200; Nearest town: Cedar City; Notes: Group site: $55. GPS: 37.591355, -112.903665

31 • Cedar Springs

Total sites: 21; RV sites: 21; Central water; Vault toilets; No showers; RV dump; Reservations accepted; Max length: 45ft; Open Apr-Sep; Tent & RV camping: $25; Elev: 6129ft/1868m; Tel: 435-889-3000; Nearest town: Dutch John. GPS: 40.908936, -109.450439

32 • Cherry

Total sites: 28; RV sites: 28; Central water; Vault toilets; No showers; No RV dump; Reservations accepted; Open May-Sep; Tent & RV camping: $23; Elev: 5282ft/1610m; Tel: 801-226-3564; Nearest town: Springville; Notes: 4 group sites: $115-$155. GPS: 40.168705, -111.476704

33 • Chicken Creek

Total sites: 7; RV sites: 7; No water; Vault toilets; Reservations not accepted; Open May-Nov; Tent & RV camping: Free; Elev: 6125ft/1867m; Nearest town: Levan. GPS: 39.530000, -111.774000

34 • China Meadows

Total sites: 9; RV sites: 9; No water; Vault toilets; Reservations not accepted; Stay limit: 14 days; Open Jun-Oct; Tent & RV camping: $16; Elev: 9406ft/2867m; Tel: 307-782-6555; Nearest town: Mountain View. GPS: 40.931114, -110.403468

35 • Christmas Meadows

Total sites: 11; RV sites: 11; Central water; Vault toilets; No showers; No RV dump; Reservations accepted; Stay limit: 14 days; Open Jun-Oct; Tent & RV camping: $21; Elev: 8839ft/2694m; Tel: 307-789-3194; Nearest town: Evanston. GPS: 40.824396, -110.802154

36 • City Creek

Total sites: 5; RV sites: 5; Potable water; Vault toilets; No showers; No RV dump; Reservations accepted; Max length: 24ft; Open May-Sep; Tent & RV camping: Fee unknown; Elev: 7540ft/2298m; Tel: 435-896-9233; Nearest town: Beaver; Notes: Group sites. GPS: 38.269726, -112.311266

37 • Clear Creek

Total sites: 12; RV sites: 12; Central water; Vault toilets; No showers; No RV dump; Reservations not accepted; Stay limit: 14 days; Open Jun-Oct; Tent & RV camping: Free; Elev: 6312ft/1924m; Tel: 208-678-0439; Nearest town: Burley. GPS: 41.953483, -113.321782

38 • Cobblerest

Total sites: 18; RV sites: 18; Potable water; Vault toilets; No showers; No RV dump; Reservations not accepted; Stay limit: 7 days; Open Jun-Sep; Tent & RV camping: $21; Elev: 8333ft/2540m; Tel: 435-783-4338; Nearest town: Kamas. GPS: 40.594482, -110.975342

39 • Cold Springs

Total sites: 9; RV sites: 9; No water; Vault toilets; Reservations not accepted; Tent & RV camping: Free; Elev: 9152ft/2790m; Tel: 435-896-9233; Nearest town: Salina. GPS: 38.782456, -111.643283

40 • Cottonwood (SFRD)

Total sites: 18; RV sites: 18; No water; Vault toilets; Reservations not accepted; Stay limit: 7 days; Open Apr-Oct; Tent & RV camping: Free; Elev: 6594ft/2010m; Tel: 801-798-3571; Nearest town: Nephi. GPS: 39.780366, -111.723377

41 • Cottonwood (SLRD)

Total sites: 3; RV sites: 3; No toilets; Reservations not accepted; Stay limit: 7 days; Tent & RV camping: $14; Elev: 6119ft/1865m; Tel: 801-733-2660; Nearest town: Salt Lake City. GPS: 40.501555, -112.559697

42 • Currant Creek

Total sites: 98; RV sites: 98; Central water; Flush toilets; No showers; RV dump; Reservations accepted; Max length: 32ft; Stay limit: 7 days; Open Jun-Sep; Tent & RV camping: $23; Elev: 7848ft/2392m; Tel: 435-654-0470; Nearest town: Heber City; Notes: 4 group sites: $90-$120. GPS: 40.331399, -111.066636

43 • Dalton Springs

Total sites: 16; RV sites: 16; Central water; Vault toilets; No showers; No RV dump; Reservations not accepted; Max length: 30ft; Open May-Sep; Tent & RV camping: $10; Elev: 8386ft/2556m; Tel: 435-637-2817; Nearest town: Monticello. GPS: 37.873914, -109.432817

44 • Deep Creek

Total sites: 17; RV sites: 17; No water; Vault toilets; Reservations not accepted; Max length: 30ft; Open May-Sep; Tent & RV camping: $12; Elev: 7730ft/2356m; Nearest town: Manila. GPS: 40.855824, -109.729974

45 • Deer Haven

Total sites: 10; RV sites: 10; Central water; Flush toilets; No showers; No RV dump; Reservations not accepted; Generator hours: 0600-2200; Open May-Sep; Tent & RV camping: $17; Elev: 9176ft/2797m; Tel: 435-865-3200; Nearest town: Cedar City; Notes: Reservable group site $65-$205. GPS: 37.574116, -112.910502

46 • Deer Run

Total sites: 13; RV sites: 13; Central water; Flush toilets; Showers; RV dump; Reservations accepted; Max length: 25ft; Open Apr-Oct; Tent & RV camping: $25; Elev: 6207ft/1892m; Tel: 435-889-3000; Nearest town: Dutch John. GPS: 40.905701, -109.444214

47 • Devils Canyon

Total sites: 42; RV sites: 42; Central water; Vault toilets; No showers; No RV dump; Reservations accepted; Max length: 35ft; Open all year; Tent & RV camping: $10; Elev: 7093ft/2162m; Tel: 435-587-2041; Nearest town: Blanding. GPS: 37.738858, -109.406363

48 • Diamond

Total sites: 50; RV sites: 50; Central water; Vault toilets; No showers; No RV dump; Reservations accepted; Max length: 32ft; Open May-Oct; Tent & RV camping: $24; Elev: 5236ft/1596m; Tel: 801-226-3564; Nearest town: Thistle; Notes: 7 group sites: $50-$190. GPS: 40.072122, -111.428203

49 • Doctor Creek

Total sites: 30; RV sites: 30; Central water; Flush toilets; No showers; RV dump; Reservations accepted; Max length: 22ft; Open May-Sep; Tent & RV camping: $15; Elev: 8924ft/2720m; Tel: 435-638-1069; Nearest town: Loa; Notes: 2 reservable group sites: $100. GPS: 38.527965, -111.743433

50 • Dripping Springs

Total sites: 23; RV sites: 23; Central water; Flush toilets; No showers; No RV dump; Reservations accepted; Max length: 45ft; Open all year; Tent & RV camping: $18; Elev: 6145ft/1873m; Tel: 435-889-3000; Nearest town: Dutch John; Notes: 4 group sites: $95-$115, No water in winter - $5. GPS: 40.923558, -109.360253

51 • Duck Creek

Total sites: 54; RV sites: 54; Potable water; Flush toilets; No showers; RV dump; Reservations accepted; Max length: 32ft; Open May-Sep; Tent & RV camping: $19; Elev: 8638ft/2633m; Tel: 435-865-3200; Nearest town: Cedar City; Notes: Group site $115. GPS: 37.520621, -112.698352

52 • East Fork Bear River

Total sites: 7; RV sites: 7; No water; Reservations not accepted; Stay limit: 14 days; Tent & RV camping: $18; Elev: 8309ft/2533m; Tel: 307-789-3194; Nearest town: Evanston. GPS: 40.912889, -110.829167

53 • East Park

Total sites: 21; RV sites: 21; Central water; Vault toilets; No showers; No RV dump; Reservations not accepted; Max length: 25ft; Open Jun-Sep; Tent & RV camping: $12; Elev: 9052ft/2759m; Tel: 435-789-1181; Nearest town: Vernal. GPS: 40.783019, -109.553264

54 • Elk Horn

Total sites: 6; RV sites: 6; Central water; Vault toilets; No showers; No RV dump; Reservations not accepted; Open Jun-Sep; Tent & RV camping: $8; Elev: 9820ft/2993m; Tel: 435-836-2811; Nearest town: Loa; Notes: Group site: $35. GPS: 38.463768, -111.456071

55 • Ferron Reservoir Northeast

Total sites: 6; RV sites: 6; Central water; Vault toilets; No showers; No RV dump; Reservations not accepted; Max length: 22ft; Open May-Oct; Tent & RV camping: $10; Elev: 9498ft/2895m; Tel: 435-384-2372; Nearest town: Ferron. GPS: 39.145866, -111.449602

56 • Ferron Reservoir South

Total sites: 7; RV sites: 7; Central water; Vault toilets; No showers; No RV dump; Reservations not accepted; Max length: 22ft; Open May-Oct; Tent & RV camping: $10; Elev: 9489ft/2892m; Tel: 435-384-2372; Nearest town: Ferron. GPS: 39.138425, -111.453058

57 • Ferron Reservoir West

Total sites: 14; RV sites: 14; Central water; Vault toilets; No showers; No RV dump; Reservations accepted; Max length: 22ft; Open May-Oct; Tent & RV camping: $10; Elev: 9495ft/2894m; Tel: 435-384-2372; Nearest town: Ferron; Notes: Group site: $40. GPS: 39.142730, -111.455298

58 • Firefighter's Memorial

Total sites: 94; RV sites: 94; Central water; Flush toilets; No showers; RV dump; Reservations accepted; Max length: 45ft; Open May-Sep; Tent & RV camping: $24; Elev: 6864ft/2092m; Tel: 435-789-1181; Nearest town: Dutch John. GPS: 40.892653, -109.454951

59 • Fish Creek

Total sites: 7; RV sites: 7; No water; Vault toilets; Reservations not accepted; Open May-Sep; Tent & RV camping: $7; Elev: 7697ft/2346m; Tel: 435-637-2817; Nearest town: Scofield. GPS: 39.774000, -111.203000

60 • Flat Canyon

Total sites: 12; RV sites: 12; Central water; Vault toilets; No showers; No RV dump; Reservations accepted; Open Jun-Sep; Tent & RV camping: $10; Elev: 8884ft/2708m; Tel: 435-384-2372; Nearest town: Fairview; Notes: Group site: $50. GPS: 39.646201, -111.259767

61 • Forks of Huntington

Total sites: 5; RV sites: 5; Central water; Vault toilets; No showers; No RV dump; Reservations not accepted; Open May-Sep; Tent & RV camping: $10; Elev: 7700ft/2347m; Tel: 435-384-2372; Nearest town: Huntington; Notes: Reservable group site: $40. GPS: 39.500731, -111.160091

62 • Friendship

Total sites: 5; RV sites: 5; No water; Vault toilets; No showers; No RV dump; Reservations accepted; Stay limit: 7 days; Open May-Sep; Tent & RV camping: $12; Elev: 5459ft/1664m; Tel: 435-755-3620; Nearest town: Logan; Notes: Group site: $50. GPS: 41.660749, -111.665259

63 • Frying Pan

Total sites: 11; RV sites: 11; Central water; Flush toilets; No showers; No RV dump; Reservations accepted; Open May-Sep; Tent & RV camping: $15; Elev: 9078ft/2767m; Tel: 435-638-1069; Nearest town: Loa; Notes: 1 group site $70. GPS: 38.608887, -111.679688

64 • Gooseberry (Fishlake)

Total sites: 13; RV sites: 13; Central water; Vault toilets; No showers; No RV dump; Reservations not accepted; Open Apr-Nov; Tent & RV camping: $10; Elev: 7894ft/2406m; Nearest town: Salina; Notes: Group site $20. GPS: 38.802843, -111.685251

65 • Gooseberry Reservoir

Total sites: 16; RV sites: 16; No water; Vault toilets; Open Jun-Sep; Tent & RV camping: $10; Elev: 8435ft/2571m; Tel: 435-384-2372; Nearest town: Fairview. GPS: 39.711624, -111.293841

66 • Granite Flat

Total sites: 52; RV sites: 52; Central water; Vault toilets; No showers; No RV dump; Reservations accepted; Stay limit: 7 days; Open May-Sep; Tent & RV camping: $24; Elev: 6745ft/2056m; Tel: 801-785-3563; Nearest town: Cedar Hills; Notes: 3 group sites: $$255-$290, No water-tank filling allowed. GPS: 40.488505, -111.653123

67 • Greendale West

Total sites: 8; RV sites: 8; Central water; Vault toilets; No showers; No RV dump; Reservations accepted; Max length: 45ft; Open May-Sep; Tent & RV camping: $20; Elev: 7014ft/2138m; Tel: 435-889-3000; Nearest town: Dutch John. GPS: 40.882615, -109.460911

68 • Greens Lake

Total sites: 20; RV sites: 20; Potable water; Vault toilets; No showers; No RV dump; Reservations accepted; Max length: 45ft; Open May-Sep; Tent & RV camping: $20; Elev: 7474ft/2278m; Tel: 435-784-3445; Nearest town: Dutch John; Notes: 1 group site $70. GPS: 40.873291, -109.537354

69 • Guinavah-Malibu

Total sites: 39; RV sites: 39; Central water; Flush toilets; No showers; No RV dump; Reservations accepted; Stay limit: 7 days; Open May-Oct; Tent & RV camping: $22; Elev: 5085ft/1550m; Tel: 801-435-3620; Nearest town: Logan; Notes: 2 group sites: $145-$170. GPS: 41.761963, -111.699463

70 • Hades

Total sites: 14; RV sites: 14; No water; Vault toilets; Reservations accepted; Open May-Sep; Tent & RV camping: $10; Elev: 7434ft/ 2266m; Tel: 435-738-2482; Nearest town: Hanna. GPS: 40.534180, -110.873535

71 • Hayden Fork

Total sites: 9; RV sites: 9; Central water; Vault toilets; No showers; No RV dump; Reservations not accepted; Stay limit: 14 days; Tent & RV camping: $18; Elev: 8871ft/2704m; Tel: 307-789-3194; Nearest town: Evanston. GPS: 40.829633, -110.853542

72 • High Creek

Total sites: 2; RV sites: 2; No water; Vault toilets; Reservations not accepted; Stay limit: 7 days; Open May-Oct; Tent & RV camping: Free; Elev: 5600ft/1707m; Tel: 435-755-3620; Nearest town: Logan. GPS: 41.976000, -111.735000

73 • Honeycomb Rocks

Total sites: 21; RV sites: 21; Central water; Vault toilets; No showers; No RV dump; Reservations not accepted; Open May-Sep; Tent & RV camping: $13; Elev: 5735ft/1748m; Nearest town: Enterprise. GPS: 37.517090, -113.856445

74 • Hoop Lake

Total sites: 44; RV sites: 44; Central water; Vault toilets; No showers; No RV dump; Reservations not accepted; Stay limit: 14 days; Open Jun-Nov; Tent & RV camping: $18; Elev: 9218ft/ 2810m; Tel: 307-789-3194; Nearest town: Mountain View WY. GPS: 40.924449, -110.124936

75 • Hope

Total sites: 26; RV sites: 26; No water; Vault toilets; Reservations accepted; Stay limit: 7 days; Open May-Oct; Tent & RV camping: $24; Elev: 6631ft/2021m; Tel: 801-785-3563; Nearest town: Orem. GPS: 40.301854, -111.615214

76 • Indian Creek Group

Total sites: 7; RV sites: 7; Central water; Vault toilets; No showers; No RV dump; Reservations accepted; Open Jun-Oct; Tent & RV camping: $3; Elev: 8780ft/2676m; Tel: 801-756-8616; Nearest town: Huntington; Notes: 7 reservable group sites: $30-$50, Individual sites available if not in use. GPS: 39.442543, -111.238806

77 • Intake

Total sites: 5; RV sites: 5; No water; No toilets; Reservations not accepted; Stay limit: 7 days; Tent & RV camping: $14; Elev: 6378ft/1944m; Tel: 801-733-2660; Nearest town: Salt Lake City. GPS: 40.497694, -112.571421

78 • Iron Mine

Total sites: 26; RV sites: 26; Central water; Vault toilets; No showers; No RV dump; Reservations accepted; Open May-Sep; Tent & RV camping: $10; Elev: 7552ft/2302m; Tel: 435-738-2482; Nearest town: Hanna; Notes: 1 group site $25. GPS: 40.553575, -110.886683

79 • Joe's Valley

Total sites: 46; RV sites: 46; No water; Vault toilets; Reservations accepted; Max length: 22ft; Open May-Oct; Tent & RV camping: $10-18; Elev: 7123ft/2171m; Tel: 435-384-2372; Nearest town: Orangeville. GPS: 39.295356, -111.292157

80 • Kaler Hollow

Total sites: 4; No water; Vault toilets; Reservations not accepted; Open May-Sep; Tents only: Free; Elev: 9022ft/2750m; Tel: 435-789-1181; Nearest town: Vernal. GPS: 40.702112, -109.614724

81 • Kents Lake

Total sites: 30; RV sites: 30; Central water; Vault toilets; No showers; No RV dump; Reservations accepted; Max length: 60ft; Open Jun-Sep; Tent & RV camping: $14; Elev: 8894ft/2711m; Tel: 435-438-2436; Nearest town: Beaver. GPS: 38.236572, -112.459961

82 • King Creek

Total sites: 37; RV sites: 37; Central water; Flush toilets; No showers; RV dump; Reservations not accepted; Max length: 45ft; Stay limit: 14 days; Generator hours: 0600-2200; Open May-Sep; Tent & RV camping: $17; Elev: 7982ft/2433m; Tel: 435-676-2676; Nearest town: Panguitch. GPS: 37.609131, -112.260498

83 • Lake Canyon

Total sites: 9; RV sites: 9; No water; Vault toilets; Reservations accepted; Open Jun-Oct; Tent & RV camping: $20-30; Elev: 8963ft/2732m; Tel: 435-384-2372; Nearest town: Fairview; Notes: 5 group sites: $40-$60. GPS: 39.575664, -111.258165

84 • Lake Hill

Total sites: 10; RV sites: 10; Central water; Vault toilets; No showers; No RV dump; Reservations accepted; Open Jun-Sep; Tent & RV camping: $10; Elev: 8428ft/2569m; Tel: 435-283-4151; Nearest town: Ephraim; Notes: 2 group sites: $30-$40. GPS: 39.327416, -111.499333

85 • LeBaron Lake

Total sites: 13; RV sites: 13; No water; Vault toilets; Reservations accepted; Open Jul-Sep; Tent & RV camping: $10; Elev: 9963ft/ 3037m; Tel: 435-438-2436; Nearest town: Beaver. GPS: 38.224352, -112.402527

86 • Ledgefork

Total sites: 73; RV sites: 73; Central water; Vault toilets; No showers; No RV dump; Reservations accepted; Max length: 75ft; Stay limit: 7 days; Open Jun-Oct; Tent & RV camping: $24; Elev: 7740ft/2359m; Tel: 801-226-3564; Nearest town: Oakley. GPS: 40.742491, -111.098815

87 • Lewis M Turner

Total sites: 10; RV sites: 10; Central water; Vault toilets; No showers; No RV dump; Reservations not accepted; Stay limit: 7 days; Open Jun-Sep; Tent & RV camping: $20; Elev: 6414ft/1955m; Tel: 435-755-3620; Nearest town: Garden City. GPS: 41.885010, -111.572754

88 • Lilly Lake

Total sites: 14; RV sites: 14; Central water; Vault toilets; No showers; No RV dump; Reservations not accepted; Stay limit: 7 days; Tent & RV camping: $23; Elev: 9948ft/3032m; Tel: 435-783-4338; Nearest town: Kamas. GPS: 40.681168, -110.939883

89 • Little Cottonwood

Total sites: 14; RV sites: 14; Central water; Flush toilets; No showers; No RV dump; Reservations accepted; Max length: 40ft; Open May-Sep; Tent & RV camping: $16; Elev: 6463ft/1970m; Tel: 435-438-2436; Nearest town: Beaver. GPS: 38.256899, -112.543814

90 • Little Lyman Lake

Total sites: 10, RV sites: 10, Central water, No showers, No RV dump; Reservations not accepted; Stay limit: 14 days; Tent & RV camping: $16; Elev: 9314ft/2839m; Tel: 307-789-3194; Nearest town: Mountain View WY. GPS: 40.934409, -110.613921

91 • Little Mill

Total sites: 36; RV sites: 36; No water; Vault toilets; Reservations accepted; Max length: 30ft; Stay limit: 7 days; Open May-Oct; Tent & RV camping: $24; Elev: 6214ft/1894m; Tel: 801-785-3563; Nearest town: American Forks; Notes: Group site: $185. GPS: 40.450195, -111.670898

92 • Little Reservoir

Total sites: 8; RV sites: 8; Central water; Vault toilets; No showers; No RV dump; Reservations not accepted; Max length: 40ft; Open May-Sep; Tent & RV camping: $12; Elev: 7346ft/2239m; Tel: 435-896-9233; Nearest town: Beaver. GPS: 38.260984, -112.489468

93 • Little Rock

Total sites: 1; RV sites: 1; No water; No toilets; Reservations not accepted; Open May-Sep; Tent & RV camping: $5; Elev: 8100ft/2469m; Tel: 435-637-2817; Nearest town: Huntington. GPS: 39.547358, -111.168333

94 • Lodge

Total sites: 10; RV sites: 10; Central water; Vault toilets; No showers; No RV dump; Reservations not accepted; Stay limit: 7 days; Tent & RV camping: $20; Elev: 5538ft/1688m; Tel: 435-755-3620; Nearest town: Logan. GPS: 41.778564, -111.621826

95 • Lodgepole (Central)

Total sites: 55; RV sites: 49; Central water; Flush toilets; No showers; RV dump; Reservations accepted; Stay limit: 7 days; Open May-Oct; Tent & RV camping: $23; Elev: 7710ft/2350m; Tel: 801-226-3564; Nearest town: Heber City; Notes: 2 group sites: $175-$335. GPS: 40.312087, -111.259508

96 • Lodgepole at Flaming Gorge

Total sites: 35; RV sites: 35; Central water; Flush toilets; No showers; RV dump; Reservations accepted; Max length: 22ft; Open May-Sep; Tent & RV camping: $18; Elev: 8117ft/2474m; Tel: 435-889-3000; Nearest town: Dutch John. GPS: 40.811634, -109.466297

97 • Loop

Total sites: 13; RV sites: 13; No water; Reservations not accepted; Stay limit: 7 days; Tent & RV camping: $14; Elev: 7342ft/2238m; Tel: 801-733-2660; Nearest town: Salt Lake City. GPS: 40.484071, -112.606085

98 • Lost Creek

Total sites: 35; RV sites: 35; Central water; Vault toilets; No showers; No RV dump; Reservations accepted; Stay limit: 7 days; Open Jun-Sep; Tent & RV camping: $23; Elev: 9987ft/3044m; Tel: 801-226-3564; Nearest town: Kamas. GPS: 40.680914, -110.933045

99 • Lower Bowns

Total sites: 2; RV sites: 2; No water; Vault toilets; No showers; No RV dump; Reservation required; Tent & RV camping: $12; Elev: 7434ft/2266m; Tel: 435-836-2811; Nearest town: Torrey; Notes: 1 Group site $45. GPS: 38.106131, -111.276529

100 • Lower Canyon

Total sites: 6; RV sites: 6; No water; No toilets; Tent & RV camping: Free; Elev: 7128ft/2173m; Tel: 435-783-4338; Nearest town: Kamas. GPS: 40.628795, -111.177702

101 • Lower Meadows

Total sites: 25; RV sites: 25; Central water; Vault toilets; No showers; No RV dump; Reservations accepted; Generator hours: 0800-2200; Open May-Sep; Tent & RV camping: $23; Elev: 5325ft/1623m; Tel: 801-999-2103; Nearest town: Ogden. GPS: 41.286621, -111.645264

102 • Lower Narrows

Total sites: 3; RV sites: 3; No water; No toilets; Reservations not accepted; Stay limit: 7 days; Tent & RV camping: $14; Elev: 6890ft/2100m; Tel: 801-733-2660; Nearest town: Stockton. GPS: 40.491621, -112.591882

103 • Lower Provo River

Total sites: 10; RV sites: 10; Central water; Vault toilets; No showers; No RV dump; Reservations not accepted; Stay limit: 7 days; Open May-Oct; Tent & RV camping: $18; Elev: 7418ft/2261m; Tel: 435-783-4338; Nearest town: Kamas. GPS: 40.593111, -111.116683

104 • Lucerne Valley

Total sites: 143; RV sites: 143; Elec sites: 75; Central water; Flush toilets; Showers; RV dump; Reservations accepted; Max length: 45ft; Open Apr-Sep; Tent & RV camping: $20; Elev: 6066ft/1849m; Tel: 435-784-3445; Nearest town: Manila; Notes: Group site: $140. GPS: 40.983541, -109.591715

105 • Mackinaw

Total sites: 44; RV sites: 44; Central water; Flush toilets; Showers; No RV dump; Reservations accepted; Stay limit: 10 days; Generator hours: 0600-2200; Open May-Sep; Tent & RV camping: $15; Elev: 8914ft/2717m; Tel: 435-638-1069; Nearest town: Loa; Notes: 4 group sites: $30. GPS: 38.555420, -111.716797

106 • Magpie

Total sites: 16; RV sites: 16; Central water; Vault toilets; No showers; No RV dump; Reservations not accepted; Generator hours: 0800-2200; Open May-Dec; Tent & RV camping: $20; Elev: 5256ft/1602m; Tel: 801-625-5112; Nearest town: Ogden. GPS: 41.270437, -111.666087

107 • Mahogany Cove

Total sites: 7; RV sites: 7; Potable water; Vault toilets; No showers; No RV dump; Reservations not accepted; Open May-Sep; Tent & RV camping: $12; Elev: 7526ft/2294m; Tel: 435-438-2436; Nearest town: Beaver; Notes: Group site $70, Individual sites available if no group use. GPS: 38.269364, -112.485762

108 • Manns

Total sites: 8; RV sites: 8; No water; Vault toilets; Reservations not accepted; Open Apr-Sep; Tent & RV camping: $12; Elev: 6158ft/1877m; Tel: 435-784-3445; Nearest town: Manila. GPS: 40.924857, -109.709071

109 • Manti Community

Total sites: 8; RV sites: 8; No water; Vault toilets; No showers; No RV dump; Reservations accepted; Open May-Oct; Tent & RV camping: $10; Elev: 7512ft/2290m; Tel: 435-283-4151; Nearest town: Manti; Notes: 1 group site $40. GPS: 39.253668, -111.541328

110 • Maple Bench

Total sites: 10; RV sites: 10; Central water; Vault toilets; No showers; No RV dump; Reservations not accepted; Stay limit: 16 days; Open May-Oct; Tent & RV camping: $21; Elev: 5899ft/1798m; Tel: 801-798-3571; Nearest town: Payson. GPS: 39.962981, -111.691831

111 • Maple Canyon

Total sites: 12; RV sites: 12; No water; Vault toilets; Reservations accepted; Open May-Sep; Tent & RV camping: $10; Elev: 7041ft/2146m; Tel: 435-637-2817; Nearest town: Moroni; Notes: Group site: $40. GPS: 39.556338, -111.686537

112 • Maple Grove

Total sites: 16; RV sites: 16; Central water; Vault toilets; No showers; No RV dump; Reservations not accepted; Open May-Sep; Tent & RV camping: $15; Elev: 6499ft/1981m; Tel: 435-743-5721; Nearest town: Scipio; Notes: Reservable group site: $50-$90. GPS: 39.016557, -112.089458

113 • Maple Hollow

Total sites: 6; RV sites: 4; Central water; Vault toilets; No showers; No RV dump; Reservations not accepted; Open May-Sep; Tent & RV camping: Free; Elev: 7031ft/2143m; Tel: 435-743-5721; Nearest town: Holden. GPS: 39.061151, -112.170831

114 • Maple Lake

Total sites: 7; RV sites: 7; No water; Vault toilets; Reservations not accepted; Stay limit: 16 days; Open May-Oct; Tent & RV camping: $24; Elev: 6447ft/1965m; Tel: 801-798-3571; Nearest town: Payson. GPS: 39.957000, -111.693000

115 • Marsh Lake

Total sites: 28; RV sites: 28; Central water; Vault toilets; Reservations accepted; Stay limit: 14 days; Open May-Sep; Tent & RV camping: $21; Elev: 9383ft/2860m; Tel: 307-782-6555; Nearest town: Mountain View; Notes: Group site: $60, Dump station 1.5 mile at Stateline Reservoir. GPS: 40.952145, -110.395835

116 • Mason Draw

Total sites: 5; RV sites: 5; No water; Vault toilets; Reservations not accepted; Open May-Sep; Tent & RV camping: $5; Elev: 8268ft/2520m; Tel: 435-637-2817; Nearest town: Moab. GPS: 38.543000, -109.303000

117 • Meeks Cabin

Total sites: 24; RV sites: 24; Potable water; Vault toilets; No showers; No RV dump; Reservations not accepted; Stay limit: 14 days; Tent & RV camping: $24; Elev: 8714ft/2656m; Tel: 307-789-3194; Nearest town: Mountain View. GPS: 41.006266, -110.584071

118 • Mill Hollow

Total sites: 26; RV sites: 15; Central water; Vault toilets; No showers; No RV dump; Reservations accepted; Max length: 16ft; Stay limit: 7 days; Open Jun-Oct; Tent & RV camping: $21; Elev: 8842ft/2695m; Tel: 801-226-3564; Nearest town: Woodland. GPS: 40.490514, -111.103721

119 • Mirror Lake

Total sites: 78; RV sites: 78; No water; Vault toilets; Reservations accepted; Stay limit: 7 days; Open Jul-Sep; Tent & RV camping: $23; Elev: 10016ft/3053m; Tel: 435-783-4338; Nearest town: Kamas. GPS: 40.700684, -110.884277

120 • Monte Cristo

Total sites: 45; RV sites: 45; Central water; Flush toilets; No showers; No RV dump; Reservations not accepted; Max length: 39ft; Stay limit: 7 days; Open Jun-Sep; Tent & RV camping: $23; Elev: 8909ft/2715m; Tel: 801-625-5112; Nearest town: Woodruff; Notes: 2 reservable group sites: $210. GPS: 41.462959, -111.497642

121 • Moon Lake

Total sites: 54; RV sites: 54; Central water; Flush toilets; No showers; No RV dump; Reservations accepted; Max length: 22ft; Open May-Sep; Tent & RV camping: $20; Elev: 8150ft/2484m; Tel: 435-738-2482; Nearest town: Duchesne. GPS: 40.569092, -110.510254

122 • Moosehorn

Total sites: 33; RV sites: 33; No water; Vault toilets; No showers; No RV dump; Reservations accepted; Stay limit: 7 days; Open Jul-Sep; Tent & RV camping: $23; Elev: 10312ft/3143m; Tel: 435-783-4338; Nearest town: Kamas. GPS: 40.697266, -110.891846

123 • Mount Timpanogos

Total sites: 27; RV sites: 27; Central water; Flush toilets; No showers; No RV dump; Reservations accepted; Max length: 20ft; Stay limit: 7 days; Open Jun-Oct; Tent & RV camping: $24; Elev: 6920ft/2109m; Tel: 801-885-7391; Nearest town: Orem. GPS: 40.406083, -111.606289

124 • Mustang Ridge

Total sites: 70; RV sites: 70; Central water; Flush toilets; Showers; No RV dump; Reservations accepted; Max length: 45ft; Open May-Sep; Tent & RV camping: $25; Elev: 6109ft/1862m; Tel: 435-889-3000; Nearest town: Dutch John; Notes: Group site: $140. GPS: 40.927246, -109.439941

125 • Navajo Lake

Total sites: 27; RV sites: 16; Central water; Flush toilets; No showers; No RV dump; Reservations accepted; Max length: 22ft; Stay limit: 14 days; Open May-Sep; Tent & RV camping: $19; Elev: 9094ft/2772m; Tel: 435-865-3200; Nearest town: Cedar City. GPS: 37.520709, -112.789445

126 • Nizhoni

Total sites: 25; RV sites: 25; Central water; Vault toilets; No showers; No RV dump; Reservations accepted; Open May-Oct; Tent & RV camping: $10; Elev: 7812ft/2381m; Tel: 435-587-2041; Nearest town: Blanding; Notes: 2 group sites: $50. GPS: 37.781000, -109.539000

127 • Oak Creek

Total sites: 10; RV sites: 7; Central water; Vault toilets; No showers; No RV dump; Reservations accepted; Stay limit: 14 days; Generator hours: 0600-2200; Open May-Sep; Tent & RV camping: $12; Elev: 6061ft/1847m; Tel: 435-743-5721; Nearest town: Oak City; Notes: 4 group sites: $30-$60. GPS: 39.352459, -112.260743

128 • Oak Creek

Total sites: 9; RV sites: 9; Central water; Vault toilets; No showers; No RV dump; Reservations not accepted; Max length: 25ft; Generator hours: 0600-2200; Open May-Sep; Tent & RV camping: $12; Elev: 8888ft/2709m; Tel: 435-896-9233; Nearest town: Teasdale. GPS: 38.088834, -111.342031

129 • Oak Grove

Total sites: 7; RV sites: 5; No water; Vault toilets; Reservations not accepted; Open May-Oct; Tent & RV camping: $2-4; Elev: 6528ft/1990m; Tel: 435-652-3100; Nearest town: Leeds. GPS: 37.316862, -113.452991

130 • Oaks Park

Total sites: 11; RV sites: 11; Central water; Vault toilets; Reservations not accepted; Max length: 20ft; Open Jun-Sep; Tent & RV camping: Free; Elev: 9262ft/2823m; Tel: 435-789-1181; Nearest town: Vernal. GPS: 40.742089, -109.623605

131 • Old Folks Flat

Total sites: 8; RV sites: 8; Central water; Flush toilets; No showers; No RV dump; Reservations accepted; Open May-Oct; Tent & RV camping: $10; Elev: 8123ft/2476m; Tel: 801-756-8616; Nearest town: Huntington; Notes: 5 reservable group sites: $30-$75. GPS: 39.539000, -111.159000

132 • Oowah

Total sites: 11; No water; Vault toilets; No showers; No RV dump; Reservations not accepted; Open Jun-Sep; Tents only: $5; Elev: 8842ft/2695m; Nearest town: Moab. GPS: 38.502671, -109.272236

133 • Panguitch Lake North

Total sites: 47; RV sites: 47; Central water; Flush toilets; No showers; RV dump; Reservations accepted; Max length: 22ft; Open May-Sep; Tent & RV camping: $23; Elev: 8389ft/2557m; Tel: 435-865-3200; Nearest town: Panguitch; Notes: Group site: $55. GPS: 37.702351, -112.656904

134 • Panguitch Lake South

Total sites: 18; Potable water; Flush toilets; No showers; RV dump; Reservations not accepted; Open May-Sep; Tents only: $14; Elev: 8409ft/2563m; Tel: 435-865-3200; Nearest town: Panguitch. GPS: 37.700151, -112.655196

135 • Paradise Park

Total sites: 15; RV sites: 15; No water; Vault toilets; Reservations not accepted; Max length: 25ft; Open Jun-Sep; Tent & RV camping: $5; Elev: 9993ft/3046m; Tel: 435-789-1181; Nearest town: Lapoint. GPS: 40.666323, -109.913874

136 • Payson Lakes

Total sites: 108; RV sites: 108; Central water; Flush toilets; No showers; No RV dump; Reservations accepted; Stay limit: 16 days; Open May-Oct; Tent & RV camping: $23; Elev: 7995ft/2437m; Tel: 801-226-3564; Nearest town: Payson; Notes: 2 group sites: $155-$220. GPS: 39.930322, -111.642672

137 • Perception Park

Total sites: 14; RV sites: 14; Central water; Vault toilets; No showers; No RV dump; Reservations not accepted; Stay limit: 7 days; Generator hours: 0800-2200; Open May-Sep; Tent & RV camping: $23; Elev: 5344ft/1629m; Tel: 801-625-5112; Nearest town: Ogden; Notes: Reservable group sites $235, Designed for physically challenged. GPS: 41.288764, -111.641201

138 • Pine Lake

Total sites: 33; RV sites: 33; Central water; Vault toilets; No showers; No RV dump; Reservations accepted; Max length: 22ft;

Open May-Sep; Tent & RV camping: $15; Elev: 8255ft/2516m; Tel: 435-826-5499; Nearest town: Bryce Canyon; Notes: 4 group sites: $45-$90. GPS: 37.744229, -111.950891

139 • Pine Valley Rec Area - Crackfoot

Total sites: 22; RV sites: 17; Central water; Vault toilets; No showers; No RV dump; Reservations not accepted; Max length: 50ft; Generator hours: 0600-2200; Open May-Sep; Tent & RV camping: $17; Elev: 6890ft/2100m; Tel: 435-652-3100; Nearest town: Pine Valley. GPS: 37.374185, -113.466044

140 • Pine Valley Rec Area - Dean Gardner

Total sites: 24; RV sites: 24; Central water; Vault toilets; No showers; No RV dump; Reservations not accepted; Max length: 30ft; Generator hours: 0600-2200; Open May-Sep; Tent & RV camping: $17; Elev: 6775ft/2065m; Tel: 435-652-3100; Nearest town: Pine Valley. GPS: 37.377722, -113.476009

141 • Pine Valley Rec Area - Ebenezer Bryce

Total sites: 19; RV sites: 19; Central water; Vault toilets; No showers; No RV dump; Reservations not accepted; Max length: 45ft; Generator hours: 0600-2200; Open May-Sep; Tent & RV camping: $17; Elev: 6900ft/2103m; Tel: 435-652-3100; Nearest town: Pine Valley. GPS: 37.373783, -113.461586

142 • Pine Valley Rec Area - Yellow Pine

Total sites: 6; RV sites: 6; Central water; Vault toilets; No showers; No RV dump; Reservations not accepted; Max length: 25ft; Generator hours: 0600-2200; Open May-Sep; Tent & RV camping: $17; Elev: 6722ft/2049m; Tel: 435-652-3100; Nearest town: Pine Valley. GPS: 37.380242, -113.479862

143 • Pioneer

Total sites: 18; RV sites: 18; Central water; Vault toilets; No showers; No RV dump; Reservations not accepted; Stay limit: 7 days; Tent & RV camping: $20; Elev: 5230ft/1594m; Tel: 435-755-3620; Nearest town: Hyrum. GPS: 41.628174, -111.693359

144 • Piute

Total sites: 47; RV sites: 47; Central water; Vault toilets; No showers; RV dump; Reservations not accepted; Open May-Sep; Tent & RV camping: $10; Elev: 8855ft/2699m; Tel: 435-638-1069; Nearest town: Loa. GPS: 38.617854, -111.652737

145 • Pleasant Creek

Total sites: 16; RV sites: 16; Central water; Vault toilets; No showers; No RV dump; Reservations not accepted; Open May-Sep; Tent & RV camping: $12; Elev: 8625ft/2629m; Tel: 435-896-9233; Nearest town: Torrey. GPS: 38.102405, -111.336141

146 • Pole Creek Lake

Total sites: 19; RV sites: 19; No water; Vault toilets; Reservations not accepted; Open May-Sep; Tent & RV camping: $5; Elev: 10272ft/3131m; Tel: 435-722-5018; Nearest town: Whiterocks. GPS: 40.678467, -110.059814

147 • Ponderosa (Uinta)

Total sites: 23; RV sites: 23; Central water; Vault toilets; No showers; No RV dump; Reservations accepted; Stay limit: 16 days; Open May-Sep; Tent & RV camping: $23; Elev: 6293ft/1918m; Tel: 801-798-3571; Nearest town: Nephi. GPS: 39.766073, -111.713801

148 • Posey Lake

Total sites: 21; RV sites: 21; Central water; Vault toilets; No showers; No RV dump; Reservations accepted; Max length: 24ft; Open all year; Tent & RV camping: $11; Elev: 8688ft/2648m; Tel: 435-826-5499; Nearest town: Escalante; Notes: Group site $45. GPS: 37.935394, -111.694205

149 • Potters Pond

Total sites: 19; RV sites: 19; No water; Vault toilets; Reservations accepted; Open Jun-Sep; Tent & RV camping: $10; Elev: 9005ft/2745m; Tel: 435-384-2372; Nearest town: Huntington; Notes: 2 group sites $30-$40. GPS: 39.450753, -111.268867

150 • Preston Valley

Total sites: 9; RV sites: 9; Central water; Vault toilets; No showers; No RV dump; Reservations not accepted; Open May-Oct; Tent & RV camping: $20; Elev: 5220ft/1591m; Tel: 435-755-3620; Nearest town: Logan. GPS: 41.773425, -111.654283

151 • Red Banks

Total sites: 12; RV sites: 12; Central water; Vault toilets; No showers; No RV dump; Reservations not accepted; Stay limit: 7 days; Open Jun-Oct; Tent & RV camping: $20; Elev: 6358ft/1938m; Tel: 435-755-3620; Nearest town: Garden City. GPS: 41.898926, -111.564941

152 • Red Canyon

Total sites: 37; RV sites: 37; Central water; Flush toilets; Showers; RV dump; Reservations not accepted; Max length: 32ft; Stay limit: 14 days; Generator hours: 0600-2200; Open May-Oct; Tent & RV camping: $20; Elev: 7290ft/2222m; Tel: 435-676-2676; Nearest town: Panguitch; Notes: Group site: $50-$100. GPS: 37.742676, -112.309082

153 • Red Canyon (Ashley)

Total sites: 8; RV sites: 8; Central water; Vault toilets; No showers; No RV dump; Reservations accepted; Open May-Sep; Tent & RV camping: $20; Elev: 7395ft/2254m; Tel: 435-784-3445; Nearest town: Dutch John. GPS: 40.889343, -109.559029

154 • Redman

Total sites: 39; RV sites: 39; Central water; Flush toilets; No showers; No RV dump; Reservations accepted; Max length: 30ft; Stay limit: 7 days; Open Jul-Sep; Tent & RV camping: $26; Elev: 8317ft/2535m; Tel: 801-733-2660; Nearest town: Murray; Notes: 2 group sites - $130-$175. GPS: 40.615273, -111.588783

155 • Renegade

Total sites: 62; RV sites: 62; Central water; Flush toilets; No showers; No RV dump; Reservations accepted; Stay limit: 7 days;

Open May-Oct; Tent & RV camping: $23; Elev: 7658ft/2334m; Tel: 801-226-3564; Nearest town: Heber City; Notes: Long-term rentals available, Concessionaire. GPS: 40.119491, -111.159597

156 • Reservoir

Total sites: 5; RV sites: 5; Central water; Vault toilets; No showers; No RV dump; Reservations not accepted; Max length: 15ft; Open May-Sep; Tent & RV camping: $5; Elev: 7950ft/2423m; Tel: 435-722-5018; Nearest town: Roosevelt. GPS: 40.575384, -110.325523

157 • River Bend

Total sites: 1; RV sites: 1; No water; No toilets; Reservations not accepted; Open May-Sep; Tent & RV camping: $3; Elev: 7126ft/2172m; Tel: 435-636-3500; Nearest town: Huntington. GPS: 39.437756, -111.133604

158 • Riverview

Total sites: 19; RV sites: 19; Central water; Vault toilets; No showers; No RV dump; Reservations not accepted; Max length: 20ft; Open May-Sep; Tent & RV camping: $10; Elev: 8028ft/2447m; Tel: 435-722-5018; Nearest town: Altonah. GPS: 40.590332, 110.336182

159 • Rosebud ATV

Total sites: 4; RV sites: 4; No water; Vault toilets; Reservations accepted; Open Jun-Sep; Tent & RV camping: $20; Elev: 8534ft/2601m; Notes: 4 double sites, water 1 mile away. GPS: 38.100596, -111.326053

160 • Salina Creek Second Crossing

Total sites: 28; RV sites: 22; No water; Vault toilets; No showers; No RV dump; Reservations not accepted; Open Mar-Oct; Tent & RV camping: Free; Elev: 7275ft/2217m; Tel: 435-896-9233; Nearest town: Salina. GPS: 38.937869, -111.543251

161 • Sawmill Hollow

Total sites: 6; RV sites: 4; No water; Vault toilets; No showers; No RV dump; Max length: 30ft; Tent & RV camping: Free; Elev: 6207ft/1892m; Tel: 801-798-3571; Nearest town: Mapleton. GPS: 40.141000, -111.341000

162 • Shady Dell

Total sites: 20; RV sites: 20; Central water; Vault toilets; No showers; No RV dump; Reservations not accepted; Stay limit: 7 days; Open Jun-Oct; Tent & RV camping: $21; Elev: 8074ft/2461m; Tel: 435-654-0470; Nearest town: Kamas. GPS: 40.591797, -111.011963

163 • Shingle Creek ATV

Total sites: 21; RV sites: 21; Potable water; Vault toilets; No showers; No RV dump; Reservations not accepted; Stay limit: 7 days; Open May-Oct; Tent & RV camping: $18; Elev: 7497ft/2285m; Tel: 435-783-4338; Nearest town: Kamas. GPS: 40.615715, -111.132215

164 • Singletree

Total sites: 31; RV sites: 31; Central water; Flush toilets; No showers; RV dump; Reservations accepted; Max length: 32ft; Open May-Oct; Tent & RV camping: $12; Elev: 8255ft/2516m; Tel: 435-896-9233; Nearest town: Torrey; Notes: 2 group sites: $50. GPS: 38.162434, -111.331178

165 • Skull Creek

Total sites: 17; RV sites: 17; No water; Vault toilets; No showers; No RV dump; Reservations accepted; Max length: 30ft; Open May-Sep; Tent & RV camping: $12; Elev: 7434ft/2266m; Tel: 435-784-3445; Nearest town: Dutch John. GPS: 40.864905, -109.526508

166 • Smith-Morehouse

Total sites: 34; RV sites: 34; Central water; Vault toilets; No showers; No RV dump; Reservations accepted; Stay limit: 7 days; Open May-Sep; Tent & RV camping: $24; Elev: 7644ft/2330m; Tel: 435-783-4338; Nearest town: Oakley. GPS: 40.768031, -111.107141

167 • Smithfield

Total sites: 6; RV sites: 6; Central water; Vault toilets; No showers; No RV dump; Reservations not accepted; Stay limit: 7 days; Open May-Sep; Tent & RV camping: $20; Elev: 5482ft/1671m; Tel: 435-755-3620; Nearest town: Heber City. GPS: 41.870399, -111.753995

168 • Soapstone

Total sites: 32; RV sites: 32; Central water; Vault toilets; No showers; No RV dump; Reservations accepted; Stay limit: 7 days; Open May-Oct; Tent & RV camping: $23; Elev: 7920ft/2414m; Tel: 435-783-4338; Nearest town: Kamas. GPS: 40.578369, -111.026611

169 • Soldier Creek

Total sites: 160; RV sites: 160; Central water; Flush toilets; No showers; RV dump; Reservations accepted; Open May-Oct; Tent & RV camping: $15-23; Elev: 7674ft/2339m; Tel: 435-654-0470; Nearest town: Heber City; Notes: Long-term rentals available, Concessionaire. GPS: 40.152733, -111.051206

170 • South Fork

Total sites: 43; RV sites: 43; Central water; Vault toilets; No showers; No RV dump; Reservations accepted; Max length: 22ft; Stay limit: 7 days; Generator hours: 0800-2200; Open May-Sep; Tent & RV camping: $23; Elev: 5295ft/1614m; Tel: 801-625-5112; Nearest town: Huntsville. GPS: 41.281696, -111.654018

171 • South Fork

Total sites: 6; RV sites: 6; No water; Vault toilets; Reservations not accepted; Tent & RV camping: Free; Elev: 9688ft/2953m; Nearest town: Vernal. GPS: 40.734967, -109.739576

172 • Spirit Lake

Total sites: 24; RV sites: 24; No water; Vault toilets; Reservations not accepted; Max length: 30ft; Open May-Sep; Tent & RV camping: $14; Elev: 10207ft/3111m; Tel: 435-789-1181; Nearest town: Manila. GPS: 40.837438, -110.000379

173 • Spring

Total sites: 3; RV sites: 3; Central water; Vault toilets; No showers; No RV dump; Reservations not accepted; Stay limit: 7 days; Tent & RV camping: $12; Elev: 5584ft/1702m; Tel: 435-755-3620; Nearest town: Logan. GPS: 41.661984, -111.653988

174 • Spring Hollow

Total sites: 12; RV sites: 12; Central water; Vault toilets; No showers; No RV dump; Reservations accepted; Stay limit: 7 days; Open May-Oct; Tent & RV camping: $22; Elev: 5033ft/1534m; Tel: 801-226-3564; Nearest town: Logan; Notes: 2 group sites: $70-$140. GPS: 41.752735, -111.716653

175 • Spruces

Total sites: 92; RV sites: 92; Central water; Flush toilets; No showers; No RV dump; Reservations accepted; Stay limit: 7 days; Open May-Sep; Tent & RV camping: $26; Elev: 7438ft/2267m; Tel: 435-649-7534; Nearest town: Salt Lake City; Notes: Group sites: $180, No pets. GPS: 40.642179, -111.637703

176 • Spruces (Navajo Lake)

Total sites: 28; RV sites: 25; Central water; Flush toilets; No showers; No RV dump; Reservations not accepted; Generator hours: 0600-2200; Open May-Sep; Tent & RV camping: $17; Elev: 9075ft/2766m; Tel: 435-865-3200; Nearest town: Cedar City; Notes: Also walk-to sites, 3 walk-to sites. GPS: 37.518715, -112.774349

177 • Stateline Reservoir

Total sites: 41; RV sites: 41; Central water; Vault toilets; No showers; RV dump; Reservations accepted; Open May-Sep; Tent & RV camping: $21; Elev: 9252ft/2820m; Tel: 307-782-6555; Nearest town: Mountain View. GPS: 40.981884, -110.384703

178 • Stillwater

Total sites: 17; RV sites: 17; Central water; Vault toilets; No showers; No RV dump; Reservations accepted; Stay limit: 14 days; Open Jun-Oct; Tent & RV camping: $21; Elev: 8510ft/2594m; Tel: 307-789-3194; Nearest town: Evanston; Notes: 4 group sites $70-$80. GPS: 40.868896, -110.835449

179 • Strawberry Bay - Loop F

Total sites: 47; RV sites: 47; Central water; Flush toilets; No showers; Reservations accepted; Open May-Oct; Tent & RV camping: $23; Elev: 7618ft/2322m; Tel: 801-226-3564; Nearest town: Provo. GPS: 40.185091, -111.158096

180 • Strawberry Bay - Loop G

Total sites: 59; RV sites: 59; Central water; Flush toilets; No showers; Reservations accepted; Open May-Oct; Tent & RV camping: $23; Elev: 7634ft/2327m; Tel: 801-226-3564; Nearest town: Provo. GPS: 40.181986, -111.156582

181 • Strawberry Bay - Loops A-E

Total sites: 175; RV sites: 175; Elec sites: 26; Water at site; Flush toilets; No showers; Reservations accepted; Open May-Oct; Tents: $23/RVs: $23-36; Elev: 7628ft/2325m; Tel: 801-226-3564; Nearest town: Provo; Notes: $10 Elec fee, 1 group site $200. GPS: 40.175939, -111.171908

182 • Strawberry Bay - Overflow

Total sites: 72; RV sites: 72; Central water; Flush toilets; No showers; Reservations not accepted; Open May-Oct; Tent & RV camping: $23; Elev: 7697ft/2346m; Tel: 801-226-3564; Nearest town: Provo. GPS: 40.179788, -111.178281

183 • Sulphur

Total sites: 21; RV sites: 21; Central water; Vault toilets; No showers; No RV dump; Reservations accepted; Stay limit: 14 days; Open May-Oct; Tent & RV camping: $21; Elev: 9104ft/2775m; Tel: 307-789-3194; Nearest town: Evanston WY; Notes: Group site: $60. GPS: 40.788873, -110.884809

184 • Sunglow

Total sites: 6; RV sites: 6; Central water; Flush toilets; No showers; No RV dump; Reservations accepted; Generator hours: 0600-2200; Open all year; Tent & RV camping: $12; Elev: 7287ft/2221m; Tel: 435-836-2811; Nearest town: Bicknell; Notes: Group site $30, No water in winter. GPS: 38.342035, -111.519529

185 • Sunrise

Total sites: 26; RV sites: 26; Central water; Vault toilets; No showers; No RV dump; Reservations accepted; Max length: 22ft; Stay limit: 7 days; Open Jun-Oct; Tent & RV camping: $20; Elev: 7615ft/2321m; Tel: 435-755-3620; Nearest town: Garden City. GPS: 41.919605, -111.461689

186 • Swift Creek

Total sites: 13; RV sites: 13; Central water; Vault toilets; No showers; No RV dump; Reservations not accepted; Tent & RV camping: $8; Elev: 8153ft/2485m; Tel: 435-722-5018; Nearest town: Altamont. GPS: 40.601074, -110.347900

187 • Tanners Flat

Total sites: 34; RV sites: 34; Central water; Flush toilets; No showers; No RV dump; Reservations accepted; Max length: 35ft; Stay limit: 7 days; Open Jun-Oct; Tent & RV camping: $26; Elev: 7293ft/2223m; Tel: 435-649-7402; Nearest town: Sandy; Notes: 4 group sites $105-$175. GPS: 40.572394, -111.699051

188 • Taylors Fork ATV

Total sites: 11; RV sites: 11; Central water; Vault toilets; No showers; No RV dump; Reservations not accepted; Stay limit: 7 days; Open May-Oct; Tent & RV camping: $14; Elev: 7418ft/2261m; Tel: 435-783-4338; Nearest town: Kamas. GPS: 40.620014, -111.137581

189 • Te-ah

Total sites: 42; RV sites: 42; Central water; Flush toilets; No showers; RV dump; Reservations accepted; Max length: 32ft; Open May-Sep; Tent & RV camping: $17; Elev: 9203ft/2805m; Tel: 435-865-3200; Nearest town: Cedar City; Notes: 1 group site $40. GPS: 37.533676, -112.818909

190 • Timpooneke

Total sites: 27; RV sites: 27; Central water; Vault toilets; No showers; No RV dump; Reservations accepted; Max length: 16ft; Stay limit: 7 days; Open Jun-Oct; Tent & RV camping: $24; Elev: 7576ft/2309m; Tel: 801-885-7391; Nearest town: American Forks; Notes: 1 group site $115, 9 equestrian sites. GPS: 40.431947, -111.645916

191 • Tinney Flat

Total sites: 13; RV sites: 13; Central water; Vault toilets; No showers; No RV dump; Reservations accepted; Stay limit: 16 days; Open May-Sep; Tent & RV camping: $23; Elev: 7192ft/2192m; Tel: 801-798-3571; Nearest town: Santaquin; Notes: 3 group sites: $115. GPS: 39.900527, -111.727811

192 • Tony Grove

Total sites: 33; RV sites: 33; No water; Vault toilets; No showers; No RV dump; Reservations accepted; Max length: 35ft; Stay limit: 7 days; Open Jul-Sep; Tent & RV camping: $22; Elev: 8081ft/2463m; Tel: 435-755-3620; Nearest town: Logan. GPS: 41.891186, -111.640694

193 • Trial Lake

Total sites: 60; RV sites: 60; Central water; Vault toilets; No showers; No RV dump; Reservations accepted; Stay limit: 7 days; Open Jul-Sep; Tent & RV camping: $23; Elev: 9879ft/3011m; Tel: 435-783-4338; Nearest town: Kamas. GPS: 40.681624, -110.950247

194 • Tushar

Total sites: 24; RV sites: 24; Central water; Flush toilets; No showers; No RV dump; Reservations accepted; Open Jun-Sep; Tent & RV camping: $12; Elev: 8691ft/2649m; Tel: 435-438-2436; Nearest town: Beaver; Notes: Group fee: $50-$160. GPS: 38.238026, -112.469397

195 • Twelve Mile Flat

Total sites: 14; RV sites: 14; No water; Vault toilets; No showers; No RV dump; Reservations accepted; Open Jun-Sep; Tent & RV camping: $7-12; Elev: 10118ft/3084m; Tel: 435-283-4151; Nearest town: Mayfield; Notes: Group site $40. GPS: 39.123032, -111.487814

196 • Twin Lake

Total sites: 21; RV sites: 21; No water; Vault toilets; Reservations accepted; Open May-Oct; Tent & RV camping: $10; Elev: 7211ft/2198m; Tel: 435-283-4151; Nearest town: Mayfield; Notes: Group site $30. GPS: 39.118654, -111.604125

197 • Twin Ponds

Total sites: 13; RV sites: 13; No water; Vault toilets; No showers; No RV dump; Reservations not accepted; Tent & RV camping: Free; Elev: 9098ft/2773m; Tel: 435-896-9233; Nearest town: Salina. GPS: 38.786458, -111.640573

198 • Uinta Canyon

Total sites: 24; RV sites: 24; No water; Vault toilets; Reservations not accepted; Max length: 22ft; Tent & RV camping: $5; Elev: 7634ft/2327m; Nearest town: Roosevelt. GPS: 40.623291, -110.143799

199 • Unicorn Ridge

Total sites: 5; RV sites: 5; No water; Vault toilets; Reservations not accepted; Open May-Oct; Tent & RV camping: Free; Elev: 7591ft/2314m; Nearest town: Spanish Fork. GPS: 40.029454, -111.281752

200 • Upper Meadows

Total sites: 9; RV sites: 9; Central water; Vault toilets; No showers; No RV dump; Reservations not accepted; Stay limit: 7 days; Open May-Sep; Tent & RV camping: $20; Elev: 5361ft/1634m; Tel: 801-625-5112; Nearest town: Ogden. GPS: 41.291000, -111.636000

201 • Upper Narrows

Total sites: 6; RV sites: 6; No water; Vault toilets; Reservations not accepted; Stay limit: 7 days; Open Jun-Oct; Tent & RV camping: $14; Elev: 6965ft/2123m; Tel: 801-733-2660; Nearest town: Salt Lake City; Notes: Group site $45-$80. GPS: 40.491541, -112.594503

202 • Upper Six Mile Ponds

Total sites: 5; RV sites: 5; No water; Vault toilets; Reservations not accepted; Open Jun-Oct; Tent & RV camping: Free; Elev: 8986ft/2739m; Nearest town: Sterling; Notes: Rough road, 4x4 recommended. GPS: 39.188436, -111.540601

203 • Upper Stillwater

Total sites: 11; RV sites: 11; Central water; Flush toilets; No showers; No RV dump; Reservations accepted; Open May-Sep; Tent & RV camping: $10; Elev: 8061ft/2457m; Tel: 435-789-1181; Nearest town: Mountain Home; Notes: Group site: $30. GPS: 40.555894, -110.700582

204 • Vernon Reservoir

Total sites: 10; RV sites: 10; No water; Vault toilets; Reservations not accepted; Stay limit: 16 days; Open Apr-Dec; Tent & RV camping: Free; Elev: 6191ft/1887m; Tel: 801-798-3571; Nearest town: Vernon. GPS: 39.991743, -112.385556

205 • Wandin

Total sites: 4; RV sites: 4; No water; Vault toilets; Reservations not accepted; Max length: 15ft; Tent & RV camping: $5; Elev: 7795ft/2376m; Nearest town: Roosevelt. GPS: 40.630702, -110.153772

206 • Warner Lake

Total sites: 20; RV sites: 20; No water; Vault toilets; No showers; No RV dump; Reservations accepted; Open Jun-Sep; Tent & RV camping: $10; Elev: 9436ft/2876m; Tel: 435-636-3360; Nearest town: Moab; Notes: Group site $50. GPS: 38.519524, -109.277145

207 • Washington Lake

Total sites: 45; RV sites: 45; No water; Vault toilets; No showers; No RV dump; Reservations accepted; Stay limit: 7 days; Open Jul-Sep; Tent & RV camping: $23; Elev: 10007ft/3050m; Tel: 435-654-0470; Nearest town: Kamas; Notes: 5 group sites $130-$190. GPS: 40.679014, -110.961644

208 • West Marsh Lake

Total sites: 17; RV sites: 17; Central water; Vault toilets; Reservations accepted; Stay limit: 14 days; Open Jun-Sep; Tent & RV camping: $21; Elev: 9354ft/2851m; Tel: 307-782-6555; Nearest town: Mountain View; Notes: Group site: $60, Dump station 1.5 mile at Stateline Reservoir. GPS: 40.955502, -110.396994

209 • White Bridge

Total sites: 29; RV sites: 29; Central water; Flush toilets; No showers; RV dump; Reservations accepted; Max length: 32ft; Open May-Sep; Tent & RV camping: $17; Elev: 7881ft/2402m; Tel: 435-865-3200; Nearest town: Panguitch. GPS: 37.745827, -112.587909

210 • Whiterocks

Total sites: 21; RV sites: 21; Central water; Vault toilets; No showers; No RV dump; Reservations not accepted; Max length: 25ft; Open May-Sep; Tent & RV camping: $8; Elev: 7510ft/2289m; Tel: 435-789-1181; Nearest town: Whiterocks. GPS: 40.619388, -109.941458

211 • Whiting

Total sites: 26; RV sites: 26; Central water; Flush toilets; No showers; No RV dump; Reservations accepted; Stay limit: 16 days; Open May-Sep; Tent & RV camping: $23; Elev: 5532ft/1686m; Tel: 801-798-3571; Nearest town: Mapleton; Notes: 2 group sites: $220-$440, 3 sites equipped for horses, RVs may NOT fill water tanks. GPS: 40.131495, -111.527386

212 • Willow Lake

Total sites: 10; RV sites: 10; No water; Vault toilets; Reservations accepted; Open Jun-Sep; Tent & RV camping: $7; Elev: 9649ft/2941m; Tel: 435-384-2372; Nearest town: Ferron. GPS: 39.134811, -111.381332

213 • Willows

Total sites: 17; RV sites: 17; Central water; Vault toilets; No showers; No RV dump; Reservations not accepted; Max length: 40ft; Stay limit: 7 days; Generator hours: 0800-2200; Open May-Sep; Tent & RV camping: $20; Elev: 5371ft/1637m; Tel: 801-625-5112; Nearest town: Ogden. GPS: 41.291695, -111.633153

214 • Willows

Total sites: 8; RV sites: 8; No water; Vault toilets; Reservations not accepted; Open Apr-Sep; Tent & RV camping: $12; Elev: 6165ft/1879m; Tel: 435-784-3445; Nearest town: Manila. GPS: 40.925959, -109.714713

215 • Wolf Creek

Total sites: 3; RV sites: 3; Central water; Vault toilets; No showers; No RV dump; Reservations not accepted; Stay limit: 7 days; Open Jun-Sep; Tent & RV camping: $18; Elev: 9471ft/2887m; Tel: 435-783-4338; Nearest town: Heber City; Notes: 2 reservable group sites $115-$200. GPS: 40.482476, -111.033555

216 • Wolverine ATV

Total sites: 7; RV sites: 6; No water; Vault toilets; No showers; No RV dump; Reservations not accepted; Tent & RV camping: $16; Elev: 9101ft/2774m; Tel: 801-466-6411; Nearest town: Peoa. GPS: 40.845957, -110.814671

217 • Wood Camp

Total sites: 6; RV sites: 6; No water; Vault toilets; No showers; No RV dump; Reservations not accepted; Stay limit: 7 days; Open May-Oct; Tent & RV camping: $20; Elev: 5377ft/1639m; Tel: 435-755-3620; Nearest town: Logan. GPS: 41.797363, -111.645020

218 • Yankee Meadow

Total sites: 29; RV sites: 29; Central water; Vault toilets; No showers; No RV dump; Reservations not accepted; Open May-Sep; Tent & RV camping: $15; Elev: 8520ft/2597m; Tel: 435-865-3200; Nearest town: Cedar City. GPS: 37.760232, -112.760014

219 • Yellow Pine (Ashley)

Total sites: 11; RV sites: 11; Central water; Flush toilets; No showers; RV dump; Reservations accepted; Max length: 36ft; Open May-Sep; Tent & RV camping: $10; Elev: 7555ft/2303m; Tel: 435-738-2482; Nearest town: Mountain Home; Notes: 1 group site $30. GPS: 40.536416, -110.639975

220 • Yellow Pine (Wasatch)

Total sites: 33; RV sites: 33; Central water; Vault toilets; No showers; No RV dump; Reservations not accepted; Max length: 25ft; Stay limit: 7 days; Open May-Oct; Tent & RV camping: $18; Elev: 7293ft/2223m; Tel: 435-783-4338; Nearest town: Kamas. GPS: 40.630859, -111.173828

221 • Yellowstone

Total sites: 4; RV sites: 4; Central water; Vault toilets; No showers; No RV dump; Reservations not accepted; Open May-Sep; Tent & RV camping: $10; Elev: 7661ft/2335m; Tel: 435-722-5018; Nearest town: Mountain Home; Notes: Reservable group site: $30. GPS: 40.542425, -110.336645

Vermont

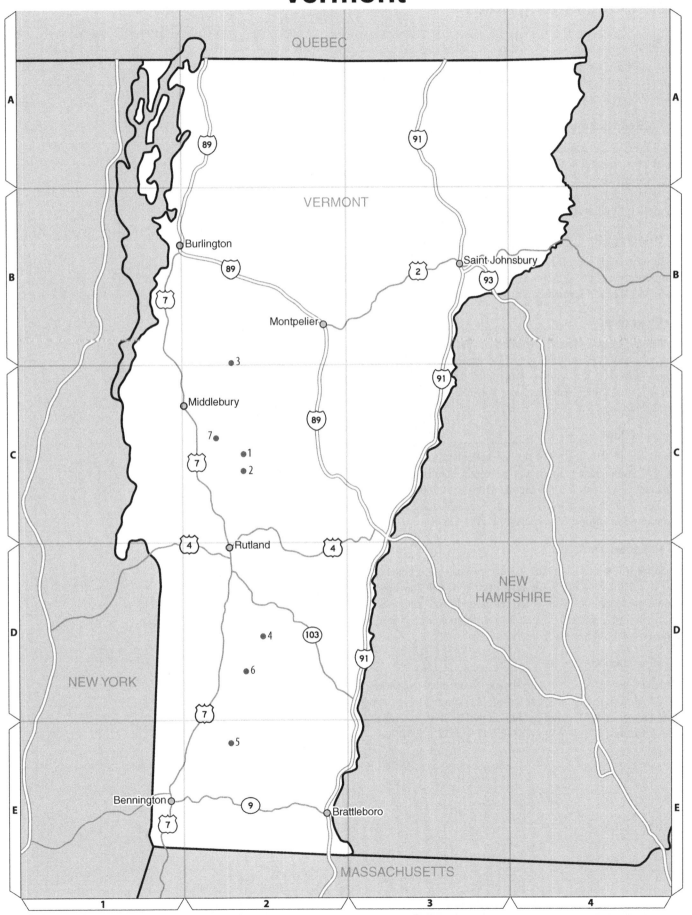

Vermont Camping Areas

1 • Bingo

Total sites: 10; RV sites: 10; No toilets; Stay limit: 14 days; Open Apr-Dec; Tent & RV camping: Free; Elev: 1317ft/401m; Tel: 802-388-4362; Nearest town: Robinson. GPS: 43.875324, -72.913288

2 • Chittenden Brook

Total sites: 17; No water; Vault toilets; No showers; No RV dump; Reservations accepted; Stay limit: 14 days; Generator hours: 0600-2200; Open May-Oct; Tents only: $15; Elev: 1765ft/538m; Tel: 802-767-4261; Nearest town: Rochester; Notes: Not recommended for RVs. GPS: 43.825684, -72.909912

3 • Downingville

Total sites: 1; RV sites: 1; No toilets; Stay limit: 14 days; Tent & RV camping: Free; Elev: 1532ft/467m; Nearest town: Downingville. GPS: 44.137614, -72.966192

4 • Greendale

Total sites: 11; RV sites: 11; No water; Vault toilets; Reservations not accepted; Stay limit: 14 days; Generator hours: 0600-2200; Open May-Oct; Tent & RV camping: $10; Elev: 1791ft/546m; Tel: 802-362-2307; Nearest town: Weston. GPS: 43.354492, -72.826172

5 • Grout Pond

Total sites: 17; RV sites: 6; Central water; Vault toilets; No showers; No RV dump; Reservations not accepted; Stay limit: 14 days; Open all year; Tent & RV camping: $16; Elev: 2260ft/689m; Tel: 802-362-2307; Nearest town: Stratton; Notes: No large RVs, Road not plowed in winter. GPS: 43.046074, -72.952078

6 • Hapgood Pond

Total sites: 28; RV sites: 28; Central water; Vault toilets; No showers; No RV dump; Reservations not accepted; Stay limit: 14 days; Open May-Oct; Tent & RV camping: $20-22; Elev: 1535ft/468m; Tel: 802-362-2307; Nearest town: Manchester; Notes: No large RVs. GPS: 43.253653, -72.892582

7 • Moosalamoo

Total sites: 19; RV sites: 19; Central water; Vault toilets; No showers; No RV dump; Reservations accepted; Stay limit: 14 days; Open May-Oct; Tent & RV camping: $15; Elev: 1585ft/483m; Tel: 802-388-4362; Nearest town: Ripton. GPS: 43.918612, -73.025721

Virginia

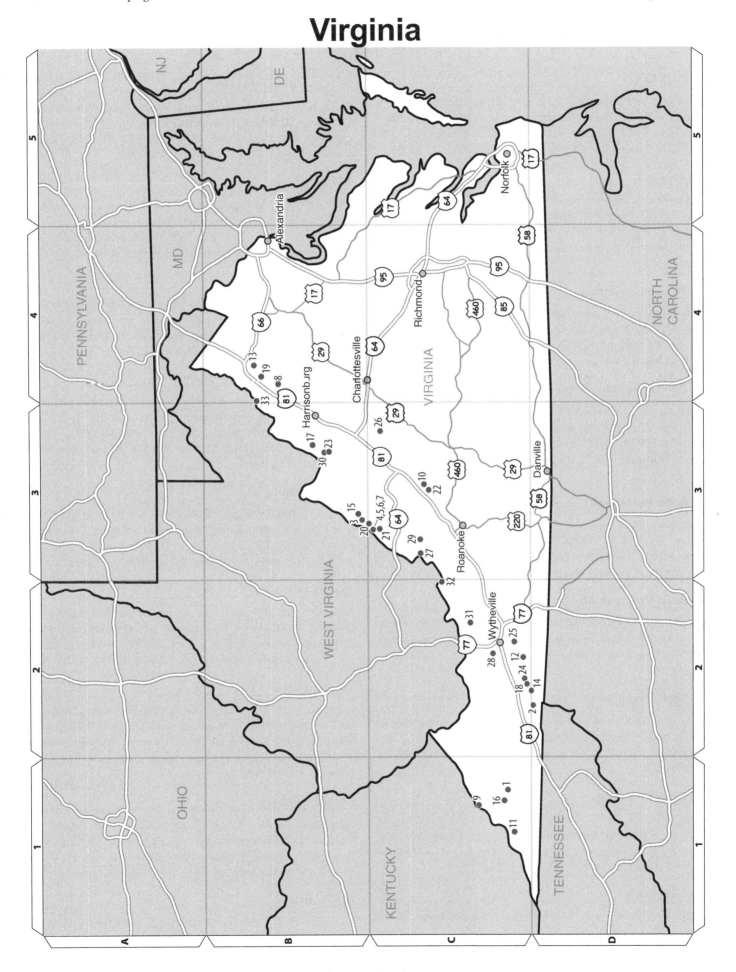

Virginia Camping Areas

1 • Bark Camp

Total sites: 34; RV sites: 34; Elec sites: 9; Central water; Flush toilets; Showers; No RV dump; Reservations not accepted; Open May-Sep; Tent & RV camping: $18-23; Elev: 2877ft/877m; Tel: 276-679-8370; Nearest town: Coeburn. GPS: 36.867697, -82.523363

2 • Beartree

Total sites: 90; RV sites: 90; Central water; Flush toilets; Showers; RV dump; Reservations accepted; Open Apr-Oct; Tent & RV camping: $24; Elev: 3143ft/958m; Tel: 276-388-3642; Nearest town: Damascus; Notes: Group site: $55. GPS: 36.668259, -81.678972

3 • Blowing Springs

Total sites: 40; RV sites: 40; Central water; Vault toilets; No showers; RV dump; Reservations not accepted; Open Mar-Sep; Tent & RV camping: $12; Elev: 1811ft/552m; Tel: 540-839-2521; Nearest town: Covington. GPS: 38.069092, -79.884521

4 • Bolar Mountain - Sugar Ridge

Total sites: 35; RV sites: 30; Central water; Flush toilets; Showers; RV dump; Reservations accepted; Open May-Nov; Tents: $16-18/RVs: $23-78; Elev: 1646ft/502m; Tel: 540-839-2521; Nearest town: Warm Springs; Notes: Group site: $165. GPS: 37.984053, -79.967817

5 • Bolar Mountain #1

Total sites: 41; RV sites: 41; Elec sites: 20; Central water; Flush toilets; Showers; RV dump; Reservations accepted; Open May-Nov; Tents: $16/RVs: $18; Elev: 1670ft/509m; Tel: 540-839-2521; Nearest town: Warm Springs. GPS: 37.985352, -79.970459

6 • Bolar Mountain #2

Total sites: 16; RV sites: 16; Elec sites: 5; Water at site; Flush toilets; Showers; RV dump; Open May-Oct; Tents: $16/RVs: $18; Elev: 1575ft/480m; Nearest town: Warm Springs. GPS: 37.979415, -79.986099

7 • Bolar Mountain #3

Total sites: 32; RV sites: 32; Elec sites: 6; Water at site; Flush toilets; Showers; RV dump; Open May-Sep; Tents: $16/RVs: $18; Elev: 1565ft/477m; Nearest town: Warm Springs. GPS: 37.976791, -79.985102

8 • Camp Roosevelt

Total sites: 10; RV sites: 10; Central water; Flush toilets; No showers; RV dump; Reservations not accepted; Open May-Oct; Tent & RV camping: $10; Elev: 1266ft/386m; Tel: 540-984-4101; Nearest town: Luray. GPS: 38.731906, -78.517929

9 • Cane Patch

Total sites: 35; RV sites: 35; Elec sites: 7; Central water; Flush toilets; Showers; RV dump; Open May-Sep; Tents: $12/RVs: $12-17; Elev: 1690ft/515m; Tel: 276-796-5832; Nearest town: Pound. GPS: 37.100888, -82.677886

10 • Cave Mountain Lake

Total sites: 40; RV sites: 40; Central water; Flush toilets; Showers; RV dump; Reservations accepted; Open Apr-Oct; Tent & RV camping: $18; Elev: 1270ft/387m; Tel: 540-291-2188; Nearest town: Lexington. GPS: 37.568574, -79.540596

11 • Cave Springs

Total sites: 37; RV sites: 37; Elec sites: 9; Central water; Flush toilets; Showers; RV dump; Reservations not accepted; Open May-Sep; Tents: $12/RVs: $17; Elev: 1627ft/496m; Tel: 276-546-4297; Nearest town: Big Stone Gap. GPS: 36.800537, -82.923474

12 • Comers Rock

Total sites: 6; RV sites: 6; Central water; Vault toilets; No showers; No RV dump; Reservations not accepted; Open Apr-Oct; Tent & RV camping: $5; Elev: 3766ft/1148m; Tel: 800-628-7202; Nearest town: Speedwell. GPS: 36.763428, -81.223389

13 • Elizabeth Furnace - Family

Total sites: 35; RV sites: 35; Central water; Flush toilets; Showers; RV dump; Reservations not accepted; Open all year; Tent & RV camping: $16; Elev: 829ft/253m; Tel: 540-984-4101; Nearest town: Front Royal; Notes: $10 Oct-Apr - limited services. GPS: 38.924507, -78.331606

14 • Grindstone

Total sites: 108; RV sites: 108; Elec sites: 60; Water at site; Flush toilets; Showers; RV dump; Reservations accepted; Open May-Nov; Tents: $24/RVs: $24-32; Elev: 3724ft/1135m; Tel: 276-388-3983; Nearest town: Troutdale. GPS: 36.687883, -81.542115

15 • Hidden Valley

Total sites: 31; RV sites: 31; Central water; Vault toilets; No showers; No RV dump; Reservations not accepted; Open Mar-Dec; Tent & RV camping: $12; Elev: 1804ft/550m; Tel: 540-839-2521; Nearest town: Warm Springs. GPS: 38.098768, -79.821744

16 • High Knob

Total sites: 13; RV sites: 13; Central water; Flush toilets; Showers; No RV dump; Reservations not accepted; Max length: 16ft; Open May-Sep; Tent & RV camping: $10; Elev: 3698ft/1127m; Tel: 276-679-1754; Nearest town: Norton; Notes: Group site: $25. GPS: 36.890306, -82.622992

17 • Hone Quarry

Total sites: 26; RV sites: 26; Central water; Vault toilets; No showers; No RV dump; Reservations not accepted; Open all year; Tent & RV camping: $5; Elev: 1946ft/593m; Tel: 540-432-0187; Nearest town: Harrisonburg. GPS: 38.462746, -79.135584

18 • Hurricane

Total sites: 30; RV sites: 30; Central water; Flush toilets; Showers; No RV dump; Open Apr-Oct; Tent & RV camping: $18; Elev:

2923ft/891m; Tel: 800-628-7202; Nearest town: Sugar Grove. GPS: 36.723094, -81.489375

19 • Little Fort

Total sites: 11; No water; Vault toilets; No showers; No RV dump; Reservations not accepted; Open all year; Tents only: Free; Elev: 1365ft/416m; Tel: 540-984-4101; Nearest town: Fort Valley. GPS: 38.867231, -78.444056

20 • McClintic Point

Total sites: 21; RV sites: 21; No water; Vault toilets; Open Mar-Dec; Tent & RV camping: $12; Elev: 1663ft/507m; Tel: 540-839-2521; Nearest town: Warm Springs; Notes: Group site: $85. GPS: 38.014631, -79.920428

21 • Morris Hill

Total sites: 58; RV sites: 58; Central water; Flush toilets; Showers; No RV dump; Reservations accepted; Open May-Sep; Tent & RV camping: $18; Elev: 2083ft/635m; Tel: 540-962-2214; Nearest town: Covington. GPS: 37.933435, -79.970313

22 • North Creek

Total sites: 16; RV sites: 16; Central water; Vault toilets; No showers; No RV dump; Reservations not accepted; Max length: 22ft; Open Mar-Nov; Tent & RV camping: $12; Elev: 1201ft/366m; Tel: 540-291-2188; Nearest town: Buchanan. GPS: 37.541793, -79.584499

23 • North River

Total sites: 9; RV sites: 9; No water; Vault toilets; Reservations not accepted; Open all year; Tent & RV camping: $5; Elev: 1867ft/569m; Tel: 540-432-0187; Nearest town: Stokesville. GPS: 38.339211, -79.206031

24 • Raccoon Branch

Total sites: 20; RV sites: 20; Elec sites: 7; Central water; Flush toilets; No showers; RV dump; Reservations accepted; Open Apr-Nov; Tents: $16/RVs: $16-22; Elev: 2769ft/844m; Tel: 800-628-7202; Nearest town: Sugar Grove. GPS: 36.747803, -81.424805

25 • Raven Cliff

Total sites: 20; RV sites: 20; No water; Vault toilets; Reservations not accepted; Open Apr-Oct; Tent & RV camping: $5; Elev: 2254ft/687m; Tel: 800-628-7202; Nearest town: Cripple Creek. GPS: 36.836139, -81.068654

26 • Sherando Lake

Total sites: 65; RV sites: 29; Elec sites: 29; Central water; Flush toilets; Showers; RV dump; Reservations accepted; Open Apr-Oct; Tent & RV camping: $22-28; Elev: 1903ft/580m; Tel: 540-291-2188; Nearest town: Lyndhurst. GPS: 37.919633, -79.008176

27 • Steel Bridge

Total sites: 3; No water; Vault toilets; Reservations accepted; Open Apr-Dec; Tent & RV camping: Fee unknown; Elev: 1729ft/527m; Tel: 540-552-4641; Nearest town: Paint Bank; Notes: 3 group sites: Free. GPS: 37.601423, -80.218647

28 • Stony Fork

Total sites: 54; RV sites: 54; Elec sites: 9; Water at site; Flush toilets; Showers; RV dump; Reservations accepted; Open Apr-Nov; Tents: $14/RVs: $20-24; Elev: 2434ft/742m; Tel: 800-628-7202; Nearest town: Wytheville. GPS: 37.010056, -81.181408

29 • The Pines

Total sites: 12; RV sites: 12; Central water; Vault toilets; No showers; No RV dump; Reservations not accepted; Max length: 16ft; Open Apr-Nov; Tent & RV camping: Free; Elev: 1896ft/578m; Tel: 540-552-4641; Nearest town: New Castle. GPS: 37.605216, -80.076455

30 • Todd Lake

Total sites: 36; RV sites: 36; Central water; Flush toilets; Showers; No RV dump; Reservations not accepted; Max length: 18ft; Open May-Nov; Tent & RV camping: $18; Elev: 1992ft/607m; Tel: 540-432-0187; Nearest town: Stokesville. GPS: 38.365723, -79.211670

31 • Walnut Flats

Total sites: 8; RV sites: 8; Central water; Vault toilets; No showers; No RV dump; Reservations not accepted; Open Apr-Dec; Tent & RV camping: Free; Elev: 2457ft/749m; Tel: 540-552-4641; Nearest town: Holly Brook. GPS: 37.198227, -80.886911

32 • White Rocks Camp

Total sites: 50; RV sites: 50; Central water; Flush toilets; No showers; RV dump; Reservations not accepted; Open Apr-Nov; Tent & RV camping: $8; Elev: 2999ft/914m; Tel: 540-552-4641; Nearest town: Simmonsville. GPS: 37.430107, -80.492676

33 • Wolf Gap

Total sites: 9; RV sites: 9; Central water; Vault toilets; No showers; No RV dump; Open all year; Tent & RV camping: Free; Elev: 2300ft/701m; Tel: 540-984-4101; Nearest town: Columbia Furnace. GPS: 38.924412, -78.689182

Washington

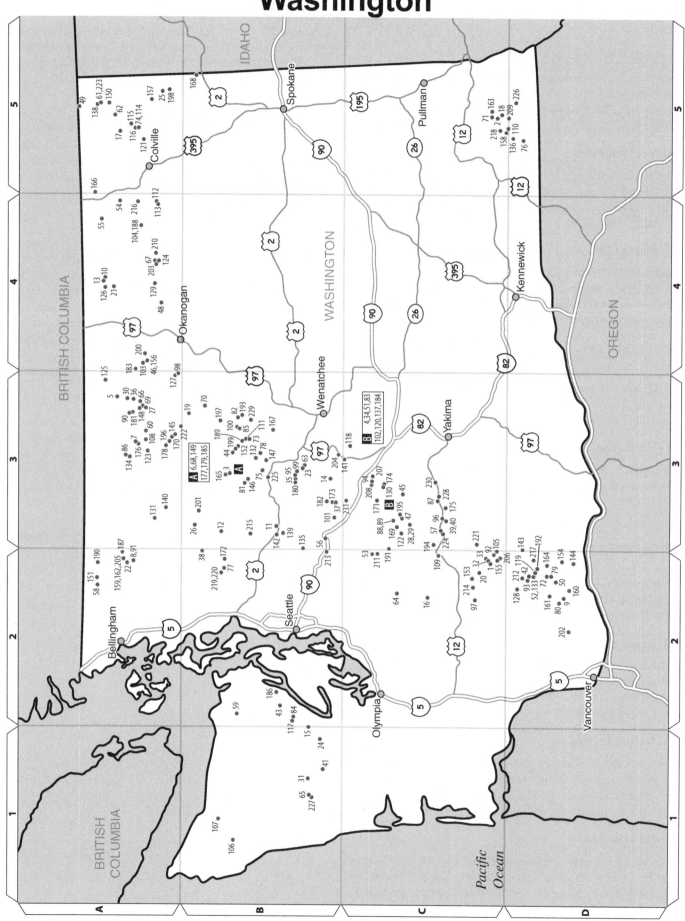

Washington Camping Areas

1 • Adams Fork

Total sites: 22; RV sites: 22; No water; Vault toilets; Reservations accepted; Max length: 45ft; Open May-Sep; Tent & RV camping: $16; Elev: 2697ft/822m; Tel: 360-497-1100; Nearest town: Randle; Notes: Group sites: $35-$45. GPS: 46.339101, -121.646541

2 • Alder Thicket

Total sites: 5; RV sites: 5; No water; Vault toilets; Open May-Oct; Tent & RV camping: Free; Elev: 5141ft/1567m; Tel: 509-843-1891; Nearest town: Pomeroy. GPS: 46.258932, -117.567041

3 • Alpine Meadows

Total sites: 4; RV sites: 4; No water; Vault toilets; Reservations not accepted; Max length: 20ft; Tent & RV camping: $14; Elev: 2707ft/825m; Tel: 509-548-2550; Nearest town: Leavenworth; Notes: Very rough road - high-clearance vehicle may be needed. GPS: 48.046578, -120.833922

4 • American Forks

Total sites: 16; RV sites: 16; No water; Vault toilets; Reservations not accepted; Max length: 30ft; Open May-Sep; Tent & RV camping: $10; Elev: 2789ft/850m; Tel: 509-653-1401; Nearest town: Cliffdell. GPS: 46.976074, -121.158691

5 • Andrews Creek

Total sites: 4; RV sites: 2; No water; Vault toilets; Reservations not accepted; Tent & RV camping: Free; Elev: 3037ft/926m; Tel: 509-996-4003; Nearest town: Winthrop. GPS: 48.783460, -120.108347

6 • Atkinson Flat

Total sites: 11; RV sites: 4; No water; Vault toilets; Reservations not accepted; Max length: 20ft; Open Jun-Sep; Tent & RV camping: $14; Elev: 2615ft/797m; Tel: 509-548-2550; Nearest town: Leavenworth; Notes: Very rough road - high-clearance vehicle may be needed. GPS: 48.000409, -120.816870

7 • Ballard

Total sites: 7; RV sites: 7; No water; Vault toilets; Reservations not accepted; Max length: 28ft; Open May-Sep; Tent & RV camping: $8; Elev: 2536ft/773m; Tel: 509-996-4003; Nearest town: Winthrop. GPS: 48.658477, -120.544554

8 • Bayview

Total sites: 24; RV sites: 24; No water; Vault toilets; Open May-Sep; Tent & RV camping: $15-17; Elev: 742ft/226m; Tel: 541-338-7869; Nearest town: Sedro-Woolley. GPS: 48.675096, -121.676641

9 • Beaver

Total sites: 23; RV sites: 23; Central water; Flush toilets; No showers; No RV dump; Reservations accepted; Max length: 25ft; Open May-Sep; Tent & RV camping: $20; Elev: 1116ft/340m; Tel: 509-395-3400; Nearest town: Carson; Notes: Group site $100. GPS: 45.853406, -121.955136

10 • Beaver Lake

Total sites: 11; RV sites: 11; Central water; Vault toilets; No showers; No RV dump; Reservations not accepted; Open May-Oct; Tent & RV camping: $8; Elev: 2792ft/851m; Tel: 509-486-2186; Nearest town: Wauconda. GPS: 48.849858, -118.968346

11 • Beckler River

Total sites: 27; RV sites: 27; Central water; Vault toilets; No showers; No RV dump; Reservations accepted; Open May-Sep; Tent & RV camping: $17-19; Elev: 1112ft/339m; Tel: 360-677-2414; Nearest town: Skykomish. GPS: 47.734619, -121.332275

12 • Bedal

Total sites: 21; RV sites: 21; No water; Vault toilets; Reservations accepted; Open May-Sep; Tent & RV camping: $15-17; Elev: 1272ft/388m; Tel: 360-436-1155; Nearest town: Granite Falls. GPS: 48.096951, -121.387348

13 • Beth Lake

Total sites: 14; RV sites: 13; Central water; Vault toilets; No showers; No RV dump; Reservations not accepted; Open May-Sep; Tent & RV camping: $8; Elev: 2868ft/874m; Tel: 509-486-2186; Nearest town: Tonasket. GPS: 48.859269, -118.984619

14 • Beverly

Total sites: 10; RV sites: 10; No water; Vault toilets; Reservations not accepted; Open all year; Tent & RV camping: $8; Elev: 3205ft/977m; Tel: 509-852-1100; Nearest town: Cle Elum; Notes: No fees 10/1-5/15. GPS: 47.378174, -120.883789

15 • Big Creek

Total sites: 23; RV sites: 23; Central water; Vault toilets; No showers; No RV dump; Reservations not accepted; Max length: 36ft; Stay limit: 14 days; Open May-Sep; Tent & RV camping: $20; Elev: 1001ft/305m; Tel: 360-765-2200; Nearest town: Hoodsport. GPS: 47.494498, -123.211182

16 • Big Creek (Gifford)

Total sites: 27; RV sites: 27; Central water; Vault toilets; No showers; No RV dump; Reservations accepted; Max length: 22ft; Open May-Sep; Tent & RV camping: $18; Elev: 1857ft/566m; Tel: 360-497-1100; Nearest town: Ashford. GPS: 46.735628, -121.970332

17 • Big Meadow Lake

Total sites: 17; RV sites: 17; Central water; Vault toilets; No showers; No RV dump; Reservations not accepted; Stay limit: 14 days; Generator hours: 0600-2200; Open May-Sep; Tent & RV camping: Free; Elev: 3428ft/1045m; Tel: 509-738-7700; Nearest town: Ione. GPS: 48.726164, -117.562668

18 • Big Springs

Total sites: 10; RV sites: 5; No water; Vault toilets; Reservations not accepted; Open all year; Tent & RV camping: Free; Elev: 5066ft/1544m; Tel: 541-278-3716; Nearest town: Pomeroy. GPS: 46.231099, -117.543764

19 • Black Pine Lake

Total sites: 23; RV sites: 23; Central water; Vault toilets; No showers; No RV dump; Reservations not accepted; Max length: 30ft; Stay limit: 14 days; Open Apr-Oct; Tent & RV camping: $12; Elev: 4137ft/1261m; Tel: 509-996-4003; Nearest town: Twisp. GPS: 48.313477, -120.274414

20 • Blue Lake Creek

Total sites: 11; RV sites: 11; No water; Vault toilets; Reservations accepted; Max length: 22ft; Open May-Sep; Tent & RV camping: $12; Elev: 1949ft/594m; Tel: 360-497-1100; Nearest town: Randle. GPS: 46.403632, -121.736681

21 • Bonaparte Lake

Total sites: 28; RV sites: 28; Central water; Vault toilets; No showers; No RV dump; Reservations not accepted; Open May-Oct; Tent & RV camping: $12; Elev: 3620ft/1103m; Tel: 509-486-2186; Nearest town: Tonasket; Notes: Group site: $50. GPS: 48.794778, -119.057269

22 • Boulder Creek

Total sites: 8; RV sites: 8; No water; Vault toilets; Reservations accepted; Max length: 24ft; Open May-Sep; Tent & RV camping: $15-17; Elev: 1020ft/311m; Tel: 360-856-5700; Notes: Group site: $70, No large RVs. GPS: 48.714355, -121.691895

23 • Bridge Creek

Total sites: 6; RV sites: 6; Central water; Vault toilets; No showers; No RV dump; Reservations not accepted; Max length: 19ft; Tent & RV camping: $19; Elev: 2102ft/641m; Tel: 509-548-2550; Nearest town: Leavenworth; Notes: Reservable group site $100. GPS: 47.562918, -120.782445

24 • Brown Creek

Total sites: 20; RV sites: 12; Central water; Vault toilets; No showers; No RV dump; Reservations not accepted; Max length: 21ft; Stay limit: 14 days; Open all year; Tent & RV camping: $14; Elev: 620ft/189m; Tel: 360-765-2200; Nearest town: Shelton; Notes: 6 sites open all winter. GPS: 47.413177, -123.318668

25 • Browns Lake

Total sites: 18; RV sites: 18; No water; Vault toilets; Reservations not accepted; Max length: 20ft; Stay limit: 14 days; Generator hours: 0600-2200; Open all year; Tent & RV camping: $16; Elev: 3399ft/1036m; Tel: 509-447-7300; Nearest town: Usk. GPS: 48.436523, -117.196045

26 • Buck Creek

Total sites: 29; RV sites: 26; No water; Vault toilets; Reservations accepted; Max length: 20ft; Open May-Sep; Tent & RV camping: $15-17; Elev: 1253ft/382m; Tel: 541-338-7869; Nearest town: Darrington. GPS: 48.267188, -121.332144

27 • Buck Lake

Total sites: 9; RV sites: 9; No water; Vault toilets; Reservations not accepted; Max length: 25ft; Stay limit: 14 days; Open May-Sep;

Tent & RV camping: $8; Elev: 3272ft/997m; Tel: 509-996-4003; Nearest town: Carlton. GPS: 48.605942, -120.202005

28 • Bumping Lake Lower

Total sites: 17; RV sites: 17; Central water; No toilets; No showers; No RV dump; Reservations accepted; Max length: 50ft; Open May-Sep; Tent & RV camping: $18; Elev: 3451ft/1052m; Tel: 509-653-1401; Nearest town: Yakima. GPS: 46.861387, -121.300921

29 • Bumping Lake Upper

Total sites: 40; RV sites: 39; Central water; Vault toilets; No showers; No RV dump; Reservations accepted; Max length: 30ft; Open May-Sep; Tent & RV camping: $20; Elev: 3478ft/1060m; Tel: 541-338-7869; Nearest town: Cliffdell. GPS: 46.855464, -121.304523

30 • Camp 4

Total sites: 5; No water; Vault toilets; Reservations not accepted; Max length: 16ft; Stay limit: 14 days; Tents only: $8; Elev: 2424ft/739m; Tel: 509-996-4003; Nearest town: Winthrop; Notes: Trailers not recommended. GPS: 48.715106, -120.125036

31 • Campbell Tree Grove

Total sites: 31; RV sites: 21; No water; Vault toilets; Reservations not accepted; Max length: 16ft; Open May-Sep; Tent & RV camping: Free; Elev: 1188ft/362m; Tel: 360-288-2525; Nearest town: Humptulips. GPS: 47.480937, -123.688034

32 • Cat Creek

Total sites: 5; RV sites: 5; No water; Vault toilets; Open May-Sep; Tent & RV camping: Free; Elev: 2753ft/839m; Tel: 360-497-1100; Nearest town: Randle. GPS: 46.348408, -121.624807

33 • Cat Creek Chimney Site

Total sites: 10; RV sites: 10; No water; Vault toilets; Max length: 35ft; Open May-Sep; Tent & RV camping: Fee unknown; Elev: 2874ft/876m; Tel: 360-497-1100; Nearest town: Randle. GPS: 46.353805, -121.618185

34 • Cedar Springs

Total sites: 14; RV sites: 14; Central water; Vault toilets; No showers; No RV dump; Reservations accepted; Max length: 22ft; Open May-Sep; Tent & RV camping: $16; Elev: 2756ft/840m; Tel: 509-653-1401; Nearest town: Cliffdell. GPS: 46.971191, -121.162842

35 • Chatter Creek

Total sites: 12; RV sites: 12; Central water; Vault toilets; No showers; No RV dump; Reservations not accepted; Tent & RV camping: $18; Elev: 2743ft/836m; Tel: 509-548-2550; Nearest town: Leavenworth; Notes: Group site: $100. GPS: 47.608000, -120.886000

36 • Chewuch

Total sites: 16; RV sites: 16; Central water; Vault toilets; No showers; No RV dump; Reservations not accepted; Max length:

35ft; Stay limit: 14 days; Open May-Oct; Tent & RV camping: $12; Elev: 2293ft/699m; Tel: 509-996-4003; Nearest town: Winthrop. GPS: 48.677307, -120.129764

37 • Cle Elum River

Total sites: 14; RV sites: 14; Central water; Vault toilets; No showers; No RV dump; Reservations not accepted; Open May-Sep; Tent & RV camping: $18; Elev: 2300ft/701m; Tel: 509-852-1100; Nearest town: Cle Elum; Notes: Reservable group site $115. GPS: 47.349764, -121.104569

38 • Clear Creek

Total sites: 13; RV sites: 13; No water; Vault toilets; Reservations accepted; Open May-Sep; Tent & RV camping: $15-17; Elev: 630ft/192m; Tel: 360-436-1155; Nearest town: Darrington. GPS: 48.220215, -121.571777

39 • Clear Lake North

Total sites: 36; RV sites: 36; No water; Vault toilets; Reservations not accepted; Max length: 22ft; Open May-Sep; Tent & RV camping: $10; Elev: 3064ft/934m; Tel: 509-653-1401; Nearest town: Naches. GPS: 46.633946, -121.267531

40 • Clear Lake South

Total sites: 31; RV sites: 31; Central water; Vault toilets; No showers; No RV dump; Reservations not accepted; Max length: 22ft; Open May-Sep; Tent & RV camping: $10; Elev: 3064ft/934m; Tel: 509-653-1401; Nearest town: Naches. GPS: 46.627686, -121.267822

41 • Coho

Total sites: 55; RV sites: 46; Central water; Flush toilets; No showers; RV dump; Reservations accepted; Max length: 36ft; Open May-Sep; Tents: $20/RVs: $25; Elev: 882ft/269m; Tel: 360-765-2200; Nearest town: Montesano; Notes: Group sites: $25-$45. GPS: 47.389648, -123.603760

42 • Cold Spring Indian

Total sites: 12; RV sites: 12; No water; Vault toilets; Reservations not accepted; Tent & RV camping: Free; Elev: 4185ft/1276m; Tel: 509-395-3400; Nearest town: Trout Lake. GPS: 46.084754, -121.758225

43 • Collins

Total sites: 16; RV sites: 10; No water; Vault toilets; Reservations not accepted; Max length: 21ft; Open May-Sep; Tent & RV camping: $14; Elev: 351ft/107m; Tel: 360-765-2200; Nearest town: Brinnon. GPS: 47.682711, -123.019192

44 • Cottonwood

Total sites: 25; RV sites: 25; Central water; Vault toilets; No showers; No RV dump; Reservations not accepted; Max length: 20ft; Tent & RV camping: $10; Elev: 3150ft/960m; Tel: 509-784-4700; Nearest town: Entiat; Notes: Limited sites - fire damage. GPS: 48.020574, -120.642210

45 • Cottonwood (Naches)

Total sites: 4; RV sites: 4; Central water; Vault toilets; No showers; No RV dump; Reservations accepted; Max length: 22ft; Open all year; Tent & RV camping: $16; Elev: 2316ft/706m; Tel: 509-653-1401; Nearest town: Cliffdell. GPS: 46.906982, -121.025879

46 • Cottonwood (Tonasket)

Total sites: 3; RV sites: 3; Central water; Vault toilets; No showers; No RV dump; Reservations not accepted; Open May-Sep; Tent & RV camping: $8; Elev: 2808ft/856m; Tel: 509-486-2186; Nearest town: Conconully. GPS: 48.586926, -119.763644

47 • Cougar Flat

Total sites: 12; RV sites: 8; Central water; Vault toilets; No showers; No RV dump; Reservations accepted; Max length: 20ft; Tent & RV camping: $16; Elev: 3140ft/957m; Tel: 509-653-1404; Nearest town: Cliffdell; Notes: Also walk-to sites. GPS: 46.916499, -121.231108

48 • Crawfish Lake

Total sites: 19; RV sites: 14; No water; Vault toilets; Reservations not accepted; Max length: 18ft; Open May-Sep; Tent & RV camping: Free; Elev: 4547ft/1386m; Tel: 509-486-2186; Nearest town: Riverside. GPS: 48.484619, -119.216064

49 • Crescent Lake

Total sites: 3; RV sites: 3; No water; Vault toilets; Stay limit: 14 days; Generator hours: 0600-2200; Open May-Sep; Tent & RV camping: Free; Elev: 2713ft/827m; Tel: 509-446-7500; Nearest town: Metaline Falls. GPS: 48.988564, -117.311432

50 • Crest Camp

Total sites: 3; RV sites: 1; No water; Vault toilets; Tent & RV camping: Fee unknown; Elev: 3547ft/1081m; Tel: 509-395-3400; Nearest town: Carson; Notes: On Pacific Crest Trail. GPS: 45.909247, -121.802613

51 • Crow Creek

Total sites: 15; RV sites: 15; No water; Vault toilets; Reservations not accepted; Max length: 30ft; Tent & RV camping: $10; Elev: 2772ft/845m; Tel: 509-653-1401; Nearest town: Naches; Notes: Discover Pass ($10/day or $30/year) required, Sno-Park permit required if camping between 11/01 and 05/01. GPS: 47.016042, -121.137167

52 • Cultus Creek

Total sites: 50; RV sites: 50; No water; Vault toilets; Reservations not accepted; Max length: 32ft; Open Jun-Sep; Tent & RV camping: $10; Elev: 4016ft/1224m; Tel: 509-395-3400; Nearest town: Trout Lake. GPS: 46.047607, -121.755127

53 • Dalles

Total sites: 45; RV sites: 45; Central water; Vault toilets; No showers; No RV dump; Reservations accepted; Open May-Sep; Tent & RV camping: $19-21; Elev: 3570ft/1088m; Tel: 360-825-6585; Nearest town: Enumclaw. GPS: 47.104293, -121.577857

54 • Davis Lake

Total sites: 4; RV sites: 4; No water; Vault toilets; Stay limit: 14 days; Generator hours: 0600-2200; Open all year; Tent & RV camping: Free; Elev: 4528ft/1380m; Tel: 509-738-7700; Nearest town: Colville. GPS: 48.738738, -118.228761

55 • Deer Creek Forest Camp

Total sites: 9; RV sites: 9; No water; Vault toilets; Reservations not accepted; Stay limit: 14 days; Generator hours: 0600-2200; Open all year; Tent & RV camping: $5; Elev: 4728ft/1441m; Tel: 509-775-7400; Nearest town: Orient. GPS: 48.864848, -118.395571

56 • Denny Creek

Total sites: 23; RV sites: 23; Elec sites: 8; Central water; Flush toilets; No showers; No RV dump; Reservations accepted; Open May-Sep; Tents: $20-22/RVs: $20-26; Elev: 2297ft/700m; Tel: 425-888-1421; Nearest town: North Bend; Notes: Group site $35-$85. GPS: 47.412138, -121.442136

57 • Dog Lake

Total sites: 8; RV sites: 8; No water; Vault toilets; Reservations not accepted; Max length: Trlr-20ft/RV-24ft; Open Jun-Sep; Tent & RV camping: $8; Elev: 4196ft/1279m; Tel: 509-653-1401; Nearest town: Naches. GPS: 46.655000, -121.360000

58 • Douglas Fir

Total sites: 29; RV sites: 29; Central water; Vault toilets; No showers; No RV dump; Reservations accepted; Open May-Sep; Tent & RV camping: $19-21; Elev: 1000ft/305m; Tel: 360-599-2714; Nearest town: Glacier. GPS: 48.901637, -121.916298

59 • Dungeness Forks

Total sites: 10; No water; Vault toilets; Stay limit: 14 days; Open May-Sep; Tents only: $14; Elev: 1070ft/326m; Tel: 360-765-2200; Nearest town: Sequim; Notes: Steep access road. GPS: 47.971732, -123.111424

60 • Early Winters

Total sites: 12; RV sites: 12; Central water; Vault toilets; No showers; No RV dump; Reservations not accepted; Max length: 32ft; Open May-Oct; Tent & RV camping: $8; Elev: 2175ft/663m; Tel: 509-996-4003; Nearest town: Winthrop. GPS: 48.598087, -120.439991

61 • East Sullivan

Total sites: 38; RV sites: 38; Central water; Vault toilets; No showers; No RV dump; Reservations accepted; Generator hours: 0600-2200; Open May-Sep; Tent & RV camping: $18; Elev: 2658ft/810m; Tel: 509-446-7500; Nearest town: Metaline; Notes: Group site: $75. GPS: 48.839781, -117.280981

62 • Edgewater

Total sites: 20; RV sites: 20; Central water; Vault toilets; No showers; No RV dump; Reservations accepted; Generator hours: 0600-2200; Open May-Sep; Tent & RV camping: $20; Elev: 2106ft/642m; Tel: 509-446-7500; Nearest town: Ione. GPS: 48.754483, -117.405590

63 • Eightmile

Total sites: 45; RV sites: 45; Central water; Vault toilets; No showers; No RV dump; Reservations accepted; Max length: 50ft; Open May-Oct; Tent & RV camping: $22; Elev: 1923ft/586m; Tel: 509-548-2550; Nearest town: Leavenworth. GPS: 47.550778, -120.764757

64 • Evans Creek ORV

Total sites: 23; RV sites: 23; Central water; Vault toilets; No showers; No RV dump; Reservations not accepted; Generator hours: 0800-2200; Open May-Oct; Tent & RV camping: Fee unknown; Elev: 3616ft/1102m; Tel: 360-825-6585; Nearest town: Wilkeson. GPS: 46.940059, -121.940076

65 • Falls Creek

Total sites: 31; RV sites: 21; Central water; Flush toilets; No showers; No RV dump; Reservations accepted; Max length: 16ft; Open May-Sep; Tent & RV camping: $25; Elev: 233ft/71m; Tel: 360-288-2525; Nearest town: Quinault. GPS: 47.469321, -123.845766

66 • Falls Creek

Total sites: 7; RV sites: 7; Central water; Vault toilets; No showers; No RV dump; Reservations not accepted; Max length: 18ft; Stay limit: 14 days; Tent & RV camping: $8; Elev: 2228ft/679m; Tel: 509-996-4003; Nearest town: Winthrop. GPS: 48.635166, -120.155407

67 • Ferry Lake

Total sites: 9; RV sites: 9; No water; Vault toilets; Reservations not accepted; Generator hours: 0600-2200; Open May-Oct; Tent & RV camping: $6; Elev: 3468ft/1057m; Tel: 509-775-7400; Nearest town: Republic. GPS: 48.523062, -118.810748

68 • Finner Creek

Total sites: 3; RV sites: 3; Central water; Vault toilets; No showers; No RV dump; Reservations not accepted; Max length: 30ft; Tent & RV camping: $14; Elev: 2589ft/789m; Tel: 509-548-2550; Nearest town: Leavenworth. GPS: 47.953383, -120.772385

69 • Flat Camp

Total sites: 12; RV sites: 12; Central water; Vault toilets; No showers; No RV dump; Reservations not accepted; Max length: 36ft; Stay limit: 14 days; Open May-Oct; Tent & RV camping: $8; Elev: 2582ft/787m; Tel: 509-996-4003; Nearest town: Carlton. GPS: 48.614746, -120.195801

70 • Foggy Dew

Total sites: 12; RV sites: 12; No water; Vault toilets; Reservations not accepted; Max length: 25ft; Stay limit: 14 days; Open May-Oct; Tent & RV camping: $8; Elev: 2251ft/686m; Tel: 509-996-4003; Nearest town: Carlton. GPS: 48.205591, -120.195899

71 • Forest Boundary

Total sites: 6; RV sites: 6; No water; Vault toilets; Reservations not accepted; Tent & RV camping: Free; Elev: 4465ft/1361m; Tel: 541-278-3716; Nearest town: Pomeroy. GPS: 46.293000, -117.557000

72 • Forlorn Lakes

Total sites: 25; RV sites: 25; No water; Vault toilets; Reservations not accepted; Max length: 18ft; Open Jun-Oct; Tent & RV camping: $10; Elev: 3766ft/1148m; Tel: 509-395-3400; Nearest town: Trout Lake. GPS: 45.960627, -121.754844

73 • Fox Creek

Total sites: 16; RV sites: 16; Central water; Vault toilets; No showers; No RV dump; Reservations not accepted; Max length: 28ft; Tent & RV camping: $10; Elev: 2080ft/634m; Tel: 509-784-4700; Nearest town: Ardenvoir. GPS: 47.925293, -120.510986

74 • Gillette

Total sites: 30; RV sites: 30; Central water; Vault toilets; No showers; No RV dump; Reservations accepted; Stay limit: 14 days; Generator hours: 0600-2200; Open May-Sep; Tent & RV camping: $20; Elev: 3173ft/967m; Tel: 509-738-7700; Nearest town: Ione. GPS: 48.612257, -117.535463

75 • Glacier View

Total sites: 23; RV sites: 23; Central water; Vault toilets; No showers; No RV dump; Reservations not accepted; Max length: 15ft; Tent & RV camping: $20; Elev: 1903ft/580m; Tel: 509-548-2550; Nearest town: Leavenworth. GPS: 47.824207, -120.808631

76 • Godman

Total sites: 8; RV sites: 3; No water; Vault toilets; Tent & RV camping: Free; Elev: 5702ft/1738m; Tel: 509-843-1891; Nearest town: Pomeroy. GPS: 46.100000, -117.786000

77 • Gold Basin

Total sites: 87; RV sites: 87; Central water; Flush toilets; Showers; No RV dump; Reservations accepted; Open May-Sep; Tent & RV camping: $26-28; Elev: 1155ft/352m; Tel: 360-436-1155; Nearest town: Granite Falls; Notes: Group sites: $205. GPS: 48.077393, -121.737305

78 • Goose Creek

Total sites: 29; RV sites: 29; Central water; Vault toilets; No showers; No RV dump; Reservations not accepted; Tent & RV camping: $14; Elev: 2264ft/690m; Tel: 509-548-2550; Nearest town: Leavenworth. GPS: 47.838691, -120.647821

79 • Goose Lake

Total sites: 18; No water; Vault toilets; Reservations not accepted; Open Jul-Oct; Tents only: $10; Elev: 3287ft/1002m; Tel: 509-395-3400; Nearest town: Trout Lake; Notes: RVs not recommended. GPS: 45.939799, -121.758072

80 • Govt Mineral Springs

Total sites: 5; RV sites: 5; No water; Vault toilets; Reservations not accepted; Max length: 18ft; Open May-Sep; Tent & RV camping: $5; Elev: 1280ft/390m; Tel: 509-395-3400; Nearest town: Carson. GPS: 45.882297, -121.995962

81 • Grasshopper Meadows

Total sites: 5; RV sites: 5; No water; Vault toilets; Reservations not accepted; Max length: 30ft; Tent & RV camping: Fee unknown; Elev: 2093ft/638m; Tel: 509-548-2550; Nearest town: Leavenworth. GPS: 47.941000, -120.926000

82 • Grouse Mt

Total sites: 4; No water; Vault toilets; Reservations not accepted; Tents only: Free; Elev: 4459ft/1359m; Tel: 509-682-4900; Nearest town: Chelan. GPS: 47.988683, -120.310512

83 • Halfway Flat

Total sites: 11; RV sites: 11; Central water; Vault toilets; No showers; No RV dump; Reservations accepted; Open May-Sep; Tent & RV camping: $10-18; Elev: 2543ft/775m; Tel: 509-653-1436; Nearest town: Naches. GPS: 46.980112, -121.095801

84 • Hamma Hamma

Total sites: 15; RV sites: 15; No water; Vault toilets; Reservations not accepted; Max length: 21ft; Stay limit: 14 days; Open May-Sep; Tent & RV camping: $14; Elev: 689ft/210m; Tel: 360-765-2200; Nearest town: Lilliwaup. GPS: 47.595657, -123.123072

85 • Handy Springs

Total sites: 1; No water; Vault toilets; Reservations not accepted; Tents only: Free; Elev: 6348ft/1935m; Tel: 509-682-4900; Nearest town: Chelan. GPS: 47.979177, -120.412465

86 • Harts Pass

Total sites: 5; No water; Vault toilets; Reservations not accepted; Open Jul-Oct; Tents only: $8; Elev: 6204ft/1891m; Tel: 509-996-4000; Nearest town: Mazama. GPS: 48.720565, -120.670116

87 • Hause Creek

Total sites: 42; RV sites: 42; No water; Vault toilets; No showers; No RV dump; Reservations accepted; Max length: 30ft; Open May-Sep; Tent & RV camping: $18; Elev: 2559ft/780m; Tel: 509-653-1401; Nearest town: Naches. GPS: 46.674561, -121.079590

88 • Hells Crossing East

Total sites: 10; RV sites: 6; Central water; Vault toilets; No showers; No RV dump; Reservations accepted; Max length: 20ft; Open May-Sep; Tent & RV camping: $14; Elev: 3287ft/1002m; Tel: 541-338-7869; Nearest town: Cliffdell. GPS: 46.965778, -121.263983

89 • Hells Crossing West

Total sites: 8; RV sites: 6; Central water; Vault toilets; No showers; No RV dump; Reservations accepted; Max length: 20ft; Open May-Sep; Tent & RV camping: $14; Elev: 3265ft/995m; Tel: 541-338-7869; Nearest town: Cliffdell. GPS: 46.965198, -121.266752

90 • Honeymoon

Total sites: 5; RV sites: 5; No water; Vault toilets; Reservations not accepted; Max length: 22ft; Stay limit: 14 days; Open May-Oct; Tent & RV camping: $8; Elev: 3337ft/1017m; Tel: 509-996-4003; Nearest town: Winthrop. GPS: 48.696751, -120.264828

91 • Horseshoe Cove

Total sites: 36; RV sites: 34; Central water; Flush toilets; No showers; No RV dump; Reservations accepted; Open May-Sep; Tent & RV camping: $19-21; Elev: 833ft/254m; Tel: 360-856-5700; Nearest town: Burlington; Notes: 3 group sites: $70. GPS: 48.669739, -121.679071

92 • Horseshoe Lake

Total sites: 11; RV sites: 11; No water; Vault toilets; Reservations not accepted; Max length: 16ft; Open Jul-Sep; Tent & RV camping: $12; Elev: 4173ft/1272m; Tel: 360-497-1100; Nearest town: Randle. GPS: 46.309814, -121.567139

93 • Huckleberry Access

Total sites: 3; RV sites: 3; Central water; Vault toilets; No showers; No RV dump; Max length: 32ft; Open May-Oct; Tent & RV camping: Free; Elev: 4216ft/1285m; Tel: 509-395-3400; Nearest town: Trout Lake. GPS: 46.091084, -121.799871

94 • Icewater Creek

Total sites: 14; RV sites: 14; No water; Vault toilets; Reservations not accepted; Tent & RV camping: $18; Elev: 2822ft/860m; Tel: 509-852-1100; Nearest town: Cle Elum. GPS: 47.113000, -120.904000

95 • Ida Creek

Total sites: 10; RV sites: 10; Central water; Vault toilets; No showers; No RV dump; Reservations not accepted; Max length: 30ft; Tent & RV camping: $19; Elev: 2648ft/807m; Tel: 509-548-2550; Nearest town: Leavenworth. GPS: 47.607617, -120.847819

96 • Indian Creek

Total sites: 39; RV sites: 39; Central water; Vault toilets; No showers; No RV dump; Reservations accepted; Max length: 32ft; Open May-Sep; Tent & RV camping: $20; Elev: 3002ft/915m; Tel: 541-338-7869; Nearest town: Naches. GPS: 46.644287, -121.242188

97 • Iron Creek

Total sites: 98; RV sites: 98; Central water; Vault toilets; No showers; No RV dump; Reservations accepted; Max length: 42ft; Open May-Sep; Tent & RV camping: $20; Elev: 1224ft/373m; Tel: 360-497-1100; Nearest town: Randle. GPS: 46.430664, -121.986084

98 • J-R

Total sites: 6; RV sites: 6; No water; Vault toilets; Reservations not accepted; Max length: 25ft; Stay limit: 14 days; Open Apr-Sep; Tent & RV camping: $8; Elev: 3944ft/1202m; Tel: 509-996-4003; Nearest town: Okanogan. GPS: 48.387828, -119.900848

99 • Johnny Creek

Total sites: 65; RV sites: 65; Central water; Vault toilets; No showers; No RV dump; Reservations not accepted; Max length: 50ft; Tent & RV camping: $19-22; Elev: 2464ft/751m; Tel: 509-548-2550; Nearest town: Leavenworth. GPS: 47.599303, -120.817072

100 • Junior Point

Total sites: 5; No water; Vault toilets; Reservations not accepted; Tents only: Free; Elev: 6424ft/1958m; Tel: 509-682-4900; Nearest town: Chelan. GPS: 47.994379, -120.400309

101 • Kachess

Total sites: 152; RV sites: 152; No water; No toilets; Reservations accepted; Max length: 32ft; Open Jun-Sep; Tent & RV camping: $21; Elev: 2269ft/692m; Tel: 509-852-1100; Nearest town: Easton; Notes: Group site: $115. GPS: 47.355196, -121.244578

102 • Kaner Flat

Total sites: 49; RV sites: 49; Central water; Flush toilets; No showers; No RV dump; Reservations accepted; Max length: 30ft; Open May-Sep; Tent & RV camping: $12; Elev: 2812ft/857m; Tel: 509-653-1401; Nearest town: American River. GPS: 47.011382, -121.129520

103 • Kerr

Total sites: 13; RV sites: 13; No water; Vault toilets; Reservations not accepted; Open May-Sep; Tent & RV camping: $8; Elev: 3182ft/970m; Tel: 509-486-2186; Nearest town: Conconully. GPS: 48.611454, -119.788275

104 • Kettle Crest

Total sites: 2; RV sites: 2; No water; Vault toilets; No showers; No RV dump; Reservations not accepted; Stay limit: 14 days; Generator hours: 0600-2200; Open all year; Tent & RV camping: Free; Elev: 5467ft/1666m; Tel: 509-447-3129; Nearest town: Kettle Falls; Notes: Suitable for equestrian use, Sno-Park permit required if camping between 11/01 and 05/01. GPS: 48.608652, -118.476856

105 • Killen Creek

Total sites: 9; RV sites: 9; No water; Vault toilets; Reservations not accepted; Max length: 22ft; Open Jul-Sep; Tent & RV camping: $12; Elev: 4468ft/1362m; Tel: 360-497-1100; Nearest town: Randle. GPS: 46.294801, -121.548949

106 • Klahanie

Total sites: 20; RV sites: 20; No water; Vault toilets; Reservations not accepted; Max length: 21ft; Open May-Sep; Tent & RV camping: $10; Elev: 479ft/146m; Tel: 360-374-6522; Nearest town: Klahanie. GPS: 47.963396, -124.305507

107 • Klahowya

Total sites: 56; RV sites: 56; Central water; Vault toilets; No showers; No RV dump; Reservations not accepted; Max length: 30ft; Stay limit: 14 days; Open May-Sep; Tent & RV camping: $17; Elev: 856ft/261m; Tel: 360-288 2525; Nearest town: Sappho. GPS: 48.065908, -124.113121

108 • Klipchuck

Total sites: 46; RV sites: 46; Central water; Vault toilets; No showers; No RV dump; Reservations not accepted; Max length: 34ft; Stay limit: 14 days; Open May-Oct; Tent & RV camping: $12;

Elev: 2992ft/912m; Tel: 509-996-4003; Nearest town: Mazama. GPS: 48.597866, -120.513455

109 • La Wis Wis

Total sites: 122; RV sites: 115; Central water; Flush toilets; No showers; No RV dump; Reservations accepted; Max length: 24ft; Open May-Sep; Tent & RV camping: $20; Elev: 1368ft/417m; Tel: 360-497-1100; Nearest town: Packwood; Notes: Large RVs not recommended. GPS: 46.674843, -121.586464

110 • Ladybug

Total sites: 7; RV sites: 7; No water; Vault toilets; Reservations not accepted; Open all year; Tent & RV camping: $8; Elev: 3438ft/1048m; Tel: 509-843-1891; Nearest town: Pomeroy; Notes: No fees/services Dec-Mar. GPS: 46.198788, -117.670236

111 • Lake Creek (Entiat)

Total sites: 19; RV sites: 19; Central water; Vault toilets; No showers; No RV dump; Reservations not accepted; Max length: 25ft; Tent & RV camping: $10; Elev: 2260ft/689m; Tel: 509-784-4700; Nearest town: Ardenvoir. GPS: 47.936671, -120.516386

112 • Lake Ellen East

Total sites: 15; RV sites: 15; No water; Vault toilets; Reservations not accepted; Stay limit: 14 days; Generator hours: 0600-2200; Open May-Sep; Tent & RV camping: $6; Elev: 2293ft/699m; Tel: 509-738-7700; Nearest town: Kettle Falls. GPS: 48.502274, -118.247387

113 • Lake Ellen West

Total sites: 15; RV sites: 15; No water; Vault toilets; Reservations not accepted; Stay limit: 14 days; Generator hours: 0600-2200; Open May-Sep; Tent & RV camping: $6; Elev: 2234ft/681m; Tel: 509-738-7700; Nearest town: Kettle Falls. GPS: 48.496272, -118.263412

114 • Lake Gillette

Total sites: 14; RV sites: 14; Central water; Vault toilets; No showers; No RV dump; Reservations not accepted; Stay limit: 14 days; Generator hours: 0600-2200; Open May-Sep; Tent & RV camping: $18; Elev: 3189ft/972m; Tel: 509-738-7700; Nearest town: Ione. GPS: 48.612551, -117.539039

115 • Lake Leo

Total sites: 8; RV sites: 8; Central water; Vault toilets; No showers; No RV dump; Reservations not accepted; Stay limit: 14 days; Generator hours: 0600-2200; Open May-Sep; Tent & RV camping: $18; Elev: 3215ft/980m; Tel: 509-738-7700; Nearest town: Colville. GPS: 48.649769, -117.497163

116 • Lake Thomas

Total sites: 16; RV sites: 8; Central water; Vault toilets; No showers; No RV dump; Reservations not accepted; Stay limit: 14 days; Open May-Sep; Tent & RV camping: $18; Elev: 3228ft/984m; Tel: 509-738-7700; Nearest town: Ione. GPS: 48.623779, -117.535645

117 • Lena Creek

Total sites: 13; RV sites: 13; Central water; Vault toilets; No showers; No RV dump; Reservations not accepted; Max length: 21ft; Stay limit: 14 days; Open May-Sep; Tent & RV camping: $14; Elev: 745ft/227m; Tel: 360-765-2200; Nearest town: Lilliwaup. GPS: 47.599366, -123.151822

118 • Lion Rock Spring

Total sites: 3; RV sites: 3; No water; Vault toilets; Reservations not accepted; Max length: 22ft; Open Jun-Oct; Tent & RV camping: Free; Elev: 6260ft/1908m; Tel: 509-852-1100; Nearest town: Ellensburg. GPS: 47.251369, -120.581709

119 • Little Goose

Total sites: 6; No water; Vault toilets; Reservations not accepted; Tents only: Free; Elev: 4049ft/1234m; Tel: 509-395-3400; Nearest town: Trout Lake. GPS: 46.037811, -121.713962

120 • Little Naches

Total sites: 21; RV sites: 21; Central water; Vault toilets; No showers; No RV dump; Reservations accepted; Max length: 32ft; Open May-Sep; Tent & RV camping: $14; Elev: 2615ft/797m; Tel: 509-653-1401; Nearest town: Cliffdell. GPS: 46.989985, -121.098032

121 • Little Twin Lakes

Total sites: 20; RV sites: 20; No water; Vault toilets; Generator hours: 0600-2200; Open May-Sep; Tent & RV camping: Free; Elev: 3750ft/1143m; Tel: 509-738-7700; Nearest town: Colville. GPS: 48.574777, -117.645809

122 • Lodgepole

Total sites: 34; RV sites: 34; Central water; Vault toilets; No showers; No RV dump; Reservations accepted; Max length: 20ft; Open May-Sep; Tent & RV camping: $18; Elev: 3596ft/1096m; Tel: 541-338-7869; Nearest town: American River. GPS: 46.915978, -121.384016

123 • Lone Fir

Total sites: 27; RV sites: 27; Central water; Vault toilets; No showers; No RV dump; Reservations not accepted; Max length: 36ft; Stay limit: 14 days; Open May-Oct; Tent & RV camping: $12; Elev: 3625ft/1105m; Tel: 509-996-4003; Nearest town: Mazama. GPS: 48.580322, -120.625244

124 • Long Lake

Total sites: 12; RV sites: 12; Central water; Vault toilets; No showers; No RV dump; Reservations not accepted; Stay limit: 14 days; Generator hours: 0600-2200; Open all year; Tent & RV camping: $8; Elev: 3320ft/1012m; Tel: 509-775-7400; Nearest town: Republic. GPS: 48.500838, -118.810169

125 • Long Swamp

Total sites: 2; RV sites: 2; No water; Vault toilets; Reservations not accepted; Open Jun-Sep; Tent & RV camping: $5; Elev: 5541ft/1689m; Tel: 509-486-2186; Nearest town: Twisp. GPS: 48.854977, -119.946295

126 • Lost Lake

Total sites: 19; RV sites: 19; Central water; Flush toilets; No showers; No RV dump; Reservations not accepted; Open May-Sep; Tent & RV camping: $12; Elev: 3875ft/1181m; Tel: 509-486-2186; Nearest town: Wauconda; Notes: Group site: $40-$80. GPS: 48.852051, -119.052246

127 • Loup Loup

Total sites: 25; RV sites: 25; Central water; Vault toilets; No showers; No RV dump; Reservations not accepted; Max length: 35ft; Stay limit: 14 days; Open May-Oct; Tent & RV camping: $12; Elev: 4134ft/1260m; Tel: 509-996-4003; Nearest town: Trout Lake. GPS: 48.395996, -119.901123

128 • Lower Falls

Total sites: 44; RV sites: 44; Central water; Vault toilets; No showers; No RV dump; Reservations accepted; Max length: 60ft; Open May-Oct; Tent & RV camping: $15; Elev: 1640ft/500m; Tel: 360-449-7800; Nearest town: Northwoods. GPS: 46.156286, -121.879205

129 • Lyman Lake

Total sites: 4; RV sites: 4; No water; Vault toilets; Open Jun-Sep; Tent & RV camping: Free; Elev: 2930ft/893m; Tel: 509-486-2186; Nearest town: Tonasket. GPS: 48.526111, -119.024979

130 • Manastash Camp/Sno-Park

Total sites: 14; RV sites: 14; No water; Vault toilets; Reservations not accepted; Open Jun-Nov; Tent & RV camping: $5; Elev: 4341ft/1323m; Tel: 509-852-1100; Nearest town: Ellensburg. GPS: 47.034743, -120.953608

131 • Marble Creek

Total sites: 23; RV sites: 23; No water; Vault toilets; Reservations accepted; Open May-Sep; Tent & RV camping: $15-17; Elev: 1234ft/376m; Tel: 360-856-5700; Nearest town: Marblemount. GPS: 48.534418, -121.272404

132 • Meadow Creek

Total sites: 4; RV sites: 4; No water; No toilets; Reservations not accepted; Max length: 30ft; Tent & RV camping: Free; Elev: 2280ft/695m; Tel: 509-548-2550; Nearest town: Leavenworth. GPS: 47.867438, -120.693655

133 • Meadow Creek Indian

Total sites: 3; RV sites: 3; No water; Vault toilets; Tent & RV camping: Free; Elev: 4139ft/1262m; Tel: 509-395-3400; Nearest town: Trout Lake. GPS: 46.069309, -121.756569

134 • Meadows

Total sites: 14; No water; Vault toilets; Reservations not accepted; Tents only: $8; Elev: 6286ft/1916m; Tel: 509-996-4000; Nearest town: Mazama; Notes: Very narrow road - no trailers. GPS: 48.708169, -120.674852

135 • Middle Fork

Total sites: 38; RV sites: 38; Central water; Vault toilets; No showers; No RV dump; Reservations accepted; Open May-Sep; Tent & RV camping: $15-17; Elev: 1112ft/339m; Tel: 425-888-1421; Nearest town: North Bend; Notes: 2 group sites $69. GPS: 47.554000, -121.537000

136 • Midway

Total sites: 5; RV sites: 5; No water; Vault toilets; Reservations not accepted; Open all year; Tent & RV camping: $8; Elev: 5149ft/1569m; Tel: 509-843-1891; Nearest town: Pomeroy; Notes: No fees/services Dec-Mar. GPS: 46.166658, -117.763064

137 • Milk Pond

Total sites: 5; RV sites: 5; No water; Vault toilets; Tent & RV camping: Free; Elev: 2989ft/911m; Tel: 509-653-1401; Nearest town: Cliffdell. GPS: 46.987000, -121.063000

138 • Mill Pond

Total sites: 10; RV sites: 10; Central water; Vault toilets; No showers; No RV dump; Reservations not accepted; Max length: 20ft; Generator hours: 0600-2200; Open May-Sep; Tent & RV camping: $24; Elev: 2661ft/811m; Tel: 509-446-7500; Nearest town: Metaline. GPS: 48.854401, -117.290516

139 • Miller River

Total sites: 18; RV sites: 18; Central water; Vault toilets; No showers; No RV dump; Reservations not accepted; Open May-Sep; Tent & RV camping: $14; Elev: 1099ft/335m; Tel: 541-338-7869; Nearest town: Miller River; Notes: Reservable group site $273, 6-ton weight limit on access road. GPS: 47.690204, -121.394063

140 • Mineral Park

Total sites: 21; RV sites: 21; No water; Vault toilets; Reservations accepted; Open May-Sep; Tent & RV camping: $13-15; Elev: 1447ft/441m; Tel: 360-856-5700; Nearest town: Marblemount. GPS: 48.463135, -121.165039

141 • Mineral Springs

Total sites: 6; RV sites: 6; No water; Vault toilets; Reservations not accepted; Tent & RV camping: $18; Elev: 2753ft/839m; Tel: 509-852-1100; Nearest town: Cle Elum; Notes: Reservable group site $80. GPS: 47.290154, -120.699695

142 • Money Creek

Total sites: 25; RV sites: 25; Central water; Vault toilets; No showers; No RV dump; Reservations accepted; Open May-Sep; Tent & RV camping: $19-21; Elev: 915ft/279m; Tel: 541-338-7869; Nearest town: Skykomish; Notes: 6-ton weight limit on access road, Near RR. GPS: 47.729004, -121.408203

143 • Morrison Creek

Total sites: 12; No water; Vault toilets; Reservations not accepted; Open Jun-Oct; Tents only: Free; Elev: 4738ft/1444m; Tel: 509-395-3402; Nearest town: Trout Lake; Notes: Rough road - RVs not recommended. GPS: 46.129594, -121.516730

144 • Moss Creek

Total sites: 17; RV sites: 14; Central water; Vault toilets; No showers; No RV dump; Reservations accepted; Max length: 32ft; Open May-Sep; Tent & RV camping: $16; Elev: 1444ft/440m; Tel: 509-395-3400; Nearest town: White Salmon. GPS: 45.794247, -121.634552

145 • Mystery

Total sites: 4; RV sites: 4; No water; Vault toilets; Reservations not accepted; Max length: 30ft; Stay limit: 14 days; Open Apr-Oct; Tent & RV camping: $8; Elev: 2897ft/883m; Tel: 509-996-4003; Nearest town: Twisp. GPS: 48.402027, -120.471718

146 • Napeequa Crossing

Total sites: 5; RV sites: 5; No water; Vault toilets; Reservations not accepted; Max length: 30ft; Tent & RV camping: Fee unknown; Elev: 2041ft/622m; Tel: 509-548-2550; Nearest town: Leavenworth. GPS: 47.920462, -120.894839

147 • Nason Creek

Total sites: 73; RV sites: 73; Central water; Vault toilets; No showers; No RV dump; Reservations accepted; Open May-Sep; Tent & RV camping: $23; Elev: 1939ft/591m; Tel: 509-763-7020; Nearest town: Coles Corner. GPS: 47.798943, -120.715262

148 • Nice

Total sites: 3; RV sites: 3; No water; Vault toilets; Reservations not accepted; Max length: 30ft; Stay limit: 14 days; Tent & RV camping: $8; Elev: 2756ft/840m; Tel: 509-996-4003; Nearest town: Winthrop. GPS: 48.632028, -120.221462

149 • Nineteenmile

Total sites: 4; RV sites: 4; No water; Vault toilets; Reservations not accepted; Max length: 30ft; Tent & RV camping: $14; Elev: 2598ft/792m; Tel: 509-548-2550; Nearest town: Leavenworth; Notes: Very rough road - high-clearance vehicle may be needed. GPS: 48.019666, -120.827204

150 • Noisy Creek

Total sites: 19; RV sites: 19; Central water; Vault toilets; No showers; No RV dump; Reservations accepted; Generator hours: 0600-2200; Open May-Sep; Tent & RV camping: $20; Elev: 2644ft/806m; Tel: 509-446-7500; Nearest town: Metaline; Notes: Group site: $67. GPS: 48.790355, -117.284428

151 • Nooksack River

Total sites: 4; RV sites: 4; No water; Vault toilets; Tent & RV camping: Fee unknown; Elev: 1272ft/388m; Nearest town: Glacier. GPS: 48.905463, -121.845241

152 • North Fork

Total sites: 8; RV sites: 8; No water; Vault toilets; No showers; No RV dump; Reservations not accepted; Max length: 28ft; Tent & RV camping: $10; Elev: 2756ft/840m; Tel: 509-784-4700; Nearest town: Entiat. GPS: 47.989023, -120.580696

153 • North Fork

Total sites: 32; RV sites: 30; Central water; Vault toilets; No showers; No RV dump; Reservations accepted; Max length: 32ft; Open May-Sep; Tent & RV camping: $18; Elev: 1503ft/458m; Tel: 360-497-1100; Nearest town: Randle. GPS: 46.451201, -121.787257

154 • Oklahoma

Total sites: 22; RV sites: 22; Central water; Vault toilets; No showers; No RV dump; Reservations accepted; Max length: 22ft; Open May-Aug; Tent & RV camping: $16; Elev: 1791ft/546m; Tel: 509-395-3400; Nearest town: Cook. GPS: 45.872313, -121.623184

155 • Olallie Lake

Total sites: 5; RV sites: 5; No water; Vault toilets; Reservations not accepted; Max length: 22ft; Open Jul-Sep; Tent & RV camping: $12; Elev: 4298ft/1310m; Tel: 360-497-1100; Nearest town: Randle. GPS: 46.289242, -121.619278

156 • Oriole

Total sites: 10; RV sites: 8; Central water; Vault toilets; No showers; No RV dump; Reservations not accepted; Open May-Sep; Tent & RV camping: $8; Elev: 2920ft/890m; Tel: 509-486-2186; Nearest town: Conconully. GPS: 48.593983, -119.772278

157 • Panhandle

Total sites: 13; RV sites: 13; Central water; Vault toilets; No showers; No RV dump; Reservations accepted; Generator hours: 0600-2200; Open May-Sep; Tent & RV camping: $20; Elev: 2096ft/639m; Tel: 509-447-7300; Nearest town: Newport. GPS: 48.509692, -117.271344

158 • Panjab

Total sites: 3; No water; Vault toilets; Reservations not accepted; Open all year; Tents only: $8; Elev: 3012ft/918m; Tel: 509-843-1891; Nearest town: Pomeroy; Notes: No fees/services Dec-Mar. GPS: 46.205649, -117.707150

159 • Panorama Point

Total sites: 15; RV sites: 15; Central water; Vault toilets; No showers; No RV dump; Reservations accepted; Open May-Sep; Tent & RV camping: $17-19; Elev: 709ft/216m; Tel: 360-856-5700; Nearest town: Concrete. GPS: 48.723409, -121.671084

160 • Panther Creek

Total sites: 32; RV sites: 32; Central water; Vault toilets; No showers; No RV dump; Reservations accepted; Max length: 25ft; Open May-Sep; Tent & RV camping: $18; Elev: 988ft/301m; Tel: 509-395-3400; Nearest town: Carson. GPS: 45.820314, -121.877338

161 • Paradise Creek

Total sites: 42; RV sites: 42; Central water; Vault toilets; No showers; No RV dump; Reservations accepted; Max length: 25ft; Open May-Sep; Tent & RV camping: $18; Elev: 1634ft/498m; Tel: 509-395-3400; Nearest town: Carson. GPS: 45.948893, -121.935065

162 • Park Creek

Total sites: 12; RV sites: 12; No water; Vault toilets; Reservations accepted; Open May-Sep; Tent & RV camping: $13-15; Elev: 892ft/272m; Tel: 360-856-5700; Nearest town: Concrete. GPS: 48.734863, -121.665771

163 • Pataha

Total sites: 3; RV sites: 2; No water; Vault toilets; Reservations not accepted; Open all year; Tent & RV camping: Free; Elev: 3993ft/1217m; Tel: 509-843-1891; Nearest town: Pomeroy; Notes: No services Dec-Mar. GPS: 46.292000, -117.514000

164 • Peterson Prairie

Total sites: 27; RV sites: 27; Central water; Vault toilets; No showers; No RV dump; Reservations accepted; Max length: 32ft; Open Jun-Sep; Tent & RV camping: $16; Elev: 3041ft/927m; Tel: 541-338-7869; Nearest town: Trout Lake. GPS: 45.968461, -121.659451

165 • Phelps Creek

Total sites: 13; RV sites: 13; No water; Vault toilets; Reservations not accepted; Max length: 30ft; Tent & RV camping: $14; Elev: 2789ft/850m; Tel: 509-548-2550; Nearest town: Leavenworth. GPS: 48.069454, -120.848994

166 • Pierre Lake

Total sites: 16; RV sites: 16; No water; Vault toilets; Reservations not accepted; Stay limit: 14 days; Generator hours: 0600-2200; Open all year; Tent & RV camping: $6; Elev: 2014ft/614m; Tel: 509-738-7700; Nearest town: Orient. GPS: 48.904053, -118.139893

167 • Pine Flats

Total sites: 6; RV sites: 6; Central water; Flush toilets; No showers; No RV dump; Reservations not accepted; Max length: 28ft; Tent & RV camping: $8; Elev: 1719ft/524m; Tel: 509-784-4700; Nearest town: Entiat; Notes: Reservable group site $60. GPS: 47.758628, -120.425108

168 • Pioneer Park

Total sites: 17; RV sites: 17; Central water; Vault toilets; No showers; No RV dump; Reservations accepted; Open May-Sep; Tent & RV camping: $20; Elev: 2132ft/650m; Tel: 509-447-7300; Nearest town: Newport. GPS: 48.213025, -117.053999

169 • Pleasant Valley

Total sites: 12; RV sites: 12; Central water; Vault toilets; No showers; No RV dump; Reservations accepted; Open May-Sep; Tent & RV camping: $16; Elev: 3406ft/1038m; Tel: 541-338-7869; Nearest town: Cliffdell. GPS: 46.942627, -121.325439

170 • Poplar Flat

Total sites: 16; RV sites: 16; Central water; Vault toilets; No showers; No RV dump; Reservations not accepted; Max length: 30ft; Stay limit: 14 days; Open May-Oct; Tent & RV camping: $12; Elev: 3028ft/923m; Tel: 509-996-4003; Nearest town: Twisp. GPS: 48.421631, -120.498779

171 • Quartz Mt

Total sites: 3; RV sites: 3; Max length: 22ft; Tent & RV camping: Free; Elev: 6116ft/1864m; Nearest town: Ellensburg. GPS: 47.076645, -121.079628

172 • Red Bridge

Total sites: 16; RV sites: 16; No water; Vault toilets; Reservations accepted; Open May-Sep; Tent & RV camping: $15-17; Elev: 1430ft/436m; Tel: 360-436-1155; Nearest town: Granite Falls. GPS: 48.070601, -121.651781

173 • Red Mountain

Total sites: 10; RV sites: 10; No water; Vault toilets; Reservations not accepted; Open May-Oct; Tent & RV camping: $14; Elev: 2313ft/705m; Tel: 509-852-1100; Nearest town: Cle Elum. GPS: 47.366455, -121.102539

174 • Riders Camp

Total sites: 5; RV sites: 5; No water; Vault toilets; Reservations not accepted; Tent & RV camping: $5; Elev: 4206ft/1282m; Tel: 509-852-1100; Nearest town: Ellensburg. GPS: 47.029255, -120.934953

175 • Rimrock Peninsula

Total sites: 60; RV sites: 60; No water; Vault toilets; Reservations not accepted; Tent & RV camping: $8; Elev: 3077ft/938m; Tel: 509-653-1401; Nearest town: Naches. GPS: 46.633862, -121.146835

176 • River Bend

Total sites: 5; RV sites: 5; No water; Vault toilets; Reservations not accepted; Max length: 30ft; Stay limit: 14 days; Open May-Oct; Tent & RV camping: $8; Elev: 2716ft/828m; Tel: 509-996-4003; Nearest town: Mazama. GPS: 48.652344, -120.553912

177 • Riverbend

Total sites: 6; RV sites: 6; No water; Vault toilets; Reservations not accepted; Max length: 30ft; Open Jun-Sep; Tent & RV camping: $14; Elev: 2530ft/771m; Tel: 509-548-2550; Nearest town: Leavenworth. GPS: 47.962417, -120.786351

178 • Road's End

Total sites: 4; RV sites: 4; No water; Vault toilets; Reservations not accepted; Max length: 16ft; Stay limit: 14 days; Open Jun-Oct; Tent & RV camping: $8; Elev: 3917ft/1194m; Tel: 509-996-4003; Nearest town: Twisp. GPS: 48.461394, -120.577396

179 • Rock Creek

Total sites: 4; RV sites: 4; No water; Vault toilets; Reservations not accepted; Max length: 30ft; Open Jun-Sep; Tent & RV camping: $14; Elev: 2536ft/773m; Tel: 509-548-2550; Nearest town: Leavenworth. GPS: 47.970330, -120.789683

180 • Rock Island

Total sites: 22; RV sites: 22; Central water; Vault toilets; No showers; No RV dump; Reservations not accepted; Tent & RV camping: $18; Elev: 2815ft/858m; Tel: 509-548-2550; Nearest town: Leavenworth. GPS: 47.608433, -120.917594

181 • Ruffed Grouse

Total sites: 4; RV sites: 4; Central water; Vault toilets; No showers; No RV dump; Reservations not accepted; Max length: 35ft; Stay limit: 14 days; Open May-Oct; Tent & RV camping: $8; Elev: 3196ft/974m; Tel: 509-996-4003; Nearest town: Twisp. GPS: 48.680899, -120.258405

182 • Salmon La Sac

Total sites: 69; RV sites: 69; Central water; Vault toilets; No showers; No RV dump; Reservations accepted; Max length: 32ft; Open May-Sep; Tent & RV camping: $21; Elev: 2415ft/736m; Tel: 509-852-1100; Nearest town: Cle Elum. GPS: 47.401580, -121.099234

183 • Salmon Meadows

Total sites: 7; RV sites: 7; Central water; Vault toilets; No showers; No RV dump; Reservations not accepted; Tent & RV camping: $8, Elev: 4488ft/1368m; Tel: 509-486-2186; Nearest town: Omak. GPS: 48.658531, -119.841833

184 • Sawmill Flat

Total sites: 23; RV sites: 23; Central water; Vault toilets; No showers; No RV dump; Reservations accepted; Max length: 24ft; Open May-Sep; Tent & RV camping: $18; Elev: 2556ft/779m; Tel: 509-653-1401; Nearest town: Naches. GPS: 46.974365, -121.096436

185 • Schaefer Creek

Total sites: 10; RV sites: 10; No water; Vault toilets; Reservations not accepted; Max length: 30ft; Open Jun-Sep; Tent & RV camping: $14; Elev: 2497ft/761m; Tel: 509-548-2550; Nearest town: Leavenworth. GPS: 47.974000, -120.802000

186 • Seal Rock

Total sites: 41; RV sites: 41; Central water; Vault toilets; No showers; No RV dump; Reservations not accepted; Stay limit: 14 days; Open Apr-Sep; Tent & RV camping: $18; Elev: 115ft/35m; Tel: 360-765-2200; Nearest town: Brinnon. GPS: 47.708963, -122.890311

187 • Shannon Creek

Total sites: 19; RV sites: 19; Central water; Vault toilets; No showers; No RV dump; Reservations accepted; Open May-Sep; Tents: $15-19/RVs: $15-17; Elev: 902ft/275m; Tel: 360-856-5700; Nearest town: Burlington. GPS: 48.739789, -121.599784

188 • Sherman Overlook

Total sites: 10; RV sites: 10; Central water; Vault toilets; No showers; No RV dump; Reservations not accepted; Max length: 20ft; Stay limit: 14 days; Generator hours: 0600-2200; Open all year; Tent & RV camping: $6; Elev: 5148ft/1569m; Tel: 509-738-7700; Nearest town: Kettle Falls. GPS: 48.605418, -118.463326

189 • Silver Falls

Total sites: 14; RV sites: 14; Central water; Vault toilets; No showers; No RV dump; Reservations not accepted; Max length: 35ft; Open May-Sep; Tent & RV camping: $12; Elev: 2480ft/756m; Tel: 509-784-4700; Nearest town: Entiat; Notes: Reservable group site $60. GPS: 47.958496, -120.537354

190 • Silver Fir

Total sites: 20; RV sites: 20; Central water; Vault toilets; No showers; No RV dump; Reservations accepted; Open May-Sep; Tent & RV camping: $17-19; Elev: 2008ft/612m; Tel: 360-599-2714; Nearest town: Maple Falls. GPS: 48.905946, -121.700461

191 • Silver Springs

Total sites: 55; RV sites: 55; Central water; Flush toilets; No showers; No RV dump; Reservations accepted; Open May-Sep; Tent & RV camping: $20-22; Elev: 2740ft/835m; Tel: 360-825-6585; Nearest town: Greenwater; Notes: 5 double sites. GPS: 46.993652, -121.531250

192 • Smokey Creek

Total sites: 3; No water; Vault toilets; Reservations not accepted; Tents only: Free; Elev: 3668ft/1118m; Tel: 509-395-3400; Nearest town: Trout Lake. GPS: 46.030785, -121.687629

193 • Snowberry

Total sites: 7; RV sites: 7; Central water; Vault toilets; No showers; No RV dump; Reservations not accepted; Tent & RV camping: $10; Elev: 2030ft/619m; Tel: 509-682-4900; Nearest town: Chelan; Notes: Small group site: $20. GPS: 47.958324, -120.289999

194 • Soda Springs

Total sites: 6; RV sites: 6; No water; No toilets; Reservations not accepted; Max length: 18ft; Open all year; Tent & RV camping: Free; Elev: 3224ft/983m; Tel: 360-497-1100; Nearest town: Packwood; Notes: No services in winter. GPS: 46.704269, -121.481736

195 • Soda Springs

Total sites: 26; RV sites: 26; Central water; Vault toilets; No showers; No RV dump; Reservations accepted; Max length: 30ft; Open May-Sep; Tent & RV camping: $18; Elev: 3035ft/925m; Tel: 509-653-1401; Nearest town: Cliffdell. GPS: 46.925781, -121.214355

196 • South Creek

Total sites: 4; RV sites: 4; No water; Vault toilets; Reservations not accepted; Max length: 30ft; Stay limit: 14 days; Open May-Oct; Tent & RV camping: $8; Elev: 3186ft/971m; Tel: 509-996-4003; Nearest town: Twisp. GPS: 48.437861, -120.529241

197 • South Navarre

Total sites: 4; RV sites: 4; No water; Vault toilets; Reservations not accepted; Tent & RV camping: Free; Elev: 6463ft/1970m; Tel: 509-682-4900; Nearest town: Chelan. GPS: 48.107487, -120.339647

198 • South Skookum Lake

Total sites: 25; RV sites: 25; Central water; Vault toilets; No showers; No RV dump; Reservations not accepted; Stay limit: 14 days; Generator hours: 0600-2200; Open May-Sep; Tent & RV camping: $18; Elev: 3547ft/1081m; Tel: 509-447-7300; Nearest town: Usk. GPS: 48.392175, -117.184521

199 • Spruce Grove

Total sites: 2; No water; Vault toilets; Reservations not accepted; Open all year; Tents only: Free; Elev: 2926ft/892m; Tel: 509-784-4700; Nearest town: Entiat. GPS: 48.004503, -120.604471

200 • Sugarloaf

Total sites: 4; RV sites: 4; No water; Vault toilets; Reservations not accepted; Open May-Sep; Tent & RV camping: $8; Elev: 2424ft/739m; Tel: 509-486-2186; Nearest town: Conconully. GPS: 48.594482, -119.697221

201 • Sulphur Creek

Total sites: 18; RV sites: 18; No water; Vault toilets; Reservations accepted; Open May-Sep; Tent & RV camping: $17; Elev: 1726ft/526m; Tel: 360-436-1155; Nearest town: Darrington; Notes: Group site: $25. GPS: 48.248264, -121.193362

202 • Sunset Falls

Total sites: 18; RV sites: 10; No water; Vault toilets; Reservations accepted; Max length: 22ft; Open May-Sep; Tent & RV camping: $12; Elev: 1073ft/327m; Tel: 360-449-7800; Nearest town: Yacolt. GPS: 45.818302, -122.252246

203 • Swan Lake

Total sites: 25; RV sites: 21; Central water; Vault toilets; No showers; No RV dump; Reservations not accepted; Stay limit: 14 days; Generator hours: 0600-2200; Tent & RV camping: $10; Elev: 3734ft/1138m; Tel: 509-775-7400; Nearest town: Republic. GPS: 48.513042, -118.834451

204 • Swauk

Total sites: 21; RV sites: 21; Central water; Vault toilets; No showers; No RV dump; Reservations not accepted; Open May-Sep; Tent & RV camping: $18; Elev: 3196ft/974m; Tel: 509-852-1100; Nearest town: Cle Elum. GPS: 47.329004, -120.654993

205 • Swift Creek

Total sites: 50; RV sites: 50; Central water; Vault toilets; No showers; No RV dump; Reservations accepted; Open May-Sep; Tent & RV camping: $19-21; Elev: 843ft/257m; Tel: 541-338-7869; Nearest town: Concrete; Notes: 2 group sites: $140. GPS: 48.728214, -121.657684

206 • Takhlakh

Total sites: 54; RV sites: 44; No water; Vault toilets; Reservations accepted; Max length: 22ft; Open Jul-Sep; Tent & RV camping: $18; Elev: 4423ft/1348m; Tel: 360-497-1100; Nearest town: Trout Lake. GPS: 46.278267, -121.600266

207 • Taneum

Total sites: 13; RV sites: 13; Central water; Vault toilets; No showers; No RV dump; Reservations not accepted; Open May-Sep; Tent & RV camping: $18; Elev: 2556ft/779m; Tel: 509-852-1100; Nearest town: Cle Elum. GPS: 47.108695, -120.856139

208 • Taneum Junction ORV

Total sites: 15; RV sites: 15; No water; Vault toilets; Reservations not accepted; Open May-Nov; Tent & RV camping: $5; Elev: 2851ft/869m; Tel: 509-852-1100; Nearest town: Cle Elum. GPS: 47.112000, -120.933000

209 • Teal

Total sites: 7; RV sites: 7; No water; Vault toilets; Open all year; Tent & RV camping: Fee unknown; Elev: 5689ft/1734m; Tel: 509-843-1891; Nearest town: Pomeroy; Notes: No services Dec-Mar. GPS: 46.189000, -117.572000

210 • Ten Mile

Total sites: 5; RV sites: 5; No water; Vault toilets; Reservations not accepted; Open May-Sep; Tents only: $6; Elev: 2112ft/644m; Tel: 509-775-7400; Nearest town: Republic. GPS: 48.517581, -118.738081

211 • The Dalles

Total sites: 45; RV sites: 45; No water; Vault toilets; Reservations accepted; Max length: 40ft; Open May-Sep; Tent & RV camping: $19-21; Elev: 2293ft/699m; Tel: 541-338-7869; Nearest town: Greenwater. GPS: 47.068335, -121.576783

212 • Tillicum

Total sites: 15; RV sites: 15; No water; Vault toilets; Reservations not accepted; Max length: 18ft; Open Jul-Sep; Tent & RV camping: $5; Elev: 3888ft/1185m; Tel: 360-449-7800; Nearest town: Trout Lake. GPS: 46.123291, -121.779785

213 • Tinkham

Total sites: 47; RV sites: 47; Central water; Vault toilets; No showers; No RV dump; Reservations accepted; Open May-Sep; Tent & RV camping: $17-21; Elev: 1529ft/466m; Tel: 541-338-7869; Nearest town: North Bend. GPS: 47.402832, -121.567871

214 • Tower Rock

Total sites: 21; RV sites: 21; Central water; Vault toilets; No showers; No RV dump; Reservations accepted; Max length: 22ft; Open May-Sep; Tent & RV camping: $18; Elev: 1240ft/378m; Tel: 360-497-1100; Nearest town: Randle. GPS: 46.445557, -121.866943

215 • Troublesome Creek

Total sites: 25; RV sites: 25; Central water; Vault toilets; No showers; No RV dump; Reservations accepted; Open Jun-Sep; Tent & RV camping: $17-19; Elev: 1356ft/413m; Tel: 360-677-2414; Nearest town: Index. GPS: 47.898178, -121.402865

216 • Trout Lake

Total sites: 5; No water; Vault toilets; No showers; No RV dump; Reservations not accepted; Tents only: Free; Elev: 3123ft/952m; Tel: 509-738-7700; Nearest town: Kettle Falls. GPS: 48.624498, -118.240203

217 • Trout Lake Creek

Total sites: 17; No water; Vault toilets; Reservations not accepted; Tents only: $10; Elev: 2185ft/666m; Tel: 509-395-3400; Nearest town: Trout Lake. GPS: 46.056428, -121.611867

218 • Tucannon

Total sites: 18; RV sites: 15; No water; Vault toilets; Reservations not accepted; Open all year; Tent & RV camping: $8; Elev: 2694ft/821m; Tel: 509-843-1891; Nearest town: Pomeroy; Notes: No fees/services Nov-Feb. GPS: 46.242903, -117.688108

219 • Turlo

Total sites: 18; RV sites: 18; Central water; Flush toilets; No showers; No RV dump; Reservations accepted; Open Apr-Sep; Tent & RV camping: $17-19; Elev: 1034ft/315m; Tel: 360-436-1155; Nearest town: Granite Falls. GPS: 48.091788, -121.783487

220 • Verlot

Total sites: 26; RV sites: 26; Central water; Flush toilets; No showers; No RV dump; Reservations accepted; Open Apr-Nov; Tent & RV camping: $19-21; Elev: 1007ft/307m; Tel: 360-436-1155; Nearest town: Granite Falls. GPS: 48.089785, -121.777559

221 • Walupt Lake

Total sites: 42; RV sites: 27; Central water; Vault toilets; No showers; No RV dump; Reservations accepted; Max length: 40ft; Open Jun-Sep; Tent & RV camping: $18; Elev: 3980ft/1213m; Tel: 541-338-7869; Nearest town: Randle; Notes: Also walk-to sites, 6 walk-to sites on lakeshore. GPS: 46.423584, -121.473877

222 • War Creek

Total sites: 10; RV sites: 10; Central water; Vault toilets; No showers; No RV dump; Reservations not accepted; Max length: 25ft; Stay limit: 14 days; Open May-Oct; Tent & RV camping: $8; Elev: 2559ft/780m; Tel: 509-996-4003; Nearest town: Twisp. GPS: 48.367676, -120.398193

223 • West Sullivan

Total sites: 10; RV sites: 10; Central water; Vault toilets; No showers; No RV dump; Reservations accepted; Generator hours: 0600-2200; Open May-Sep; Tent & RV camping: $20; Elev: 2625ft/800m; Tel: 509-446-7500; Nearest town: Metaline. GPS: 48.839316, -117.285775

224 • White Pass Lake

Total sites: 10; RV sites: 10; No water; Vault toilets; Reservations not accepted; Max length: 20ft; Open Jun-Sep; Tent & RV camping: $8; Elev: 4442ft/1354m; Tel: 509-653-1401; Nearest town: Naches. GPS: 46.644486, -121.380960

225 • White Pine

Total sites: 5; RV sites: 5; No water; Vault toilets; Open May-Sep; Tent & RV camping: Free; Elev: 2369ft/722m; Tel: 509-548-2550; Nearest town: Leavenworth. GPS: 47.789091, -120.872694

226 • Wickiup

Total sites: 7; RV sites: 7; No water; Vault toilets; Tent & RV camping: Free; Elev: 5968ft/1819m; Tel: 509-843-1891; Nearest town: Pomeroy; Notes: No services Dec-Mar. GPS: 46.137000, -117.435000

227 • Willaby

Total sites: 21; RV sites: 19; Central water; Flush toilets; No showers; No RV dump; Reservations accepted; Max length: 16ft; Open Apr-Oct; Tent & RV camping: $25; Elev: 276ft/84m; Tel: 360-288-2525; Nearest town: Quinault; Notes: Also walk-to sites, 2 walk-to sites. GPS: 47.460449, -123.861328

228 • Willows

Total sites: 16; RV sites: 16; Central water; Vault toilets; No showers; No RV dump; Reservations accepted; Max length: 20ft; Open May-Sep; Tent & RV camping: $14; Elev: 2474ft/754m; Tel: 509-653-1401; Nearest town: Naches. GPS: 46.672607, -121.039795

229 • Windy Camp

Total sites: 2; Central water; Vault toilets; No showers; No RV dump; Tents only: Free; Elev: 5965ft/1818m; Tel: 509-682-4900; Nearest town: Chelan. GPS: 47.899071, -120.331957

230 • Windy Point

Total sites: 15; RV sites: 15; Central water; Vault toilets; No showers; No RV dump; Reservations accepted; Max length: 22ft; Open May-Sep; Tent & RV camping: $14; Elev: 2077ft/633m; Tel: 541-338-7869; Nearest town: Naches. GPS: 46.693060, -120.907220

231 • Wish Poosh

Total sites: 34; RV sites: 34; Central water; Flush toilets; No showers; No RV dump; Reservations accepted; Open May-Sep; Tent & RV camping: $14; Elev: 2284ft/696m; Tel: 509-852-1100; Nearest town: Cle Elum. GPS: 47.279933, -121.088678

West Virginia

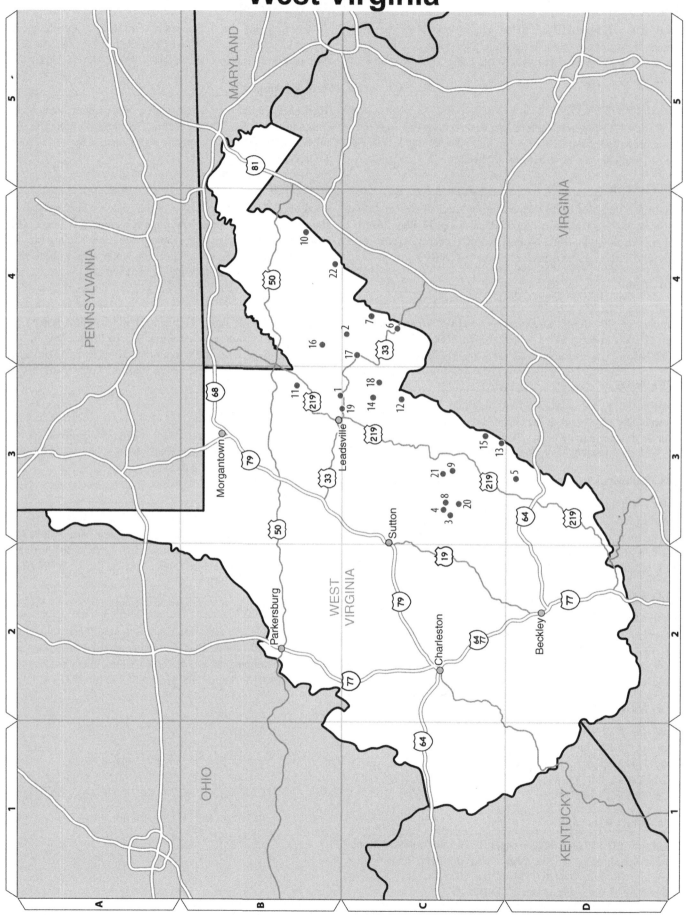

West Virginia Camping Areas

1 • Bear Heaven

Total sites: 8; No water; Vault toilets; Reservations not accepted; Stay limit: 14 days; Open Apr-Nov; Tents only: $10; Elev: 3445ft/ 1050m; Tel: 304-478-2000; Nearest town: Elkins. GPS: 38.928949, -79.675647

2 • Big Bend

Total sites: 46; RV sites: 46; Central water; Flush toilets; No showers; RV dump; Reservations accepted; Stay limit: 14 days; Open Apr-Oct; Tent & RV camping: $22-23; Elev: 1234ft/376m; Tel: 304-358-3253; Nearest town: Petersburg. GPS: 38.889160, -79.239502

3 • Big Rock

Total sites: 5; RV sites: 5; Central water; Vault toilets; No showers; No RV dump; Reservations not accepted; Stay limit: 14 days; Open Mar-Nov; Tent & RV camping: $10; Elev: 2251ft/686m; Tel: 304-846-2695; Nearest town: Richwood; Notes: No large RVs. GPS: 38.296109, -80.523824

4 • Bishop Knob

Total sites: 54; RV sites: 54; Central water; Vault toilets; No showers; No RV dump; Reservations not accepted; Max length: 40ft; Stay limit: 14 days; Open Apr-Nov; Tent & RV camping: $8; Elev: 3150ft/960m; Tel: 304-846-2695; Nearest town: Dyer. GPS: 38.337731, -80.489029

5 • Blue Bend

Total sites: 21; RV sites: 21; Central water; Flush toilets; Showers; No RV dump; Reservations accepted; Open Mar-Nov; Tents: $16/ RVs: $16-20; Elev: 1998ft/609m; Tel: 304-536-2144; Nearest town: White Sulphur Springs; Notes: Group site: $25. GPS: 37.921365, -80.267422

6 • Brandywine Lake

Total sites: 46; RV sites: 46; Central water; Flush toilets; Showers; RV dump; Reservations not accepted; Open May-Nov; Tent & RV camping: $18; Elev: 2034ft/620m; Tel: 540-432-0187; Nearest town: Brandywine; Notes: No large RVs, $8 in off-season. GPS: 38.599609, -79.200928

7 • Camp Run

Total sites: 9; RV sites: 9; No water; Vault toilets; Reservations not accepted; Open all year; Tent & RV camping: Free; Elev: 1716ft/ 523m; Tel: 540-432-0187; Nearest town: Milam; Notes: Rough road. GPS: 38.747117, -79.109119

8 • Cranberry

Total sites: 30; RV sites: 30; Central water; Vault toilets; No showers; No RV dump; Reservations not accepted; Max length: 40ft; Stay limit: 14 days; Open Mar-Nov; Tent & RV camping: $10; Elev: 2598ft/792m; Tel: 304-846-2695; Nearest town: Dyer. GPS: 38.325439, -80.441895

9 • Day Run

Total sites: 12; RV sites: 12; Central water; Vault toilets; No showers; No RV dump; Reservations not accepted; Stay limit: 14 days; Open Mar-Nov; Tent & RV camping: $8; Elev: 3117ft/950m; Tel: 304-799-4334; Nearest town: Marlinton. GPS: 38.287618, -80.215737

10 • Hawk

Total sites: 15; RV sites: 15; Central water; Vault toilets; No showers; No RV dump; Reservations not accepted; Max length: 16ft; Open Apr-Dec; Tent & RV camping: Free; Elev: 1363ft/415m; Tel: 540-984-4101; Nearest town: Intermont. GPS: 39.116244, -78.499712

11 • Horseshoe

Total sites: 21; RV sites: 18; Central water; Vault toilets; No showers; No RV dump; Reservations accepted; Open May-Sep; Tents: $15/RVs: $15-20; Elev: 1768ft/539m; Tel: 304-478-2481; Nearest town: Parsons; Notes: Group sites available - $20-$85. GPS: 39.180386, -79.601185

12 • Island

Total sites: 12; RV sites: 10; No water; Vault toilets; Reservations not accepted; Open Apr-Nov; Tent & RV camping: $10; Elev: 2998ft/914m; Tel: 304-456-3335; Nearest town: Bartow; Notes: Also walk-to sites, 2 walk-to sites. GPS: 38.579109, -79.704029

13 • Lake Sherwood

Total sites: 153; RV sites: 153; Central water; Flush toilets; Showers; RV dump; Reservations accepted; Open Mar-Nov; Tents: $16/ RVs: $20; Elev: 2684ft/818m; Tel: 304-536-2144; Nearest town: White Sulphur Springs. GPS: 38.007259, -80.010093

14 • Laurel Fork

Total sites: 15; RV sites: 15; Central water; Vault toilets; No showers; No RV dump; Reservations not accepted; Open Apr-Dec; Tent & RV camping: $8; Elev: 3120ft/951m; Tel: 304-456-3335; Nearest town: Elkins. GPS: 38.739990, -79.693359

15 • Pocahontas

Total sites: 8; RV sites: 8; Central water; Vault toilets; No showers; No RV dump; Reservations not accepted; Stay limit: 14 days; Open Mar-Nov; Tent & RV camping: $8; Elev: 2523ft/769m; Tel: 304-799-4334; Nearest town: Marlinton. GPS: 38.102051, -79.966553

16 • Red Creek

Total sites: 12; RV sites: 12; Central water; Vault toilets; No showers; No RV dump; Reservations not accepted; Stay limit: 14 days; Open Apr-Nov; Tent & RV camping: $11; Elev: 3878ft/1182m; Tel: 304-257-4488; Nearest town: Petersburg. GPS: 39.031738, -79.316406

17 • Seneca Shadows

Total sites: 78; RV sites: 38; Elec sites: 13; Central water; Flush toilets; Showers; No RV dump; Reservations accepted; Stay limit: 14 days; Open Apr-Oct; Tents: $17/RVs: $22-30; Elev: 1834ft/

559m; Tel: 304-567-3082; Nearest town: Riverton; Notes: Group site: $65. GPS: 38.828154, -79.385544

18 • Spruce Knob Lake

Total sites: 42; RV sites: 29; Central water; Vault toilets; No showers; No RV dump; Reservations accepted; Stay limit: 14 days; Open Apr-Oct; Tents: $13-16/RVs: $16; Elev: 4055ft/1236m; Tel: 304-567-3082; Nearest town: Riverton. GPS: 38.707275, -79.588135

19 • Stuart

Total sites: 26; RV sites: 26; Elec sites: 26; Central water; Flush toilets; Showers; RV dump; Reservations accepted; Open Apr-Oct; Tent & RV camping: $30; Elev: 2346ft/715m; Tel: 304-636-5070; Nearest town: Elkins; Notes: Group site: $55-$130. GPS: 38.917480, -79.770996

20 • Summit Lake

Total sites: 33; RV sites: 33; Central water; Vault toilets; No showers; No RV dump; Reservations not accepted; Stay limit: 14 days; Open Apr-Nov; Tent & RV camping: $10; Elev: 3527ft/1075m; Tel: 304-846-2695; Nearest town: Richwood. GPS: 38.248646, -80.444052

21 • Tea Creek

Total sites: 28; RV sites: 28; Central water; Vault toilets; No showers; No RV dump; Reservations not accepted; Stay limit: 14 days; Open Apr-Nov; Tent & RV camping: $10; Elev: 3028ft/923m; Tel: 304-799-4334; Nearest town: Marlinton. GPS: 38.341872, -80.232626

22 • Trout Pond

Total sites: 36; RV sites: 36; Elec sites: 11; Central water; Flush toilets; Showers; RV dump; Reservations accepted; Open Apr-Nov; Tents: $22/RVs: $27; Elev: 1995ft/608m; Tel: 304-897-6450; Nearest town: Wardensville. GPS: 38.953771, -78.733634

Wisconsin

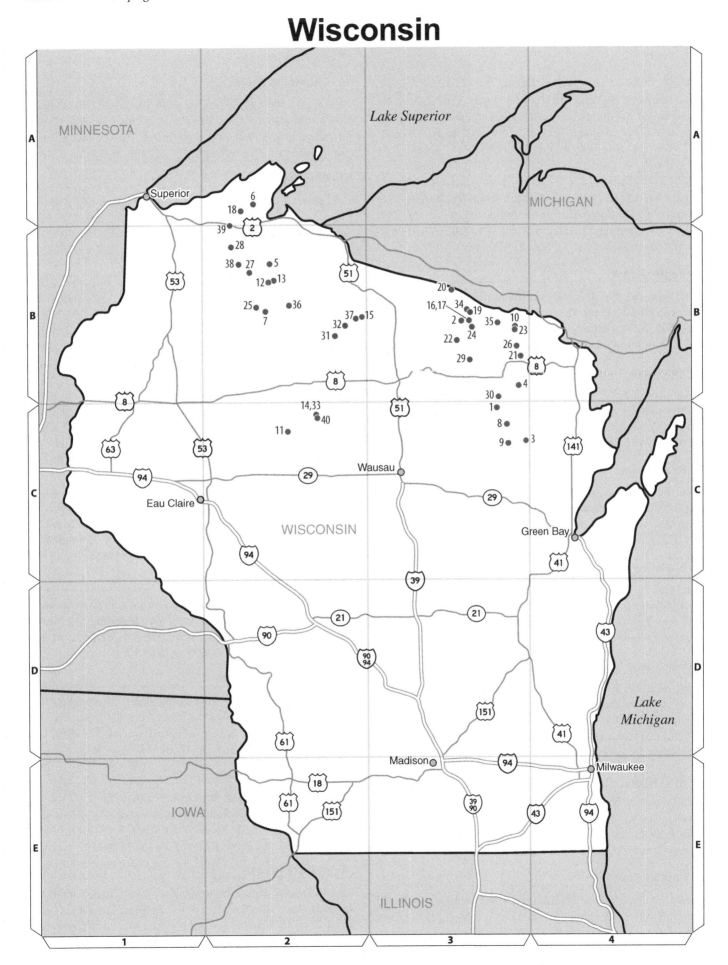

Wisconsin Camping Areas

1 • Ada Lake

Total sites: 19; RV sites: 19; Central water; Vault toilets; No showers; No RV dump; Reservations not accepted; Open May-Oct; Tent & RV camping: $15; Elev: 1709ft/521m; Tel: 715-674-4481; Nearest town: Wabeno. GPS: 45.370445, -88.731153

2 • Anvil Lake

Total sites: 17; RV sites: 13; Central water; Vault toilets; No showers; No RV dump; Generators prohibited; Open May-Oct; Tent & RV camping: $15; Elev: 1752ft/534m; Tel: 715-479-2827; Nearest town: Eagle River. GPS: 45.936523, -89.060791

3 • Bagley Rapids

Total sites: 30; RV sites: 30; Central water; Vault toilets; No showers; No RV dump; Reservations not accepted; Open May-Oct; Tent & RV camping: $15; Elev: 958ft/292m; Tel: 715-276-6333; Nearest town: Lakewood. GPS: 45.157604, -88.465838

4 • Bear Lake

Total sites: 27; RV sites: 21; Central water; Vault toilets; No showers; No RV dump; Reservations accepted; Open May-Oct; Tent & RV camping: $15; Elev: 1384ft/422m; Tel: 715-674-4481; Nearest town: Laona. GPS: 45.514102, -88.529479

5 • Beaver Lake

Total sites: 10; RV sites: 5; Central water; Vault toilets; No showers; No RV dump; Reservations accepted; Max length: 30ft; Open May-Oct; Tent & RV camping: $15; Elev: 1460ft/445m; Tel: 715-264-2511; Nearest town: Mellen. GPS: 46.301270, -90.897705

6 • Birch Grove

Total sites: 16; RV sites: 14; Central water; Vault toilets; No showers; No RV dump; Reservations not accepted; Max length: 35ft; Open May-Sep; Tent & RV camping: $15; Elev: 1135ft/346m; Tel: 715-373-2667; Nearest town: Washburn. GPS: 46.686035, -91.060547

7 • Black Lake

Total sites: 29; RV sites: 26; Central water; Vault toilets; No showers; No RV dump; Reservations accepted; Max length: 45ft; Open May-Oct; Tent & RV camping: $15; Elev: 1421ft/433m; Tel: 715-264-2511; Nearest town: Hayward; Notes: Also walk-to sites, 3 walk-to sites. GPS: 45.988525, -90.929199

8 • Boot Lake

Total sites: 32; RV sites: 26; Central water; Vault toilets; No showers; No RV dump; Reservations accepted; Open May-Nov; Tent & RV camping: $18; Elev: 1352ft/412m; Tel: 715-276-6333; Nearest town: Mountain. GPS: 45.267012, -88.646001

9 • Boulder Lake

Total sites: 89; RV sites: 89; Elec sites: 23; Central water; Flush toilets; Showers; RV dump; Reservations accepted; Max length: 45ft; Open May-Oct; Tent & RV camping: $15-20; Elev: 1129ft/344m; Tel: 715-276-6333; Nearest town: Langlade. GPS: 45.141201, -88.635138

10 • Chipmunk Rapids

Total sites: 6; RV sites: 6; Central water; Vault toilets; No showers; No RV dump; Reservations not accepted; Open Apr-Nov; Tent & RV camping: $15; Elev: 1444ft/440m; Tel: 715-479-2827; Nearest town: Florence. GPS: 45.892832, -88.557319

11 • Chippewa

Total sites: 78; RV sites: 76; Central water; Flush toilets; Showers; RV dump; Reservations accepted; Max length: 35ft; Open May-Sep; Tent & RV camping: $15-18; Elev: 1289ft/393m; Tel: 715-748-4875; Nearest town: Medford. GPS: 45.222457, -90.705954

12 • Day Lake

Total sites: 55; RV sites: 52; Central water; Vault toilets; No showers; No RV dump; Reservations accepted; Max length: 45ft; Open May-Oct; Tent & RV camping: $18; Elev: 1466ft/447m; Tel: 715-264-2511; Nearest town: Clam Lake; Notes: Blueberry/Heron loops closed. GPS: 46.181192, -90.903699

13 • East Twin Lake

Total sites: 10; RV sites: 8; Central water; Vault toilets; No showers; No RV dump; Reservations accepted; Max length: 30ft; Open May-Oct; Tent & RV camping: $15; Elev: 1466ft/447m; Tel: 715-264-2511; Nearest town: Clam Lake. GPS: 46.192627, -90.859863

14 • Eastwood

Total sites: 21; RV sites: 21; Central water; Vault toilets; No showers; No RV dump; Reservations accepted; Open May-Sep; Tent & RV camping: $15; Elev: 1470ft/448m; Tel: 715-748-4875; Nearest town: Medford. GPS: 45.332031, -90.444824

15 • Emily Lake

Total sites: 11; RV sites: 8; Central water; Vault toilets; No showers; No RV dump; Reservations not accepted; Open May-Oct; Tent & RV camping: $15; Elev: 1585ft/483m; Tel: 715-762-2461; Nearest town: Park Falls. GPS: 45.964600, -90.010010

16 • Franklin Lake North

Total sites: 37; RV sites: 37; Central water; Vault toilets; No showers; No RV dump; Reservations accepted; Open May-Oct; Tents: $15/RVs: $15-18; Elev: 1758ft/536m; Tel: 715-479-2827; Nearest town: Eagle River. GPS: 45.940598, -88.985699

17 • Franklin Lake South

Total sites: 40; RV sites: 40; Central water; Vault toilets; No showers; No RV dump; Reservations accepted; Open May-Oct; Tents: $15/RVs: $15-18; Elev: 1736ft/529m; Tel: 715-479-2827; Nearest town: Eagle River. GPS: 45.930416, -88.994124

18 • Horseshoe Lake

Total sites: 9; RV sites: 9; No water; Vault toilets; Reservations not accepted; Open Apr-Nov; Tent & RV camping: $12; Elev: 1296ft/395m; Tel: 715-373-2667; Nearest town: Ino; Notes: Group site: $25, Horse ties. GPS: 46.642391, -91.183953

19 • Kentuck Lake

Total sites: 31; RV sites: 31; Central water; Vault toilets; No showers; No RV dump; Reservations accepted; Open May-Nov; Tent & RV camping: $15-18; Elev: 1742ft/531m; Tel: 715-479-2827; Nearest town: Eagle River. GPS: 45.992920, -88.980469

20 • Lac Vieux Desert

Total sites: 31; RV sites: 31; Central water; Vault toilets; No showers; No RV dump; Reservations not accepted; Open May-Oct; Tent & RV camping: $15; Elev: 1693ft/516m; Tel: 715-479-2827; Nearest town: Eagle River. GPS: 46.136031, -89.156127

21 • Laura Lake

Total sites: 41; RV sites: 38; Central water; Vault toilets; No showers; No RV dump; Reservations accepted; Max length: 30ft; Open May-Oct; Tent & RV camping: $15; Elev: 1509ft/460m; Tel: 715-674-4481; Nearest town: Laona. GPS: 45.701746, -88.502792

22 • Laurel Lake

Total sites: 12; RV sites: 12; Central water; Vault toilets; No showers; No RV dump; Reservations accepted; Open May-Oct; Tent & RV camping: $15; Elev: 1670ft/509m; Tel: 715-479-2827; Nearest town: Eagle River. GPS: 45.815918, -89.110596

23 • Lost Lake

Total sites: 27; RV sites: 27; Central water; Vault toilets; No showers; No RV dump; Reservations accepted; Open May-Oct; Tent & RV camping: $15; Elev: 1542ft/470m; Tel: 715-479-2827; Nearest town: Tipler. GPS: 45.883789, -88.558350

24 • Luna - White Deer

Total sites: 37; RV sites: 37; Central water; Vault toilets; No showers; No RV dump; Reservations accepted; Open May-Oct; Tent & RV camping: $15-18; Elev: 1736ft/529m; Tel: 715-479-2827; Nearest town: Eagle River. GPS: 45.899658, -88.962158

25 • Moose Lake

Total sites: 15; RV sites: 11; Central water; Vault toilets; No showers; No RV dump; Reservations accepted; Max length: 40ft; Open May-Sep; Tent & RV camping: $15; Elev: 1417ft/432m; Tel: 715-264-2511; Nearest town: Hayward; Notes: Also walk-to sites, 4 walk-to sites. GPS: 46.017578, -91.017090

26 • Morgan Lake

Total sites: 18; RV sites: 18; Central water; Vault toilets; No showers; No RV dump; Reservations accepted; Open May-Oct; Tent & RV camping: $15; Elev: 1470ft/448m; Tel: 715-479-2827; Nearest town: Florence; Notes: Group site: $35. GPS: 45.772217, -88.543945

27 • Namekagon Lake

Total sites: 34; RV sites: 34; Central water; Vault toilets; No showers; No RV dump; Reservations accepted; Max length: 45ft; Open May-Oct; Tent & RV camping: $18; Elev: 1444ft/440m; Tel: 715-264-2511; Nearest town: Cable. GPS: 46.244629, -91.086670

28 • Perch Lake (Drummond)

Total sites: 16; RV sites: 15; Central water; Vault toilets; No showers; No RV dump; Reservations not accepted; Max length: 35ft; Open May-Oct; Tent & RV camping: $15; Elev: 1234ft/376m; Tel: 715-373-2878; Nearest town: Drummond. GPS: 46.404535, -91.268991

29 • Pine Lake

Total sites: 12; RV sites: 12; Central water; Vault toilets; No showers; No RV dump; Reservations not accepted; Open May-Sep; Tent & RV camping: $15; Elev: 1654ft/504m; Tel: 715-276-6333; Nearest town: Laona. GPS: 45.685961, -88.991583

30 • Richardson Lake

Total sites: 26; RV sites: 25; Central water; Vault toilets; No showers; No RV dump; Reservations accepted; Open May-Nov; Tent & RV camping: $15; Elev: 1598ft/487m; Tel: 715-276-6333; Nearest town: Laona. GPS: 45.441650, -88.713623

31 • Sailor Lake

Total sites: 25; RV sites: 25; Central water; Vault toilets; No showers; No RV dump; Reservations accepted; Max length: 35ft; Open May-Oct; Tent & RV camping: $15; Elev: 1542ft/470m; Tel: 715-762-2461; Nearest town: Park Falls; Notes: Also walk-to sites, 3 walk-to sites. GPS: 45.841693, -90.275804

32 • Smith Rapids

Total sites: 11; RV sites: 11; No water; Vault toilets; No showers; No RV dump; Reservations accepted; Open Apr-Oct; Tent & RV camping: $15; Elev: 1545ft/471m; Tel: 715-748-4875; Nearest town: Park Falls; Notes: 7 sites for equestrian use. GPS: 45.909996, -90.173962

33 • Spearhead Point

Total sites: 27; RV sites: 24; Central water; Vault toilets; No showers; No RV dump; Reservations accepted; Open May-Oct; Tent & RV camping: $15-18; Elev: 1391ft/424m; Tel: 715-748-4875; Nearest town: Medford. GPS: 45.327637, -90.444824

34 • Spectacle Lake

Total sites: 33; RV sites: 31; Central water; Vault toilets; No showers; No RV dump; Reservations accepted; Open May-Oct; Tent & RV camping: $15-18; Elev: 1772ft/540m; Tel: 715-479-2827; Nearest town: Eagle River. GPS: 46.008301, -89.011230

35 • Stevens Lake

Total sites: 6; RV sites: 6; No water; Vault toilets; Reservations not accepted; Max length: 40ft; Open May-Oct; Tent & RV camping: $15; Elev: 1555ft/474m; Tel: 715-479-2827; Nearest town: Florence. GPS: 45.925084, -88.713741

36 • Stockfarm Bridge

Total sites: 8; RV sites: 8; Central water; Vault toilets; No showers; No RV dump; Reservations accepted; Open May-Oct; Tent & RV camping: $15; Elev: 1483ft/452m; Tel: 715-264-2511; Nearest town: Glidden. GPS: 46.037515, -90.715335

37 • Twin Lakes

Total sites: 17; RV sites: 17; Central water; Vault toilets; No showers; No RV dump; Reservations accepted; Open May-Oct; Tent & RV camping: $15; Elev: 1594ft/486m; Tel: 715-762-2461; Nearest town: Park Falls. GPS: 45.955526, -90.071987

38 • Two Lakes

Total sites: 94; RV sites: 83; Central water; Vault toilets; No showers; RV dump; Reservations accepted; Open May-Oct; Tent & RV camping: $21; Elev: 1388ft/423m; Tel: 715-739-6334; Nearest town: Washburn; Notes: Also walk-to sites, 7 walk-to sites, Dump fee: $10/campers/$25 unregistered campers. GPS: 46.292132, -91.196771

39 • Wanoka Lake

Total sites: 20; RV sites: 19; Central water; Vault toilets; No showers; No RV dump; Reservations not accepted; Max length: 35ft; Open May-Nov; Tent & RV camping: $15; Elev: 1116ft/340m; Tel: 715-373-2667; Nearest town: Washburn. GPS: 46.543533, -91.283115

40 • West Point

Total sites: 15; RV sites: 15; Central water; Vault toilets; No showers; No RV dump; Reservations not accepted; Open all year; Tent & RV camping: $15; Elev: 1384ft/422m; Tel: 715-748-4875; Nearest town: Medford. GPS: 45.318191, -90.438158

Wyoming

SOUTH DAKOTA

NEBRASKA

WYOMING

COLORADO

MONTANA

IDAHO

UTAH

Sheridan

Cheyenne

Casper

Rawlins

Rock Springs

Thermopolis

Cody

Jackson

Highways: 80, 85, 16, 20, 25, 90, 26, 220, 287, 120, 14, 191, 30, 83, 131

Site numbers visible on map: 6, 21, 105, 18, 26, 39, 47, 1, 29, 15, 120, 69, 70, 71, 72, 91, 66, 84, 56, 107, 95, 10, 46, 96, 97, 116, 74, 117, 13, 20, 11, 55, 62, 78, 82, 118, 128, 77, 34, 20, 134, 115, 67, 36, 31, 13, 68, 123, 61, 122, 80, 81, 102, 28, 127, 101, 112, 100, 92, 93, 111, 99, 5, 58, 114, 75, 79, 139, 41, 32, 9, 12, 138, 63, 27, 60, 59, 76, 73, 65, 23, 44, 38, 133, 8, 90, 106, 35, 125, 30, 33, 57, 16, 98, 40, 49, 130, 87, 50, 45, 135, 89, 136, 3, 131, 52, 94, 110, 4, 24, 103, 25, 48, 64, 53, 37, 119, 86, 85, 43, 121, 22, 83, 109, 00, 54, 51, 104, 124, 349, 129, 2, 1, 19, 42, 17, 132, 140, 126

Wyoming Camping Areas

1 • Allred Flat

Total sites: 32; RV sites: 32; Central water; Vault toilets; No showers; No RV dump; Reservations not accepted; Max length: 22ft; Open May-Sep; Tent & RV camping: $10; Elev: 6814ft/2077m; Tel: 307-739-5500; Nearest town: Smoot. GPS: 42.489502, -110.962402

2 • Alpine

Total sites: 16; RV sites: 16; Central water; Vault toilets; No showers; No RV dump; Reservations accepted; Max length: 22ft; Open May-Sep; Tents: $12/RVs: $12-24; Elev: 5705ft/1739m; Tel: 208-523-1412; Nearest town: Alpine; Notes: Group sites: $50. GPS: 43.197042, -111.041419

3 • Angles

Total sites: 4; RV sites: 4; Central water; Vault toilets; No showers; No RV dump; Open Jun-Sep; Tent & RV camping: $5; Elev: 8602ft/2622m; Tel: 307-739-5500; Nearest town: Jackson; Notes: Food storage order 04-00-104. GPS: 43.825442, -110.201607

4 • Atherton Creek

Total sites: 21; RV sites: 21; Central water; Vault toilets; No showers; No RV dump; Reservations not accepted; Open May-Sep; Tent & RV camping: $15; Elev: 6978ft/2127m; Tel: 307-739-5500; Nearest town: Jackson. GPS: 43.636963, -110.523193

5 • Bald Mountain

Total sites: 15; RV sites: 15; Central water; Vault toilets; No showers; No RV dump; Reservations accepted; Stay limit: 14 days; Open Jun-Sep; Tent & RV camping: $16; Elev: 9101ft/2774m; Nearest town: Lovell. GPS: 44.805908, -107.858887

6 • Bearlodge

Total sites: 8; RV sites: 8; No water; Vault toilets; No showers; No RV dump; Reservations not accepted; Stay limit: 10 days; Open all year; Tent & RV camping: $14; Elev: 4675ft/1425m; Nearest town: Aladdin. GPS: 44.655000, -104.327000

7 • Beartooth Lake

Total sites: 21; RV sites: 21; Central water; Vault toilets; No showers; No RV dump; Reservations not accepted; Max length: 32ft; Stay limit: 16 days; Open Jul-Sep; Tent & RV camping: $15; Elev: 8963ft/2732m; Tel: 307-527-6921; Nearest town: Cody; Notes: Food storage order 04-00-104. GPS: 44.943705, -109.590529

8 • Big Game

Total sites: 16; RV sites: 16; No water; Vault toilets; Reservations accepted; Max length: 32ft; Open Jun-Sep; Tent & RV camping: $10; Elev: 5919ft/1804m; Tel: 307-527-6921; Nearest town: Wapiti; Notes: Food storage order 04-00-104. GPS: 44.461914, -109.605469

9 • Big Sandy

Total sites: 12; RV sites: 12; No water; Vault toilets; Reservations not accepted; Max length: 22ft; Open Jun-Sep; Tent & RV camping: $7; Elev: 9124ft/2781m; Tel: 307-739-5500; Nearest town: Boulder. GPS: 42.687829, -109.270774

10 • Bobbie Thompson

Total sites: 16; RV sites: 12; Central water; Vault toilets; No showers; No RV dump; Reservations not accepted; Tent & RV camping: $10; Elev: 8727ft/2660m; Tel: 307-745-2300; Nearest town: Saratoga; Notes: No longer a designated CG but dispersed camping allowed. GPS: 41.156892, -106.255284

11 • Bottle Creek

Total sites: 11; RV sites: 11; Central water; Vault toilets; No showers; No RV dump; Reservations not accepted; Max length: 16ft; Stay limit: 14 days; Open Jun-Oct; Tent & RV camping: $10; Elev: 8747ft/2666m; Tel: 307-745-2300; Nearest town: Encampment. GPS: 41.174682, -106.900458

12 • Boulder Lake

Total sites: 15; RV sites: 15; No water; Vault toilets; Reservations not accepted; Max length: 100ft; Open Jun-Sep; Tent & RV camping: $7; Elev: 7333ft/2235m; Tel: 307-367-4326; Nearest town: Boulder. GPS: 42.857201, -109.617225

13 • Boulder Park

Total sites: 32; RV sites: 32; Central water; Vault toilets; No showers; RV dump; Reservations accepted; Max length: 22ft; Open Jun-Sep; Tent & RV camping: $17; Elev: 7989ft/2435m; Tel: 406-587-9054; Nearest town: Ten Sleep. GPS: 44.163272, -107.253051

14 • Bow River

Total sites: 13; RV sites: 13; Central water; Vault toilets; No showers; No RV dump; Reservations not accepted; Max length: 32ft; Tent & RV camping: $10; Elev: 8591ft/2619m; Tel: 307-745-2300; Nearest town: Elk Mountain. GPS: 41.513503, -106.371114

15 • Brooklyn Lake

Total sites: 19; RV sites: 19; No water; Vault toilets; Max length: 22ft; Tent & RV camping: $10; Elev: 10659ft/3249m; Tel: 307-745-2300; Nearest town: Centennial. GPS: 41.373779, -106.246582

16 • Brooks Lake

Total sites: 13; RV sites: 13; No water; Vault toilets; Reservations not accepted; Max length: 32ft; Open Jun-Sep; No tents/RVs: $10; Elev: 9068ft/2764m; Tel: 307-455-2466; Nearest town: Dubois; Notes: Hard sided camping only. GPS: 43.751044, -110.004671

17 • Buckboard Crossing

Total sites: 46; RV sites: 46; Elec sites: 14; Central water; Flush toilets; Showers; No RV dump; Reservations accepted; Max length: 45ft; Open May-Sep; Tent & RV camping: $20-28; Elev: 6112ft/1863m; Tel: 435-784-3445; Nearest town: Green River; Notes: 8 sites with electric, Fee showers. GPS: 41.248954, -109.601870

18 • Campbell Creek

Total sites: 6; RV sites: 6; No water; Vault toilets; Reservations not accepted; Max length: 22ft; Stay limit: 14 days; Open Jun-Aug;

Tent & RV camping: $10; Elev: 8018ft/2444m; Tel: 307-358-4690; Nearest town: Douglas. GPS: 42.455311, -105.835949

19 • Cave Falls

Total sites: 23; RV sites: 23; Central water; Vault toilets; No showers; No RV dump; Reservations not accepted; Open Jun-Sep; Tent & RV camping: $10; Elev: 6207ft/1892m; Tel: 208-557-5900; Nearest town: Ashton ID. GPS: 44.130843, -111.014876

20 • Circle Park

Total sites: 10; RV sites: 10; Central water; Vault toilets; No showers; No RV dump; Reservations accepted; Stay limit: 14 days; Open Jun-Sep; Tent & RV camping: $16; Elev: 8107ft/2471m; Tel: 406-587-9054; Nearest town: Buffalo. GPS: 44.282764, -106.990528

21 • Cook Lake

Total sites: 32; RV sites: 32; No toilets; Reservations not accepted; Open all year; Tent & RV camping: $18; Elev: 4862ft/1482m; Tel: 605-673-9200; Nearest town: Sundance; Notes: $10 mid-Sep to mid-May. GPS: 44.594262, -104.411833

22 • Cottonwood Lake

Total sites: 18; RV sites: 18; Central water; Vault toilets; No showers; No RV dump; Reservations not accepted; Tent & RV camping: $10; Elev: 7530ft/2295m; Tel: 307-739-5500; Nearest town: Afton; Notes: Horse corrals, Reservable group site $35. GPS: 42.640229, -110.816899

23 • Crazy Creek

Total sites: 16; RV sites: 16; No water; Vault toilets; No showers; No RV dump; Reservations not accepted; Max length: 28ft; Stay limit: 16 days; Open May-Sep; Tent & RV camping: $10; Elev: 6939ft/2115m; Tel: 307-527-6921; Nearest town: Cooke City MT; Notes: Food Storage Order 04-00-104, Not ADA-accessible. GPS: 44.942524, -109.775604

24 • Crystal Creek

Total sites: 6; RV sites: 6; Central water; Vault toilets; No showers; No RV dump; Reservations not accepted; Max length: 24ft; Open May-Sep; Tent & RV camping: $12; Elev: 7014ft/2138m; Tel: 307-739-5500; Nearest town: Jackson; Notes: 2 overflow sites can take 32ft rigs. GPS: 43.610736, -110.431379

25 • Curtis Canyon

Total sites: 11; RV sites: 11; Central water; Vault toilets; No showers; No RV dump; Reservations not accepted; Max length: 24ft; Open May-Sep; Tent & RV camping: $15; Elev: 7041ft/2146m; Tel: 307-739-5500; Nearest town: Jackson. GPS: 43.512451, -110.661377

26 • Curtis Gulch

Total sites: 6; RV sites: 6; Central water; Vault toilets; No showers; No RV dump; Reservations not accepted; Max length: 22ft; Open May-Oct; Tent & RV camping: $10; Elev: 6683ft/2037m; Tel: 307-745-2300; Nearest town: Douglas. GPS: 42.407354, -105.623326

27 • Dead Indian

Total sites: 10; RV sites: 10; No water; Vault toilets; Reservations not accepted; Max length: 32ft; Stay limit: 16 days; Open all year; Tent & RV camping: $10; Elev: 6014ft/1833m; Tel: 307-527-6921; Nearest town: Cody; Notes: Food storage order 04-00-104. GPS: 44.753416, -109.418004

28 • Dead Swede

Total sites: 22; RV sites: 22; Central water; Vault toilets; No showers; No RV dump; Reservations accepted; Stay limit: 14 days; Open Jun-Sep; Tent & RV camping: $18; Elev: 8471ft/2582m; Tel: 406-587-9054; Nearest town: Dayton. GPS: 44.688965, -107.447021

29 • Deep Creek

Total sites: 12; RV sites: 12; Central water; Vault toilets; No showers; No RV dump; Reservations not accepted; Max length: 22ft; Stay limit: 14 days; Open Jul-Sep; Tent & RV camping: $10; Elev: 10108ft/3081m; Tel: 307-326-5258; Nearest town: Arlington. GPS: 41.459004, -106.272645

30 • Deer Creek

Total sites: 6; RV sites: 6; No water; Vault toilets; Reservations not accepted; Max length: 16ft; Stay limit: 16 days; Open all year; Tent & RV camping: Donation; Elev: 6447ft/1965m; Tel: 307-527-6921; Nearest town: Cody; Notes: Food storage order 04-00-104, Not ADA-accessible. GPS: 44.158457, -109.619461

31 • Deer Park

Total sites: 7; RV sites: 7; Central water; Vault toilets; No showers; No RV dump; Reservations not accepted; Stay limit: 14 days; Open Jun-Sep; Tent & RV camping: $16; Elev: 8914ft/2717m; Tel: 307-674-2600; Nearest town: Ten Sleep. GPS: 44.244559, -107.222858

32 • Dickinson Creek

Total sites: 15; RV sites: 15; No water; Vault toilets; Reservations not accepted; Max length: 20ft; Stay limit: 16 days; Open Apr-Oct; Tent & RV camping: Free; Elev: 9354ft/2851m; Tel: 307-332-5460; Nearest town: Ft. Washakie; Notes: Tribal fishing license required if on nearby reservation land. GPS: 42.835693, -109.057617

33 • Double Cabin

Total sites: 14; RV sites: 14; Central water; Vault toilets; No showers; No RV dump; Reservations not accepted; Max length: 32ft; Stay limit: 16 days; Open May-Sep; Tent & RV camping: $15; Elev: 8077ft/2462m; Tel: 307-527-6241; Nearest town: Dubois; Notes: Food storage order 04-00-104. GPS: 43.806233, -109.560665

34 • Doyle

Total sites: 19; RV sites: 18; Central water; Vault toilets; No showers; No RV dump; Reservations accepted; Open Jun-Sep; Tent & RV camping: $16; Elev: 8182ft/2494m; Tel: 406-587-9054; Nearest town: Buffalo. GPS: 44.072585, -106.987182

35 • Eagle Creek

Total sites: 20; RV sites: 20; Central water; Vault toilets; No showers; No RV dump; Reservations not accepted; Max length:

40ft; Stay limit: 16 days; Open May-Sep; No tents/RVs: $15; Elev: 6490ft/1978m; Tel: 307-527-6921; Nearest town: Wapiti; Notes: Food storage order 04-00-104, Hard-side units only. GPS: 44.471680, -109.888672

36 • East Fork

Total sites: 12; RV sites: 12; Central water; Vault toilets; No showers; No RV dump; Reservations not accepted; Stay limit: 14 days; Open Jun-Sep; Tent & RV camping: $14; Elev: 7634ft/2327m; Tel: 307-674-2600; Nearest town: Big Horn. GPS: 44.595931, -107.208718

37 • East Table Creek

Total sites: 20; RV sites: 20; Central water; Vault toilets; No showers; No RV dump; Reservations not accepted; Max length: 30ft; Open May-Sep; Tent & RV camping: $15; Elev: 5830ft/1777m; Tel: 307-739-5500; Nearest town: Hoback Junction. GPS: 43.211670, -110.807373

38 • Elk Fork

Total sites: 13; RV sites: 13; No water; Vault toilets; Reservations not accepted; Max length: 22ft; Stay limit: 16 days; Open all year; Tent & RV camping: $10; Elev: 5988ft/1825m; Tel: 307-527-6921; Nearest town: Cody; Notes: Food storage order 04-00-104, No fee/no services Oct-Apr. GPS: 44.462891, -109.629395

39 • Esterbrook

Total sites: 12; RV sites: 12; No water; Vault toilets; Reservations not accepted; Max length: 22ft; Stay limit: 14 days; Open all year; Tent & RV camping: $10; Elev: 6333ft/1930m; Tel: 307-358-4690; Nearest town: Douglas; Notes: No fee in winter - no water. GPS: 42.425222, -105.324637

40 • Falls

Total sites: 54; RV sites: 54; Central water; Vault toilets; No showers; No RV dump; Reservations not accepted; Max length: 32ft; Stay limit: 16 days; Open Jun-Sep; Tent & RV camping: $15-20; Elev: 8357ft/2547m; Tel: 307-455-2466; Nearest town: Dubois; Notes: Food storage order 04-00-104. GPS: 43.706445, -109.971104

41 • Fiddlers Lake

Total sites: 20; RV sites: 20; Central water; Vault toilets; No showers; No RV dump; Reservations not accepted; Max length: 40ft; Stay limit: 16 days; Tent & RV camping: $15; Elev: 9416ft/2870m; Tel: 307-332-5460; Nearest town: Lander. GPS: 42.629691, -108.881472

42 • Firehole Canyon

Total sites: 37; RV sites: 37; Potable water; Flush toilets; Showers; RV dump; Reservations accepted; Open May-Sep; Tent & RV camping: $20; Elev: 6079ft/1853m; Tel: 801-226-3564; Nearest town: Rock Spring. GPS: 41.350596, -109.445167

43 • Forest Park

Total sites: 13; RV sites: 13; Central water; Vault toilets; No showers; No RV dump; Reservations not accepted; Max length: 30ft; Open May-Sep; Tent & RV camping: $10; Elev: 6975ft/2126m; Nearest town: Alpine. GPS: 42.831299, -110.689941

44 • Fox Creek

Total sites: 33; RV sites: 33; Elec sites: 27; Water at site; Vault toilets; No showers; No RV dump; Reservations not accepted; Max length: 32ft; Stay limit: 16 days; Open Jul-Sep; Tent & RV camping: $20; Elev: 7090ft/2161m; Tel: 307-527-6921; Nearest town: Cody. GPS: 44.976612, -109.833924

45 • Fremont Lake

Total sites: 54; RV sites: 54; Potable water; Vault toilets; No showers; No RV dump; Reservations accepted; Max length: 32ft; Open May-Sep; Tent & RV camping: $12; Elev: 7530ft/2295m; Tel: 307-367-4326; Nearest town: Pinedale; Notes: Group site: $35. GPS: 42.946149, -109.792327

46 • French Creek

Total sites: 11; RV sites: 11; Central water; Vault toilets; No showers; No RV dump; Reservations not accepted; Max length: 20ft; Open all year; Tent & RV camping: $10; Elev: 7792ft/2375m; Tel: 307-326-5258; Nearest town: Saratoga; Notes: No fees/services Oct-Apr. GPS: 41.226683, -106.480591

47 • Friend Park

Total sites: 11; RV sites: 8; No water; Vault toilets; Reservations not accepted; Max length: 22ft; Tent & RV camping: $10; Elev: 7556ft/2303m; Tel: 307-358-4690; Nearest town: Douglas; Notes: Also walk-to sites, 3 walk-to sites. GPS: 42.256138, -105.484929

48 • Granite Creek

Total sites: 51; RV sites: 51; Central water; Vault toilets; No showers; No RV dump; Reservations not accepted; Open May-Sep; Tent & RV camping: $15; Elev: 6831ft/2082m; Nearest town: Hoback Junction. GPS: 43.359131, -110.445313

49 • Green River Lake

Total sites: 52; RV sites: 52; Central water; Vault toilets; No showers; No RV dump; Reservations not accepted; Open Jul-Sep; Tent & RV camping: $12; Elev: 8064ft/2458m; Tel: 307-367-4326; Nearest town: Pinedale; Notes: Reservable group site $35, Food storage order 04-00-104. GPS: 43.311768, -109.859863

50 • Half Moon Lake

Total sites: 17; RV sites: 17; No water; Vault toilets; Reservations accepted; Open May-Sep; Tent & RV camping: $7; Elev: 7648ft/2331m; Tel: 307-367-4326; Nearest town: Pinedale; Notes: Food storage order 04-00-104. GPS: 42.936881, -109.761537

51 • Hams Fork

Total sites: 13; RV sites: 13; Central water; Vault toilets; No showers; No RV dump; Reservations not accepted; Open May-Sep; Tent & RV camping: $7; Elev: 7995ft/2437m; Tel: 307-828-5100; Nearest town: Kemmerer. GPS: 42.250732, -110.730469

52 • Hatchet

Total sites: 9; RV sites: 9; Central water; Vault toilets; Reservations not accepted; Max length: 24ft; Open all year; Tent & RV camping: $12; Elev: 6886ft/2099m; Nearest town: Moran Junction; Notes:

No service/no fee in winter, Food storage order 04-00-104. GPS: 43.824103, -110.353564

53 • Hoback

Total sites: 12; RV sites: 12; Central water; Vault toilets; No showers; No RV dump; Reservations not accepted; Max length: 32ft; Open May-Sep; Tent & RV camping: $15; Elev: 6230ft/1899m; Tel: 307-739-5400; Nearest town: Hoback Junction. GPS: 43.279704, -110.597651

54 • Hobble Creek

Total sites: 18; RV sites: 18; Central water; Vault toilets; No showers; No RV dump; Reservations not accepted; Max length: 30ft; Open Jun-Sep; Tent & RV camping: $7; Elev: 7369ft/2246m; Tel: 307-828-5100; Nearest town: Kemmerer; Notes: Corrals available. GPS: 42.398246, -110.783021

55 • Hog Park

Total sites: 17; RV sites: 17; Central water; Vault toilets; No showers; No RV dump; Reservations accepted; Max length: 30ft; Stay limit; 14 days; Open Jun-Oct; Tent & RV camping: $10; Elev: 8524ft/2598m; Tel: 307-326-5258; Nearest town: Encampment. GPS: 41.025981, -106.863193

56 • Holmes

Total sites: 11; RV sites: 11; Vault toilets; Reservations not accepted; Tent & RV camping: Fee unknown; Elev: 9678ft/2950m; Nearest town: Laramie; Notes: Not maintained. GPS: 41.217716, -106.273552

57 • Horse Creek

Total sites: 9; RV sites: 9; Central water; Vault toilets; No showers; No RV dump; Reservations not accepted; Max length: 32ft; Stay limit: 16 days; Open May-Sep; Tent & RV camping: $15; Elev: 7740ft/2359m; Tel: 307-455-2466; Nearest town: Dubois; Notes: Not ADA-compliant, Food storage order 04-00-104. GPS: 43.666666, -109.635365

58 • Hugh Otte

Total sites: 8; RV sites: 8; No water; Vault toilets; Reservations not accepted; Stay limit: 16 days; Tent & RV camping: Free; Elev: 7056ft/2151m; Tel: 307-332-5460; Nearest town: Lander; Notes: Horse corral. GPS: 42.732432, -108.849298

59 • Hunter Peak

Total sites: 10; RV sites: 10; Central water; Vault toilets; No showers; No RV dump; Reservations accepted; Max length: 32ft; Open May-Sep; Tent & RV camping: $15; Elev: 6634ft/2022m; Tel: 307-527-6921; Nearest town: Clarks Fork; Notes: Food storage order 04-00-104. GPS: 44.885276, -109.655263

60 • Island Lake

Total sites: 20; RV sites: 20; Central water; Vault toilets; No showers; No RV dump; Reservations not accepted; Max length: 32ft; Stay limit: 16 days; Open Jul-Sep; Tent & RV camping: $15; Elev: 9541ft/2908m; Tel: 307-527-6921; Nearest town: Cody; Notes: Food storage order 04-00-104. GPS: 44.941382, -109.538894

61 • Island Park

Total sites: 10; RV sites: 10; Central water; Vault toilets; No showers; No RV dump; Reservations accepted; Open Jun-Sep; Tent & RV camping: $17; Elev: 8573ft/2613m; Tel: 406-587-9054; Nearest town: Ten Sleep. GPS: 44.205444, -107.236011

62 • Jack Creek

Total sites: 16; RV sites: 16; Central water; Vault toilets; No showers; No RV dump; Reservations not accepted; Max length: 22ft; Open all year; Tent & RV camping: $10; Elev: 8433ft/2570m; Tel: 307-326-5258; Nearest town: Saratoga; Notes: No fees/services Oct-May. GPS: 41.283313, -107.120419

63 • Jack Creek

Total sites: 7; RV sites: 7; No water; Vault toilets; Reservations not accepted; Max length: 32ft; Open all year; Tent & RV camping: Donation; Elev: 7572ft/2308m; Tel: 307-527-6921; Nearest town: Meeteetse; Notes: Very rough road last 3 miles, Not ADA-compliant, Food storage order. GPS: 44.110045, -109.351875

64 • Kozy

Total sites: 8; RV sites: 8; No water; Vault toilets; Reservations not accepted; Open May-Sep; Tent & RV camping: $15; Elev: 6401ft/1951m; Tel: 307-739-5400; Nearest town: Bondurant. GPS: 43.270168, -110.513831

65 • Lake Creek

Total sites: 6; RV sites: 6; No water; Vault toilets; Max length: 22ft; Stay limit: 16 days; Open Jun-Sep; Tent & RV camping: $10; Elev: 7008ft/2136m; Tel: 307-527-6921; Nearest town: Clarks Fork; Notes: Food storage order 04-00-104. GPS: 44.921356, -109.706989

66 • Lake Owen

Total sites: 38; RV sites: 38; Central water; Vault toilets; No showers; No RV dump; Reservations not accepted; Max length: 22ft; Stay limit: 14 days; Tent & RV camping: $10; Elev: 8999ft/2743m; Tel: 307-745-2300; Nearest town: Foxpark. GPS: 41.146484, -106.100830

67 • Lakeview

Total sites: 20; RV sites: 11; Central water; Vault toilets; No showers; No RV dump; Reservations accepted; Open Jun-Sep; Tent & RV camping: $18; Elev: 8556ft/2608m; Tel: 406-587-9054; Nearest town: Ten Sleep. GPS: 44.176941, -107.215965

68 • Leigh Creek

Total sites: 11; RV sites: 11; Central water; Vault toilets; No showers; No RV dump; Reservations accepted; Max length: 40ft; Open May-Sep; Tent & RV camping: $16; Elev: 5417ft/1651m; Tel: 406-587-9054; Nearest town: Ten Sleep. GPS: 44.080528, -107.314515

69 • Libby Creek - Aspen

Total sites: 8; RV sites: 8; Potable water; Vault toilets; No showers; No RV dump; Reservations not accepted; Max length: 22ft; Open May-Sep; Tent & RV camping: $10; Elev: 8606ft/2623m; Tel: 307-745-2300; Nearest town: Centennial. GPS: 41.318668, -106.160802

70 • Libby Creek - Pine

Total sites: 6; RV sites: 6; Potable water; Vault toilets; No showers; No RV dump; Reservations not accepted; Max length: 22ft; Open May-Sep; Tent & RV camping: $10; Elev: 8652ft/2637m; Tel: 307-745-2300; Nearest town: Centennial. GPS: 41.319632, -106.162826

71 • Libby Creek - Spruce

Total sites: 8; RV sites: 8; Potable water; Vault toilets; No showers; No RV dump; Reservations not accepted; Max length: 16ft; Open May-Sep; Tent & RV camping: $10; Elev: 8573ft/2613m; Tel: 307-745-2300; Nearest town: Centennial. GPS: 41.319306, -106.158437

72 • Libby Creek - Willow

Total sites: 16; RV sites: 16; No water; Vault toilets; Reservations not accepted; Max length: 22ft; Open May-Sep; Tent & RV camping: $10; Elev: 8665ft/2641m; Tel: 307-745-2300; Nearest town: Centennial. GPS: 41.320542, -106.166375

73 • Lily Lake

Total sites: 8; RV sites: 8; No water; Vault toilets; Reservations not accepted; Max length: 22ft; Stay limit: 16 days; Open all year; Tent & RV camping: Donation; Elev: 7700ft/2347m; Tel: 307-527-6921; Nearest town: Cooke City (MT); Notes: Snow may hamper winter access. GPS: 44.945000, -109.714000

74 • Lincoln Park

Total sites: 12; RV sites: 12; Central water; Vault toilets; No showers; No RV dump; Reservations not accepted; Max length: 32ft; Stay limit: 14 days; Open all year; Tent & RV camping: $10; Elev: 8114ft/2473m; Tel: 307-326-5258; Nearest town: Saratoga; Notes: No services/no fees Oct-May. GPS: 41.373554, -106.514147

75 • Little Popo Agie

Total sites: 4; RV sites: 1; No water; Vault toilets; Reservations not accepted; Max length: 16ft; Stay limit: 16 days; Tent & RV camping: Free; Elev: 8802ft/2683m; Tel: 307-332-5460; Nearest town: Lander. GPS: 42.607848, -108.857318

76 • Little Sunlight

Total sites: 5; RV sites: 5; No water; Vault toilets; Reservations not accepted; Stay limit: 16 days; Tent & RV camping: Free; Elev: 6952ft/2119m; Tel: 307-527-6921; Nearest town: Cody; Notes: Not ADA-compliant, Food storage order 04-00-104. GPS: 44.718000, -109.591000

77 • Lost Cabin

Total sites: 19; RV sites: 19; Central water; Vault toilets; No showers; No RV dump; Reservations accepted; Open Jun-Sep; Tent & RV camping: $17; Elev: 8218ft/2505m; Tel: 406-587-9054; Nearest town: Buffalo. GPS: 44.146823, -106.953639

78 • Lost Creek

Total sites: 13; RV sites: 13; Central water; Vault toilets; No showers; No RV dump; Reservations not accepted; Max length: 22ft; Open all year; Tent & RV camping: $10; Elev: 8816ft/2687m; Tel: 307-745-2300; Nearest town: Encampment; Notes: No services/no fees Oct-Jun. GPS: 41.141602, -107.075928

79 • Louis Lake

Total sites: 9; RV sites: 9; No water; Vault toilets; Reservations not accepted; Max length: 24ft; Stay limit: 16 days; Tent & RV camping: $10; Elev: 8594ft/2619m; Tel: 307-332-5460; Nearest town: Lander. GPS: 42.592449, -108.843566

80 • Lower Paintrock Lake

Total sites: 15; RV sites: 15; Central water; Vault toilets; No showers; No RV dump; Reservations not accepted; Stay limit: 14 days; Open Jun-Sep; Tent & RV camping: $15; Elev: 9242ft/2817m; Tel: 307-674-2600; Nearest town: Shell. GPS: 44.394382, -107.383872

81 • Medicine Lodge Lake

Total sites: 13; RV sites: 13; Central water; Vault toilets; No showers; No RV dump; Reservations not accepted; Open Jun-Sep; Tent & RV camping: $15; Elev: 9275ft/2827m; Nearest town: Shell. GPS: 44.400563, -107.387528

82 • Middle Fork

Total sites: 9; RV sites: 9; Central water; Vault toilets; No showers; No RV dump; Reservations accepted; Open May-Sep; Tent & RV camping: $18; Elev: 7533ft/2296m; Tel: 406-587-9054; Nearest town: Buffalo. GPS: 44.301555, -106.950974

83 • Middle Piney Lake

Total sites: 5; RV sites: 5; No water; Vault toilets; Reservations not accepted; Tent & RV camping: Free; Elev: 8917ft/2718m; Nearest town: Big Piney; Notes: Rough road. GPS: 42.603328, -110.564412

84 • Miller Lake

Total sites: 7; RV sites: 7; Central water; Vault toilets; No showers; No RV dump; Reservations not accepted; Max length: 22ft; Stay limit: 14 days; Tent & RV camping: $10; Elev: 9094ft/2772m; Tel: 307-745-2300; Nearest town: Laramie. GPS: 41.069348, -106.155917

85 • Moose Flat

Total sites: 10; RV sites: 10; Central water; Vault toilets; No showers; No RV dump; Reservations not accepted; Max length: 30ft; Open May-Sep; Tent & RV camping: $10; Elev: 6427ft/1959m; Tel: 307-654-0249; Nearest town: Alpine; Notes: Free off-season - no services. GPS: 42.971714, -110.769273

86 • Murphy Creek

Total sites: 10; RV sites: 10; Central water; Vault toilets; No showers; No RV dump; Reservations not accepted; Max length: 30ft; Stay limit: 16 days; Open May-Sep; Tent & RV camping: $7; Elev: 6237ft/1901m; Tel: 307-886-5300; Nearest town: Alpine; Notes: 1 70' pull-through. GPS: 43.072266, -110.835938

87 • Narrows

Total sites: 19; RV sites: 19; Central water; Vault toilets; No showers; No RV dump; Reservations accepted; Open May-Sep; Tent & RV camping: $12; Elev: 7900ft/2408m; Tel: 307-367-4326; Nearest town: Pinedale; Notes: Food storage order 04-00-104. GPS: 43.103271, -109.940918

88 • Nash Fork

Total sites: 27; RV sites: 27; Central water; Vault toilets; No showers; No RV dump; Reservations not accepted; Max length: 22ft; Tent & RV camping: $10; Elev: 10230ft/3118m; Tel: 307-745-2300; Nearest town: Centennial. GPS: 41.358643, -106.233643

89 • New Fork Lake

Total sites: 15; RV sites: 15; No water; Vault toilets; Reservations not accepted; Open Jun-Sep; Tent & RV camping: $7; Elev: 7835ft/2388m; Tel: 307-367-4326; Nearest town: Pinedale; Notes: Reservable group site $35, Food storage order 04-00-104. GPS: 43.083008, -109.967041

90 • Newton Creek

Total sites: 31; RV sites: 31; Central water; Vault toilets; No showers; No RV dump; Reservations not accepted; Max length: 40ft; Stay limit: 16 days; Open May-Sep; Tent & RV camping: $15; Elev: 6266ft/1910m; Tel: 307-527-6921; Nearest town: Cody; Notes: Food storage order 04-00-104, Hard-side units only, Not ADA compliant. GPS: 44.452217, -109.757546

91 • North Fork

Total sites: 60; RV sites: 60; No water; Vault toilets; Reservations accepted; Max length: 30ft; Open Jun-Oct; Tent & RV camping: $10; Elev: 8547ft/2605m; Tel: 307-745-2300; Nearest town: Centennial. GPS: 41.324463, -106.156738

92 • North Tongue

Total sites: 12; RV sites: 12; Central water; Vault toilets; No showers; No RV dump; Reservations accepted; Stay limit: 14 days; Open Jun-Sep; Tent & RV camping: $17; Elev: 7884ft/2403m; Tel: 406-587-9054; Nearest town: Dayton. GPS: 44.780029, -107.533691

93 • Owen Creek

Total sites: 7; RV sites: 7; Central water; Vault toilets; No showers; No RV dump; Reservations accepted; Max length: 45ft; Open Jun-Sep; Tent & RV camping: $17; Elev: 8465ft/2580m; Tel: 406-587-9054; Nearest town: Burgess Jct. GPS: 44.704655, -107.500399

94 • Pacific Creek

Total sites: 8; RV sites: 8; No water; Vault toilets; Reservations not accepted; Open May-Oct; Tent & RV camping: $10; Elev: 7034ft/2144m; Tel: 307-739-5500; Nearest town: Jackson; Notes: Food storage order 04-00-104. GPS: 43.939921, -110.442754

95 • Pelton Creek

Total sites: 16; RV sites: 16; Potable water; Vault toilets; No showers; No RV dump; Reservations not accepted; Max length: 16ft; Tent & RV camping: $10; Elev: 8258ft/2517m; Tel: 307-745-2300; Nearest town: Laramie. GPS: 41.073391, -106.303591

96 • Pickaroon

Total sites: 8; RV sites: 8; No toilets; Reservations not accepted; Max length: 16ft; Stay limit: 14 days; Open Jun-Sep; Tent & RV camping: Free; Elev: 7448ft/2270m; Tel: 307-745-2300; Nearest town: Laramie. GPS: 41.126000, -106.431000

97 • Pike Pole

Total sites: 6; No water; No toilets; Reservations not accepted; Max length: 16ft; Stay limit: 14 days; Open Jun-Sep; Tents only: Free; Elev: 7460ft/2274m; Tel: 307-745-2300; Nearest town: Laramie. GPS: 41.129305, -106.426689

98 • Pinnacles

Total sites: 21; RV sites: 21; Central water; Vault toilets; No showers; No RV dump; Reservations not accepted; Max length: 32ft; Stay limit: 16 days; Open Jun-Sep; Tent & RV camping: $15; Elev: 9150ft/2789m; Tel: 307-455-2466; Nearest town: Dubois; Notes: Hard sided campers only, Food storage order, Not ADA compliant. GPS: 43.754258, -109.996443

99 • Porcupine

Total sites: 16; RV sites: 16; Central water; Vault toilets; No showers; No RV dump; Reservations accepted; Open Jun-Sep; Tent & RV camping: $17; Elev: 8806ft/2684m; Tel: 406-587-9054; Nearest town: Lovell. GPS: 44.831595, -107.858279

100 • Prune Creek

Total sites: 21; RV sites: 21; Central water; Vault toilets; No showers; No RV dump; Reservations accepted; Open Jun-Sep; Tent & RV camping: $18; Elev: 7716ft/2352m; Tel: 406-587-9054; Nearest town: Dayton. GPS: 44.769395, -107.469242

101 • Ranger Creek (Paintrock)

Total sites: 10; RV sites: 10; Central water; Vault toilets; No showers; No RV dump; Reservations not accepted; Open Jun-Sep; Tent & RV camping: $16; Elev: 7707ft/2349m; Tel: 406-587-9054; Nearest town: Big Horn; Notes: Reservable group site $75-$145. GPS: 44.545929, -107.500241

102 • Ranger Creek (Tongue)

Total sites: 11; RV sites: 11; Central water; Vault toilets; No showers; No RV dump; Reservations not accepted; Stay limit: 14 days; Open Jun-Sep; Tent & RV camping: $14; Elev: 7707ft/2349m; Tel: 307-674-2600; Nearest town: Big Horn. GPS: 44.600505, -107.218599

103 • Red Hills

Total sites: 5; RV sites: 5; Central water; Vault toilets; No showers; No RV dump; Reservations not accepted; Max length: 30ft; Stay limit: 16 days; Open May-Sep; Tent & RV camping: $15; Elev: 7034ft/2144m; Tel: 307-739-5400; Nearest town: Jackson. GPS: 43.611408, -110.437492

104 • Reunion Flat

Total sites: 4; RV sites: 4; Central water; Vault toilets; No showers; No RV dump; Reservations not accepted; Open May-Sep; Tent & RV camping: $12; Elev: 6909ft/2106m; Nearest town: Driggs; Notes: 3 reservable group sites $50. GPS: 43.757307, -110.951781

105 • Reuter Canyon

Total sites: 24; RV sites: 24; Central water; Vault toilets; No showers; No RV dump; Reservations accepted; Open May-Sep; Tent & RV camping: $14; Elev: 5466ft/1666m; Tel: 605-574-4402; Nearest town: Sundance; Notes: Free Sep-May. GPS: 44.425922, -104.423934

106 • Rex Hale

Total sites: 30; RV sites: 30; Elec sites: 6; Central water; Vault toilets; No showers; No RV dump; Reservations accepted; Max length: 40ft; Open May-Sep; Tents: $15/RVs: $15-20; Elev: 6152ft/1875m; Tel: 307-527-6921; Nearest town: Cody; Notes: Food storage order 04-00-104. GPS: 44.454352, -109.730896

107 • Rob Roy

Total sites: 65; RV sites: 65; Central water; Vault toilets; No showers; No RV dump; Reservations not accepted; Max length: 35ft; Tent & RV camping: $10; Elev: 9590ft/2923m; Tel: 307-745-2300; Nearest town: Laramie. GPS: 41.216087, -106.253221

108 • Ryan Park

Total sites: 42; RV sites: 42; Central water; Vault toilets; No showers; No RV dump; Reservations accepted; Open Jun-Sep; Tent & RV camping: $10; Elev: 8474ft/2583m; Tel: 307-326-5258; Nearest town: Saratoga; Notes: Group site $100. GPS: 41.326008, -106.492299

109 • Sacajawea

Total sites: 17; RV sites: 17; Central water; Vault toilets; No showers; No RV dump; Reservations not accepted; Max length: 22ft; Open Jun-Sep; Tent & RV camping: $7; Elev: 8386ft/2556m; Tel: 307-276-3375; Nearest town: Big Piney. GPS: 42.617397, -110.533716

110 • Sheffield

Total sites: 5; RV sites: 5; Vault toilets; Reservations not accepted; Max length: 25ft; Open May-Sep; Tent & RV camping: $10; Elev: 6879ft/2097m; Nearest town: Jackson; Notes: Must ford creek to reach CG, Not recommended for large RVs. GPS: 44.093231, -110.663017

111 • Shell Creek

Total sites: 15; RV sites: 15; Central water; Vault toilets; No showers; No RV dump; Reservations accepted; Open May-Sep; Tent & RV camping: $17; Elev: 7618ft/2322m; Tel: 406-587-9054; Nearest town: Greybull. GPS: 44.550654, -107.515246

112 • Sibley Lake

Total sites: 20; RV sites: 20; Elec sites: 14; Central water; Vault toilets; No showers; No RV dump; Reservations accepted; Open Jun-Sep; Tents: $16/RVs: $16-20; Elev: 8008ft/2441m; Tel: 406-587-9054; Nearest town: Dayton. GPS: 44.759033, -107.438965

113 • Silver Lake

Total sites: 17; RV sites: 17; Central water; Vault toilets; No showers; No RV dump; Reservations not accepted; Open Jul-Sep; Tent & RV camping: $10; Elev: 10490ft/3197m; Nearest town: Centennial. GPS: 41.311648, -106.359852

114 • Sinks Canyon

Total sites: 14; RV sites: 9; Central water; Vault toilets; No showers; No RV dump; Reservations not accepted; Max length: 20ft; Open May-Sep; Tent & RV camping: $15; Elev: 6903ft/2104m; Tel: 307-332-5460; Nearest town: Lander. GPS: 42.736683, -108.836672

115 • Sitting Bull

Total sites: 41; RV sites: 41; Central water; Vault toilets; No showers; No RV dump; Reservations accepted; Open all year; Tent & RV camping: $16; Elev: 8674ft/2644m; Tel: 406-587-9054; Nearest town: Ten Sleep. GPS: 44.191647, -107.212079

116 • Six Mile Gap

Total sites: 9; RV sites: 9; Central water; Vault toilets; No showers; No RV dump; Reservations not accepted; Max length: 32ft; Open May-Oct; Tent & RV camping: $10; Elev: 7802ft/2378m; Tel: 307-326-5258; Nearest town: Encampment. GPS: 41.044396, -106.399187

117 • South Brush Creek

Total sites: 20; RV sites: 20; Central water; Vault toilets; No showers; No RV dump; Reservations not accepted; Max length: 32ft; Open Jun-Oct; Tent & RV camping: $10; Elev: 8235ft/2510m; Tel: 307-326-5258; Nearest town: Saratoga. GPS: 41.344787, -106.503815

118 • South Fork

Total sites: 14; RV sites: 14; Central water; Vault toilets; No showers; No RV dump; Reservations accepted; Open May-Sep; Tent & RV camping: $18; Elev: 7690ft/2344m; Tel: 406-587-9054; Nearest town: Buffalo. GPS: 44.277175, -106.947647

119 • Station Creek

Total sites: 16; RV sites: 16; Central water; Vault toilets; No showers; No RV dump; Reservations not accepted; Open May-Oct; Tent & RV camping: $15; Elev: 5860ft/1786m; Nearest town: Hoback Junction. GPS: 43.204346, -110.834473

120 • Sugarloaf

Total sites: 16; RV sites: 16; No water; Vault toilets; Reservations not accepted; Max length: 32ft; Open Jul-Sep; Tent & RV camping: $10; Elev: 10807ft/3294m; Tel: 307-745-2300; Nearest town: Centennial. GPS: 41.353856, -106.293654

121 • Swift Creek

Total sites: 8; RV sites: 8; Central water; Vault toilets; No showers; No RV dump; Reservations not accepted; Open May-Sep; Tent & RV camping: $10; Elev: 6420ft/1957m; Nearest town: Afton. GPS: 42.725058, -110.904915

122 • Tensleep Canyon

Total sites: 5; RV sites: 5; No water; No toilets; Reservations not accepted; Tent & RV camping: Free; Elev: 4892ft/1491m; Nearest town: Ten Sleep. GPS: 44.068419, -107.368815

123 • Tensleep Creek

Total sites: 5; RV sites: 5; No water; Vault toilets; No showers; No RV dump; Open Jun-Sep; Tent & RV camping: $13; Elev: 5564ft/1696m; Nearest town: Ten Sleep. GPS: 44.084959, -107.307909

124 • Teton Canyon

Total sites: 20; RV sites: 20; Central water; Vault toilets; No showers; No RV dump; Reservations accepted; Max length: 22ft; Open Jun-Sep; Tent & RV camping: $12; Elev: 6964ft/2123m; Nearest town: Alta. GPS: 43.756576, -110.919724

125 • Threemile

Total sites: 21; RV sites: 21; Central water; Vault toilets; No showers; No RV dump; Reservations accepted; Max length: 60ft; Stay limit: 16 days; Open Jul-Sep; No tents/RVs: $15; Elev: 6713ft/2046m; Tel: 307-527-6921; Nearest town: Lake Junction; Notes: Hard-side units only. GPS: 44.496338, -109.951172

126 • Tie City

Total sites: 17; RV sites: 17; Central water; Vault toilets; No showers; No RV dump; Reservations not accepted; Max length: 32ft; Tent & RV camping: $10; Elev: 8606ft/2623m; Tel: 307-745-2300; Nearest town: Laramie. GPS: 41.250141, -105.434753

127 • Tie Flume

Total sites: 27; RV sites: 27; Central water; Vault toilets; No showers; No RV dump; Reservations accepted; Open Jun-Sep; Tent & RV camping: $18; Elev: 8366ft/2550m; Tel: 406-587-9054; Nearest town: Burgess Junction. GPS: 44.715096, -107.450733

128 • Tie Hack

Total sites: 19; RV sites: 19; Central water; Vault toilets; No showers; No RV dump; Reservations accepted; Open May-Sep; Tent & RV camping: $18; Elev: 7805ft/2379m; Tel: 406-587-9054; Nearest town: Buffalo. GPS: 44.282825, -106.943389

129 • Trail Creek

Total sites: 10; RV sites: 10; Central water; Vault toilets; No showers; No RV dump; Reservations accepted; Open May-Sep; Tent & RV camping: $12; Elev: 6722ft/2049m; Tel: 208-354-2312; Nearest town: Victor ID. GPS: 43.538574, -111.037598

130 • Trails End

Total sites: 8; RV sites: 8; Central water; Vault toilets; No showers; No RV dump; Reservations not accepted; Open Jun-Sep; Tent & RV camping: $12; Elev: 9314ft/2839m; Nearest town: Pinedale. GPS: 43.006371, -109.753064

131 • Turpin Meadow

Total sites: 18; RV sites: 18; Central water; Vault toilets; No showers; No RV dump; Reservations not accepted; Open May-Sep; Tent & RV camping: $12; Elev: 6949ft/2118m; Tel: 307-739-5500; Nearest town: Jackson; Notes: Food storage order 04-00-104. GPS: 43.854935, -110.262977

132 • Vedauwoo

Total sites: 28; RV sites: 20; Central water; Vault toilets; No showers; No RV dump; Reservations not accepted; Max length: 32ft; Tent & RV camping: $10; Elev: 8297ft/2529m; Tel: 307-745-2300; Nearest town: Buford. GPS: 41.156839, -105.376952

133 • Wapiti

Total sites: 41; RV sites: 41; Elec sites: 21; Central water; Vault toilets; No showers; No RV dump; Reservations accepted; Max length: 50ft; Stay limit: 16 days; Open May-Sep; Tents: $15/RVs: $20; Elev: 5945ft/1812m; Tel: 307-527-6921; Nearest town: Cody; Notes: Food storage order 04-00-104, $5 Elec fee. GPS: 44.465978, -109.624538

134 • West Tensleep

Total sites: 9; RV sites: 9; Central water; Vault toilets; No showers; No RV dump; Reservations accepted; Stay limit: 14 days; Open Jun-Sep; Tent & RV camping: $17; Elev: 9114ft/2778m; Tel: 406-587-9054; Nearest town: Ten Sleep. GPS: 44.258615, -107.215786

135 • Whiskey Grove

Total sites: 9; RV sites: 9; Central water; Vault toilets; No showers; No RV dump; Reservations not accepted; Open Jun-Sep; Tent & RV camping: $7; Elev: 7746ft/2361m; Tel: 307-367-4326; Nearest town: Pinedale; Notes: Food storage order 04-00-104. GPS: 43.255000, -110.026000

136 • Willow Lake

Total sites: 19; RV sites: 17; No water; Vault toilets; No showers; No RV dump; Reservations not accepted; Open Jun-Sep; Tent & RV camping: Free; Elev: 7707ft/2349m; Tel: 307-739-5500; Nearest town: Pinedale; Notes: Food storage order 04-00-104. GPS: 42.990811, -109.900115

137 • Wolf Creek

Total sites: 20; RV sites: 20; Central water; Vault toilets; No showers; No RV dump; Reservations not accepted; Max length: 62ft; Open May-Sep; Tent & RV camping: $15; Elev: 5860ft/1786m; Tel: 307-739-5400; Nearest town: Jackson. GPS: 43.198538, -110.895835

138 • Wood River

Total sites: 5; RV sites: 5; No water; Vault toilets; Reservations not accepted; Max length: 30ft; Stay limit: 16 days; Open May-Sep; Tent & RV camping: Donation; Elev: 7316ft/2230m; Tel: 307-527-6921; Nearest town: Meeteetse; Notes: Food storage order. GPS: 43.931703, -109.132183

139 • Worthen Meadow

Total sites: 28; RV sites: 28; Central water; Vault toilets; No showers; No RV dump; Reservations not accepted; Max length: 24ft; Stay limit: 16 days; Open May-Oct; Tent & RV camping: $15; Elev: 8826ft/2690m; Tel: 307-332-5460; Nearest town: Lander. GPS: 42.698798, -108.929953

140 • Yellow Pine

Total sites: 19; RV sites: 19; No water; Vault toilets; No showers; No RV dump; Reservations not accepted; Max length: 32ft; Tent & RV camping: $10; Elev: 8327ft/2538m; Tel: 307-745-2300; Nearest town: Laramie; Notes: Horse corrals. GPS: 41.254796, -105.410843

Other Public Campground Guides

Visit our website at www.roundaboutpublications.com to learn more about the titles below and other books about camping and traveling in America.

Bureau of Land Management Camping

The Bureau of Land Management Camping book describes 1,142 camping areas managed by the BLM in 11 western states. Details for each camping area include number of campsites, amenities, facilities, fees, reservation information, GPS coordinates, and more.

Free RV Camping Guides

Two books provide details about officially designated camping areas in the United States. The Free RV Camping American West edition describes 1,902 formal campgrounds and dispersed camping areas in 11 states across America's West. The Free RV Camping American Heartland edition describes 1,784 camping areas across 12 states in America's heartland. Both guides include camping areas managed by federal, state, local, and other public agencies.

RV Camping in Corps of Engineers Parks

This is the best guide to all RV-friendly camping areas operated by the Corps of Engineers. It's perfect for RV travelers because all of the hike-in, boat-in, and tent only camping areas are not included, making it very easy to locate campgrounds that can accommodate RVs. Includes details about 644 campgrounds at 210 lakes in 34 states. Corps of Engineers parks are considered by many RVers to be the best public campgrounds in the USA.

RV Camping in National Parks

This book describes all of the RV-friendly campgrounds in national parks, recreation areas, monuments, and other areas managed by the National Park Service. Included are 254 campgrounds in 90 national park areas in 31 states.

RV Camping in State Parks

RV Camping in State Parks describes camping areas in 1,644 parks in 49 states. The book provides contact information, phone numbers, directions, and GPS coordinates for each state park. It also includes activities available like boating, fishing, swimming, and hiking. Camping details include the season, number of sites, cost per night, type of hookups available, and facilities such as restrooms, showers, dump station, etc.

The Ultimate Public Campground Project

This is a 17-volume series of guidebooks that describe over 38,000 public camping areas across the United States. Included are camping areas managed by federal, state, local, and other public agencies.

Made in the USA
Las Vegas, NV
10 July 2023

74446186R00155